THE MIND OF LATIN CHRISTENDOM

THE MIND OF
LATIN CHRISTENDOM

BY

EDWARD MOTLEY PICKMAN

OXFORD UNIVERSITY PRESS

LONDON · NEW YORK · TORONTO

1937

FIRST · EDITION

THE winter of 1903 which I spent in Rome at the age of sixteen first awoke my love of history — I remember pondering
even then on how the Empire fell. During the fifteen years
following, through college and the war, a variety of other interests absorbed me, but, as I reached maturity, as my experience took shape, I turned gradually back, for a further understanding, from the present to the past. It was then that
Europe, both parent and teacher of our American world,
caught my imagination again — for Europe was Time, or at
least our Time, and I, if I were ever to learn anything, was
doomed to learn with Time as teacher.

So I set out, wandering for many years, avid but aimless.
And when, after some time, I found a direction, it was a backward one, from the seventeenth century, to the eleventh, to
the fourth. I know now that what led me back was Christianity. Whatever century I studied, whatever land, whatever
subject, there was always before me the same gigantic phenomenon. To our Western history, at any rate, Christianity
presented at once the tangible obstacle and the intangible
solution.

But I had no passion, no gift, for religion. Brought up in
the thin atmosphere of Unitarianism, faith died in me leaving
no trace. How, then, was I to understand this history of ours?
Must I become a Christian in order to be an historian? Was
I otherwise doomed to view Christianity — as Gibbon did —
in the guise of a superstition clogging the progress of mankind? Yet I also felt that an historian might possibly benefit
as well as suffer from the absence of this Creed. For history
deals with objective phenomena; therefore the historian is
bound to perceive and respect their objectivity. Only too
well do I know that I can never understand a faith I do not
hold; but my consolation, and my excuse for proceeding in
the face of this handicap, is that true Christians have so far
failed to write histories that explain history: like writers of
memoirs, they fall into anachronisms, invariably eluding the

really puzzling and decisive mysteries. They either take too much for granted or remain too blissfully unaware.

I have chosen to start with the later fourth century because it was only then that Christianity began to transform our Latin ancestors — and so us. My book, therefore, is an attempt to make our whole history since then a little more comprehensible. It is a dim introduction to ourselves, as we have been, are, and shall be. May it rouse and perhaps help others also to retell this story in their own better way.

Let not the reader suppose that this book is an adequate history of even its restricted subject. It only tries to emphasize certain matters for some reason too often eschewed. Let him not suppose that by reading this book he will learn even the accessible essentials. On the contrary, rather than read it he will do far better to read two very great works: the *Confessions* and the *City of God* of Augustine. And, if there is still time, he should read the *Life of St. Martin* by Severus — which is short and lively — and glance, with discrimination, through the *Letters* of Jerome, the *Conferences* of Cassian, Salvian *On the Government of God,* the *Letters* and *Sermons* of Pope Leo, and the very readable *Letters* of Sidonius, all of which — although in varying degrees — are available in English translations.

Among English historical works on the period Gibbon on the whole still stands alone. Dill's *Roman Society in the Last Century of the Roman Empire* is also highly recommendable. Dudden's recent book on Ambrose is businesslike and may well serve as an introduction to the present volume. Hodgkin describes the political and military events in Italy in effective detail, and Duchesne's *Histoire Ancienne de l'Eglise* is a work of real talent which the English translation does not wholly obscure. Boissier's *La Fin du Paganisme* excels even Dill's work, but there is, unfortunately, no English translation.

An apology is due for the cavalier way in which I have entered a field where highly trained scholars are wont to dig unmolested. My excuse is that I wanted to learn what things they had exhumed, in order that I might indulge in meditations on them. That some rare scholar should serve as guide is devoutly to be wished for, but since, for more than a generation now, no such scholar has stepped forward, I think it proper that others, knowing not all they should yet something, offer such guidance as they can.

For many years the resources, and above all the courtesies, of the Harvard College Library have been at my disposal; yet even now I cannot pose as a trained classicist, scientist, theologian, or medievalist. To the classicist, for instance, I betray my defects in chapters I and IV, to the scientist in chapters II and III, to the theologian in chapters V and VI, and to the medievalist in chapters VII and VIII. I can therefore only remind all these of the virtues of patience and charity, begging them to remember that, in contrast to its parts, a whole is at once less easily circumscribed and more easily punctured. No doubt a little knowledge is a dangerous thing, but it is also true that where nothing is risked nothing is won.

Since, therefore, honesty as well as modesty forbids me to wish the reader a safe voyage, may I at least wish him storms instead of fog!

E. M. P.

17 Chestnut St.,
Boston, Mass.
April 1937

CONTENTS

Chapter VI: *FREE WILL*

Chapter VII: *MONASTICISM*

Chapter VIII: *THE PAPACY*

	Spain	Britain	Aquitaine	Northeast Gaul / Provence	Italy / Africa	Dalmatia	Danube	Constantinople	Egypt / Asia Minor	Syria	Persia
260					Cyprian				PLOTINUS		
268					Pontius						Mani
276											
284										Porphyry	
292											
300							Diocletian		Paul (hermit) / Anthony (hermit)		
304					Arnobius				Arius		
312					Lactantius					Eusebius	
320								Constantine		Iamblichus	
328					Aurelius Victor						
336											
344					Firmicus Maternus						
352				Victorinus					Athanasius		
360			Hilary of Poitiers / Ausonius		Damasus		Ulfilas		Oreibasos		
368										Cyril of Jerusalem	
376	Priscillian			Optatus	Martin / Ambrosiaster			Julian	Basil	Gregory Nazianzus / Gregory of Nyssa	
384											
392				Faustus of Mileve / Rufinus	AMBROSE / JEROME					John Chrysostom	
400	Theodosius I / Prudentius			Servius						Theodore of M.	
408	PELAGIUS (+ Celestius?)		Paulinus of Nola	SEVERUS	AUGUSTINE / Macrobius		Gratian / CASSIAN				
416			Rutilius		Innocent I / Boniface		Zosimus(?)				
424			Honoratus / Vigilantius		Paulinus (of Milan) / Possidius		Claudian				
432	Orosius		Germanus / Vincent	Eucherius / Celestine	Martianus Capella / Julian of Ecl.		Eutyches		Cyril of Alexandria / Nestorius		
440			Prosper / Lupus		LEO						
448			SALVIAN	Hilary of Arles	Maximus of Turin						
456	FAUSTUS of Riez				Patiens of Lyons						
464				Constantius of Lyons / Lucidus	Severinus (?)						
472					Claudianus Mamertus						
480			Ruric of Limoges	Sidonius	FELIX III				Zeno		
488				Remi of Rheims	Epiphanius of Pavia						
492					GELASIUS						

Year	Toleration	Evil	Cosmology	Natural Law	Politics	Justice on Earth	Free Will	Monasticism	Morals	Christology	Papacy	Church and State
260		evil in matter										
268												
276					cities fortified							
284												
292					totalitarian State							
300		evil in devil / dualism						first hermits				
308	toleration for Christians					civic virtue weakens						
316												
324										Christ a complete God		
332												
340												
348												
356	toleration debated		defence of natural law					pre-existence				
364			hierarchy of powers							Christ a created being		
372							F. W. in East	first Latin monks				theocracy looms
380					the temporal Church						State backs Rome / Petrine claim	
388			obstacle of devil				prev. grace (Milan)	monks scorned				Church defies
396			vogue of miracles			no J. on E.		fabrication of miracles?				Emperor
400	persecution by Church						predestination (Africa)					
408		man evil	divine despotism	one kind of event								universality of Church
416	paganism collapses					fame	F.W.(Pel.)		humility vs. truth			
424			astronomy			J. on E. for monks					foisting of canons	
432				miracles resisted			prev. grace (Rome)	monks triumph in Gaul			past binds future	
440			obstacle of devil		patriotism contracts				vogue of Virgin	Christ as two Persons		
448		Jehovah vs. saints			strategy of virtue	J. on E. for all		egoism		Christ a man as well?		Church loses State
456						O. T.	F. W. in Gaul	monks accepted				
464				miracles triumph								
472							predestination condemned in Gaul					
480	persecution by barbarians					temporal J. on E.						
488					Italian patriotism			fabrication of canons				Church defies State
492								monks' privileges				State ephemeral

THE MIND OF LATIN CHRISTENDOM

NOTES

(a) Two chronological charts are to be found on pages x and xi.

(b) From the abbreviated foot-note references the full biblio-graphical record may be found on pp. 657–674.

(c) The cross-references in the foot-notes are greatly amplified in the index, pp. 675–738.

CHAPTER I

THE THRESHOLD

A. THE ENLIGHTENMENT OF 373 [1]

THE city of Rome was at the centre of the Mediterranean and at the centre of the territory which she conquered and transformed into an Empire, but she remained always on the periphery of ancient civilization. Almost reversing the compass, the situation would have been nearly repeated if, in 1675, Brandenburg had conquered Europe.

So long as the great wars of conquest lasted, Rome influenced the East as much as the East influenced Rome; but with the return of normal conditions Rome was gradually submerged, first by Hellenistic, later by Oriental conceptions.[2] Even before the year 200 her two most distinguished scientists, Ptolemy and Galen, hailed respectively from Alexandria and Asia Minor, and after that year the preponderance of the East was further accentuated. Under the dynasty of the Severi, Oriental ways became the fashion in Rome; [3] the two greatest jurists, Ulpian and Papinian,[4] the two greatest philosophers, Plotinus and Porphyry,[5] the last three great scientists, Alexander of Aphrodisias, Diophantus, and Pappos,[6] all hailed from the eastern end of the Mediterranean.[7] Not one of them was a European. And the same is true of the six most influential religions of the Empire,[8] each of which, in its own way, was engaged in transforming the Roman world.

---

[1] It was in 373 that Ambrose became bishop, that Jerome decided to join the hermits of the East, and that Augustine became a Manichee: see pp. 255, 26 n. 151, & 63.

[2] Cumont 1929 [4] 7–8: as in architecture and industry; Lot 1927 161: as in jewelry, personal ornament, and dress.

[3] Cumont 1929 [4] 19.

[4] Cumont 1929 [4] 5. And perhaps Gaius too, who flourished just before 200: Ledlie 1914 5–8. On the influence of Greek legal conceptions on Roman law after 235 see Jolowicz 1932 518–30.

[5] Cumont 1929 [4] 5. Iamblichus and Sextus Empiricus might be added.

[6] Sarton 1927 I 314, 330, 337 and, on Philoponos, who flourished only after 500, see 416.

[7] On the literary talent of the time see Lot 1927 174–77.

[8] (1) Magna Mater — Asia Minor; (2) Isis — Egypt; (3) Baal — Syria; (4) Neoplatonism — Egypt and Syria (Plotinus, Porphyry, Iamblichus);

1

It is also worth observing that whereas six of the greatest Christian theologians of the years 200 to 373 were Africans,[9] eight of the ablest Emperors were born between the Danube and the Adriatic: [10] the thinkers grew up beside the hot desert, the men of action near the cold frontier. But Christians could be men of action too: Martin, the apostle of Gaul, was born of a Roman army officer stationed close to the Danube.

During these years from 200 to 373 Italy, and especially Rome, was being orientalized, while Spain, Gaul, Africa, and Britain were being Romanized. All were absorbing foreign cultures so fast that they had no surplus vitality with which to create. In the year 330 the capital of the Empire was officially transferred from Rome to Constantinople much as Brandenburg, had she conquered Europe in 1675, might in time have removed the capital of her Empire from Berlin to Paris.

We of today know that in the year 373 the western half of the Empire was about to fall; yet no one living then could reasonably have suspected this,[11] for, both physically and intellectually, her civilization seemed in many ways more advanced in that year than it had ever been before.[12]

Architecturally, for example, the Latin Empire's appearance had never been more imposing.[13] In some of the ter-

(5) Mithra & Mani — Persia; (6) Christianity — Palestine.

[9] (1) Tertullian — Carthage — fl. 210; (2) Clement — Alexandria — fl. 210; (3) Origen — Alexandria — fl. 235; (4) Cyprian — Carthage — fl. 250; (5) Arius — Alexandria — fl. 330; (6) Athanasius — Alexandria — fl. 346. Cyril of Jerusalem, Pope Damasus and Hilary of Poitiers may be added only after 350, and the greatest Greek Fathers: Basil, the Gregories, and John Chrysostom, only after 375. Lactantius was probably born in Italy but his career and reputation were wholly associated with Africa.

[10] (1) Aurelian — Pannonia — 262; (2) Claudius — Illyria — 265; (3) Carus — Dalmatia — 272; (4) Probus — Pannonia — 279; (5) Diocletian — Salona — 295; (6) Constantine the Great — Upper Moesia — 322; (7)

Constantius II — Pannonia — 367; (8) Valentinian — Pannonia — 372. These territories probably also produced the best soldiers: Lot 1927 120.

[11] Boissier 1909 II 6 192–94. Dill 1906 2 148–49 cites the *Letters* of Symmachus as evidence; and Troeltsch 1915 21 n. 1 cites *Sermon* # 81 of Augustine.

[12] It is possible, however, that the Empire's prestige abroad was on the decline by 375. In 360 is the first known case of a barbarian in the Roman service retaining his barbarian name instead of assuming a Roman name: Kurth 1919 I 125.

[13] The Christians did not begin the destruction of pagan temples until after 380: Babut 1912 213–16 & 220. Speaking of the city of Rome Lanciani 1899 47 says that 'at the beginning of the fifth century the great buildings still remained substantially

ritory — notably in Italy and Spain — there was less construction after the second century than before. Nevertheless, even in those lands, the appearance was then still as impressive as it had ever been, and in Africa, Dalmatia,[14] and Britain, construction continued very active in the fourth century. Only in Gaul had there been a serious destruction of buildings. Taking advantage of the internal disturbances of the year 275, the Franks and Alamanni had broken the Rhine frontier and sacked many of the finest cities of Gaul.[15] Only the walled cities like Trier, Autun, Lyons, and Narbonne were able to resist,[16] and urban prosperity never recovered. Many fragments of older construction have been found embedded in the walls that were built shortly after in order to prevent a recurrence of such a disaster.[17] This blight, however, had been of a year's duration only, and had not extended elsewhere. On the whole, therefore, construction continued to accumulate: [18] to the vast quantity of basilicas, theatres, arenas, baths, temples, aqueducts,[19] and private castles in town and country,[20] were now added Christian buildings,[21] and great walls too — along the frontiers and round the cities,[22] like the Aurelian wall round Rome.

The economic prosperity of this western half of the Empire was unquestionably now on the decline. Yet only in Italy can the distress have been acute. In Gaul conditions varied greatly: [23] Provence, if we except Arles, had declined; so had Autun, Lyons,[24] and Narbonne. On the other hand the valley of the Moselle, with the great frontier city of Trier at its centre, was enjoying an unprecedented prosperity,[25] while the wealth and fertility of Aquitaine, and especially of Auvergne, remained a by-word throughout the fifth century.[26] Of Spain

---

intact, and a few additional were made to the list of existing monuments.'

[14] Mommsen 1886 V 203–04.

[15] Jullian 1913 IV 599.

[16] Ibid. 600–01.

[17] Ibid. 600 n. 3.

[18] Although the *rate* of increase was presumably on the decline.

[19] Jullian 1926 VII 114 & 135 & VIII 52–54 & 222; Lot 1927 155–56.

[20] Ibid. 145.

[21] San Giorgio Maggiore in Naples

was built in 367–382, and Santa Maria Maggiore in Nocera in about 392–408: Rivoira 1925 252–53 & 259. On the city of Rome see also Duchesne 1911 III [6] 655–58, & Dufourcq L'Av. 1910 IV [5] 100–02.

[22] Lot 1927 17.

[23] Bloch 1911 334–83.

[24] Jullian 1926 VII 27 & 183.

[25] Ibid. 379, citing Ausonius.

[26] Bloch 1911 355 & 360–61; Jullian 1926 VII 90–92, 147, & 282.

we cannot be so specific, but from all accounts her prosperity continued, with a lively trade and a well developed mining industry in addition to her agriculture.[27] Probably the most flourishing Latin province during the fourth century was Proconsular Africa.[28] She had been spared the many disastrous turmoils of the third century, and it was in the fourth that camels were first imported in quantity from Egypt, contributing to an era of great economic development.[29] Of Britain we know much less, but it has been calculated that she reached the peak of her prosperity only in the first half of the fourth century.[30] Britain had never been much more than a Roman outpost; yet her agricultural capacity may be roughly gauged by the fact that in the year 358 the grain commandeered there by the army for shipment to the mouth of the Rhine required repeated crossings from London by a specially built fleet of six hundred vessels.[31]

It is an irritating but undeniable fact that civilization tends to follow wealth. Why should it not? In about the year 373 the concentrations of wealth in the West were chiefly in Rome, Roman or Proconsular Africa, Spain, Aquitaine, Arles, Trier, and along the Dalmatian coast.[32] And it was from precisely these territories that the fourth century Latin intellectual talent sprang.[33]

When Cæsar conquered the Gauls they could barely read or write, and none could understand the spoken Latin tongue. Yet within a century Latin had everywhere become the current written language; [34] after the second century, Celtic writing was confined to wills, medical receipts, and magical

---

27 Cf. Gibbon 1776 ff. ch. 31 (345).

28 Salvian *D.G.D.* VII §§ 84–87.

29 Mommsen 1886 VI 340.

30 Ward 1911 9.

31 Julian *Letter to the Athenians* 280A says 600. Zosimus *Historia Nova* III 5 § 2 says 800, but he wrote after 450.

32 On Dalmatia see Mommsen 1886 V 203–04.

33 Rome contributed Ambrosiaster, Praetextatus, Probus, Flavian, Symmachus, as well as most of the Popes of the day, including Damasus. Africa furnished Victorinus, Optatus, Faustus, Augustine, and Macrobius.

Aquitaine furnished Hilary, Ausonius, Paulinus of Nola, Sulpicius Severus, and Rutilius Namatianus. Spain furnished Pacian, Priscillian, Theodosius, and Prudentius. Dalmatia furnished Jerome and Rufinus.

34 Jullian 1920 VI 109–11. The most backward regions of Gaul were Brittany, Normandy, Rouergue, and Gévaudan: ibid. 115. Bloch 1911 385–86 says we cannot tell how fast or slowly the spoken Celtic was discarded. The fate of the lesser indigenous tongues of Gaul, Iberian, Ligurian, Aquitanian, Lusitanian, and Italiot, is even more obscure: Jullian ibid. 112.

incantations;[35] and in the course of the fourth century Latin so entirely superseded Celtic that the French language contains hardly more than half a dozen words of Celtic derivation.[36] By the year 373, in fact, Gaul, rather than Italy, was the recognized centre of Latin poetry and rhetoric. The same thing was true, although in a lesser degree, of Roman Africa. Here the native Berber tongue had retreated before the Punic, and the Punic in its turn had been eclipsed by Greek and Latin. In the early third century even the nobility of some of the provincial cities spoke only Punic,[37] but by the end of the fourth century Latin was the tongue of all but the illiterate, and Latin education, especially in science and philosophy, was here pre-eminent.[38]

The persistence of civilization was not, however, confined to the West; here there had perhaps been more progress, but only because the culture had originally been so crude. Other signs of vitality in which East and West shared jointly appear in the varied fields of warfare, jurisprudence, natural philosophy, religious toleration, education, and literature.

It seems paradoxical to say that the Roman army was never more efficient than in the years when it lost the western half of the Empire, yet this is the opinion of the military historian.[39] When we realize that the soldiers in the Roman armies were now chiefly barbarians,[40] and that the barbarians against whom they fought had had every opportunity of studying Roman military methods, such victories as those won with inferior numbers by Constantine, Valentinian, and Gratian seem hardly credible,[41] while the feats of the armies of Stilicho and Aetius [42] in the fifth century and of Belisarius in the sixth are hardly less impressive. Even under the Emperor Julian, who, although a brave, was also a headstrong general, very inferior Roman forces routed the fierce Ala-

---

[35] Ibid. 111.

[36] Dill 1906 2 407; Jullian 1920 VI 117–18 gives the words. German was currently understood along the Rhine: Steinhausen 1913 66.

[37] Mommsen 1886 VI 357; Grupp 1903 I 517.

[38] Mommsen 1886 VI 325–29. Cf. Salvian *D.G.D.* VII § 16.

[39] Young 1916 I 488–90, 502, 522–23 & 571–77. Cf. Ammianus *R.G.* XXIV 6 § 14; Dill 1906 2 288–90; & Boissier 1909 II 6 384.

[40] Steinhausen 1913 72; Lot 1927 122–23.

[41] Cf. Jullian 1926 VIII 123–24.

[42] Aetius was born in 396 and died in 454: Lot 1927 239–40 & 247–48.

manni in 357,[43] and proved their tactical superiority over the
no less warlike and much more civilized [44] Persian forces in
the disastrous but heroic campaign of 363. Whether these
feats were chiefly due to the Roman superiority in officers,
organization, discipline, equipment,[45] or tactics [46] is not easy
to determine, but in any case the underlying cause must have
been a higher intelligence. Why, if this were so, half the
Empire was conquered, is a very different question. We know
that some of the most powerfully fortified cities of the frontier
when captured by the barbarians were not defended even by
a skeleton garrison. Faulty military strategy might account
for this,[47] but faulty political control is the more usual explanation.

In the domain of jurisprudence, evolution continued for
at least two hundred years after the golden or classical age
had ended in 235. This earlier law had corresponded in
many ways to the English common law, in which a primitive
formalism grew, through long experience with actual cases,
into a system where general principles of equity tempered —
yet without supplanting — the earlier strictness. There procedure rather than substance still governed, and the act rather
than the intent; there too individual rights resisted the exigencies of public policy, respecting the freedom and sanctity
of obligations.

Anarchy followed for fifty years. Then, with the accession
of Diocletian in 285, new tendencies appeared, and although
the dates of these changes can only be in rare cases determined [48] it is generally agreed that most of them occurred
before 440. How much of the initiative was Eastern, how

[43] Ammianus *R.G.* XVI 12 §§ 2,
26 & 63: 13,000 Romans against 35,-
000 Alamanni. Cf. Orosius *H.A.P.*
VII 29 § 15; and on Gratian's victory
over them ibid. 33 § 8; & cf. Bloch
1922 288; Jullian 1926 VII 187, 193 &
196; & Lot 1927 219.
[44] The Persians were disciplined
and also armoured: Ammianus *R.G.*
XXIV 6 § 8 & XXV 1 § 12.
[45] The Germanic armies rarely
used armour: Dalton 1927 I 232–33.
[46] The barbarians with the Ro-

mans often used their own tactics:
Lot 1927 272–73. Ordinarily they
used the wedge, and when this failed
to pierce the Roman third line it was
easily surrounded: Gebhardt 1922
I [6] 55. On Roman stratagems see
Hodgkin 1892 I [2] 192. Bloch 1922
288 says the Roman superiority lay
in training and tactics.
[47] Rarely now did the Romans
concentrate more than 6000: Lot
1927 267.
[48] Jolowicz 1932 493.

much Western, is also doubtful; [49] but in any event the sixth
century *Corpus Juris* of Justinian is no more than a tardy
compilation.[50]

In considering these changes it must be remembered that
it is rather their tendency than their magnitude which is
important; for law is by its nature stolid, moving, if at all,
rather sluggishly round a centre. Certain conceptions lie at
the basis of all legal systems, so that any slightest tendency to
give these a new orientation is likely to be symptomatic of far
greater changes in the living environment. Such are, for instance, a man's right to abuse as well as use his own property; [51] the rights of buyer and seller — provided there be no
fraud — to outwit or circumvent each other; [52] respect for the
sanctity of obligations; the principle that no man shall be
enriched at the expense of another; [53] the principle of protecting the deserving and innocent and of penalizing the undeserving.[54]

Technically, the refinement of a system of law consists in
devising an ever more perfect protection of individual rights
and in enhancing the benefits which these may be allowed to
confer. Here the change after 285 from reliance on form
to reliance on substance marks a definite progress. Under
the old law, for instance, a creditor's rights could not be assigned because there was no form of action against the debtor
available to the assignee; but under the new law, since the
debtor's obligation subsisted, the assignee could bring suit.
Just before 235 the jurist Paulus had recognized the assignee's
right, but the remedy open remained indirect and inse-
cure.[55] In this case the assignability of the right enhanced
the benefit to be derived from it. Of similar effect were the
remedies now offered to secure not merely damages for breach
of contract but a specific performance under the eagle eye of
the court.[56]

The law of sales, too, was now further refined: title no
longer passed automatically with delivery but only if either

[49] Karlowa 1885 I 943–47; Jolowicz 1932 518–30.
[50] See Baviera 1912 108.
[51] Ibid. 75.
[52] Ibid. 106–07.
[53] Ibid. 77, citing Cicero and
Paulus; Jolowicz 1932 517.

[54] Baviera 1912 82.
[55] Jolowicz 1932 419, 422, & 424.
Paulus was of unknown origin but
very possibly an Italian: *Encicl. Ital.*
1933 XXVI 231.
[56] Jolowicz 1932 526.

the payment had been made or credit definitely extended; [57] and earnest money was now no longer treated as mere evidence of a contract but as a forfeit put up in case of nonperformance.[58]

A more important change than these was the new attitude towards the written document. Before 235 it had merely been so much evidence of a transaction,[59] later it might itself constitute that transaction. On the other hand a document was no longer decisive evidence of intent: [60] evidence could be introduced to show a contradictory intent. Thus in the case of a simulated transaction, evidence could now be introduced of a mutual intent that it be not real in fact.[61] The criterion became what the parties meant rather than what they said.

These changes, however, form but a small proportion of those which the new era witnessed. Far more important historically, at least, was the unmistakable tendency to subordinate the demands of individual justice to the requirements of social justice — a tendency with which our own twentieth century is already familiar. One instance is the inclination to discriminate against the creditor, arising from the laudable desire to protect those who cannot protect themselves. The danger here is that the unscrupulous can often successfully masquerade as unfit. Take the case of a bachelor who is heavily in debt. By the new law he can, by marrying, give his wife an underlying lien on his assets as security for her dowry, thereby transferring them from honest creditors to a perhaps wholly subservient wife.[62] Similarly, according to the new bankruptcy law, the bankrupt could not only avoid a prison sentence but keep such assets as he needed in order to escape destitution.[63] In the same spirit it was now enacted that a thing pledged or mortgaged as security for a loan could not be seized according to the terms of the agreement but only according to the terms laid down by the statute.[64] Each one of these laws undermined the principle of the sanctity of contracts, and, in so doing, hampered the debtor's chance to borrow cheaply.

[57] Jolowicz 1932 521.
[58] Ibid. 521–22.
[59] Ibid. 431 & 522–23.
[60] Ibid. 494.

[61] Ibid. 515.
[62] Ibid. 516 & 520.
[63] Ibid. 516–17.
[64] Ibid. 516.

In other cases the owner is the one discriminated against. A purchaser in good faith of stolen goods was, under the old law, liable to restore the goods to their rightful owner; under the new law he was protected.[65] This change was commercially expedient, but it showed little respect for the time-honoured principle of *caveat emptor,* and consequently served, at least incidentally, to protect the unscrupulous buyer and thus facilitate the disposal of stolen goods. The new law also discriminated against the owner by exempting the custodian from liability in case of theft unless he could be proved guilty of negligence.[66] Suppose the custodian says he was robbed; will it always be easy for the owner to prove collusion or negligence? These cases, which involve the penalizing of one of two supposedly innocent parties, suggest not so much a prejudice against property owners as a new confidence that the courts can cope with fraud. At the same time there remained the consolation that, if injustice were done, it would be to the rich rather than to the poor.

In another category is the case where a thief adds to the value of the thing stolen — as by making a bar of silver into an ornament. Under the old law he must restore the ornament, thereby actually enriching the owner. This seems fair enough — for it was undeniably his silver. But the later law observed that this solution conflicted with the principle that no one should be enriched at the expense of another. A penalty could be imposed on the thief in the criminal courts, but since he owned the value of his labour the owner must repay this amount [67] — which might well be enough to cover the fine and so allow the thief to escape the alternative of prison or death — a good instance, this, of the evolution from the old formalism to the new equity.[68]

But by far the greatest surface change was in the status of persons. In early Roman days the power of the *pater familias* over wife, children, and slaves was virtually unrestricted, and this power, though broken here and there, still subsisted at the beginning of the fourth century. The system, however, was actually already long obsolete, and after 323, with the added pressure of Christianity, it crumbled fast. And not only was

[65] Baviera 1912 97–98.
[66] Jolowicz 1932 529–30.
[67] Ibid. 517.
[68] Ibid. 516 & 525–26.

the status of women, children, slaves, and other dependent persons vastly improved: the Church also procured legislation adjusting such matters as marriage — with restrictions on consanguinity — divorce, concubinage, inheritance, etc. to suit her own opinions.[69] Primitive law here became modern law almost over-night.

The great jurists of the earlier or classical period undeniably laid down many of the principles out of which this new law grew; intellectually theirs was the more creative period — when the ideas were first born. The full realization of their ideas, however, in the form of co-ordinated laws and decisions, was the work of the fourth century.[70] Yet can we safely affirm that the one system was clearly superior to the other — that, as time passed, there was more perfection rather than less? Pragmatically each system was doubtless that most appropriate to its age; but to say this is to beg the question. Perhaps we may say that the later law, which cast aside the despotism of the *pater familias,* which improved the legal status of the least efficient, which preferred a discretionary equity to a rigid form, which limited freedom of contract in the public interest, and which risked indulgence to the wrong-doer in order the more surely to safeguard the innocent, was a law less primitive, more biologically evolved, less concerned with the nicety of defending pre-existing rights and more concerned with a fairer readjustment of those rights. Thus were the rights of the individual more and more sacrificed for the supposed good of the State. But this effort, when we compare it to the theological development of this time, seems by contrast more enlightened than wise. Its weakness lay in the substitution of experimental legislation based on theories of social need, in place of judicial decisions based on long practice,[71] in its reliance on divining the future instead of on reading the past. It introduced the deductive method of the reformer in place of the inductive or empirical method of the jurist.[72] By substituting a government of men for a government of laws it defied the ancient legal maxim that ' hard cases make bad laws ',[73] and by replacing individ-

---

[69] Baviera 1912 71 & 111–16; Jolowicz 1932 518–20.

[70] That is, somewhere between 235 and 426.

[71] Karlowa 1885 932; Jolowicz 1932 420.

[72] Jolowicz 525.

[73] Ibid. 516.

ualism with paternalism [74] it discouraged individual responsibility and initiative. In a word it accepted the fallacy that a State, because it is impersonal, must be impartial, and because impartial must be just. It was forgotten that human ignorance and greed prosper as much in public as in private life, that justice requires not only impartiality but wisdom, and that wisdom cannot be created by imperial appointment but only by experience, concentration, discrimination, and an inborn talent. Public office too often breeds over-confidence, which in turn breeds rashness.

With the accession of Diocletian, however, the die was cast: henceforth the Roman State, patriarchal now in power as well as age, helplessly succumbed to the allurements of a benevolent despotism.

It has been argued [75] that the later Roman law actually undermined the principle of retributive justice, and that this change was due to the incorporation into law of specifically Christian principles — that justice came to be conceived in terms of needs rather than deserts, in terms of mercy rather than of impartiality. But there is not only no evidence that any such change really did occur, there is also no evidence that Christian ideals envisaged any such revolutionary change. Not only did Christianity always differentiate civil or legal from divine justice; throughout the fourth century even that divine justice itself rewarded exclusively and emphatically according to merit. To be sure many who deserved damnation were spared through the divine mercy, but the salvation of one was never jeopardized in order to facilitate the salvation of some other. Thus, as between individuals, divine — rather more than civil — justice took pains to be meticulously fair.

Nevertheless it is certain that in the fourth century the

[74] Jolowicz 1932 446 says that after 285 the government began 'to place such burdens on its subjects, either by way of taxation or labour, that the individual appeared to be merely an instrument for the preservation of the State, and compulsory social organization reached a degree of intensity that has probably never been equalled.'
And on 517 he says that 'together with this "humane" attitude of the law, there is also found an almost pathetic confidence in the power of legislation to do away with evils of an economic character by mere prohibition, and a taste for excessive regulation by statute of matters to which fixed rules can hardly, by their very nature, be applied with success.'
[75] By Riccobono: see Baviera 1912 82.

humanitarian spirit was spreading fast in all fields: [76] a
feeling that rights, if they were to continue to command
respect, must be more fairly distributed; that, as in the case
of slavery, human rights had precedence over property rights.
But was this instinctive groping towards the humane, this
impatience with human misery, an artificial Christian importation? Why should it not have been an indigenous and
natural growth? The most conspicuous impulse was of
course Christianity; [77] at the same time it is certain that only
a change in the Roman heart could have brought about
Christianity's triumph.[78] A deep concern for the unfortunate is evident, for instance, in the legislation of that arch-
enemy of Christianity the Emperor Diocletian,[79] while it was
the Christian Constantine who repealed the law of 228 which
had deprived the father of the legal right to kill his sons.[80]
And the effort of the pagan Emperor Julian to eradicate the
immoral and brutal elements in paganism is well known.[81]
It is true that slavery was deplored by Christians, but so it
was by the group of pagans whose conversation is recorded by

[76] Dill 1906 [2] 278–81. According to
Rostovtzeff 1926 356, this spirit is
first discernible in the legislation inspired by the jurists (the greatest of
whom were Syrian) in the early third
century.
[77] Jullian 1926 VII 137–38.
[78] The Mithraic religion, so popular in the early fourth century, required an unceasing warfare against
the powers of evil and a very strict
personal morality: Cumont 1929 [4]
146–47. The Neoplatonist Porphyry
of the later third century (arch-
enemy of the Christians: Whittaker
1901 145–46, & Augustine D.C.D.
passim) wrote his most original
treatise, the De Abstinentia, to argue
that a man should not eat meat because he can live without it, and, in
killing animals, is guilty of gross injustice towards them: see especially
III §§ 18 & 26. And the early fourth
century Neoplatonist Iamblichus
recommends the study of philosophy
because it tends to promote human
sympathy and love: Whittaker 1901
132.
[79] Baviera 1912 114; Lot 1927 22–
23.
[80] Muirhead 1886 346; Baviera

1912 114–15; on other cases of his
cruelty see Jullian 1926 VII 109 n. 6
& 110 n. 7. But Fustel de Coulanges
1891 II 92 says that he mitigated
some of the worst abuses of slavery.
[81] Dill 1906 [2] 34–35, 72 & 99–100;
Duchesne 1910 II [4] 328; Carter 1911
140; Batiffol 1924 [2] 2–3; Nock 1933
159. Lot 1927 199 says that Valentinian I, the Christian Emperor who
followed Julian, was pitilessly cruel;
on the other hand Jolowicz 1932 443
says that ' in 365 Valentinian I made
it his special concern to protect the
poorer classes [plebs] against illegal
exactions both of the tax-collecting
authorities and the great landowners
[potentiores].' It may be that his
cruelty was roused by the fear of
black magic and treason, while his
heart was at the same time touched
by the misery of the poor and innocent. Moreover Lot 213 recognizes —
as does Maurice 1927 119 — that on
the whole the humanitarian preoccupation of the Christian Emperors is
revealed in their legislation. Jullian
1926 VII 274–75 & VIII 11–14 speaks
of the high quality of the fourth in
contrast to the first century Emperors.

Macrobius.[82] Both merely echoed what decent Romans had
been saying ever since Seneca.[83] Yet, although the Christians
joined the pagans in trying to mitigate slavery's abuses, they
never, officially or unofficially, agitated to secure its abolition.[84] It is true that in their crusade against the cruelties
practised in the arena Christians encountered strong pagan
opposition. But it must not be forgotten that, whereas to
Christians the games seemed to mock the memory of their
martyrs, to pagans they seemed a gesture of loyalty to Rome's
majestic past.[85] It is absurd, of course, to qualify the Christian's claim to be the great champion of human misfortune,
the great democrat[86] and humanitarian;[87] yet it must not
be forgotten that the wholesale conversions were possible
largely because towards the Christian ideal the pagan was
keenly predisposed.[88] The whole age, while outwardly dis-
integrating, was inwardly undergoing a process of moral
awakening and purification.

That the civil law was being affected, however judiciously
or injudiciously, by a humane concern for the unfortunate
is surely evidence of a persisting enlightenment. But more
remarkable evidence, perhaps, in this age of violent moral
and religious ferment was the general loyalty to the ordinary

---

[82] *Saturnalia* I § 11.

[83] Whittaker 1923 21.

[84] Carlyle 1927 I [2] 50. However,
many individuals like Melania the
Younger in 406, emancipated all their
slaves. It is said that she had 8000.
See Goyau 1921 90; Jullian 1926 VIII
164: & Dudden 1935 544.

[85] Dill 1906 [2] 55–56; Lot 1927 207.
The otherwise gentle Symmachus
tried to perpetuate the splendour of
the games because they symbolized
the splendour of the Empire: Boissier 1909 II [6] 169 & 174. Augustine's
disciple Olypius, while still a Manichee, was torn between the horror
and thrill of gladiatorial combats:
Augustine *Confessions* VI 8; although
a law of Constantine had forbidden them in 325: Jullian 1926 VII
138–40.

[86] In most pagan religions special
dispensations were sold at high
prices: Nock 1933 56–57. This was
hardly a democratic procedure.

[87] Cf. Dill 1906 [2] 56–57; & Augustine *Letter* # 133.

[88] The pagan Roman of this time
had a rather higher standard of
morality and a greater liking for un-
ostentatious living than ever before:
Dill 1906 [2] 160–61, 172 & 210; &
Boissier 1909 II [6] 191, 270 & 277.
Both writers probably had Macrobius' *Saturnalia* particularly in mind,
especially III §§ 13–17. But the
pruriency of the theatre, which ca-
tered chiefly to the lower classes, was
apparently as bad as ever: Dill 1906 [2]
56–57 & 139. Even Christianity,
moreover, showed no very intense
sympathy for the poor: Dill 1906 [2]
211; and the same was probably true
of Mithraism: Cumont 1929 [4] 145;
and of Manichæism: Burkitt 1925
59–60. Like the Neoplatonists, these
pagan cults laid stress on the duty of
the individual to avoid injuring
others rather than on the duty of
conferring positive benefits.

processes of natural law. The early Greeks, Jews, and Romans alike were ready to believe that they could, by certain
ritualistic acts, affect the will of their divinities. Such a confidence survived in some degree, and in the fourth century
even showed signs of revival; but no such change was yet
affecting the minds of cultivated men.

Plotinus, the renowned Alexandrian philosopher, who
taught with such success in Rome in about 260, attacks
those who

assert diseases to be Spirit-Beings and boast of being able to expel
them by formula: this pretension may enhance their importance
with the crowd, gaping upon the powers of magicians; but they
can never persuade the intelligent that disease arises otherwise
than from such causes as overstrain, excess, deficiency, putrid
decay.[89]

And he observes elsewhere that

Not even a God would have the right to deal a blow for the un-
warlike: the law of nature decrees that to come safe out of battle
is for fighting men, not for those who pray. The harvest comes
home not for praying but for tilling; healthy days are not for
those who neglect their health: we have no right to complain of
the ignoble getting the richer harvest if they are the only workers
in the fields, or the best.[90]

Yet the great Neoplatonist has rightfully earned the reputation of being among the most abstract and intangible of
philosophers.

Among the followers of Plotinus, however, there are signs
of degeneration. Even his own disciple Porphyry, although
he denies that animal sacrifice, or anything comparable, can
affect the wills of the beneficent gods, is inclined to think
that the demons — perhaps because of the fact that their
powers were limited — could be affected by such practices.[91]
Of the precise attitude of Iamblichus, who flourished in about
330, there is doubt; [92] but Sallust, living some forty years later,
specifically denied the power of prayers or sacrifices to influence the will of the gods, though he confessed that he did not
see how the mass of men could ever be really weaned from

[89] *Enneads* II 9 § 14.
[90] Ibid. III 2 § 8.
[91] Whittaker 1901 117–18.
[92] Whittaker ibid. 125 defends

Iamblichus from the charge of dabbling in magic; but Bidez 1930 78
thinks he took it seriously.

this superstition.[93] That the Emperor Julian, on the other hand, eagerly plunged into the weird lore of theurgy, is notorious. He was, to be sure, young and amateurish; nevertheless he was neither uncultivated nor stupid.

And as the Neoplatonists were of two minds regarding this fundamental attitude towards the supernatural, so were the Christians.[94] Among the humble, especially with the text of the Bible constantly before them, a faith that they might come to acquire a certain power over God's will, was inevitable. Yet that such a view was far from universal among Christians and not even a peculiarity to which they were unduly prone, is indicated by the attack by the Christian Firmicus Maternus of Sicily in 346 on the Phrygian propaganda which claimed that the due performance of their rites was an infallible device for causing crops to grow:

The farmer knows when he ought to plow, to sow, to reap the crops ripened by the sun, to thresh them when dried. This is the physical explanation, these are the true sacrifices which are performed in annual labour by men of sound mind; this is all that God required: that men should respect the ordained laws of the seasons in the gathering of the harvest. Why, for the sake of this, must the fictions of a miserable [god's] death be insisted on? [95]

A man's belief in his power to influence the will of the gods — and so be himself the cause of supernatural events — is more a matter of disposition and education than of any specific faith. Therefore in both Neoplatonism and Christianity the more enlightened struggled to temper the credulity of the rest.[96] It is rarely a religion that is the cause of superstition; on the contrary, a religion well organized and directed will often do much to eradicate it. But if the leaders lose either their enlightenment or their leadership, faith can grow superstitious over-night. It is not the name, but the thing, that counts. Until the end of the fourth century, certainly, the enlightened view still shone.

We might expect that a triumphant Christianity would do its utmost to discredit religious toleration. Yet for some

---

[93] Although he always viewed it with abhorrence: Maurice 1927 118–19.

[94] Whittaker 1901 136.

[95] De Errore Prof. Relig. 3 § 4.

[96] See pp. 185–92, 226 n. 28, 456–60, & 517–18 for the controversy over Martin; & cf. Cumont 1929⁴ 185.

time little or nothing was done. For one thing the idea of freedom, having been sacred to Christians for three hundred years, was not to be casually or hastily discarded. Furthermore there must have been an instinct among the more enlightened that the time for repression, although it might come later, had not come yet. If the pagans, who in 327 still constituted nine tenths of the population, were to be converted, the Christian dogma itself required elasticity rather than crystallization. The dogma was in that year still an amorphous thing, green, pliable, with a certain capacity for further growth. From Paul to Athanasius there had been a steady progress under what might be called a regime of *laissez faire*. Trusting God's sure guidance and mocking the puny laws of the State, Christianity had come to temporal as well as spiritual greatness. This growth must be allowed freely to go on.

The Romans, moreover — and the Christians were still Romans — had always been intellectually liberal; being a practical people they had always allowed those whom they conquered, so long as they acted as they were told to, to think as they liked.[97] The Christians had not been persecuted because of their philosophy; their crime was an unwillingness to do as they were told. Of this Diocletian's policy is an illustration: Mithraism and Manichæism were analogous as philosophies,[98] but because the Mithraist chose to fight the evil demons by serving in the Roman army,[99] while the Manichees shrank from all acts of physical violence,[100] Diocletian honoured the one [101] but persecuted the other.[102] The Mithraist was a good citizen; the Manichee, like the Christian, seemed a public enemy.[103]

Nor did Christianity, in succeeding to the Roman inheritance in 323, show any impatience to break with this tradition. One reason doubtless was that Athanasians and Arians were struggling for supremacy, and neither dared, as a Church, to persecute for fear of a later retaliation. When the

---

[97] Lot 1927 26. And Whittaker 1901 16 says that the Neoplatonists maintained the Hellenistic tradition of toleration.
[98] See pp. 31–33, & 63–65.
[99] Cumont 1913 [3] 39.

[100] Stoop 1909 36–37.
[101] Cumont 1913 [3] 49.
[102] Stoop 1909 34 & 37–38. See Dufourcq *L'Av.* 1910 IV[5] 52 on the Edicts of 296 & 302.
[103] Stoop 1909 38.

Emperor Constantius began to exercise physical pressure in order to promote the Arian cause, the Athanasian bishop, Hilary of Poitiers, cried out:

But now, alas, worldly considerations are the recommendations to the divine faith, and, so long as factiousness is associated with His name, Christ is revealed as if divested of His virtue. The Church, who won believers by suffering exile and imprisonment, now commands faith by threatening exile and imprisonment; she who was once consecrated by the cruelty of her persecutors now swings to and fro according to the respect shown her by her communicants. She who has become great by priests driven to flight now herself drives her own priests away. She glories in being loved by the world — she who could not be Christ's did the world not hate her.[104]

To be sure other circumstances might have suggested another view; the fact remains, nevertheless, that Christianity did cherish the principle of toleration and abandoned it only reluctantly as the need of maintaining social, and even political, cohesion among Romans made centralization and authority unavoidable. A generation after Hilary the issue was brought to a head by the activities of the Spanish heretic Priscillian. At first the Church authorities — notably Ambrose and Pope Damasus — encouraged the intervention of the State in order to check the spread of the contagion; [105] but when the State not only interfered but in 385 actually executed Priscillian and several of his followers because of their belief in Manichæan magic, this was done in the face of the opposition of Ambrose, of the new Pope Siricius, and of many independent bishops like Martin of Tours.[106]

The legislation after 323 was, except under Julian from 361 to 363, invariably Christian, but it does not follow that it was always influenced by Christian policy, even when it directly concerned religion. As we have said, the first legislation against the Manichees was under the pagan Diocletian, and the periodical re-enactment of these laws thereafter merely maintained the pagan tradition. The purpose was very evidently to check the rising popularity among the vulgar of superstitious practices — especially of irresponsible

[104] *Contra Arianos vel Maxentium* §4.
[105] Duchesne 1910 II 4 533.
[106] Ibid. 538–39; & cf. Jullian 1926 VII 299 n. 3.

prophecy [107] and magic.[108] Perhaps these were never a fully accredited element in the dogmas of any of the more important faiths, but rather excrescences which attached themselves to these bodies. Here a careful distinction must be made between mere belief in the possibility of true prophecy and magic, and the actual dabbling in these occult arts. Diocletian, for instance, was outwardly at least, a Mithraist, and the Mithraists were firm believers in both the power of demons and the art of the astrologer.[109] Yet he enacted legislation against the Manichees whose beliefs were in many ways so similar. The patriotism of the one in contrast to the quietism of the other was doubtless one reason, but it is probable that another lay in the Mithraic reluctance and the Manichæan proneness to utilize these occult powers of prophecy for irresponsible and perhaps destructive ends.[110] For fatalism in any form is dangerous. So long as it can reconcile itself with action, as in Mithraism, the danger may be averted; but so soon as it belittles action, stressing instead a negativity which must be passive, choosing rather to learn than to actualize the future, the poison of destruction is introduced and the State roused to resist.

That the attack was on this generic excrescence rather than on any specific faith is indicated by the fate which attended two Neoplatonists in the middle of the fourth century — a fate which, so far as we know, was not shared by any Manichees. In 335 a certain Sopater, disciple of the Neoplatonist Iamblichus, was put to death on a charge of magic; [111] and later, under Valens, another Neoplatonist, Maximus, was executed because he had allowed himself to be professionally consulted regarding the identity of Valens' successor.[112] The

107 Martroye 1930 672–75.

108 Maurice 1927 & Martroye 1930 *passim;* Coster 1935 12 & 15.

109 Cumont 1913 [3]: on demons 113–14 & 172, on astrology 126.

110 Mani originally proscribed magic: Stoop 1909 21–23. But a religion which preached the independent power of demons was bound to succumb to magic. In the fourth century at any rate the Manichees were regarded as the arch-magicians: Maurice 1927 116; and in 385 Priscillian was condemned as both a Mani-

chee and a magician: Stoop 1909 98, & Duchesne 1910 II [4] 536–37. Evidently this identification was not new, for Diocletian's law of 296 was entitled ' De maleficis et Manichaeis ': Stoop 1909 34 n. 1. Augustine *Contra Faustum* XIV § 11, says that ' there is an unconscious worship of idols and devils in their legends.'

On Manichæan astrology, see pp. 341 n. 36, 443–44, & 450.

111 Whittaker 1901 132.

112 Ibid. 135; & cf. Dudden 1935 160–62. For other cases see Hodgkin

saints of the sixth century in Gaul did not hesitate to intimi-
date the Merovingian kings by threats that they would invoke supernatural forces; [113] but the fourth century Roman
still clung, if rather desperately, to a natural world, and it is
probable indeed that many of the pagan creeds lost the good-
will of the State partly because, in contrast to Christianity,
they tended more and more to encourage a defiance of that
natural law [114] on which all civil, in contrast to theocratic,[115]
governments are founded. Doubtless as Christianity's re-
spectability rose that of the rival faiths fell, and they became
the havens of all the extravagant notions which they could
not, in their extremity, afford to repudiate. The debasement
of Neoplatonism, under Iamblichus and his successors, is
contemporaneous with the alliance between Christianity and
the State.[116]

Fourth century Christianity, therefore, remained true to the
Roman tradition of tolerating all beliefs, but of not tolerating
any acts which might harm the State. The Neoplatonist
Maximus was executed because he had identified himself with
a practice that promoted anarchy. For suppose that not
only the identity of Valens' successor, but also the month and
year of that succession, had appeared divulged. The vulgar,
taken in by prophecy, would be easily tempted to rally to
the support of this successor, who, one may be assured, was
already plotting to depose Valens and usurp the Imperial
Office.[117] Even if Valens himself, the Church authorities,
and other enlightened persons were wholly sceptical of such
prophecies — which they certainly were not [118] — they must

1892 I 2 210–12; & on Libanius see
Thorndike 1923 I 538.
  113 See Gregory of Tours *History*
IV § 2.
  114 Maurice 1927 110 & 115; & see
Boissier 1909 II 6 265–66 on Flavian.
  115 In the Dark Ages to come
Christendom may have been saved
from a theocratic rule because the
rulers of the West were un-Romanized barbarians, whereas the Church
remained in the control of Romans
or the descendants of Romans. Thus
each was jealous of its own traditions
and prerogatives.
  116 On Neoplatonic magic see p.
444. On Neoplatonic astrology see

Cumont 1929 4 281 line 15, 168 (on
Iamblichus), & 288 lines 12–15 & 293
lines 38–40 (on Proclus). For the
view of Macrobius — who wrote
shortly after 400 — see *Commentary*
I § 19. Cf. Maurice 1927 110.
  The Stoics were no less addicted to
astrology: Cumont 1929 4 153, 156, &
160; Maurice 1927 110.
  117 Coster 1935 16.
  118 See Dill 1906 2 20; Maurice
1927 118; & Cumont 1929 4 167,
where he cites Firmicus Maternus.
Even the famous Alexandrian astron-
omer Ptolemy, who lived in the second century, was a firm believer in
astrology: Boquet 1925 131.

have been obliged to deal sharply with such prophets in order
to restrain the madness of the people. The Christian Arnobius, living in the early fourth century, believed that the demons wielded wide powers; [119] and even the most orthodox
Christians were ready, as we shall see, to attribute real though
restricted powers to Satan. But by and large the Christian
faith was not dualistic and therefore not prone to exaggerate
the power of petty or hostile spirits. To the State, therefore,
the offence of these pagans was not at all in their superstitious
beliefs; rather it was in appropriating and capitalizing these
unseen powers. For it was generally believed, and for good
reasons, that such practices, if they could be indulged in with
impunity, must tend to disrupt effective governmental control. That law and order in government should require an
analogous law and order in nature — for which an unhampered and serene Providence seemed to offer the best prospects — may seem logically far-fetched; but psychologically
and empirically it is probably true. Government already had
quite enough flesh and blood demons to contend with, and
therefore had no relish for combat with those other demons
of the air. For, in so far as the populace should come to believe that earthly affairs were being interfered with from
above, its fear of and admiration for earthly governors must
fade. Supernatural powers certainly could not be dispensed
with — hardly a Roman conceived of such a possibility —
but this fact made it all the more important that the supernatural powers adopted for worship be of a kind most compatible with a natural government in the hands of human
beings. That to modern eyes the Christian God hardly fulfilled all the conditions that a temporal ruler could ask for,
is another matter; what to us might seem a choice of evils
must, in the fourth century, have seemed rather the more
natural choice between evil and good. The Christian idea,
of a divine justice which at times seemed to conflict with civil
justice, [120] might lead in the future to conflicts in jurisdiction,
but the risks which this involved were small in comparison
with those to be run should the Romans come to have faith
in a supernatural world in which no justice of any kind held

[119] Dufourcq *L'Av.* 1910 IV 5 53   [120] See pp. 440–41.
n. 3.

sway. It was better that an alliance between evil men and evil spirits be thought a cunning scheme designed by the good God in order that the latent evil in man be brought to light. For to the Christians the devil was, although in spite of himself, an *agent provocateur*, set, not to aid and abet the criminal but to catch him.

Persecution of the pagan cults was not wholly confined, however, to legislation against astrology and magic: on occasions over-zealous Christians interpreted these laws as a licence to destroy heathen temples and maltreat their priests.[121] Nor should it be forgotten that Roman paganism had always been the State religion, supported financially by the State and prescribing adherence to it as the badge of civic loyalty. When, therefore — in some provinces as early as 350 [122] — State financial support was withdrawn [123] and the gesture of worship before the old shrines was declared to be no longer obligatory,[124] the Roman pagan imagined that his faith was being persecuted. Yet we now know that — unless in the case of the Manichees — this was not so, at least not until after 390.[125] In the city of Rome [126] and in the rural districts,[127] moreover, no real effort was made to enforce even those laws which had been enacted; [128] and we know too that, at least until 416, pagans were freely appointed to the higher State offices, usually outnumbering the Christian appointees.[129] That serious discrimination against pagans came only

[121] Boissier 1909 II [6] 295, citing Libanius *On the Temples,* which was written in 387; Ambrose, *Letter* # 40; Dudden 1935 371–79.

[122] Boissier 1909 II [6] 196–97, citing the anonymous *Dialogue of Asclepius.*

[123] Ibid. 259, & Dudden 1935 258: citing the Edict of 382.

[124] Ibid. 260 ff.

[125] Dill 1906 [2] 32; & Boissier 1909 II [6] 296, both say 391; but Martroye 1930 699 believes that Theodosius I aimed only at the abuses of the pagan cults and that the first blanket prohibition was enacted by Arcadius in 395; & cf. Dudden 1935 403 & 441. In 379 Gratian had prohibited all heretical Christian cults, but he aimed at institutions, not at individuals: Dudden 1935 191 & 259.

[126] According to Augustine, *Confessions* V 10, there was a nucleus of Manichees in Rome in about 380, and there is no suggestion that they were in danger of persecution. But Duchesne 1911 III [4] 661, and Batiffol 1924 [2] 433, think that the danger became more serious after about 382. Cf. Boissier 1909 II [6] 234–36 & 289.

[127] Dill 1906 [2] 27–28; Boissier 1909 II [6] 297.

[128] As late as the year 400 Augustine could write in his *Contra Faustum* V § 8, ' the wonder is that the gentleness of Christian times allows such perverse iniquity to pass wholly, or almost wholly, unpunished.'

[129] See Dill 1906 [2] 47 on Rutilius Namatianus; see Lot 1927 46 on the army; see Boissier 1909 II [6] 256 & 353 on civilian offices. The last pagan

slowly and late is illustrated by the complaint of Ambrose in 384 that

a Christian widow's bequest to the priests of a temple is valid; but her bequest to the ministers of God is not.[130]

And the complaint of the pagan Symmachus, made in the same year, was not that paganism was forbidden as a faith but only that it had been deprived of its position as the official State religion.[131] It is clear, therefore, that until 416 the Christian Emperors did nothing to prohibit pagan beliefs as such, but only specific acts deemed contrary to public policy.

The Christian State moved only gradually towards a policy of repression partly because a minority has to use caution and tact, but partly too because the Christian distrust of violence had recently been vindicated by the failure of Diocletian's policy. Since the triumph of 312 had been gained wholly by the power of persuasion and example, it was naturally on this power, new to the Romans, that the Christians for some time continued to rely. The State, they believed, had only to grant them a fair field and no favour. Later — as we shall see — sentiment inevitably changed, yet never wholly: for it was the Latin Church which set the new precedent of a State emancipated from partnership with religion [132] — a precedent never thereafter, except in the papal States, entirely broken in the West. Was not this, too, a symptom of enlightenment?

In this fourth century, moreover, not only were library and educational facilities greater,[133] the variety of accessible learn-

---

outburst in Rome was in 394 under the usurper Eugenius: Dudden 1935 426–27. Not only were the elaborate ceremonies of traditional paganism then revived, but also those of Isis and Osiris, of Cybele and Mithra: Grisar 1911 I 2.

[130] Ambrose *Letter* # 18 § 4.

[131] Boissier 1909 II 6 291, citing the *Letters* of Ambrose (# 18 §§ 3, 4 & 10, & *Relatio Symmachi* § 3).

[132] Writing under the Arian Emperor Constantius in about 360 Hilary of Poitiers in *Contra Constantium* § 10 compared the Emperor's

professions of concern for the Church to the professions of Judas. Pope Zosimus was the first Pope to solicit the support of the State, perhaps by Augustine's influence — see Turmel 1931 I 119–20 — but Caspar 1930 I 360 thinks that the Church as a whole did not approve of setting such a precedent.

[133] Rand 1928 219–23; & Dudden 1935 4–5. For Gaul see Bloch 1911 395. Rostovtzeff 1926 375 says that primary education hardly began in the Empire until after the year 200.

ing and doctrine also surpassed anything that had ever previously been. A young man could study philosophy at Athens, Carthage, or Rome [134] — as did Julian, Macrobius, or Augustine — or study Christianity under Jerome in Palestine or under Ambrose in Milan. Rhetoric was best studied at Bordeaux,[135] law in Rome [136] or Beyrout; [137] were anyone interested in studying science — which almost nobody was — Alexandria offered every facility, for the science of the ancient world lay there intact.[138] To be sure the personal instruction of a great teacher was on many subjects no longer to be had: Julian at Athens could find no Socrates or Plato to guide his enthusiasms. Indeed there was probably a great deal of really bad instruction. Nevertheless an enterprising student had little to complain of; he was free to study anything he liked, to express any opinion he chose, and, conveniently at his disposal, lay the accumulated thought and discovery of the whole ancient world.

Finally, and above all, after the third century, with its civil and foreign disturbances and the literary and intellectual sterility of the West,[139] the later fourth century appeared as an important and even brilliant renaissance; and this not to the Christian only but to the pagan too. What Roman nobles, for example, had, for many generations past, attained the distinction and influence of a Prætextatus, a Flavian, a Symmachus? Since when had such talented history been written as we find in the mutilated *History* of Aurelius Victor,[140] or such sound learning as in the great *Commentary on*

[134] Lot 1927 190.

[135] Dill 1906 2 164.

[136] Levy 1929 233; & Dudden 1935 20. Also Autun: Levy 1929 235. In the West generally the study of law was at this time very much alive: ibid. 236–39.

[137] Lot 1927 190; Cumont 1929 4 5; Jolowicz 1932 469.

[138] Oreibasos, the most famous doctor after Galen, studied his medicine at Alexandria in about 350: Pagel 1915 129. The libraries of Alexandria may have suffered in 273 as well as in 46 B.C., but apart from these no serious damage is recorded

until the pillage by the Christians in 389 or 391: *Encycl. Brit.* 1910 XVI 11 546.

[139] Tertullian — fl. 210, Cyprian — fl. 250 and Lactantius — fl. 310, are the only exceptions. All three of these were Christians of Proconsular Africa.

[140] Of Aurelius Victor, born in Leptis, south of Carthage, in about 325, Monceaux 1894 422–24 says: 'Toujours le philosophe domine et juge les faits de l'histoire. Aurélius Victor était aussi un écrivain original. Comme les grand prosateurs de son pays, comme saint

Virgil by Servius?[141] The scientific understanding of a Macrobius [142] or a Martianus Capella was as eclectic as their Platonic philosophy, but in neither is the material debased, and both well bear comparison with any analogous Latin writer of the previous three hundred years. Nor need there be any apology for the pagan poetry of an age which produced in quick succession an Ausonius, a Rutilius, a Claudian. There was infinitely more originality in the Christian writing of this time, but Roman paganism was never conspicuous for its originality, and the texts written from 370 to 425 far excel anything produced since the Age of the Antonines. As late as 376 Symmachus was still indulging in optimism:

Truly we live in a century which loves virtue, when men of talent have no one to blame but themselves if they do not win eminence.[143]

Yet this only refers to the humble contribution of a dying paganism; imagine then the exaltation of the Christian! [144]

Augustin, son contemporain, il a un style à la fois bizarre et puissant. Il dispose d'un riche vocabulaire, et ne se laisse guère arrêter par la grammaire ou des scrupules de goût. Il aime le relief, la couleur, et y sacrifie tout. Il sait voir et faire voir. Souvent, d'un trait, d'une anecdote, il peint un personnage et le rend vivant. Quelques-uns de ses portraits, par exemple ceux de Trajan, de Titus et de Sévère, sont esquissés de main de maître. . . . Il a de l'âpreté, du mordant, peu de goût, un réalisme assez cru, un sens aigu du pittoresque, de la force et de l'audace. A côté d'incohérences dont les abréviateurs seuls sont responsables, il montre bien du talent dans certains fragments des *Césars:* si son Histoire des Empereurs nous était parvenue intacte, sans doute l'Afrique aurait en lui son Tacite.'

141 Of Servius, born in Mauretania in about 350, Monceaux 1894 411–12 says:
' Il sut choisir, apprécier, classer ce qu'il empruntait; et il y ajouta le résultat de ses longues études personnelles. Ainsi s'est formé peu à peu ce précieux commentaire, où la plus vaste et la plus solide érudition se coordonne avec aisance sous la main d'un homme d'esprit et de goût, et où le style, toujours élégant et ferme, s'égaie assez souvent de notes plus personnelles, de quelques brusqueries d'expressions: répertoire inépuisable de renseignements curieux sur la langue courante, sur les vieilles traditions grecques et italiques, sur la religion et l'ancienne organisation de Rome.'

142 On Macrobius see pp. 205–10.

143 *Letters* III # 43.

144 Of this late fourth century revival Boissier 1909 II[6] 431 says:
' L'invasion a surpris la littérature du IVe siècle quand elle était dans tout son éclat. Au moment où les barbares se sont jetés sur l'empire, saint Jérôme, saint Augustin, Claudien et Symmache, Prudence et Paulin de Nole vivaient encore. Je ne puis croire qu'une société qui venait de produire à la fois tant d'hommes distingués fût aussi affaiblie, aussi décrépite qu'on le prétend, et condamnée inévitablement à

If it be decadent to cling to outlived tradition [145] — and it is, certainly, a suspicious symptom — then, Symmachus notwithstanding, there was decay in paganism. But, if this be so, must not the casting aside of that tradition as an obsolete encumbrance be a symptom of vitality? Is it out of an effete people, out of an exhausted civilization, that great transformations come? Was Italy feeble in the fifteenth century, or Germany in the sixteenth, or France in the eighteenth? Surely not. Yet none of those transformations can be compared in either magnitude or violence with that effected within the Roman Empire of the later fourth century.

For this was the age, not only of Christian poetry, fertile, and rising to greatness in Nicetas,[146] Ambrose,[147] Prudentius, and Paulinus; [148] it was above all the age that witnessed the birth and stared in wonder at the rise of the three greatest Latin Fathers: Ambrose again, Jerome, and — mightiest of all — Augustine. Although born respectively in Dalmatia, Trier on the Moselle, and Thagaste in Numidia, their parents were in each case prosperous [149] and eager enough to give their sons the best education the Empire could afford.[150] Each son showed promise in youth, each spent his earlier

---

périr. Il me semble, à voir l'élan que les lettres venaient de prendre, qu'elle aurait pu vivre encore, et que c'est un accident qui l'a perdue.'

[145] See Boissier 1909 II⁶ 165–66 & 175 on the close resemblance between the habits and mentality pictured in the *Letters* of Symmachus and those pictured in the *Letters* of Pliny the Younger. Symmachus undoubtedly did follow a conventional model; but why did he choose to follow this particular one? He must have chosen it because its taste was to his taste, because its point of view was that which still appealed to him.

[146] Nicetas was born in about 335 and became bishop of Remesiana in Moesia. He is very probably the author of the last half, and perhaps all, of the famous *Te Deum:* Kuhnmeunch 1929 273–74. He was a friend of Paulinus of Nola, and a missionary — so perhaps a native of Italy or Gaul. In any case he chose

to write in Latin. See Morin 1904 234.

[147] On the attributions of various hymns to Ambrose see Dreves 1893 14 ff. Caesarius of Arles refers to the hymn *Hic est dies verus Dei.* On *Deus, creator omnium* see Augustine *Confessions* IX 12; on *Intende, qui regis Israel* see Faustus of Riez *Letter* # 7.

[148] Jullian 1926 VIII 272–73.

[149] On Jerome see Monceaux 1932 4; on the worldly situation of Augustine's mother see his *Confessions* IX 8.

[150] Ambrose came to Rome when he was twelve years old: Carter 1911 149; Jerome also came when he was twelve: Monceaux 1932 15; Augustine did not go to Rome until he was twenty-nine, but he went to Carthage to study when he was sixteen: Alfaric 1918 23; and Carthage was then quite as much a centre of culture as Rome was.

years in experiencing and digesting what ancient civilization could teach, each, having reached maturity,[151] then passed decisively beyond it.

B. THE PAGAN PROBLEM OF EVIL

The conversion to Christianity of Ambrose, Jerome, Augustine, and many other distinguished Latin Romans completed a revolution in Western thought so overwhelming that for the next thirteen hundred years no one thought of attributing it to natural causes, so disturbing in its effects that for another two hundred years many men could only visualize it as a final and conclusive symptom of human decadence.[1] The converts themselves believed they had found ultimate truth: evidently the many other alleged truths being circulated about the Roman world could no longer carry conviction. Why was it that a belief which had satisfied Plato, a belief which had satisfied Lucretius, or Marcus Aurelius, or Apuleius, or any other belief familiar to classical antiquity, could not satisfy Ambrose, Jerome, or Augustine?

In order to get even a crude conception of why this might be, it will be necessary briefly to summarize the course of philosophical evolution in earlier times, and, in doing this, a distinction must be made between that kind of curiosity which grows out of a more violent reaction to inner than to outer experience, and that which grows out of the opposite. To the former, consciousness is a far greater mystery than the outer world: to the latter it is the other way about. The former will be satisfied with no explanation which is not moral — that is, which does not seek above all to explain good

---

[151] Ambrose was born in 339 and was called to the see of Milan in 373. Although he had not yet been baptized his election indicates that he was already a champion not only of Christianity but of orthodox Athanasianism. On Augustine see p. 63 ff. The chronology of Jerome's youth is complicated by uncertainty as to his age: the date of his birth has usually been given as 340 (Dufourcq *L'Av.* 1910 IV [5] 137 n. 1, says 338), but Monceaux 1932 xv–xxiii gives good reasons for preferring the year 347. In that case he was twenty-six when he set out for the East early in 374.

[1] Cf. Boissier 1909 II [6] 339–40 & 354–85.

and evil, pleasure and pain; [2] the latter will be satisfied with no explanation which is not mechanical — that is, which does not seek to explain matter and energy. Neither curiosity is essentially more primitive than the other, nor is the effort to reconcile and combine the two methods into a third explanation necessarily evidence of a higher intelligence: all three are merely so many methods for discovering some general law or combination of laws which seems to explain the disparate facts which the two experiences have observed.

Now the early Greeks were primarily interested to learn what nature and matter consisted of and how it functioned: whether or not it was because their outer experience was more violent than their inner, at any rate they chose this outer experience as the criterion of reality and interpreted inner experience in the light of inferences drawn from it. It was the Pythagorean school which first insisted that man's soul was as real and significant a fact as were the body and natural world which encased this soul, but it was not until Socrates that morals dared to challenge the primacy of physics and mathematics. Plato's doctrine was the first and perhaps the greatest effort to reconcile and synthesize these disparate methods, and, like most compromises, it seemed equally unsatisfactory to both the moralist and the scientist. Whereas to the latter Plato's laws of matter and energy were vitiated by moral significances, to the former his good was too ingenuously identified with mathematical and cosmological perfection. [3] It was magnificent philosophy, but it was neither good science nor good ethics. And the same thing, I think, may be said of Aristotle. [4]

Just as, after the great syntheses of Aquinas and Scotus, the courses of science and morals, as if by natural reaction, diverged, so in the century following Aristotle, while science proceeded, unencumbered by morals, to the discoveries of

---

[2] Cf. *Revelations* xxi 4: 'And God shall wipe away all tears from their eyes; and there shall be no more death, neither sorrow, nor crying, neither shall there be any more pain.'

[3] Like the good of the Pythagoreans, that of Plato was rather aesthetic harmony than moral purity. Whittaker 1901 12 says that Plato and Aristotle 'affirmed physical law in its most general principles', but 'this they subordinated to their metaphysics by the conception of a universal teleology. The teleological conception of nature [as designed for an intelligible purpose] there is good historical ground for attributing also to Socrates.'

[4] See Lot 1927 191.

Euclid, Aristarchus, Archimedes, and Apollonius, morals too burst their metaphysical shackles to inaugurate the famous schools of the Pyrrhonist,[5] the Hedonist, and the Epicurean. While the care-free scientists were laying the first solid foundations of geometry, astronomy, and physics, the equally care-free moralists were subjecting to a searching and precise analysis the motives of human conduct, the basis of happiness, and the intrinsic value of conscience and virtue. Such was the condition of affairs in the Hellenistic East when, in the year 200 B.C., Rome began her conquest of it.

The earlier Romans seem to have shown no curiosity about abstract reality — whether scientific, metaphysical, moral, or spiritual; almost before they were civilized they found themselves launched on a career of political conquest which lasted several centuries, and during this time they had no leisure to speculate with any method. Their first conquests had been of people hardly more civilized than they, but in the course of the second century the great Hellenistic world fell into their laps, with the result that, almost before they realized it, the science, philosophy, and morals of the Greeks were becoming not only the badge of culture but the curriculum of the schools. What the Greeks had learned as a result of many centuries of painful experiment, the young Roman was now trying to digest in a few years of adolescent education. Now, so long as the Republic lasted, so long as the Mediterranean world was ruled by that Latin race which lived in and about the city of Rome, the man of this ruling class was still always a citizen first and foremost — this was his vocation and to this he must be trained. His duties thus required that he be a statesman, an orator, a jurist, a soldier, or an engineer, and always a father and an honest man; but they did not require that he be either a scientist, a philosopher, an artist, or a saint. So long, therefore, as it was the ambition of the Roman to be a citizen above all else, so long must the Greek education remain something of an artificial accomplishment, a luxury to be used rather for display than for real needs. Virgil imitated Homer,[6] Lucretius put the

5 Pyrrho believed that intellectual speculation was incompatible with serenity or peace of mind: Weber 1906 [5] 149.

6 Macrobius makes an extensive analysis of Virgil's debt to Homer in his *Saturnalia* III–IV, written soon after 400.

physics of Democritus into verse, Cicero imitated everybody; the plays were imitations, so were the poems.[7] Not that they were on that account without literary merit, but only that they were without intellectual significance. As Du Bellay said of the French of 1549, they were still doing too much to find the leisure for the cultivation and articulation of their own ideas.[8]

Only with the Empire and the many changes which it introduced did the individual Roman begin to feel less conscious of his civic responsibility. As, in course of time, it became clearer that the Gaul, Berber,[9] Briton, or Syrian [10] made an adequate soldier, the Syrian too a competent banker and jurist, the Gaul a good orator,[11] the Spaniard a severe moralist, the Roman felt more and more safe to indulge a leisure which allowed his natural curiosity freer play.[12] Here, however, a remarkable thing happened: for whereas Greek morals now acquired a wide vogue, Greek science made almost no impression; as the Republic died every prominent Roman was either a Stoic or an Epicurean, while the helio-geocentric issue, for instance, aroused no interest. Why was this?

One reason may be that the Romans were a practical people, and so more interested in conduct than in abstract truth, or, to put it more precisely, more interested in the truth behind the human predicament than in the truth behind conic sections and the courses of the heavenly bodies.[13] In other words they were practical enough to be most eager to know what virtue and happiness were and how they might be realized, to know why they were in this world and whether they might survive in another.[14] It was this inclination, perhaps, which attracted them to face the problems of inner experience, to weigh the Stoic against the Epicurean hypothesis,[15] to welcome the in-

---

[7] Jullian 1926 VIII 256 says Lucan was the least imitative of the Latin writers.

[8] *Deffence et Illustration* I ch. 3. And this is comparable to the injunction given before 260 by the Christians Minucius Felix, Tertullian and Cyprian: ' Non loquimur magna sed vivimus ': Kuhnmuench 1929 3–4.

[9] Jullian 1926 VIII 93.

[10] Cumont 1929 4 103. Many were also recruited from the Danube provinces: Lot 1927 120.

[11] Dill 1906 2 406.

[12] Cf. Boissier 1909 II 6 357–59.

[13] See Ambrose *Exameron* VI 7–8.

[14] Cf. Stoop 1909 2. Immortality was still generally doubted in the first century A.D.: Nock 1933 103.

[15] Both of which were found wanting in metaphysical content: Duchesne 1911 I 6 6.

troduction of that welter of Oriental religions, to examine Christianity with the rest, and at last, because Christianity seemed to furnish the best solution of their problem, to adopt it as the religion of the State.

Whatever the causes, these successive phases surely indicate some definite organic progress; a theme is being developed — what is it? Without a doubt it is the problem of evil [16] — the greatest of all human problems, that of pain and death. If not the key to the Greek intellectual genius it is at least one of its most striking characteristics that in its earlier phase it largely ignored this problem. Quite cheerfully the Ionians took it for granted that evil was inevitable, either because it was an intrinsic incident of nature [17] or because it was an illusion produced by its contrast to good.[18] Later, being more closely scrutinized, it was declared due to the grossness of the matter of which the world was made.[19] The moralists in their turn were fertile in suggestions as to how evil could be mitigated, but no further progress was made in the determination of why it existed. Yet now, in the fourth century, this, however unconsciously, was becoming the real issue, since, without a proper diagnosis, the cure must remain largely a matter of chance.

So long as the idea of an autocratic [20] Providence did not exist, these explanations of evil — as illusory non-being, as the antithesis of the good, as Fate or Chance,[21] as a property of matter — might serve. Even to the Stoics — whose God, though alleged to love man, was nothing more than nature beneficently conceived [22] — the problem of evil seemed solved by the faith that man lived in the best of all possible worlds. But with the advent and wide diffusion of Oriental doctrines

---

[16] Stoop 1909 8.

[17] Anaximander, Democritus, etc.

[18] Heraclitus, Parmenides, etc., followed in language by Plato and Plotinus: cf. Whittaker 1901 81 & 85. Such language is still used even by Christians: Jerome *Letter* # 48 § 14 (*C.S.E.L.* 54 373 line 9) says that the devil exists, ' still, because he is lost to God, he is said not to be '; and Augustine *Confessions* VII 12 says ' If things then shall be deprived of all their goodness they shall have no being at all.'

[19] The Pythagoreans, Empedocles, Plato, etc.

[20] Olympian Zeus was hampered not only by a higher Fate, but also by Hera and the rest of his fellow-Olympians.

[21] Cf. Macrobius *Saturnalia* V § 16 on Virgil's view; & see Nock 1933 100 ff.

[22] Weber 1906 [5] 143–44; Duhem 1914 II 444.

appeared the conception of God as a living person, with many of the qualities and moral ideals of a man. Disassociated, as the Stoic God was not, from the natural world, He became the symbol of man's will to be disentangled from his unmoral environment, and so became the enemy of carnal evil. Here at last was an actively, humanly benevolent God — a true Providence,[23] who refused to justify or explain away evil by metaphysical subterfuges. Why, then, did He not annihilate it? Because He was not omnipotent, because there were other forces that effectively thwarted His will.

As the fourth century opened the religion most conspicuous in the Empire was Mithraism, to which the Emperors Diocletian, Galerius, and Licinius were each devoted.[24] Indeed it was to Mithra that Licinius commended himself in that last struggle of the years 323–324 with Constantine, so that in a sense it proved the last obstacle to Christianity's triumph. This Persian cult explained reality as the effect of a war between the powers of Light and of Darkness: between the gods Ormuzd and Mithra,[25] supported by fire [26] and man's soul, and the demon Ahriman with his allies, the earth and man's body.[27] Nature was worshipped, the sun particularly,[28] but only the immaterial in nature which the god of Light had created.[29] The material part was thought of not only as a thing uncreated by that god but even as an instrument actively manipulated by the powers of Darkness in the hope of destroying all Light. The souls of men, from their serene heights in the empyrean, were precipitated into earthly bodies, at one time as if captured by an invasion of the powers of Darkness, at another as if voluntarily in order the better in this way to grapple with the enemy in his own territory.[30] The incarnated soul was therefore either a prisoner of war or an invader

23 Whether the god of Plotinus may fairly be described as a Providence is very doubtful; but Neoplatonism evolved in many ways after his death in 270: see pp. 66–67. Augustine, during his Neoplatonic phase between 382 and 387, must have believed in a God not wholly indifferent to human affairs: for in Confessions VI 5 he says that he had never doubted the existence of a one 'true and most high God' to whom

belonged 'the government of human businesses' and who had 'a care of us.'
24 Dufourcq L'Av. 1910 IV 5 50; Cumont 1913 3 49 & 210–11; Cumont 1929 4 131.
25 Cumont 1913 3 129.
26 Ibid. 114 & 129
27 Ibid. 112.
28 Ibid. 127.
29 Ibid. 118, 122 & 125.
30 Ibid. 144–45.

— always within the enemy lines. Moreover, if only in order to make the analogy to a state of war the more complete, there were not only moments of direct physical combat but also moments of diplomacy and negotiation; the demons must therefore at appropriate times be propitiated to ward off evil, and would even at times, as by deserters, traitors, or spies, be surreptitiously invoked to act against the powers of Light.[31]

This Mithraism made a particularly successful appeal to the soldiers of the Empire, and with reason: for it was a religion of action, virile and practical, even optimistic and worldly, since it taught that earthly as well as heavenly justice and felicity could be furthered by noble deeds.[32] Strength of soul as well as of body was eagerly cultivated,[33] but rather as a means than as an end — imposed, as in military discipline, less for its own sake than for the general welfare.[34] It demanded the self-discipline rather of Loyola than of Benedict; its end was rather Martha's than Mary's. It was the last active, civic religion that Rome was to know.[35]

[31] Cumont 1913 [3] 113.

[32] Ibid. 143–44.

[33] Ibid. 142.

[34] Ibid. 142–44 & 149.

[35] To Plotinus the civic virtues are preliminary to the purgative, and action is therefore deemed inferior to contemplation: *Enneads* I 1 § 12, & I 2 §§ 1 & 2. He does tolerate the exercise of courage and wits as a protection against the violence of others: *Enneads* III 2 § 8; but this is only negatively civic because, although it is resistance to oppression, it includes no positive act of initiative.

According to Whittaker 1901 130 the Neoplatonist Iamblichus, who flourished in about 330, declared tyranny to be the consequence of the people's inability to maintain law and justice themselves. This suggests a transitional stage of thought, in which the cure for tyranny lies less in resistance by courage and wits and more in the cultivation of justice — a conception that approaches the Christian.

Lot 1927 16 says that after 350 the Romans' sense of public obligation waned. Of this tendency Christianity, although perhaps not a decisive cause, was certainly a symptom.

On the attitude of Ambrose, see Carlyle 1927 I [2] 162.

The final step is, as usual, taken by Augustine. In *D.C.D.* V 21 he says ' We do not attribute the power of giving kingdoms and Empires to any save to the true God . . . whose good pleasure is always just. . . . He who gave power to Marius gave it also to Caius Caesar. . . . He who gave it to the Christian Constantine gave it also to the apostate Julian. . . . And if His motives are hid are they therefore unjust? ' See p. 568. Cf. *D.C.D.* V 19. Thus a resistance to tyranny risked being a resistance to God.

The Neoplatonist Macrobius, hardly if at all younger than Augustine, quotes with approval Cicero's passage where Scipio is told in a vision that ' there is in heaven a place, assured and fixed in advance, for those who have saved, defended or aggrandized their country, where they may enjoy an eternal felicity ': *Commentary* I § 4. But we may be permitted to suspect that this, in Macrobius, is an anachronism: to him it was rather the nobility than the utility of the deed that deserved praise and reward.

In Mithraism, therefore, evil was both an independent and an actively hostile force, and the phenomena of experience were explained as the consequence of a struggle of the rival forces of good and evil for world dominion. This may have been an entirely adequate, but it was also a most unwelcome, explanation: for it not only attributed wide powers to the demons and their worshippers but also absolved evil men from real responsibility for their malice because only their bodies, not their souls, could be to blame. And, incidentally, it reduced the prestige and power of the good God to almost contemptible proportions. For obviously a being is not a God merely because well-disposed. Unless his might was in some fair proportion to his goodness he might still be loved but could not with any conviction be worshipped. Although the Emperor Julian showed deference to Mithraism as late as 360,[36] its popularity was by then well on the wane. As a religion suitable to the needs of the Empire it had been tried and found wanting.

Another explanation of reality in high repute as the fourth century opened was the Neoplatonic, which was merely the current variation of the traditional Greek conception inherited from Plato.[37] Christianity itself was at this time being much influenced by Greek thought, and Origen, who first had tried to make Christianity philosophically lucid,[38] shared his Alexandrian origin with his younger contemporary Plotinus, founder of the Neoplatonic variation in about the year 250. The God of Plotinus was no more than the old Greek abstraction of goodness or perfection — hardly more than another, more tenuous God superimposed above the divine

---

It might not prove vain to investigate the parallel phenomenon of the sacrifice to the gods. Porphyry, *De Abstinentia, passim,* and the anonymous author of the *Dialogue of Asclepius* (written before 350), both demand that sacrifices be only by a devotion of the mind, without actual bloodshed by animal sacrifice: Boissier 1909 II [6] 196, & Whittaker 1923 10. And whereas in Mithraism animal sacrifice was vital: Cumont 1913 [3] 171 & 190–92, to the Manichees it seemed an abomination: Stoop 1909 46–47 & 130 n. 2. Of course the Christians agreed with Porphyry and the Manichees. May it not be, therefore, that only so long as action could seem intrinsically — and not merely extrinsically — virtuous, does the instinct subsist that the sacrifice must be of something physical?

[36] Bidez 1930 79.

[37] Whittaker 1901 107, 111–12 & 122–23. Although after Plotinus oriental conceptions began to be appropriated: see Porphyry *De Abstinentia* II §§ 39–42.

[38] See pp. 52–53.

Nature of the Stoics.[39] According to his system there was, in contrast to God, an unformed matter, uncreated by God because a nothing and so uncreatable, and yet negative only in the moral and not in the cosmic sense, for its power of resistance was serious:

Matter . . . must be evil in its own kind. For in matter we have no mere absence of means or of strength; it is utter destruction — of sense, of virtue, of beauty, of pattern, of Ideal principle, of quality. This is surely ugliness, utter disgracefulness, unredeemed evil.[40]

But why should there be this evil matter? Plotinus does his best to explain the inexplicable:

Why does the existence of a principle of Good necessarily comport the existence of a principle of Evil? Is it because the All necessarily comports the existence of Matter? Yes: for necessarily this All is made up of contraries: it could not exist if Matter did not. The nature of this Cosmos is, therefore, a blend; it is blended from the Intellectual-Principle and from Necessity: what comes into it from God is good; evil is from the Ancient Kind which, we read, is the underlying matter not yet brought to order by the Ideal-Form.[41]

All this is, if you like, Plato warmed over; nevertheless the consequence was the re-entry of Platonism into the intellectual arena.

The real world of Plotinus, therefore, is the effect of the contact and conflict between these two mutually exclusive and hostile forces. It arises from the nature of God's goodness which, by definition, must desire to extend its jurisdiction and influence. God does this by the emanation from his own being, without diminution of himself, of other beings made of his own being. Among these are human souls. Separated now from God — and so divine and yet distinct from him — they tend instinctively to turn from the exclusive contemplation of their maker and to act as if different from him:

In a weary desire of standing apart they find their way, each to a place of its very own. This state long maintained, the soul is a deserter from the All; its differentiation has severed it; its vision

[39] See Macrobius *Commentary* I § 17 on the God whom ' Jovem vetates vocaverunt.'

[40] *Enneads* II 4 § 16, & cf. § 24.
[41] Ibid. I 8 § 7.

is no longer set in the Intellectual; it is a partial thing, isolated,
weakened, full of care, intent upon the fragment; severed from
the whole, it nestles in one form of being; for this it abandons all
else . . . for a thing buffeted about by a worldful of things.[42]

This, if we may call it so, is the sacrifice that goodness makes
in order to wean this evil nothingness from itself and transform it into something. It is therefore, in another sense, the
very goodness of the soul which obliges it to turn from divinity
to itself and so towards matter, for such is the irresistible law
by which the soul, like all else, is governed:

To this power we cannot impute any halt, any limit of jealous
grudging; it must move for ever outward until the universe
stands accomplished to the ultimate possibility. All, thus, is produced by an inexhaustible power giving its gift to the universe,
no part of which it can endure to see without some share in its
being.[43]

The soul is therefore the slave of a natural impulse to diffuse
its own goodness, and cannot do other than good:

Unwisdom, then, is not due to the soul, and, in general — if we
mean by Fate a compulsion outside ourselves — an act is fated
when it is contrary to wisdom. But all our best is of our own
doing.[44]

Which tempts Augustine to the observation that

These fellows would be light, indeed, not in the Lord but in
themselves; imagining the nature of the soul to be the same that
God is.[45]

These souls of Plotinus thus became the victims of their
own pride, automatically falling from heaven the more they
neglected to contemplate it, and, as they fell, acquiring the
various human passions that were floating in the spheres between heaven and earth.[46] In due course they received human
bodies, and ample time and opportunity then to repent of

---

42 Ibid. IV 8 § 4.
43 Ibid. IV 8 § 6.
44 Ibid. III 1 § 10. And Macrobius Commentary II § 12 cites without disapproval the words of the Stoic
Cicero: 'This sensible form is not
you: the soul of man, this is the real
man, and not this external figure
which the finger can point at. Know
then that you are God.'

45 Confessions VIII 10.
46 Cf. Enneads IV 8 §§ 2, 4 & 5; &
see an elaborate exposition of this
process in Macrobius Commentary I
§§ 11 & 12. On the Mithraic conception see Cumont 1913³ 145–46; on
the Manichæan see Leo Letter # 15
§ 10, and Wesendonk 1922 35.

their folly, and to strive to live in this body as purely as they had before this incarnation. Plotinus believed that this soul, on the death of its body, passed into another, purer or less pure according to the degree of its repentance and renunciation,[47] and he believed that this soul, even after attaining such virtue as to be again received into the bosom of the All, was at some future time liable once more to seek its freedom and so fall again.[48] Thus the nature of things prescribed cycles of destiny, obliging the soul periodically to be tempted, to fall, to repent, to redeem itself, to be tempted and fall again.

But Porphyry, his disciple, living in the late third century, rejected not only the cyclical theory but also that of the transmigration of souls into other bodies.[49] What, then, was to happen to the soul of a bad man when his body died? Being by nature immortal and yet unworthy of reincorporation in the All, it was likely to become an active and mischievous Presence. It was therefore an easy matter for Porphyry to identify such souls with those demons [50] already so familiar to and dreaded by the early Roman and later Mithraist. Yet to Porphyry the power of these demons was mild: although they are the cause of ' pestilence, sterility, earthquakes, excessive dryness and the like ', and can also greatly inflame the evil passions of men, they cannot ' attack a pure soul, because it is dissimilar to them '.[51] Here was a serious modification of Neoplatonic doctrine: the rebellious soul particles which had detached themselves in a conceited desire to become wholes had previously acted in all innocence and could not have acted otherwise.[52] But to Porphyry these souls had become so contaminated by matter that even after the death of their bodies they continued in their bad habits. Their pride having led them not only into suffering but also into sin, this contamination became a part of the very soul itself. Here — perhaps under Christian influence — was the beginning of a Fall involving a change in the soul's very status: pride leading not only to suffering but to sin, and being, therefore, itself an evil.

[47] Enneads I 8 § 10, & IV 3 § 9.
[48] According to Augustine D.C.D. X 30.
[49] According to Augustine D.C.D. X 30, & XII 20.
[50] De Abstinentiâ II §§ 37-43. On the Roman Platonic tradition see the ridicule heaped on Apuleius (of about 200 A.D.) by Augustine in D.C.D. IX 3-11.
[51] De Abstinentia II §§ 40 & 43.
[52] See Plotinus Enneads IV 8 § 6.

On the other hand Porphyry elaborated one peculiarly Greek doctrine which directly contradicted Christianity: the whole of reality, from God to man to matter, was a single process of becoming, of organic biological growth. Man was simply the least imperfect of the animals, and, if Porphyry rejected the supposition of Plotinus that a good soul on death entered a more immaterial body and a bad soul the body of a beast, he recognized that the beast's mind, although inferior to man's, was also rational.[53] He recalled with delight how, to the ancient allegation of Chrysippus that animals were created for the sake of man, Carneades had mischievously rejoined that if either were made for the other it was clearly the man for the dragon. For, said Porphyry, if utility is the criterion of a thing's reason for being, clearly

we were generated for the sake of the most destructive animals such as crocodiles, whales, and dragons. For we are not in the least benefited by them; but they seize and destroy men that fall in their way and use them for food.[54]

Since, therefore, the theory of Chrysippus and the Christians, that these animals like the rest of creation exist only for man's advantage, is contradicted by observed facts, it seemed safer to Porphyry to stick to the old Greek doctrine of natural rights for all rational beings, whether human or not, as each an integral and significant part of nature. How inconsistent, then, to advocate justice towards cruel men and deny it to devoted beasts: [55]

since justice pertains to rational beings . . . how is it possible to deny that we should also act justly towards beasts? [56]

To Porphyry, evidently, man — whether soul, body, or soul and body — was simply one of many intrinsically important elements of reality: if man was at or near the centre, this was not because the rest of reality existed on account of him, but rather because in the hierarchy of nature he was neither very high nor very low.

There were, therefore, profound differences between the Mithraic and Neoplatonic systems. The Mithraic imagined a chronic regime of lawless violence, the good and the bad assaulting each other with an identical ferocity; the Neoplatonic imagined instead a biological law of nature, to which the good God and the good soul were as helplessly bound as were the evil body and its matter. That the good were positive and the evil negative forces suggested the ultimate triumph of good, but this was because of a blind and inexorable process of becoming, and not because of any personal will, divine or human. And there was also this further difference: for to the Mithraists all things were either wholly light or wholly darkness, two contradictory and antagonistic elements; whereas to the Neoplatonists there was every intermediate degree of half-light, high-light and shadow of being in every stage of becoming. To the Mithraist, man was virtually a contradiction in terms, being composed of two elements quite incompatible; to the Neoplatonist, man was an intermediate order of being in which the positive and negative elements, in about equal quantities, fused in a perfectly natural way. The two elements produced a harmony, morally and divinely imperfect, but biologically perfect.

Yet for all its scientific merit this Neoplatonic system clung to the psychological defect of the Mithraist and of all pagan systems in general: it persisted, however delicately, in identifying matter with evil. This conception goes back at least as far as the Pythagoreans, who thought man's soul so superior to anything else in the world that it must be of another nature. And, since man had an instinctive admiration for his own soul, he naturally identified it with the good and blamed matter for all the evil.

Now the peculiar characteristics of this injurious matter were its heaviness and deadness, and these, contrasted with the lightness and vitality of divinity, thus came to be thought the very qualities and attributes of evil. And this in turn suggested that matter was probably the very substance which the Good was least capable of skilfully manipulating.[57] The greatest known concentration of matter was the earth,[58] and it seemed more than a coincidence that this earth was appar-

---

[57] For the soul emanates only indirectly from God through many intermediary emanations, and it was to be inferred that God's control was less complete over each successive emanation: see *Enneads* IV 8 § 3; & Macrobius *Commentary* II § 12.

[58] Reymond [1927] 174. Cf. Anaxagoras and the Atomists.

ently situated at the centre of a universe spatially composed chiefly of very light and active, if not actually spiritual, substances. Out of this was evolved the idea of a physical hierarchy — from fire, to air, to water, to earth.

Of these substances fire was the lightest and most active. Furthermore, fire produced heat and light, and these were the very qualities associated with that sun which was the cause of all earthly life.[59] If the sun — and so heat and light — were good, then matter and weight, darkness and cold, were evil. The cults of the Syrian Baal [60] and of the Persian Mithra [61] both centred, therefore, on sun worship, and to the latter the great reality was a titanic struggle between the powers of light and of darkness. Similarly, to the later Manichees, who owed so much to Mithraism,[62] light was the quality that unified divinity.[63] In this struggle, as in that not dissimilar Neoplatonic struggle between ideal-form [64] and matter, fire holds the key position among substances as the sun holds this position in the firmament. Its heat, a humble quality communicated to the earth to maintain material growth, is in contrast to its light, by which it communicates with divinity. On this conception of fire as the substance which connects heaven and earth, observe the subtle elaboration of Plato by Plotinus:

At the second circuit from the earth [says Plato] God kindled a light; he is speaking of the sun which, elsewhere, he calls the all-glowing and, again, the all-gleaming: thus he prevents our imagining it to be anything else than fire, though of a peculiar kind; in other words it is light, which he distinguishes from flame as being only modestly warm: this light is a corporeal substance, but from it shines forth that other 'light' which, though it carries the same name, we pronounce incorporeal, given forth from the first as its flower and radiance, the veritable 'incandescent body.' [65]

Thus what men know as fire is connected with the divine substance by means of the corporeal light of the sun; and it was from such a metaphysics that the Neoplatonic science and religion dangled helplessly. If, however, it was a fanciful, it

[59] Cf. Macrobius *Saturnalia* I § 17.
[60] Cumont 1929 [4] 123–24 & 330.
[61] Cumont 1913 [3] 193–94 & 257.
[62] Cumont 1929 [4] 131.
[63] Wetter 1915 122–23. Thus breaking down an astrological polytheism.

[64] Iamblichus and the Emperor Julian both worshipped the sun: Bidez 1930 ch. 12.
[65] *Enneads* II 1 § 7.

was also a majestic and even a sublime conception: it continued to hold the imagination of the Christians long after as well as before the death of paganism, and it was a Neoplatonic — and perhaps even a Mithraic — as well as a Christian vision which Dante was to immortalize in the closing cantos of the *Paradiso*.

Antiquity had thus been brought up on the conception of a hierarchy of substances: from God, His intermediaries and the human soul, to fire, air, water, and earth; and good and evil existed in each of these in proportion to the degree of their corporeality. Recalling again that the earlier Greeks were physicists, and that the philosophers, as their disciples, evolved their theories out of those of their masters, it becomes clear that their doctrine of morals was a thing tacked onto their physics and derived from it. It is true that after Aristotle many of the Greeks shook themselves free from the yoke of science, seriously cultivating independent theories of morals; but these were never effectively incorporated into any philosophic system, so that if a Roman wished to study Greek philosophy his only recourse was to the 'scientific' systems of Plato and Aristotle. The Christian Gospels were to have no difficulty in demolishing Greek morals; [66] but the Bible remained vague and unconvincing not only as science but as philosophy, and Christianity's victory under Constantine must inevitably remain emotional and intuitional rather than intellectual so long as it was unable to formulate a philosophy that could hold its own against that of the Greeks. It was to this gigantic task of giving Christian morals, if not a scientific and dialectic, at least an intellectual and philosophic frame, that the Christian theologians had to devote themselves.

C. CHRISTIAN REVELATION

Christianity was merely a faith in the truth of the biblical revelation: that the God there described was the real God and that man and the visible world were created by Him.

[66] Of the Pyrrhonists, Hedonists, and Epicureans, as listed p. 28 n. 5.

On this bare fact the success or failure of the new doctrine must depend, for the rest of it was as unoriginal as it was incidental. In the Mithraic and Neoplatonic systems there was, as we have seen, a Fall of a sort. There was also one in the Phrygian cult.[1] And in Mithraism there was even a Redemption.[2] The Syrian,[3] Mithraic,[4] and Neoplatonic [5] cults could each boast of a Trinity, and the Syrian even of a Mother and Son.[6] Everywhere there were angels and demons,[7] divine Incarnations,[8] Passions and Resurrections,[9] First Judgments and Last Judgments,[10] Heavens,[11] Purgatories [12] and Hells,[13] Anti-Christs [14] and resurrections of the body,[15] Last Suppers and Holy Communions.[16] And everywhere there were expiations and purgations of the soul.[17] At this time, indeed, such things seemed to be in the very air men breathed.

Most — if not all — of them, however, were matters rather of form than of substance, like the conventional dress that reveals nothing of the wearer's true nature. For with religions as with men, the further we get from form and the nearer to substance the fewer are the resemblances and the more striking the differences. It is only to us that Chinamen all look alike. Undeniably Christianity was conventional in regard to those many doctrines that mattered very little; it was, however, original in regard to the one doctrine — of God's relation to man — that mattered a great deal. It is true, to be sure, that whereas the Christian Bible has

1 Cumont 1929 4 60–61.
2 Cumont 1913 3 138–39.
3 Cumont 1929 4 114.
4 Cumont 1913 3 110 & 130. On the Manichæan variation see Stoop 1909 26, Wesendonk 1922 52, & Burkitt 1925 43–44 & 61–62.
5 Whittaker 1901 35–38.
6 Cumont 1929 4 55–56 & 122.
7 Cumont ibid. 59; Cumont 1913 3 112.
8 Saintyves 1907 221 n. 3; Whittaker 1901 137 citing Celsus according to Origen. Nock 1933 236–37 distinguishes, however.
9 Whittaker 1901 137; Cumont 1929 4 55–56, 72, 90–91, & 101; Nock 1933 234.
10 Cumont 1913 3 145 & 148; & see Claudian In Rufinum II lines 476–78.
11 The Orphic cult taught of a heavenly reward: Nock 1933 26. The now current belief, even among pagans, in the immortality of the soul was probably induced by a feeling that the soul was not enough prized, or even noticed, by men. It was therefore the part of wisdom and virtue to prize it, which was justifiable only if this act of prizing it was proved justified by its permanence and so by its ultimate reality: cf. Macrobius Commentary I § 11.
12 Wesendonk 1922 35; Burkitt 1925 43.
13 Cumont 1913 3 145; Wesendonk 1922 36–37; Burkitt 1925 65–66.
14 Cumont 1913 3 147.
15 Ibid. 147–48; Cumont 1929 4 92.
16 Cumont 1913 3 139; Cumont 1929 4 37 & 65.
17 Cumont 1929 4 35–36, 64, 84–86, & 111–12.

been preserved to us in its entirety, the sacred texts of most of the other religions, in so far as they may once have existed, are now lost — probably for ever.[18] We are therefore judging on inadequate and so perhaps misleading evidence in assuming that no other Oriental religion had a text at all comparable to the Bible, and consequently that the nature of the other Gods was never more than vaguely and abstractly conceived. Yet certainly from the little we know of these other Gods they were either legendary beings — often a jumble of naturalistic and mythological conceptions, projections of nature or of man himself[19] rather than sublimations of these — or else abstractions such as the Cause, by emanation or infusion, of Good.[20] Growing up, as Christians did, under the influence of Greek speculation, they acquired the habit of saying that their God too was only to be identified by His perfect unknowability, that His nature could be defined only by a series of definitions of what He was not;[21] yet no one could spend an hour reading the Bible without seeing that in fact nothing could be farther from the truth. For even to any properly brought up Christian child God was intimately known. It has been said that the picture which the Old Testament gives of Him is sometimes embarrassingly life-like;[22] certainly the picture of Him in the Gospels, in the guise of a man, is one of the most vivid and human ever written. Indeed that Christians have so often felt incompetent to describe their God is rather because He had already been so completely described that nothing more could possibly be added.[23]

---

[18] On the literature of the Manichees see Stoop 1909 v, & Dufourcq GMR 1910 IV 120 ff.

[19] On the God of the Manichees see Stoop 1909 12–14; Burkitt 1925 40 & 49; & Augustine Confessions V 3, where he speaks of the Manichees as 'changing thus the glory of the incorruptible God into an image like to corruptible man, and to birds, and to four-footed beasts and creeping things.'

On the association — by Plotinus, Porphyry, and Macrobius — of the Neoplatonic God with natural and sexual powers see Whittaker 1923 26.

[20] On the Mithraic God see Cumont 1913 [3] 169. On the Neoplatonic God see Whittaker 1901 passim; & Macrobius Commentary I § 2.

[21] See Plotinus Enneads VI 7 § 38; Augustine D.C.D. X 12–13. On the attitude of Augustine see Jones 1923 95.

[22] As in Exodus xix–xxxiv or Leviticus xxiv. Augustine D.C.D. XXII 2 explains what God's anger is.

[23] Cassian De Institutis VIII 3 says that if the Old Testament is to be taken literally God sleeps, is angry, stands, sits, is ignorant and forgetful, has 'hair, head, nostrils, eyes, face, hands, arms, fingers, belly and feet . . . which, indeed, is shocking to

Now, as we have seen, the search of the fourth century Roman was for a religion which should satisfactorily reconcile a benevolent and omnipotent God with a real and persistent evil. Until he found this solution the Roman could not relax, for now, in the year 300, philosophy was no longer, as in Cicero's day, a matter of urbane finish, but of vital necessity. Now there was no longer a dalliance with culture but a grappling with life and death — the practical Roman now craved a solution and would allow neither tradition nor logic to stand in his way.[24]

Why must God be benevolent? Because, were He not so, He must be identified with the blind Fate or Fortune which, as Augustine was soon to observe, can only be worshipped in the hope of receiving more than one deserved.[25] Why must God be omnipotent? Because, were His control over matter or evil deities incomplete, our trust in Him must be more a pious wish than a conviction. The Neoplatonic God whose will was constantly being frustrated by matter, or the Mithraic God whose will was constantly being frustrated by demons,[26] was inevitably little more than another of those well-disposed ' spirits ' of paganism, who might or might not be able to answer one's prayers. Why must evil be assumed to exist? Because it did exist, and, on the practical Roman, the philosophers' talk of evil as an illusion made no impression.

But why, if God were benevolent and omnipotent, did He not at once purge the world of all evil? This was the great stumbling block, and, as one religion after another was tried and analyzed, the solution seemed still to be as far away as ever. But where there is sufficient will to be rid of a dilemma there will, sooner or later, be a way. It will not be a philosophic way, because philosophy is fettered by logic; it must be a human way and a human revelation, and only after this revelation can philosophy perhaps be of service in designing a logical facade. This relevation was Christ's, because through him it was first indicated to men how a benevolent

---

think of.' Yet Augustine was only one of many who said that everything in the Bible must be taken as literally as well as symbolically true.
[24] Cf. Stoop 1909 2 & 8; Nock 1933 114–15 & 119–21.

[25] *D.C.D.* IV 18.
[26] Cf. Cumont 1913 [3] 106–08. And on the Manichees see Augustine *Confessions* V 10.

and almighty God could rule a world of evil. But it was not done by logic, rather it was done in the teeth of logic.[27] God the Father was Jehovah — more conspicuous for His omnipotence than for His benevolence;[28] God the Son was Christ who helplessly died on the Cross because he loved men. Yet these two Gods were one God.[29] As a philosophy the conception was wretched: even a student would be mortified to propound such a doctrine, for it betrayed a failure to grasp the first principles of rational thought. But the doctrine did not come in a philosophical treatise, it came instead in a huge and wonderful book which revealed a whole real world. That the revelation revealed a paradox simply proved the reality of paradox — in itself a revelation of the first order. I think it was Pascal, rather than Ambrose,[30] Augustine, or Scotus,[31] who first had the wit fully to recognize the reality of the contradiction. Even the mystics, though they accepted it, did not rationalize it. Scholastics, in trying to rid Christianity of this problem, have merely shown that they were incapable of disassociating the flesh and blood of religion from the dry bones of dialectic.[32]

Of course paradox has no intrinsic merit, its advantage depends wholly on how far it promotes a better understanding of reality. If the world seems at any given time to be paradoxical, then, unless it be declared so, further discovery is obstructed. Astronomy was hampered for thousands of years because it insisted that the only perfect motion was circular; physics was hampered in much the same way because no one could imagine that motion was as natural to a body as rest.[33] Through the Christian revelation that a benevolent and almighty God does rule over a world of evil, discoveries fol-

---

[27] On the alleged rationalism of the Manichees see Stoop 1909 6–7 & 108. Neoplatonism was, relatively speaking, extremely rational.

[28] In spite of the fact that Jehovah is more merciful in the later books of the O.T.

[29] On the paradox of Christ's two natures see especially Leo Letters # 28 § 3, # 35 § 2, & # 59 § 5.

[30] On his dislike of logic and hence of Aristotle, see Dudden 1935 14–15 & 558.

[31] Who had a much more gran-

diose conception than Aquinas of God's omnipotence.

[32] A distinguished authority on Catholic theology has told me that almost every final decision of the Church to this day on a matter of dogma has favoured the more paradoxical view.

[33] Philoponos, an early sixth century Alexandrian, asserted that motion was as natural to bodies as rest: Sarton 1927 I 416; & Gerland 1913 141–45. But this view does not seem to have gained any currency.

lowed which in a few generations transformed man's whole understanding of himself. If the Christian hypothesis of paradox be an error, it has nevertheless been one so fruitful to mankind that every other error — of Plato, of Copernicus, of Darwin — pales by comparison. And yet, being a paradox, it is not very easily explained.

The Bible had shown that evil existed in spite of God's benevolent omnipotence. Therefore, since He presumably did not require evil, He doubtless merely acquiesced in it, and this, necessarily, for good reasons whose existence man had not hitherto suspected. What might this reason be? The answer which the Bible gave could hardly have been made more obvious: God fostered man's virtue, and was doing what He could to increase it. Then was God perhaps not omnipotent? For surely His efforts had so far met with but very dubious success. Might it not be, then, that although the Christian God was omnipotent over nature, matter, and demons, He was not omnipotent over man? Or was it not rather that He here refrained from exercising His power? But were He able in fact to exercise it and yet did not, He would be wanting in benevolence. Here is the supreme delicacy of Christian doctrine: we emphasize God's omnipotence and His benevolence contracts, or we emphasize His benevolence and His omnipotence suffers. Through the effort to keep this paradox in equilibrium the Christian has been able to penetrate psychological depths of which no pagan had ever had any conception.[34]

The secret, in so far as it may be detected, seems to be this: God is not so much the King as the Father of men — and therefore He has for them a father's pride. Unlike the benevolent despot, He does not simply seek to promote general contentment, He seeks to rear men with such a character and virtue as men should have. He who only rears his son to be happy is but a poor father; the true parent is a creator, producing a new power at great trouble and risk.[35] The Neoplatonists and Mithraists conceived of a God who created men out of Himself — by an emanation — and who re-

---

[34] A fanciful analogy to God's omnipotence, His benevolence, and evil, would be the legislative, executive, and judicial powers of a State.

[35] Cf. *Genesis* vi 6, & *Exodus* xxxii 14.

warded them by ultimately re-absorbing and so destroying
them. But the Christian God, in creating man, was creating
something new. Why did He not create man perfect? Because if He did He would not be creating, but be merely
copying Himself.

Nor was it merely one new nature that He thus created;
for each individual soul was a separate and independent creation.[36] Each obscure and lonely soul was a new thing — itself
to all eternity; not a mere emanation or effect of procreation,
but a thing-in-itself. Each man was endowed with a special
will and special passions to be plagued by, each was given a
rational mind and delicate emotions, and tossed into a real
world to fight his own fight with the weapons at his disposal.[37] God might conceivably have created men with
smooth rational minds, without emotions and passions, without the will to sin. Such beings were not worth creating.
He did not simply want a supernatural world full of monoto-
nous virtue and happiness; He wanted instead a dynamic, even
a dramatic world, no matter whether supernatural or natural,
of actively, positively virtuous men. He wanted you virtuous, me virtuous, yet without our ceasing to be you and me.
Might not God be at once benevolent and almighty without
being satisfied merely to create a world of paper dolls?[38]

As the Old Testament so amply testifies, it was a bold, even
a rash experiment. Adam, through his free will and passions,

---

[36] Plotinus, to be sure — see *Enneads* VI 7 §§ 9–12 — believed that
there was an original Idea or Form
to correspond to each individual
thing. But as these things included
every pebble and blade of grass as
well as every soul the notion offered
cold comfort.

[37] Observe how in *Confessions* VI
7 & 9 Augustine imagines God to
have used ingenious and painstaking
devices in order to lead the young
Alypius towards conversion. The
first steps were merely to wean him
from a love of the Circensian Games
to a serious devotion to the Manichees, and to teach him how easily
justice can miscarry. For each move
made by man God has His counter-
move, as a rider might handle a frac-
tious horse.

[38] Many of the earlier theologians,
to be sure, among them Irenæus —
Rivière 1905 166–67; Tixeront 1924
I 9 260; and Gregory of Nyssa: Uberweg 1915 II 10 133 — thought that
God was incapable of producing beings more perfect than Adam. Yet,
if this were so, how could God have
made it no longer possible for the
angels to sin? True, they might have
sinned yet refrained from doing so;
this entitled them to a reward as it
entitled human saints. Such views
must be connected with the view that
God was somehow bound by a higher
Justice or Fate: see pp. 54–55. The
view I give in the text is rather that
of Augustine. Among his predecessors Hippolytus had flatly denied
that God was unable to create perfection if He chose: Rivière 1905 128.

was liable to will to sin; therefore eventually he did sin, and the Fall, from a contingency, became a reality. That God risked this Fall was evidence that He respected man; that God was still willing to redeem him was evidence that He loved man.[39] Of this love Christ was the herald and symbol.

Was it a new conception of human nature which brought about a new conception of God, or was it rather the Revelation of the new God which revealed a new human nature? It is impossible to say, for each reacted so directly on the other that the identity of the original spark must for ever remain lost in obscurity. All we can ever know is that out of the action and reaction grew up a novel yet mature doctrine, involving the hypothesis of a new God and a new man and therefore of a totally new relation between the two.

From a strictly religious point of view the most significant effect was the stimulus which Christianity gave to mystic contemplation — that ' experimental perception of the presence of God in the soul '.[40] Far from being an exclusively Christian discovery, this experience was common to most of the other Oriental cults and it had already been a feature of the doctrine of Plotinus.[41] And technically, indeed, Christianity was here at a disadvantage; for its doctrine emphasized the essential difference between the human and the divine soul. Nevertheless, the intimate knowledge of God derived from the Bible was unique: here as nowhere else was something tangible that could be loved. The Neoplatonist was obliged to love a Being at once unknown and himself; the Christian could love a Being who was neither unknown nor himself.[42]

Although this ' experimental perception ' was, and still is, the normal goal of Christianity, few, even of the most pious and assiduous, have ever attained it in this life; yet the few who have say it is an experience which no other in life can

---

[39] It was not consonant with the rarified majesty of the Neoplatonic God to love in any human sense: see Plotinus *Enneads* VI 8 § 15.

[40] Butler 1924 17.

[41] Cf. *Enneads* VI 9 *passim*. Stoop 1909 19 says that there is also an element of this mysticism in Manichæism.

[42] An identity of essence and substance in contrast to an image which, even if it rise by virtue from a contingent to an actual moral affinity, becomes only a likeness and never an identity: see p. 438 n. 13.

parallel. Augustine attained it; so did Gregory the Great,
Bernard,[43] Francis, Teresa, John of the Cross, and many
more. Through their records, inarticulate as they inevitably
must be, they have ever been, to those gifted with such perceptions, what Dante and Shakespeare are to the man of
letters, what Bach and Mozart are to the musician.

Fortunately, however, all human experiences differ only
in degree: what one man can feel vividly and deeply any
other can feel too in a humbler way. And the better one man
leads, the better the rest can follow. Pagan philosophy had
assumed a fundamental rift between body and soul, between
matter and spirit, between God and the tangible world. This
conception was now obsolescent and doomed. For Christianity now suggested a new alignment of forces, a new equilibrium, in which body, matter, and the tangible world were
unceremoniously relegated to a subordinate role. Evil and
good there still were, and the goodness was still God, but the
evil, formerly an outer and alien thing, was now an inner
and personal. The Pythagoreans had been so impressed by
the significance of the soul that they associated it with Good;
the Christians were so impressed by its significance that they
saw in it, not the source of good only, but the source of evil
as well. To them the struggle which reality revealed was not
a cosmic thing with each man an incidental and indecisive
participant, but an infinite number of individual things with
each man at the very centre of that struggle.

But if this tangible world, with its bodies and other matter,
was relegated to a subordinate role, to what was it subordinate? To the human soul evidently, which was the sole object of God's creation. As Ambrose said,

[Man] is the consummation of the whole work, the cause of the
world, for whose sake all things were made.[44]

Blithely oblivious to the observation of Carneades that man
was more appropriately created for the sake of the dragon
than the dragon was for man, Ambrose relapses into a more
vulgar and unenlightened view of the nature of beasts:

[43] See Butler 1924 on Augustine,
Gregory, & Bernard. I hesitate to include Ambrose in spite of Rand 1928
70 ff. & Dudden 1935 495 n. 5.

[44] *Letter* # 43 § 19; & cf. Dudden
1935 475 notes 6–8.

Although they are irrational they still acknowledge reason, taking advantage of that discipline which nature has not given them. Furthermore wild beasts, seeing man's gentleness, grow gentle under his rule. Often have they closed their jaws, recalled by the sound of the human voice. We have seen hares caught without injury by the harmless fangs of dogs, and even lions, if they hear man's voice, letting their prey escape; leopards and bears even, urged on and recalled by the sound of that voice.[45]

Now all this is more or less true, but by an irony of logic it tends rather to show that man was created that the beast might lead a less irrational life, it does nothing to show why the lion, leopard, and bear were created for man's sake — unless for his entertainment in the circus. At a later time more plausible explanations were to be given of why everything in nature was created for man's benefit. The interesting thing about the argument of Ambrose is the revelation of so vivid a faith that he could carelessly distort the facts of common observation in support of that faith. He was so sure that all nature was significant only in its relation to man that no argument in support of it could be fallacious. For this Christian Revelation was inconceivably momentous, revolutionizing not only the traditional conception of God but also of nature and of man. This man was the premeditated creation of God's will and the rest of the creation was merely an incident. The antinomy was no longer between God and nature but between God and man.

The relationship between God and man was therefore doubly intimate, for while God's affinity with the world was still through what was good in man, His concern for the world was no less concentrated on the evil in man. The problem of evil, instead of being dissipated throughout the various phenomena of nature, was concentrated within the human soul, and God's concern for the triumph of the Good could only be with that triumph in each individual. Unworried now by cosmic difficulties — a rebellious devil or a recalcitrant matter — the new Roman God need no longer be distracted by any consideration of cosmic welfare. For He had so created the world that only the individual soul had any significance. Souls alone were capable of arousing His

45 *Letter* # 43 § 16.

solicitude. The behaviour of the humblest man was therefore hardly more important to the man himself than it was to God, so that man's intimacy was based not only on the Bible picture of God but, more specifically, on the knowledge that this God was deeply concerned about him. The Christian — unlike the Greek — believed that God could requite man's love, and that this love of God in turn fed that of man. It was precisely because God did not have to govern that He had the leisure to love. To such a God, man could pour his heart out, confident of His attention, confident that He had no other care than to listen and console. It was because the evil of the world was now concentrated in man's soul that God must watch over it with undivided concentration, nursing and guiding it, as does a parent a child. And the more God seemed to care for man the more man cared for Him.

So long as the Roman believed his soul to be divine he must hold his head high before God, to prove himself worthy of his noble blood; he must be stiff, must not betray his weakness, must play a part. Only now, as he learned that his soul was the antithesis of God, that it was the cause of all the misery inside himself and of much of the misery outside, only now could the stout soul of the Roman reveal its true humanity, only now could it weep and love, be weak and yet not blush:

None of all this do these Platonic writings contain. Those leaves can show nothing of this face of pity, those tears of confession, that sacrifice of thine, a troubled spirit, a broken and a contrite heart. . . . No man sings there ' Shall not my soul wait upon God, seeing from him cometh my salvation? For he is my God and my Salvation, my Defence; I shall be no more moved.' No man in those books hears him calling, ' Come unto me all ye that labour '; yea, they scorn to learn of him because he is meek and lowly in heart. For these things hast thou hid from the wise and prudent, and hast revealed them unto babes.[46]

This was how, to Augustine, Christianity introduced the heart into human philosophy. It was precisely because the soul was its own feeble self that it was a heart and so a real man that could sin and suffer, that could also be grateful and

[46] *Confessions* VII 21. Cf. Guitton 1933 91 on the pride of Plotinus.

charitable, humble and contrite. By conceiving of himself as a complete entity, with the heart as his essence, man now attained a new dignity: for as he grew less proud he grew more conscious of himself. No longer now did he imagine himself a mere errant particle of divinity entangled in the mortifying garb of the flesh; instead he saw himself as a new and unique thing-in-itself. He felt infinitely small, infinitely foolish and feeble, but at least he knew, as had hardly a Roman before him, that he was himself.

And he would be himself for ever, in a life everlasting. For as Jerome said even of the saints:

Glorious indeed they shall be, and graced with angelic splendour, but they will still be human; the apostle Paul will still be Paul, Mary will still be Mary.[47]

No man is divine or will ever become so, but some day he may in a measure deserve God's love, and — so deserving — live with Him in peace and for ever.

D. CHRISTIAN PHILOSOPHY

This belief in Revelation was a matter of faith, of love; a thing which touches the heart can be felt but not argued. Yet man is so constituted that he is tempted to argue — as over the beauty of a woman or a song — though in his heart he is sure of the folly of it. And so it was with the new faith: men arose who, graced with the change of heart, so longed to make others share that they strove to give reasons, reasons that seemed as superfluous as they were true. How prove the beauty of the woman or the song; yet how deny their beauty?

Reasons were first given by the Jews of Alexandria as the new faith spread there in the second century from Palestine. The reasoners were the Gnostics, who believed they could fit Revelation into the familiar Platonic frame. If we may define heresy as a belief contrary to familiar tradition this Gnostic doctrine was the first serious Christian heresy: for Jehovah was identified with the demiurge linking the mercy

[47] *Letter* # 75 § 2.

of true divinity with the chaos of matter through a justice that repelled.[1] Irenaeus, of Smyrna and later bishop of Lyons, had ably defended orthodox tradition against these Platonizing Christians, but the philosophic current proved strong, and with the coming of Origen — a devout Christian but also an Alexandrian — philosophy became an integral part of the Christian teaching and theology began.

The Gnostics had tried to fit Revelation into a Platonic frame; Origen reversed the technique, seeking to fit Platonism into the frame of Revelation. His effort, however, creditable as it was, only produced a doctrine alien to both.[2] Thus as a Christian Origen declared that God had created matter,[3] but as a Greek philosopher he called matter eternal.[4] In the same way he explained the Redemption as a way of appeasing God's wrath; [5] but he also described it as a way of freeing man from the clutches of the devil.[6] He denied that the human soul had ever before been incarnated,[7] but he thought it was now incarnated as a penalty for earlier misbehaviour.[8] He said that man's free will required punishment for his sins; [9] yet he believed these punishments remedial and so never for eternity.[10] He admitted that grace was indispensable to salvation; [11] but he thought it must be bestowed in proportion to merit and therefore as a matter of justice rather than of mercy.[12] Although he recognized that both faith and works were indispensable to salvation,[13] he believed that the highest virtue came only through knowledge.[14] Consequently, while he considered that free will, and not matter, was the cause of evil in men,[15] he supposed that matter was the prime

[1] Tixeront 1924 I [9] 198–99. Turmel 1931 I 29–34 suspects that our text of the *Epistle to the Romans* has been doctored by them. Irenæus, who lived at the height of the Gnostic heresy, preferred to rely on the traditional and familiar doctrine of the Church rather than on Scripture, because he thought Scripture had been too much tampered with: Dufourcq 1904 [3] 112–20; & Tixeront 1924 I [9] 205–06 & 241–42.

[2] Duchesne 1911 I [6] 357.

[3] Tixeront 1924 I [9] 491.

[4] Ibid. 310.

[5] Ibid. 315–16.

[6] Ibid.

[7] Ibid. 326.

[8] Dufourcq *L'Av.* 1910 IV [5] 153–54; Duchesne 1911 I [6] 354–55; Tixeront 1924 I [9] 311.

[9] Rivière 1905 377–79; & cf. Dufourcq *L'Av.* 1910 IV [5] 154.

[10] Duchesne 1911 I [6] 355; Tixeront 1924 I [9] 325–28.

[11] Tixeront 1924 I [9] 317.

[12] Cf. Dufourcq *L'Av.* 1910 IV [5] 154.

[13] Tixeront 1924 I [9] 317–18.

[14] Ibid.

[15] Uberweg 1915 II [10] 106. Or at least of the differences between men: Tixeront 1924 I [9] 311; & cf. 329.

obstacle to knowledge and so to the highest virtue.[16] Origen is today commonly ranked as the most influential Christian theologian before Augustine; [17] yet it is clear that he had only made a rather embarrassing beginning.

The value of Origen lay rather in the abundance than in the concatenation of his ideas. Later generations had this vast treasure to draw upon, and if some, like his younger contemporary Plotinus, drew on the old ideas,[18] others drew on the new ideas and used them to refute the old ones. Thus Origen furnished the melting-pot out of which grew the maturer systems of later times.[19] So long as the persecutions lasted abstract speculation remained a luxury, but with the prospect, after Constantine,[20] that Christianity must shortly become the religion, not of a select few, but of all, the need of laying indestructible foundations became imperative. It was no longer a personal faith to die for but a State religion to rule by.

The Christian must now explain evil not only to himself but to the whole pagan world. Faith explained nothing except to him who had it, and such a person really needed no explanations. He believed that God, who was Truth, had told him what he must think and do, and that it was superfluous, and therefore impertinent, to ponder over the hows and whys. As the child must trust the father, as the sheep must trust the shepherd, so must man trust God. The pagan, however, was importunate: why, he asked, did God allow Adam to sin, why did He so severely punish him, why were Adam's descendants forced to share his penalty, why did God choose to redeem man by the cruel Passion? As the pagans asked these questions and the Christians tried to answer them, ten other thorny questions would arise for each one answered. With the ever wider propagation of the faith many men became Christians who had a taste for such speculations, so that as time went on more and more of the questioning was done by the Christians themselves.

---

16 Tixeront 1924 I 9 303.
17 Ibid. 329.
18 Plotinus, also from Alexandria, was about twenty years younger than Origen. Cf. Porphyry *Life of Plotinus* §§ 3 & 14.

19 Tixeront 1924 I 9 297 & 329–30.
20 On the conversion of Constantine to Christianity see p. 138 ns. 7 & 8.

Of the cause of the Fall Irenæus had offered an early explanation which gave general satisfaction: if God's creations had been perfect they would have been duplicates of Himself, which was absurd.   Therefore He had only the alternative of creating living things with a free will they could abuse, or of not creating any living thing at all.[21]   Since, moreover, God deliberately willed to create such imperfection He must have had beneficent reasons, must, by means of His fore-knowledge, have been sure that all would turn out ultimately for the best.[22]

Meanwhile, however, Adam abused this free will, and, as a penalty, he and his descendants were abandoned by God to the clutches of the devil.   It was believed that during this dark period man had retained his free will not to sin, but that he was so handicapped by the physical penalties imposed — of toil, suffering, and death — that he could not avoid sinning.   And since at that time God was chary of His grace, of pardons for repentance, of strength with which to resist future temptations, only a few were saved.[23]

This seemed an excessive penalty; but the impression was confirmed by the startling violence of the Redemption.   Why, when God wished to redeem man from his plight, was His mere will not adequate?   Evidently there was some obstacle to be overcome, some law of Fate or Nature, or some living being hostile not only to man but to Christ.   Yet to admit Fate was pagan; to admit the devil's independent power was Manichæan; to admit the wrath of God was Gnostic.

It was Irenæus here again who pointed towards the right solution.   Though his language was loose and his reasoning incomplete his instinct was faultless.   To him God was just because He knew that without justice there can be no mercy.   Therefore the Fall had somehow to precede the Redemption.   God showed His mercy by choosing — in the Person of His Son — to assume the burden of man's guilt on Himself by

[21] See pp. 35–36, & 95.

[22] Presumably on the theory that good could only come out of evil: Turmel 1931 I 41.

[23] Turmel 1931 I 35–79 *passim* says that up to Augustine only a few, like Origen, assumed a guilt as well as a weakness, and only a few, like Justin, Theophilus of Antioch, Clement, Lactantius, Eusebius of Cæsarea and Theodore of Mopsuestia denied even the penalty of weakness.   Therefore the majority recognized the penalty, but as a weakness and not as a guilt.

becoming, and dying as, a man. Thus, innocent, He had suffered, thereby paying the debt demanded by justice of those who had not paid the full penalty of their sin. This vicarious expiation becomes comprehensible only if the debt be regarded in a material rather than in a moral sense. Justice is the creditor who demands payment of his debt: that another than the debtor pays this debt is immaterial. For once the creditor had received back what he loaned, the debtor is freed.

But who was this creditor? Was it justice, the Father, or the devil? It was no one of them because it was all three.[24]

Irenæus had been wise not to press the analysis further. Under the stimulus of Origen, however, the theologians became bolder. That Christ had made the supreme sacrifice in order to satisfy himself or even his Father seemed absurd; that he had done this in order to satisfy an impersonal and abstract justice seemed no less absurd; that he had done this in order to satisfy the demands of his natural enemy the devil seemed therefore almost self-evident. Irenæus had characterized Christ's Atonement as a ransom, and therefore as something paid to one enjoying a real though illegal possession. Origen [25] and many later [26] had also seen things in this light. But in the course of the fourth century some came to regard the devil's dominion as not only real but also legal, God being somehow bound by the terms of a contract. This was ticklish doctrine, for it suggested a reversion to the Neoplatonic conception of a Good and an Evil held by a higher power in equilibrium; yet some of the theologians were seduced by it.[27] Most notable of these was Ambrose, the great bishop of Milan, whose weakness for Neoplatonic hypotheses as derived from Origen led him into many dubious speculations. Thus of the Atonement he says:

If we were redeemed not by the corrupt metals, silver and gold, but by the precious blood of our Lord Jesus Christ, from whom, pray, were we bought unless from him who had originally bought us with the price of our sinful inheritance? Without doubt he

---

24 Rivière 1905 125–26 & 375–77; Tixeront 1924 I 9 265–67.
25 Rivière 1905 377–81.
26 Lactantius: Turmel 1931 I 53; Athanasius: Rivière 1905 144, &

Tixeront 1921 II 6 152; Rufinus: Bethune-Baker 1933 5 342.
27 Jerome: Tixeront 1921 II 6 297; Gregory of Nyssa: Rivière 1905 384–86, & cf. Turmel 1931 I 353–54.

demanded that price as the condition upon which he would release from slavery those whom he was holding bound. The price
of our freedom, moreover, was the blood of the Lord Jesus, which
of necessity had to be paid to that one to whom we had been sold
on account of our sins. Until, therefore, this price had been paid
for all men — which had to be paid by the shedding of the blood
of the Lord that all might be absolved — it was necessary that
there be shed the blood of individual men.[28]

Although many, including Gregory of Nyssa, shared this
theory of the Pact, many too were shocked by it. One of
these was Gregory of Nazianzus:

To whom, indeed, and why was this blood shed for us, this noble
and precious blood of a God become our priest and our victim?
We had been, to be sure, the prisoners of the devil because we
had been sold by our sin and had spurned felicity. If now a ransom is paid only to him who had custody of the prisoners, to
whom then, I ask you, and why, was the blood of Jesus Christ
offered? If it be to the devil, what sacrilege! How can anyone
suppose that he should have received not merely a ransom from
God, but God Himself as that ransom — thereby offering him so
generous a price in exchange for the tyranny, that the devil could
not justly detain us?

The passage goes on to reject the alternative suggestion of
Cyril of Jerusalem [29] that the Atonement was in order to
appease the wrath of God, concluding rather feebly that it
was

because humanity had to be sanctified by the humanity of God,
that He might deliver us Himself, and overcome the tyrant, and
draw us to Himself by the mediation of His Son who also arranged
this to the honour of the Father whom it is manifest that He obeys
in all things.[30]

Which is as much as to say that God died as a man in order to
honour Himself, or else that the Father was by nature incapable of redeeming man except by a magic sacrifice —
theories which are both discreditable to divinity. These later
theologians would have done better to follow Irenæus and
let well enough alone.[31]

[28] *Letter* # 72 §§ 8–9. And cf.
Letter # 41 § 7, & *Expos. Evang. sec.
Lucam* VII §§ 114–17.
[29] Rivière 1905 167–68, & cf. Tixeront 1921 II [6] 152–55. This conception is to be found in an exaggerated
form in Bossuet and Bourdaloue: see
Rivière 1905 8–9.
[30] *Oration* # 45 § 22.
[31] Cf. Bethune-Baker 1933 [5] 344.

There was, moreover, a further difficulty to all these solutions: since the devil must have known what the consequences would be if he killed the innocent Christ, how was he prevailed upon to accept such a ransom? The usual explanation [32] was that he had been trapped by Christ's perfect disguise as a man and so as a sinner. The legal analogy was an irrevocable agency terminated by the agent's abuse of the power delegated to him. To the objection of some that the breach was invalidated because the principal had fraudulently induced it, Gregory of Nyssa replied that justice required that one who had acquired his power by fraud be also deprived of it by fraud,[33] in other words, that the devil's power, although valid in law, had never been valid in equity.[34]

Need we be surprised at these efforts to reduce theology

In earlier times the Redemption was commonly regarded as a mere Revelation or teaching: on the Apostolic Fathers see Turmel 1931 I 333–36; on Justin see Bethune-Baker 1933 [5] 331; on the *Epistle to Diognetus* of about the year 200 see Rivière 1905 110–11; on Clement of Alexandria see Turmel 1931 I 348; on Tertullian, Arnobius, and Lactantius see Rivière 1905 214–24.

Later a popular theory was that the Redemption was primarily a magical infusion, through the Incarnation, of all human beings with an element of divinity: on Hippolytus see Rivière 1905 129, & Turmel 1931 I 339; on Athanasius see Rivière 1905 146–50, Tixeront 1921 II [6] 151, & Bethune-Baker 1933 [5] 346–47.

No less popular was the idea of the Redemption as a blood-ransom paid to the devil. This view was held by Origen: Rivière 1905 377–79. On Athanasius' opinion of this view see Turmel 1931 I 352–53. This idea, of expiation by an innocent where adequate satisfaction — as by penance — could not be obtained from the wrong-doer, was a familiar one to the Romans. Human sacrifice was still practised by many of the frontier races — as in Britain when Cæsar went there: *B.G.* VI 16, and by the Saxons.

[32] This is what is commonly known as the 'mouse-trap theory': see Augustine *Sermon #* 130 § 2. On Origen see Rivière 1905 380–81; on Athanasius see Turmel 1931 I 352; on Hilary see Tixeront 1921 II [6] 298; on Pacian of Barcelona see Rivière 1905 401, & Tixeront 1921 II [6] 298; on Gregory of Nazianzus see Rivière 1905 420–21; on Gregory of Nyssa see ibid. 385, & Tixeront 1921 II [6] 298; on Ambrosiaster see Rivière 1905 402, & Tixeront 1921 II [6] 298; on Ambrose see Rivière 1905 419, Tixeront 1921 II [6] 298, & Bethune-Baker 1933 [5] 343; on John Chrysostom see Rivière 1905 396–97 & 417; on Theodore of Mopsuestia see ibid. 427.

[33] Rivière 1905 386; & Turmel 1931 I 354. This certainly raised a nice point of law: if the devil's right was voidable in equity on account of fraud, equity could be appealed to; but it is hard to see how a valid contract could be voided on the ground of an anticipatory breach where the principal has himself tricked his agent into the commission of an *ultra vires* act.

On how the devil was caught according to the wrath of God theory — where the devil was helpless — see pp. 83–84.

[34] Which was evidently the view of Irenæus: Rivière 1905 376, & Tixeront 1924 I [9] 266–67. In other words, God could not afford to arouse any suspicion, however ungrounded, that He had in any degree treated the devil unfairly.

to legal terms? In that Greek philosophy to which the Gnostics and Origen — as well as Plotinus — had clung, reality was seen in terms of blind natural forces; to the Mithraists reality seemed a lawless struggle between the two living forces of Good and Evil. But in place of these the Christians were now trying to explain reality in terms of justice. In their efforts to avoid both natural science and primitive personifications they had recourse to the jurisprudence of the Empire: to them reality was neither physics nor war, but justice. The eternal conflict between good and evil was being fought neither in nature nor on the field of battle, but in a court of law.[35]

It is possible, furthermore, that this disposition to interpret reality in terms of law and order may have led the Imperial government to look upon Christianity with favour. It was the plain task of Emperors to discredit chance and violence, and in the Jehovah of the Old Testament they could easily fancy that they saw a likeness of themselves. Whether or not this affinity between the exigencies of a government and the revelations of a religion actually did foster the memorable alliance under Constantine may be a matter of doubt. Nevertheless it was surely not by chance that the first great age of Roman jurisprudence under Julianus and Gaius coincided with the first great age of Christian theology under Justin and Irenæus; and that the age of the greatest jurists, Paulus, Ulpian, and Papinian, was also that of Clement, Tertullian, and Origen.[36] And, just as ancient law closed with the codification under Theodosius II, so did the theology of the Fathers close with Augustine.[37] A distinguishing character-

[35] On the legalism of Ambrose, see Dudden 1935 557. To defy logic and then superimpose law on paradox was an experiment that Ambrose's disciple Augustine dared not emulate.

[36] On Origen's legalistic approach to theology see Rivière 1905 377–78.

[37] With Diocletian the Emperor's will became sovereign and the law was subordinated to it; consequently the power and prestige of the jurist declined, and young men who wished to exercise their legal talents to the full found in theology a more profit-

able subject-matter. For in this new field theory, while still conditioned by the actualities of human nature, was not conditioned by the practical exigencies of the State. Furthermore the civil law had evolved to a high degree of perfection, whereas theology was still in many ways unformed. If born two hundred years earlier such men as Ambrose or Augustine, while accepting the Christian faith, might nevertheless have preferred their lay careers — Ambrose in the public service, Augustine as a professor of rhetoric

istic of Roman law was its philosophic approach; a no less distinguishing characteristic of Roman Christianity was its legal approach. The two converging lines lead us to the heart of the genius of that time.

Christ's sacrifice had redeemed mankind. Did this mean that all men would ultimately be saved? Origen and many others who followed his teaching thought so,[38] but the sounder doctrine of Irenæus was later revived which limited the benefits of the Redemption to those who took the virtuous initiative of choosing to be baptized.[39] For these alone were cleansed of the devil and infused with the grace which absolves the penitent and gives him the strength to resist the temptations to come.

There was a difficulty here, however. If grace were conferred only for merit the unbaptized could acquire merit — for otherwise they could never choose to be baptized.[40] Yet it was fairly clear that the Redemption did not automatically restore all mankind to the original status of Adam, for, were this so, the rite of baptism, which professed to do this very thing, was superfluous. Merit consisted in the love of God,

---

following the path of Cicero. Cf. *Confessions* V 13, VIII 6, & IX 2. According to Rivière 1933 ³ 26 & 72, Augustine's own way of expounding a theological point is often juristic.

[38] On Origen's predecessor and master, Clement of Alexandria, see Tixeront 1924 I ⁹ 295–96; on Origen and Arnobius see ibid. 325–28 & 459; on Martin see Severus' *Life of Martin* 22; on Gregory of Nyssa see Tixeront 1921 II ⁶ 199; on Jerome see ibid. 341. Gregory of Nazianzus could never make up his mind: ibid. 199–200. Cyril of Jerusalem and John Chrysostom urged that prayers be said for the damned because of a presumption that their punishment would in this way be gradually mitigated: ibid. 200. Ambrosiaster thought that at least those who had openly spurned the faith when it had been fairly offered to them would never be saved — although the devil himself very likely would be: ibid.

340. Basil also thought that some would be eternally damned, but he acknowledged that most Christians preferred to follow the doctrine of Origen: ibid. 198–99.

[39] On Irenæus see Turmel 1931 I 40–41; on Cyprian of Carthage see ibid. 50.

[40] This view, that men still had free will apart from baptism, seems to have been generally held until about the year 375: on Origen see Dufourcq *L'Av.* 1910 IV ⁵ 154; on Eustathius, Diodorus, and Theodore of Mopsuestia see Tixeront 1921 II ⁶ 8–9; on Gregory of Nazianzus, Gregory of Nyssa, and John Chrysostom see ibid. 145–47. And, of the Latins: on Hilary of Poitiers see Tixeront 1921 II ⁶ 282–83; on Optatus of Mileve see Harnack 1904 XIV 416 lines 25–26; on Rufinus see Turmel 1931 I 107–08. And cf. ibid. 94 bottom.

and how was one still uncleansed — with the devil still inside him — to love God? Since the regeneration came only through baptism, Ambrose was tempted to conclude that the unbaptized could not love God, could not acquire merit. How, then, were they ever induced to seek baptism? Obviously through a grace freely given, irrespective of merit; and, since many did not seek this baptism, Ambrose must further conclude that these had been predestined not to be baptized and hence not to be saved.

Only by baptism, therefore, did man regain the precious grace of a free will not to sin. Of this Adam and his descendants had been deprived, so that the Fall had been not only in physical but in spiritual status — a degeneration not of the body only but also of the soul and will. Baptism, however, did restore the original status: the Christian, quite like the innocent Adam, received again the grace of a free will which enabled him to resist sin, and thus to acquire, if he chose, that merit which inevitably drew down, as its just reward, the final grace that saved.[41]

Without denying that this view of Ambrose arose out of a careful scrutiny of Scripture, it seems likely that its triumph now — and later — was partly occasioned by outward changes. For until the end of the persecutions in 312 a willingness to be baptized was, apart from a stoic martyrdom, the great sacrifice and therefore the great merit. During that long period few can have thought that the will to be baptized was caused by divine grace rather than by human merit. And such further merits as might be acquired thereafter — as by martyrdom — could properly be regarded as works of

---

[41] This theory of Ambrose — that the unbaptized could do nothing to be baptized, since the very wish to be was a free grace conferred by God irrespective of individual merits — obliged Christians for the first time to face the vital problem of original sin. For, until Ambrose, adults were believed to have this free choice, so that, if they died unbaptized, it was their own fault. They had sinned as responsible adults and done nothing, as they might have, to procure absolution. It is true that infants who died unbaptized were declared damned, but because they had not sinned in their own persons, they were thought to go rather to an intermediate place — a limbo — where they did not suffer: see Dudden 1935 644. But according to Ambrose adults who died unbaptized were condemned to eternal suffering, yet unavoidably. How could this be unless men inherited not only an irresistible disposition to sin but also a pre-existing guilt — and hence a punishment justly due at birth? See generally Tixeront 1921 II⁶ 144 & 281; & Bethune-Baker 1933⁵ 305–06.

supererogation, or beyond the minimum that God required.[42]
Soon after 312, on the other hand, baptism became a means
to worldly advancement: to wish to become a Christian must
then seem less meritorious than, having become one, to live
as a Christian should. Being baptized seemed too often a
matter of chance; living as a good or bad Christian seemed
quite definitely a matter of free choice.[43]

But how could it be said that God wished to save all if He
made no apparent effort to save those who died unbaptized?
Did this mean that He wished to save only as many as He
could? If so there was still some alien power acting to frustrate Him. Now the *Apocalypse* had hinted very broadly at
the shortcomings of the Redemption; [44] and Origen,[45] Ambrosiaster,[46] and Gregory of Nazianzus [47] explained how,
according to the Old Testament, God had made one or more
earlier efforts to redeem man which had each proved abor-
tive. Had the Redemption, then, perhaps not achieved everything that Christ might have wished? Tertullian said it had
lessened rather than extinguished the independent power of
the devil.[48] Gregory of Nyssa, explaining that suffering arose
out of the struggle of the soul to free itself from the body,
laid the blame for the world's miseries on matter.[49] Ambrose
says that when the soul is freed of its body it acquires a new
vigour.[50] And finally Theodore of Mopsuestia, youngest of
the Greek theologians before Augustine, declares that the
soul, by being rid of its body, is rid also of the evil that is
attached to it.[51] Thus, even if the devil was not still under

[42] Because the acid test of martyrdom proved devotion to a degree
that the lesser trials of others, who
were nevertheless also saved, did not.
Cf. pp. 362 n. 35, 383–84, 414, & 423.

[43] Another reason for declaring
baptism indispensable to salvation
was the prevalent habit of postpon-
ing it. For baptism wiped out all
past sins, whereas after baptism only
one mortal sin would be officially
forgiven: Tixeront 1921 II[6] 187 &
321–22; & Poschmann 1928 I 58 ff;
see p. 594; & cf. Augustine *Confessions* I 11. If one unbaptized believed that it lay in his own power
to be baptized whenever he chose, he
was too likely to postpone it; whereas

if he was convinced that the wish
came from the outside, as an unearned and therefore lucky divine
grace, he would be likely to judge
that he had better take advantage of
any present wish, fearful that such a
wish might never again be vouchsafed him.

[44] Cf. Tixeront 1924 I[9] 107–08.

[45] Duchesne 1911 I[6] 355.

[46] Rivière 1905 401.

[47] Ibid. 177.

[48] Tixeront 1924 I[9] 405.

[49] Cherniss 1930 56.

[50] *De Excessu Fratris* II § 3.

[51] Turmel 1931 I 76. Theodore
was born in 350 and died in 428.

serious suspicion, matter was; even without the serpent there was still the apple.[52]

And why, after all, should this not be? Since the old Adam, for all the grace in him, had been so easily seduced, would all the graces showered on us by the Redemption — and all the privileges and barriers designed to protect us — prove adequate to forestall recurrences of that memorable disaster? [53] Man was still weighed down by the burden of an ancient wrong.[54] What was the cause of this? Might it not even be because, as Tertullian had averred, the devil and his minions stalked the earth as hitherto, and kept it vile?

These earlier theologians had grappled boldly with the problem of evil; but they had not resolved it.

[52] Certainly the ascetic current, frankly hostile to matter, was as strong as ever during the fourth century. On monasticism see ch. VII. The vogue of chastity, at least, was on the increase: (a) the clergy were forbidden to live with their wives or marry: Duchesne 1911 I [6] 531–32; (b) Mary was declared not only to have conceived, but to have died, as a virgin: Tixeront 1921 II [6] 330–31, & 1924 I [9] 411–12.

[53] If the devil had originally acquired his dominion by violence, might he not re-acquire such dominion, by another *coup d'Etat?* That God would have any reason again to enter into a legal compact with the devil was unlikely. And yet, if those who died unbaptized were damned precisely as men were damned during the pre-Redemption era, could it be said that the devil had been shorn of all his powers?

[54] Observe that baptism did not remove any of the penalties imposed on Adam: physically the burden of original sin subsisted in its entirety, an embarrassing fact to which the theologians hesitated to call attention. See, however, Ambrosiaster *Commentaria . . . ad Roman.* V § 12. The unbaptized, indeed, were spiritually rather worse off — certainly in comparison with the Patriarchs and Prophets. The baptized were technically better off spiritually; but this depended a great deal on how much more was now expected of them.

CHAPTER II

AUGUSTINE

A. Augustine's Pagan Phase

AUGUSTINE, the greatest theologian and probably the greatest Roman of the Empire, was born at Tagaste in 354. His parents were inconspicuous but well-to-do; the mother, Monica, a devout Christian, the father a pagan whose ambition induced him to give his son the best education that Proconsular Africa could provide. Before many years this son had become a promising teacher of rhetoric, training the young lawyers in that eloquence which was then so essential to their success. But Augustine was also of a speculative turn of mind — from the beginning a searcher after truth — and when not yet twenty years old was already an initiate in the persecuted sect of the Manichees.[1] What was this new sect?

The Manichees had grown out of an effort to reconcile Mithraism with the already triumphant Christianity. Hardly known before the early fourth century they began, after about 340,[2] to recruit their numbers from the wholly un-Christian Mithraists, and in the later half of that century became a menace not only to Christian orthodoxy but even to the State. Fundamentally they retained the frank dualism of the Mithraists,[3] but the prominence of the devil in the Christian theology of this time made plausible a reconciliation with the doctrine of Christ. Although they repudiated Jehovah and declared the Old Testament a work of the devil, they condescended to give Christ the honour of a rank next below that of their Persian founder Mani — successive prophets launched in a gigantic combat against the powers of evil.[4]

---

[1] See Augustine's *Confessions* I–III; & cf. ibid. VIII 7.

[2] Stoop 1909 62–68 chooses 350, Wesendonk 1922 51 chooses 330, as the time when Manichæism began to exert an important influence within the Empire.

[3] Stoop 1909 26–33 etc., stresses the oriental and Greek character of the Manichæan doctrine; Burkitt 1925 66–94 stresses its Greek and Christian character; Cumont 1929 4 131 says it was heir to the cardinal doctrines of the Mithraists.

[4] On their attitude towards the Bible see Augustine *Confessions* V 11, *Contra Faustum passim*, & *D.C.D.* XI 13.

Matter and demons were still, as in Mithraism, the sources of evil, for as Augustine described it,

I believed evil to have been a kind of substance, and [that it] had a bulk of earth belonging to it, either deformed or gross, which they called earth, or else thin and subtle (like the body of the air), which they imagine to be some ill-natured mind gliding through the earth.   For I know not what imperfect piety constrained me to believe that the good God never created any evil nature.[5]

It was therefore easy to believe further

that man is evil on account of the nature of the race of darkness which . . . was an object of dread to God; [6]

and that men were condemned to a miserable incarnation

not for any fault of their own, but for being irremediably contaminated by the pollution against which they were sent by the Father to contend; [7]

which explains how Augustine could logically suppose

that it was not we ourselves that sinned, but I know not what other nature in us; and it much delighted my proud conceit to be set outside of fault; and when I had committed any sin not to confess I had done any . . . but I loved to excuse myself, and to accuse I know not what other corruption that I bare about me, and that was not I.[8]

That the essential evil of this earth and mind obliged man to sin — against God's will and his own — was virtually the old Mithraic teaching; yet there had also been a positive side to Mithraism: a faith in the natural capacity of man, by fighting gallantly against evil, to overcome it; and this the Manichees abandoned.   Instead, a new strategy was now recommended, whereby self-discipline, which had been a mere means to the Mithraists, became itself the end.[9]   The social fatalism which Christianity had popularized was appropriated: since man could do nothing to improve the carnal world, the heroic deeds of the Mithraist were useless; the only task within man's power was, by a repudiation of his body, to

[5] *Confessions* V 10. And cf. ibid. VII 2; & Burkitt 1925 31, 51, & 95.
[6] *Contra Faustum* XIX § 24.
[7] Ibid. V § 7.

[8] *Confessions* V 10.
[9] Stoop 1909 10; & Burkitt 1925 4, 39, & 99–100.

purify his soul and set it free.[10]   This, however, was a struggle
of the soul, not to master itself and so its body, but to escape
from a body that defied it — rather a retreat from than an
assault upon evil.

Consequently the Manichees, while avoiding the Mithraic
way of Martha, also avoided the way of Mary; instead they
chose the old puritanical way of the Stoics and Neoplatonists
who sought for virtue in renunciation.   For, so long as the
body is identified with evil, so long will the struggle be inevitably negative — to resist and contract, to repress and submit — so long will there be only elimination and impoverishment.   He who hates the body hates man, and he who hates
man hates life.   Thus is life easy to repudiate — but evil not
so easy.

Therefore, in spite of their attachment to the other-
worldliness of the Gospels, the Manichees were doomed to
fail because they could not shake off the age-long identity of
the body with evil and of the soul with God.[11]   So long as
man believed he could repudiate his body, so long could he
believe that his sins were not his sins but rather those imposed
on him by the body in which the devil had encased him.[12]
Could he only psychologically divest himself of this carnal
vestment he must be spotless and divine.   That he had
achieved this state was the delusion of the Manichæan ' Elect ',
with the result that his pride was open and shameless.[13]   As
if pride must be a virtue because it was not carnal!   And
further, what else than a negative virtue was this sinlessness?
For, as the process of purification advanced, the man receded
— with his sin faded his individuality.   The sublimation of
virtue, and the reward, were the virtual annihilation of the
soul through its absorption into the huge mass of the Light-
Substance.[14]

[10] Duchesne 1911 I 6 561; & Burkitt 1925 32 & 62–63. Stoop 1909 37
& 39 contrasts this view with that of
the Mithraists. The Manichæan
' Elect ' or ' Perfect ', in contrast to
the ordinary members, could not
marry, engage in agriculture or commerce, or kill — even by breaking the
branch of a tree: Stoop 1909 40 & 46–
47. Cf. Augustine Contra Faustum
V § 1.

[11] Cf. Jerome Ad Pammachium
§ 21.
[12] See p. 97.
[13] Augustine Confessions V 3, 10 &
13; & Burkitt 1925 46.
[14] Burkitt 1925 39, 60, 66 & 99–
100. On what this mass or substance
was see Augustine Confessions V 10:
' moles corporum ', ' duas moles ',
' subtile corpus '.

For nine years [15] Augustine held this belief, but soon after his arrival in Rome he renounced it, his pride tapering off into scepticism:

For there rose a conceit in me that those philosophers which they call Academics, should be wiser than the rest, for that they held men ought to make a doubt upon everything, and decreed that no truth can be comprehended by man.[16]

And from Greek doubt was but a short step to Greek philosophy and so to Neoplatonism. Even to Plotinus evil had been conceived as a negative thing, as a passive obstacle hindering God in His efforts to diffuse His perfection. In contrast to the Mithraists and Manichees, therefore, matter, although producing an evil effect, was not caused by any evil intent. Here the conflict was not against another Being but only against privation or absence of Being. Thus matter seemed less a thing to annihilate and more a thing to ameliorate.

The Neoplatonists also taught Augustine that God was not even a very light and ethereal substance, for He was a spiritual substance and therefore outside both time and space. Thus, as Augustine later testified, already then he had

become certain that Thou wert both infinite and yet not diffused over either finite or infinite places.[17]

Furthermore, Neoplatonism had in the meanwhile been radically affected by Christian influences. Plotinus had said that matter was uncreated and that the human soul was a detached particle of God, yet now, in about 383 — or 130 years later — Augustine records that in

certain books of the Platonists, translated out of Greek into Latin . . . I read, not indeed in the self-same words, but to the very same purpose, persuaded by many reasons and of several kinds, that *In the beginning was the Word, and the Word was with God, and that Word was God; and the same was in the beginning with God. All things were made by Him, and without Him was* nothing made *(John* i 1–3) . In that which was made *was life, and the life was the light of men* (ibid. 4) . *And the light shined in the darkness, and the darkness comprehended it not* (ibid. 5) . And for that the soul of man, though it *gives testimony of the light,*

15 *Confessions* III 11, & V 3 & 6.   17 *Confessions* VII 20.
16 Ibid. V 10; & cf. *Enchiridion* 20.

yet itself is not that light (ibid. 8) ; but the Word, God Himself, is
*that true light that lighteth every man that cometh into the world;
and that He was in the world, and the world was made by Him,
and the world knew Him not* (ibid. 9–10) .[18]

Evidently at some time before 383 Neoplatonism was already
teaching, not only that the Word was God, but also that matter was created by God and that the human soul was not a
part of Him.

No doubt there was at this time more than a single school
of Neoplatonic thought; nevertheless such vital changes as
these were cannot but remind us that any doctrine, however
solidly constructed, is so sensitive and delicate that an apparently slight modification here and there, even if innocently conceived, may prove ample to upset it.   And so here:
if God created matter it must be somehow subsidiary and subject to Him.   And to the extent that He can and does manipulate it the effect must somehow prove salutary to all who seek
the Good.   Similarly if the soul is merely an imperfect image
of God, He must have created it too as something imperfect.
Yet by these two changes the antinomy conceived by the
Greeks between the material body and the spiritual soul was
destroyed: each was merely so much created imperfection.
In these imperfections evil of course lay, but in which?   Since
God had not created evil, it must have arisen through change.
But matter, being dead, had no will, and, having no will,
could not change.   The soul, on the other hand, having a
will, could change, and so be the cause of evil.   Even as a
particle of God this soul was thought to have sinned and
fallen; how much the more susceptible to sin must a soul be,
created merely in the divine image?   And, if the soul was
really the cause of sin, might it not be that God had created
matter rather to cleanse than to smirch it?   According to
Plotinus the world-purpose of the incarnation of souls was
to purify that flesh.   But if the flesh was made by God might
not the design rather have been that it purify the soul?

Appointed to teach rhetoric at Milan in 384 Augustine first
came upon Ambrose the bishop, whose eloquence entranced

---

[18] *Confessions* VII 9; & cf. *D.C.D.*
XIV 5, written in about 420: ' The
Platonists, indeed, are not so foolish
as, with the Manichees, to detest our
present bodies as an evil nature; for
they attribute all the elements of
which this visible and tangible world
is compacted, to God their Creator.'

him.[19] It was his first personal contact with enlightened
Christianity.[20] From Ambrose he first learned that the ungainly material of the Old Testament might be taken in a
symbolic instead of a literal sense, and might in this way be
reconciled to the New.[21] And his sympathy was the more
easily won because Ambrose, devout and orthodox Christian
though he was, clung to the older view that the flesh offers a
serious impediment to virtue:

Let us consider then how the creature hath been made subject to
vanity, not indeed willingly, but by the divine ordinance, which
has appointed that our souls should be united to our bodies on
account of their hopes, in order that, hoping for good, they should
make themselves worthy of a heavenly recompense [22]

which is a doctrine none the less Neoplatonic because the
words are in part those of Saint Paul.[23] For, as Ambrose
said elsewhere,

Every soul, therefore, seeing herself shut up in the prison-house
of the body, if she be not debased by her connexion with this
earthly habitation, groans under the burden of the body to which
she is joined; for the corruptible body presseth down the soul.[24]

This is again Saint Paul,[25] with the addition of *The Wisdom
of Solomon;* [26] but it is also Greek and pagan.[27]

For Augustine, therefore, Ambrose provided a stepping-
stone; from paganism to Truth. But, useful — even indispensable — as Ambrose was, he proved unsatisfactory, for he
did nothing to explain evil. This Neoplatonic Christianity
was emotionally seductive but intellectually vulnerable; it
sought to show that evil really did not exist when in fact
everyone knew that it did. For the only suggested source
of evil was this 'creature . . . made subject to vanity, not
indeed willingly.' To be sure these souls had had an irresistible urge to become important, and for this pride in them-

19 *Confessions* V 13. And cf. Dudden 1935 I 327.
20 Cf. *Confessions* V 10: 'quia non
erat catholica fides, quam esse arbi-
trabar.'
21 Ibid. 14. And cf. quotations in
Turmel 1931 I 64–65.
22 *Letter* # 34 § 5.
23 *Romans* viii 20.

24 *Letter* # 34 § 4.
25 II *Corinthians* v 4.
26 ix 15.
27 He denies that the flesh is the
author of sin: *De Jacob* I § 10, for it
is rather the soul's vanity. But he
thinks that the flesh greatly aggra-
vates the soul's sinfulness.

selves — which was hardly more than self-respect — they had
been plunged into an innocent matter for purgation. Yet
before the eyes of all there persisted a trafficking in evil infinitely surpassing any exaggerated self-respect. This evil
could still be called a nothing; [28] yet the fact remained that
this nothing was the cause of all human misery. In Ambrose,
evidently, the heart had been so intoxicated by the beauty of
the new God that his mind became the willing slave of his
love. In his exhilaration he failed to see that his optimism,
though it was purifying him, offered the pessimist no fair
solution. He was of those who never see evil because they
prefer not to look.

Augustine, on the other hand, was during all this time
specifically groping for a doctrine that would explain the
magnitude of the evil in the world,[29] and he was not to be
put off even by the honeyed eloquence of Ambrose who
thought the extent of evil grossly exaggerated. Indeed it was
Augustine's very consciousness and hatred of evil that made
him so love God. Yet if God too regarded evil as insignificant and ephemeral, He was hardly the God whom Augustine
so longed to love.

It was during these years when Augustine was on the verge
of his conversion that he first learned of Victorinus. This
Victorinus had been, as Augustine now was, a distinguished
rhetorician and Neoplatonist; in about 355 when at the
height of his fame, with his statue already in the Roman
Forum, he had created a sensation by publicly acknowledging Christianity.[30] Now in a work of his, written shortly
after his conversion, Augustine must [31] have read this passage:

It is the soul which, being free, has, by the abuse of its free will,
violated the power bestowed on it. It is trapped by a foolish
greed and lust rather than by pride.[32]

---

[28] In his *Enchiridion* 11 Augustine
says: ' For what is that which we call
evil but absence of good? ' But is not
the corollary just as plausible, that
good is nothing more than the absence of evil?
[29] *Confessions* VII 3, 5, 7, & 12.
[30] Ibid. VIII 2. And cf. Monceaux 1894 402–05; & Labriolle 1934
340.

[31] For the deep impression made
on Augustine by the career and conversion of Victorinus, see his *Confessions* VIII 2. And cf. Duchesne 1911
III 4 121 n. 1.
[32] *Ad Justinum Adimantum* § 16
(of about 357–370).

If Victorinus could thus advance in perception why should
not Augustine? Granted that the soul, no longer now a part
of God, had been not only proud but greedy and lustful, was
it not less likely that either God or necessity was the cause?
Yet Augustine, during those decisive months between his
conversion in August 386 and his baptism at Easter 387, was
still in a quandary. For in November 386 [33] he wrote to a
friend:

When either God, or nature, or necessity, or our own will, or
some or all of these together (for the matter is very obscure, but
you have undertaken to explain it) has cast us into this world
as if upon some stormy sea — and, it might seem, at random —
how many may know on what to lean or by which way to return?
Unless by chance some storm, which to the dull appears adverse,
should throw together even the unwilling and resisting — lost and
wandering — on the longed-for shore.[34]

That his conversion was the result of a violent change of heart
there cannot be a doubt — for to deny that already then he
knew and loved God as he was ever after to know and love
Him is to challenge the veracity of his *Confessions*.[35] It may
be questioned, however, whether, already then, he knew himself and so man as he was later to know him, and whether he
yet understood the whole relation between God and man as
he was later to understand it. He had learned what humility was, but not yet what it taught.

B. Augustine from 387 to 400

In the year 387, at the age of thirty-three, Augustine, the
brilliant young African rhetorician, formally renounced the
pagan way of life and was baptized into the Christian faith.
What was its peculiar appeal to such a man as he then was?
Observe that at this age of thirty-three he was still too young
to have known bodily pain not due to intemperance, already
too prosperous to have smarted from the world's cruelty or

[33] Turmel 1931 I 88.
[34] *De Beata Vita* § 1.
[35] *Confessions* VII 9–17, & VIII 18–
IX 6.

indifference. As, therefore, he sinned in his worldly life and remorsefully repented, only to sin again and repent again, he perceived that the misery he suffered was not being caused by aerial demons or evil men, that it was not being caused by outward circumstances beyond his control.[1] The only dangerous demons were those men with whom he had deliberately chosen to associate; the only evil circumstances were also those that he had chosen. He could quite as well have chosen other men, other circumstances. Doubtless in his periods of remorse he had observed the many occasions when he had been cold-blooded and ruthless, envious, proud, and unjust. What caused these sins? Was it not preposterous to blame demons or other men, nature or his humble body, for outrages manifestly committed by him? What flagrant hypocrisy for his soul to blame other factors when it alone was to blame!

He pondered the Christian explanation of how evil entered the world. If the Fall were merely allegory it was no better than any of the current pagan myths — which really explained nothing. But suppose the story of the Fall were literal; suppose Adam really had existed, with a free will, and had, by abusing it, vitiated his divinely created nature? Might not this perhaps be the key which would unlock the mystery of evil?

Most of the earlier Christians had asserted that the Redemption had restored man to the felicitous condition of the innocent Adam;[2] for it was awkward to admit that Christ's sacrifice had done less good than Adam's sin had done harm. And yet, should the story of *Genesis* by any chance be literally true,[3] Adam was at first immune to labour, to suffering, even to a bodily death, whereas the holiest living Christian was still subject to all three. And, if man's bodily status was still that of the Fall, so in many ways was his spiritual status: the innocent Adam was fully instructed in the ways of God and

---

[1] Cf. *Confessions* VI 6.

[2] Irenæus: Tixeront 1924 I 9 260, & Bethune-Baker 1933 5 334–35; Hippolytus: Tixeront 1924 I 9 416–17; Cyril of Jerusalem: Rivière 1905 168; Athanasius: Bethune-Baker 1933 5 347, citing *Orat. contra Arian.* II § 68; and even John Chrysostom:

Rivière 1905 185, citing *In Joan. Hom.* XXVI §§ 1–2.

[3] As early as 395 Augustine seems to have taken it literally: *De Libero Arbitrio* III § 31. But he does not recognize the corporeality of Adam's body until after 400: Tixeront 1921 II 6 461.

all His sciences,[4] and he was not only free to repress any
bodily desire, he was free of that desire itself.[5] Yet the holiest
Christian was still steeped in ignorance of God's ways, and his
bodily desire was so urgent that it was not within his power to
repress it.

Evidently, then, the Redemption had not restored man
to the status of the innocent Adam, and, since God is just,
this could only be because man, even now, was still guilty.
It had already been suggested by Ambrose that since the
benefits of the Redemption operated only through baptism,
the unbaptized had had no free will to wish to be baptized,
so that, whether they were or not, it was by God's will.[6] Thus
those who died unbaptized, unless innocent infants,[7] were
punished for sins which they had no power to avoid. But
Augustine further observed that even the innocent infants
were liable to suffering and death; these too, therefore, were
being punished, and this could not be merely because they
had inherited a weakness which obliged them to sin, for they
were too young to sin. It must therefore be because they inherited not only a weakness or inclination to sin but also an
unexpiated guilt, as if they already had sinned.[8]

Now Ambrose had introduced Augustine not only to the
idea of a symbolical interpretation of *Genesis,* but also to the
Neoplatonic conception of the pre-existence of souls.[9] Accordingly Adam's Fall might conceivably be interpreted as
that of all souls, sinning while disembodied and each in its
turn incarnated as a remedial punishment. Augustine had
accepted this explanation for a time,[10] but as he swung away
from Neoplatonism he rejected it, adopting instead the theory
called traducianist, according to which the polluted soul of
Adam subsisted in all his descendants:

If God created a single soul out of which come the souls of all
men, who can say that it did not sin when that first man sinned?[11]

[4] Tixeront 1921 II 6 462–63.
[5] *D.C.D.* XIV 10, 24, & 26.
[6] See pp. 59–60.
[7] Because they had not personally
sinned, but merely inherited a defect, the doctrine up to Augustine
was that they went, not to hell, but
to a neutral limbo: Turmel 1931 I
66–67.

[8] See the mature exposition in
Contra sec. Juliani Respons. V § 64.
And see Tixeront 1921 II 6 470–71.
[9] Turmel 1931 I 69.
[10] Ibid. 89–90.
[11] *De Libero Arbitrio* III § 56.

See, therefore, how hard it was for Augustine to shake himself free of the accumulated thought of antiquity: for this
traducianism, no less than the idea of pre-existence, was a
naturalistic conception — just, if at all, not because humanly
fair but because biologically inevitable. It ran counter both
to the legal idea of a humane equity and to the Christian
idea of an even more humane mercy. Both civil bankruptcy [12] and religious absolution were based on the assumption that a soul, even in the course of its maturity, can change
into something new and better, that it is therefore not fair
to saddle man for ever with the burden of his past misdeeds.

Until about 397 [13] Augustine was sure of only two things:
the omnipotence and benevolence of God, and the stupidity
and malice of men. His faith in God was based on his intuition of the power of Good; his conviction about men was
based on his close scrutiny of himself. He became a Christian
because he found that the Bible specifically taught these two
facts. Henceforth his task was to explain the whole of reality
— as man could experience it — in terms of these two certainties. Now the Bible taught that during the period after
the Fall the gulf between God and man had been wide;
clearly, then, the Redemption had been an effort by God to
re-establish an effective contact between them. How successful had it proved? The earlier Christians had taken
a sanguine view, believing that it had restored to man a full
free will to acquire virtue and merit.[14] Certain Latins, however, and particularly Ambrose, had recently explained that
this was restored only by baptism.

This doctrine of Ambrose must have had a special appeal
for Augustine. Hitherto he had understood that Christians
— in contrast to Manichees or Neoplatonists — must believe
in a universal free will, whereas in himself he felt none. Of
his state of mind a few years before his baptism he writes,

[12] See p. 8 n. 63.

[13] Tixeront 1921 II [6] 461, a work
which has the *imprimatur* of Catholic orthodoxy, says: ' En général, et
sauf de légères exceptions, on ne se
trompera pas trop en partageant à
ce point de vue sa vie littéraire en
deux périodes, l'une de recherches
auxquelles se mêlent quelques hési-
tations et qui va de l'an 386 à l'an
397, date de sa consécration épisco-
pale; l'autre de possession définitive
de la doctrine, et qui se confond avec
la durée de son épiscopat, 397–430:
cette possession, on le comprend,
n'excluant pas d'ailleurs un certain
progrès de lumière, effet heureux du
choc des idées dans la controverse.'

[14] See pp. 59 n. 38, & 380–82.

As for continency, I supposed it to be in the liberty of our own
power, which I for my part felt that I had not; being so foolish
withal, that I knew not it was written, that no man can preserve
his chastity unless Thou give it.   And Thou verily wouldst have
given it if with cordial groanings I should have knocked at Thine
ears, and with a settled faith have cast my cares upon Thee.[15]

And shortly after, emboldened no doubt by the moral support of Ambrose, he is already in a slightly different [16] state
of mind — he is surer that he cannot do what he freely wills,
is trusting more to his own feelings and less to the doctrine
as commonly taught:

I now knew as well that I had a will, as that I had a life: and
when therefore I did either will or nill anything, I was most sure
of it, that I and no other did will and nill: and there was the
cause of my sin, as I perceived presently.   But what I did against
my will, that I seemed to suffer rather than to do: that I judged
not to be my fault, but my punishment; whereby I, holding Thee
most just, quickly confessed myself to be not unjustly punished.[17]

Whether he then hoped that, once baptized, he would — as
Ambrose was alleging — feel himself rid of this impediment,
he does not tell us; but if he did he must soon after have been
disabused.   For if, after baptism, he felt infinitely lighter,
happier and wiser, felt a virtue in him that he had not felt before, he also felt that this was not his doing but God's.   He
seemed changed only because he had found God.

Even the doctrine of Ambrose, therefore, now seemed only
half true.   For if baptism relieved man neither of toil, suffering, death, nor ignorance, why assume that it does relieve
the burden on the will?   Who or what has ever led us to
believe that baptism in any way restored man's fallen status?
Does it do more than drive the devil out and let the Spirit
in?   Baptism restores, not free will, then, but only a preliminary grace.   Curiously enough it was in 397, the very

[15] *Confessions* VI 11.
[16] *Felt* is merely ' eram conscius ';
judged is ' judicabam '.
[17] *Confessions* VII 3.   In his *De
Prædest. Sanctorum* § 8, written in
429, he says that he had not believed
in free will since 397.   Yet in his
Confessions of 399 he says he doubted
it before 387!   Perhaps for a time

after baptism he felt obliged to believe in at least a post-baptismal free
will.   Then, in 397, he became a
bishop and in this same year his master Ambrose died.   Only then did he
feel free to voice an opinion which
he had secretly held since 387 and
doubtless since he first became a
Manichee.

year of Ambrose's death, that Augustine first formulated the doctrine of predestination, and he does this without any suggestion that baptism affects this fallen status:

God comes to the help of, or abandons, whom He chooses, since those He helps and those He abandons belong to the same lump of sinners.[18]

And two years later he is as specific as he is concise: speaking of the proud, he says,

These may please themselves, but Thee do they displease highly; not only for pleasing themselves in things not good as if they were good, but also for so doing in Thy good things as if they were their own; or as if Thine yet as given them for their own merits; or, if also as proceeding from Thy mere grace, yet not in a neighbourly spirit, but as grudging it to others.[19]

He here describes first those who do evil proudly, as if they were doing good; secondly, those who do good proudly, as if the cause were their own merit; thirdly, those who do good proudly, as if the immediate cause were grace, yet as if conferred because of their own merit; lastly, those who do good proudly, recognizing that grace alone and not any merit of theirs is the cause, yet somehow preening themselves that this grace should fall, however undeservedly, on them. The whole future controversy over grace and free will is outlined in this one packed sentence: listed in order are the Epicureans, the Pelagians, the Semi-Pelagians,[20] and lastly Augustine himself.[21]

Moreover the sentence further reveals why Augustine felt compelled to go so far: for he perceives how, even if men accept his doctrine of predestination, they will somehow eke out a pretext for pride. Yet this pride is a sin, everywhere and always, the more so not only because the pagans admired it but also because it is the most insidious of sins and the most difficult to be rid of.[22] Yet if we shall admit that man can ever acquire any merit at all he could justly take pride in

[18] '. . . ex eadem massa sint peccatorum': *De Diversis Quaest.* qu. 2 § 17. And cf. Tixeront 1921 II [6] 490. On the use of the word *massa* see Buonaiuti 1917 117–25.

[19] *Confessions* X 39. And cf. ibid. VII 21, & IX 13.

[20] Including the post-baptismal doctrine of Ambrose.

[21] See pp. 127–32, & 394–98.

[22] Cf. *Confessions* X 36.

his accomplishment, and thus, in a sense, sin justly. Therefore Augustine never tired of insisting that, as he truly believed, man was born — and lived and died — a guilty wretch, whose only hope lay, not in himself, but in the free grace which God might, or might not, choose to bestow. For were man given the slightest encouragement to believe that he had, or might have, the capacity to earn any merit, however slight, of his own, how should he be truly humble, how confess and repent, how beg rather for mercy than justice, how stem his horrid pride? Moreover, if we are to admit that man is something, how are we to believe that God is all?

With this conception, so fantastic and even repulsive, yet so salutary and even logical, Augustinian theology approached its final and majestic maturity. Great as Augustine otherwise was, great as had been his predecessors, had it not been for this gigantic effort to pierce the mystery of man's dilemma, Christianity and Western civilization could never have become what they did become, ancient thought could never have been so utterly shattered. For this tight coupling of God's omnipotence with man's impotence, of God's nobility with man's baseness, cast man completely at God's feet. Sinful, miserable, ignorant, helpless, man's only hope now was to make a full confession of his sins, repent of them, and try to touch God's heart. To the pagan a grovelling suppliant; to himself a confessor at last of bitter truth.

It was thus that Augustine, by his doctrine of predestination, was able to inaugurate an analysis of man's psychological constitution unparalleled in any previous age. For the faith that God, full of love and mercy, yet hating evil with the full force of His majesty, found only evil impulses in man's heart, transformed the whole conception of prayer and so of man's relation to the Almighty. The Neoplatonic God neither loved man nor could help him if He would; the God of the earlier Christians, though He loved man, would only help him to the extent man helped himself; but the God of Augustine did not merely love man, He would help him, however little he deserved it, all He could. In the one Fate ruled, in the other justice, in the third mercy.

To the earlier Christians like Ambrose, as to Augustine, God was a Person who could read every thought and sub-

conscious desire in man's heart. Since nothing could be hid
it was best not to try any hiding.[23] But if man's salvation
depended on the merit he acquired? How could man then
resist, in his confession, an undue emphasis on meritorious
behaviour and, in the case of evil behaviour, an undue
emphasis on extenuating circumstances? But this was not
prayer, for it was not supplication but argument. It promoted not self-knowledge but self-deception. True prayer
is not to demand justice but to beg mercy.[24] Only so could
man penetrate to the darkest recesses of his conscience, pry
out, recognize and analyze his sin, and, knowing it as it actually was, hate and repudiate it. This acid discipline in
self-knowledge, acquired only through a merciless and mortifying examination of conscience,[25] has now been a matter of
common knowledge for fifteen hundred and more years; but
on the Roman of the year 400 the effect was overpowering.
Augustine's own description is classic:

Too late came I to love Thee, O Thou Beauty both so ancient
and so fresh, yea too late I came to love Thee. And behold, Thou
wert within me, and I out of myself where I made search for

[23] In *Confessions* X 2 he says, ' And
from Thee, O Lord, unto whose eyes
the bottom of man's conscience is
laid bare, what could be hidden in
me though I would not confess it?
For so should I hide Thee from me,
not myself from Thee.'

And in ibid. 5, ' Although no man
knows the things of a man but the
spirit of man which is in him; yet is
there something of man, that the
very spirit of man that is in him,
knoweth not. But Thou knowest all
of him, Who hast made him.'

[24] It has been said that a true
scientist is one who, at sunrise, is
naturally conscious that it is the
earth which is revolving and not the
sun which is rising. So it might be
said that a true Christian is one who,
when praying, is naturally conscious
that he is not affecting the will of
God. But the general run of Christians could not be expected to pray
in this way: cf. pp. 158–59.

[25] Plotinus and Porphyry both
urged the importance of self-knowledge: Whittaker 1901 112–13. But
this self-knowledge was of a soul that

was assumed to be divine — and
hence man's better self. The Christians, on the other hand, and
Augustine particularly, urged a self-
knowledge of man's baser self.

In *Letter* # 28 § 6, of 395, to
Jerome, Augustine says, ' I catch occasional sight of my faults, but I prefer to hear of them from better men,
lest, after censuring myself, per-
chance rightly, I fall again into self-
flattery and think that my judgment
of myself was more finical than fair.'

In *Confessions* X 37 he says, ' Behold, O Truth, in Thee I see that I
ought not so much for mine own
sake to be moved at mine own
praisies as for the good of my neighbour. And whether so I be, I know
not. For I know less of myself in
this, than of Thee. I beseech now, O
my God, discover me unto myself.'

And in ibid. 38 he says, ' And with
a greater vanity does a man glory
oftentimes of his contemning of vain-
glory; for which reason he cannot
now be said to glory in his contempt
of vain-glory: for he does not truly
contemn it, who glories at it.'

Thee; I ugly rushed headlong upon those beautiful things Thou hadst made. Thou indeed wert with me, but I was not with Thee.[26]

In another passage he analyzes the obstacles confronting men in this search — their carelessness and cowardice:

For a happy life is a rejoicing in the truth; for this is a joying in Thee, who art the Truth, O God my Light, the Health of my countenance, and my God. This is the blessed life that all desire; this life which alone is blessed do all desire; to joy in the truth is all men's desire. I have had experience of divers that would deceive, but not a man that would willingly be deceived. . . . Wherefore then joy they not in it? Why are they not happy? Even because they are more strongly taken up with other things which have more power to make them miserable than that hath to make them happy which they remember so little of. For there is a dim glimmering of light unput-out in men: [27] let them walk, let them walk, that the darkness overtake them not.[28] . . . Therefore do they hate the truth, for the sake of that thing which they love instead of truth. They love truth when it enlightens them, but they hate it when it reprehends them. For because they would not willingly be deceived and fain would deceive, do they love it when it discovers itself, but hate it when it discovers them.[29]

This discovery — of the truth that reprehends: that man is fundamentally selfish, brutal, and proud, and that to believe himself otherwise is miserable self-deception [30] — destroyed the whole mentality of the ancient world which was founded on self-respect.[31]

C. Augustine's Mature Doctrine

Not until after the year 400 did Augustine concentrate on the problem of the Fall. Since God could not create anything evil His creations of the angels, of matter, of man, were each

---

26 *Confessions* X 27.
27 Might this possibly be an echo of the theory of the pre-existence of souls?
28 From *John* xii 35.
29 *Confessions* X 23.
30 See *Confessions* VIII 7: 'Thou

now settedest me before mine own face, that I might discern how filthy, and how crooked, and sordid, and bespotted, and ulcerous I was.'
31 Cf. Dudden 1935 531 on Aristotle's disdain of the humble. The passage in Cleanthes' *Hymn* of about

perfect in their kind. But, just as the angels had free will and many of them abused it, so did man have free will and the first man, Adam, abused it. Therefore, just as the devil thereby vitiated his nature, transforming it into something hateful, so did Adam; each, by his free will, turned perfection into imperfection,[1] order into disorder.[2] God had, to be sure, made evil a potentiality or contingency, but since it depended wholly on the devil's and man's initiative to actualize this evil they could fairly be held to blame.

Of the nature of Adam's sin Augustine is specific:

Even in that one sin . . . a number of distinct sins may be observed, if it be analyzed as it were into its separate elements. For there is in it pride, because man chose to be under his own dominion rather than under the dominion of God; and blasphemy, because he did not believe God; and murder, for he brought death on himself; and spiritual fornication, for the purity of the human soul was corrupted by the seducing blandishments of the serpent; and theft, for man turned to his own use the food he had been forbidden to touch; and avarice, for he had a craving for more than should have been sufficient for him; and whatever other sin can be discovered on careful reflection to be involved in this one admitted sin.[3]

By sinning, Adam incurred guilt and therefore a just punishment:

Sinners are ordained to punishment; which ordination is punishment because it is not conformable to their nature, but it is justice because it is conformable to their fault.[4]

This punishment was partly physical, exposing man to toil, suffering and death, and partly spiritual, depriving man of the knowledge of God and of the free will to acquire merit.

---

250 B.C. is closer to the Christian conception than any later independent pagan expression: ' Nothing is made, is produced, except by thee, barring the evil which arises out of the heart of the evil man.' Quoted by Dourif 1863 98–99.

[1] That is, absolute imperfection, because a degeneration from itself. This was quite different from the relative imperfection conceived by Plato and Plotinus. To Plotinus man was imperfect, but only in the sense that his being was incomplete; to Augustine man was by nature perfect because he had been created by God, but was now actually imperfect because his perfect nature had been transmogrified by the evil use he had made of his free will: see Tixeront 1921 II [6] 371.

[2] De Natura Boni § 23 (of 404).

[3] Enchiridion 45. Ambrose spoke of both pride and sensuality: Dudden 1935 615.

[4] De Natura Boni § 7.

At this point he is careful to insist that the soul's incarnation in flesh was in no way the cause of the sin, and that even the corruption of the flesh was wholly a consequence of that sin:

> For the corruption of the body, which weighs down the soul, is not the cause but the punishment of the first sin; and it is not the corruptible flesh that made the soul sinful, but the sinful soul that made the flesh corruptible.[5]

The cause of Adam's own plight evidently offered no difficulty, for he had no one to blame for it but himself. To explain why his descendants should thereafter share his plight was, however, most difficult. Any Roman knew that in a primitive or clan society descendants were commonly held guilty of the crimes of their ancestors — at least to the third and fourth generations;[6] but the trend of Roman law and opinion had for a long time now been towards a diametrically opposite conception.

Why must Augustine assume an inherited guilt then? Simply because no impartial observer could deny that the descendants of Adam were, even now, still under the bitter regime of suffering and death, and, in the case of infants, for no conceivable fault of their own. The earlier theologians had evaded this embarrassment, talking airily of how, by baptism, this guilt was wiped away; but Augustine, for all his faith in God and Revelation, could not ignore the blunt fact that many even baptized infants suffered miserably and died.

In addition to these penalties there was another — the most terrible of all — of eternal damnation after a miserable earthly life. Baptism could avert this in the few cases where the infant died before growing up — and for all adults it transformed damnation from a certainty to an uncertainty. But baptism could do nothing to mitigate the severity of the other punishments imposed during life on earth. A part of the punishment subsisted therefore — a daily reminder that man was still paying the penalty for Adam's sin. This punishment was just because God imposed it. But why was it just?

The traditional explanation, borrowed from paganism, was

---

[5] *D.C.D.* XIV 3.
[6] *Exodus* xx 5. Cf. *Enchiridion* 46, where Augustine interprets Eze-kiel xviii 5-9 & 14-17 as a prophecy of the New Testament. And cf. ibid. 47.

based on the assumption of the pre-existence of souls. They had somehow sinned before their earthly incarnations. But Augustine soon realized that neither the Bible nor human experience offered any evidence of such a pre-existence. Instead he accepted the traducianist theory, according to which God, in creating Adam, ' created a single soul out of which come the souls of all men.' [7] These souls were somehow kept dormant until God saw fit to incarnate them.[8] But this theory not only required a symbolic rather than a literal interpretation of *Genesis,* it also failed to explain how Christ's human soul could have been undefiled.[9] At least by 415, therefore, Augustine had discarded this traducianist theory too.[10] There remained the creationist theory, according to which the soul, although created after the parents' copulation, became morally soiled by contact with the lust-defiled womb.[11] This explained why, of all human souls, Christ's alone was undefiled; but it was so patently unjust that, rather than accept it, Augustine preferred to remain for the rest of his life in a quandary [12] — one of the major penalties he paid for the sake of intellectual honesty. At all costs he would hold to his faith that God was just, and hold to his conviction that even baptized infants suffered: their guilt was no less certain because he could not learn the how or why.

Augustine offered still another proof of the existence of an inherited guilt:

Why, therefore, in man does lust offer a resistance to the soul which in the case of animals it does not, unless because it is appropriate to the nature of the animal but only to the punishment of man? For how is it that the thing which should not exist does exist, or which should not resist does resist, unless there has been sin? [13]

That after the Fall man was no longer the perfect thing that God created seemed therefore to be proved in several ways: by the suffering of apparently innocent infants, and by the struggle of the mature human soul against the assaults of

<hr>

[7] See p. 72 n. 11.
[8] *De Genesi ad Litteram* VII §§ 22, 24, & 28 (of 401–415).
[9] Tixeront 1921 II [6] 377.
[10] Ibid. 477–78; & quotations in Turmel 1931 I 148–50.

[11] This was the view of Ambrose: see p. 384 n. 16.
[12] *Retractationum* I 1 § 8. And cf. Turmel 1931 I 218–23.
[13] *Contra sec. Juliani Respons.* IV § 41.

lust. That animals suffer neither physical nor mental anguish Augustine, in spite of Porphyry, seems to have taken serenely for granted. He thus glibly evaded the grave issue which much later, from Descartes to Bayle, shook the foundations of the Christian structure.[14] This error of Augustine's, which was due to no intellectual dishonesty but merely to a too superficial observation of the humbler parts of nature, was one reason why he could cling to, yet without solving, the mystery of original sin.[15] By casting overboard all the Neoplatonic ballast he gained an insight into human nature which no ancient before him had had; but by focusing all significant reality on man as a centre he so discredited the natural sciences that their revival was postponed until almost the eighteenth century.[16] For the final triumph of the Fall as the explanation of the human predicament, made secure by the genius of Augustine, destroyed the Greek conception of the natural world.

After the Fall the Redemption. Countless passages in Augustine reflect the influence of the current theological explanation; over and over again he speaks of the Passion as a ransom, a substitution, a satisfaction, a propitiation, an expiation, a sacrifice.[17] It is evident that he accepted the belief that Christ's execution as a criminal somehow lightened the burden of man's guilt, the blood of an innocent having paid a part of the debt. But to whom or to what was this sacrifice made? To the Father, to the devil, or to some independent law of justice?

The Gnostic suggestion that the Father represented justice and the Son mercy, and that the Son had died in order to melt His Father's heart, although it had enticed Cyril of Jerusalem,[18] received only scorn from Augustine:

Was it indeed so that when God the Father was wroth with us, He saw the death of His Son for us, and was appeased towards

14 Pickman 1932 234–41.

15 For if Augustine had realized that animals suffered much as men do he must have revised his whole conception of the divine plan. Their punishment could be just only if they had been guilty.

16 Miall 1912 x; & add the names of Leibnitz and Bayle.

17 Rivière 1905 256–57; Tixeront 1921 II 6 382.

18 See p. 56 n. 29.

us? Was then His Son already so far appeased towards us that He even deigned to die for us; while the Father was still so far wroth that except His Son died for us He would not be appeased? . . . Pray, unless the Father had already been appeased, would He have delivered up His own Son, not sparing Him for love of us? . . . Therefore both the Father and the Son and the spirit of both, work all equally and harmoniously.[19]

In whatever sense the Father may at one time have been wroth with man, He was appeased at the moment of the Redemption. Even then there was still wrath between man and God, but it was not God's towards man, it was man's towards God. Rather it was unregenerate man who must be appeased.[20]

Did Augustine then think that Christ's sacrifice had been to the devil? Such an alternative seemed to him equally preposterous, for God did not

dismiss man from the law of His own power when He permitted him to be in the power of the devil; since even the devil himself is not separated from the power of the Omnipotent, as neither from His goodness.[21]

The devil, indeed, continues to exist at all only because God continually wills that he shall; if God should cease so to will the devil would cease to exist,

since the devil's nature subsists only by the supreme Creator, who gives being to all that in any form exists.[22]

Actually the devil was no more than the jailer, under orders to keep his prisoners in custody. His possession of them was legal but was revocable at will.

At the same time, however, Augustine was fond of saying [23] that by the Redemption the devil had been enticed and trapped, the bait set being Christ,[24] the first sinless man since the created Adam. For the devil, supposing this man

[19] *De Trinitate* XIII § 15.
[20] Rivière 1933 [3] 167, 191, & 351–54.
[21] *De Trinitate* XIII § 16. And cf. Rivière 1933 [3] 34, 65–66, 83–85, & 134.
[22] *D.C.D.* XXII 24 (*D. & K.* II 610 lines 20–21). And cf. Tixeront 1921 II [6] 370.
[23] As in *Sermons* # 130 § 2, # 134

§§ 4–6, # 263 §§ 1–2, & # 344 § 4. See Turmel 1931 I 362–63 for French translations of these passages. Cf. Rivière 1933 [3] 117–18.
[24] Rivière 1933 [3] 320–38. And cf. ibid. 137–46 on whether Augustine thought the devil was merely deceived or was rather pig-headed.

to be like all the other descendants of Adam, had tempted him. His custody of man, however, had been granted on the implied condition that he should hold only the guilty — a single miscarriage of justice and this right was forfeited.[25] That Christ should thus trick the devil seemed hardly consonant with His dignity; but He evidently had no alternative. For although God or Christ could prevent the devil from doing what He did not wish him to do, He could not oblige him to do what he did not wish to. God could annihilate but could not reform him. The reason was that the devil, unlike matter and even animals, had a will which was none the less real because evil. Like unregenerate man, the devil too was a thing-in-itself, to be controlled, therefore, negatively by violence but positively by artifice. The idea recalls the old proverb:

A man may well bring a horse to water, but he cannot make him drink without he will.[26]

God must therefore be resourceful, fertile in expedients, for often, in order to control both demons and man, He must alternately bully and cajole, frighten and encourage, flatter and deceive. The Redemption, so far as the devil was concerned, seemed to Augustine a case of pious fraud.

Augustine's predecessors would have been only too glad to be rid of the abhorrent theories of a wrathful Father or an independent devil, but only if some equally plausible and more agreeable explanation were offered in their stead. This was the task that now challenged Augustine's genius.[27]

One possible way out was based on the assumption of some cosmic law of justice, by which not only the devil but God also was bound. If it could be reasonably assumed that all mankind must share a common destiny — blessed so long as their total sins did not outweigh their total virtues, damned so long as their total sins tipped the scales in their favour — it could be argued that the punishment inflicted on the innocent human Christ, because He was at the same time God, had sufficed to redress the balance in favour of innocence and virtue, thereby setting all the guilty free. This, forty years earlier, had been the theory of Cyril of Jerusalem:

---

25 Rivière 1933 ³ 138, 154 & 388.   27 Cf. Rivière 1933 ³ 210–11 & 354–
26 John Heywood *Proverbes* I 11.   58.

The injustice done by the sinners was not as great as the justice done by Him who died for us; our sins together were not worth so much as was the virtue of Him who delivered up His soul for us.[28]

Fundamentally, however, this theory was a primitive one, harking back to an age which practised human sacrifice of an innocent, or imposed revenge on others of the same family or tribe where the wrongdoer could not himself be caught. Hostages are a modern survival, where the primitive instinct of treating a hostile people as a moral unit is brought to life again. To an enlightened Roman,[29] however, as to a modern, the idea that justice is satisfied because the punishment of an innocent leads to a pardon of the guilty is repellent. For two wrongs cannot make a right.

Such a theory of justice was intelligible at all only if it be granted that the devil had had a real legal claim on men. For if, as Ambrose supposed, the devil were analogous to a creditor who holds man as security till his debt of sin is paid, it could be argued that Christ, by His innocent death, had paid the debt and thereby released the security. Man, to be sure, the original debtor, had sacrificed nothing; therefore as between Christ and man there had been the antithesis of justice. To the devil, on the other hand, full justice had been done: for he, as creditor, had no just cause to complain that his debt had been paid by Christ instead of by the original debtor. Augustine denied, however, that the devil had any rights, either as creditor or otherwise; therefore in his eyes the only satisfaction the Redemption could offer was to a primitive communal justice which ignored all individual considerations. To such a conception Augustine could make polite acknowledgment; but he could not accept it as a real solution.[30]

It could be argued much less crudely, however, that such wholesale justice becomes enlightened if considered in terms of human affections: as where a guilty son may be justly pardoned in order to stay the grief of his innocent mother, or where an innocent hostage is punished in order to sadden

---

[28] *Catech.* # XIII § 33 *(P.G.* 33 813A).

[29] Cf. Gibbon 1776 ff. ch. 19 (282).

[30] In 390 Ambrose excommuni-cated Theodosius I for inflicting on the inhabitants of Thessalonica precisely this kind of justice: see Dudden 1935 381–83.

the guilty.   Some such situation is envisaged in *Genesis* xviii
32, where Jehovah promises Abraham that He will spare the
city of Sodom if He can find ten of its inhabitants innocent.
Because he finds only Lot, however, He proceeds with His
destruction.   Evidently Lot's innocence, unlike Christ's, was
not enough to save the guilty; indeed he was even punished
himself, by the loss of wife, home, and all his relatives except
two daughters.   According to this theory the Redemption
was comprehensible provided Christ died in order to appease
His Father's wrath: for how, after such a manifestation of
obedience, courage, humility, and love, could the Father's
heart stay hard?   The justice of leaving unregenerate man in
bondage was outweighed by the injustice of allowing Christ's
sacrifice to prove vain.   But this assumes that very divergence
of will and disposition between Father and Son which
Augustine emphatically repudiated.   Were there no such
divergence the Father must have been as eager to pardon
unregenerate man as the Son was; in which case this pardon
could quite as well have been extended by fiat and the painful
Redemption eschewed.   For it was inconceivable that even a
God would choose to submit to the indignities and pain of the
Redemption merely in order to soften His own heart!

Augustine, moreover, despised the affection of the innocent for the guilty.   Above all he was certain that no God
would ever stoop to such sentimentality.   Mercy did not consist in the pardon of the unregenerate guilty, but in the pardon of the grief-stricken and remorseful penitent.   It was
precisely the failure of Origen to understand true mercy
which led him to believe that God would ultimately pardon
even the guilty.   Naturally God could pardon evil men —
if He chose.   But to Augustine it was obvious that He did
not choose.

Therefore man clearly had to be worth pardoning before
being pardoned.   How was God to make him worth pardoning?   Notice Augustine's description of the devil as hardly
more than a symbol of human sin; [31] the idea was not his, but
the use of it was his.   For in that case emancipation from the
devil meant emancipation from sin, and it must follow that
pardon must be unjust so long as sin subsisted and punish-

[31] Rivière 1933 [3] 18 & 27-28.

ment unjust so soon as the sin ceased. Furthermore Augustine insists that in the sequence of the Redemption man's contrition precedes his pardon.[32] Therefore unless there should be contrition first there could be no pardon; and, once there had been contrition, pardon must automatically follow because of God's mercy. In both cases we see how the contrition is the essential and the pardon the unessential. How, then, did Augustine think that the Redemption produced this contrition?

Athanasius [33] and Gregory of Nyssa [34] had argued that the Incarnation had magically impregnated every individual human being with a sense of shame at the magnitude and vileness of his sin. But why, then, Augustine argued, was it necessary that Christ not only become, but die as, a man? An innocent's death might be needed to induce divine pardon, but why to infuse human contrition? Furthermore, whether this contrition was induced by the Incarnation or by the Passion, the process in either case recalled that of sympathetic magic, Christ having somehow become all men [35] rather as an effigy was thought to become a designated group of individuals. That such a process would automatically induce the requisite contritions smacked far too much of archaic superstition, suggesting that God had resorted to magic in order to circumvent a higher power. For why, otherwise, did He not simply induce such contritions by fiat? The roundabout procedure might be good divine politics: in order to impress the superstitious populace; but to enlightened persons who could grasp the implications of Omnipotence the dependence of grace on such a sacrifice pre-supposed the dependence of the Christian God on the hoary Fate of the pagans. Clearly the bestowal of grace was somehow coincident with the Redemption — for the gift was itself of a faith in that Redemption [36] — but that the sacrifice was in any sense the cause of that gift seemed to Augustine very doubtful. Surely the cause of both was rather the omnipotent will of God, which could quite as well have willed either one without also willing the other. That the Patri-

---

[32] Ibid. 187. Cf. pp. 393-94.
[33] See p. 56 n. 31.
[34] Tixeront 1921 II 6 149-50.
[35] Ambrose thought this: Dudden

1935 610-11. But the devil's defeat was a necessary preliminary to such magic.
[36] *Enchiridion* 118.

archs and Prophets received the grace of a faith in the Redemption before it occurred was conceivable — for divinity operated outside of time. But it was one thing to suppose that God was outside of time in act as well as in will, and quite another to suppose Him deficient in omnipotence.

Christ nevertheless had an obstacle to overcome, which was neither the Father, the devil, nor any higher power either moral or physical. What was it? According to the earlier theologians, God, in order to humiliate as well as dispossess the devil, had had to resort to artifice: there the evil will of the devil had been a definite obstacle. But to Augustine the devil was hardly more than a personification of the evil will of men — as of Judas and the rest who brought the Passion to pass. God did not care to reform the devil because He had no love for sin; but God did care to reform man because He loved that part of man that was not sin. God might have reformed man by the same infusion of virtue that He had already given the angels who had chosen not to fall.[37] But He wanted man to have an indispensable if minute part in winning his own security. It was because God not only loved but respected man, because He valued each man as an individual entity, that He preferred instead the far more arduous but ultimately more rewarding course of trying — by bullying and cajolery, by frightening and encouraging, by flattery and deceit — to induce man to try to reform himself.

Two discredited African theologians of the early fourth century, Arnobius and Lactantius, had said that the real purpose of the Redemption was in order to teach men to love God.[38] It was this theory that, nearly a hundred years later, their great fellow-countryman was now to revive. What, then, according to Augustine, was the true divine strategy?

First he explains why the Redeemer had to be a God: since a God was certainly equally able to redeem men in any other way [39] — as by fiat — that He nevertheless chose to redeem them by dying proved not only how much He loved them but also that His sole purpose in dying was in order to

---

[37] *Enchiridion* 28 & 57. Cf. Ambrose *De Fide* III §§ 19–20.
[38] Rivière 1905 214–24; Tixeront 1924 I 9 416–17; & cf. p. 56 n. 31.

[39] Rivière 1905 248; Tixeront 1921 II 6 381; & Bethune-Baker 1933 5 350–51.

teach them how much He loved them.[40]   Consequently the
Redemption had no cosmological, physiological, or magical,
but merely a psychological, purpose; and its effect was not produced by any inner infusion of virtue but merely by the
natural reaction of men's autonomous inner disposition to
an external stimulus.

Among Augustine's many reasons why Christ had also to
be a man, we find an identical preoccupation with this didactic or psychological aspect.   One reason, which he never
tired of reiterating, was that God wished to teach men the
innocence and dignity of the flesh.[41]   Another was His wish
that men observe the contrast between the innocent Son's
ready obedience to the Father and the irresolution [42] and
disobedience [43] of guilty men.   But lastly and above all it
seemed to Augustine that Christ had assumed a human nature in order to teach men that to God alone was the power,
and that it was therefore the sole task of men to fight evil
not outwardly but inwardly, not by violence but by humility,
not by hate but by love.[44]   Speaking of his state of mind just
before his conversion he recalls how

I, not yet humble enough, did not apprehend my Lord Jesus
Christ, who had made Himself humble; nor did I yet know what
lesson that infirmity of His would teach us.[45]

It was only later that the importance of Christ's lesson became clear to him:

It pleased God that in order to rescue man from the grasp of the
devil, the devil should be conquered, not by power, but by righteousness; and that so also man, imitating Christ, should seek
to conquer the devil by righteousness, not by power.   Not that
power is to be shunned as though it were something evil; but the
order must be preserved whereby righteousness is before it.   For
how great can possibly be the power of mortals?   Therefore
let mortals cleave to righteousness; power will be given to im-
mortals.[46]

[40] Rivière 1905   258; Bethune-
Baker 1933 [5] 349–51.
[41] See p. 50 n. 46.
[42] Rivière 1905 254.
[43] Turmel 1931 I 376; Rivière
1933 [3] 354–58.
[44] Rivière 1905 258–59.
[45] *Confessions* VII 18.

[46] *De Trinitate* XIII § 17.   In *Enchiridion* 53 he says that 'All the
events, then, of Christ's crucifixion
. . . were so ordered that the life
which the Christian leads here might
be modelled upon them.'   Cf. Rivière
1905 258–59.

Evidently the more deeply Augustine probed the mystery of the Redemption the more doubtful he became of the validity of any of the traditional or current explanations, and the more convinced he became that the solution lay not in any intrinsic effect of Incarnation or Passion, but in the extrinsic effect of the whole proceeding on the mind and will of man. The Redemption was, therefore, a Revelation more in deeds than in words. The real marvel was that Christ practised what He preached.

The extent to which Augustine conceived Christianity in psychological rather than in cosmological or other terms is very remarkably illustrated in his account of two priests, each of whom had contradicted the story of the other. Augustine thereupon sent them to the famous tomb of Felix, at Nola, enjoining both to swear there that they were telling the truth. His purpose in this was, as he put it,

to compel the guilty to confess, either by judgment or through fear of judgment.[47]

He was not here specifically doubting whether God would there pass miraculous judgment; at the same time he was confident that the fear of both priests that God would do this must exert such pressure on their consciences that the truth would come out. Like that of the Redemption, the utility of the miracle was not physical but psychological.[48]

Moreover there was another potent argument: Christ had been willing to die in order to help the ignorant guilty: but there was no indication that He intended ever to die again in order to help the instructed guilty. Therefore the purpose of His death was to instruct.

That such was Augustine's real view seems also to be corroborated by his belief that some of the Patriarchs and Prophets of the Old Testament had been saved. For, after speaking of Christ's Incarnation, he observes that

it was by faith in this mystery, and by godliness of life, that purification was attainable even by the saints of old, whether before the Law was given to the Hebrews (for God and the angels were even then present as instructors) , or in the periods under the Law.[49]

---

[47] *Letter* # 78 § 3. Quoted more fully p. 221 n. 42.

[48] See p. 219.
[49] *D.C.D.* X 25.

These men were saved,[50] not because of the Redemption, but because of their faith in its coming, because of the instruction they had received. Why, then, did God not choose to grace more of the Hebrews in this way, if He was thus able to grace a few? Since the Redemption was so emphatically intended to instruct men, it seemed natural to infer that the defect of the pre-Redemption era was an inadequate instruction. In other words the faith in God's omnipotence and mercy was then so feeble, and man's love of God so tenuous, that if God had tried to bestow grace at all liberally He risked filling men with such over-confidence that their still feeble wills would not co-operate. And since Augustine conceived of all men as morally equal,[51] their over-confidence would make grace invariably ineffectual and not a single one would be saved. For Augustine was emphatic that the co-operation of the human will was essential if grace was to be effective:

Nobody can be helped who does not make some effort of his own.[52]

The soul cannot receive and possess these gifts . . . except by yielding its own consent.[53]

God not only could but did pardon by fiat, but He pardoned only the contrite,[54] and He chose to promote contrition, not

[50] Although, as Augustine says in *Enchiridion* 109, 'during the time that intervenes between a man's death and the final resurrection, the soul dwells in a hidden retreat where it enjoys rest or suffers affliction according to what it was alloted while living in the flesh.' The Patriarchs and Prophets were therefore already enjoying that rest before the Redemption, while even the post-Redemption saints have as yet received nothing more.

[51] Relying on *I Corinthians* iv 7: 'For who maketh thee to differ from another?'

[52] *De Pecc. Meritis* II § 6, quoted p. 398.

[53] *De Spiritu et Littera* § 60, quoted p. 399.

[54] The current doctrine of adult baptism corroborated this: it does not wipe out either the inherited guilt or the personal sin unless the baptized is — or until he shall be — contrite: Tixeront 1921 II⁶ 404–06.

And see Ambrose *Letter* # 51 § 11: 'If we shall have sinned the Lord Himself . . . does not show mercy unless there is penitence.' Moreover in martyrdom and other conspicuous cases of contrition pardon of both the guilt and the sins results apart from baptism — provided there was no fair opportunity to receive it: ibid. 410; & also Ambrose, acc. to Dudden 1935 420 & 644. One who professes contrition but postpones baptism may fairly be assumed to be shamming. Therefore all the truly contrite infallibly receive pardon, while all the uncontrite do not receive it.

Infant baptism, that *enfant terrible* of Christian theology, here again resists Augustine's every assault: contrition being inconceivable, baptism here becomes decisive: ibid. 405 & 409.

In much the same way Augustine taught that whereas the sacrament of communion accentuated the virtue

by grace only, but also by the help of ingenious devices calculated to rouse men from their lethargy.

Aided only by the meagre Revelation of the Old Testament God had dared to bestow grace only occasionally; the Redemption was therefore resolved upon in order that His grace might be effectually bestowed on a more generous scale. Yet to Augustine even the Redemption did not make it safe for God to bestow His grace on all: for even these instructed men, should they observe the completeness of God's generosity, would, by their over-confidence, so weaken their wills that they could no longer furnish the indispensable quantity of co-operation. Then again, just as before the Redemption, there would be the danger that no one could be saved. God could now save many more than before, but He could not yet save all. Of course God could, had He chosen to, have made men wholly and irretrievably righteous by the universal bestowal of a grace which would be effective apart from the co-operation of the human will. But God did not choose to bestow any such grace because He preferred that men be obliged to exercise their own natural wills, preferred to respect their integrity as human beings. And God can safely do this because

even what is done in opposition to His will does not defeat His will. For it would not be done did He not permit it . . . nor would a good Being permit evil to be done unless because in His omnipotence He can turn evil into good.[55]

Conceived in this fashion, everything — including the Redemption — becomes a spiritual drama concerned exclusively with the mutual relations of God and man as distinct entities, with the sin of man as the sole obstacle to be overcome and the Redemption, with its Incarnation and Passion, as the best means of overcoming it.[56]

---

of the contrite it aggravated the sin of the hypocrite: ibid. 417.

Do not suppose that Augustine was sceptical of physiological effects: for to him the grace of God, most potent of all powers, was often physiological. But he was instinctively sceptical of the alleged physiological influence of concrete acts initiated by men: whether the act be the Crucifixion, baptism, communion (Ambrose was less particular: see Dudden 1935 644 & the quotations in Coulange 1927 87–96 & 101–02), contact with a relic, or prayer. He was, in other words, distrustful of magic.

[55] *Enchiridion* 100.

[56] Rivière 1933 [3] 170 says: ' Dans la vue historique du plan divin qui relie ces différents chapitres du *Con-*

According to Augustine's predecessors the purpose of the Redemption had been cosmological: to shake man loose from the control of some supernatural power which held him in bondage.   Man's destiny had seemed at the mercy of conflicting cosmic powers.   Therefore Christ had died in order to overcome certain obstacles: God's wrath, the devil's possession, or some abstract justice or Fate.   But according to Augustine the Redemption's purpose was intimately moral [57] and individual: to shake man loose from the bondage of his own individual degeneration.   In order to do this God must wheedle and coax, admonish and exhort, and cap all this with an instruction so sensational and moving that man's will, with the help of grace, must repent its past misdeeds and resolve for the future to seek virtue.

According to Augustine, therefore, the Redemption was a most peculiar affair: no less than all the other affairs related in the Old Testament it had been quite literally true; its significance, however, was not literal.   That it seemed a real sacrifice or expiation was because of skilful stage-craft. To be sure Christ really was a man, really did die as a man dies; but not at all for the reasons alleged.   Although the death was literally true, the expiation was only theatrically true: for the plot was simulated and the purpose disguised. The whole affair, indeed, was a pious fraud, practised on man just as it was on the devil; but it was so ingeniously contrived and so well acted that even Augustine, on many occasions, spoke as if he too had been taken in.[58]   This was because he still wanted to be taken in — knowing that God intended him to be, for his own good — but in his heart he knew only too well that he had bared the underlying truth.

For he had become convinced that, so long as God should choose to tolerate the integrity of the human will, so long

---

tra Faustum, ainsi que dans la synthèse dogmatique de l'*Enchiridion,* il saute aux yeux que l'économie de la Rédemption se ramène à un drame spirituel, qui se déroule tout entier entre Dieu et nous, avec le péché comme seul obstacle à vaincre et le sacrifice du Christ comme unique moyen d'y parvenir.'

[57] Rivière 1905 257–58.

[58] Which is perhaps why Turmel,

impatient of orthodox interpretations, can argue that Augustine thought the Redemption a real sacrifice to an independent devil: 1931 I 360–80; and why Tixeront 1921 II [6] 382, & Rivière 1933 [3] 348–64, subservient to orthodox interpretations, can argue that Augustine thought the Redemption a real sacrifice to the Father, was it useless for Him merely to be just and merciful: He must so act as to prove to the most dull and benighted, to the most weak and malicious, that He actually was so.   To be sure in proceeding as He did He encouraged a cosmological — and therefore a false — conception of the pre-Redemption era — a sop He could well afford in order to win the credulity of the unweaned pagan.   Revelation had made it clear to all that since the Redemption there had been no other dualism than that between God's faith in man and man's lack of faith in God.   Augustine, however, was the first to discern that this was not merely the present and latest alignment of forces but the exclusive and eternal.   To him the only impediment to God's will — and even this was self-imposed and revocable at His pleasure — was that very human soul which God most loved.[59]

Yet the outlook was not on that account the more encouraging.   Between man and the old death there was now a more generous grace.   But of what help would it be?   Of no earthly help, most evidently, for labour and misfortune, suffering and death,[60] were as much the lot of man now as they ever had been.   Yet of ultimate help, surely — if only one were fortunate enough to be among the chosen.   No man, though, could raise a finger to force a bestowal of this grace: it must come, or not come, wholly as God, not man, disposes.   Ambrose had said that baptism alone gave man the free will to sin or not to sin; Augustine said man never regained this power of the innocent Adam.   For all that is good in man comes straight from God.

Why, indeed, should this grace be at the disposal of human initiative?   How should God be thought a machine handing

[59] Cf. Guitton 1933 93, who argues that Augustine scraped off the Neoplatonic accretions of Christianity, returning to the undefiled Jewish sources — notably to the doctrine contained in the *Wisdom of Solomon.*

[60] Observe again the didactic explanation: referring to his *De Pecc. Meritis* of 412, he says in *D.C.D.* XIII 4 of about 417: 'There it was said that the parting of body and soul was left, though its connection with sin was removed, for this reason, that if the immortality of the body followed immediately upon the sacrament of regeneration, faith itself would thereby be enervated.   For faith is then only faith when it waits in hope for what is not yet seen in substance.'

out favours automatically according to merits independently acquired? Man, moreover, is incapable of merit: he has no free will not to sin, even after baptism, but only the feeble if indispensable will to grasp and accept God's grace when this is tendered. Nor can he even do anything to keep that grace once it has been given.[61] For to God alone is the power. Let man pray, then, with his whole heart and soul; not that he has any reason to think that any prayer or thought or deed of his can swerve the divine will; yet he has been taught God's infinite mercy and may hope.[62] For man should know that he is a horrid thing, and should not grieve over his lot but over his sins. Let him not whine and grumble; let him instead be grateful that God sees in him some potential good and so loves that good that He may choose to save him.

Of course God might have created a good which could not turn itself into evil, for

Good can exist without evil.[63]

But, if such an incorruptible good had been created, man could not have been; so man should be grateful to God that He chose to create a world in which evil as well as good could exist, and so man as well as God. Therefore whatever the motive, the fact is certain that God

judged it better to bring good out of evil than not to permit any evil to exist.[64]

Nor can we doubt that God does well even in the permission of what is evil. For He permits it only in the justice of His judgment. And surely all that is just is good. Although, therefore, evil, in so far as it is evil, is not a good, yet the fact that evil as well as good exists, is a good. For if it were not a good that evil should exist, its existence would not be permitted by the omnipotent Good, who without doubt can as easily refuse to permit what He does not wish, as bring about what He does wish.[65]

---

[61] See pp. 396–98.
[62] His idea of the power of prayer seems to have changed with time: in 399 (*Confessions* VI 11) he wrote (see p. 74) 'And Thou verily wouldst have given it, if with cordial groanings I should have knocked at Thine ears, and with a settled faith have cast my cares upon Thee.'
In about 424 (*D.C.D.* XXI 24) he

wrote: ' But she [the Church] is heard in the case of those only who, though they oppose the Church, are yet predestined to become her sons through her intercession.' See, however, Tixeront 1921 II 6 490–91.
[63] *Enchiridion* 14 (' quamvis bona sine malis possint ').
[64] Ibid. 27.
[65] Ibid. 96.

In other existences God has created good without evil — as
in heaven. Or evil without good — as in hell. But in this
present world and life God has chosen so to order things
that good depends on evil, can only come out of evil.[66] For

the very pleasures of our human life do we procure by preceding
difficulties: nor these only which fall upon us unlooked for and
against our wills, but even purposed by us and desired. There
is no pleasure at all in eating and drinking unless the pinching
of hunger and thirst go before it. Drunkards eat certain saltish
meats, with purpose to procure a thirsty hotness in the mouth,
which, whilst the drink quenches, the pleasure is procured. The
order also it is, that the spouse already affianced uses not instantly to be given to her sweetheart: for fear that when he is an
husband he should less esteem of her for being so soon obtained,
whom while he was a wooer he sighed not after, thinking her too
long delayed. This is observable in such joy as is dishonest, and
to be abhorred; seen also in that joy which is consented to, and
lawful; seen likewise in the most sincere honesty of friendship;
seen lastly in Him who was dead, and afterwards revived; who
was lost and is found. The greatest joy is everywhere ushered in
by the greatest painfulness.[67]

And elsewhere Augustine calls as a witness a pagan, Crantor,
quoted by Cicero, to discredit the cause so dear to the pagans:

For to be quite free from pain while we are in this place of misery
is only purchased, as one of the world's literati perceived and remarked, at the price of blunted sensibilities both of mind and
body.[68]

No evil seemed present while Adam lived in the Garden of
Eden. Yet it was there, and by God's will, for God judged it
better so. Surely it was a most real and terrifying free will
that God had bestowed on Adam: the will whereby he might,
whenever he chose, so vitiate his own — and so all subsequent
— human nature, that even the supreme sacrifice of the God-
Christ could only partially repair the damage. That original
sin subsisted, therefore, could not be a matter of doubt.

---

[66] Irenæus had already said as
much, but he had applied it only in
order to justify the pre- and not the
post-Redemption era: Turmel 1931
I 41–42. Lactantius in his turn had
applied it, but only in order to explain why God had put good souls
into evil bodies: ibid. 52, citing *De
Ira Dei* §§ 15–20.
[67] *Confessions* VIII 3.
[68] *D.C.D.* XIV 9. Cf. p. 320.

By the Neoplatonists matter had been indicted, by the Manichees the devil, by the Gnostics even God Himself. The earlier Christian theologians had in their turn indicted man's soul. They had failed to convict, however, and, so long as there was no conviction, the indictments against matter, the devil, and even against God Himself, subsisted. Which, then, was the real culprit, which was the real cause of the evil in the world? Until Augustine the decision remained doubtful, but it was now at last resolved. For Augustine had not merely indicted the soul, he had convicted it — and with such decisive arguments that all doubts were resolved. It followed that now for the first time the indictments pending against matter, the devil, and the Father could with safety be quashed. Many before Augustine had seriously doubted their guilt, but, the true culprit not having then been fully exposed, suspicion had remained. Their innocence could be proved only by proving the guilt of another.

That God was not morally responsible had always, in spite of the periodical recrudescence of the wrath-of-God theory, been strongly suspected. That the devil was responsible Augustine was now most emphatically to deny:

Must we say then that the one [who succumbs to evil] was tempted by a secret suggestion of the evil spirit? As if it were not by his own will that he consented to this suggestion and to any inducement whatsoever! [69]

Nor was he less emphatic in championing the innocence of matter:

There is no need, therefore, that in our sins and vices we accuse the nature of the flesh to the injury of the Creator, for in its own kind and degree the flesh is good; but to desert the Creator good, and live according to the created good, is not good, whether a man choose to live according to the flesh, or according to the soul, or according to the whole human nature, which is composed of flesh and soul, and which is therefore spoken of either by the name of flesh alone, or by the name soul alone. For he who extols the nature of the soul as the chief good, and condemns the nature of the flesh as if it were evil, assuredly is fleshly both in his love of the soul and hatred of the flesh; for these feelings arise from human fancy, not from divine truth.[70]

[69] *D.C.D.* XII 6.   [70] Ibid. XIV 5; & cf. ibid. XII 4.

Here was the crucial discovery. Long ago had the Gnostic view been discredited, while its heir the wrath-of-God theory, though still offered as a desperate hypothesis, was popular with no one. More recently, because of the Manichæan exaggeration, the theory of the devil's independent power had lost favour, Ambrose having sought to merge it into a general conception of justice. But a suspicion of matter's guilt lay at the bottom of that Greek philosophy which had impregnated the whole Mediterranean world. Tertullian had been able to acquit matter only by making the devil to blame.[71] But with Origen fear of matter sank more deeply than ever into the Christian mind, hypnotizing not only the monks like Basil and Jerome, who were multiplying daily, but also men so sane and judicious as Ambrose.

Happily it was just at this moment that the tide turned: it was in 396 that Jerome repudiated Origen,[72] it was in 397 that Ambrose died, and it was in the years 399 to 401 that the Neoplatonic Christianity of Origen, which had dominated almost everywhere for about one hundred and fifty years,[73] was now formally condemned, at Alexandria, at Rome, and finally by the Emperor.[74] If a coincidence it was certainly an auspicious one that the years 395 to 399 were also those during which Augustine, by finally condemning the soul, acquitted once and for all that matter which had been impeding the progress of Christian theology no less effectively than it was said to impede the Neoplatonic God.

Like all discoveries it was so simple once it had been adequately explained. For how, even if God had not created it, could matter be evil? And, since God did create it, how could it sin and so change its nature into evil? By itself this

[71] Tixeront 1924 I 9 403–04.
[72] Tixeront 1921 II 6 341.
[73] Ibid. I 9 329 on Origen: ' C'est le fleuve débordé qui, dans l'abondance de ses eaux, roule à la fois le limon qui féconde et le sable qui rend stérile. Mais, heureux ou funeste, les théologiens de l'antiquité jusqu'à saint Augustin en Occident, et même après en Orient, ont à peu près tous subi directement ou indirectement l'influence du grand alexandrin; ils ont souvent accepté ses principes et développé ses idées.

Même ceux qui l'ont combattu se sont servis des armes qu'il leur fournissait.'
Among those who thought Origen not only orthodox but authoritative were not only such earlier fourth century theologians as Eusebius of Cæsarea, Pamphilus, Athanasius, and Evagrius, but also Basil and the two Gregories in the later fourth century: see Butler 1898 I 177; & Harnack 1911 XX 11 273c.
[74] Tixeront 1921 II 6 336.

matter is a dead thing, a blind and negative thing, whereas evil is a live thing, cunning and active. Let us suppose that the human soul may some day become divine and perfect, is that a reason for assuming it to be so now? Because it associates itself with a poor dead thing may it on that account blame that thing for all its own evil thoughts and deeds? This is pure sham: why bear a grudge against the innocent matter of this world, a substance which cannot possibly have any relation to either good or evil? The heart of man is not miserable and evil because immersed in this bodily and earthly life, but in spite of it; and in hell, though disembodied, man will be much worse off. For matter, the creation of God for the sake of man, is in its own humble way quite perfect:

How can I tell of the rest of creation, with all its beauty and utility, which the divine goodness has given to man to please his eye and serve his purposes, condemned though he is, and hurled into these labours and miseries? Shall I speak of the manifold and various loveliness of sky and earth and sea; of the plentiful supply and wonderful qualities of the light; of sun, moon and stars; of the shade of trees; of the colours and perfume of the flowers; of the multitude of birds, all differing in plumage and song; of the variety of animals, of which the smallest in size are often the most wonderful — the works of ants and bees astonishing us more than the huge bodies of whales? Shall I speak of the sea, which itself is so grand a spectacle, when it arrays itself as it were in vestures of various colours, now running through every shade of green, and again becoming purple or blue? . . .
How grateful is the alternation of day and night! How pleasant the breezes that cool the air! How abundant the supply of clothing furnished us by trees and animals! Who can enumerate all the blessings we enjoy? If I were to attempt to detail and unfold only these few which I have indicated in the mass, such an enumeration would fill a volume. And all these are but the solace of the wretched and condemned, not the rewards of the blessed.[75]

But if there is no evil inherent in nature and so none in the body, the evil they appear to cause must in fact arise from the bad use to which they are put, and they are therefore not the source of, but only mirrors reflecting, an evil originating elsewhere.

Now God has arranged that this should be. Therefore

[75] *D.C.D.* XXII 24.

contact of the soul with the flesh is good for the soul,[76] but is bad for the flesh since it vitiates it.[77] Thus it is that the soul's contact with the flesh and the world is indispensable to its true regeneration, for this life on earth is a Purgatory where the latent evil may be exposed to the light, where through contact with the earth the soul may be cleansed and toughened. As the soul treats its bodily servant well or ill, so is the soul itself washed or sullied.[78]

So Augustine reasoned, so he expounded and preached; and so too was his Roman blood able to cling loyally to the world of earth which had long served him and his race so faithfully. Unlike the Stoics, Manichees, and Neoplatonists, unlike the monk Jerome,[79] unlike the lordly bishop Ambrose, who all in one or another way fought the body because it was the body, Augustine kept his faith in it — as a humble being serving a humble end. For had not God created it for the sake of man? If Augustine warned against self-indulgence in riches,[80] patriotism,[81] marriage,[82] friendship,[83]

---

[76] Cf. *D.C.D.* IX 17, quoted p. 107.
[77] Cf. Ibid. XIV 3, quoted p. 80. And in ibid. XII 3 he says: ' Vice, therefore, is contrary to God, as evil is to good. Further, the nature it vitiates is a good, and therefore to this good also it is contrary. But while it is contrary to God only as evil to good [because it cannot hurt Him], it is contrary to the nature it vitiates, both as evil and as hurtful.'
[78] Cf. Victorinus, quoted p. 69 n. 32.
[79] Cf. Jerome *Letters* # 39 § 7, & # 122 § 3.
[80] In *Contra Adimantum* XX § 20 Augustine says of wealth: ' Who does not understand here that it is not wrong to possess these things, but wrong only to love them and put one's hopes in them, and to prefer and even strive after them rather than for truth, justice, wisdom, faith, a clear conscience, love of God and one's neighbour? '
[81] In his *Confessions* X 36, of 399, he speaks slightingly of government: ' Because now certain offices of human society make it necessary both to be loved and feared of men, even therefore doth the adversary of

our true blessedness lay hard at us, everywhere spreading in his snares Well done, well done.' This he said while still in the heat of his conversion and discoveries, whereas in *D.C.D.* I 15, written about fifteen years later, he speaks of the conduct of Regulus with undisguised admiration, calling it a ' very noble example.' Boissier 1909 II 6 389 says that his behaviour in those difficult years of the early fifth century ' a toujours été celle d'un ardent patriote, et sa fidélité pour le prince, qu'il ne sépare pas de la patrie, ne s'est pas démentie un instant.' See also ibid. 391–92 & 396, citing Augustine *Letters* # 198, 199, & 228.
[82] ' And concerning wedlock, Thou didst advise me to a better course than that was which Thou leftest me a free choice in ': *Confessions* X 30. And cf. his *De Bono Conjugali passim.* See Boissier 1909 II 6 362–67 on the general problem of celibacy at this time.
[83] Augustine was rather perplexed than mortified at the strength of his love for a friend: *Confessions* IV 4–9; and for his mother: ibid. IX 12.

food, drink,[84] and even music,[85] it was not because these affections were carnal, but because they were purely extrinsic and incidental, yet tended to wean us from the love of God. Indulgence in logic, in mathematics, science or rhetoric was, for this same reason, no more commendable. For, if this lay and carnal world, improperly used, was sure to actualize the evil in man's soul, properly used it must serve rather as a help than as a hindrance. For to what purpose was this life designed if not in order that man might thereby at least initiate his moral regeneration? In matter, consequently, lay rather the cure than the cause of the disease.

At the opposite extreme were the later pagan creeds according to which each soul was a soldier, acting under military orders and obliged, whether he liked it or not, to enter battle in order to bring victory to his commander. Some soldiers might serve willingly and smartly, others reluctantly and slackly, but in either case their fight was against an enemy outside themselves. The Augustinian Christian, on the other hand, was fighting no external enemy — for God had none — but only his own interior unworthiness. Since God had no cosmic cause not yet won, no Christian could fight for it; to fight the sin in his own soul was the extent of his obligation. Whatever other tasks God might wish performed He was ready to perform Himself. Both pagan and Augustinian must seek the purification of their own souls; but, whereas to the pagan this was a means by which the outer world might be reclaimed for the kingdom of God, to the Augustinian this purification was an end in itself. As it was, therefore, each individual soul, and not conglomerate matter, that was the root of evil, so the enemy of man, as of God, was no longer physiological environment but psychological inheritance.[86]

---

[84] Cf. Possidius *S. Augustini Vita* 22.

[85] He analyzes his pleasure in hearing music in *Confessions* X 33.

[86] It is incidentally true that Christianity, and especially that of Augustine, was an eclectic compromise between the Platonist schools which repudiated matter, and the Epicurean which cherished it. But, to assume that this is a manifestation of blind organic and evolutionary forces, while a plausible hypothesis, is a purely gratuitous one. Some day scholars will perhaps prove that a mechanical evolution in human ideas is a law of nature. Nevertheless, if man is ever going to prove this, or anything else of the sort, he must start by a humble and even tedious examination of the individual elements — multifarious and chaotic — of which the whole historical fabric is made up. No one can hope to

The importance of this Augustinian doctrine is not easily to be overestimated, for it contradicted the most fundamental tenet of classical speculation. Hitherto the war had been between God and a hostile nature, between man's soul and its environment — which was a pioneer conception of things. Henceforth the war was simply between God and the evil in man's soul. It is hard to say which this new view changed most radically, the old view of nature or the old view of man; but in either case it was here if anywhere that in a philosophic sense, antiquity ended and modern times began. For Europe did not break the spell of Augustine till the eighteenth century.

D. AUGUSTINE ON SCIENCE

Augustine's diagnosis and localization of the evil that was besetting man produced at one and the same time a new God, a new man, and a new world. He said the discovery made him happy because it was the truth. It was a truth, certainly, and one so fundamental that it entirely contented him, but it was not the whole truth — certainly not about nature, and possibly not even about man.

Of any great truth it will be said that it is revolutionary, and this will be true; but it will be so chiefly because it intoxicates those who first grasp it, thereby revolutionizing them. Augustine, for example, believed that Christianity, through its disclosure of the true nature of God, also disclosed each of the manifold processes of nature, since — assuming that a God such as he conceived had created and was now controlling nature — His purpose in causing this or that to happen ought without too much difficulty to be inferred. It was just this which Aquinas would not so easily believe:

---

understand Augustine, or anyone else, as a scientific phenomenon until long after he has understood him empirically — as a living and loving human being. Perhaps he was a mechanism, but, if so, he was a mechanism so much more complex than any mechanism we have ever imagined, that for practical purposes such a hypothesis can only lead us into folly.

his conception of nature was such that he felt the need of using logic and learning at least to corroborate, and, if necessary, to contradict, what intuitive inference might suggest.[1] And of course in the last three hundred years science has shown nature to be very different from what Augustine supposed, without in the least undermining the great mystical, ethical, and psychological truths which he used as his premise. And there is another inference of Augustine's which now appears unwarranted: that man, because he was made in God's image, might come to know God's final purpose. Yet the explanation of this rash conclusion lies in the very fact of his discovery: on the one hand he discovered true humility, which, one might suppose, ought to encourage the belief that man is not capable of learning eternal truth; on the other hand this discovery was manifestly itself an eternal truth and so an enticement to believe that from it the many other eternal truths might infallibly be inferred. He had thus recognized the virtue and consolation of ethical humility only at the cost of his intellectual humility. For now, in contrast to his state of mind before 387, he was sure he was right, sure that his explanation of reality must be the true explanation. Here then was another revolutionary discovery: that man is capable of understanding the nature and final purpose of reality. With it the Dark and Middle Ages, with it the Renaissance and Reformation, budded and bloomed. That there might be such a virtue as intellectual humility no more occurred to the humanists than to Calvin and the Jesuits. There were, to be sure, philosophic sceptics, like Occam, Nicolas d'Autrecourt, Raimon de Sabiunde, and Montaigne, who doubted man's intellectual capacity to find truth except by simple faith. But these, as Pascal reveals in his own case, were as consoled by their intuitions as they were discontented with their arguments. It was not until the earlier eighteenth century, bounded by Bayle and Voltaire, that man's incapacity to grasp truth by any methods was first generally recognized and acknowledged.[2] Perhaps the vic-

---

[1] Cf. Duhem 1914 II 412–13.

[2] Francisco Sanchez, the Portuguese Jew physician born in about 1550, seems to have been a sceptic of faith as well. Vanini too was an atheist — at least he was burnt at the stake in 1635 on that supposition. But neither of these men attracted any following. Charron, born in 1541, Bruno, born in 1550, and Du

tory over ethical pride has been won, but the struggle against
intellectual pride is just beginning: for if Augustine, in the
full flush of his discovery, supposed that he could explain
nature through man, there have been times, certainly in the
later nineteenth century, when the wisest men, reverting to
the method of the early Greeks, believed they could explain
man through nature.

Augustine had discovered a new nature. May we on that
account conclude that he opened the door to a new era in
science? His mind, being of the highest order, unquestionably perceived truths most salutary and enlightening to science — he could touch no subject without infusing it with
something of his own brilliance — yet he was not of a strictly
scientific cast of mind:

For although, with a cruel zeal for science, some medical men
who are called anatomists have dissected the bodies of the dead,
and sometimes even of sick persons who have died under their
knives, and have inhumanly pried into the secrets of the human
body in order to learn the nature of the disease and its exact seat
and how it might be cured; yet those relations of which I speak,
and which form the concord — or, as the Greeks call it, the *harmony* — of the whole body, outside and in, as of some instrument,
no one has been able to discover because no one has been auda-
cious enough to seek for them.[3]

Here is the weak spot in Augustine's intellectual armour: he
was an experimentalist, but he was also rather a psychologist
than a natural scientist, drawing his conclusions from repeated observations of live men and not of corpses. He admits that his conversion to the true faith was possible only
because of the preliminary enlightenment received through
the false faiths of paganism; that it was through his pagan
understanding of so many of the parts that he was finally enabled to perceive the whole. In the ardour of his conversion
he insists that recognition of Christianity is indispensable to
virtue. But he also insists that, although no sublimation of
pagan error could itself produce virtue, it was an indispensable preliminary to a later acceptance of truth. Why, then,

---

Vair, born in 1556, can none of them   [3] *D.C.D.* XXII 24.
be so regarded.

was Augustine unwilling to tolerate pagan dissections of the
corpse in order that the Christian harmony of the living body
be some day revealed?   Partly because he was not greatly
interested even in the living body; but partly too, I think,
because doubt, to him, was rather a pain than a pleasure. He
had long doubted only in order that in the long run he
might banish all doubt. But experiment pre-supposes doubt;
therefore his experiment too was a pain, a painful yet indispensable means to a happy end.   With the end finally
achieved the means became not only superfluous but repugnant. It could serve only to remind him of a past mortification that he longed to forget. His was the psychology of
any convert, aggravated by the self-confidence of genius.
Having no doubts himself he could not respect the doubts
of others.

In their investigation of truth the anatomists were employing a technique analogous to that which he had employed with such fruitful results.   Just as the errors of the
philosophers had guided him to his truth, so must the errors
of the anatomists guide them, or others coming after them,
to their truth. Yet this is what Augustine flatly denied. He
did so partly because he disliked dissection, partly because
he disliked doubt; but may he not also have done so partly
because he had a faith that his own momentous discovery —
of the nature of God and His relation to man — could be
used as a short cut even to this incidental truth of the body's
harmony? We cannot say; but we can say that Augustine's
intellectual evolution teaches the fallibility even of human
genius, teaches how, if doubt breeds other doubts, so certainty breeds other certainties. But if it teaches that creation breeds exclusion it also teaches that doubt breeds nothing at all.   This does not mean that science and faith
are incompatible, but merely that genius is not omnis-
cience.

Just as a brilliant scientific mind, while incapable of offering religion any constructive criticism, can often expose
certain errors which no religious mind could itself have perceived, so a brilliant religious mind can help to indicate certain encumbrances which impede the progress of science.
To the extent that dissection was a proper medical procedure

Augustine's contempt for it was calculated rather to harm than to help. On the other hand his masterly demonstration that matter was dead [4] and without moral significance was capable of doing science a real service. That it did not do this at once was due to external circumstances which rendered any immediate progress, in either religion or science, impracticable. Nevertheless it is not unlikely that the renaissance of science in the seventeenth century — a revulsion from the biological [5] world of Aristotle — was facilitated by the Christian hypothesis which Augustine proved. For, if the scientist had not then had full confidence in the deadness of matter, an incipient physics would not have roused his curiosity and mathematics would have seemed a sterile pursuit. Had matter not then been regarded as susceptible of analysis by a mathematical and physical technique, the scientific experiments which inaugurated our modern era might have had to await an age equipped to handle the far more intricate technique of bio-chemistry.

Another scientific contribution, negative too, but promising, followed from his refutation of Neoplatonism. The Platonic school had long successfully maintained that matter must be evil because it was to be found at the maximum distance from God: the earth being at the centre of the universe and God encircling the celestial periphery, it was the least directly under His control. Manipulating the universe from this periphery,[6] the centre must be the least affected and so retain the maximum capacity to thwart His designs. But, protests Augustine, how then does water get into the high clouds, why are the heavenly bodies so close to God, and why are there volcanoes, why fires in the houses of men? And, above all, why are there then souls in bodies?

For Aristotle said that the soul was a fifth body, while Plato denied that it was a body at all. . . . What then does it do in an earthly body? What does this soul, which is finer than all else, do in such a mass of matter as this? What does the lightest

---

[4] On the contrary pagan view see Augustine *D.C.D.* IV 11. But Augustine was not always consistent, see *D.C.D.* XI 27 on how ' even the lifeless bodies . . . protect their existence.'

[5] See p. 215 n. 20.

[6] See Macrobius *Commentary* I § 17, where he quotes Cicero with approval.

of substances do in this ponderosity?   This swiftest substance in such sluggishness. . . . Behold with what arguments human infirmity, possessed with vanity, contradicts the omnipotence of God! [7]

It seemed most clear, on the contrary, that the corporeal was often close to God and the incorporeal far away.

The biblical revelation was thus in many ways a mere corroboration of what ordinarily acute lay observation should have, yet had not, made clear.   Chiding the Neoplatonists who refused to accept Christ's divinity, Augustine says,

For him you despise on account of the body he took of a woman and the shame of the cross; for your lofty wisdom spurns such low and contemptible things, and soars to more exalted regions.[8]

And yet,

Though His incarnation showed us nothing else, these two wholesome facts were enough: that true divinity cannot be polluted by flesh, and that demons are not to be considered better than ourselves because they have not flesh.[9]

Two further considerations clinch the matter so far as Christians are concerned.   Why are the devils in hell given merely aerial bodies if not to show that it is not matter which is the cause of evil and suffering? [10]   And if the body be the source of humiliation and sorrow why will the souls of the blessed regain their bodies at the crack of doom? [11]   The Neoplatonists had taught that evil was inherent in matter and that the universe was so designed that whereas dense matter — that is, earth and water — gravitated towards the centre, the lighter substances — air and fire — sought to approach the periphery.   Thus were their physics and astronomy derived from their philosophy and at its mercy.   But, as Augustine showed, that philosophy in fact did not explain, but rather contradicted, observed facts.[12]   According to the

[7] D.C.D. XXII 11.   According to Duhem 1914 II 410, Augustine here misrepresents Aristotle's conception; but the error is excusable because he was wholly concerned to refute Plato, with whose opinions he was familiar.
[8] D.C.D. X 28.
[9] Ibid. IX 17.

[10] Ibid. VIII 15 & 22; & XXI 3.
[11] Ibid. XIII 19; & XXII 11.
[12] Augustine had studied a good deal of astronomy, concluding that the theories then current were all hopelessly subjective and therefore unreliable: Dufourcq L'Av. 1910 IV 5 230 n. 1.

Neoplatonic hypothesis, the sun, moon,[13] planets, and stars must necessarily be composed of fire or some even less corporeal substance — it forbade that their degree of corporeality should rival that of the earth — but according to the Christian hypothesis there was no reason for such assumptions. This scientific statement was negative certainly, but at least it opened the way, as Neoplatonism did not, to a new conception of the corporeal universe based, not on philosophy, but on simple observation. That not only the area or extension,[14] but also the mass or corporeality, of the sun was far greater than that of the earth was, for instance, a conclusion to which any Christian might safely come, but no Neoplatonist could suppose this without repudiating his faith. In the same way the helio-centric theory of Aristarchus and Copernicus could seem to the Christian a symbol designed by God to emphasize man's frailty; [15] but to the Neoplatonist that theory seemed to threaten his whole philosophic structure.[16] The Renaissance resistance to Copernicus [17] was due to an Aristotelian-scholastic [18] loyalty to Greek philosophy; the Augustinians, whether Catholic or Protestant, could well regard him with indifference.[19]

Augustine had thus opened the door to a new era in science. The trouble was that, instead of waiting for a scientist to pass through it, in his impatience he insisted on passing through it himself. For this we cannot wholly blame him: he had observed how Greek philosophy had seriously distorted science and how perfectly, on the contrary, the well-

[13] Macrobius *Commentary* I § 19 says that the moon, 'although a much denser body than the rest of the celestial spheres, is much more rarified than the earth is.'

[14] Macrobius *Commentary* I § 20 admits that the diameter of the sun was 140,000 stadia, that of the earth only a little over 80,000, but he supposed the density of the sun to be infinitely less and therefore its mass or weight.

[15] As it later did to Cardinal de Bérulle (born in 1575): Bremont 1921 III 24.

[16] In spite of the importance they attached to the sun: Macrobius *Commentary* I § 20 & II § 4, & *Saturnalia* I §§ 17–23. Because the importance

of the sun depended on its absence of base matter. In the hierarchy of substances from earth, to water, to air, to fire, the earth was at the bottom and the sun at the top.

[17] From the year 1543 until nearly 1650.

[18] Dufourcq *L'Av.* 1910 IV 5 230 n. 1 says that the Platonists, in contrast to the Aristotelians, were inclined to be sceptical of such categorical hypotheses as that of Ptolemy. It is certainly true that Macrobius, at least, was as little cock-sure as he was sceptical.

[19] Augustine *De Genesi ad Litteram* II § 10 says the planets can move even if the outer heaven does not.

known scientific facts coincided with Revelation. Christianity therefore not only revealed the true God and the true man but the true outer world. Here was Truth, and it remained only to work out the detailed explanation of everything by inference from the major premises.

Now these were the Christian God and the Christian man and the intimate relations connecting the two. Since to Augustine God had created the universe foreknowing that Adam would sin and the Fall therefore ensue, it was clear that this universe was appropriately designed, not only to rejoice the good Adam but to facilitate the regeneration of the bad. The present purpose of nature, therefore, was to help wipe out the evil that man had contracted by the Fall. An anthropocentric conception of the world is anything but a Christian, much less an Augustinian, invention: it is probably common to all civilizations in similar stages of evolution. It is therefore not a coincidence that, in one form or another, it is to be found in Plato, the Stoics,[20] Pliny,[21] and the Manichees,[22] as well as in the Bible and Augustine. But although to the pagans, man was the key to reality, they conceived of a recurrent or cyclical sequence of events [23] whose divine course was either being chronically impeded by the sluggishness of matter or chronically disturbed by meddlesome or malignant deities, while God held aloof, serenely veiled in the majestic obscurity of His unknowability. To most pagans, certainly, man seemed at the centre of a Purpose,[24] but exactly what this was and how effectively and expeditiously it was being realized, admittedly defied the ingenuity of their sharpest intellects.

The Christians, on the other hand, far from being content to believe that God had created the natural world and man for a purpose about whose exact nature they were in doubt, were ready to believe that they knew exactly why these were created. This the pagan had been too modest to insist on. To the early Roman, man was an animal so superior that he could form political states, create noble works of art, and learn the ways and uses of physical nature, but why this was

---

[20] Fuller 1912 30.

[21] Singer 1931 59.

[22] The cosmological warfare was for the possession of man's soul.

[23] See pp. 36 n. 48, & 119–20.

[24] Cf. Rutilius Namatianus *De Reditu Suo* (of 416) II lines 31–40.

so he could never properly determine. To the later Roman, whether Stoic, Neoplatonist, or Manichee, man seemed no less superior, but, since his mastery of the physical world was so deplorably inadequate,[25] he concluded that the divine order of things was being disturbed by either the activity of a rebellious Satan or the sluggish passivity of an obstinate matter. He, better than his ancestors, knew the ways of God and heaven; of earthly matters, however, his ignorance subsisted. He therefore consoled himself by alleging their insignificance. But to the Christian, and especially to Augustine with his sense of God's omnificence, divine rule was as meticulous on earth as it was in heaven: the true explanation of specific events might escape man's comprehension, but of the general scheme and of the end towards which all things tended he could have no doubt. For to him the physical world had been created by God as an instrument for the tempering of man's soul. By means of it God tempted, rewarded, and chastised; by means of it too He communicated His grace.

To the early pagan the prime virtues were civic because the world was intrinsically significant; to the later pagan the prime virtues were ascetic because the world was insignificant;[26] but to the Christian the prime virtues were those which a pure love engenders because the world, although significant, was only extrinsically so. Therefore to the Christian, as to the early pagan, the physical world was not to be abjured but to be accepted: as Augustine said, 'in its own kind and degree the flesh is good.'[27] Or, as he says elsewhere,

This is the order of concord, that a man, in the first place, injure no one, and, in the second, do good to everyone he can reach.[28]

[25] To the Mithraists man's opportunity to weaken the powers of Darkness was while he was on earth. Indeed that was why he was incarnated. But after 340 the religions of other-worldliness predominated.

[26] Even Symmachus, old-fashioned pagan though he was, praises piety in contrast to earthly fame: *Letters* III # 6. By piety he probably meant virtuous behaviour, but he could hardly have explained in what concrete ways it should be practised or to what end.

Macrobius *Commentary* I § 4 & II § 17 makes a clumsy effort to reconcile Cicero's view with Neoplatonism.

To the Christian theological virtues of faith, hope, and charity, Porphyry had added only truth: see Whittaker 1901 109. Unless truth be counted a civic virtue, he added none.

[27] See p. 97, quoting *D.C.D.* XIV 5.

[28] *D.C.D.* XIX 14.

Now this latter duty, superimposed upon the first, is the positive that must follow the negative, and this good — as Christ's example amply proved — included the satisfaction of many fleshly wants, food to the hungry, clothing to the naked, comfort to the sorrowful, health to the sick — and even life to the dead.

If, however, the physical or natural world had no intrinsic but only an extrinsic significance, its phenomena must be re-interpreted. It was clear that domestic animals were created in order to furnish man with the necessities of life: food, clothing, and power.[29] Trees provided shade and material for building shelters, crops provided food, certain herbs provided medicines,[30] perhaps the oceans were created as barriers to prevent men from stumbling onto the earthly paradise. But there remained much the larger part of natural phenomena which could not be explained so literally and yet which necessarily was created only for man's benefit. The explanation was found in symbolism, a device by which a concrete thing was saddled with an abstract and usually didactic significance. What was number for? What were the stars for, and why were there planets, and why seven planets? God had created nothing without an ethical and didactic reason. Such ideas were not confined to Christians; not only Ambrose,[31] Jerome,[32] Augustine,[33] and Cassian,[34] but the Mithraists,[35] and the Neoplatonists too, like Macrobius,[36] believed that the number 7 was of special significance; it was generally supposed, for instance, that the seven planets were created in order to recall to man's memory that his life consisted of seven ages, and that the virtues also were of this number.[37]

This faith — that almost everything existed rather in order to be recognized by man as the symbol of something else

---

[29] Cf. Augustine's citation of Genesis i 28 in Confessions XIII 23.
[30] Cf. Jerome Contra Jovinianum II §§ 5 & 6; & Ambrose Exameron III §§ 38–41.
[31] Letter # 44.
[32] Letter # 53 § 2.
[33] Confessions XIII 28; De Pecc. Meritis II § 57; D.C.D. XI 30.

[34] Conlationes V passim.
[35] Cumont 1913 ³ 121–22.
[36] Commentary I § 6. On the mania of Iamblichus see Lot 1927 191.
[37] Cf. Kurth 1919 II 302. The number 12 was also popular: it fitted the Apostles and the signs of the Zodiac: see Leo Letter # 15 § 13.

than for its own sake — resulted in an explanation of the
world which was more complete and consistent than anything imagined before or since, but it sounded the death knell
of unprejudiced investigation in the physical world. In western Europe symbolism began to lose its prestige only after
the middle of the thirteenth century, at the very moment
when science first began to reassert its prerogatives.

By the year 400, therefore, this tendency to explain everything symbolically was running riot throughout the Roman
Empire.[38] There seemed no end to its possibilities, nothing
that it could not explain. Numbers, herbs, animals,[39] precious stones, qualities of density, shape, and colour, words and
names — all these were henceforth interesting and real only
in so far as they were significant of something else. And
natural events which were in any way unusual or variable,
such as storms, floods, droughts, plagues, heavenly conjunc-
tions, eclipses, and comets,[40] were each observed only in order
to learn of what they were a premonition, of what they were
a consequence — always as symbols.

The Christians no doubt had a special excuse: Christ had
himself regarded the Old Testament as a symbolic prefigur-
ing of his Incarnation, consequently the Christian was obliged
to read his Jewish history as if something symbolic; [41] and,
with this precedent and this habit, it was not unnatural that
he should be led to scrutinize the events being enacted before his own eyes in the same state of mind. And more than
this, Christ taught largely in parables, that is, by stories which
were left to the disciples to find the symbolic meaning of if

[38] For luxuriant pagan allegory in
Africa see Martianus Capella (fl.
about 425?) and F. P. Fulgentius (fl.
about 485).

[39] See on Ambrose, Dudden 1935
476.

[40] See Dill 1906 2 41. Ambrose
thought comets were portents: *Letter*
51 § 14. Augustine said that
comets were produced by demons:
D.C.D. II 25.

[41] The Sicilian Christian, Firmicus
Maternus, writing in 346, spoke as if
all the motley pagan beliefs must be
believed literally true, or else rejected utterly. In the West the Bible
was not subjected to symbolic inter-

pretation before Hilary of Poitiers
in 358: Lot 1927 433; & Rand 1928 85.

Ambrose encouraged such interpretations and in this way overcame
one of Augustine's chief difficulties:
Confessions V 14. In ibid. VI 3, 4 &
11, & VII 1 he says that Christianity
had long been distasteful to him because, if man was made in God's
image, He must be a material thing.
In 412 Augustine explains his principle of biblical exegesis: ' Now that
is not the sole meaning of the passage *the letter killeth but the spirit
giveth life,* which merely prescribes
our not taking in a literal sense any
figurative phrase which in the proper

they could.[42] Believing, as the Christian did, that the Old Testament revealed truth through symbols,[43] that the New Testament parables did as much, and believing too that God created everything in nature for its effect on man, it was inevitable that he should take natural phenomena as ethical symbols. Of all the Christians, Jerome was the most cool-headed: he sounded a warning against the abuse of allegorical interpretation, both in the Bible and in nature.[44] He explained faulted rocks as the result of some early outburst of the divine wrath,[45] but he avoided the inference that the rocks had also been faulted for didactic reasons — in order that man might for ever after be reminded of the power of that wrath. His explanation was perhaps wrong, but at least it was an effort to study geology in terms of time.

If, however, the Christians had symbolism thrust upon them, the pagans showed no greater capacity to resist its fascination. Christianity was fast conquering men's minds by its explanation of all reality; since it now controlled the State its attitude must tend to grow less tolerant. This common danger impelled many of the pagan cults to forget their differences and to try to unite their forces by patching together a syncretic religion in which each of the threatened religions would furnish some of the ingredients. A merger on so colossal a scale, to be accomplished quickly to meet an emergency, must use heroic methods: the individual Gods, doctrines, and rituals had to be fused without regard for pious sensibilities. To resort to the magic of symbolism seemed their best chance, and it was to this task that the fourth century Neoplatonists and other pagans devoted themselves.[46] Long before, Greek mythologies had been interpreted, as by Plato, to be mere symbols and personifications of the various processes of nature, and to Porphyry, in the

---

meaning of its words would only produce nonsense, but it also signifies that we should regard the underlying sense of the figurative terms': *De Spiritu et Littera* § 6.

[42] The parable is, of course, occasionally explained, as in *Matt.* xiii.

[43] In *Contra Faustum* VI § 2 Augustine distinguishes the moral precept: ' Thou shalt not covet ' from

the symbolic precept: ' Thou shalt circumcise every male '.

[44] Rand 1928 117–18. And Jerome refused to recognize *Revelations* as canonical: Charles 1911 XXIII [11] 213.

[45] Brewster 1927 125–26.

[46] Boissier 1909 II [6] 225–26; & Bidez 1930 69.

later third century, this was an adequate interpretation. But, with the temporal triumph of Christianity under Constantine in the early fourth, the need for a more systematic fusion of pagan beliefs — for a more united paganism — became imperative. Thus to Julian, a Neoplatonic contemporary of Ambrose, the myth of Attis — who, forsaking Cybele his benefactress, disobediently marries an earthly nymph and is castrated, only to be led upward again by Cybele into heavenly glory — is no longer, as to Porphyry, a symbol of spring vegetation which is injured before it bears its fruit, but a symbol of the soul's perpetually recurring departure from and return to the Neoplatonic God.[47] From a naturalistic it becomes a theological symbol. A particularly drastic suggestion, which the Christian, Firmicus Maternus,[48] in 346 subjects to exhaustive ridicule, was that, since the Phrygian beliefs symbolized earth, the Egyptian water, the Syrian and Punic air, and the Persian fire, each cult was but a part of the true pagan cult honouring the four elements.[49] A similar effort of this kind was undertaken in the early fifth century by Macrobius, who devotes a series of chapters of his *Saturnalia* to a proof that almost every god worshipped by pagan antiquity was really only a personification of some attribute of the sun.[50]

Thus the ancient world, pagan and Christian alike, collapsed in an orgy of symbolism.

Neoplatonism had shown no respect for the integrity of science because it felt obliged to make the natural world serve as the handmaid of its philosophy: even though science might indicate otherwise, a concentration of matter at the centre of the universe had to be assumed. But there is no evidence

---

[47] *Oration* V 165B & C, 167, 168A, & 171B.

[48] On what is known of him see Thorndike 1923 I 525 ff.

[49] See Cumont 1929⁴ 189 who observes further: 'Ce système est certainement emprunté aux théologiens païens. Dans le péril commun qui les menace, les cultes autrefois rivaux se sont réconciliés et se regardent comme des divisions d'une même église, dont leurs clergés forment, si j'ose dire, les congrégations. Chacun d'eux est consacré particulièrement à l'un des éléments dont la combinaison forme l'univers; leur ensemble constitue la religion panthéiste du monde divinisé.' Dill 1906² 100 says that Julian 'dreamt of regenerating the ancient worship by borrowing a dogmatic theology from Alexandria, an ecstatic devotion from Persia, a moral ideal from Galilee.'

[50] I §§ 17–23.

that Christianity treated science with any more respect: it did not, to be sure, try to dictate what must be the location and distribution of matter, but this was only because it had no immediate incentive to do so. Christianity did not refrain out of respect for the integrity of science but merely out of indifference to the conclusion. To other conclusions it might be anything but indifferent. Philosophies and theologies arise and prosper, not because of their ability to distort, but rather because of their ability to tally with, the science then current. Friction cannot therefore occur so long as a later science does not reveal the fallacies of the old and so of the theology which this old had engendered. Neoplatonism was hampered by dependence on the science Plato knew; [51] Christianity, still pliable and immature in the fourth century, was not so committed. Through alliance with the science then current, Christianity could make it a source of strength — each seemed to corroborate the other. But this does not mean that Christianity had any more respect for science. This respect demands a faith in the truth, not merely of what is already discovered, but of what may in the future be discovered, and of such a faith no Roman, whether Christian or pagan, had a particle.[52]

Other ages and civilizations have shown this respect for science; why then did the Roman Empire of the fourth century, in many ways so highly evolved, not show it? And why, above all, did Augustine, otherwise so enlightened, regard the outer world and its behaviour as merely an ephemeral adjunct of the spiritual conflict waged in the soul of man? The only plausible reason is that by the year 400 pure science had been virtually at a standstill for six hundred years, so that its truths seemed stale and obvious, familiar and so insignifi-

---

[51] Manichæan science was under far greater handicaps: Stoop 1909 13-14.

[52] Augustine, for instance, made no effort to emancipate himself from the current assumption that the planets and stars moved only because a physical force was being constantly applied to them — presumably by a divinity: ' For were He to withdraw His efficacious power from things, they should be able neither to go on and complete the periods assigned to their measured movements, nor should they even continue in the possession of that nature they were created in ': *D.C.D.* XXII 24. Philoponos, who later envisaged the law of inertia of bodies, was a Christian, but this means little since all sixth century Alexandrians must have been Christians — at their peril. See Sarton 1927 I 416 & 421-22. See pp. 1 n. 6, 44 n. 33, & 215 n. 19.

cant. During these centuries there had been various advances in applied science,[53] but these merely extended the application of known laws, they revealed no new ones and so no new angles from which reality could be surveyed.

Now, as is well known, science and theology are, if not irreconcilable enemies, at least natural rivals — if reason does not prove this, history does. And this is because they offer two mutually exclusive methods for the discovery of truth. Both are empirical, both are — we may hope — sound; and, although neither has yet demonstrated as much as its devotees have hoped, no third method has yet been devised that can rival either of them.

It was in the Hellenistic world of the third century B.C. that the scientific method first conspicuously won its independence — it was an age of empiricism, of the free observation of nature unhampered by pre-conceived doctrines: the prevailing ethics was that of the Hedonists, the science that of the physicists, the philosophy that of the Cynics and Epicureans. And, during the three hundred years which followed, conditions remained substantially unchanged. Until the first diffusion of the Oriental religions in about the year 100 A.D., no specifically religious belief was generally familiar, and none of any kind had monopolized attention or devotion. True, there was a variety of superstitious beliefs and practices, but not one of these carried really wide or deep devotion. At the same time the science which was then known enjoyed such free currency among men as only a Roman Empire could provide. Among men of enlightenment perhaps no philosophy rivalled that of Epicurus. By its denial of all supernatural explanations of inexplicable phenomena it seemed to provide an ideal soil for the growth of scientific curiosity and achievement. Never, it would seem, either before or since, has the opportunity been greater for the progress of the scientific method; and yet, in the year 100 A.D., pure science was still substantially where it had been when Epicurus first lived and spoke.

It was in about this year 100 A.D. that the Oriental cults

[53] Water mills, for instance, in the fourth century: Lot 1927 118 & 423. And cf. in general ibid. 194.

made their first serious western inroads.[54]   Spreading from
their various points of origin, they gradually impregnated
the whole Empire.   Why did they spread so fast if not because men were by that time discouraged with the scientific
method?   A new method could not teach them less and might
teach them more.   It is an extraordinary record, this growth
of religion from 100 to 400 A.D. — the decline and fall of the
State is no more unique and dramatic.   What a variety of
stages, how orderly, even how scientific, an evolution!   Before the year 100 the Stoics and Epicureans; [55] after that
year the Egyptian and Phrygian cults; in the third century
the Syrian and Persian-Mithraic cults; in the fourth the Manichæan, the Neoplatonic,[56] and finally the Christian conception.   Unfortunately only the Christian has left us a detailed
record of its growth — a steady evolution from Paul to Augustine.   Yet each of the others must have had analogous
evolutions, analogous contacts with contiguous cults, analogous intricacies of action and reaction.

If science was already in disrepute in the year 100 A.D.
what possible respect could it hope to attract in the year 400?
As the Christian looked back he could descry the first shift
from science to theology three hundred years earlier.   How
fruitful must this shift have seemed!   Pure science, after at
least four hundred years of fair trial, had added very little to
man's knowledge even of this world; religion, on the other
hand, after only three hundred years' trial, had advanced
from the sterile theories of the Stoics and Epicureans to the
dizzy peak of Augustinian theology.   Augustine wrote no
formal treatise on the evolution of religion, but over and
over again he explains how, but for the various Greek and
Oriental doctrines, men would have been neither morally
nor intellectually qualified to grasp the Revelation.[57]   To
the thoughtful men of his day the advance of religion from

[54] According to Lot 1927 433 the
Greeks were first attracted to oriental
mysticism during the first century
A.D.

[55] Whittaker 1901 43 says: ' by the
Epicureans and Stoics everything
that can be spoken of at all was regarded as a body, or a quality or
relation of body, or else as having
no other being than " nominal." '

[56] Neoplatonism had originated in
Alexandria in about 225, but was not
known in Rome until after 250:
Whittaker 1901 33.   It was not triumphant as a philosophy in Athens
until about 400: ibid. 156.

[57] See Augustine Confessions VII
20.

100 to 400 seemed quite as marvellous and conclusive as seems today to similar men the scientific advance from Galileo to Einstein. And in each case the elapsed time was very nearly three hundred years.

E. AUGUSTINE ON HISTORY

To Augustine the Christian revelation disclosed a new theology and philosophy, a new ethics and psychology, a new science. But even with all this he was not content: it must teach a new history too. It was already much to understand why God must be both benevolent and omnipotent, why man must be guilty and miserable, why nature was created as it in fact was; there remained, nevertheless, the problem of how and why man and nature have evolved: what caused the growth of Greek science and philosophy, why the Jews were made the Chosen People, what laws and purposes so extended and glorified the Roman State,[1] what the explanation might be of pestilences, persecutions, heresies, and barbarian invasions. The world had moved, was still moving, and Augustine must know whither and why.

Just as Greek philosophy had impeded her science, so had it precluded the development of any philosophy of history. Not theology only, but philosophy too, can tyrannize. From the Greeks' premise that matter was the source of evil they inferred that it was also the source of corruption — of the contingent and ephemeral. It was, apparently, the Pythagorean school — of Philolaus or some of his disciples, with Aristotle later in collusion — which first conceived of a fundamental distinction between the super- and sub-lunar worlds.[2] Beyond the moon lay the world of the incorporeal and incorruptible, below it the world of the corporeal and so corruptible.[3] The upper world, being eternal, was the

[1] *D.C.D.* V 16. And cf. Leo *Sermon* # 82 § 2.

[2] Philolaus was born in about 474 B.C., Aristotle in 384 B.C.: see Reymond [1927] 165–66. Duhem 1914 II 453 says that the Christian

emancipation of the sub-lunar from the tyranny of the super-lunar world was of great advantage to science.

[3] See Macrobius *Commentary* I § 21.

real world, the lower, being ephemeral, was the realm of
the unreal; or, to use familiar medieval terms, the upper
world was real, the other nominal.   Thus the Idea of Horse,
as a universal concept, was real because it might and did
exist in the mind of God and other deities above, but the
individual and material horses existing below, simply because
formerly not real and ultimately not to be real, were not real
even now.[4]   But if by definition the corruptible was not
real, matter was not, and so neither evil nor corporeal
motion.   Thus neither was change real, nor what we call
history.

But, since reality merely meant incorruptibility, might
there not nevertheless be some evolution of corruptibility —
from one kind of ephemeral state to another?   Possibly, but
this, said the Greeks, can have no permanent effect, must
therefore be insignificant and probably dictated rather by
chance than by reason.   That the corruptible, sensible world
could never really evolve in any philosophical sense seemed to
be astronomically corroborated by the orderly recurrence of
the Great Year, in which — through the precession of the
equinoxes — the heavenly bodies in course of time must return to precisely the same apparent positions that they had
formerly occupied — a matter actually of 25,817 years, but
then very variously calculated.[5]   To men who believed that
all the motion and life in the universe was transmitted from
beyond the outermost stars it was inconceivable that, if the
heavenly bodies answered to a cyclical law, human bodies
should not also.   Thus even Plotinus, who denied that the
positions of the heavenly bodies caused earthly events, admitted that these, being subject to the same law as was man,
foretold — if man could but read their secrets — what the
future held in store.[6]   This cyclical theory, advanced by Plato
and systematized by the Stoics and Platonists who followed
him,[7] was closely connected with the belief in the transmigra-

[4] This Greek conception was, of
course, shared by many Christians.
Thus Jerome *Letter* # 15 § 4 says
' all things created, although they appear to be, are not. For there was a
time when they were not, and that
which once was not may again cease
to be.'

[5] An earlier calculation had been
432,000 years: Cumont 1929 [4] 164.
[6] See Macrobius *Commentary* II
§ 3; & Whittaker 1901 71–72.
[7] On Plato see a passage in Augustine *D.C.D.* XIII 19.   On Plotinus'
view of cycles see Whittaker 1901
74–75, & *Enneads* IV 8 § 5, & V 7 § 2.

tion of souls.[8] Some even assumed, not only that a soul must dwell in many kinds of animal bodies in the course of any Great Year, but must, in all subsequent Great Years, inhabit precisely the same bodies in precisely the same order.[9] Thus everything, both statically and dynamically, will repeat itself identically and interminably.[10]

But might not the pagan, though denying the reality of the corporeal world and though affirming the law of recurring cycles, nevertheless conceive of a law governing the evolution of the world and man within this ephemeral cycle? He might, and usually did, but, since nothing of a decisive nature was accomplished, since it must all be sooner or later done over again, the nature of these changes was only of academic interest.[11] There were plenty of evolutionary traditions — among the Greeks [12] as well as the Hebrews — from a barbarous to a civilized state, but the tendency was to ascribe the changes rather to the inefficiency of the Gods than to any pre-ordained and vital divine determination. For irregular change of itself suggested an incomplete divine guidance.

This was the real difficulty confronting the pagans: the end or final cause of things was pre-ordained and predetermined, the goodness of Nature could probably be relied upon to see that everything turned out right in the long run: but, because matter was an obstacle, many of the detailed events occurred rather by chance than design. This did not mean that these details were uncaused [13] but rather that their causes,

---

According to Augustine *D.C.D.* XII 20, Porphyry rejected the theory of cycles. On Iamblichus see Whittaker 1901 125. Macrobius *Commentary* II § 10 argued from the low degree of culture still existing and from the limited records of the past that the cycle was a brief one, periodically wiped out by floods. He thought that only the Egyptians avoided this destiny.

[8] Whereby Origen and Rufinus justified infant damnation: see Jerome *Letters* # 124 § 8, & # 130 § 16. Cf. pp. 72 n. 9, & 80–81.

[9] Particularly the Stoics: see Whittaker 1901 74; & Heussi 1930 13–14.

[10] According to Duhem 1914 II

449–51 Origen reconciled the cyclical theory with free will by supposing analogous rather than identical repetitions.

[11] Guitton 1933 359.

[12] Macrobius *Commentary* II § 10 gives the conventional pagan account. See Boissier 1909 II 6 284 on Ambrose's refutation of the Rousseau-like 'back to nature' argument of the pagan Symmachus.

[13] Plotinus *Enneads* III 1 § 1 says that everything that happens has a cause, which may be not only matter or God but also human will. But all the myriad causes are effects of a single originating cause, which is Nature.

since they did not proceed directly from the divine will of Nature, were far too various to be understood. Plotinus, the master-mind of later paganism, explains this clearly:

> But what of chastisements, poverty, illness, falling upon the good outside of all justice? . . . Such misfortunes do not answer to reasons established in the nature of things; they are not laid up in the master-facts of the universe, but are merely accidental sequents: a house falls, and anyone that chances to be underneath is killed, no matter what sort of man he be: two objects are moving in perfect order — or one if you like — but anything getting in the way is wounded or trampled down. Or we may reason that the undeserved stroke can be no evil to the sufferer in view of the beneficent interweaving of the All.[14]

Even to Plotinus, therefore, man's earthly life seemed largely at the mercy of a blind chance or destiny: the divine Good guarantees his soul ultimate rescue from the trials of the flesh, but, so long as he remains in the flesh, his environment has no relation to him or to the Good — it is a natural, inevitable evil which he can neither destroy nor understand. Thus the course of history has been casual; and, since it might quite as well have taken many other courses, it has not only no relation to him or to Goodness, but none to the future. Cause here still governs, but it is both blind and infinitely complex. It is only the super-sensible world that can be known.

What may the cult of Mithra have done to break down this conception of the world as ephemeral, recurrent, insignificant, and yet infinitely complex? By regarding the world as a battleground between the forces of good and evil, it granted, if not an ultimate reality, at least a significance to matter such as the Platonists had denied. This battle on earth was a real battle, on which, perhaps, the future of God's rule depended. A victory by God and those fighting for Him might result in the permanent annihilation of evil and so of matter, but, at least until annihilated, evil and so matter were real. This made the study of history important, but it did nothing to make it easy — there were too many unknown quantities. God, being the Good, might be known; so too, being evil, might the devil. But in addition to these factors there were men, some fighting on one side, some on the other. And finally there was the composite universe — a confusion of

14 *Enneads* IV 3 § 16.

spirit and matter, each unit perhaps obeying its own law unless and until checked by a sovereign force. Here, therefore, were five independent forces in conflict, and, if we count each individual man as a separate, though subordinate, agent, an infinite number. How was it to be determined what share any one of them might have in producing events? How could the reactions of these conflicting forces on each other be calculated, as to either past, present, or future events? Where the future thus lay at the mercy of several disparate and conflicting sovereignties no true philosophy of history was conceivable.

But the Manichæan heresy — that compound of Neoplatonism, Mithraism, and Asiatic Christianity [15] — probably did something to simplify the problem. For, whereas the Mithraist had faith in man's capacity to affect worldly affairs for good as well as for evil, the Manichee either shrank from the world as inevitable evil [16] or else compacted with its demon rulers. The good soul on earth in a certain sense was good, but it could not do good so long as it remained at the mercy of its material body in a world of matter. The Christian, Mark of Gaza, thus describes this view as he had known it in the year 400: they acknowledge nativities, he says,

and the science of the stars, in order that they may sin without fear; holding that the commission of sins is not in us, but comes from the necessity of fate.[17]

According to the Manichees, therefore, man is categorically eliminated as the original cause of anything: incarnated, he is at the mercy of the devil and matter; once freed of his body, he again becomes a mere particle of the divine Light.[18] The number of agencies is presumably reduced,[19] but, since the Manichee was a dualist, he still admitted two original causes.[20] The devil, to be sure, was doomed to ultimate defeat, but even God could perhaps not foreknow how long or bitter the struggle would prove, how long or severe would be His reverses. Consequently this pseudo-Christian God, although

[15] Burkitt 1925 72–95.
[16] Ibid. 64–65.
[17] Quoted by Burkitt 1925 8.
[18] Ibid. 39.
[19] In *Contra Adimantum* § 11

Augustine says they believed ' in a numerous family of gods ', but these were doubtless as unfree in will as men were.
[20] See pp. 63 n. 3, & 64 n. 6.

able to know the ultimate end towards which all things tended, was nevertheless helpless to know, because He could not control, the means by which that end was to be wrought.[21]

To this problem — which had been the despair of antiquity — Augustine now offered a bold, even a desperate solution. Other Gods had been benevolent; it was, therefore, to be a peculiar distinction of the Christian God that He was omnificent as well. And, since He was so, it must follow that every other energy, factor, agency, or being was wholly impotent. Of every tiniest and most inconspicuous event the Christian must be able truly and literally to say, ' it is God's will '. To Augustine everything was therefore equally and completely a divine miracle: man, and the method of his propagation, perhaps the most extraordinary,[22] but every other slightest natural phenomenon hardly less so. There was no conflict, no real distinction, between the powers of God and those of nature, man, or demons, and everything that happened was at once a natural and a supernatural phenomenon:

A portent, therefore, happens, not contrary to nature, but contrary to what we know of nature.[23]

He does not deny the existence of natural laws any more than he denies the activity displayed by living men, or angels, or demons; he merely denies that their operation has any other cause than God's will. Each is no more than an instrument, an amanuensis, a puppet of God.[24] To grant the least exception to this principle would be to play into the hands of the pagans, for with the smallest limitation on God's omnipotence His impotence begins.

The Greeks had evolved no philosophy of history because the events of the carnal world were unreal; the Mithraists and Manichees had evolved none because those events, though real, were caused by forces too varied or conflicting for human analysis; the first to evolve one were the Christians, because

---

[21] Cf. Augustine *Contra Faustum* V § 7.

[22] *D.C.D.* XII 23.

[23] Ibid. XXI 8. Although for practical purposes Augustine occasionally distinguishes, as where, *D.C.D.* III 15, he concludes that the obscuration of the sun at the hour of the Crucifixion was to all intents and purposes contrary to nature. On his catalogue of miracles in *D.C.D.* XXII 28 see p. 221.

[24] On the demons see *D.C.D.* II 23, & XXII 24.

they worshipped an omnipotent God.[25] This God had revealed Himself and His holy purposes; therefore to the degree that man could learn, by love and meditation, to read God's will, he could read history — the past, the present, perhaps the future too.

In an open letter of 384 written to refute the arguments of the pagan Symmachus, Ambrose said,

Our ancestral rites, he says, should be preserved. But what if all things have become better? The world itself, which at first was compacted by the gathering together of the elemental seeds through the vast void, an unconsolidated sphere, or was obscured by the thick darkness of the yet unordered work, was it not afterwards endowed with the forms of things which constitute its beauty, and were not the heaven, sea and earth distinguished from each other? The earth, rescued from dripping darkness, was amazed at its new sun. In the beginning too the day shines not, but as time goes on it is bright and warm with the increase of light and heat.[26]

And he proceeds,

Let them say then that all things ought to have continued as at first; that the world once covered with darkness is now displeasing because it shines with the beams of the sun. And how much better it is to have dispelled the darkness of the mind than that of the body, and that the beam of faith has shone forth than that of the sun. So then the early stages of the world as of all else have been unsettled, that the venerable age of hoary faith might follow. Let those who are affected by this find fault with the harvest too, because it ripens late; or with the vintage, because it is in the fall of the year; or with the olive, because it is the latest of fruits.[27]

Augustine is in certain passages more concrete:

---

[25] In the second century the Christians Meliton and Irenæus had supposed that it was Christianity that had led to the *Pax Romana*. It was only in about 235 that Origen in Alexandria and Julianus Africanus advanced the theory that this *Pax Romana* had been brought about by God in order to facilitate the diffusion of Christianity: Dufourcq 1905 198 n. 1. On Julianus see Troeltsch 1915 19. Church historians, notably Eusebius of Cæsarea in the early fourth century, assume that events are caused by God, but they do not profess to explain systematically how this was to be historically demonstrated. For the view of Augustine's near contemporary (six years older) Prudentius, see *Contra Symmachum* II lines 578–636, & *Peristephanon* II lines 275–76.

[26] *Letter* # 18 § 23.

[27] Ibid. § 27.

The teachings of the philosophers are not the commandments of the gods, but the discoveries of men who, at the prompting of their own speculative ability, made efforts to discover the hidden laws of nature, and the right and wrong in ethics, and in dialectic what was consequent according to the rules of logic, and what was inconsequent and erroneous. And some of them, by God's help, made great discoveries; but when left to themselves they were betrayed by human infirmity and fell into mistakes. And this was ordained by divine Providence that their pride might be restrained, and that by their example it might be pointed out that it is humility which has access to the highest regions.[28]

And he is convinced that since there has been a steady evolution in understanding, so will there continue to be one. Expounding *Matthew* v 38–9

Ye have heard that it hath been said, *an eye for an eye and a tooth for a tooth*.[29] But I say unto you that you resist not evil; but whosoever shall smite thee on thy right cheek, turn to him the other also,

Augustine anticipates the supposedly novel evolutionary conception of the nineteenth century:

For since at first carnal men burned to revenge themselves far out of proportion to the injury inflicted on them, the first rule of mercy was laid down for them, that the revenge should on no account exceed the measure of the original injury.[30]

Now if divine revelation itself has been gauged according to expediency, varying as has human enlightenment that it might not fall on barren soil, it is the duty of Christians no less than of others to exercise their intelligences in order that they may prove themselves the more qualified to comprehend the infinite wisdom of God. Thus, technical revelation aside, it is none the less imperative that the effort to comprehend be never relaxed:

If it is considered unseemly to emend anything that Plato has touched, why did Porphyry himself make emendations, and these not a few? [31]

[28] *D.C.D.* II 7.
[29] *Exodus* xxi 24.
[30] *Contra Adimantum* § 8; & cf.

ibid. § 17 on the contrast between *Exodus* xxiii 22–24 & *Matt.* v 44.
[31] *D.C.D.* X 30.

Actually, were it not for the effort of Plato to improve on his predecessors, and of Porphyry to improve on Plato, the human race might never have been ripe for the second and supreme Revelation. But for Porphyry's effort, defective as it was, the doctrine of Christ must have spread more slowly, might even have been postponed.

Finally Augustine is happy to be able to explain the causes of the glory of Rome:

Therefore it was not only for the sake of recompensing the citizens of Rome that her empire and glory had been so signally extended, but also that the citizens of that eternal city [the zealous Christians] during their pilgrimage here, might diligently and soberly contemplate those examples, and see what a love they owe to the supernal country on account of life eternal, if the terrestrial country was so much beloved by its citizens on account of human glory.[32]

Augustine loved the Greek philosophers, and he loved the civic devotion of his Roman ancestors.[33] God being the truth as he saw it, and the justice, he believed that God had rewarded them, as he himself would have liked to reward them. History was thus no longer the creature either of a blind Fate or of ineffective, petty, or malignant deities, but was a systematic moral evolution whose processes lent themselves, if not to scientific, at least to psychological, and so to intellectual, investigation. The premise, to be sure, was teleological, and the sources were experienced human intuition checked by an alien and Oriental text; we ought perhaps to call it pseudo-science; but just as surely as astrology had to precede astronomy, magic precede physics,[34] alchemy precede chemistry, so this Augustinian conception of history — of everything moving slowly and smoothly towards a preordained end — was the necessary preliminary to the modern conception of astronomical, geological, biological, and human evolution. The Christians were the first to tackle, however awkwardly, the great problem of man in time.[35]

In evolving a philosophy of history Augustine had an ad-

[32] D.C.D. V 16.
[33] Ibid. I 15 & 24; & Duchesne 1911 III 4 197–98.
[34] Cf. Cumont 1929 4 179.
[35] See especially Guitton 1933 359.

Cf. Troeltsch 1915 19, & Heussi 1930 8–14. Nock 1933 113 says that most of the ancients doubted progress, usually imagining, indeed, a congenital decline.

vantage over most other Christians because of his doctrine of predestination.[36] We must not, he said, confuse this doctrine — as Cicero did [37] — with that of God's foreknowledge. For all Christians agreed that God knows what is going to happen, not because He makes it happen, or because He infers the future from a close scrutiny of past and present complexities, but simply because He is outside of time and can therefore know events as if they were all occurring simultaneously:

He moves things temporal without Himself moving in time.[38]

Of a past sequence men can themselves have such an impression. As with the layman seeing a picture, so with the musician hearing a composition: although at any given instant he can concentrate on only one point, he can, in retrospect, be instantaneously conscious of the whole work.[39] It was evidently in some such way, according to the Christians, that God could see and hear the future.

But this does not preclude free will, for God's knowledge is merely of choices already made. It is true that God can in this way know how everything is going to turn out, and true, therefore, that He willed this ultimate end. At the same time He may be causing it to come out so, indirectly, by the mere act of Creation, thereafter so delegating His power that man's free will became a contributory cause of things. In such a case God will know how it is all going to turn out almost as we do who see a play over again. But He does not on that account cause these happenings — any more than we cause the second performance.[40] So all Christians agreed about God's foreknowledge; the doubt concerned His power.

Plotinus, whose opinion always held the respect of Christians, seems to have based this phase of his philosophy on the

[36] In *De Pred. Sanctorum* § 19 Augustine speaks of ' predestination, which cannot exist without foreknowledge, although foreknowledge may exist without predestination.'

[37] Cf. *D.C.D.* V 9 & 10.

[38] Ibid. X 12.

[39] In what is probably an early nineteenth century forgery Mozart is made to write: ' I can survey it [his composition] like a fine picture or a beautiful statue, at a glance. Nor do I hear in my imagination the parts successively, but I hear them as it were all at once.' See Holmes 1878 212 for the letter in translation.

[40] On Cassian see Loofs 1906 III 196 line 45; on Boethius, *De Consol.* V ch. 6.

law of probabilities, assuming that Being or Good was chronically conquering Non-being or Evil, so that the losses suffered
by Good were comparable to the casualties suffered by a
victorious army.   Recall his observation that 'such misfortunes do not answer to reasons established in the nature
of things; they are not laid up in the master-facts of the
universe, but are merely accidental sequents.'[41]   They
might be compared to the rising atoms within a falling
body.

Yet Plotinus believed in an iron-clad destiny, that is, in a
multitude of secondary causes which followed inevitably from
one single original cause.[42]   His system might be compared to
an engine the degree of whose waste of fuel energy can be accurately calculated beforehand.   But if Plotinus, in spite of his
assumption that there is only one original cause, was obliged
to admit the existence of 'accidental sequents', how could
those Christians who admitted some degree of human free
will and so a variety of original causes, avoid a similar admission of 'accidental sequents' which must inevitably derogate
from God's omnipotence?   For it is the essence of man's free
will that he can be an original cause, an entity, within his
humble sphere, whose will is as uncaused as is God's.   There
is thus no longer, as with Plotinus, a clash of secondary causes
pre-ordained by a one original cause, but a clash of original
causes with each other, which in this case requires that God
be constantly obliged to change His plans,[43] acting according
rather to circumstances than to any pre-arranged scheme.
For the nature of His act must be subsequent to and dependent upon the initiating will of man.   Further than this, original causes were being created every instant by millions of
men, so that it was hard to conceive that even God could
instantly and simultaneously redress all these new situations.
Since the spatial insignificance of the earth and so of man in
comparison with the celestial sphere was as vividly felt in the

[41] See p. 121 n. 14. Boissier 1909
II [6] 399 says the Stoic view was comparable.
    [42] In *Enneads* III 1 § 1 he says:
' Causelessness is quite inadmissible '
and that ' the general cause of all is
Nature.' Cf. ibid. III 4 § 6, & IV 3
§ 13. Even the ' accidental sequent '

has a cause — probably that furthest
removed from those Firsts among the
Eternals which alone ' cannot be referred to outside Causes ': ibid. III 1
§ 1.
    [43] Cf. Tixeront 1924 I [9] 311 on
Origen.

year 400 [44] as in the time of Pascal,[45] it was natural to suspect that what might in the eyes of God seem an insignificant divergence from ordained procedure might seem a huge divergence in the eyes of men. It was thus conceivable not only that a man might fall, or a city, but that a whole people be in jeopardy, before God should set Himself to redress matters. For to Him such divergences might seem nothing more than ' accidental sequents ' of man's free will.[46]

Furthermore, if God was in fact obliged to redress a situation created by the initiative of others, there remained the question of how He should redress it. The simplest method was surely a miraculous intervention, whereby He would correct the errors which had accumulated, in the same way that a man resets his watch. To those Christians, therefore, who believed in real human free will, a metaphysical distinction could be made between the miraculous and the natural event. By some such reasoning as this it was possible to save man's freedom and so self-respect without derogating from God's substantial omnipotence.

Now it was to precisely this Christian doctrine that Augustine was opposed because it contradicted two of his deepest convictions: the first that God was — at least since the Fall — absolutely omnificent, the second, in which the Fall corroborated his personal experience,[47] that man, as he now existed, was incapable, of his own accord, of willing a virtuous act. That Adam, before the Fall, had been given a free will, Augustine was obliged to admit; but that his descendants, even after the Redemption, had again received one, he emphatically denied. For, after all, if man's will be recognized as something, how could God's be recognized as everything? God's potency can only begin where that of man ends, and where potency implies merit, God would merely share the totality of merit with man.

This raises the second point: if man can really acquire merit he may justly feel pride in his achievement, and once

---

[44] Cf. Ambrose *Exameron* IV 25–27. Macrobius *Commentary* I § 16 speaks of ' terra quae tota puncti locum pro caeli magnitudine vix obtinet.'

[45] See Brunschwicg ed. 1921 XII 73–82.

[46] This may be why Augustine, unlike Ambrose and other earlier Fathers, urged submission even to an unjust ruler: cf. Carlyle 1927 I [2] ch. 14.

[47] See Gilson 1929 200.

he is allowed to think he is something he will soon think he is everything.[48]   Men may thus, as we have seen,

> please themselves, but Thee do they displease highly: not only for pleasing themselves in things not good, as if they were good, but also for so doing in Thy good things as if they were their own: or as if Thine, yet as given them for their own merits: or, if also as proceeding from Thy mere grace, yet not in a neigh-bourly spirit, but as grudging it to others. In all these perils and travails, and others of the like kind, Thou seest a trembling of my heart.[49]

To deny that God was everything and man nothing seemed to Augustine little else than an affirmation of paganism.

Here, however, a distinction is to be observed: Augustine thought it safe to admit that man's will was free in the sense that he could will good freely if he chose; but he insisted that man was not free to actualize the good he might will — was not free to translate pious wishes into realities. He might wish that he did not covet his neighbour's goods but this could not stop him from coveting them.[50] A man who willed evil could translate it into actuality — his depravity was quite sufficient for that — but only if he received grace could he actualize a will to virtue.[51] Moreover, having received this grace which he had necessarily done nothing to merit, he was constrained to be virtuous because the grace was irresistible. Now, no more than before, was he free, as Adam had been, to love or hate, to be good or bad: he must love and be good.

But, even were all this true, was God's control over events on this account necessarily complete? Suppose that a man did receive grace, had he not still a choice between the vari-ous acts of virtue? Might he not still choose between the life of a hermit and that of a bishop, choose between Mary's and Martha's way? This was improbable, because grace might come by a propitious juxtaposition of outward circum-stances [52] or by an inner illumination, or by both: in any case

---

[48] Since pride was the prime cause of Adam's sin it is the root of all evil: see ibid. 187–88; & cf. *Galatians* vi 3.

[49] *Confessions* X 39, quoted on p. 75 n. 19.

[50] See Gilson 1929 192 & 199; & cf. *Confessions* VIII 9, & IX 1; & *D.C.D.* V 10, where Augustine speaks of 'him who willed, but was not able

to accomplish what he willed.' A more thorough account of Augus-tine's doctrine of predestination is on pp. 394–400.

[51] See p. 395.

[52] On God's manipulation of out-ward circumstances, see Augustine's explanation of how He handled Alypius: *Confessions* VI 7 & 9; and

God's hand followed him like his shadow, directed his slightest step. Suppose, however, that a man is denied grace, has he
not still a choice of evil courses? May he not choose to rape
rather than to kill, to indulge rather his sloth than his ambition? Since this man was destined never to receive grace,
could God nevertheless be thought of as directing his course
towards perdition? Yet, were the man thus free, God must
be obliged to arm Himself against contingencies created by
human initiative, His will being thus dependent on, and so
subject to, the will of an evil man, and such an initiative in
man Augustine most emphatically will not allow:

Scripture . . . shows us that not only men's good wills, which
God Himself converts from bad ones, and, when converted by
Him, directs to good actions and eternal life, but also those which
follow the world, are so entirely at the disposal of God that He
turns them whithersoever He wills and whensoever He wills — to
bestow kindness on some and to heap punishment on others.[53]

But is it not repulsive to conceive of God meticulously
directing the lives of men whom He has already irrevocably
destined to damnation? Might He not at least have the
delicacy of leaving them to their own devices? Perhaps this
was rather awkward, but there was nevertheless no way to
evade the ugly hypothesis without giving evil men an initiative to which God must conform His subsequent determination. Moreover there was a positive as well as this negative
reason: a man might, apparently, choose the lesser of two
evil courses and, although no such act is theologically meritorious and so an approach to eternal rewards, it may well
have merit enough to induce God to grant him some earthly
reward:

Now, therefore, with regard to those to whom God did not purpose to give eternal life . . . if He had also withheld from them
the terrestrial glory of that most excellent empire, a reward would
not have been rendered to their good arts — that is, their virtues
— by which they sought to attain so great a glory. For as to those
who seem to do some good that they may receive glory from men,
the Lord also says, *Verily I say unto you, they have received their
reward.*[54]

---

of how He handled Augustine: ibid.   [53] *De Gratia et Lib. Arbit.* § 41.
VII 20.   [54] *D.C.D.* V 15.

But in order to render this reward God is obliged to devise appropriate outward circumstances quite as meticulously as where He is guiding a man towards salvation. A scintilla of free will is here admitted, but it requires only a slight disposition in order to inaugurate God's guidance of his earthly career. Let us, however, suppose instead a pure villain — one who only refrains from rape in order to kill: God is likely to inaugurate his eternal punishment during his life, but He may, on the contrary, give him an earthly glory, in order to prove, as He did in the case of Marius,[55] that a people who worship demons are liable to be ruled by them. Or God may need a villain as a cog in His machinery of outward circumstances, designed to guide those destined for salvation. Suppose such a man somehow roused from sloth to ambition so that he becomes a notorious tyrant. To Augustine his choice may well have been forced by God — for the edification, chastisement, or tempering of the tyrant's victims.[56] Denied grace himself, he is nevertheless requisitioned to assist in conferring the graces which God has destined for others. There is thus a tiny space left for the free will to do evil, but hardly does the evil will stir before God charges Himself with the wretch's destiny.

It is therefore because God is conceived as an omnipresent and omnificent despot that His subjects cannot truly call their souls their own. Augustine might admit that this was unfortunate — but so was the Fall unfortunate, and God's omnipotence is not to be tampered with merely because man is ready to clutch at any straw which will save a remnant of his pagan self-respect. To Augustine, man had already been flattering himself quite long enough.

We can see now why, of the many pagan and Christian writers before 450, the only ones to expound a philosophy of history were Augustine, and his devoted disciple Orosius.

It was a strange world to which the genius of Augustine had given birth, yet is it, after all, a stranger one than that which the genius of modern science has disclosed? Of the two experiences, the inner and the outer, which has taught man the more about reality? It is clear enough that

[55] *D.C.D.* II 23.   [56] Ibid. V 21.

Christianity, though unintentionally, did much harm to that branch of science which depends on the unprejudiced observation of outer nature,[57] but it seems an open question whether it did not in the long run do good to science as a whole.   Actually Augustine was quite as empirical as any modern physicist; the difference is that he chose to draw his conclusions about the universe from his observation rather of man's psychology than of nature's physiology.   Augustine's method, indeed, much more resembled that of the early Greek physicists than it did the stricter philosophical method of Plato and Aristotle, for this latter was based, not on biting experience, but on certain dialectical assumptions — of perfection, harmony, incorruptibility, eternity, etc.   And, if this be so, it becomes clearer why the Middle Ages, intoxicated by a dialectic which outran their experience, chose to use Plato and Aristotle to illuminate the biblical revelation, and why the real Augustinian revival was postponed until the return of the empirical method in the Renaissance.

F. Decline and Decadence

Yet, because the greatness of Christianity was not temporal but spiritual, its triumph boded ill for the State.   Its final victory was only gained in the later fourth century; in the early fifth the western half of the Empire collapsed, and it is undeniable that the victory contributed to that fall.   To the Christians the Empire lived in sin and must die before it could be reborn.[1]   It is true that many of them mourned the

[57] One prejudice against unprejudiced observation was raised by its evident simplicity.   Because it was relatively easy to observe idly and yet accurately, it was thought relatively unimportant: for God demanded difficult things of men.   Many medieval scholastics felt that the very difficulty of studying the super-sensuous world was evidence of its importance and fruitfulness.   Thus Hugo of Saint Victor (a Saxon who flourished in about 1150) argues the superiority of logic over observation on the ground that logic has only very recently been mastered by man: *Erud. Didasc.* I § 12.

[1] For cases of where people, upon conversion, abandoned their civil occupations and employments, see, besides the many *Letters* of Jerome, Augustine's *Confessions* VIII 6, & IX 1, 2 & 8.   On Orosius and Salvian see Duchesne 1911 III⁴ 608.

fall and hoped, and even prayed, that it might be averted; on the other hand few troubled to raise a temporal hand to forestall it.[2]   Already the cloud of predestination was darkening the bright new teleological sky: the natural wish to save the State into which they have been born must, like other temporal inclinations — to friendship, self-respect, and prosperity — be repressed: for God was apparently ordaining otherwise and men could only submit humbly to His will.

On the other hand it is equally impossible to maintain that Christianity was a symptom of decadence.[3]   Ambrose, Augustine, and Bossuet were here more nearly right than Gibbon. For these three said that Rome had come into being in order that out of it Christianity might spring, and this, because it respects the law of cause and effect, is an evolutionary conception at bottom.   As we have said, Ambrose and Augustine had, each in his own way, outgrown ancient civilization as he found it; each had learned that man was in fact something more than antiquity had supposed.   Not that they belittled Plato or Aristotle, not that they did not relish Cicero, Virgil, and Horace; on the contrary they admired them — much as we do; they believed that these pagans had spoken wisely, that they had had premonitions of what Christ should re-

[2] Salvian, writing as late as 445, was still preaching the virtue of weakness and non-resistance: see pp. 367–70. Auvergne was one of the few Gallic territories to resist the barbarian invaders, yet in the midst of that resistance, in 474, bishop Sidonius of Clermont declares that their chief hope lies in prayers: *Letters* VII # 1.

[3] The issue is squarely raised by Cumont 1929 [4] 38:
'A mesure qu'on descend vers la fin de l'Empire, les volontés semblent s'amollir et les tempéraments s'énerver. On trouve de moins en moins cette robuste santé de caractères qui, incapable d'une aberration durable, n'éprouvent pas le besoin d'être guidés et réconfortés; on voit se répandre ce sentiment de déchéance et de fragilité qui suit les égarements de la passion; la même faiblesse, qui conduit au crime, pousse à en chercher l'absolution dans des pratiques extérieures de l'ascétisme, et l'on vient aux prêtres des cultes orientaux, comme aux médecins de l'âme, demander des remèdes spirituels.'
Since Cumont does not except Christianity from this condemnation it is clear that he is still true to the nineteenth century conception of decadence — that of Darwinism, the Empire-builders, and Nietzsche. Yet to regard nervous temperaments, highly sensible of their fragility and in need of spiritual consolations, as so many signs of decadence, is hardly substantiated by the historical evidence. For how, even if we choose to condemn the cathedral of Chartres and Francis of Assisi as Christian manifestations, are we to explain our admiration for Shakespeare? And was it not during the sixteenth and seventeenth centuries — which so glorified Augustine — that our modern science was born?

veal; and they felt, again much as we still do, that, but for
the instruction offered by these pagans,[4] mankind would not
have known enough adequately to appraise and prize the
Revelation.   For to these Fathers of wide education and experience Christianity was not true merely because the Prophets had foretold it, or because of Christ's or any other
miracles, or because they seemed to have had visions of or com-
munications with God — these served merely as corroborative
evidence.[5]   To them Christianity was true because it alone explained them, and explained human life as they had experienced it.   Platonism had explained Plato and life, to Plato;
to Augustine it explained Plato, but it explained neither life
nor Augustine.[6]

[4] Cf. *Confessions* VII 20.

[5] Augustine says repeatedly that
we must believe in order to understand, but does not this mean ' in
order adequately and satisfactorily to
understand '?   Through understanding, Aristotle was attracted to the
doctrine of Plato just as Augustine
was attracted to Christianity; the difference was that whereas Aristotle
felt free to emend Plato, Augustine
felt constrained to follow the Bible
blindly.   Yet it is an open question
whether the emendations of Plato
by Aristotle were more radical than
the interpretations of the Bible by
Augustine.   That, however, is not
here material: the point is that each
chose a certain text because it seemed
the explanation that best fitted experienced reality.   To Aristotle, who
sought reality in a biological harmony, Plato must appeal; to Augustine, who sought reality in the paradox of a human nature that can wish
to be virtuous without being able to
become so, Christ's revelation must
appeal.

The intellectual character of
Augustine's conversion is indicated
by a passage in *Confessions* V 3.
Speaking there of the time when
Manichæism was beginning to disturb him, he says: ' But in his
[Mani's] writings I was commanded
to believe all, but it did not answer
unto those reasons which had been
found true, both by mine own calcu-
latings and eyesight; from all of
which his was quite contrary.'   And
commenting on the disputations between Manichee and Catholic he said
that at that time ' although the
Catholic party seemed to me not to
be overthrown, yet it appeared not
to be altogether victorious ': ibid. V
14.   Cf. Dudden 1935 330–31.
That his approach was intellectual
rather than emotional does not make
it the less likely that grace was the
cause of his conversion: for why
might not Augustine have received
grace in the form of an unusually
acute intellectual sensibility?

[6] Cf. Harnack 1897 III[3] 99 n. 1;
& Jones 1913 89.

CHAPTER III

MIRACLES

A. THE NEW VIRTUES

DURING the fourth century, while the enlightenment — and so the aspirations — of the Romans had continued to advance, their institutions and organization fell into a decline. It was as if there were two antagonistic wills, the one individual the other national, the one ideally desirable the other actually necessary. In a new way valour was again conquering discretion.

This had not always been so. The Roman virtues associated with the age of the Republic had evolved out of primitive and international needs: to ensure the survival of the State in its struggle against rival States. This called for a military civilization, with a cohesion that could produce the maximum strength by forbidding waste of energy. The virtues that this engendered were courage, energy, and loyalty, for the end was not a social or individual but a military perfection.

In this stage of Rome's development it had been the State that set the ideal standard, surpassing the individual and tending, therefore, to raise a man, as citizen, above himself. Under the Empire, however, with the security it gradually brought, the individual could afford to aspire to higher virtues, directed now towards private instead of public harmony. New virtues arose to meet the new situation: instead of physical courage, energy, and loyalty, men preferred to cultivate gentleness, charity, and modesty. And, as they preferred to inspire spiritual affection instead of physical respect, to inspire love instead of fear, to make life agreeable as well as safe, the old military virtues lost their prestige, began to be viewed with condescension. In the Middle Ages, following the suggestion of the Cluny monks,[1] Christians came to realize that unless superimposed upon a solid foundation of civic

[1] Taylor 1914 I 2 297–98.

virtue,[2] the more fragile Christian virtues could not impose
a general respect. Out of this realization grew the institutions
of knighthood and the Military Orders. But the Romans of
the Empire did not appreciate this and therefore tended to
deplore the very State that had produced them. In the earlier
time even the noblest Roman aspired only to be worthy of his
State, but the time came now when the noble Roman instead
aspired to transcend it.[3]

This new movement began with exaggerations. No sooner
did physical life seem safe than it began to seem contemptible;
to supply the growing demand for a world that was more
than flesh appeared the Neoplatonists — whose founder Plotinus 'seemed ashamed of being in the body'[4] — and the
many Oriental cults, Christianity among them, all of which
taught a subordination of the present, tangible life to a future,
intangible one. As symbol of this world the State, which
had once been an end in itself, became the chief obstacle to
the realization of the end. From the chosen instrument it
became the foe of human aspirations. The obstinacy of the
martyrs was directed less against pagan theology than against
the worship of the State.

Mithraism was probably favoured by Diocletian because
it offered a compromise calculated to appease the rising thirst
for other-worldliness. To induce the Romans to fight, the
incentive of protecting the State against alien, barbarian
marauders was not enough; the incentive must now be more
abstract and this need Mithraism supplied through its theology of an international warfare against the powers of evil.
No less a personage than the devil himself could now seem a
worthy foe. The fight was no longer for physical survival
against a ring of hostile powers but for the spiritual survival
of righteousness. To be worth fighting for, the State had to
be imagined a symbol of that righteousness — not, as earlier,
an end in itself, but as a direct means to a quite different end.
The incentive is analogous to that which was to inspire the
medieval Crusaders.

At the same time Diocletian tried to revive the prestige of

2 'These are the four cardinal virtues — temperance, prudence, justice
and fortitude': Ammianus *R.G.* XXV
4 § 1.

3 Fustel de Coulanges 1891 II 219–
21.

4 Porphyry *Life of Plotinus* § 1.

the State by means of an elaborate legislative programme [5] which should reorganize the machinery of government and artificially regulate every phase of civic life, including the economic and moral. But, because it was in fact the State that was defective, this intensification of State activity served only to aggravate the disequilibrium, increasing the power of the very element that was in discredit.

It was in 324,[6] just forty years after the accession of Diocletian, that Constantine became sole Emperor. His mother was a Christian;[7] as the rival of Diocletian's party it was not unnatural that Constantine should appeal for the support of that faith which the Mithraists had most feared and persecuted. This Christianity, moreover, might easily have seemed to offer the one remedy the decrepit State required. For Christ taught that the regeneration of society, and so of the State, could only come through individual purification. That the change must come rather from within than from without seemed corroborated by the evident inadequacy of Diocletian's energetic reforms. With the old civic patriotism dead the vices of the State could only be checked by checking the power of the State, and the new virtues now seeking to become articulate could be fostered only by the diffusion of a religion belittling civic objectives. Because the citizen was already balking at the new tyranny of regulation, the more the State demanded the less it got; the more desperately it courted devotion the more it created distrust. Seeing, therefore, that evil was invulnerable so long as assaulted from without, Constantine inferred that it was vulnerable only to assaults from within.[8]

In a sense, therefore, this turning to Christianity for help was a final act of Roman patriotism. It seemed to offer the last hope of salvaging the State and so the civilization it had bred. The change it effected, however, was for some time a matter merely of degree, the flood of legislation continuing

---

[5] Lot 1927 22 says 'Aucun autre empereur ne nous a laissé un aussi grand nombre de rescrits ou d'édits: douze cents. L'esprit en est des plus louable.'

[6] Ibid. 38–39.

[7] On his mother Helena see Jullian 1926 VII 97. His father may

have died one (in 306): Dufourcq L'Av. 1910 IV [5] 64–65, but this is uncertain: see Jullian ibid. n. 7.

[8] There is an abundance of conjecture about Constantine's motives in championing Christianity: cf. Lot 1927 31–43.

unabated and perhaps often aggravating the difficulties by
further regulation of moral conduct. By a law of Constantine, for instance, the death penalty was imposed for adultery.
This not only involved that taking of life which Christians
shrank from; it probably had but small effect as a deterrent.
Before the end of the century, at all events, the futility of
such legislation must have been very generally recognized.
Jerome reports how

Every day the blood of adulterers is shed, adulteries are condemned; yet lust is raging and rampant in the very presence of
the laws, the symbols of authority and the courts of justice.[9]

Which leads him to conclude, according to the old proverb,
that

Where there is the most law there is the most evil.

Evidently the higher a law aspired the more impracticable it
was to enforce.

If faith in the efficacy of civil law died only reluctantly in
the course of the fourth century, nevertheless throughout
this same period, beginning with the Council of Nicæa in 325,
much progress was being made in the construction of a wholly
new system of law, appropriately designed to suit the new disposition of mind. This was the canon law of the Church.
Even though it was rather instinctively than consciously
evolved in order to save Roman civilization, the fact remains
that it alone saved the little that was saved. And there is the
curious additional fact that it was the bishop of Rome who
became head of the Church. Was this not chiefly because his
rule seemed most likely to remain true to the traditions of
Roman civilization? Was this not somehow a triumph for
the blunt moral integrity of the Latin over the speculative
extravagances of the East?

With the gradual prestige acquired by the Christian-Latin
bishop over a State grown oriental, canon law began to challenge the supremacy of civil law. The ascendency of Ambrose over successive Emperors is characteristic.[10] Super-im-
posed upon the civil law this canon law was soon to acquire
the mastery and the old law to be gradually subordinated to
it.[11] A wholly new theory of government was thus inaugu-

---

[9] Jerome *Contra Jovinianum* I
§ 36.

[10] See pp. 266, 546, & 554-55.

[11] See pp. 554-55, 596, & 636.

rated, according to which every human imperfection became criminal and every punishment spiritual. The executive was no longer the Emperor and his State, but instead each man and his conscience. If the State were destined to be saved this salvation must come, not by more legislation and a stricter police enforcement, but rather by more divine grace and a closer voluntary co-operation. If there were to be any triumphs these must be of each individual over his baser self. If the walls of Roman civilization were not to fall they must be shored up from within by the infusion of a strengthening grace.

The new law of the canons evolved in order to combat the new sins — a new enemy called for a new strategy. The old Roman sins had been cowardice, laziness, treason — the sins of soldiers; the new sins were cruelty, obscenity, gluttony, avarice, and pride — compatible with a soldier's efficiency and so with a soldier's repute, but incompatible with his repute as a man. The Romans had become reluctant to fight because it was both unnecessary and disagreeable — they had learned to prefer more delicate pleasures.[12] Therefore as the soldiers' virtues lost in esteem, their vices gained in repulsiveness. Their roots, however, still ran deep in the Roman soil, and upon Christianity devolved the task of pulling them out. It was by its dedication to this work that it first disarmed the hesitating Roman and then won his devoted allegiance.

Under a military regime cruelty, being so often necessary, was not thought an evil. For up to a certain point the soldier must, like the surgeon, be callous to suffering, even to suffering deliberately induced. Thus if torture, for instance, were legitimate in order to extract secrets from prisoners of war, it could not seem wholly illegitimate when applied in order to extract secrets from those other enemies of the State, the criminal suspects. In a rougher age, moreover, no one felt squeamish about torturing such persons in public. Out of this rude custom grew many of the cruel sports to be witnessed in the arena, where not only criminals suffered but

12 On the mercy, chastity and temperance of the Emperor Julian, see Ammianus *R.G.* XXV 4 §§ 8, 2 & 4.

even professional gladiators, who fought to the death to keep alive the Roman love of military valour.

It may well be that the cruelties to which the Christian martyrs were subjected inaugurated the arena's fall in prestige. It could be argued that the prisoner of war and the gladiator had chosen their rude vocation, and that this was true too of the criminal suspect. But the sufferings were imposed on the Christian martyrs only because they protested against those cruelties. Because they would not sacrifice to the bloodthirsty pagan gods they were themselves bled.[13] To plead the cause of mercy may be rash but it can never be criminal.

The Christians' triumph put an end only to their own sufferings; it did not otherwise change the law. When, just after 400, the Christian Prudentius described the tortures inflicted on the martyrs[14] these had ceased a century earlier; yet it is likely that the details were derived rather from his own observations of contemporary criminal procedure than from documents or oral tradition. For in 405 the law still prescribed torture in such cases, just as it had in 312 or 324.

Nor was torture resorted to only as a punishment of the condemned; it was inflicted with no less ingenuity on suspects — in order either to extract a damaging confession or to implicate other persons. Witness, as late as 420, the burning sarcasm of Augustine:

What shall I say of torture applied to the accused himself? He is tortured in order to discover whether he is guilty, so that, though innocent, he suffers most undoubted punishment for a crime that is still doubtful, not because it is proved that he committed it, but because it is not ascertained that he did not commit it. Thus the ignorance of the judge frequently involves an innocent person in suffering. And what is still more unendurable — a thing indeed to be bewailed and, if that were possible, watered with fountains of tears — is this, that when the judge puts the accused to the question, that he may not unwittingly put an innocent man to death, the result of this lamentable ignorance is that this very person, whom he tortured in order that he might not condemn him if innocent, is condemned to death both tortured and innocent. For if he has chosen, in obedience to the philosophical instructions to the wise man, to quit this

---

[13] Cf. Eusebius *Eccl. Hist.* VIII 8, & *Martyrs of Palestine passim.*   [14] Cf. *Peristephanon* V lines 100–269.

life rather than endure any longer such tortures, he declares that
he has committed the crime which in fact he has not committed.
And when he has been condemned and put to death, the judge
is still in ignorance of whether he has put to death an innocent
or a guilty person, though he put the accused to the torture for
the very purpose of saving himself from condemning the innocent; and consequently he has both tortured an innocent man in
order to discover his innocence, and has put him to death without discovering it.[15]

What is Augustine's remedy?   None, of a temporal kind:

If such darkness shrouds social life, will a wise judge take his seat
on the bench or no?   Beyond question he will.   For . . . these
numerous and important evils he does not consider sins; for the
wise judge does these things, not with any intention of doing
harm, but because his ignorance compels him, and because human society claims him as a judge.   But though we therefore
acquit the judge of malice, we none the less condemn human life
as miserable.[16]

Almost on a level with the virtue of mercy the Christian
put that of chastity, and, had any of us lived in those days,
we must easily have seen why.   For the obscenity so prevalent
in Roman tradition was countenanced, even encouraged, by
the public authorities.[17]   Modern sceptics may wonder that
Christians became so early entangled in the dogmas relating
to the virginity of Mary, which they were now saying she had
preserved in spite of Christ's birth.[18]   But why wonder that
Christians sought to glorify the chastity of women, sought to
glorify it by insistence that even motherhood might not im-
pair virginity?   Superficially this savours of primitive folk
lore; actually it was a flaming symbol of revulsion against the
prostitution of sex.

It was precisely because modesty, which is near kin of
chastity, was now being widely cultivated, that Roman criminal law devised tortures which should cause anguish to decency as well as to flesh.   Of the martyrdoms described by

[15] *D.C.D.* XIX 6.
[16] Ibid.
[17] Cf. Prudentius *Peristephanon* X
lines 141–215 & 1056–90, and Augustine *D.C.D.* VI 9, on the obscenities
with which the pagan rites had become encrusted.
[18] Ambrose *Letter* # 42 § 4, to

Pope Siricius, says that 'persons deluded by perversity are said to be declaring that Mary conceived, but did
not give birth, as a virgin.' According to Augustine one such person was
Jovinian: (Migne *P.L.* 23 207 § 3).
See Dudden 1935 394.

Eusebius he was often himself an eye-witness; of the rest he had abundant and fresh report:

> Women tied by one foot were hoisted aloft by a kind of pulley, and swung through the air, their bodies completely naked down to the least covering; and thus they presented this most disgraceful, cruel, and inhuman of all spectacles to the whole company of onlookers.[19]

> And others in Pontus . . . endured in their privy parts and bowels sufferings that were disgraceful, pitiless, unmentionable, which the noble and law-abiding judges devised with more than usual eagerness, displaying their cruelty as if it were some great stroke of wisdom.[20]

That where mere physical pain did not cause the martyr to flinch resort was often had to the more subtle torture of shame, Prudentius also testifies. In his fictitious embellishment of the martyrdom of Agnes he describes how, when torture failed, the threat of rape was substituted:

> Then says the savage tyrant: ' it may be easy to bear punishment by overcoming torture and spurning life as cheap, nevertheless the modesty of consecrated virginity is held dear. Therefore, unless she bow her head to the altar and beg Minerva's pardon that a virgin should persist in despising a virgin, I am resolved that she be driven into a public brothel. All the youth will rush in and find fresh game for their wanton sports.' [21]

Pope Damasus [22] and bishop Ambrose,[23] both hard-headed men of the world, were, in their memorials of Agnes, no less emphatic than Prudentius that her glory as a martyr was almost eclipsed by her glory as a virgin. We may be inclined to think that Jerome's mania for chastity was something freakish, induced by a psychological distortion. Quite apart, however, from his real genius as a scholar, from his brilliant success as a missionary among the Roman nobility, it will, I think, be more judicious to explain Jerome as a phenomenon rather of history than of medicine. True, he was not like other men — even of his own time — but this was chiefly because he was, in every way, much bigger than they. No less than Ambrose

[19] *Eccl. Hist.* VIII 9 § 1.
[20] Ibid. 12 §§ 6–7.
[21] *Peristephanon* XIV lines 21–30.
Cf. Victor of Vita *H.P.A.P.* III § 22.

[22] Franchi de' Cavalieri 1899 10–20.
[23] *De Virginitate* I § 2.

or Augustine, Jerome, if he is to be judged, must be scrutinized rather with telescope than microscope.

And, as it was of cruelty and mercy, of obscenity and modesty, so it was of gluttony and fasting, of drunkenness and
sobriety. That most Romans ate and drank [24] immoderately
and yet without shame or remorse, is a commonplace; it is less
generally recognized that the ascetic excesses, the often repulsive mortifications of the flesh, in which some Christians indulged, was much less an expression of rational conviction
than an angry protest against the grossness then prevalent.
There were, no doubt, other reasons for this excess: the instinct that because the spirit is superior to the flesh it is therefore incompatible with it, or the natural desire not to be
outdone by the other ascetic sects which taught that matter
was offensive to God. But a larger, deeper reason lay in the
revulsion against the complaisant attitude of even the decent
Roman towards the glutton and the drunkard.

To the virtues of mercy, chastity, and fasting may be added,
and for the same reason, the virtues of poverty and humility.
The Christian ideal of poverty did not sweep the Empire because Romans thought poverty a desirable end-in-itself. Since
the Christian was so eager to gain control over wealth, to acquire the right to dispose of its profits at discretion, his design
was evidently to limit not its use but its abuse. Wealth in
those days, as always, was in the hands of good men and bad; [25]
but, as new wealth became harder to acquire by honest than
by dishonest methods, the incentive to dishonesty increased.
The Christians were not to be the last, as they were probably
not the first, to rise in wrath against such a condition, and to
conclude that because individual riches produced evil, individual poverty would produce good.

As of poverty, so of humility — which rose to the peak of
eminence among all the virtues. Was it merely a coincidence
that a veneration for humility hardly equalled in history
evolved out of a civilization which had especially glorified
ambition and fame? The desire of the Roman of the Empire
for fame, even if posthumous [26] and a product of fraud,[27] is a

---

[24] Dudden 1935 468–69.
[25] Ibid. 465–68 & 548. And on
usury 470–74.

[26] Cf. Dill 1906 2 430–37.
[27] Cf. Salvian *Ad Eccl.* III § 60,
quoted p. 372 n. 26.

matter of merriment to us. But it was more tragic than comic
then. For it not only demoralized and corrupted the individual in search of it; the public too was debauched. Prodigal
spending to win publicity, bribery, blackmail, public offices
put up for sale: in a hundred ways the State and citizens were
being degraded because to Romans ambition remained a virtue. Can we then blame the Christian for seeking obscurity
and the cultivation of humility; can we even blame him, being as he was a Roman, if this search was at times accompanied
by a surreptitious ostentation? [28] For, without doubt, many
martyrs indulged themselves in prospects of a posthumous
earthly glory. But these were venial sins at this time, mere
incidentals to remind us that even the noblest Christians
were, as they have taught us, sons of Adam no less than we.

It must not be supposed, however, that these new Christian
virtues came into being only as a protest against the Roman
civilization of this age. On the contrary, they already existed,
were already matured and recorded in writing three hundred
years before. It was not Rome that created Christianity, but
Christianity that transformed Rome. At the same time, as
Augustine has himself elaborately explained, had Rome not
existed as she did, both in geographical extent and disposition of mind, Christianity could hardly have spread and triumphed. Nor was the faith wholly unaffected by the process
of expansion: it reconciled itself to bloodshed in warfare and
to much else that a real and enormous world found indispensable. But the compromises were made with reluctance
and as exceptions to prove the rule. There was no real compromise with principle, but only with concrete applications
of principle. And how could this be otherwise with the Bible,
Old Testament as well as New, daily read and pondered by
every Christian teacher — the Word every day freshly revealed?

The Mithraic compromise of Diocletian was a political
failure, perhaps because the needs of an inner regeneration,
while respected, were subordinated to purely temporal and
material ends. The Christian compromise of Constantine,

---

[28] Jerome *Letters* # 77 § 11, # 108
§ 3, & # 130 § 6 refers to increased
worldly renown as an inducement to
the adoption of the ascetic life.

on the other hand, while a political success,[29] proved a military failure, and this failure was perhaps because temporal and material needs were now too much subordinated to inner regeneration. Yet the Christians did not want the State to fall, and they appeared to have it in their power to save it: legislation and administration, army, courts, bureaucracy, and priesthood — all were put at their disposal. There was the will and capacity, therefore. Why was there no way?

It may be that if Christianity had had more time — it was only fifty-four years from 324 to the first great barbarian victory at Adrianople [30] — the blood transfusion might have staved off death. It may also be that paganism, which remained a political threat until the death of Julian in 363, proved too serious an obstacle. In the last decades of the fourth century, to be sure, paganism, formidable in numbers but demoralized, was dying at an incredible speed. But this dying produced a violent inner convulsion. Moreover apart from outright paganism, if the Church had had a fuller control over the Neoplatonically-minded Christians, over the Manichees, Arians, and other heretical sects, she might have dared to assume a fuller control over the State.

This would have meant a theocracy, with the ruling and priestly functions consolidated. As the successors of Theodosius, who would not have preferred Ambrose to Honorius, Leo to Ricimer, Gelasius to Odoacer? By such conjectures, however, we are falling into an anachronism, for the Latins, at least, conceived of their faith as the antithesis of the temporal State. They did not conceive of a temporal life and a temporal civilization except in terms of the individual. Not only did no one aggregation of men appear more important than any other, none appeared to have any importance at all. That we today are unable to imagine a civilization apart from a political State does not prove that no other people ever imagined this; it merely proves that we have not the imagination to see ourselves from the outside and others from the inside.

The specific key to the Christians' attitude towards the

[29] In the sense that the Christian party was, except under Julian, 361–363, never again ousted from political power.

[30] This Roman defeat of 378 seemed to Hodgkin the beginning of the death agony: 1892 I 2 275.

State was their faith not in other-worldliness but in a Providence. This earthly life was rather ephemeral than intrinsically unimportant; they did not repudiate it, therefore, as
did the more extreme sects. At the same time they did conceive of it as a Purgatory, where contingent good could be
actualized, and latent or incipient good revealed and consolidated. The Christians were the first, after the Jews, to
believe that right makes might, because theirs was the first
God who was as omnipotent as He was benevolent.

Such a conception was truer than it was false; but it was
also more sublime than true. Quite like Augustine, they mis-
took a new truth for a complete truth. The great Christian of
that day was uncannily intuitive: he sensed that it might
somehow lie within his power to regenerate himself, that his
will might be somehow free; but he also felt — and this quite
unconsciously — that he needed not only an intent but a
capacity, a worldly wisdom yet unborn. Applied to the individual this was grace; applied to the State it was Providence.
Just as, in order not merely to wish to rule over himself but
in order to actualize that wish, a man must have grace, so, by
analogy, was this true of political rule. If disasters were attributed to the wrath of God, peace and prosperity must be
no less attributed to His benignity. The Christian, therefore, renounced his worldly inheritance, not because he despised it, but because he instinctively felt himself unequal
to the task it appeared to impose. According to Possidius,
the biographer of Augustine, the citizens of Hippo, on the approach of the Vandals in 430, besought his advice. To them
he answered that he thought judicious measures should be
taken to resist their assault — just as if God had no power to
intervene, for, he said,

' We are inquiring what we ought to do in order that we be not
adjudged as tempting God by looking for divine miracles in all
things.' [31]

But this was merely to advise that the citizens act as if success
or failure depended on their action, even though they knew
all the while that their measures must prove impotent. The
city must be defended, less in order to avert the Vandal on-

[31] S. *Augustini Vita* 30 § 11.

slaught, than in order to avert the divine displeasure. Had they fought fully believing that the decision depended rather on them than on God, then too must they have incurred the divine displeasure — and in an aggravated form. Therefore they fought rather like mercenaries or slaves: as scrupulous to do the minimum required as they were unconcerned to do the maximum possible. Theirs was the state of mind of hirelings rather than partners.

And, in about 400, men's capacity to inaugurate even their own inner regeneration became a matter of doubt. If they had not even this, how could they expect to direct their common lives and so shape history?

To accuse the Christians of criminal negligence would be an anachronism; it is undeniable on the other hand that they sought to shift a responsibility which, as Romans, they had assumed, onto the shoulders of a supernatural Being not yet wholly to be differentiated from the Fate of their ancestors. But who does not, in assuming new responsibilities, neglect the old ones? The woman neglects her parents for a husband, her husband for her children, her children for a Cause. If parenthood precludes virginity, so does virginity preclude parenthood. The only State that the Christian found compatible with his aspirations was the monastery.

Perhaps there lies an historical law here, still incompletely revealed to us, which transcends even the might of Rome and of Christianity. Augustine may have had an intimation of it, for, having said that God brought the great Empire into being in order that His Revelation might be the more easily comprehended and diffused, he might logically have added that God was now bringing about its dissolution in order that man, confronted by the contrast between his aspirations and his achievements, might the more fully perceive that inner must precede outer reformation. Therefore the submission of the late Roman to this law of selection is proof not of cowardice but of courage, not of negligence but of care. Folly it may seem to us if we merely look back; but, looking with them, forward, it must rather seem antiquity's last gift to human wisdom.

B. The Demand for Miracles

In such cults as the Stoic and Neoplatonic there was an element of aristocratic exclusiveness.   True to the Greek conception of perfection in the abstract, their professed aim was for quality by isolation.[1]   They perhaps even feared that should their cults be too much diffused they would be vulgarized — as some think literature is debased by a literacy too widely diffused.   Not that they wished the common man any ill; they merely distrusted his taste.

Mithraism was apparently the first influential cult to adopt a more democratic attitude.   For it conceived of man as an agent of justice dedicated to the annihilation of all evil.   Through active, physical combat the imprisoned souls of all men ought some day to be emancipated from the flesh and so from the devil.   These Mithraists fought no doubt primarily in order to win the emancipation of their own souls; nevertheless, their victory would be incidentally that of every other man too.   This was the psychological merit of their dualism: as with an army, the fate of each was bound up closely with the fate of all.

It was out of this same humanitarian instinct that Christianity arose: since God loves all men, so, if we are truly to love God, must we love all men too.   Or at least we must love that good which is innate, if latent, in them all.   That is why mere love of God, because He is goodness, is not enough; we must also love His created good; and, as proof of this additional love, faith must be confirmed by works.   It is not enough, therefore, to wish that God be merciful as well as just.   Man must himself so deal with his fellow-creatures, both by precept and example, that the latent good in men is brought to light.   For, if men do this, God will be the less inclined to punish and the more inclined to forgive.   Among the Christians there were of course many, like the hermits and mystics, who were hardly distinguishable from the Pla-

[1] On their reluctance to diffuse their doctrine see Porphyry *Life of Plotinus* §§ 3 & 17.

tonic contemplatives; but the vast majority were reformers and missionaries.

Reformers they were; but what a contrast to the materialistic reformers of today! Their reforms were not consciously designed to promote happiness in this world — not even peace and justice except within the seclusion of the monastery. Their object was to qualify men for the joys of that other world to come, where all past injustices would vanish and justice be made eternal. Yet every Christian actually longed for a regime of justice in this world too — he even groped spasmodically towards it — and for happiness here in some small measure. Indeed it was precisely because the Roman so craved yet despaired of an earthly Utopia that he accepted the Christian revelation of the after-life.

In our modern Utopias there is an abundant solicitude for the undeserving; capital punishment is in discredit and prison reform — to say nothing of parole — is in favour; no longer now need Christians believe that there are any souls in hell. But, if such be our Utopia, it was not that of the year 400. The Pelagian Celestius, believer in man's free will, taught that no rich man can possibly be saved; [2] Ambrose declared that

Many are condemned, but few crowned; [3]

and Augustine, denier of free will, that

In comparison with those that perish few, but in their absolute number many, are delivered. [4]

Differing as they did on an essential point of Christian doctrine these three men nevertheless shared a philosophy of punishment that shocks us. The poet Prudentius, too, complacently describes the sufferings of the damned. [5] Then, varying the theme of Celestius, he proceeds to describe the reward which God is reserving for the victims of the present life:

These whom you now proudly despise, whom you regard as execrable, will soon be rid of their ulcerous limbs and be whole;

---

[2] See p. 411 n. 28.
[3] *Enarr. in Psalm.* # 40 § 7.
[4] See p. 401. *De Corr. et Gratia* § 28.

[5] *Hamartigenia* lines 823 ff.

when, at length relieved and ever free of bondage to corrupted flesh, in the prime of life they will shine in the citadel of the Father; neither dirty nor feeble, as they now for the time being appear, but resplendent with purple robes and golden crowns.[6]

Reforms vary with time, but not the reformers.

With this alluring prospect dangled before the minds of the sufferers it is no wonder that there should at times have been an over-eagerness to precipitate the transformation by a premature death. The well-known propensity of the pagan to suicide [7] was generally despised by the Christian.[8] Nevertheless, of the martyrs about to be tortured, Eusebius records that

Some of them, to escape such trials, before they were caught and fell into the hands of those that plotted against them, threw themselves down from the tops of lofty houses, regarding death as a prize snatched from the wickedness of evil men.[9]

And in several instances he tells of how Christians, longing for martyrdom, openly befriended those already accused in order that they too should be accused and thereby martyred.[10] The memory of this disposition is still fresh in the pages of Prudentius, for in three instances [11] martyrs, fearing not to be killed, pray God — and in each case to good purpose — that He refrain from sparing them. But these are isolated cases and concern martyrs only; after winning toleration Christians repressed their impatience to reach heaven and no further scandals of suicide are recorded.[12] It is remarkable, indeed, that in a world where suicide had been tolerated, even extolled, at least since the time of Socrates, and where pagan Romans as well as Manichees still resorted freely to it, Christianity, for all its doctrine of the after-life, stepped in to declare it tantamount to murder. We can see, then, how

[6] *Peristephanon* II lines 265–76.
[7] For late fourth century instances, see Dudden 1935 429, 432, 467, 472, & 513.
[8] Cf. Augustine *D.C.D.* I 19 & 23, &, on the Stoics, XIX 4.
[9] *Eccl. Hist.* VIII 12 § 2.
[10] *Martyrs of Palestine* 1 § 5g, 2 § 1, 3 § 3, 4 § 8, 5 § 3, 8 § 6, 11 §§ 15, 20, & 24–26. This practice had been frowned upon in very early times: Schäfer 1932 76.

[11] *Peristephanon* V lines 353–68, VI 112–20, & VII 36–60. And cf. ibid. III lines 151–55, & XIV 21–51 & 69–72. And cf. Augustine *D.C.D.* I 26.
[12] Rufinus *Hist. Monach.* (*P.L.* 21 413A) does record a case where a saint prays that he may soon be allowed to die. Christian women in Rome committed suicide after being raped by the Visigoths in 410: Augustine *D.C.D.* I 17.

martyrdom offered a pretty problem for the casuist: the Christian might properly long to die, might properly long to be martyred. And yet, no more than he might raise a finger to evade a death impending, might he raise a finger to induce it: he must die, like the devotee of astrology, when Destiny decreed.

A further obligation was imposed on the martyr: he must die not only passively but humbly and therefore obscurely — safe from that posthumous glory so dear to the pagan. Yet, on the other hand, as a teacher of the truth as well by example as by precept, he might hope that his death would strike the imaginations of the beholders. Theoretically this latter difficulty could be met by a faith in the impression a humble death will make; practically, however, such an impression proved vain because many others were constantly being put to death for alleging, as did the Christians, some principle or right that they cherished — and dying often with no less fortitude. Yet if no Jews, heretics,[13] magicians, or other traitors,[14] but only Catholics, were dying for the truth, it seemed incongruous that these deaths be indistinguishable. If their truth alone were the real truth would there not be some distinguishing Sign? This supposition may sound strange to modern ears, but it was a natural one in the late fourth century. The Gods of that day received or were denied worship largely according to the visibility of their power in the eye of the earthly beholder; if they did not appear to be influencing earthly affairs they perhaps were unable to do so, and in that case it was unlikely that they wielded decisive power over heavenly affairs. In fact this was precisely the weakness, pragmatically, of the Manichæan doctrine: a God who cannot direct the petty affairs of men probably cannot direct the stars.[15]

In early days martyrdom had been the great Christian event, the one to be above all cherished and remembered. Christ had himself been martyred, so had Peter, Paul, and, almost within the memory of Diocletian's contemporaries,

---

[13] The names of Silanus, a Novatian, and of Hippolytus, a schismatic, were included in the list of martyrs compiled in Rome in 354: Achelis 1899 9.

[14] See pp. 18–19.

[15] Cf. Jerome *Contra Vigilantium* § 10.

the holy bishop Cyprian of Carthage.[16] These were the great
heroes of the faith; [17] and yet, except to the few, what guarantee was there that any of these, Christ included, had died
for the truth apart from the Signs that were revealed in the
hour of their trials? These Signs had been manifested at the
Crucifixion, why should they be withheld from those who
died for Christ's sake? [18] In the absence of such a Sign there
must inevitably be a lingering suspicion of error. Thus there
was a craving for a miracle: to prove not only the holiness of
the martyr and the presence of God, but also God's power
over nature. If only a martyr were so graced he could safely
be venerated, and the most sceptical eye-witness must then
acknowledge the greatness of the new God.

There was, moreover, a psychological as well as a didactic
reason why the martyrs must reconcile themselves to a posthumous fame: having, while alive, been intensely concerned
with the earthly welfare of others, they must naturally retain
that concern after death, must wish to perpetuate their beneficence. While in the flesh they had been lavish in deeds of
mercy and charity, had perhaps even effected miraculous
cures. Should they now, when no longer sinners, when no
longer alive in the flesh but alive in heaven, find their beneficent powers impaired? As Jerome says,

When once they have entered on their life with Christ shall they
have less power than before? [19]

Were such the case their death would be a calamity instead of
a victory. The theologians did not find it easy to explain how
a soul in heaven could receive delegated powers from the
omnipotent God; [20] at the same time they had to confess that
the saint's will could not justly be frustrated, even where its
beneficence was indiscreet.[21] This embarrassment was a pen-

[16] Martin's disciple Postumianus
(see p. 180) stopped at Carthage on
his way east in about 400 in order to
'prostrate myself at the tomb of the
martyr Cyprian': Severus Dialogue I
3.

[17] See p. 175 n. 69.

[18] Prudentius Peristephanon XII
describes the martyrdoms of Peter
and Paul in Rome, but he mentions
no miracles.

[19] Contra Vigilantium § 6.

[20] On the pagan tradition that the
gods had no other distraction than to
meddle in human affairs, see Claudian Epithalamium lines 56 ff.

[21] Cf. Dufourcq L'Av. 1910 IV 5
127. Cyprian of Carthage, martyred

alty Christianity must pay for its assumption that not only the
soul's virtue but also its personality survived the body's death.

Of miracles connected with martyrdoms, Eusebius cites
two instances [22] where the official who was responsible for a
martyr's death soon after died himself. It was God, of course,
and not the martyr, who decreed this punishment; but may
He not have done this partly in order to please the martyr?
According to Prudentius, the martyr Agnes restored her
would-be seducer to life.[23] For her sake God showed him
an exceptional mercy. Eulalia, on the other hand, at the
moment of her martyrdom, spat in her tormentor's face. His
subsequent death was surely not decreed in the face of her
remonstrances.[24]

A vengeful spirit, however, was not a common [25] attribute
of holiness, particularly of holiness in heaven. The eagerness of the saints to help the living, far from being slaked,
was rather aggravated by their new blessedness. As Jerome
said,

If the Apostles and martyrs can intercede for others at a time
when, being still in the flesh, they have to be concerned for themselves, how much better can they do so after their crowns, victories and triumphs? [26]

The living were the chief objects of their solicitude, for, of
the dead, those already saved had no need of help, while those
already damned deserved none. Until 420 there were, to be
sure, certain Christians still holding to Origen's view that
even in the case of ' the wicked and unbelieving ' mercy would
prevail at the Day of Judgment. This, according to Augustine, was how they argued:

If the saints used to pray for them when still suffering from their
cruel hatred, how much more will they do so when they see them

---

in 254, imagined that some saints,
and especially the martyrs, had accumulated merit beyond that required for salvation, and that they
could — God of course consenting —
allocate this excess to the living,
either to procure them penance and
absolution during life or special
mercy at death: Bethune-Baker
1933 [5] 355.

[22] *Martyrs of Palestine* 7 § 7, & 13
§ 10.

[23] *Peristephanon* XIV lines 56–60.
[24] Ibid. III line 128.
[25] But on Jerome see p. 198 n. 28.
[26] *Contra Vigilantium* § 6. But
Jerome *Letter* # 127 § 10 says that
Pope Anastasius was no doubt removed by death ' that he might not
by his prayers seek to avert the sentence of God passed once for all.'
This was that Alaric should sack the
city of Rome. As a theologian Jerome was an opportunist.

prostrate and humble suppliants? For we cannot, they say, believe that the saints will lose their bowels of compassion when they
have attained the most perfect and complete holiness; so that they
who, when still sinners, prayed for their enemies, should now,
when they are freed from sin, withhold from interceding for their
suppliants. Or shall God refuse to listen to so many of His beloved children when their holiness has purged their prayers of
all hindrance to His answering them? [27]

Augustine's answer to these over-merciful Christians is soberly judicious: when freed from sin the saint will perceive
in how far the divine compassion differs from the human:

Their intellectual knowledge, which shall be great, shall keep
them acquainted . . . with the eternal sufferings of the lost [28]

— yet without in any way detracting from their serenity.

The whole humanitarian zeal of the saint, therefore, was
concentrated on living men. This explains the passage in
Prudentius on Cyprian, the great Carthaginian martyr:

In heaven above he reigns, nor less is present in the world, nor
quits these earthly courts, but still discourses, prophesies, instructs, expounds, exhorts.[29]

Prudentius may here have had partly in mind the influence
that the writings of Cyprian still had on men, but he could
not limit Cyprian's present power over earthly affairs to the
fortuitous preservation of his books. For this would have put
an undue premium on winning an earthly fame while alive
in order to perpetuate one's influence among men.

That Prudentius in fact had a very different kind of influence in mind is indicated by other passages of his. Invok-
ing the dead martyr Laurentius he says:

As if you were always present, you nourish your disciples of the
city, embracing them tenderly in a paternal love.[30]

[27] *D.C.D.* XXI 18. The idea of
Purgatory was still embryonic: Prudentius *Hamartigenia* lines 962–67, &
Peristephanon VI lines 160–62,
merely expresses a hope that the torments of hell will cease at the Last
Judgment. This Origen had categorically taught. Augustine says
that some of the damned will be acquitted at the Last Judgment: *D.C.D.*
XXI 13, 16 & 24. But he insists that
the Church shall not pray for those
who 'retain an impenitent heart
until death and are not converted
from enemies into sons': ibid. XXI
24.
[28] *D.C.D.* XXII 30.
[29] *Peristephanon* XIII lines 99–
103.
[30] Ibid. II lines 569–76.

And in the Passion of Agnes he is more specific:

The tomb of Agnes, brave girl, renowned martyr, lies in the home of Romulus. Buried within the very sight of the towers, the virgin watches over the safety of the citizens, and she also protects those strangers who, with pure and faithful hearts, are suppliants.[31]

In the Passion of Hippolytus Prudentius alleges a prospect of something more than earthly assistance to those who invoke the help of that martyr. In his zeal to persuade a certain bishop to celebrate as a feast day the anniversary of the martyrdom of Hippolytus — as the bishop was already celebrating those of the martyrs Cyprian, Chelidonus, and Eulalia — he says:

If you do this, may the almighty Christ heed you as you pray for the people committed to your care; may the wolf be kept out of your well-filled sheepfold, and may your flock not lose a single lamb to him; may you, O watchful shepherd, restore even me — the sick sheep that lags behind in the grassy pasture; may you fill the folds with milk-white lambs and then be taken up yourself to join the company of the blessed Hippolytus.[32]

Prudentius offers the bishop a variety of inducements, but here, in contrast to the earlier passages, the benefit which the martyr may be expected to confer concerns not only temporal but also eternal welfare. The sheepfold is a state of grace, to be maintained against the assaults of the devil. His suggestion is that veneration of Hippolytus will invite grace from heaven and so inculcate virtuous conduct during life that salvation will be earned. In another passage, in the Passion of Romanus, Prudentius ascribes a further power to the saints, the long poem concluding with this desperate invocation:

I wish that, being as I shall be on the left among the goats, I may be recognized from afar, and that, because of this invocation, the good King may say: 'Romanus is asking it; transfer this goat to Me; let him be a sheep on My right hand; let him be clothed with a fleece.'[33]

Here is further power conferred on the blessed martyr: by his prayer of intercession to God he is able not only to reform

---

[31] *Peristephanon* XIV lines 1–6.
[32] Ibid. XI lines 239–46.
[33] Ibid. X lines 1136–40; & cf. II

lines 577–84, IV lines 189–92, V lines 545–64, & VI lines 157–59.

the living so that they may earn salvation as a matter of justice but also to procure a pardon for those dead who have not repented while alive and so deserve damnation.

Prudentius was, to be sure, a layman writing poetry, one who, though without taint of heresy, has never been canonized. He was, nevertheless, a great figure in his day, widely read and admired then and for many centuries thereafter.[34] If we cannot cite his views as evidence of the official orthodoxy of the year 405, we may safely regard them as views already widely prevalent and, if not sanctioned, at least countenanced by the responsible authorities. That there was no complete incompatibility between his views and those of Rome is indicated by the inscription which was placed on the tomb of Agnes a generation earlier by Pope Damasus:

O that this holy glory, this soul of modesty, may be venerated by me, in order that, O renowned martyr, you may, I pray, heed the prayers of Damasus.[35]

Already before the end of the fourth century, therefore, the Roman Pope was recognizing that a prayer to God would be more effective if supplemented by a prayer to a martyr. Already here was the local deity of the city distracting men's concentration from an exclusive devotion to the one omnipotent God. In a sense, of course, the martyr had become indistinguishable from God, but in another sense this Agnes, in direct contrast to Neoplatonic doctrine, retained her mundane personality, retained her particular solicitude for her friends and so for her city. If the citizens of the old city rejoiced in so renowned a martyr, this was partly because they expected to receive special consideration, special mercies, which other persons in other places could not expect. To the extent that Agnes was in particular favour with God the inhabitants of the city were something of a Chosen People, the likely beneficiaries of mercies which must be denied to others. But observe one peculiarity: unless Agnes were prayed to she could do nothing; she could confer no individual favours except such as were asked for.[36] Her power therefore depended on the popularity of her cult.

[34] Kuhnmeunsch 1929 149.
[35] Quoted by Franchi de' Cavalieri 1899 10. The inscriptions of Damasus almost all use similar language: see Schäfer 1932 *passim*.
[36] Cf. the threats in quotations on

It now becomes of importance to distinguish two effects of prayer: those which could also be explained according to the current understanding of natural law, and those which were in contradiction to that understanding. If Damasus prayed to Agnes that she help him to lead a more virtuous life, and he thereupon did lead a more virtuous life, his will to do so, as expressed in his prayer, might be considered an adequate explanation. Even if he prayed that a heresy which, like that of the Arians, was plaguing him, should collapse, and if it thereupon in fact did collapse, this too could be explained by natural causes. If, on the other hand, he should pray to Agnes that all the sick of Rome be healed over-night, or that all the pagan inhabitants, but no others, be stricken until they repent and seek Christian baptism, should one or both of these things happen as prayed for there would be a manifest miracle, inexplicable by the natural law of probability and so a Sign to all men, Christian and pagan alike.

It was certainly for the first kind of help that Damasus prayed to Agnes: for a bestowal of the divine grace which should so strengthen his will to virtue that he could realize his wish. Therefore to the extent that a Christian, indifferent to earthly vicissitudes, wished only for salvation, the help he prayed for could be bestowed without doing violence to the operations of natural law. His longing to be virtuous could easily, by the sceptical, be regarded as an adequate explanation of why he became so. It was, as we shall see,[37] because the Pelagian heresy — which was to break out in the early fifth century — sympathized too much with this sceptical view, that it at once aroused a bitter controversy, and conversely it was because Augustine's theory of predestination was the only complete refutation of the ' natural ' explanation that it for a time won general approval. In the uneasiness which the Pelagian view aroused few perceived that Augustine's view was in fact just as destructive of the power of prayer as was the view of Pelagius. Yet if the Pelagian could suppose that he need not pray because he had the capacity to answer the prayer himself,[38] so the Augustinian might also be tempted to

---

pp. 183 & 185; & see Dudden 1935 308 & 311 lines 21–23.

[37] See pp. 410–11.

[38] As Jerome Letter # 133 § 5, explains.

dispense with prayer on the ground that God was unwilling to alter a course of events which He had from eternity pre-destined. The Christian doctrine of the will must, if only as a matter of expediency,[39] be so conceived that prayer is allowed a maximum of efficacy. If it was this crying need that helps to explain the passion of the antagonists in the Pelagian quarrel, it helps no less to explain why so much was made of the martyrs: where you need help it is consoling to suppose that not One only, but several — many perhaps — are in a position to give that help.

Out of this faith in the power of the dead martyr to heed prayers which, if addressed to God, might not be heeded, grew up, very gradually, the dogma of the Communion of Saints,[40] according to which, in present terminology,

all the members of the Church, in heaven, on earth, and in purgatory, are in communion with each other . . . assisting each other with their prayers and good works.[41]

The earliest Latin reference to this was written in the late fourth century by Nicetas, friend of Paulinus of Nola, and consecrated bishop of Remesiana in western Moesia. Addressing one about to be baptized, he says,

Therefore believe that in this one Church you are about to attain to the communion of saints.[42]

What, specifically, he meant by this we cannot — perhaps he could not — say. But in a general way he meant that all the baptized are beneficiaries of the good-will of the dead, as well as of the living saints. Prudentius has the martyr Fructuosus say as his last words,

I shall pray to Christ for all the people.[43]

This must mean that the heathen accept baptism and that the baptized achieve virtue. Pragmatically the imagination must inevitably be stirred by this grandiose conception: if all the saints in heaven are praying to Christ for our salvation, the

---

[39] See p. 77 n. 24.
[40] Cf. Dufourcq *L'Av.* 1910 IV 5 127–28.
[41] Apostle's Creed, ninth article.
[42] As quoted by Morin 1904 212, where he discusses the general problem.
[43] *Peristephanon* VI line 84. Fructuosus had been bishop of Tarragona: Dufourcq *L'Av.* 1910 IV 5 31.

force so engendered must seem irresistible. And, in addition, by judicious prayers to the individual saint, influential either because of his universal fame, like Peter or Paul, or, like Agnes, because of her local fame as virtually the guardian of her native city Rome, special advantages might be procured.

All these miracles, however, were spiritual in nature, and, being such, were at once impossible either to prove or to disprove. A Christian might try to demonstrate that they were explicable only by supernatural causes; a sceptic might try to prove them natural. But neither could present a single argument of any validity, the true causes of spiritual effects being as obscure then as they still are today. In the case of miracles of a material nature, on the other hand, there was room for legitimate argument: a physical occurrence must, in order to pass as miraculous, contradict some then accepted natural law. The less well natural law was understood the more frequently, manifestly, would contradictions to it occur. Thus the God of Thunder survived only so long as thunder was believed to be a supernatural phenomenon; comets remained divine portents only so long as their orbits remained unknown. Such miracles must invariably raise the same doubt: is the event the effect of some natural process which has so far evaded human analysis, or is it an unnatural and so a divine process? The acceleration of modern science — both in physics and in anthropology — has induced many of us to prefer the first explanation; ignorance of such sciences induced the ancients to prefer the second. Augustine, indeed, as we have hinted,[44] was perhaps the first man of antiquity to offer an intelligible compromise.

Primitive religion consisted largely in the analysis of the so-called miracle: an event which appeared to be supernatural was assumed to be in some way a manifestation of a God's will, and it was the duty of the priests to scrutinize it, generalize from it, and thus accumulate a store of knowledge which would reveal the will of the deity. Did this miracle indicate that God was exhorting, rewarding, chastising, warning the people, or was He merely correcting the direction towards which events were tending? The task of the priests was not an easy one and, not unlike other specialists, they often dis-

[44] See p. 123; & cf. p. 216.

agreed among themselves. In the interpretation of the Old
Testament the Christian priest found himself in an analogous
labyrinth. God, for instance, had chastised Adam and Eve;
but was their sin against obedience or humility or chastity? [45]
And, as often as not, the absence of a miracle had to be explained. Why, for instance, did God deal so gently with the
murderer Cain? [46] Resort could of course be had to symbolic
interpretation, but although this was the most fertile line of
approach it was not always the most conclusive. Many events
of the Old Testament were clearly and even satisfactorily explained in the text itself, but many remained unexplained —
to tax the ingenuity of the learned.

At the close of the fourth century a world was still
conceived in which miracle and natural event occasionally
clashed because God must correct the vagaries of natural law
in order to readjust events according to His will. To the
Christian the growth of the Roman State appeared to have
been achieved without doing much violence to nature, the
Jews, on the other hand, had lived in a world full of miracles.
Rome and Christianity being now amalgamated, a corresponding mixture of natural event and miracle was likely.[47]
Miracles would occur at least as often as God thought the
Christians would benefit by them. Consequently the Christians were eager to detect any evidence of significant phenomena, and, because these would naturally have a Christian
character, we need not be surprised to find that many of the
miracles described by Prudentius are suspiciously reminis-
cent of biblical wonders.[48]

There is not the slightest reason to think, however, that the
Christian was more ready than his pagan [49] or other contemporaries to credit an alleged miracle. For credulity and
scepticism were then — as they still are — matters rather of
disposition than of faith. And the very fact that the Christian
had the miraculous world of the Bible imposed on him en-

[45] *Enchiridion* 45, quoted p. 79,
gives Augustine's mature belief. Cf.
D.C.D. XIII 20 & 21, & XIV 10.
[46] See *Genesis* iv 11, 16 & 17.
[47] Cf. Augustine *D.C.D.* XXII beginning of 8.
[48] *Peristephanon* II 381–84, V 473–
84, & VI 112–20.

[49] Claudian *In Eutropium* I lines
494–96, exclaims — rhetorically yet intending to be taken seriously — :
' What marriage, what harvest, will
be fruitful . . . under a Consul
[Eutropius the eunuch] stricken with
sterility! ' Cf. Nock 1933 83–98.

abled him the more easily to dispense with that fairy world of pagan deities, both good and bad, each constantly striving to outwit the rest. For to Christians there was but one almighty God, whose will could never be seriously thwarted, by demons, subordinates, living men or nature — for God had Himself designed each one of these to serve as His passive instruments. The more omnificent God was, the less need He had to do violence to nature. As in the human microcosm, it was surprising, not when the will to raise the arm caused the arm to rise, but when the will failed to raise it.

Such, roughly, was the state of mind in which the Christians witnessed the martyrdoms, heard the accounts of them, repeated and recorded them, celebrated and honoured them.

C. Miracles of the Martyrs

The first Latin record of a martyrdom is that of Cyprian's death at Carthage in 258, written soon after by his disciple Pontius. Already here there is a miracle of a sort: Cyprian dreams that he is condemned and that he is accorded the single day's respite that he asks for. His martyrdom in fact occurred exactly one year after that dream.[1] By interpreting the day as symbolizing the year, Pontius makes out his case for a miracle.[2] But it is hardly of a kind either to confound the sceptic or thrill the believer. No pagan record could have been more restrained.

By far the most complete contemporary record of martyrdoms is that given by the Greek historian Eusebius, of Cæsarea in Palestine. Born in 260, he was a mature eye-witness of many of the martyrdoms suffered under Diocletian and his immediate successors.[3] In his various accounts the miraculous episodes are few and far between. Inserted in his *Chronicle* for the year 312 is an account of how the martyr Quirinus, having been cast into a river with a mill-stone tied to his neck, continued to float for some time while he ha-

---

[1] Cf. Ambrose *De Officiis* I § 41.   [3] Cureton 1863 vii–viii.
[2] *Vita Cypriani* §§ 12 & 13.

rangued the by-standers, sinking only after he had prayed to God that he be allowed to sink.[4] But since Quirinus was martyred in Pannonia while Eusebius was living in Cæsarea this miracle is based on hearsay evidence which Eusebius merely repeats.

His *Martyrs of Palestine,* by contrast, is largely a first-hand account: in it he lists the names of fifty martyrs who were executed either in his presence or in his immediate vicinity, and in a good many cases gives detailed descriptions; yet, in contrast to later records of this kind, he mentions only three miracles. Moreover, of these three, one, where Romanus continued to talk after his tongue had been cut out,[5] occurred at Antioch while Eusebius was living at Cæsarea, and was therefore also a case of hearsay.[6] It is likely, of course, that something unexpected and inexplicable occurred in these two hearsay cases of Quirinus and Romanus: why otherwise should miracles be reported in these and none in the hundreds of others occurring during the same period under analogous circumstances? Nevertheless the two remaining miracles which Eusebius witnessed himself are of greater interest. In the first case the body of the martyred Aphianus, having been cast into the sea with stones tied to each foot, was not long afterwards tossed up on the beach during a severe earthquake.[7] In the second case, having told of how the bodies of many martyrs were cast out and devoured by wild beasts, he proceeds:

When, therefore, things had continued in this manner for many days, there happened a prodigy which will scarcely be believed. The atmosphere was perfectly calm and clear, when all of a sudden many of the columns of the porticos in the city emitted spots as it were of blood, while the market-places and the streets became sprinkled and wet as with water, although not a single drop had fallen from the heavens.[8]

---

[4] Quoted by Dufourcq *G.M.R.* 1907 II 223. And Eusebius *Eccl. Hist.* VIII 7 §§ 2–5 describes how loath the wild beasts often were to set on martyrs exposed at Tyre under Diocletian. In his many accounts of martyrdoms in this *Eccl. Hist.* he records only one other miracle in connexion with them: IV 15 §§ 10–39, and this in spite of the fact that many of his accounts are at second hand, culled from hearsay or tradition. For miracles not connected with martyrdoms see III 39 § 9, V 5 §§ 1–6, V 7 §§ 3–5, VI 9 § 3, VI 29 §§ 3–4, & VII 17.

[5] *Martyrs of Palestine* 2 § 2.

[6] Cureton 1863 viii.

[7] *Martyrs of Palestine* 4 § 15.

[8] Ibid. 9 §§ 12–13.

In each of these accounts Eusebius says he knows that many will be incredulous, but he protests that he saw the former wonder with his own eyes and that the latter was observed by all of the inhabitants, many of whom are still living as he writes.

For us today to argue the true nature and explanation of these wonders would be even more idle than presumptuous. That Eusebius observed something which contradicted his understanding of natural law, and that he speaks of it because he was mystified, is perfectly obvious. We may believe, either that his observation was faulty or that a natural law unknown to educated Romans of his day was in operation; but we may quite as justly believe that something occurred which would also have mystified us had we been eye-witnesses. In either case these peculiar occurrences were not fabricated by an ignorant or prejudiced person but were the report of one who was not only intellectually honest but present in person. Doubtless an Epicurean, had he witnessed what Eusebius did, would have continued to deny that anything inexplicable had occurred, but his own natural explanation would probably have been a lame one because based on an *a priori* conviction and not on the experience. A man who witnesses fifty martyrdoms and hundreds of episodes connected with these, and yet finds only two of the episodes inexplicable by natural law, certainly appears more impartial than one who sees marvels yet denies he has seen them.

The *Martyrs of Palestine* and other Greek texts of Eusebius were not translated into Latin until nearly 400.[9] Apart from Pontius on Cyprian, therefore, the nearest approach to a contemporary Latin record of martyrdoms is found in texts recording the execution of James and Marion in Numidia in 258,[10] and that of Euplus in Sicily in 303.[11] In these the simple narrative, the absence of both anachronisms and miracles, is relied on as evidence that the texts were contemporary. All we know positively is that they were in existence by the year 500, and, since almost all the martyr-texts known to have been written after 400 show striking differences from

---

[9] Rufinus translated his *Eccl. Hist.* into Latin in about 400: *P.L.* 21 222B. Jerome made the other translations.

[10] Dufourcq *G.M.R.* 1900 I 67–75.
[11] Dufourcq *G.M.R.* 1907 II 177–85.

these,[12] we may infer with good reason that they were written at a much earlier period — before there was any motive for embellishing the story.

Another group of texts describing martyrdoms can be traced back to the last quarter of the fourth century. Even if not earlier and therefore not written by eye-witnesses, they may have been based on stories told by eye-witnesses, because a witness who was twenty years old in 311 might still be alive and repeating his story fifty or more years later. In one category are the anonymous texts on the martyrdoms along the Danube: two in Moesia,[13] two in Pannonia,[14] and one in Noricum.[15] In another are the two accounts of the martyrdom of Agnes in Rome, that by Pope Damasus,[16] and so before 384, in the form of an inscription; the other by Ambrose in his *De Virginibus,* written in 377.[17] In none of these seven accounts is there any mention of a physical miracle: evidently the strange phenomena related by Eusebius were still rare, and the fashion of inventing such episodes was not yet general. On the other hand it was during these very years that Pope Damasus officially condemned the irresponsible circulation of a miraculous literature about the martyrs,[18] which indicates that before 384 there were already some less scrupulous writers who told of miracles without giving adequate evidence of their authenticity. Damasus sought to check this tendency as one discreditable to the Church and to the truth for which she was responsible.

But his effort to be conscientious proved vain. Already the martyrs were consolidating themselves as the heroes and heroines of the faith [19] — the only Gentiles who could qualify. Many of the cities could boast of containing the tombs of martyrs of their own stock, as Rome could boast of those of Laurentius, Sebastian, and Agnes.[20] These were not only Christian martyrs but Romans — local deities they came to

---

[12] Dufourcq *G.M.R.* 1900 I *passim.*
[13] Dasius: Dufourcq *G.M.R.* 1907 II 251–55; & Julius: ibid. 245–48.
[14] Pollion: ibid. 238–40; & Irenæus: ibid. 241–43.
[15] Florian: ibid. 229–34.
[16] Franchi de' Cavalieri 1899 10.
[17] I §§ 5–9.
[18] Dufourcq *G.M.R.* 1900 I 377.
[19] See p. 175 n. 69.
[20] Dufourcq *G.M.R.* 1900 I 28 n. 2.

be because they had been fellow-citizens. Peter and Paul too,
were buried in Rome,[21] but they were Jews; and, furthermore,
they belonged to all Christendom, were in no sense the exclusive property of that one city.[22]

There is no need to wonder how the cult of these local
martyrs originated, for devotion at their tombs must have
begun on the day of their burial and continued ever after.
In those days every Christian who venerated these tombs
seemed to come into personal contact with the martyr. For
such persons, before any others, the martyr would do everything he could. Prayers said at the tomb of Peter or of Paul
were too much like prayers to God, but those said at the
tomb of a Roman were as if to a friend — who was not only
less busy, but who would give less consideration to general
expediency and justice and more to loyalty, affection, and
even to discreet flattery.

So did the martyr cults survive, and, as the Christians mul-
tiplied, the tombs became the centres of a devotion which
attracted crowds.[23] Soon the caves of the catacombs became
impossibly small and churches were hastily constructed in
order that the bodies of the more renowned and popular
martyrs might be transferred to these.[24] When Prudentius
was in Rome in about 402 the martyr who had most recently
come into vogue was Hippolytus.[25] Not only was his cave
incapable of containing the multitude which came to celebrate the anniversary of his martyrdom but even the open
field about it could not contain the crowd.[26] And, in 403,
Jerome hears reports of how

For all its gilding the Capitol is beginning to look dingy. Every
temple in Rome is covered with soot and cobwebs. The city is
stirred to its depths and the people pour past their half-ruined
shrines to visit the tombs of the martyrs.[27]

Obscure so long as they lived, for some time after their
deaths remembered by only the pious few, the martyrs were

[21] Schäfer 1932 17–23.
[22] Dufourcq G.M.R. 1907 II 94–95.
[23] Cf. Jerome's description in his
Commentary on Ezekiel XII §40
(P.L. 25 375A).
[24] Cf. Peristephanon XI lines 215–
26. On the splendour of these
churches see Jerome Letters # 52
§ 10, # 60 § 12, & # 130 § 14.

[25] On the historical Hippolytus see
Bonwetsch 1900 VIII 127 lines 37 ff.;
& cf. Damasus' inscription: Schäfer
1932 57.
[26] Peristephanon XI lines 189–214.
[27] Letter # 107 § 1.

now fast becoming famous. Yet nothing was really known about them, either of their parentage, station in life, reputation and career, or trial and death.[28] Here was a glaring incongruity, and it has been plausibly assumed that as the faithful crowded round the tombs they asked the guardians — priests or others — to tell them some details of the lives and trials: whether they were rich or poor, nobles or plebeians, clerics or laymen, young or old; whether their conspicuous virtue was learning, charity, humility, or chastity; and, finally, how they were accused, tried, executed. When the guardians declared their ignorance in these matters there was disappointment. The visitor had often come some distance on a pilgrimage to the now famous shrine. How was it possible that a martyr so renowned should have no history, that his life, obviously so remarkable, should not be known even to those attendant at his tomb? If nothing was known, why was he especially to be venerated, why did he better deserve commemoration than any obscurest martyr whose very name had been lost? Under these circumstances it is probable that the guardians, guides, or others whom the reputation of the martyr especially concerned, succumbed to the temptation of answering these questions by inferring certain facts which were likely apart from actual knowledge. And, once the habit of embellishing a story had been formed, the emulative instinct would be roused. Each enthusiastic and inventive mind would fill up some awkward gap in the record.[29]

A good example is the story, already partly quoted, of the child-martyr Agnes. There is no contemporary record; our earliest information comes from Damasus and Ambrose, both of whom wrote in about 377. Since Agnes presumably faced death unflinchingly, both naturally praised her fortitude. But both more particularly praised her chastity.[30] Why should a girl be so glorified because still a virgin? Apparently because, just as the vulgar pagan praised woman only for her seductive beauty, the good Christian praised her only for her chastity. But this need to drag chastity in left the

[28] Dufourcq G.M.R. 1907 II 157.
[29] Cf. Dufourcq G.M.R. 1900 I 272–73; & Schäfer 1932 163–66.

[30] *Agnes* is close to the Greek word ἀγνος, meaning chaste: Schäfer 1932 77.

story at loose ends: for there can be no heroism without resistance to temptation.[31]

In 405 Prudentius wrote a much longer account of Agnes. As before, her chastity is emphasized at the expense of her fortitude, but Prudentius gives a reason: she had been threatened with rape. We have quoted the passage [32] describing how the judge, finding her impervious to torture, orders her to be offered as a prey to the first youth who shall present himself. Thereupon a youth quickly advances, but he is at once struck down by a bolt from heaven.[33] There had been no miracles in the accounts of Damasus and Ambrose. Observe carefully why Prudentius introduces one. Agnes, to prove her mettle, must be put in imminent danger of rape, and this danger, once incurred, could be averted only by a power superior even to a Roman judge. A miracle therefore offered at once the most dramatic and the only plausible solution. In some such way the story grew, from perhaps a bare knowledge of Agnes' age and sex,[34] by an irresistible logic.[35]

Another case of embellishment is that of Romanus, whose sermon after his tongue had been cut out was briefly recorded by Eusebius.[36] Prudentius, writing on Romanus less than one hundred years later, makes his story more than eight times as long.[37] No other miracles are related, but the original miracle is elaborated at great length and the tongueless Romanus is made to deliver a long argument on the merits of Christianity and demerits of paganism, all of which must have been pure invention.

Yet Prudentius had his own code of veracity: only three of his poems record actual physical miracles, and, of these, two are taken from the authentic contemporary accounts of Eusebius. These were in the cases of Romanus and Quirinus.

---

[31] In § 9 Ambrose said, 'how many desired her in marriage.' But this was hardly a dramatic temptation.

[32] See p. 143 n. 21.

[33] *Peristephanon* XIV lines 46–49. Jerome *Letter* # 130 § 5, written in 414, refers to her humiliation but not to any miracle.

[34] What embellishment there was between 312 & 377 is uncertain.

[35] On the further elaboration of the Agnes legends see Schäfer 1932 79–81.

[36] See p. 163 n. 5.

[37] 1140 lines of about six Latin words, as against sixty-seven lines of about twelve English words.

The third, by far the most miraculous of all, describes the martyrdom of Vincent,[38] and it is interesting to observe that Vincent was one of the few Spanish martyrs Prudentius referred to. Being a Spaniard himself, Prudentius probably derived his episodes from the popular local tradition,[39] in which a miraculous world was taken for granted. In the other cases he consulted either written texts [40] or else the more learned ecclesiastical tradition; here, however, he utilized the unself-conscious and irresponsible faith of the people among whom Vincent had lived and died a hundred years before.[41]

Prudentius tells of many other miracles, but they are on the borderline of the natural. A strange light is the commonest type,[42] seen sometimes by all,[43] sometimes by only a few.[44] Or there is a strange odour, sweet to some, foul to others.[45] On the whole his treatment of the miraculous may be taken as characteristic of his time. He welcomes any report of a miracle which confirms his faith; nevertheless he betrays no conscious aim to invent and so to deceive.[46] Occasionally, as in Agnes, he specifies that ' so, at least, the story runs ',[47] but this qualification is not interposed because of any doubt that miracles of the kind really occurred, it is merely inserted where the particular episode seemed not too well attested. It is interesting to notice that two of his stories are

---

[38] Prison miraculously illuminated: *Peristephanon* V lines 269–70; his stocks shattered: ibid. 270–71; potsherds soften: ibid. 277–80; sweet fragrance: ibid. 277–80; angel appears: ibid. 283–304; jailer hears singing: ibid. 317–24.

[39] Dufourcq *G.M.R.* 1907 II 154–55. There is a noticeable resemblance between the miracles attributed to Felix by Paulinus of Nola in *Carmen* XV lines 177–86, written before 395, and those attributed to Vincent by Prudentius after 400. Were these coincidences or did the traditions about Vincent inspire Paulinus? Paulinus not only married a Spaniard but lived there for some time immediately after his conversion.

[40] According to Schäfer 1932 58 his story of Hippolytus seems to have been taken from Seneca's *Phaedra*,

where the same tragedy overtakes Hippolytus.

[41] Duchesne 1911 III [4] 17 says: ' Dans la religion chrétienne, le culte des saints, des reliques, des images, est un apport du populaire. Il est dans la nature des choses que la religion se ressente un peu de ceux qui la pratiquent. Pourquoi le populaire n'y aurait-il pas mis son empreinte? Les penseurs y mettaient bien la leur, et c'était une empreinte plus dangereuse.'

[42] *Peristephanon* I, II, V, VI & XIV.

[43] Ibid. V.

[44] Ibid. II.

[45] Ibid.

[46] In his account of Cyprian Prudentius *Peristephanon* XIII adds no wonders to the natural account of Eusebius.

[47] Cf. *Peristephanon* XIV line 57.

based on paintings [48] — whether contemporary with the event or not we cannot tell.   Neither pictures a miracle, but we have no right, on that account alone, to suppose such a source more authentic than many of his others.   On the whole we may judge that while Prudentius made the most of the episodes told to him — what poet would not? — he invented no others.   As a Christian who felt his faith deeply it was natural that he believe what others said to its credit yet that he at the same time refrain from indulging his poetic fancies as the pagan poets did.[49]   He was as honest as he was uncritical.

In speaking of spiritual effects we referred not only to those produced by the martyrs during their lives but also to those which they continued to produce after their deaths: answers to prayers for grace during life and for mercy after death. Now just as it seemed impossible that the spiritual power of the martyr could be circumscribed or diminished by death, so it must be of his physical power.   Faith in such powers was important, not only in order to hearten the Christian but also in order to confound the pagan.   For pagans were playing with magic as much as ever, perhaps more; and, since strange things happened even at pagan rites, the only practicable way of belittling these phenomena was by producing others more remarkable to eclipse them.   No Christian denied the well-authenticated pagan miracle, but he declared it the work of demons.[50]   If these demons were not to be respected and appeased, as pagan and Manichee believed they should be, Christian miracles must be alleged which should surpass and confound them, in order to prove that the power of demons, even on earth, was merely subsidiary to that of God and His good agents.   Though life on earth was but an ephemeral prelude to the life everlasting and was therefore only designed as a prelude, nevertheless, even on this earth, the power of God was the controlling power and that of the demons was merely to do such mischief as God Himself permitted.   That the demons, posing as Gods, were allowed to perform feats

[48] *Peristephanon* IX lines 9-20, & XI lines 123-44.
[49] Ibid. X lines 216-20.

[50] Cf. Augustine *D.C.D.* II 25, X 16-18, XVIII 18, & XXI 6.

apparently miraculous, merely proved the Christian conten-
tion that demons can easily outwit all those who will not place
their faith in Christ.

Now such a faith, though in contrast to certainty, is at least
an expectancy, and often an eager one. After death, of course,
the expectancy would become certainty, but this often seemed
an intolerably long time to wait. Was it not natural that
God, in His mercy, should on occasion satisfy something of
that expectancy during mortal life, reinforcing the faith He
asked for with an occasional Sign? Did Christ intend to reveal Himself only to Jews? Prudentius said that Romanus
had been taunted by his accuser:

Truly this Christ of yours, whom you avow to have been crucified,
never existed.[51]

That Christ should not choose miraculously to save Romanus
from death was understandable: His kingdom was not of this
world. But it was hard to believe that the taunt must pass unchallenged. For although He may be reluctant to govern
He is surely eager to teach.

It was one thing, however, for the Christian to expect a
miracle, quite another to have it in fact occur, and occur so
often that no reasonable doubts could remain. Yet we have
every reason to believe that it did occur, over and over again:
the sick would visit the martyr's tomb, pray, weep, touch
either an actual bone of the corpse or else some object which
had been closely in contact with it,[52] and would, time and time
again, arise cured! [53] Why could the Christian martyrs cure
better [54] than pagan deities? It was faith in the infinite mercy
of God, a faith impossible for the Neoplatonist worshipping
the imperturbable One, for the Manichee worshipping the
God of heaven alone, for the pagan worshipping Jupiter or
others. The Christian need expect no true justice on earth,
but he knew that God ruled that earth, and knew too that
God's mercy was unbounded. Why should God not want to

---

[51] *Peristephanon* X lines 584–85.
[52] Cf. Ambrose *Letter* # 22 § 9.
[53] Cf. ibid.; & Jerome *Vitae S.
Hilarionis* §§ 14–17, 37, etc.; & Prudentius *Peristephanon* I lines 33 ff. &
100–20, & XI lines 177–82.

[54] Cassian *Conlationes* VIII 19, &
XV 1 & 6 admits that, through pacts
with demons, evil men can acquire
healing powers.

be merciful, not want to alleviate the miseries of those who loved Him? And so God did cure them, not always but often; cured those who felt sure that they deserved to be cured, who knew they were asking no more than was right and fair.

The power of the faith cure is not to be judged by our present experience of it. Roman doctors were not useless, were perhaps as successful in healing as any doctors up to 1800; but what they could do was infinitely little compared to what can be done today.[55] And, apart from cure, they were quite as helpless in relieving pain — not to mention the surgeon's helplessness in causing it. Prudentius says:

> Nor does it matter whether fire and cords [of torture] rage
> Or bitter weakness racks the sufferer,
> Since often sickness can attack with greater savagery.
> Tormenting hooks can never pierce the body with such cruelty
> As does the dagger driven in by dreadful pleurisy;
> Nor is the skin by scorching metal-plate so burned
> As fever with its black bile can consume the veins,
> Or, spreading over, bake the outer skin,
> Or, by its blistering heat, bring boils out,
> Making one feel as if seared by scorching branding-irons.
> You think me miserable because I hang stretched out
> By twisted elbows, because my feet are torn,
> Because my joints keep tune with my crackling nerves:
> Yet so do those cry out that their bones are breaking
> Whom knotty gout and rheumatism torture.
> You all abhor the cruel hands of the torturer;
> But are the hands of doctors kindlier
> When the Hippocratic butchery begins?
> They cut the palpitating viscera and, while fresh blood
> Still stains the scalpel, the putrid matter is scraped off.[56]

The horrors of torture led Augustine to condemn, not the judge, but human life;[57] for he too was aware that human cruelty did not surpass the misery caused by the sickness that no man caused. The intensity of Augustine's faith in another world enabled him to view the miseries of the present life as an ephemeral and so incidental evil. But to others it could not seem so — for year after year of such torture was long, unbearably long. It was hard to believe that the good God would so afflict the truly penitent and virtuous, hard to be-

55 Cf. Augustine *D.C.D.* XXII 24.   57 See p. 142 n. 16.
56 *Peristephanon* X lines 481–500.

lieve that such sufferings were not rather a penance imposed for past sins, to last only until the change of heart should come. So the greater the consciousness of virtue the greater the confidence in the efficacy of the prayer, and it was this complete confidence, based on an innate instinct of what true mercy must be, that so often provided the cure.

Because the ancients, like all the earlier peoples — and also like the very modern — believed in a physics of both matter and spirit, they supposed that the cure, though communicated by spirit, was more easily communicated to the body through another body.[58] A spiritual curative power seemed somehow stored up in the relic, to be released if the prayer were acceptable. It was not denied, of course, that a human body could be cured directly by a spiritual force — since God could do what He chose — but such a miracle was less explicable and so less likely than one effected through the medium of the relic.[59] Then there was also the glorious but subordinate position of the martyr to be considered: if he could procure permission to effect a cure apart from contact with one of his relics not only would his power too much resemble God's, the petitioner would also not need to do him other honour than to pray to him; whereas, if the relic must serve as intermediary, a pilgrimage to that relic was necessary, a sacrifice which, incidentally, could not fail to flatter the martyr and so predispose him to accede to the prayer.

In the late fourth century this doctrine of the relic was still in a formative stage, the spontaneous creation of individuals. Damasus vaguely countenanced it,[60] though there was no official sanction of it by subsequent Popes. But the doctrine grew, regardless of sanctions — nothing could have stopped its growth — for the cures which resulted seemed amply to prove the correctness of the hypothesis. There was one inconvenience, however: the relics of martyrs were to be found in only a few places. Rome could boast of several, but many other cities could boast of none. Later it became a common

---

[58] This theory is said to be at the basis of all the sacraments.

[59] See pp. 91 n. 54, & 200.

[60] Pope Damasus nowhere specifies what prayers will be answered or whether physical contact is essential, but he may have had a suspicion that burial close to a martyr's corpse might improve a sinner's chances of salvation: Schäfer 1932 46–47; & cf. ibid. 158.

practice to divide the corpse, thereby multiplying the localities where a single martyr could cure; but this practice had not yet begun, for it was still thought that such a separation might jeopardize an effective resurrection of the body.[61]

By the year 386 Rome was already deriving worldly advantage from the number of martyrs' bodies she possessed. As this was an advantage to the Roman so it was a disadvantage to others, who must, if they hoped to have their prayers answered, journey to Rome. Even so, there might be a question of whether a Roman martyr would give them quite the same consideration as native Romans. It is this doubt that Prudentius wishes to dispel where he says of Agnes,

Buried within the very sight of the towers, the virgin watches over the safety of the citizens: and she also protects those strangers who, with pure and faithful heart, are suppliants.[62]

Even this assurance, however, did not make up for the disadvantage of being obliged to go to Rome in order to benefit by the virtue of Agnes. Some other cities than Rome had martyrs' tombs that effected great wonders; why should one city be so much better off than another? [63]

It was in the year 386 [64] that Ambrose, then the great bishop of Milan, wrote to his sister to give her news of a wonderful event. He begins,

For after I had dedicated the basilica [at Milan] many, as it were, with one mouth began to address me, and said: 'Consecrate this as you did the Roman basilica.' And I answered: 'Certainly I will, if I find any relics of martyrs.' And at once a kind of prophetic ardour seemed to enter my heart.[65]

He has an excavation made in front of the chancel screen and two corpses of great stature and in perfect preservation are uncovered.[66] Miraculous cures accompany every phase of the discovery. Their names being found to be Protasius and Gervasius,

Old men now repeat that they once heard the names of these martyrs and even their titles.[67]

[61] Cf. Eusebius *Eccl. Hist.* V 1 §§ 62–63; & *Peristephanon* VI lines 136–41, & XI lines 135–52.

[62] *Peristephanon* XIV lines 3–6. See p. 156 n. 31.

[63] Dufourcq *G.M.R.* 1907 II 58–59.

[64] Ibid. 40–41.

[65] *Letter # 22* § 1.

[66] Ibid. § 2.

[67] Ibid. § 12.

How great was the rejoicing of all, and how great the discom-
fiture of the Arians, who tried in vain to discredit the whole
affair.[68] Ambrose writes triumphantly:

Who are we to esteem as the princes of the people but the holy
martyrs?   Amongst whose number Protasius and Gervasius, long
unknown, are now enrolled, who have caused the Church of
Milan, barren of martyrs hitherto, now, as the mother of many
children, to rejoice in the distinctions and instances of her own
sufferings.[69]

Shortly after this event Ambrose had two martyrs dug up
in Bologna under suspiciously similar circumstances.[70]   And
it was in about this same year 393 that Paulinus, the Aquitanian noble, came to live at Nola where he became bishop
and where he popularized the cult of Felix,[71] who as bishop
in 250 had suffered persecution by the Emperor Decius.
Felix, since he had died of old age, was not technically a martyr but merely a *confessor*.[72]   But he was on that account none
the less honoured by Paulinus and the citizens of Nola.[73]
Thus, by the early years of the fifth century, when Prudentius
wrote, the cult of the martyrs — and of a few *confessors* —
was already well under way, so that Prudentius, by honouring their names and deeds and present powers, was doing no
more than to echo the enthusiasm of the faithful.   And, as
the number of relics increased, so did the number of cures;
and, as the number of cures increased, so did the number of
the converts.   Already was Catholicism no longer a dream of
justice and happiness in another world; it had become, for
thousands upon thousands, a faith by means of which not virtue only, and so the solace of a clear conscience, but also
health, and so the comfort of physical well-being, could be
won in this world without in any degree lessening the chance
of a higher, fuller, and more durable happiness in the world
to come.

[68] Ibid. §§ 16 & 17.
[69] Ibid. § 7; & cf. Dudden 1935
299–308.
[70] Dufourcq *G.M.R.* 1907 II 51; &
Dudden 1935 316–19.
[71] Dufourcq ibid. 158.

[72] Kuhnmeunsch 1929 204–05.
The Latin word is *continentes*:
Duchesne 1910 II 4 529; & cf. ibid.
1911 III 6 531.
[73] Dufourcq *G.M.R.* 1907 II 158.

D. Miracles of the Confessors

The martyrs might well be, as Ambrose had said, the princes of the people. No Catholic wished, or would have been able, to dim their glory. But after the year 312 the days of martyrdom were gone; [1] if Christianity were to continue to produce heroes a new career must be carved for them. The example of Christ must still be followed, but how? Of the martyrs, only a courageous faith was required; henceforth, in order still to prove that faith, there had to be the evidence of good works. [2] The most obvious career was in the fast evolving hierarchy of the Church. But this, in comparison with the self-effacement of the martyr, might seem too worldly an ambition. [3] The career of the foreign missionary occasionally offered a middle course between worldliness and self-denial — Eusebius tells of a certain Pantænius who set out for India [4] — but at a time when half the Romans were still pagan the foreign mission was premature.

Eventually monasticism was to solve this problem, and happily. [5] But its beginnings were crude. The first monks were the hermits [6] of the desert, too many of whom were merely oriental ascetics with a Christian veneer. [7] Ignorant that ' in its own kind and degree the flesh is good ', [8] they macerated their bodies by fasting and hardship; [9] forgetting

---

[1] Although in Rome in about 400 the martyr Almachius, hurling himself by way of protest between two fighting gladiators, was killed by them: Butler & Thurston 1926 I 9–10. Cf. pp. 301–03, 524, & 627–28.

[2] Dufourcq L'Av. 1910 IV 5 129–31.

[3] Cassian Conlationes I 20 § 5 (written in about 423) warns against the wiles of the devil, as ' when he incites a man to desire the holy office of the clergy under the pretext of edifying many people.' And cf. Eucherius De Laude Eremi § 1 (of 426–9).

[4] Eccl. Hist. V 10 §§ 2–3. Ulfilas worked only among his own people.

[5] Cf. Goux 1856 13–14.

[6] The words hermit and anchorite are substantially synonymous, although the anchorite was not necessarily a religious recluse and he might live, though secluded, near or in a city.

[7] See p. 65.

[8] See p. 97 n. 70.

[9] Rufinus Hist. Monach. (P.L. 21), written in about 403, tells of those who would not eat cooked food: 411D; who drank a minimum of water for fear of inducing phantasms in the mind just as wine rouses passions in the body: 457C & 449A & B; and who for three years on end stood upright until told by God to desist: 433D–434A.

that without mercy and charity there can be no love of God, they shrank from all intercourse except with beasts.[10]   Even Jerome, though he did not quite practise what he preached, was seduced by their theory of simplification, for he says:

A monk's task is not to teach but to lament: to mourn either for himself or for the world, and with terror to anticipate our Lord's advent.   Knowing his own weakness . . . he is afraid of stumbling. . . . I confess my weakness.   I would not fight in the hope of victory lest some time or other I lose the victory.   If I flee I avoid the sword; if I stand I must either win or fall.   But what need is there for me to let go certainties for uncertainties?   Either with my shield or with my feet I must shun death.   You who fight may either be overcome or win.   When I flee I do not conquer because I flee; rather I flee in order to be sure that I be not overcome.   There is no safety in sleeping with a serpent beside one. Possibly he will not bite me, yet it is possible that after a time he may.[11]

This is the philosophy, if not of cowardice, at least of Stoic contraction; it was not the Christian, not even really Jerome's, way.   But it was the way of the more renowned of the early hermit monks.[12]

Yet these monks succeeded in making a great stir in the world, being advertised so well that they became famous during their lives; and their alleged miracles were taken to be an adequate guarantee of their holiness.[13]   Of the two earliest, Paul and Anthony, who were both born in about 250 [14] and lived about a hundred years, the latter became the more famous because in 359 [15] the great Alexandrian bishop Athanasius wrote his *Life* and so spread his fame throughout the Greek speaking world.   Already in this first *Life* there is such an abundance of the miraculous as is not to be found in the fifty accounts of martyrs by Eusebius, written nearly fifty years earlier.   Athanasius knew Anthony intimately and got the stories, therefore, at first hand.[16]   But the peculiarity is that many of the miracles occurred to Anthony when he was

[10] Cf. Severus *Dialogue* I 17; Rufinus *Hist. Monach.* (*P.L.* 21 391B) says of one of the hermits: ' the more he absented himself from human cares and conversation the closer God was to him.'

[11] *Contra Vigilantium* §§ 15 & 16.

[12] Cf. Duchesne 1910 II [4] 491–92 & 494.

[13] See pp. 152, & 507.

[14] *The Book of Saints* 1921 26 & 210.

[15] Robertson 1892 188.

[16] Cf. *Vita S. Antonii* § 91.

quite alone,[17] and could, therefore, have been related only by
him. And, since he fasted excessively and had a great many
visions,[18] we are bound to suspect that he was subject to hal-
lucinations; especially in those not infrequent cases where he
was beset either by demons,[19] or by wild beasts [20] such as
hyenas [21] and centaurs.[22] His cures of the sick and possessed,
on the other hand, we cannot doubt, for witnesses here were
abundant. And as much may be said of his power of telepathy.[23] Of the two physical miracles, one, where a silver
platter lying in his path in the desert vanishes as he scorn-
fully passes it by,[24] must have been reported by him alone as
no one was with him at the time. But in the other case,
where, in the presence of others, he prays and a spring gushes
forth,[25] Athanasius may have had the testimony of some or all
the onlookers. Of course we cannot affirm that any or all
these miracles were either imagined or invented, but it seems
likely that Anthony did a good deal of ingenuous boasting,
and that his impeccable honesty served to impose his own
credulity on others, and even on so enlightened a man as
Athanasius. This *Life* marks the beginning of the vogue for
the hermit, introduces the contemporary holy man as the first
serious rival of the historical martyr.

Less than fifteen years later, or before 374, this Greek *Life*
was translated into Latin [26] and the fame of the hermit began
to spread in the West.[27] And, as a companion piece, Jerome,
who had reached Jerusalem in 374, now followed with a *Life*
of the other hermit, Paul, so that the two *Lives* must both have
reached the West in about the same year 375. This story of
Paul by Jerome is most ungainly, reflecting, no doubt, the
ungainliness of Paul: his austerities and misanthropy are
spasmodically interlarded with accounts of the miraculous
behaviour of animals. In one case — which Athanasius does
not mention — Anthony, on his way to seek out the retreat
of Paul — for hermits did occasionally deign to consort with
each other —

17 Cf. Severus *Dialogue* I 24.
18 *Vita S. Antonii* § 10.
19 Ibid. §§ 8 & 13.
20 Ibid. § 9.
21 Ibid. § 52.
22 Ibid. § 53.

23 Ibid. §§ 59 & 60.
24 Ibid. § 11.
25 Ibid. § 54.
26 Robertson 1892 189.
27 Augustine *Confessions* VIII 6.

beholds a creature of mingled shape, half horse, half man, called by the poets Hippo-centaur. At the sight of this he arms himself by making on his forehead the sign of salvation, and then exclaims, 'Hello! Where in these parts is a servant of God living?' The monster after gnashing out some kind of outlandish utterance, in words broken rather than spoken through his bristling lips, at length finds a friendly means of communication, and, extending his right hand, points out the way desired.[28]

Jerome goes on to tell of how a raven brought Paul his daily ration of half a loaf of bread,[29] and of how, as he lay dying, two lions appeared and, unbidden, proceeded to dig his grave with their paws.[30]

Paul is said to have died in 342, so that Jerome heard his story within a generation. Legends can grow fast, but in this case legend is not the explanation, for Athanasius had already written his *Life* of Anthony within three years of his death and with personal knowledge of the man.[31] That queer things were happening in the Thebaid desert was, to the men of that day, a certainty. The miraculous world so vivid and active in the time of Christ, but in apparent abeyance since then, was now reviving in Egypt by the power of the holiness of the hermits. This was good news to Christians, and they honoured the hermits accordingly.

In about 389 [32] Jerome wrote still another biography of a hermit, the *Life* of Hilarion, who died in 371. This Hilarion is not the misanthropist that Paul and Anthony were, but, if he is more sociable, he is also more disconcerting. He not only effects many cures,[33] he also triples the crop of a vineyard,[34] keeps off a pirate ship,[35] gets a serpent to crawl into a fire and be burnt.[36] If his two predecessors were chiefly Stoics, he is chiefly a magician:

Another story relates to Italicus, a citizen of the same town [Gaza]. He was a Christian and kept horses for the circus to contend against those of the Duumvir of Gaza who was a votary of the

---

[28] *Vita S. Pauli* § 7.
[29] Ibid. § 10.
[30] Ibid. § 16.
[31] Israël 1880 130, 137, 145, & 153 argues that the credulity in Jerome's *Lives* exceeds that in Athanasius' *Life of Anthony*, but it must be remembered that Athanasius, unlike

Jerome, relied on a good deal of first hand information.
[32] Cavallera 1922 I 130–33.
[33] See pp. 171–73.
[34] *Vita S. Hilarionis* § 27.
[35] Ibid. § 41.
[36] Ibid. § 39.

idol god Marnas. This custom, at least in Roman cities, was as old as the days of Romulus, and was instituted in commemoration of the successful seizure of the Sabine women. The chariots raced seven times round the circus in honour of Consus in his character of the God of Counsel. Victory lay with the team which tired out the horses opposed to them. Now the rival of Italicus had in his pay a magician to incite his horses by certain demoniacal incantations, and to keep back those of his opponent. Italicus therefore came to the blessed Hilarion and besought his aid not so much for the injury of his adversary as for protection of himself. It seemed absurd for the venerable old man to waste prayers on trifles of this sort. He therefore smiled and said, ' Why do you not rather give the price of the horses to the poor for the salvation of your soul? ' His visitor replied that his office was a public duty, and that he acted not so much from choice as from compulsion, that no Christian man could employ magic, but would rather seek aid from a servant of Christ, especially against the people of Gaza who were enemies of God, and who would exult over the Church of Christ more than over him. At the request therefore of the brethren who were present he ordered an earthenware cup out of which he was wont to drink to be filled with water and given to Italicus. The latter took it and sprinkled it over his stable and horses, his charioteers and his chariot, and the barriers of the course. The crowd was in a marvellous state of excitement, for the enemy in derision had published the news of what was going to be done, and the backers of Italicus were in high spirits at the victory they promised themselves. The signal was given; the one team flies towards the goal, the other sticks fast: the wheels are glowing hot beneath the chariot of the one, while the other scarce catches a glimpse of their opponents' backs as they flit past. The shouts of the crowd swell to a roar, and the heathens themselves with one voice declare Marnas conquered by Christ. After this the opponents in their rage demanded that Hilarion as a Christian magician should be dragged to execution. This decisive victory and several others which followed in successive games of the circus caused many to turn to the faith.[37]

In the very early fifth century [38] an Aquitanian, Postumianus, returned from a voyage to the East and substantiated the stories of the miracles wrought by the hermits. Most of these, including the cases of tamed animals,[39] are of the usual sort, but there is one which is as disquieting as it is new:

[37] *Vita S. Hilarionis* § 20.
[38] In the year 404 according to Monceaux 1926 15.
[39] As in Severus *Dialogue* I 13–16. For modern evidence of the relative ease with which the African lion may be domesticated, see E. F. V. Wells *Lions, Wild and Friendly* London 1933.

A holy man who possessed a marvellous power of being able to banish evil spirits from the bodies of their victims, worked wonderful miracles almost every day, not alone by his presence and words; sometimes mere scraps of his hairshirt or letters written by him sufficed to heal those who were possessed. As a consequence, immense numbers of persons came to him from all parts. And I do not here refer to persons of low estate; prefects, counts and governors of high and varied dignity came to prostrate themselves before his threshold. Saintly bishops even, laying aside their episcopal authority, frequently sought his blessing. . . .

Alas, in course of time, little by little, the homage and the adulation so constantly paid to the holy man awoke in him the besetting sin of vanity. He felt the insidious growth of pride within his soul, and he struggled against it hard and long. But it seemed impossible to exterminate the evil completely, though he was fully aware of its existence while he continued to exercise his gift of healing. His power over devils was known by all and by no means could he avoid his frequent visitors. And all the while the hidden venom grew and festered in his soul; and he who, with a mere wave of the hand, was able to banish evil spirits from the bodies of his fellow men, was powerless to free himself from the miserable sin of pride.[40]

This marks a further step in the evolution of the miracle: Hilarion, because of his remarkable holiness, had been able to work miracles at will, even to the point of procuring victories in chariot races. This was dangerously close to familiar pagan magic — the only difference being in the character of the magician. But the story of Postumianus destroys even this last barrier, for the magician here possesses a power which was independent of any present goodness.[41] Any pagan magician might plausibly allege that he too had once been extraordinarily virtuous, and that this was why he had these special powers. Doubtless this Christian still exercised these powers for beneficent ends, but many a pagan magician could allege no less. The danger was, as any of the contemporaries of this holy man could see, that since he was himself no longer in a state of grace he might, at any moment, exercise his powers in order to do harm. Playing with magic was playing with fire.

---

[40] Severus *Dialogue* I 20.
[41] Thereby contradicting Jerome's statement that ' A good tree does not bear evil fruit, nor an evil tree good fruit, so long as they continue in their goodness and badness ': *Contra Jovinianum* II §25. Rufinus *Hist. Monach.* I (*P.L.* 21 401D–402A)

A hard and fast line between the miraculous and the magical is not easy to draw because the difference is only one of degree. Observe, however, that the wonders occurring at the deaths of the martyrs seemed to occur through no conscious wish of theirs: the body does not sink, the corpse remains intact,[42] the thunderbolt strikes. The martyrs are passive; the initiative comes from elsewhere. This is also true of some of the hermit wonders; but in others — and this is an important distinction — the initiative passes from God to the man. No martyr could fail to perform a miracle, because he never tried. But the confessor, since he often did try, was in a very delicate position: he could afford to fail only very occasionally. We here approach the domain of magic, because it is a power that can be counted on often enough to appear reliable. Failure of an attempted cure could be partially explained by the patient's lack of faith rather than by any diminution of the healing power. Still, it was an unwelcome explanation, as any explanation of failure is bound to be. The great saint was one who could overcome this resistance. This magic was analogous to grace: [43] a constant current of power, but effective only if in contact with another if feebler virtuous power. In this principle, however, lay the seeds of danger: since the miracle was chiefly designed to glorify the saint his merit must be magnified, and the simplest way of doing this was to minimize the merit and hence the co-operation of the patient or suppliant. The acid test of a saint's merit would then be his capacity to confer a supernatural benefit on a sinner. The story told by Postumianus, however, goes even a step further by suggesting that one who from virtue has relapsed into sin can transmit his past virtue. This is an opening wedge to a magic as crass as any known to paganism.

To this danger signal Paulinus, the holy bishop of Nola,[44] adds another: in his poem of 399 [45] in honour of the confessor Felix, who had lived more than a century earlier, he tells of

---

tells an analogous tale, but, as the pride waxes, the reward turns sour.

[42] See pp. 162–63 on Quirinus & Aphianus.

[43] The routine cases were the sacraments, as of baptism, commun-ion, or ordination. A man was thought to become an Emperor *ipso facto* by an analogous magical rite: see Jullian 1926 VIII 7.

[44] See p. 175 n. 71.

[45] Lagrange 1877 316.

how a peasant who had long venerated Felix as his special
protector arose one day to find his precious yoke of oxen
stolen from his barn.   Here, in the cultivated language of
Paulinus, is the prayer with which the peasant, after describing the circumstances and seriousness of his loss, asks Felix
to find the oxen and return them:

Restore these same animals; I shall not accept any others.   Nor
shall I go to other districts in search of them — I have a right to
get them back here: they must be restored at this threshold where
I, as a suppliant, constrain you yourself and cling to you; why
should I seek, and where should I seek, I who have no idea who
the thieves are? My debtor is right here, I hold the guardian himself on account of the theft; and this guardian, O Saint, is you —
answerable to me, cognizant of them: it is you that I hold; you
know where they are, you who by the light of Christ see all things,
even those hidden, who discern what is far removed, and comprehend, God surrounding you, where all things are.   And for this
reason the hidden thieves and their retreats, wherever these may
be, are not concealed from you, nor can these thieves evade you,
because a Hand is on them already.   God is one everywhere,
Christ's right hand is gentle to the faithful, but punishes the
wicked.   Therefore restore my oxen to me and lay hold of the
thieves.

I do not demand them as defendants; let them go, for I am not,
O Saint, ignorant of your methods: you do not requite evil deeds,
you prefer to correct the wicked by forgiving rather than ruin
them by chastisements.   Let this, therefore, be our covenant:
separate what is yours from what is mine in this way: through
you what is useful to me shall be kept from harm; mercy shall
rightly claim what is yours; and let your verdict be evenly bal-
anced: for your part free the guilty, for mine restore my oxen.
There you have the terms; let no subordinate of yours be a cause
of delay; hasten to relieve me of so much anxiety.   For I am determined not to give way in anything or leave this doorpost until
you shall have come to my help; unless you hasten I shall die on
this threshold.   In that case, returning my oxen which you recovered too late, you will not find me.[46]

Needless to say, in a wonderfully short time the oxen were
safely back in their stalls.

The stories told by Jerome and Postumianus have shown
us how, in the hands of the untutored and unscrupulous, the

---

[46] *Carmen* XVIII lines 284-312.

miracle can degenerate into magic. To this abuse of Christianity to serve commercial or egotistical ends Paulinus' story records a further debasement of the miraculous: a virtual threat by the distracted peasant to discredit the reputation of his patron saint unless there were a prompt compliance. Thus the power of the dead saint does not depend wholly on God's will, or even on the saint's own private judgment. Instead it depends also on how often the saint in fact performs the miracle that is asked of him. Many of the requests, without being actually sinful, might be purely temporal and financial; yet the saint's reputation for particular holiness tends to depend on the frequency with which he accedes to such material demands. For, if he is too strict, he risks a neglect by boycott: a saint who will grant only such favours as God Himself might well bestow, must reconcile himself to impending oblivion. That a peasant should conceive of the utility of Felix's holiness in this light is not unnatural; what does startle is the readiness of Paulinus, urbane and cultivated as he was, to credit and circulate such a story. For it taught that it was to the suppliants' advantage to importune their saints.

Only a few years later, in about 403,[47] appeared a fuller account in Latin, by the priest Rufinus of Aquileia, of the wonders done by the hermits of the Egyptian desert. The isolated testimony of an Athanasius and a Jerome is here corroborated on a vast scale. Rufinus seems to allege that he himself witnessed these wonders in the course of a journey down the Nile in the winter of 394-5, and, although he is probably recording the journey of another,[48] there is no reason for doubting the general authenticity of the testimony. The wonders recorded here are bewildering both in their abundance and variety: dragons stand guard at a monastery gate,[49] hermits cross rivers immersed above the waist and yet dry,[50] on the backs of crocodiles [51] or through the air — wafted

[47] Pauly-Wissowa 1914 1195.
[48] The original was probably in Greek: see ibid. See also Krüger 1906 XVII 201 lines 34-41; Carl Schmidt 1898 13-27; Cuthbert Butler 1898 & 1904 I 277. Butler thinks that the original Greek was written by a certain Timotheus, archdeacon of Alexandria. But see *P.L.* 21 420A & 426A where the writers allege their ignorance of Greek. Were these interpolations by the translator Rufinus?

[49] *P.L.* 21 421A.
[50] Ibid. 438A.
[51] Ibid. 430B–D.

by an invisible power,[52] food [53] — and once at Easter even a
sumptuous banquet [54] — is dispensed from heaven, the sun
is arrested in his course,[55] dead men speak from their tombs [56]
or are recalled to life,[57] one hermit is able to move at an infinite speed.[58]   Cures,[59] prophecies,[60] hypnotism,[61] the constant presence of ministering angels [62] and mischievous demons,[63] are everyday phenomena; one hermit, Apollonius,
hears God speaking to him to urge that he leave his isolation
for a preaching tour among men.   Apollonius appearing to
hesitate, God seeks to win his obedience by the promise that

everything you ask of God will be vouchsafed you.[64]

Another hermit, Paul, simple-minded but holy, finding his
prayers were not curing a madman,

indignant as a child might be, is alleged to have said to the Lord,
'Truly I shall not eat today unless you cure him', whereupon at
once, as if by a tender master, he was given satisfaction by God.[65]

Not content to importune the saints, the self-assurance of
these hermits emboldens them to strike sharp bargains even
with God.

So far the confessors of the West had been rather mythical
figures, like Felix of Nola, whose reputation was chiefly due
to the miracles occurring at his tomb.[66]   There had been no
living personality to rival the fast growing reputations of the
Eastern hermits.   But the West had not long to wait: in
the year 395 [67] appeared a *Life* by Sulpicius Severus, an Aqui-

---

52 Ibid. 457A. Done that he might
not have to blush at taking off his
clothes in order to swim.
53 Ibid. 401D, 406C, 423B–C, &
431C.
54 Ibid. 416A–C.
55 Ibid. 424A–D.
56 Ibid. 423D–424A, & 450A–451A.
57 Ibid. 452A–C.
58 Ibid. 425B–C.
59 Ibid. 411B–D, 432B, & 459A.
60 Ibid. 393C, 404D–405A, 415D–
416A, 428A–B. For cases of mental
telepathy, see 417D, 433A–B, 434D–
435A, & 442C–443A.

61 Ibid. ch. VI & 414A–B.
62 Ibid. 411D–412B.
63 Ibid. 399–401, 417A–C, 428D–
429A, etc.
64 Ibid. 410D–411B.
65 Ibid. 459B.
66 For the miracles told of him
during his life, see *Carmen* XV lines
177–86 & 238–57, & *Carmen* XVI lines
66–70 & 95–119.
67 Duchesne 1911 III 4 164; Monceaux 1926 14.

tanian noble, of the holy Martin, bishop of Tours. So great was the success of the book that within a few years Martin was becoming the great popular hero of the Latin West, fast gaining the renown [68] which was to make him the pride of all Gaul and ultimately the national saint of France.[69]

Martin was born in Pannonia in about 325,[70] the son of a Roman army officer. His youth was spent in Pavia; later he entered the army in his turn, but after a time was violently converted to Christianity and as soon as he could resign his commission left for Gaul to seek the guidance of the famous Hilary, bishop of Poitiers. In about 369 Hilary died and two years later [71] Martin was consecrated bishop of Tours, an office that he continued to hold with ever increasing renown till his death in 397.

Severus, his biographer, seems to have been an aristocrat of Toulouse.[72] Born in about 355, in 391 [73] the fame of Martin drew him to Tours, and in 395 appeared the biography [74] which made Martin famous throughout the Empire. The beauty of Martin's character, his gentleness, charm, and deep love of men as well as of God, introduces a new note into the spirit of Christianity. ' O truly blessed man ', says Severus,

utterly without malice, judging no one, condemning none, never returning evil for evil. Against all injury he was armed with the most extraordinary patience. He, the head, the bishop, allowed himself to be insulted by miserable clerics. And never . . . in so far as was possible, did he exclude them from his all-pervading charity.[75]

Where is any sorrow-stricken soul whose affliction he did not share? How many scandals caused his heart to burn within him! How often has he wept for the dead! . . . He was in truth a man apart, endowed with special gifts of pity, mercy and charity.[76]

And the story is told [77] how, one day,

[68] See Severus *Dialogue* I 23.
[69] Monceaux 1926 7.
[70] Ibid. 19–20 says 316, while other scholars prefer 335. But Severus *Dialogue* II 7 says that Martin was 61 years old during the regime of Maximus, and this was from 383–387.
[71] Ibid. 29 says in 371.
[72] Duchesne 1911 III [4] 168. Severus was living there in 404: *Letter* # 3.

[73] Monceaux 1926 14 says that Severus was in broken health when he journeyed to Tours between 391 and 395 to visit Martin. Severus was a close friend of Paulinus of Nola, who was born in 353.
[74] There is an English translation, by Mary Caroline Watts, N. Y. 1928.
[75] *Life of Martin* 26.
[76] *Letter* # 2.
[77] By Severus, but on the author-

dogs were after a hare. The poor beast was exhausted after a long chase and we were in a great open plain with no cover of any kind; there was no chance of escape, and the wretched creature was already doomed; doubling desperately it evaded death to the last possible moment. The tender-hearted saint took pity on the poor hunted thing. He ordered the hounds to cease their pursuit and to leave their prey. Instantly they ceased to run.[78]

It was because Martin so loved men that he supposed the evil in them to be something alien to their true nature.

It was never a difficult matter to obtain pardon from Martin.[79] On one occasion the priest Brictio had insulted him. Upon this,

addressing himself to the guilty man and also to the rest of us, the saint related how he had watched the two devils when they had excited the priest and added that the insults had not hurt him because he knew full well who had caused them to be spoken.[80]

There is a faint Manichæan echo in Martin's eagerness to acquit man of his evil acts and to blame the devil instead. Actually, however, his sweet nature transcends all habitual dogmas, for he dares hope, not merely as Manichee and even Catholic did, for the punishment or at least the segregation of evil, but for its complete annihilation. Addressing himself to the devil he says:

' If thou, unfortunate one, would but cease to pursue mankind, if today, now that the judgment day is nigh, thou wouldst repent thee of thy misdeeds, I am so sure of the mercy of the Lord Jesus Christ that I would promise thee pardon and peace.' [81]

What a contrast to the sternness of the Hebrew doctrine:

Ye serpents, ye generation of vipers, how can ye escape the damnation of hell? [82]

Two women shall be grinding at the mill; the one shall be taken and the other left.[83]

If any man come to me, and hate not his father, and mother, and wife, and children, and brethren, and sisters, yea, and his own life also, he cannot be my disciple.[84]

---

ity of Gallus, another of Martin's disciples.

[78] *Dialogue* III 9.
[79] Ibid. 15.
[80] Ibid.

[81] *Life of Martin* 22.
[82] *Matt.* xxiii 33.
[83] Ibid. xxiv 41.
[84] *Luke* xiv 26.

Too many Christians, like Augustine, loved men because God asked them to; Martin loved God the more because God asked him to love man.   On one occasion Martin agreed to communicate with the bishops who had forced the execution of Priscillian, in consideration of the Emperor's promise not to persecute Priscillian's followers. ' In so doing,' Gallus says,

he chose for one hour to yield up his principles rather than abandon many unfortunate beings to a dreadful fate.[85]

Martin was willing to give ten devils the kiss of peace in order to save a misguided sect from physical suffering.   In giving in so utterly to his love of man there was perhaps an element of self-indulgence, and, in his fear of hurting, an element too of materialism.   But however weak, philosophically speaking, however simple and even childish, Martin enriched Christianity, making it more tender and gentle than it had been.[86] In its lofty righteousness Martin had detected a note of irritability; he soothed it; and, in their gratitude, the Gauls chose him as their national saint.

Yet how are we ever to grasp the incongruities and paradoxes of this life?   This most holy and lovable Martin was also — at least among the Latins — the first Christian magician, the first professional wonder-worker.   But if the cause of this weird partnership is obscure, the effect of it is most apparent: henceforth that physical power over men which had formerly been associated with Emperors and armies was to be associated instead with Christian virtue.   The people need no longer worry that civil government was breaking down; for the instrument by which God guided events was not the material institution but the spiritual individual.   To the State succeeded the saint.

Some of the miracles of Martin as related by Severus reveal rather the simplicity of Severus than the power of Martin.   In one case Martin prophesies that

at the outset, Maximus would indeed be the victor, but shortly afterwards he would perish,[87]

[85] *Dialogue* I 13.

[86] Although Martin was about thirty years older than Augustine, his fame began only with the publication of Severus' *Life* in 395, only a few years before Augustine became a conspicuous figure.

[87] *Life* 20.

which was the likely career of any late fourth century Gallic usurper. And elsewhere Severus concludes that

Martin, then, had had for long a sure presentiment of his approaching death.[88]

He relates how, on another occasion, Martin, perceiving some ducks devouring their prey with voracity,

ordered the birds to leave. . . . He addressed the birds in the imperious tone of voice that he was wont to use when putting demons to flight. At once all the ducks gathered themselves together in a group, and together they all departed from the river.[89]

In such cases a natural explanation is transparently likely.

In another kind of case, however, hypnotic control seems to have been applied:

When Martin was one day on the road he met by chance the funeral procession of a pagan who was being conveyed to the grave with the usual superstitious rites. . . . Martin feared the rites of profane sacrifice. . . .

Therefore with hand outstretched towards the oncoming band, Martin made the sign of the cross, bidding the people stand still and lay down their burden. There ensued a wonderful sight. The unfortunate creatures, at first, were as though turned to stone. Then, when they sought to proceed, not being able to advance, they turned round and round and pirouetted in a laughable fashion. Finally, vanquished, they laid the corpse that they were carrying on the ground. Overcome with astonishment, looking from one to the other, they silently asked themselves what had befallen them.

In the meantime the Blessed One had perceived that it was a matter of a funeral train and not of a sacrifice. At once he raised his hand again and gave them back their freedom and allowed them to carry away the corpse. Thus when he chose he forced them to stop; and when he so pleased he permitted them to proceed.[90]

That Martin, with ' his long, hanging pallium made of coarse skins ' [91] and his ' imperious tone of voice,' [92] was able to frighten these peasants, does not seem so incredible to us as it did to Severus.

Severus alleges only one clear physical miracle. In that

---

[88] *Letter* # 3 § 6.
[89] Ibid. § 8.
[90] *Life* 12.

[91] *Dialogue* II 3.
[92] *Letter* # 3 § 8.

case the pagans of a certain town, being angered by Martin's preaching, decided, in order to prove his power, to cut down their sacred tree in such a way that it must fall on the spot where they had bound him. If it did not strike him they agreed to be converted.

The great pine tree had grown to one side and it seemed certain that, in falling, it would crash in the direction towards which it leaned.

But, just as it begins to fall, it

seems to be caught backwards by some unseen power and it falls in quite the opposite direction to which it had inclined, so that the peasants, who had gathered in what appeared to be so safe a place, have a narrow escape from being crushed to death.[93]

The peasants were so impressed that, according to Severus, almost every pagan of the district hastened to embrace the new faith.

These stories of Martin are vouched for by Severus himself. He does not say whether he was an eye-witness or was told of them by Martin or some other, but he implicitly assumes full responsibility for them.[94] This *Life,* as we have said, appeared in about 395, and it was about ten years later that he published the *Dialogues,* the first book recording the Eastern hermit stories of Postumianus, the second and third books recording further miracles of Martin as related to Severus by his friend Gallus. This Gallus was not an Aquitanian but a Gaul,[95] presumably from the neighbourhood of Tours, less cultivated than Severus but quite as ardent an admirer of Martin and quite as authentic a witness of the wonders that had occurred. If Severus had not believed the stories told by Gallus he would not have written those dialogues; at the same time the source is now not Severus the Aquitanian aristocrat but Gallus the humble disciple from Tours.

Gallus has a serpent story to match the duck story of Severus:

A serpent slipped into the river and swam towards the bank on which we were seated. ' In the name of the Lord ' said Martin

93 *Life* 13.
94 Cf. *Life* 25.
95 *Dialogue* I 27.

' I command you to return.' Instantly, even as the saint spoke, the venomous reptile turned and swam back, before our eyes, to the opposite bank. We all stood amazed at the sight, and Martin said, with a deep sigh: ' the serpents hear me, but men hear me not! ' [96]

He also has a story of weather-control to match any that the pagan magicians of his time were boasting of:

The estates of Auspicius, moreover, were usually visited by more terrible storms than were any other districts. Martin prayed fervently, and completely delivered the whole countryside from the terrible scourge with which it had been for so long afflicted. During the twenty years which still remained of Martin's earthly life, no one, in those parts, suffered any further ill from hailstones. This was undoubtedly no affair of chance, but was entirely owing to the intervention of Martin.[97]

One of Martin's most engaging traits was his sociability. It is Postumianus who tells of how

Martin conversed every day of his life with angels.[98]

But it remained for Gallus to testify further that

When demons sought him out, Martin always recognized them and accosted them by their names. Mercury was very frequent and disturbing in his attacks, but the saint declared that Jupiter was heavy, stupid, and dull.[99]

In a world created by God out of His love for men there seemed, to Martin, to be nothing to hate,[100] no one who did not in some way reflect and symbolize the goodness of his Creator. Jupiter, the God of stupid people, would naturally be conceived of as stupid too. Christian charity invited Martin to forgiveness, and evil was more easily forgiven if ascribed rather to ignorance and stupidity than to cunning and malice.[101]

That Gallus was often an eye-witness of the wonders he describes is shown by his story of the serpent, which ' swam towards the bank on which we were seated.' [102] On the occa-

---

[96] Ibid. III 9.
[97] Ibid. 7.
[98] Ibid. I 25.
[99] Ibid. II 13.
[100] He recalls no one so much as Francis of Assisi.

[101] Cf. *Life* 22 quoted p. 187, on Martin's eagerness to prevail on the devil to repent.
[102] See p. 190.

sion of a wholly extraordinary cure he appears also to have been present:

> One of the household slaves was badly bitten by a serpent. . . . The poison had already spread throughout the man's whole body; the skin was perceptibly swollen over all the veins, and the vital organs were frightfully inflamed. Martin stretched forth his hand and touched each limb in turn, and then laid a finger on the little wound left by the serpent's sting. And then occurred the marvel. . . . We could clearly trace the poison hurrying along the veins of the slave's body towards Martin's finger; and from the tiny wound the venom mixed with blood flowed freely. . . . The slave rose up a sound man.[103]

This, although technically a cure, is virtually a physical miracle: that is, a phenomenon contradicting what we too know of natural law. And Gallus relates several similar wonders. One case is more ludicrous than impressive:

> Some of the possessed had their feet in the air, but strange to say their garments never fell down, doubtless out of a regard for decency.[104]

Another case, however, takes us wholly out of the realm of nature and into that of magic:

> There was a certain enormous pillar surmounted by an idol. Martin desired to overthrow it but possessed nothing with which to carry out his desire. Accordingly, as usual, he had recourse to prayer. Lo! in the sky there appeared forthwith, and this is an accredited fact, a similar pillar, which, descending, fell upon the idol, whereupon the whole huge mass of stone was reduced to powder.[105]

To the wonders credited to the martyrs, in Palestine, in Pannonia, and in Spain, were now added the more vivid because contemporaneous wonders of the confessors, first in the Eastern desert, now too in Western Gaul. As the theology of Latin Christianity had come from the Empire's centre, in Italy and Africa,[106] so the magic of Christianity came from the fringes of the Empire, from territories only distantly in touch with the Latin Roman civilization of that time. Everywhere the miracle was accepted as a theoretical possibility, but only

103 *Dialogue* II 2.
104 Ibid. III 6.
105 Ibid. 9.

106 From Ambrose and Augustine and from the Roman papacy.

in a few places had there yet been experience of such a thing. The medical cure, of course, was a matter of daily occurrence; this was in a special category, since failures were even more frequent than cures, but the physical miracle, which defied not only their known laws of nature but also ours, was, in the year 405, still a *parvenu* that had its way to make.

E. THE SCEPTICS

In Book I of the *Dialogues* of Severus Postumianus has no sooner ended his account of the wonders performed by the Eastern hermits than Severus comes to the defence of his hero Martin:

> Most surely you have told us wonderful acts, and I am far from desiring to belittle your holy men.   Still, I must confess that I have heard no single word which denotes in any way Martin's inferiority.   And, moreover, I venture to state that no other can profitably to himself be compared with this great man.   And we must also reflect that any comparison made between him and the hermits, or even the anchorites, is by no means a fair comparison.   For these men are free from all hindrances, and only Heaven and the angels bear witness to the miracles which are told of them.   Martin, on the other hand, lived in the midst of men, in the world, among the people.[1]

This is not a chivalrous observation.   Postumianus had just been describing the great acclaim with which Severus' *Life of Martin* was being received in the East;[2] it was hardly the moment for Severus to insinuate doubts regarding the veracity of Postumianus' Eastern informants.   And if Severus doubted these stories might not others be tempted to retaliate by doubting his?

Faced by an entirely authentic record of Martin, and separated from these alleged events by over fifteen hundred years, we are really helpless to profess doubts unless we can find other texts of equal authenticity to confirm our scepticism.   By a curious chance it happens, however, that this very text that alleges the miracles at the same time testifies to a

---

[1] *Dialogue* I 24.   [2] Ibid. 23.

widespread contemporary doubt of their truth. First there is this episode told by Severus himself:

I was told . . . of the remark made by a certain individual, which must surely have been suggested to him by the Old Enemy. Why, enquired this man, was this same Martin, who had restored the dead to life and who had saved houses from the flames, why was he himself recently injured in a fire in which he nearly perished amid cruel sufferings? [3]

And this is what Postumianus says to Severus:

I now repeat with horror a remark which I recently heard, to the effect that some wretched man (I do not know his name) had said that you, in your beautiful book, had made many false statements. And that remark is scarcely human, no, it savours of the devil. To speak thus is not merely to deny Martin, but it implies a refusal to believe in the authenticity of the Gospels. For, as is well known, Our Lord has Himself declared that miracles similar to those worked by Martin may be worked by all the faithful. And so to deny that Martin has worked miracles is to deny the words of Christ. But these wretched, degenerate, and slothful men blush to perceive that Martin has done what they themselves are incapable of doing. They prefer rather to deny his miracles than to confess their own unworthiness. [4]

This 'wretched man' was evidently a Christian, and evidently too, from the later reference to other 'wretched, degenerate, and slothful men', he was not the only one who was sceptical. And Postumianus evidently thought it impious to doubt any of the miracles attributed to Martin — even though this doubt might be, not of Martin's own credibility, but only of the value of the informant's testimony. Any intimation that Severus might, in one or two cases, have been misinformed was, to Postumianus, tantamount to a denial, not only of Martin's virtue and good faith, but also of the truth of Christ's revelation. By this outburst of intolerance the testimony of Postumianus suffers seriously.

Let us now see what Gallus tells us. Referring in *Dialogue* III to the marvels he had related the day before — in *Dialogue* II — he says,

I intend to subjoin to every description of a miracle the names of reliable witnesses, of living men, to whom any who may be in-

[3] *Letter # 1 § 2.*   [4] *Dialogue I 26.*

credulous can have recourse. I am forced to this on account of
the incredulity of many, who, I am told, have difficulty in believing all that I related yesterday. . . . This digression is needful
by reason of the annoying and persistent incredulity of certain
persons.[5]

From this it is clear that, even within the select circle of
Severus at Toulouse [6] — even among those first told and so
supposedly most disposed to believe — there were some who
doubted and frankly said so.

These, however, were sceptics living in Toulouse in the
year 404. They had very inadequate means for weighing the
evidence — barely more than we have. Is there then no trace
of sceptics who were living in Tours in Martin's lifetime?
One such trace does exist, the story, told by Gallus, of Brictio:

Brictio, who, before he became a priest, had possessed nothing of
his own . . . this Brictio now kept horses and purchased slaves.[7]

A coarse, vulgar person no doubt; but one who nevertheless, as we shall see in a moment, was not negligible. Gallus
proceeds to tell us that

Martin . . . was now, so Brictio declared, in his old age falling
a prey to vain superstition, and was merely the dupe of silly notions and misleading visions.[8]

But why should we listen to this offensive Brictio? For two
reasons. In the first place Severus pictures the saintly old
man in daily intercourse with angels. Now Martin was probably already over sixty-five [9] when Severus first journeyed
to Tours to see him in 391.[10] Many of the stories may have
concerned an earlier period; both Postumianus and Gallus
may have known him as he was before 391; nevertheless, it
is possible that Brictio's accusation had a foundation.

There is, however, a much better reason for taking Brictio's
statement seriously. Gallus says that

afterwards this same Brictio was frequently denounced for many
and grave faults. But the bishop would never consider deposing
this priest. Martin could never bear to avenge any personal in-

5 Ibid. III 5.   8 Ibid.
6 Duchesne 1911 III [4] 168.   9 See p. 186 n. 70.
7 *Dialogue* III 15.   10 Monceaux 1926 14 & 29.

juries: as he was often heard to say, ' If Christ could tolerate Judas surely I can put up with Brictio '.[11]

Presumably, therefore, Martin and Brictio were never reconciled. Yet it was precisely this Brictio who, in 397, was elected to succeed him.[12] There was no question at that time of a political appointment, by Roman or other authority, and we must therefore conclude that, at least throughout the later years of Martin's episcopate, there was a powerful opposition party within the Church which, at his death, assumed control.[13] And, besides, it is significant that, in the years immediately following, we find the most ardent admirers of Martin, not in Tours, but in Toulouse.

It is true that Severus' *Life of Martin* was already written and published before 397; [14] the miracles were therefore recorded before resentment had been aroused by Brictio's election. But there was already hostility between the parties before then, and Severus may well have written what he did on that account. In any case we may fairly envisage the addition of the *Dialogues* to the *Life* as inspired not only by a veneration for Martin and a wish to prove his superiority over the hermits,[15] but also by a desire to avenge the humiliation to Martin's memory caused by the election of Brictio — by a determination to prove to the Christians of Gaul that Tours had repudiated the greatest saint yet produced within the Empire. Of the quarrel with the Brictio faction Duchesne has said, ' everything that Sulpicius Severus wrote was with this controversy in mind.' [16]

Yet the revenge of Martin's party was sweet: this small group of texts on the miracles of Martin had an immediate and enduring success. Within seven years — if we may believe Postumianus [17] — it was known throughout the Roman-Christian world, in the East as well as in the West. Martin thereby became in Christian tradition just what Severus, in writing his book, intended that he should: the greatest miracle-worker not only of Gaul but of the whole Christian world.[18] What were the real wonders that he wrought we

11 *Dialogue* III 15.
12 Duchesne 1911 III 4 165.
13 Ibid.
14 See p. 185 n. 67.

15 *Dialogue* I 26, & III 2 & 17.
16 Duchesne 1911 III 4 165.
17 *Dialogue* I 23.
18 Monceaux 1926 88–94.

shall never know, but the wonders the book wrought were
incalculable: for through it, more than through any other
single influence, the idea of the saint as a wonder-worker took
root in the West.   And although, technically, we must suspect
a good deal of fabrication, we cannot doubt that Martin himself was a saintly and masterful figure.   More perhaps than
anything else, it was the memory of this Martin, of Pannonia,
Pavia, and Tours, that was gradually to bridge the gulf now
soon to yawn between Augustine and the barbarians.

Associated — we do not know how closely — with Severus
and his disciples at Toulouse,[19] was a certain priest, Vigilantius, hailing from southern Aquitaine.[20]   He had also — perhaps when in Barcelona — become the friend of Paulinus of
Nola.[21]   In 396 this Vigilantius had gone to Palestine fortified with a letter from Paulinus to Jerome; but he there quar-
relled with Jerome, taunting him with certain heretical propensities,[22] and, on his return home, he began to stir up a
variety of controversies.   By 404 he had gathered together
a group who sympathized with him, including some of the
bishops of his vicinity,[23] and in that year he wrote a treatise,
now lost, incorporating his views.[24]   With most of these we
have no concern here: they included marriage for deacons,
a judicious and piecemeal charity, a condemnation of the
monk's evasion of responsibilities, objection to the burning
of tapers — either at sunrise or at night [25] — but, above all, resentment against the growing cult of the saints.   Two years
later, in 406, Jerome answered Vigilantius in a typical invec-
tive which tells us almost all we know about him.[26]   Jerome
dealt with each of the disputed propositions of Vigilantius in
turn, but particularly with that one which concerns the saints
and which also particularly concerns us.

[19] Duchesne 1911 III 4 168.

[20] Convenae was perhaps the modern town of Martres: Jülicher 1908
XX 630 lines 46–48.

[21] Duchesne 1911 III 4 168. See
p. 175 n. 71. Shortly after his violent conversion in about 385, Paulinus left Bordeaux for Barcelona,
where he was ordained priest, passing
on to Nola only in 393.

[22] Duchesne 1911 III 4 169.

[23] Ibid. 170; Jülicher 1908 XX 629
lines 30–34.

[24] Jülicher ibid.

[25] Jerome Contra Vigilantium §§ 2,
13–14, 15–16 & 4, respectively.

[26] See bibliography in Jülicher
1908 XX 628 lines 4–14.

Vigilantius probably did not reject the miracles then daily occurring at the tombs of the saints — had he dared to do this Jerome would have told us; but he did cast doubt on them indirectly by his argument that miracles were only designed in order to overcome the resistance of the incredulous.[27]   The intimation must have been that the biblical miracles had occurred only for such a purpose.   Now, if this were so, real believers who invited miracles through prayers or ritual were not acting with proper piety.   In asking for some other gift in addition to faith they were asking for too much.   And there may have been a further insinuation: if God allows miracles only in order to inculcate faith, those alleged miracles that seem to aim at more may well instead be tricks of the devil, leading men on by cunning deceptions.   In other words, the more illicit the purpose of the miracle the less likely it is to be one.   For any miracle calculated to effect a material advantage is in flat contradiction to the words ' My kingdom is not of this world.'

Whether an alleged miracle really is one depends further on the person to whom the prayer which invites it is addressed: for Vigilantius did not believe that dead saints could pray and so intercede in answer to the prayers of men.   Jerome says to Vigilantius:

In your pamphlet you say that while we live we are able to pray for each other, but that after we have died the prayer of no one for another will be heard; and in particular since the martyrs, beseeching vengeance for their blood, were not able to get any satisfaction.[28]

Vigilantius had evidently cited *Revelations* vi 10:

And they [the martyrs] cried out with a loud voice, saying ' How long, O Lord, holy and true, dost thou not judge and avenge our blood on them that dwell on the earth?'

Jerome, however, simply parries this text with others.   He seems to think that no saint can be happy in heaven unless he

---

[27] Jerome *Contra Vigilantium* § 10 says: ' Let us grant that signs are for the incredulous who, since they have refused to believe through preaching and instruction, must be led to the faith by signs, and that the Lord produced these signs for the sake of the faithless; yet not for this reason are the signs to be reviled because these men were without faith, rather are they the more admirable because they are of such power that they can tame the hardest hearts and compel them to believe.' Cf. Cassian *Conlationes* XV 3.

[28] Jerome ibid. § 6.

can get vengeance wreaked on those who persecuted him on earth, and that, unless the saint can pray to God that He wreak such vengeance and unless God hear and heed that prayer, the earthly persecutor may never be punished. Such a conception is a sorry commentary on Jerome as a theologian. For why should a saint in heaven wish a vendetta? And why should God be just only when importuned?

But even if we assume, says Vigilantius, that the saints in heaven can and in fact do occupy their leisure in such ways, is it not absurd to suppose further that their souls haunt either their tombs or any other places on earth, so that they will more readily hear and heed the prayers of the living when offered in one place rather than in another? Jerome thus sarcastically addresses Vigilantius:

You say that the souls of the apostles and martyrs reside either in the bosom of Abraham, or in some cool spot, or below the altar of God, and that they cannot, leaving their tombs, be present wherever they choose. For, being of senatorial dignity forsooth, they are to be found, not among criminals in a foul prison, but in the free and honourable confinement of the Fortunate Isles and Elysian Fields.[29]

And a little later Jerome purports to quote Vigilantius' own words:

Do the souls of the martyrs then love their tombs, flutter about them so that they are constantly present — lest perhaps some sinner might present himself and they, if absent, would not be able to hear him?[30]

Catholic physics was at this time not yet crystallized. In the miracles told by Severus of Martin we observe that in certain cases, as of impending shipwreck[31] or other emergency, a mere prayer to a saint might suffice to avert disaster. Reliance on mere prayer, however, was risky, and it was therefore far safer to carry some relic of a saint on one's person — such a talisman having a definite physical power to communicate virtue, acquired through an earlier physical contact with the saint's own virtue. Whether the psychological effect

---

29 Ibid.
30 Ibid. § 8.
31 *Dialogue* III 14.

of the relic's virtue was on God's wrath, the saint's vanity, or the suppliant's sincerity might be a matter of doubt. Whatever the mechanics might be, the belief was that without the automatic physical power exercised by the relic there was a double risk: either the suppliant might lack the necessary contrition or the saint might lack the necessary alertness.

In these emergencies the relic and prayer alone were thought adequate because there was nothing more that a suppliant could then do. But since a portable relic must be small its power was thought greatly inferior to that possessed by the prime relic, which was the corpse itself. Therefore as often as the suppliant had both the leisure and the ability, it seemed natural that the saint should expect him to make some real sacrifice as a proof of his sincerity. Here an act of charity or abstinence would be helpful, but the safest course was a pilgrimage [32] to the spot where the corpse of the saint was, where physical contact could be made with those material objects which had in turn been in physical contact with the saint's soul during his earthly life. In this fourth century, when the corpses of the saints were still kept intact,[33] the whole physical virtue of the saint was concentrated at this single point. The sick man who could get to the tomb and pray there, hour after hour and day after day, believed he would gradually become so impregnated with the virtue emanating from it that the evil disease within him must, after a time, be overcome and consumed.

Here was a Catholic physics of which Vigilantius would take no account. This does not mean, however, that this was a new kind of physics first conceived by Catholics or even by Christians: on the contrary, untutored Roman Catholics were merely appropriating the current physics of the untutored Roman pagans who believed that by certain physical concatenations or formulas a certain physical effect could, almost automatically, be produced. The primitive laboratory

---

[32] On the records of fourth century pilgrimages see Dufourcq *L'Av.* 1910 IV[5] 128 n. 1: all those recorded are to the Holy Land — from Bordeaux in 333, from Brescia in 370, and from Spain in 388. Many certainly went to Rome as pilgrims, but from how far away we do not know:

see p. 166. Postumianus visited the tomb of Cyprian at Carthage on his way from Gaul to the East in about 400: *Dialogue* I 3. Gregory of Nyssa (born in about 334) was hostile to pilgrimages: Dufourcq ibid.

[33] See p. 174 n. 61.

was a curious mixture of a traditional hypothesis seemingly corroborated by empirical success.   Sometimes that success was due to real, although uncomprehended, physical laws; again it was due to real, although uncomprehended, psychological laws.   Here, as quoted by Jerome, is the complaint of Vigilantius:

Why is it necessary that you not only venerate with so great honour, but even adore this I know not what which you carry in a small urn? [34] . . . Why do you in adoration kiss ashes bound up in a cloth? . . . And in what follows we see introduced into the Church under pretext of religion what is very like the rite of the pagans; even with the sun shining masses of tapers are lit, and everywhere they adore and kiss I know not what bit of ashes wrapt in a costly cloth and put in an urn.   Men of this sort do great honour, indeed, to the most blessed martyrs, supposing that they must be glorified by most cheap tapers, to those martyrs whom the Lamb, who sits on the central throne in all the brilliance of His majesty, Himself glorifies.[35]

Jerome and Vigilantius were not at odds simply because, although both Catholics, they differed in their interpretation of the Bible; rather they differed because Jerome was a Roman who believed in magic and Vigilantius was a Roman who did not.   Nor should this surprise us: for the fundamental transformation effected by Christianity was in the understanding not of physics but of love.   Here, in this rather incidental problem of Christian theology, intellectually enlightened Romans — whether pagan or Christian — shared one view, while the more credulous shared the other.   In this fact there is nothing derogatory to Christianity: that its revelation was complete in the sense that it revealed the true laws of physics as well as the true laws of the heart, is a claim no responsible Christian has ever made.   And, since there had been no such revelation, no Christian could be blamed for adapting the old pagan physics to the new Christian situation, and thus utilizing the relic in order to strengthen the tie binding men to the new God.   That Vigilantius and others balked merely reminds us that these may have found other, less material, ways of effecting this essential contact.

[34] Was it the pagans or the Christians who burnt the martyrs' corpses? Cf. Eusebius *Eccl. Hist.* V 1 § 62.

[35] Jerome *Contra Vigilantium* § 4.

At the turn of the century we see Jerome in the East championing the wonders told of the hermits; in Tours we see Brictio momentarily triumphant over the memory of Martin; in Aquitaine we see the views of Jerome and Severus challenged by Vigilantius; from Spain Prudentius is about to journey to Rome, with his story of Vincent already accepted and all on the alert to learn what he might of the wonders done in Italy. What was the state of affairs there?

The attitude of Pope Damasus, who had died in 384, was one of moderation: on the one hand he had taken pains to carve on the tombs of many of the martyrs a variety of bad verses — which often wound up with a prayer that they help him to salvation; [36] on the other hand, he deliberately ignored the many stories already cropping up of the alleged wonders these martyrs had performed.[37] Much as he cherished their memory and longed for their help, he was not ready to sacrifice historical truth in the name of edification — to countenance the dissemination of uncorroborated stories merely because they would, if believed, promote the worldly interests of faith. Since faith was truth it must respect the truth. He did not reject the stories as false; he merely ignored them until or unless it could be proved that they were true.[38]

Ambrose, the public official and man of action who had died in 397, was not so squeamish. Caring even more for results [39] than for principles, he deceived himself — and so of course others — in the interest of a noble expediency. Ambrose was a romantic; in contrast to Augustine he allowed the intoxicating fumes of the new Revelation to cloud his judgment.

Infinitely less engaging and arresting was the court poet Claudian who, although born in Egypt, was probably of Ital-

[36] See *Damasi Epigrammata* ed. Max Ihm 1895; & Schäfer 1932 160.

[37] Of the twenty-six inscriptions by Damasus carved in order to preserve the memories of the Roman martyrs and other holy persons, the only suggestion of a miracle — beyond the hope expressed of a future spiritual intercession — is an episode in the inscription for Eutychius: ' One drowsy night dreams filled the mind [of Damasus], and the hiding-place that contained the bones of this innocent man revealed itself [to him] ': Schäfer 1932 101.

[38] Ibid. 160 says: ' Wir wissen dass Damasus hier und da sein Misstrauen der von ihm wiedergegebenen Tradition gegenüber nicht verschweigt.' He evidently accepted current stories readily if they were not miraculous, but rejected equally well accredited miracles: ibid. 162.

[39] On Ambrose's practical attitude see Dudden 1935 535–37 & 554.

ian extraction.[40]   Nominally a Christian — as his conventional poem *De Salvatore* [41] indicates — at heart he was always a pagan,[42] and the new faith was merely a convenience,
that he might not lose the favour of the imperial court in
Ravenna.   One poem of his which is of particular interest
opens thus:

By the ashes of St Paul and the shrine of revered St Peter,
Do not pull my verses to pieces General James.
May St Thomas then prove a buckler to protect thy breast
And St Bartholomew bear thee company to the wars;
May the blessed saints then prevent the barbarians from crossing
    the Alps
And Suzanna endow thee with her strength;
Thus, should any savage foe seek to swim the Danube,
Let him be drowned in it like the swift chariots of Pharaoh;
Then too may an avenging javelin strike the Getic hordes
And the favour of Thecla guide the armies of Rome.[43]

Claudian is apparently poking fun at the credulity of a certain James, a cavalry officer, who, in order to achieve his military successes, was inclined to rely rather on the saints than
on his own wits.   The thing is neither funny nor profound,
but it does suggest that the court of Ravenna was, in the year
401,[44] still pagan enough to enjoy a joke at the Christian who
took his saints too seriously.   It might be argued that it is not
so much the saints that are ridiculed as the service for which
James implores their intercession; but I think that if this
were so Claudian would have expressed himself differently.
A strong suspicion remains that in the aristocratic and fashionable circles of Ravenna the saints were still the object of
jibes rather than of prayers.

In the Africa of this day there were many Manichees, influential enough to win the adherence of the young Augustine
and to hold it during the nine years from 373 to 382.   The
leader of the sect was a certain Faustus, of Mileve near Cirta,
and, just as we know the opinions of Vigilantius only through

---

[40] *Encycl. Brit.* 1910 VI [11] 463D.
[41] *Carmina   Minorum   Corpusculum* # 40.
[42] More than ten years after the
death of Claudian Augustine spoke
of 'the poet Claudian, although an
alien from the name of Christ' etc.:

[D.C.D.] V 26.   And Orosius writing
in 417 calls Claudian 'a most stubborn pagan': *H.A.P.* VII 35 § 21.
[43] *Carmina   Minorum   Corpusculum* # 50.
[44] Birt 1892 lxii.

Jerome's attack on him, so we know the opinions of Faustus
only through Augustine's attack on him [45] — a long work was
this *Contra Faustum Manichæum*, written in the year 400
and largely concerned with their conflicting arguments regarding the divinity of the Old Testament. Augustine pre-
sents the arguments of Faustus at some length and as if in
Faustus' own language; he certainly tried to be fair and his
nine years as a member of the sect thoroughly qualified him
to expound its real tenets. If we have not the real Faustus
here we at least have a skilful imitation of him.

Book XX is the most interesting one to us. In it Faustus
is represented as arguing that the Manichæan doctrine, with
its frank dualism, is the only really novel religion: pagans,
Jews, and Catholics alike holding to the theory of a single
principle governing the world — the pagans being, no doubt,
the Stoics and Neoplatonists. The essence of this monistic
conception, says Faustus,

is that all things, good and evil, mean and glorious, fading and
unfading, changeable and unchangeable, material and divine,
have only one principle. In opposition to this my belief is that
God is the principle of all good things, and *Hyle* [which is matter]
of the opposite. *Hyle* is the name given by our master in divinity
to the principle or nature of evil. The pagans accordingly think
it right to worship God with altars, shrines, images, sacrifices and
incense. Here also my practice differs entirely from theirs: for I
look on myself as a reasonable temple of God, if I am worthy to
be so; and I consider Christ His Son as the living image of His
living majesty; and I hold a mind well cultivated to be the true
altar, and pure and simple prayers to be the true way of paying
divine honours and of offering sacrifices. Does this constitute a
mere schism with the pagans? . . .[46]
In a schism little or no change is made from the original; as for
instance you, in your schism from the Gentiles, have brought with
you the doctrine of a single principle, for you believe that all
things are of God. The sacrifices you change into love feasts, the
idols into martyrs to whom you pray as they do to their idols.
You appease the shades of the departed with wine and food. You
keep the same holidays as the Gentiles: for example, the calends
and solstices. In your way of living you have made no change.
. . . The fact is there are only two sects, the Gentiles and ourselves.[47]

    45 Augustine mentions him in   46 *Contra Faustum* XX § 3.
Confessions V 3, 5, & 13.   47 Ibid. § 4.

Augustine effectively demolishes most of the philosophical part of the argument, showing on the one hand how close to dualism the Neoplatonic conception was, and on the other how different in conception was the Catholic veneration of the martyrs from the pagan worship of heterogeneous deities. Only it would seem that on this latter point the issue was not fully met: for, however anxious Augustine certainly was to distract attention from the martyrs —

whom we regard with the same affectionate intimacy that we feel towards holy men of God in this life — [48]

the fact was that the fast growing Catholic population was not so easily weaned of its pagan habits. Had the Catholic authorities not been tolerant of the popular enthusiasm for the martyrs, the popular enthusiasm for Catholicism might have suffered. Like Vigilantius, Faustus refused to recognize that every success, however noble, has its price. These two men were, by disposition, Protestants; they lacked the wisdom of Augustine which, like all wisdom, included worldly wisdom.

The two most enlightened Roman circles of the year 400 were those described by Macrobius [49] in his Neoplatonic *Saturnalia* and by Augustine in his *Confessions*. It cannot be accidental that while these circles were both Italian and even Roman, both the writers were African. Our last picture of enlightened antiquity is therefore an African picture; there was the last stronghold of both philosophy and ethics, of science and psychology.

Nor can it be accidental that to both the Neoplatonist and the Christian the paramount conception was of One God — of a centralization of power as best adapted to explain a world of order. For, with a multiplicity of gods, each with his own axe to grind, how could there be order in the natural world? Such divine government might still be hierarchical, with a Jupiter, a One, or a Jehovah in legal control, but, to the extent that the power of the Master was not complete, the teleo-

[48] Ibid. § 21.
[49] Macrobius flourished between about 384 and 423.

logical end in view might be approaching only circuitously, by cancelling one error against another. Hence it may well be that the contrasting monotheistic conception was at this time being induced by a vivid consciousness of a natural law, by the inference that the observed ineluctability of events was consistent only with the harmony of a single will.

Just as Augustine's doctrine of predestination was evolved out of a conviction that man's will is governed by a power outside itself, so the Neoplatonic doctrine expounded by Macrobius was evolved out of a conviction that the motion of things is governed from without. Each saw reality as ordered, the one by a supernatural Mind, the other by an organic device. But both see a Law that governs, a Law which no other power, natural or supernatural, can in the least affect or deflect. Whether the Will seem relatively human or inhuman, that Will is the only Will, the only Cause.

Macrobius was not original as a scientist, he was not born in the right age for such good fortune; but his learning was vast, his understanding superior, and his astronomy well bears comparison with that of any Latin of an earlier age.[50] Granted that his sources of information were chiefly Greek,[51] at least he knew where the best information was to be had and knew enough, having found it, to recognize its merit. Taken as a whole, of course, the Macrobian explanation of reality is incomparably inferior to that given by Augustine; if it shares much of the Augustinian enlightenment it has no share of the talent. Perhaps on only one point is Macrobius definitely superior: his understanding of cosmology and astronomy is as solid, for its day, as that of Augustine is tenuous. Not that Augustine held views of a more primitive kind; it was rather that on such matters as these he was never able really to concentrate. Being unable to see what significance they might have in his theological system, he unconsciously dismissed their problems as academic.[52]

This is not the place to give any extended exposition of

---

[50] The only Latin predecessors of Macrobius who seem to have been his equals in understanding of astronomy were Vitruvius (fl. under Augustus) and Seneca (fl. under Tiberius): Boquet 1925 105, 118, & 121.

[51] That is, from the Greek speaking Eastern half of the Empire.

[52] Fortified by his suspicion that the current astronomical hypotheses were largely guess-work.

Macrobian science; at the same time the *Commentary*, since it was written by an African contemporary of Augustine and was widely read by the very Roman aristocracy which was still the decisive intellectual force in the West, may not be wholly ignored. For it indicates what, in the year 400, was the scientific knowledge that the pagan could pit against the rising tide of theological faith. At least it serves to show, I think, that decline in understanding of the outer world cannot have been one of the causes of the reaction from it. During the later fifth and following centuries this understanding did decline — at a fearful rate — but this decline did not set in until after Catholicism had become fully ensconced.

One point of cosmology should be observed: whereas Augustine denies that the antipodes are inhabited — for if so Christ did not reveal Truth to all mankind [53] — Macrobius is certain that they are inhabited, and for this reason: the temperate zone is climatically as suited to men in the south as in the north. If we deny inhabitants to the south temperate zone — either because we have never been there or because they must soon fall off — they may, with equal logic, deny us.[54] We may well ask, why did no one explore beyond the equator in order to see for himself? The reason of both writers, as of most of antiquity, was their belief that the intervening equatorial region was too hot for human life to endure.

Of the minuteness of the earth in comparison with the sky Macrobius has no illusions:

The earth is, in comparison with the sky, a mere measure of quantity, that is, a point which cannot be divided [into anything smaller].[55]

Furthermore, in the face of Aristotle and Ptolemy, and following rather an old Egyptian belief,[56] he argues that the planets Venus and Mercury revolve round the sun as a centre, instead of round the earth; [57] and, that this is not an isolated

---

[53] ' But as to the fable that there are antipodes, that is to say, men on the opposite side of the earth where the sun rises when it sets on us and who walk with their feet opposite ours, that is on no account credible ': *D.C.D.* XVI 9.

[54] *Commentary* II § 5. Lucretius had denied that the antipodes were inhabited: Boquet 1925 112.
[55] *Commentary* II § 9. Ptolemy had said no less: Boquet 1925 127.
[56] Berry 1898 99.
[57] *Commentary* II § 4.

opinion, is shown by an identical statement in the work of another African of that day, Martianus Capella.[58] Now this view, which was not approached again until the fifteenth century [59] and which then proved the opening wedge to the overthrow of the Ptolemaic system, is not to be found in Augustine or, so far as I know, in any Christian writer of this time. Man having been set as master over the rest of creation, the Christian did not relish the idea that any planets should revolve, not round man's earth, but round the Neoplatonic sun.

But Macrobius goes even further than this. The theory of Aristotle and Ptolemy was that all motion was transmitted by a First Mover to the outer sphere of fixed stars, and that this outer sphere in its turn moved the next one inside it, and so on down to the moon. Macrobius accepts this theory in general,[60] but he has noticed that the planets, and so the spheres to which these correspond, do not in fact follow the outer sphere but on the contrary have motions of their own which at times run directly counter to the outer motion. Doubtless they are chiefly drawn by the great outer sphere, but they must also be under the influence of something else. What might this be? Enumerating each sphere in turn, he says,

Next the fierce and bloody meteor of Mars, next, almost at the centre of this region, the sun dominates — chief, king, and regulator of the other celestial torches, intelligence and regulating principle of the whole world.[61]

Why, since the sun is almost at the centre — that is, almost half-way between the outer sphere and the earth — and since it is by so much the largest, should it not be the sun which

---

[58] *De Nuptiis* VIII § 857. Vitruvius is apparently the only other Latin writer to allege this: Boquet 1925 105. Capella flourished somewhere between 410 and 439: *Encicl. Ital.* 1930 VIII 832; Monceaux 1894 445–46. Thus Capella probably wrote after Macrobius had written his *Commentary* and could therefore have taken the idea from it, although that idea was probably fairly current in the Africa of this time. Copernicus got this idea from Capella, but this may merely mean that he first ran across it there: Berry 1898 99.

[59] That is, if we can regard the view of Nicholas of Cusa (1401–1464) as comparable. Cusa is supposed to have believed that the earth, sun, and other planets all revolved round a point in space as their common axis: Gerland 1913 223.

[60] *Commentary* II § 4: ' ergo orbis altissimus, et ut in immensum patens, et ut spiritu eo fortiori, quo origini suae vicinior est, incitatus.'

[61] Ibid. I § 17.

gives to the planets their individual motions contrary to that
of the outer sphere?

Each planet must traverse a given space before reaching its point
of maximum distance from the sun. Having reached that point
beyond which it cannot go, it appears to recede, and, when it has
reached the point fixed for its retrograde motion, it again goes
forward.[62]

We may smile as we please at the many extravagances in the
pagan beliefs of that day, nor are we naturally sympathetic
with the notions of the fourth century syncretists who merged
Neoplatonism with sun-worship. That sun-worship was actually induced by the Copernican instincts of the astronomers
we certainly may not affirm; at the same time it seems likely
that the fourth century sun-worshippers were getting very
close to Copernican ideas. The heliocentric theory of Aristarchus was then surely available and known.[63] A slight shift
of emphasis, a single mind of talent, might have drawn the
African Neoplatonists into the fertile way leading to Copernicus and so, perhaps, to Galileo. Macrobius says:

According to certain others whose opinion seems the more probable, the stars which we call fixed have, like the planets, a motion
of their own as well as one in common with the sky. But, because
of the immensity of the outermost sphere, they take an incredible
number of centuries to make one cycle in their course; hence their
motion is not perceptible to man, because the span of human life
is not long enough to admit the detection of a mere small fraction
of so slow a cycle of motion.[64]

Macrobius cannot here have in mind the variations in the
positions of the fixed stars caused by the earth's orbit,[65] for
these variations are annual; nor can he have in mind the variations in their apparent velocities due to the precession of the
equinox, for this would still be a common motion in the sense
that each fixed star would still be in the same position in re-

---

[62] Ibid. § 20.
[63] There is at least no evidence
that it was ever really lost.
[64] *Commentary* I § 17. Dufourcq
L'Av. 1910 IV 5 177 n. 1, says that
this conception, originating with
Hipparchus and adopted by Ptolemy,
was also accepted by Origen. Macrobius was therefore probably following a concrete Alexandrian tradition.

[65] These variations of course
actually occur whether the orbit of
the earth be taken into account or
not. Since Macrobius did not think
that the earth moved, in an orbit or
otherwise, he cannot merely have
meant that the fixed stars changed
their positions relative to the earth.

lation to all the others. This would hardly constitute ' a motion of their own as well as a common motion.' Moreover his analogy is specifically to the planets and so involves definite changes in the relative positions of the fixed stars to each other. This does not assume a difference in distance from the earth and so an indeterminate and even infinite thickness of the sphere of fixed stars, but does destroy the concept of that sphere as a solid in which each star is embedded like so many raisins in a cake. I cannot see that even Galileo, with his telescope, went further than this; [66] certainly until Halley in 1718 there was no successful demonstration of it.[67]

Thus A'ugustine, the most distinguished Catholic of his time, grew up in an environment where also flourished the most talented Manichee and the most talented Neoplatonist of the age. It took Augustine nine years to appreciate the folly of Faustus' doctrine; it took Latin Europe over a thousand years to appreciate certain of Macrobius' astronomical hypotheses. Therefore before considering the attitude of Augustine towards miracles it is well to realize how different were the Carthaginian circles he frequented in his youth from the military circles where Martin was educated.

F. Augustine on Miracles

The conventional Catholic theory of the miracle is best exemplified by Jerome. Although primarily a scholar and an ascetic, he also dabbled, if with small success, in theology He attacked Pelagius [1] and he attacked Origen,[2] his learning was prodigious,[3] his opinions were usually sound,[4] but he had no originality; he was fertile in revealing new facts but sterile

---

66 Berry 1898 164.
67 Ibid. 255.

1 In *Dialogus adversus Pelagianos.*
2 In *Apologia adversus libros Rufinum.*
3 His greatest achievement was of course his Latin translation, from the original Hebrew and Greek, of the Bible — the Vulgate version — and hi great Commentaries on this.

4 Although harping on the lewd ness of marriage was surely in ba taste.

in conceiving new hypotheses. He could judiciously weigh two conflicting opinions advanced by others but he could not formulate any of his own. He could learn and teach, but, being without imagination, he could not invent.

Consequently his explanation of the miracle is just what we should expect:

When both the original text and the other expounders agree with equal authority, the difficulty is not in the Scriptural text but in the meaning. For what mortal would believe that a boy of eleven could engender a son? And many other things are said in Scripture which seem incredible and yet are true. For nature cannot prevail against the Lord of nature.[5]

The true explanation is that when anything is done against nature it is a manifestation of God's might and power. And, in order to show plainly that in these great signs our attention is called, not to a change in nature, but to the almighty power of God, he who by faith had walked on water began to sink for want of it and would have done so had not the Lord lifted him up.[6]

This is not even a view peculiar to Christianity, but rather the traditional and conventional view of antiquity. Originally Fate had been sovereign, ruling even over the gods, and the ancient mythology had in a sense been the story of how some god had gradually learned to manipulate and guide that Fate, bending it more and more to his will. The personal divinity had learned how in some measure to obstruct, suspend, and correct the blind and independent course of Destiny which was ever moving on, oblivious of justice or of any rational end. Fate is the unmanned ship, and this god a captain who harnesses the force of wind and wave, of sail and keel, driving her as he chooses. But since these forces are not his creatures he must subdue them to his will — tack into a head wind, heave to in a gale, lay on with the oars when the wind fails. The Christians' faith in their God's control over nature was heightened by their faith that He had Himself created it: this was a further step in the evolution of the teleological concept. Nevertheless, to Jerome as to most other Christians, nature was thought a separate entity, with powers which God had originally infused but which now operated automatically. Nature was a tool skilfully designed

---

[5] *Letter* # 72 § 2 (of 398).   [6] Ibid. # 108 § 24 (of 404).

for a purpose, but still a tool that could only effect that purpose if handled with unremitting care. To Jerome, therefore, the Christian miracle was hardly more than the pagan miracle under a new name: it was still a revelation of the power of a personal God to control the vagaries of an impersonal Fate.

That Augustine's conception, unlike Jerome's, should mark a departure from the conventional view of antiquity need not surprise us: for from his insistence on God's omnificence he was bound to conclude that no other power than God could possibly be the cause of any — even the most commonplace — event. Therefore:

> Not even the devil himself is outside of God's government, since the devil's nature subsists only by the supreme Creator, who gives being to all in any form that exists.[7]

> The power delegated to the demons at certain appointed and well-adjusted seasons, that they may give expression to their hostility . . . is found to be not merely harmless but even useful to the Church.[8]

Ordinary man, too, was of course eliminated as a factor by the doctrine of predestination: whether through the medium of divine grace or his own evil propensities, he was inexorably moved by God.[9] But particularly important to us is Augustine's extension of this assumption to include the martyrs and other saints. When, between 415 and 426, he was writing his *City of God,* the stories of Athanasius and Jerome, of Prudentius, Paulinus, and Severus, of Postumianus and Rufinus, were already old favourites, and in many places churches had been, or were being, built to honour a saint and to house the multitudes who hoped there to receive special favours and mercies. Under such circumstances Augustine might well have felt embarrassed: to him the virtues of the martyrs were merely so many manifestations of the might of the divine grace; their characters, their courage, their merits, were gifts arbitrarily bestowed on souls by themselves wholly undeserving.[10] The

---

[7] *D.C.D.* XXII 24 *(D. & K.* II 610 lines 19–21).

[8] Ibid. X 21; & cf. *De Trinitate* XIII § 16.

[9] See pp. 129–32.

[10] See pp. 397–98.

Church, in sanctioning the veneration of such men, was in fact encouraging hero-worship, was countenancing the false and insidious notion that a man might be something — and perhaps a great deal — more than a nothing.[11]   Such a story as that related by Postumianus, of the hermit who kept his magical powers after succumbing to pride,[12] was not of a kind to allay Augustine's anxiety.   In the course of a Sermon on the martyr Fructuosus he had said:

Whenever a certain person spoke to him, and begged that he keep him in mind and pray for him, he answered, ' I am bound to pray for the catholic Church in its full extension from east to west.' For who, indeed, prays for individuals?   Yet he who prays for all ignores no individual.[13]

Now if this be so, a suppliant wastes his breath in asking for personal help — at best he can ask only for help in behalf of all Catholics indiscriminately.   Conversely, Augustine says elsewhere,

His saints, inspired by His holy will, desire many things that never happen.   They pray, as for certain individuals; they pray in a pious and holy manner; but what they request He does not perform, even though He Himself by His own Holy Spirit has wrought in them this will to pray.[14]

The martyr or saint, therefore, is distinguishable from other men only in so far as he is indistinguishable from God:

For they are not our gods, but their God is our God.   Certainly we honour their reliquaries as the memorials of holy men of God who strove for the truth even to the death of their bodies. . . . But . . . whatever honours the religious may pay in the places of the martyrs, they are but honours rendered to their memory.[15]

The churches which had been, or were about to be, dedicated to this or that martyr, were undeniably built for them, but wholly as symbols of God's grace and not at all as symbols of human merit.   And in one passage Augustine seems actually to disparage the martyrs:

If the Decii [of old] dedicated themselves to death, consecrating themselves in a form of words as it were that, falling, and pacify-

[11] See pp. 75 n. 19, & 130 n. 49.
[12] See pp. 180–81.
[13] *Sermon* # 273 § 2.   Cf. p. 159 n. 43.
[14] *D.C.D.* XXII 2.
[15] Ibid. VIII 27.

ing by their blood the wrath of the gods, they might be the means of delivering the Roman army; if they did this, let not the holy martyrs carry themselves proudly, as though they had done some meritorious thing for a share in that country where are eternal life and felicity.[16]

To be a true saint one must be humble; but this humility, difficult enough to achieve under the most favourable circumstances, would be impossible if it were believed that merit caused that humility. Never was more wholesome doctrine expounded, for to Augustine the omnificence of God was chiefly predicated on the Christian reverence for humility.

Augustine must, of course, shrink from an open controversy which would rouse such men as Severus against him. Therefore he spoke without heat. But he did not mince his words. If he must err, let this be on the side of Neoplatonism rather than of polytheism.

By denial of the devil's power Augustine refuted the Manichees; by denial of man's — and even the martyrs' — power he refuted the pagans and Pelagians; [17] but he had also, by a denial of nature's power, to refute the Neoplatonists. Therefore of God he says:

were He to withdraw His efficacious power from things, they would not be able either to go on and complete the periods assigned to their measured movements, or even to continue in possession of that nature they were created in.[18]

In order to understand what Augustine meant here we must recall the antique conception of the laws of motion, which was based on the explanation given by Aristotle.

Today we are wholly familiar with that law according to which a body, once in motion, because of its inertia continues in motion except in so far as some obstacle retards it. Air is the most familiar obstacle; where there is none, as in the heavens, the planets continue at a constant speed for the very reason that there is nothing to stop them. This seems so obvious an explanation that it is hard to bear in mind that it

---

[16] *D.C.D.* V 18. And cf. his *De Cura pro Mortuis Gerenda* § 19: 'The dead are not able by their own nature to affect the affairs of the living.'

[17] Paulinus of Nola and Severus were both for a time seduced by the Pelagian doctrine.

[18] *D.C.D.* XXII 24 (*D. & K.* II 610 lines 27–30), quoted p. 115 n. 52; & cf. Tixeront 1921 II [6] 375.

was first successfully propounded by Galileo,[19] and that antiquity held Aristotle's very different conception. That old view was based on the gratuitous assumption that rest is natural to bodies,[20] on which account they move only so long as they are impelled from without: thus the hurled spear moves only so long as the air currents, rushing in to fill the vacuum left in its wake, drive it on by this impact.[21] This was why Aristotle taught that each planet was embedded in a solid sphere, and that, as this sphere moved the planet, so was it moved itself by the friction of the sphere immediately outside it. Motion, therefore, implied power constantly operative, and this was supplied by the famous First Mover which, without itself moving, moved the outermost sphere of the fixed stars — which in turn moved the sphere next inside it and thereby transmitted the initial power by successive stages to the earth.

It is easy to see how, out of this theory, grew not only the propensity to believe in astrology or the power of the heavenly bodies to direct human affairs, but also the belief in a single supreme power, physically if not absolutely the cause of all motion and so of all change — and so of all life. The Epicureans, said Augustine,

alleged that human affairs did not have the care of the gods,[22]

but, so long as it was supposed that all motion depended on the constant application of an external heavenly power, their intuition, however acute, was in defiance of the laws of physics as then understood. The claim of the fifth century Epicureans that God might long ago have abdicated [23] was not heeded, therefore, until revived by Descartes [24] in the light of Galileo's demonstration. Of course, even according to the Aristotelian theory, a body could continue to move for a time after the motive power had been withdrawn, but, should this

[19] Although Philoponos, an Alexandrian born in about 475, had an intuition of the Galilean theory: see Gerland 1913 141–42; Reymond 1925 201; & Sarton 1927 422; as did also Occam in about 1323: *Quaestiones et Decisiones in IV Libros Sententiarum* II qu. 26; & cf. p. 208 n. 59 on Nicholas of Cusa.

[20] Except that certain bodies move, as when rising or falling, because they are seeking to regain their natural positions.

[21] Reymond [1927] 189.

[22] *D.C.D.* XVIII 41.

[23] See Salvian *D.G.D.* I § 20, quoted p. 346 n. 71.

[24] See Maugain 1909 158.

in fact occur, the heavenly bodies would move ever more slowly, each day, month, and year being longer than the last. Since tradition and observation, however, showed that this had never occurred and was not now occurring, it seemed evident that a power was being constantly applied; otherwise a planet, like a cast spear, must, in a short time, cease to move. In the light of this change it becomes fairly clear, I think, why the vogue of astrology, of Aristotle's physics, and of Augustine's philosophy ended together, almost simultaneously, in the third quarter of the seventeenth century.[25]

But if God is equally and exclusively the cause of every event, no one event can be more or less miraculous than any other: if there is in fact only one kind of event, all events must be equally miraculous and therefore equally unmiraculous. That this is indeed Augustine's view appears from a passage where he is arguing for the probable truth of Varro's statement that to the planet Venus there once

occurred so strange a prodigy that she changed her colour, size, form, and course, which never happened before or since.

For he observes that

so great an author as Varro would certainly not have called this a portent had it not seemed to be contrary to nature. For we say that all portents are contrary to nature; but they are not so. For how is that contrary to nature which happens by the will of God, since the will of so mighty a Creator is certainly the nature of each created thing? A portent, therefore, happens not contrary to nature, but contrary to what we know of nature.[26]

This is a thrust, not only at the pagans, but also at those Christians who felt a little too smug about their knowledge of the laws of nature, and who, therefore, were too ready to assume that any event which was inexplicable to them was on that account also contrary to those laws. And, not satisfied with this thrust, he strikes next at those Epicureans who refused to believe any story which could not be reconciled with their feeble understanding of nature:

as if divine power cannot bring to pass in an object anything else than what their own experience has shown them to be its nature.[27]

---

[25] Pickman 1932 226–29 & 241–43.   [27] Ibid.
[26] D.C.D. XXI 8.

This view of Augustine's, therefore, was a wholly rational and even profound inference from what he had learned of human nature — including what he had learned of the vanity as well as of the stupidity of scientists.

And Augustine here allowed history, as well as his own observation of human nature, to enlighten him: referring to a legend of the time of Romulus he says,

> For an eclipse of the sun had also happened; and this, by the ignorant multitude who did not know that it was brought about by the fixed laws of the sun's course, was attributed to the divine power of Romulus.[28]

From this episode out of the past he needed only to infer that present, like past, comprehension was no more than relative ignorance. As the multitude of that earlier day were mystified by an eclipse, so in his day were they no less mystified by such phenomena as comets.[29] Intrinsically, therefore, the present criterion was no better than the early one: a miracle was not to be measured by anything so feeble as current understanding.

Augustine next goes on to say that, bad as this test must be, the test which is in fact usually applied is even less sensible: for this is not according to any real understanding of the process, but rather according to the frequency or rarity of the occurrence. Thus an everyday occurrence, however inexplicable, is on that account alone regarded as natural. Speaking of the creation of Adam, and of Eve from a bone taken from Adam's side, he says,

> But this seems fabulous rather than true to men, who measure by customary and everyday works the power and wisdom of God, whereby He understands and produces without seeds even seeds themselves; and because they cannot understand the things which at the beginning were created, they are sceptical regarding them — as if the very things which they do know about human propagation, conception and births, would seem less incredible if told to those who had no experience of them; though these very things, too, are attributed by many rather to physical and natural causes than to the work of the divine mind.[30]

28 Ibid. III 15.
29 Seneca was almost alone among the ancients in arguing that comets, like the planets, had orbits and would therefore return at predetermined times: Boquet 1925 118 & 121.
30 D.C.D. XII 23.

Or, as he later repeats the idea,

Even the very things which are most commonly known as natural would not be less wonderful — or less effectual to excite surprise in all who beheld them — were it not that men are accustomed to admire nothing except what is rare.[31]

He is also impressed by the fact that, although all men are obviously of like nature, it is rather when two men look alike that there are exclamations of surprise. Actually

the unlikeness is the more wonderful consideration of the two. . . . And yet, because the very rarity of things is that which makes them wonderful, we are filled with much the greater wonder when we are introduced to two men so like that we either always or frequently mistake in endeavouring to distinguish between them.[32]

He also uses inanimate objects as illustrations: the magnet is of course one instance.[33] Another is lime, which

itself cold to the touch . . . yet has a hidden store of fire. . . . The marvellous thing is, that this fire is kindled when it is extinguished. For in order to disengage the hidden fire the lime is moistened or drenched with water, and then, though it be cold before, it becomes hot by that very application which cools what is hot.[34]

Most picturesque is this question:

But who can explain the strange properties of fire itself, which blackens everything it burns, though itself bright; and which, though of the most beautiful colours, discolours almost all it touches and feeds upon? [35]

Augustine knew as well as anyone else that fire had once been worshipped as divine, even as by many the sun was in his day. Why was it not divine? Because it was once rare and is now common shall we conclude that it was once divine yet is now natural? But there is one greatest marvel of all, and at the same time beyond all others the least explicable:

Whatever marvel happens in this world it is certainly less marvellous than this whole world itself — I mean the sky and earth, and all that is in them — and these God certainly made.[36]

[31] *D.C.D.* XXI 8.
[32] Ibid.
[33] Ibid. XXI 4.
[34] Ibid.
[35] Ibid.
[36] Ibid. X 12.

To this ingenious doctrine of the single kind of event there is a curious corollary: for it is evident that God, who has planned that everything come to pass as it in fact has, must have intended that mankind should mistake what was in fact miraculous for something natural, or, to put it the other way, should take what was not different in kind from all other events for something very special and peculiar. Augustine must therefore determine if he could why God had done this.

In the case of the eclipse, quoted above, which, ' by the ignorant multitude . . . was attributed to the divine power of Romulus ', God must have wished to deceive them, and for some good reason, which, though Augustine does not say so, was probably that the Romans might the more readily submit to that orderly civil government out of which the greater Rome, pre-ordained cradle of Christianity, should in time evolve. But if Augustine does not here, in regard to the pre-Redemption era, trouble to analyze the divine intent, in another passage he lays down, very lucidly, the reason why, after the Redemption, the apparent or, as he terms it, the visible miracle was still so liberally employed:

God, who made the visible heaven and earth, does not disdain to work visible miracles in heaven and earth, that He may thereby awaken the soul which is immersed in things visible to worship Himself, the Invisible.[37]

Within this miracle doctrine, however, lurks danger: if it should become generally recognized — as it already was by Augustine — that events were miraculous only in so far as they were rare, God could no longer awaken man's drowsy soul by a rare event. In such an eventuality it could be plausibly argued that, since the object of the apparent miracle was to teach the ignorant of God's omnificence, it would cease the moment this lesson had been learned. Yet such an argument would be most dangerous because it happens that the more man understands God's omnificence the more likely he is to misunderstand His nature. At least if we may take Descartes [38] as the continuator of Augustine we observe that a God who is the cause of everything soon comes to be every-

[37] Ibid. Cf. the view of Vigilantius, see p. 198 n. 27.
[38] See Pickman 1932 229; & cf.

Maimonides (c. 1185) Guide for the Perplexed 37 prop. 6.

thing: He who moves nature is nature, He who moves man's will is man's will.[39] A God who chooses to reveal Himself as independent of checks and balances invites the logician, at any rate, to flirt with the pantheism of a Spinoza.

Such was Augustine's theoretical view of the miracle. Does it suggest what his practical view was likely to be? That is, regarding his credulity or incredulity when confronted with concrete cases? Logically his view encouraged a detached and judicious attitude: for, as it did not induce a fear that the inexplicable occur,[40] neither did it induce a fear that it might not.[41] That he followed this logic in practice is evident from a letter of his, written in 404, dealing with a controversy between two of his clergy. Since there was no other evidence than their mutually contradictory statements,

I fixed upon the following as a means of discovering the truth. Both pledged themselves in a solemn compact to go to a holy place, where the more awe-inspiring works of God might much more readily make manifest the evil of which either of them was conscious, and compel the guilty to confess, either by judgment or through fear of judgment. God is everywhere, it is true, and He that made all things is not contained or confined to dwell in any place; and He is to be worshipped in spirit and in truth by His true worshippers, in order that, as He hears in secret, He may also in secret justify and reward. But in regard to the answers to prayer which are visible to men, who can search out His reasons for appointing some places rather than others to be the scene of miraculous interpositions? To many the holiness of the place in which the body of the blessed Felix is buried is well known, and to this place I desired them to repair; because from it we may receive more easily and reliably a written account of what may be discovered in either of them by divine interposition. For I myself know how, at Milan, at the tomb of the saints, where demons are brought in a most marvellous and awful manner to confess their deeds, a thief who had come thither intending to deceive by perjuring himself, was compelled to own his theft, and to restore what he had taken away; and is not Africa also full of the bodies of holy martyrs? Yet we do not know of such things being done in any place here. Even as the gift of healing and the gift of discerning of spirits are not given to all saints [I *Cor.* xii 9–10 & 30],

---

[39] See pp. 75–76, 129–32, & 400.
[40] Such as the Epicureans harboured.
[41] Such as most Christians harboured.

as the apostle declares; so it is not at all the tombs of the saints that it has pleased Him who divideth to each severally as He will, to cause such miracles to be wrought.[42]

I quote this at such length partly in order to show how open-minded Augustine was. He showed no slightest inclination to believe in any apparent miracle unless there were concrete evidence. But I quote partly too in order to call attention to the passage 'and compel the guilty to confess, either by judgment or through fear of judgment.' He seems here to recognize that in many cases the apparent miracle may in fact be caused by fear and so be what to the sceptic was a wholly natural phenomenon. But whether or not this was the true explanation did not matter to him, and not only because the truth would in either case be revealed, but also because in either case the result would be a direct effect of God's will.

This quotation, moreover, throws light on the speed at which the cult of the martyrs was progressing: in 404 Africa is already 'full of the bodies of holy martyrs', yet he does not know of any 'miraculous interpositions' having been effected there. But in Book XXII chapter 8 of his *City of God,* written in, or barely before 426, he tells of how some relics of the martyr Stephen, brought to Hippo only two years before, had already effected about seventy miraculous cures. And ten of them he describes in some detail. It is unlikely, however, that these led Augustine to attribute any innate healing power to the relic. In the first place three of the ten occur, not in the presence of the relics, but merely at a memorial or shrine set up in honour of the martyr; [43] in the second place Augustine describes eight [44] other medical cures effected without the help of Stephen or any other martyr or saint: in two cases the cure comes after contact with earth brought from Jerusalem, in two more it follows baptism, in two others it follows a simple prayer to God. There is some reason to think that these latter cures all occurred before the coming of the relics of Stephen.[45] If so we have an illustra-

---

[42] *Letter* # 78 § 3.

[43] The Council of Carthage of 401, canon # 17, forbids any *memoria martyrum* except where there are relics of the martyr or where it is certain that he was born, or where he suffered death: Hefele 1908 II [2] 129.

[44] The cases included possession, raising of the dead (cf. *Sermon* # 324), paralysis, hæmorrhoid, cancer, hernia, blindness, a boil, and a stone.

[45] At least these are the first to be related, and one or two are certainly

tion of how cures which had formerly been effected by a variety of methods became, in due course, the special prerogative of relics.   In one of the cases, at any rate, where the cure was effected by simple prayers to God, Augustine and his friend Alypius ' were not yet priests, though already servants of God ', which fixes the date as about 390.   Here is the substance of the account:

Who but a very small number are aware of the cure which was wrought upon Innocentius, ex-advocate of the deputy prefecture, a cure wrought at Carthage, in my presence, and under my own eyes? . . . He was being treated by medical men for fistulae, of which he had a large number intricately seated in the rectum.   He had already undergone an operation, and . . . had suffered long-continued and acute pain; yet among the many folds of the gut one had escaped the operators so entirely that, though they ought to have laid it open with the knife, they never touched it.

A second operation had therefore to be performed, and

such was the terror his former pains had produced, that he made no doubt he would die in the hands of the surgeons.   They comforted him, and exhorted him to put his trust in God, and nerve his will like a man.   Then we went to prayer; but while we, in the usual way, were kneeling and bending to the ground, he cast himself down, as if someone were hurling him violently to the earth, and began to pray; but in what a manner, with what earnestness and emotion, with what a flood of tears, with what groans and sobs that shook his whole body and almost prevented him from speaking, who can describe!   Whether the others prayed, and had not their attention wholly diverted by this conduct, I do not know.   For myself, I could not pray at all.   This only I briefly said in my heart: ' O Lord, what prayers of Thy people dost Thou hear if Thou hearest not these? ' . . . The dreaded day dawned.   The servants of God were present, as they had promised to be; the surgeons arrived; all that the circumstances required was ready; the frightful instruments are produced; all look on in wonder and suspense.   While those who have most influence with the patient are cheering his fainting spirit, his limbs are arranged on the couch so as to suit the hand of the operator; the knots of the bandages are untied; the part is bared; the surgeon examines it, and, with knife in hand, eagerly looks for the sinus that is to be cut.   He searches for it with his eyes; he feels

---

not records of recent occurrences. Whereas those connected with Ste-

phen must all have occurred in the preceding two years.

for it with his finger; he applies every kind of scrutiny; he finds a perfectly firm cicatrix! [46]

To be consistent, Augustine must have believed that this cure was effected, not in defiance of nature, but in accordance with some natural process not yet comprehensible to man. But since this natural process, like any other, was identical with the divine process, the mechanics employed, whether material or spiritual, did not rouse his curiosity. For he knew that even those matters which scientific men professed to understand, they in fact did not. Augustine was of course constantly aware of the mysterious phenomena of light,[47] heat, gravitation, etc., but he was equally aware that in confessing his ignorance of their essence he was wiser than his more presumptuous contemporaries. His lack of real curiosity in these matters was, no doubt, rather temperamental than logical, but was the curiosity of others, like Macrobius let us say, less temperamental?

How, then, did Augustine view the apparent physical miracle which was not in the form of a cure? There are, of course, an enormous number related in the Bible, and all of them, since Augustine asserted the literal truth of the Old Testament record, had to be accepted without question as true. Nevertheless, whenever a 'natural' explanation is practicable Augustine prefers it — as where he discusses the great age attributed to Methuselah. After citing the accounts given by Virgil and Pliny of men far stronger and longer lived than any now known, he goes on

and even that same Pliny tells us that there is still a nation in which men live two hundred years. If, then, in places unknown to us, men are believed to have a length of days which is quite beyond our own experience, why should we not believe the same of times distant from our own? Or are we to believe that in other places there is what is not here, while we do not believe that in other times there has been anything but what is now? [48]

But the difficulty presented by Methuselah's great age does not seem to us greater than some others that Augustine accepted without hesitation:

[46] *D.C.D.* XXII 8.   [48] *D.C.D.* XV 9.
[47] Cf. *Sermon* # 277 § 10.

We read in the divine books that even the sun itself stood still when a holy man, Joshua the son of Nun, had begged this from God until victory should finish the battle he had begun; and that it even went back, in order that the promise of fifteen years added to the life of king Hezekiah might be sealed by this additional prodigy.[49]

Here, because he has no way of investigating in order to prove or disprove, he readily believes; at the same time, whenever he can investigate, he does, even where the wonder occurred at the supreme moment of the Crucifixion. The text of *Matthew* xxvii 45 reads

Now from the sixth hour there was darkness over all the land until the ninth hour.

Observe that a miracle is only implied. Augustine might, therefore, conscientiously admit the fact and yet accept it as an eclipse of the same sort that had deceived the Romans in the time of Romulus. Investigating with a clear conscience, therefore, he nevertheless concludes that

when the Lord was crucified . . . this . . . obscuration of the sun did not occur by the natural laws of the heavenly bodies because it was then the Jewish Passover, which is held only at full moon, whereas natural eclipses of the sun happen only at the moon's last quarter.[50]

Suppose the Crucifixion had in fact occurred during the last quarter: Augustine must then have ascertained how much the Jews knew about eclipses. Moreover, even if he found that they did understand them, the coincidence would nevertheless be a terrifying one.

The cool-headed fairness of Augustine is nowhere more manifest than in his treatment of pagan miracles. Of these he says that doubtless

the greater part are merely illusions practised on the senses — as the drawing down of the moon, ' that it may ' as Lucan says ' shed a stronger influence on the plants.' [51]

And in regard to the lamp in the temple of Venus he says that

to this inextinguishable lamp we may add a host of marvels wrought by men or by magic — that is, by men under the influ-

---

[49] *D.C.D.* XXI 8.   [51] Ibid. X 16.
[50] Ibid. III 15.

ence of devils or by devils directly — for such marvels we cannot
deny without impugning the truth of the sacred Scriptures that
we believe.[52]

For this same reason, and because the facts were well accredited and uncontroverted, he accepts the story

that the ship in which the image of the Phrygian mother stood,
and which could not be moved by a host of men and oxen, was
moved by one weak woman who attached her girdle to the vessel
and drew it, as proof of her chastity; that a vestal, whose virginity
was questioned, removed the suspicion by carrying from the Tiber
a sieve full of water without any of it dropping.[53]

Augustine believed these wonders because he could not conscientiously deny them; but, having accepted them, he proceeds to use them as one more argument for the truth of Christianity. Having analyzed this power of magic, he concludes

if this be so, how much more able is God to do those things which
to sceptics are incredible, though to His power easy! [54]

These physical miracles, whether biblical or pagan, had
already long been traditional. The former now had the
guarantee of a holy revelation, but the latter enjoyed a prestige which, to the loyal Roman, was hardly less secure. Both
kinds, therefore, belong to a special category of wonder quite
different from the miracle — either recently effected, or recently related — where the instinct of loyalty to tradition was
absent. Of those which had occurred some time before but
were only now gaining currency, the alleged wonders related of
the martyrs formed the larger part. Augustine's attitude here
is non-committal. Frankly admitting the inherent probability that the martyrdoms were accompanied by extraordinary
manifestations, he nevertheless takes pains to emphasize the
wholly negative part played in them by the martyrs themselves. Occasionally, as in one of his Sermons on Vincent,
he will refer, if rather vaguely, to some strange phenomenon
— as that Vincent's corpse floated rather than sank [55] — but
all his emphasis, constantly reiterated, is on God as the ex-

[52] Ibid. XXI 6.
[53] Ibid. X 16. The first of these
stories is also told by Jerome in Contra Jovinianum I § 41.
[54] D.C.D. XXI 6.

[55] Sermon # 276 § 4. And cf. Sermon # 324 where a prayer to a
memorial to Stephen revives a dying
baby.

clusive and initiating cause.   Thus not only is the faith which
induces the martyrs to confront, but also the courage which
enables them to bear, the tortures and death, are powers actually infused by God irrespective of the martyr's own will:

> He who supposes that Saint Vincent was capable of doing these
> things by his own strength, is greatly in error.   For he who be-
> lieves himself capable of such feats, although his patience seems
> to have prevailed, has in fact been overcome by pride.[56]

> For when may corruptible dust hold out in the face of such mon-
> strous torments, except the Lord be dwelling within him? [57]

I cannot help feeling that Augustine's natural readiness to
accept the fast growing stories was seriously dampened by his
suspicion that many of them were circulated chiefly in order
to glorify a local martyr.   He was therefore willing to accept
them, but only with reluctance, laying as little stress on them
as he dared.   It is certainly significant, for instance, that
although Severus' *Life of Martin* was immensely popular
throughout the Empire during the last thirty years of Augustine's life, he nowhere mentions Martin or the book.[58]

The moment Augustine considers contemporary miracles,
moreover, he becomes actively critical:

> For my own part, I do not wish all the marvels I have cited to be
> rashly accepted, for I do not myself believe them implicitly, save
> those which have either come under my own observation, or
> which anyone can readily verify — such as the lime which is heated
> by water and cooled by oil. . . . But of those which I have cited,
> yet which I have not myself seen but only read about, I have been
> unable to find trustworthy witnesses from whom I could ascertain
> whether they are facts, except in the case of that fountain in which
> burning torches are extinguished and extinguished torches lit,
> and of the apples of Sodom, which are ripe to appearance but are
> filled with dust.   And indeed I have not met with any who said
> they had seen that fountain in Epirus, but only with some who
> knew there was a similar fountain in Gaul not far from Grenoble.
> The fruit of the trees of Sodom, however, is not only spoken of in
> books worthy of credit, but so many persons say they have seen
> it that I cannot doubt the fact.[59]

[56] *Sermon # 274.*
[57] Ibid. # 276 § 1.
[58] Babut 1912 11–13.   Nor did
Jerome, although he lived until 420,
mention either Martin or Severus'
Life of Martin: ibid. 10–11.
[59] *D.C.D.* XXI 7.

I cannot find that Augustine anywhere says he was present at any other miracle than a cure. In one case he believes in the story of a ring that became mysteriously detached from a girdle which the while remained tightly knotted; but he believes wholly on the faith of another, and partly because

the lady is distinguished, nobly born, married to a nobleman. She resides at Carthage. The city is distinguished, the person is distinguished, so that inquirers cannot fail to obtain satisfaction.[60]

Before Augustine's death in 430 the readiness of Christians to believe almost any miraculous tale which argued in their favour, was already an accomplished fact. How much of this was due to thoughtless ardour, how much to a wish to find some premature escape in this world from the horrors they professed to despise, how much to a survival of the pagan belief in the chronic intervention of demi-gods in the affairs of men — these things we cannot wholly know. Nevertheless it would be a mistake to suppose that before 430 Christians were already living in a miraculous world. Some of the monks perhaps were, and some ardent converts like Severus, and many, if not most, of the simple-minded. If, on the other hand, there were a few who kept their heads as well as Augustine, the Church and the responsible members still lived in a natural world and reacted naturally to it. That what we may, for want of a fitter term, call superstition, increased during the last centuries or decades of the western Empire, is not for me to say. If there can be no religion without such superstition, then there can perhaps be no deep intuition without its accompanying illusions. But this is only saying that human enlightenment is, for many centuries yet to come, doomed to imperfection. In order to attain the lofty conceptions which Christianity offered the ancient world, some incidental sacrifices were inevitable. Man's progress, even at best, is awkward and one-sided. A thing done for the first time cannot be done with that grace which comes only with painful repetition.

But to come back to Augustine: I venture to think that it

[60] Ibid. XXII 8 (*D. & K.* II 578, lines 28–31). In another case in the same chapter prayer brings a poor man a fish with a golden ring in its belly. This is hardly a physical miracle. Moreover such a phenomenon was familiar in pagan legend: Nourry 1907 134–36.

was his very urbanity that tempted him to accept so many of these hearsay stories; that it was precisely his wide and remorselessly analyzed personal experience which taught him the vanity of arbitrary scepticism. Those cures which he relates, for instance — most of which are probably explicable through auto-suggestion — were doubtless real cures. They are quite mystifying enough even to the hard-headed modern physician. Often Augustine had observed the Epicurean witnessing such wonders and still refusing to believe; often he had observed the intellectual dishonesty of persons who denied before, as well as after, the event. He had doubtless observed, too, as many of us have, that stupid and uneducated people are not only the most gullible but also the most sceptical: having no powers of discrimination they judge a problem, not on its specific merits, but according to some preconceived and often irrelevant prejudice. He knew that unless one were willing to have faith in the judgment of other men, in the records of other ages, no enlightenment was possible. His problem — and it is still ours — was not whether to believe on faith, but rather what to believe on faith — and when and whom.

CHAPTER IV

THE BISHOPS

A. THE AILING STATE

IN THE year 300 Christianity was a persecuted minority sect; in the year 400, although still in a minority,[1] it was the State religion and already without a serious rival. This century marks another great change: in the year 300 Rome was the capital of the whole Empire; in the year 400 she was hardly even the capital of the Latin half. This latter change needs a word of explanation.

As oriental influence came more and more to guide the destinies of the Empire, pouring its culture over the West and finally drawing the capital to Constantinople,[2] Rome — and so Italy — gradually lost both her economic privileges[3] and her prestige.[4] Until the death of Constantine in 337 the Empire had remained Latin,[5] and its true centre, therefore, still Rome; thereafter the East reverted to its original Hellenistic and oriental nature,[6] re-affirming its own civilization; while the West — now a homogeneous because Latinized organism — was diffusing and intensifying a different culture: one highly coloured by the East,[7] yet fundamentally occidental.

It is an elementary fact that the centre of a whole cannot be the centre of either of its halves; therefore Rome, formerly at the geographical centre of a single organism, now found

[1] 'Au cours du Ve siècle, les Païens de majorité passent minorité': Lot 1927 47.

[2] Diocletian began to reside in Nicomedia in 284; Constantine founded Constantinople in 324: Lot 1927 24 & 40–42.

[3] Hartmann 1923 I² 33–34.

[4] Steinhausen 1913 I² 64.

[5] Lot 1927 43, says of Constantine in 324: 'La Rome nouvelle, dans sa pensée devait être toute romaine. Il y transporta une partie du Sénat et fit bâtir des palais pour les vieilles familles qu'il y attira. Les lois furent toutes romaines. La langue de la cour, des bureaux, fut le latin.'

[6] Ibid. Only in the early fifth century does the Greek language begin to be more usual than the Latin at the court of Constantinople: ibid. 320.

[7] To the philosophies and religions may be added the importance of the Syrian and Jew in trade. See Salvian *D.G.D.* IV § 69 on the Syrians in Gaul in about 445.

herself at the peripheries of two.[8]   And as this city, half orientalized, lost her political, she also lost her intellectual supremacy — even within the Latin half.   While the Hellenistic and oriental element was attracted towards Ravenna
because her harbour faced the East — causing her to become
the Western capital in 424 [9] — the Latin element also tended
to move elsewhere: southward to Africa, northward to Milan [10] and Aquileia, northwestward into Gaul.   The first
Italian immigration into Gaul had been along the Mediterranean coast, from Frejus, Marseilles, and Narbonne, into
Spain; [11] later it turned inland, from Arles westward to Toulouse and Bordeaux,[12] and northward up the Rhone.

The southern coast had been the first to be conquered by
Rome, partly because she needed this strip in order to connect
Italy with Spain by land, partly too because the inhabitants of
this region were rather Iberians and Ligurians [13] than Celts
— a Mediterranean and not a northern people.   It was not
until seventy years later, in 54 B.C., that Cæsar conquered the
rest of Gaul.   Therefore the province of Narbonne, from
Toulouse to the Alps, ever remained the truly Roman part
of Gaul, and, as the Greek East gradually returned to its own
oriental ways, this *Gallia Narbonensis* grew to be more and
more the centre of Latin civilization.   Here were the great
cities of Marseilles and Arles, and these, it will be seen, are
almost precisely at the centre of a circle drawn to include
Italy's foot, Proconsular Africa, southwestern Spain, the wall
of Britain, and the upper Danube.

Northwest of Narbonne lay Aquitaine, bounded by the
Pyrenees, the Atlantic, and the southwestern watershed of the
Loire.   Its three largest cities were Bordeaux, which grew up
only after the Roman conquest, and the more purely Celtic
Clermont and Poitiers.   North and east of Aquitaine lay
Gaul proper, extending from the still barbarous coastlines
of Brittany and Normandy to the lower Seine and Marne —
with Paris on its northerly edge — and including Burgundy,

[8] Lot 1927 213 says that the Empire
' se scinde en deux, *pars Orientis pars
Occidentis*, dès la fin du [IIIe] siècle.'
Although the Greek language never
wholly lost its prestige: Jullian 1926
VIII 256–59.

[9] Hartmann 1923 I [2] 175.
[10] Dill 1906 [2] 146; Lot 1927 24 &
234.
[11] Jullian 1920 VI 348–53.
[12] Ibid. 377.
[13] Ibid. 1920 III [2] 24.

the heart of Celtic civilization,[14] as far as Lyons.   It was in
this Burgundy, containing the sources of many of Gaul's
largest rivers and with Autun as its capital, that the great
work of Romanization had been achieved.   Thence feebler
tentacles ran west down the Loire to Nantes, northwestward
through Paris and Rouen and northward through Rheims
and Boulogne to Britain.   And finally, after about 260, a
main route developed northeastward down the Moselle: here
lay Trier which, as the military capital of the West, became,
in the fourth century, second in political importance only to
Rome.   Beyond Trier, again, on the Rhine, were the great
city encampments of Cologne and Mainz, guarding the most
vulnerable stretch of the Rhine frontier.[15]   Here there had
been few native Celts [16] or Germans; [17] consequently this
Moselle-Rhine region became more Roman than any other
part of Gaul except Narbonne.[18]   Not that it became Italian,
as the city of Narbonne had become even before Cæsar; Roman now designated the races of the Empire, for her soldiers
and merchants were as likely to be Syrians as Celts.[19]   All the
greater Gallic cities became cosmopolitan: Arles, Bordeaux,
Lyons, and Autun,[20] as well as Trier, Cologne, and Mainz.
Only the smaller ones, like Sens, Chalon-sur-Saône, and Dijon
in Burgundy, or like Poitiers, Clermont, Vienne, Rheims,
or Metz, retained characteristics distinctively Celtic.   On the
whole, however, Roman ways superseded native ways; the
territories least affected were precisely those that were most
isolated and backward: the Cevennes,[21] Brittany and Normandy,[22] Flanders, Brabant, Hainaut, and the Ardennes.[23]
Each of these had been a land of forests and peasants, and
such each remained.

The centres of education and culture were Marseilles, still
the centre of Greek culture, to which the Scythian Cassian
came shortly after 400 to introduce Egyptian monasticism,[24]

[14] Ibid. 1920 VI 416–30.
[15] Ibid. 486–48 & 497.
[16] Ibid. 492 & 495–96.
[17] Ibid.
[18] Ibid. 488.
[19] There are traces of Egyptians at
Nimes: ibid. 342.
[20] Arles: ibid. 324; Bordeaux:
ibid. 387; Lyons: ibid. 521–3; Autun:
ibid. 424.

[21] Jullian 1920 VI 337 & 391–94.
[22] Ibid. 409–11 & 437–38.
[23] Bloch 1911 375–79; Jullian 1920
VI 463–65. At the mouth of the
Rhine the Salian Franks, numbering
only a few thousand men (Jullian
1926 VIII 376) had been allowed to
settle in about 297 (ibid. VII 86) as
allies of the Empire.
[24] See p. 474.

Toulouse,[25] which produced Severus [26] and Rutilius,[27] Bordeaux,[28] which produced Ausonius [29] and Paulinus of Nola,[30] and finally, farther north, Autun, where the young Celts gathered to imbibe the Latin culture.[31] The contrast between the Roman culture of north and south is apparent from the observation of Gallus of Tours to Severus and his friend Postumianus:

I tremble when I reflect that I, a poor Gaul, will be required to converse at length with two gentlemen of Aquitaine, for my rustic mode of speech will surely grate unpleasantly on your refined ears.[32]

Had Gallus studied at Autun he might not have been so modest; yet even so the artificiality of his refinement would probably have betrayed his origin.

Important as the Roman roads were in the Romanization of Gaul, it seems clear that the river valleys continued to serve as the chief arteries of communication.[33] Why otherwise should Bordeaux, which hardly existed before Cæsar's day, have become one of Gaul's largest cities? Here were exchanged the metals of Spain and Britain for goods shipped from the farthest ends of the Empire.[34] This business was transacted at Bordeaux because the Garonne ran down to the sea from Toulouse where roads met from Narbonne and Arles. The importance of the Rhone needs no comment, nor that of the Moselle. The importance of Burgundy was originally due to the Celtic concentration there; but the same cause which produced that concentration maintained it throughout Roman times: its strategic position near the headwaters of the Loire, Seine, Marne, Meuse, Saône, and Moselle.

It appears that Gaul may, for our purposes, be conveniently divided into two almost equal halves, by drawing a line from Bordeaux, through Sens — on the upper Seine — to Cologne

25 Jullian 1920 VI 358.
26 See p. 186 n. 72.
27 L.C.L. ed. Minor Latin Poets 753; & Labriolle 1934 471.
28 An uncle of Ausonius was professor at Toulouse: Dill 1906 2 173.
29 Ibid. 167.
30 Ibid. 181; & Jullian 1926 VIII 264.

31 Jullian 1920 VI 123–24 & 425–26.
32 Severus Dialogue I 27.
33 Jullian 1926 VIII 205–06. And cf. Dalton 1927 I 151–56.
34 Jullian 1920 VI 379–80.

on the Rhine.   The whole northwesterly half was relatively primitive and un-Romanized, with few cities and these either Celtic or on the Boulogne artery, the whole southeasterly half — except for the mountainous Cevennes — a land as civilized and populous, as Romanized and prosperous, as any in the Empire.[35]   It was, therefore, on the integrity of this half of Gaul, as much as on that of Italy, that the safety of the Latin Empire must depend.

It may be that this Latin trend from Italy to Gaul was a real source of danger to the fourth century Empire.   There was hardly more reason why Gaul should now obey Rome than Rome obey Gaul.   Had the barbarians not overrun the West until a hundred years later it is conceivable that they might then have encountered some city, like Lyons[36] or Arles,[37] as the acknowledged Latin-Roman capital — capable of organizing the whole West to resist.[38]   But in the year 400 the change was not complete: although the Gallo-Roman no longer trusted the Empire he did not yet trust himself,[39] and there was, consequently, neither individual, institution, nor territory equipped to organize military resistance on an imperial scale.   This partially explains the large number of usurpers who arose in these years: smaller or larger territorial groups had become convinced that if only they could organize independently they might stave off the impending disintegration; and when the imperial government strove to defeat them the only result was civil war.[40]   The West was thus becoming a house divided against itself.[41]   The irony is that

[35] Jullian 1913 IV 600–05, thinks that Gaul after the Frankish-Burgundian invasions of 275–276 became a shadow of her former self, and his description in vols. V & VI is of the Gaul of before that date.   Undeniably the destruction in those years was tremendous, undeniably the great cities never again recovered their size or magnificence (cf. p. 236); nevertheless Gaul's recuperative powers — if we may trust Dill and Boissier who both studied fourth century Gaul minutely — must have been hardly less tremendous, as Jullian 1926 VII 90–92, admits.

[36] Cf. Bloch 1911 346–54; Bayet 1911 86; Jullian 1920 VI 516.

[37] Ausonius, in *Ordo urbium nobilium* X § 2, speaks of *Gallula Roma Arelas*.   In the fourth century Spain was ruled by the praetorian prefect of the Gauls, who resided at Trier: Lot 1927 322.   The Council held at Arles in 315 was of all the western Churches: Turner 1911 178.

[38] Cf. Dalton 1915 I xvii.

[39] See Jullian 1926 VIII 380.

[40] The battle of Mursa in 351, in which Constantius defeated the usurper Magnentius, resulted in terrific casualties: Jullian 1926 VII 154–56.

[41] Duchesne 1911 III⁴ 583–602. Cf. Sidonius *Letters* I # 7 § 5 on 'the Greek emperor.'

it was a last successful assertion of imperial over local sovereignty — the withdrawal of the imperial troops on the Rhine to reinforce those fighting Alaric in Italy [42] — which precipitated the *débâcle*. Had Gaul been able to keep them and command them, the Rhine might have been held. Had these troops been Gauls, this might have happened; instead they were men from every province and race of the Empire. Such men might fight for a usurper who paid them well, rather than for Rome and her Emperor, but why should they fight for Gaul?

This geographical phase, however, was only one among the many of the crisis; for the rest we merely know enough of the times to see the complications, we do not know enough to order them into sequences of cause and effect. The apparent and therefore hypothetical causes of Rome's fall are legion, but we do not yet understand the processes of history well enough to say with any confidence which of the many symptoms were the fundamental and decisive ones. Vaguely we can say that the immediate cause was military, that the cause behind this was political,[43] and we can say, even more vaguely, that the deeper causes were moral,[44] religious,[45] psychological,[46] geographical,[47] economic,[48] racial,[49] and even organic;[50] we can go on, to cite specific evidence and draw wise inferences, yet we strike no bottom short of a resort to the teleological theory of Augustine.

We cannot here do more, therefore, than state very briefly the conditions at the moment of the collapse, when the Empire's political organization, clogged by an intricate and cumbersome system of administrative law, was cracking, tottering, and about to fall. As the fourth century drew to a close the Empire's sovereign power, ill-defined, rose and fell according rather to fortuitous circumstance than to any plan, whether

---

42 Hartmann 1923 I 2 37.
43 Ibid. 30.
44 See pp. 140–45.
45 See pp. 147–48, & 596–601.
46 A distinguished philosopher has told me he suspects that Rome fell chiefly because the Romans had become bored by their own civilization. Lot 1927 170 says that now, after nearly eight hundred years,

men first became indifferent to the beauties of Greek sculpture.
47 On the theory that the Empire was too big: see Dill 1906 2 267.
48 The popular explanation of everything nowadays: see Lot 1927 97–98.
49 But we do not know enough, as yet, of the racial components.
50 This is Spengler's theory.

well- or ill-advised. Because no civic principle or social philosophy was being followed, even in the moments between the chronic civil wars [51] legislation was arbitrary and without continuity. Nor could the bureaucracy, although still led by the aristocracy,[52] guarantee a reasonable execution of the laws in force.[53] Corruption and venality were rife and even respectably traditional. Over and above this the natural laws of agricultural, commercial, and industrial economy were not understood; [54] taxes were levied in order to allay present rather than future emergencies; and, since there was no pretence of equality before the law except within social castes, special burdens, exemptions and privileges had become the rule rather than the exception. Men of the senatorial or aristocratic class, for instance, were both forbidden to serve in the army [55] and virtually immune to heavy taxation,[56] and, since many of the higher civil offices were designedly sinecures, idleness and riches were practically forced on them; slaves, on the other hand, could be neither idle nor rich. It might perhaps be said that while it was the ambition of all to join the senatorial class — by illicit gains, pandering or flattery, even by a usurpation of power — it was the concern of the State to keep them out of it.[57] This explains the precarious position of the independent middle class, and consequently the origins of feu-

---

[51] On their frequency and intensity just before and after the year 400 see Gibbon 1776 ff. chs. 27, 29, & end of 31; & Hodgkin 1892 I [2] 824–30 & 849.

[52] Coster 1935 10 & 24–25.

[53] Fustel de Coulanges 1891 II 204–06. Sanford 1930 109 n. 31 & 145 n. 24 contrasts the laws of the Theodosian Code with the actual conditions of 445 as described by Salvian. Even though Salvian exaggerated, even though earlier enforcement had surely been stricter, there would still have been a wide discrepancy. See Salvian *D.G.D.* IV § 30, V § 30, & VII § 93.

[54] Lot 1927 21, 91 & 95.

[55] Duchesne 1911 III [4] 148; Rostovtzeff 1926 458; Dudden 1935 93. Jullian 1926 VIII 73 says that ' Tous les empereurs depuis Gallien jusqu'à Théodose, ont suivi la même politique lamentable: enfermer et pour

ainsi dire enliser le citoyen romain, Sénateur ou prolétaire, dans les besognes de la vie civile.' Thus the duties as well as the inclinations of the educated Romans held them to civil life, and this was the easier to accept because the barbarian — and especially the Frankish — officers of the Roman army proved able as well as loyal: ibid. VII 165–69, 279–81, and 312–13, & VIII 121–23.

[56] Fustel de Coulanges 1891 II 59 & 203; Dill 1906 [2] 268–69; Bloch 1922 264 & 272; Lot 1927 148, 151, & 201–02; Jullian 1926 VIII 43 n. 3 & 44. And see Salvian *D.G.D.* IV § 30, V § 30 & § 35.

[57] A law of Theodosius I forbad any of the *curiales* to join the senatorial order: Bloch 1922 281. Cf. Coster 1935 10. Laws had been enacted to make this difficult ever since Constantine: Fustel de Coulanges 1891 II 188–89.

dalism: he who was not powerful enough to give orders must take orders from those who were.[58]

Very rich men were no novelty in the later Roman Empire, but after the invasions and troubles of the later third century their way of living radically changed. Up to then they had lived in splendour in the cities, allowing agents to superintend the management of their huge and scattered estates. But city life changed rather suddenly thereafter: the ample stretches of suburban villas, parks, and gardens were cut off by fortifications which sharply differentiated the city from the countryside and crammed it into a minimum of space. The rich not only found this new city uncomfortable to live in; they also found it necessary to give their estates a closer supervision. They therefore tended to move from city to country, turning their villas into so many fortified towns.[59] Hitherto raiding bands, whether insurgents under a usurper, peasants in revolt[60] or marauding barbarians, had been able not only to destroy the crops but also to fire the buildings and carry off or kill the workers; now the buildings were protected and a nearby refuge provided for all. These changes isolated the landowner from municipal affairs — which were becoming a heavy burden — leaving him the freer to run his own affairs as he chose. Very rich men, like Paulinus of Bordeaux and Nola, who owned *fundi* in many parts of the Empire[61] must travel periodically in order to inspect them; but even in such cases the unit of possession always remained the *fundus,* a contiguous, even a compact,[62] territorial and economic entity, agriculturally — and even industrially[63] and judicially — self-sufficient.

Although these *fundi* must necessarily be situated within the territorial limits of a *civitas* with its regular local govern-

[58] Lot 1927 150–53. And see Augustine *D.C.D.* II 20, & Salvian *D.G.D.* IV § 20, & V §§ 8 & 9.

[59] Jullian 1926 VIII 188 & 222 n. 1; Lot 1927 144–45.

[60] Such as the Bagaudes: Bloch 1911 370–71 & 387; Jullian 1926 VII 51–56.

[61] See Gibbon 1776 ff. ch. 31 on the estates of Probus, which ' were scattered over the wide extent of the Roman world.' The parents of Paulinus of Nola owned at least three separate estates in Aquitaine, others in the Narbonnese, at least two in Italy — at Fundi in Latium and at Nola in Campania — and perhaps several in Spain: Lagrange 1877 9–10. Ausonius *Letter* # 24 lines 115–16 describes the properties of Paulinus as *regna*. On the estates of Melania the Younger see Jullian 1926 VIII 134–35.

[62] Bloch 1911 437 & 439.

[63] Ibid. 440.

ment, their owner, if rich enough, was able to qualify under
the law of the Empire as one of the *potentiores* or senators,
and, as such, to be emancipated from all vital connection with
the *civitas*.[64] His many *fundi* might belong to almost as many
civitates, but he was too important to be controlled by any of
them. And after 376 his status became definitely imperial.[65]
In earlier times every senator lived in Rome and had a seat in
the Senate there. But by 400 most of the provincial aristocracy had received the senatorial title by courtesy,[66] with no
right as such to sit in the Roman Senate,[67] and with only a
limited obligation to embark on the *cursus honorum*,[68] a
career which to many now seemed more costly than glorious.

Having no duties towards Rome and none towards any
civitas, they resigned themselves complacently to a squirely
life on a magnificent scale. They became the first feudal
lords. From each fortified villa they ruled over a whole community, administering justice, equipping armed men, wel-
coming their friends and driving off the obsequious tax-
collector.[69] The personnel of the *fundus* were this landlord's
own men: they had either been put, or put themselves, under
him; against him they therefore could have no redress. Nor
could the *civitas* ever proceed directly against him, for civilly
he was answerable only to the governor of his province and
criminally only to the prefect or the Emperor.[70]

By the year 400 the *fundus* was already a self-sufficient unit,
capable in many cases not only of keeping the municipal and
provincial authorities at arm's length, but even of defying the
agents and will of the Emperor.[71] As a consequence of these
immunities and this homogeneity, the *fundi* were in full prosperity as the fourth century closed,[72] and the senators, so long
as they did not quarrel among themselves, offered the one
effective check on the arbitrary rule of the Emperor.[73] They

[64] Lot 1927 145.

[65] Coster 1935 3, 5–6 & 24–25.

[66] Bloch 1911 436. The *illustres*
and *spectabiles* outranked the senators, but these titles were not hereditary: ibid. 437. Below the hereditary
clarissimi were the *perfectissimi* or
aristocracy of the *civitas*, including
primarily the *duoviri* and *ædiles*: see
p. 242; Jullian 1926 VIII 178–79.

[67] Lot 1927 144.

[68] Coster 1935 5–6. Desirable,
however, in order to maintain their
public prestige: Jullian 1926 VIII
144–46.

[69] Lot 1927 145.

[70] Coster 1935 3 ff. & 24–25.

[71] Bloch 1922 264; Coster 1935 13.

[72] Jullian 1913 IV 605; Hartmann
1923 I 2 34; Lot 1927 145 & 149.

[73] Coster 1935 13.

held all the highest offices of the State,[74] they owned a large
proportion of the private wealth; it was they — unless the
Emperor or a usurper intervened — who gave the orders;
all the rest must take them.

First among these were the tillers of the soil, of which the
lowest in status were the slaves.[75] Outright slavery was now
on the decline; not that there was any scarcity of prisoners of
war or any substantial Christian hostility to that status. Slave
labour, always notoriously inefficient,[76] could compete with
free labour only so long as slaves could be had for the asking
and be housed and fed like dogs. But the less a slave seemed
a soulless barbarian and the more he seemed a Christian Roman, the better the treatment he must be accorded. Better
treatment of the slave, however, did not eliminate loafing.
The economic solution, therefore, was to put him on his
own responsibility — to work or starve. Already there was
a higher status which allowed the slave the use of a house of
his own; at times he was even allowed a surrounding plot of
land and a share of its profits. A law of 374 forbad a slave
to be sold except with the land he worked.[77] Out of this
status was evolved a yet higher one, where the slave could
transmit these privileges to his children.[78] But complete
emancipation was rare, for whether slave, serf, or freedman,
the man remained the helpless client or dependent of his
patron or master.[79] It was in such ways that the slave rose;
we have also to see how the freeman fell.

The free and independent farmer with a moderate landed
property had prospered under the Empire. The more successful of these were the *decuriones* and magistrates of the
civitas.[80] A few had worked up into the envied ranks of the
potentiores,[81] but many more had worked down. Now it is
invariably the small capitalist who is the first victim of adverse
conditions, the first who suffers when either law or violence
begins to tyrannize.[82] And violence will often be the lesser
evil because it tends to be ephemeral — the destruction of a

[74] Fustel de Coulanges 1891 II
200–02.
[75] Ibid. 82–92 gives an admirable
description of the status.
[76] Bloch 1922 257; Lot 1927 125.
[77] Fustel de Coulanges 1891 II 94
n. 3.

[78] Bloch 1911 444–45.
[79] Fustel de Coulanges 1891 II
107–15, 123–25, & 133–34.
[80] Ibid. 151–52.
[81] Lot 1927 145.
[82] Fustel de Coulanges 1891 II 194
supposes that the *potentiores*, al-

summer; whereas law tends to be perpetual — the destruction of a generation. And so it was in later Rome: violence came once in ten years, the tax-collector annually.

It was apparently the folly of the Roman tax system that it was based not on real but on arbitrary values, on what a given property ought theoretically to produce rather than on what it at that moment could produce — that is, on assessed rather than on market values.[83] If a tax is set at a quarter of a gross income and that income is halved, the net income becomes one third of what it had been and the market value, therefore, also one third. The Empire wanted to live on the scale to which it had become accustomed,[84] and it succeeded — for a time. But no device can permanently benefit the State which does not also benefit the individual. By this tax system the State for a few years extracted an artificially high revenue, but, as this discouraged production, that revenue, while growing ever more burdensome, actually became every year somewhat less. For the State is necessarily an economic parasite, living off the fat of its subjects. Its prosperity is the longer lived, but only by a thin margin.

Thoroughly weakened and discouraged by this tax burden, the small landowner found it impossible to survive the more and more violent disturbances of the later fourth century. The State was living off his fat, leaving him none to live off of. In contrast to the *fundi* of the *potentiores* his farm was not self-sufficient; nor was he politically organized to act in concert with others in a similar plight. Unless he could increase his holdings he must watch them dwindle to nothing — with the debtor's prison at the end of the road. For he had all his eggs in one basket: if a drought came, if a market were cut off, if marauders burnt his crops, he received a blow from which he could not recover. Even if he were merely cheated he would lack the funds necessary to prosecute or defend his case in court.[85]

---

though the most dangerous of all possible creditors, became the only available money-lenders.

[83] The Emperor Julian reduced the tax rate in Gaul from 25 to 7 per thousand: ibid. 49–50. The re-assessment was made only once every fif-

teen years, with the result that no damage could lead to a reduction until the next re-assessment: Jullian 1926 VIII 34–37.

[84] Lot 1927 127.

[85] Bloch 1922 263.

It was at such a juncture — now every year more frequent — that the neighbouring *potentior* or plutocrat stepped in to offer a way out: he agreed to protect the farmer from eviction for non-payment of taxes or for any other cause, and would champion his personal rights either in or out of court; in return the farmer must convey the legal title to the property, paying a fixed rent for the beneficial use of it. The farmer retained the right to buy back this property at a sum agreed upon, but this would have been almost as undesirable as it was difficult.[86] So far this was hardly other than a life tenancy, but there were further provisions: in consideration of the right of the farmer's heirs to inherit the property on these same terms, the farmer agreed that neither he nor his heirs should ever abandon or assign their rights. He thereby bound not only himself for life but also his heirs for ever.[87] A law of Diocletian gave rigid effect to this practice, decreeing that every lease, however limited and free its terms, be an hereditary tenancy.[88] This was done in order to prevent lessees from abandoning the land at the termination of the lease and in this way putting their land out of cultivation.[89] For the owner could not have found other labourers. Thus in the name of efficiency the individual was enchained: the free farmer became a *colonus*.

Roman ways were not our ways: the status of serfdom was not so harsh as it appears. Ancient man was never fed as we have been on eulogies of freedom, to him citizenship itself was a sort of slavery, granting favours rather than rights.[90] To the ancients dependence and contentment were not incompatible terms, as the clergy and monks of this time bear witness; and it is to be observed that if the farmer bound himself and his heirs for ever, so did the landlord-plutocrat bind himself and his heirs for ever, to the farmer and his heirs! As a practical matter the landlord could divest himself of his property, as by sale, without fear of resistance from his dependents. But whether he might do this legally — according

86 For the finer distinctions of tenure see Bloch 1922 260–61.

87 Bloch 1911 445–48; Lot 1927 124–31.

88 Hartmann 1923 I 2 16.

89 Lot 1927 130. This institution of the *colonus* had long existed in the East — especially in Asia Minor, Egypt, and Greece — and it may have existed in an analogous form in Gaul before Cæsar: ibid. 125.

90 Ibid. 141.

to law [91] or to the express terms of the conveyance — is questionable, and surely he had no legal right to abandon his land and dependents without first installing an adequate substitute.[92] He was physically free, but only because he could afford to pay others to do his work for him; the serf was doubtless also free on the same terms, to get away as often as he liked provided he could pay another to do the allotted task. And probably he could assign his whole status to another, provided that other was acceptable to the landlord. Certainly this binding of the person in perpetuity was the antithesis of freedom; the longing of the average man, however, was, not to be free, but to be safe.[93]

For the time being those who owned land outright could retain their old freedom, selling, leasing, or abandoning it as they chose; [94] but if, having abandoned it, they failed to pay the taxes due, their only chance of freedom lay in flight.

It may be that in agriculture the laws rather ratified than inaugurated these new feudal relationships,[95] for these were, after all, binding only as between individuals with the State not a party. In many other vocations and callings, on the other hand, the State took the initiative, imposing restrictions and burdens revocable not by mere consent of the other contracting party but only through legislative repeal. Persons bound in this way became the serfs, not of a landlord, but of the State itself. It seems as if the State actually set out to make each of its citizens a serf. All this was done, we may well believe, with the sincere desire to benefit the State: it is a natural supposition that when conditions are getting worse the need is for more organization, more regimentation, more artificial devices to promote efficiency — for a mobilization of the whole civilian population. That this condition might be realized the State decreed a great variety of occupations hereditary: that of the soldier [96] came first, and this

[91] On the hereditary obligations of the senatorial class see Bloch 1922 283.

[92] See Goyau 1921 9 *passim*.

[93] Coster 1935 10–11, esp. n. 32. This feudal tendency acquired a particular momentum during the rule of Theodosius I: Jullian 1926 VIII 140 notes 2 & 4.

[94] Lot 1927 131. But by a law of 425 even their freedom began to be restricted: if they wished to buy more land they must buy equal areas of good and bad land, paying taxes on both: ibid.

[95] Bloch 1922 257.

[96] Since 235: Jullian 1913 IV 552 n. 7. Cf. Hartmann 1923 I 2 24–25; & Lot 1927 121.

was why Martin of Tours had to serve as his father had served before him.[97]   Next came the trades furnishing materials of war [98] — including even the miners,[99] as extractors of the raw metals.   Since regulation in one category upsets the equilibrium in allied categories, these in turn must then be regulated too.   The army needs not only fighting equipment but also food, and the city populace needs food.   We therefore find the Roman merchants [100] and shipowners [101] hereditarily bound to their callings, that the grain shipments to Rome, for instance, from Egypt, Africa, and Sicily might move regularly and in proper abundance, and beyond these the bakers [102] were similarly bound, that the chain might have no weak link.   And, since the populace must be amused as well as fed, actors,[103] musicians,[104] and the like were also bound — they and their heirs for ever.   If the State was to be efficient it must begin by being so at the top: consequently last but not least of the categories on which was imposed the hereditary yoke was the bureaucracy of public or civil servants.[105]

Particularly important was the effect of this policy of regimentation on that urban section of the *civitas* which we may call the city, and which was its seat of government.   For these cities were the real units which, with the *fundi*, constituted the Empire.   Under the early Empire municipal life was the real Roman life; Rome was merely the largest city, and each smaller one was, or tried to be, another Rome in miniature.[106] Consequently for some time they enjoyed a good deal of self-government.

First of the municipal officials were the *duoviri*, and, closely associated with them, the *ædiles*.   These four, acting as a unit, formed the executive and financial branches, and the court of first instance.[107]   Complementing these was the municipal Senate or *curia*, whose members were also locally elected. Besides having limited legislative powers this *curia* acted as

97 Severus *Life of Martin* 2.
98 Lot 1927 117.
99 Ibid. 116–17.
100 Ibid. 143.
101 Ibid. 118.
102 Ibid.
103 Ibid. 119.   Cf. Dill 1906 [2] 57.

104 Ibid.
105 Lot 1927 116; Jolowicz 1932 442–43.   And cf. in general Bloch 1922 284.
106 Lot 1927 139.
107 Ibid. 137.

a court of appeal from the decisions of the four executives. In the earlier days membership in the *curia* was an honour much sought after; it involved heavy private expense,[108] but the honour far outweighed this inconvenience, and carried with it a modest but real power.[109]

The first blow to municipal prestige and self-respect was dealt by Diocletian, who revived and transformed the imperial office of *curator*. This *curator* became in each city the inspector of finances and the court of appeal, thereby depriving the locally elected officials of all real power.[110] Henceforth to be a municipal official was more expensive and less glorious. Then came Constantine to deal the city its mortal blow by a series of merciless laws: he made the members of the *curia* or *decuriones* individually responsible — jointly and perhaps severally — for the taxes due from the whole *civitas* to the imperial treasury,[111] including those due from the haughty landlords in their fortified domains. And, because under such conditions no one would any longer choose to be a *decurio,* Constantine provided further that they could not resign and that in case of death their heirs must assume the burden.[112] By a law of 320 the *decurio* could not resign even in order to adopt an ecclesiastical career.[113] This was all very well so long as these victimized families could be bled, but the time came when there was nothing left to bleed. Of what use were these laws then? The solution was found in a law which drafted everyone enjoying a certain minimum of income — including even the despised bankers, merchants, and lawyers[114] — into a group called *curiales*, who served to replace the original *decuriones* as these became insolvent.[115] So far as we know these laws were well enforced, draining almost every modestly well-to-do[116] citizen of his last cent,

[108] Ibid. 138; Jolowicz 1932 444.

[109] Lot 1927 138.

[110] Ibid. 139. Technically the office was not then new, but its powers were: Bloch 1922 275–76. On the falling prestige of the *decurio* see a suggestion by Fustel de Coulanges 1891 II 32–34.

[111] Lot 1927 140; Jolowicz 1932 447.

[112] Hartmann 1923 I² 22; Lot 1927 140.

[113] Koeniger 1919 23; Lot 1927 146.

[114] Lot 1927 138 & 144. Most of these were freedmen and hence presumably disqualified.

[115] Ibid. 141. They were even forbidden to sell their lands or slaves without the consent of the governor of the province; and if they died childless three-quarters of their property must go into the treasury of the *curiales:* Bloch 1922 279.

[116] Jullian 1926 VIII 146–47 says

and leaving the city impotently at the mercy of the central machine. Shall we conclude that the policy of the imperial government was greedy and cunning? Much more probably it was well-meaning but obtuse.

In contrast to the State's mad thirst for revenue, there was now not only exhaustion of the soil, war damage, privilege and venality, but also — in Italy particularly [117] — a serious decline in the rural population and hence in the area of land under cultivation. This must have been chiefly due to the tax system which forced the abandonment of all lands that could not yield a fair profit over and above the assessment.[118] The poor owner might be caught and properly chastised, but this did nothing to restore his abandoned acres to cultivation and therefore did nothing to help the imperial revenue. The obvious solution was an artificial increase in the agricultural population.

For some time now the army had been recruited by obliging landowners to furnish quotas corresponding to their holdings.[119] Slaves were barred, but of the other dependents the least desirable were naturally chosen.[120] These were branded, bound to a service of from twenty to thirty years, and by a law of Constantine their sons were bound to serve in their turn. If on frontier garrison service, each soldier was allotted a tract of arable land, with a skeleton of serfs and certain exemptions from taxation.[121] Such a holding was hereditary and inalienable, making the soldier doubly a serf of the State: farming for it in peace-time, fighting for it in war.[122] His wage, apart from booty and irregular donatives, consisted in what he could earn from his land.

Whether men thus recruited, or rather impressed, made efficient farmers we do not know, but we do know that they

---

that most men of this class owned a modest *fundus* as well, of a size to maintain about thirty families — there were perhaps ten thousand such in Gaul. The financial distress of these owners must have greatly accelerated the feudal concentration in the hands of the Senators.

117 Bloch 1922 253.

118 See p. 239.

119 Early in the fourth century the *potentiores* were allowed the alternative of furnishing a money equivalent: Hartmann 1923 I 2 26.

120 Fustel de Coulanges 1891 II 143–46. But it was a simple matter to emancipate a slave with the intention of delivering him over as a recruit: Bloch 1922 289–90.

121 Ibid. 285–86.

122 Muirhead 1886 385–87; Lot 1927 123.

made miserable soldiers.[123] Furthermore, having been drawn from agriculture, the system added nothing to the number of farmers. For both reasons, therefore, Constantine inaugurated the scheme of soliciting barbarians for the army,[124] often rewarding them with Roman citizenship and subjecting them to the same regulations that applied to the native conscripts. This system not only gave the army a new strength; it also effected a real increase in the number of farmers. By the year 350 probably half the soldiers in the imperial army were barbarians.[125]

Half the army, however, constituted hardly more than one per cent of the Roman population; therefore although the scheme partly solved the military difficulty it did almost nothing to solve the economic. The next step must inevitably be the introduction of civilian barbarians to cultivate the abandoned farms as serfs. In the course of the fourth century this occurred on a considerable scale,[126] so that by 400 these barbarian immigrants constituted an important fraction of the whole population. In an earlier day the assimilation of such an alien minority would have been complete within a generation, for then the barbarians, awed by the Roman display of courage and intelligence, strove only to emulate Roman ways. But these fourth century barbarians instead learned only their own strength and Rome's weakness, and they reacted accordingly.[127]

Yet such was even the faded glamour of Rome that barbarian loyalty to her constantly surprises us.[128] Disloyalty was rather the characteristic of the native Romans. We have spoken of the mutual distrust of the different provinces; this was accentuated by the transfer of the capital to Constantinople, for how in the West could one be entirely loyal to a Hellenistic-Asiatic State? We have spoken too of the Christian indifference to the national welfare, and of how this at-

[123] Lot 1927 121–22.

[124] By allowing a money equivalent barbarian recruits could be hired who were stouter and were perhaps paid less: Bloch 1922 289.

[125] Jullian 1926 VIII 80; & cf. ibid. VII 286–90.

[126] Bayet 1911 62. The movement began under Diocletian and Constantine: Hartmann 1923 I 2 28.

[127] On the situation in the East in 399 see the oration delivered before the Emperor by Synesius of Cyrene: On Kingship chs. 14–15. Cf. Gibbon 1776 ff. ch. 30.

[128] Bloch 1922 296–99; Jullian 1926 VII 317 ff.

titude was even more pronounced among many Neoplatonists and Manichees.[129]   Probably to the pagan aristocrat in Rome the Greek capital at Constantinople and the Christian Church with her Asiatic Bible seemed his most dangerous enemies. In the year 400 it still seemed these, rather than any barbarians, who could most viciously wound the State.[130]

It is hard to say, in any given case, quite how the Christian regarded the barbarian menace, for the view of each varied according to his own particular disposition and station.   Augustine, somewhat to his mortification, clung to Rome with his heart; he may subconsciously have felt the need of a superior civilization in order to support a superior religion.   Prudentius, the Spanish aristocrat and poet, also loved Rome.[131]   The Spaniard Orosius, on the other hand, and the Gaul Salvian, both living a generation later, seemed well reconciled to the new inevitable.[132]   On the whole, the aristocrats were opposed to any change, and so, doubtless, were many of their loyal and favoured subordinates; but many of the less fortunate were lukewarm and inert — the more pious because of the iniquity or at any rate the insignificance of the Earthly City,[133] others from a faith in their helplessness to alter the divine course of affairs, and still others from a sound conviction that no change could be socially, economically, or equitably for the worse.[134]

The immediate cause of the fall was military for the simple reason that if the Empire had had enough good soldiers, no invasion could have succeeded.   To say this is of course to beg the question, but the fact remains that the western half of the Empire had, in the years of the great invasions, only about 300,000 men under arms.[135]   What may have been the popu-

129 On the internationalism of the Christians see Boissier 1906 II 6 425–26.   And cf. Newman 1858 373–75. This was equally true of the other oriental religions: Cumont 1929 4 23–24.

130 On the political rivalries of pagan, Arian and Catholic, see Bloch 1922 308.   There were, to be sure, indications of the unpopularity of the barbarian contingents: ibid. 295–96.   But probably only in cases of specific provocation.   The innumerable slaves in the great households (Dudden 1935 463), many of whom must have been born free barbarians, made these Romans intimately familiar with the barbarian character — and the barbarians with the Roman.

131 Labriolle 1934 346.

132 Boissier 1906 II 6 407.

133 Duchesne 1911 III 4 198.

134 Boissier 1906 II 6 421–23; Hartmann 1923 I 2 30–31; Onory 1931 269–70.   And see pp. 273–74.

135 Hodgkin 1892 I 2 629–30 says 350,000 men; Lot 1927 267 says 275,-

lation of this half in the year 400 is a matter of the merest guess-work. Under Augustus the lowest total estimate is fifty million, [136] and, since the East was more populous, let us say twenty million for the West. By a most generous allowance of five million net loss during the four hundred years of the Empire,[137] we have left about fifteen million,[138] and consequently, in contrast to the late war during which several nations maintained one soldier for every ten of its population, Latin Rome maintained but one for every fifty. This is hardly more than conjecture, but it at least coincides with what we know of the attitude of the average Roman towards the barbarian threat. Since, then, the army was of fair quality,[139] yet deficient in numbers and disposition,[140] the blame must attach, not to the officers and men, but to the rulers and citizens. For one reason or another they really did not care.[141]

To one who sees history in terms of politics — as Gibbon, living in the late eighteenth century, was bound to — political decadence can only mean general decadence. Hence Gibbon, and many since, have thoughtlessly inferred that because in the year 400 there was bad government, bad taxation, bad citizenship, and bad military preparedness, there must also have been bad thinking, and that Augustine and the Christians merely substituted bad theory for bad practice. It is true that degeneration of government can breed physical disaster which, if acute and prolonged enough, will kill anything, including life itself and so all thought. This is what virtually did happen in the sixth century. But if we are to condemn Augustine on the evidence of the Roman State's condition in 406, we must also condemn Aristotle because of

---

000. Jullian 1926 VIII 77 says that there were about 25,000 Roman Gauls in the army, and about 70,000 Roman soldiers quartered in Gaul in 390: ibid. 102.

[136] Lot 1927 75, citing figures of Julius Beloch. Yet Diercks 1895 I 81 believes that Spain had a maximum population of thirty millions.

[137] Speck 1906 III part II 550 says that Italy had eight millions in the year 200, and Jullian 1920 V 27 says that Gaul had nearly forty millions in the year 160. A very heavy de-

cline occurred in the disturbances of the later third century: Jullian 1926 VII 24–29; but there was also a heavy increase from 285 on: ibid. 92 & 132–33, & VIII 237–40.

[138] Dudden 1935 25 estimates the population of Rome at two million in the year 350.

[139] Although poor as compared with its former quality: Lot 1927 267.

[140] Too many were quartered in cities of the interior: Jullian 1926 VIII 100–03.

[141] See p. 234 n. 46.

the Greece of Alexander's day,[142] Galileo because his Florence was decaying, Velasquez and Calderon because they lived in and learned from seventeenth century Spain. Doubtless civilization does follow the lead of politics, but often at a respectable distance! To say that the Roman pagan, the Manichee, the Neoplatonist, and the Christian would have been wiser had they given more consideration to politics, is to say the obvious; but to say that, because the Spartans, Carthaginians, and earlier Romans did give this consideration, they chose the better part, is simply to say that the body is more to be cherished than the soul.

B. THE CHURCH'S REMEDY

What was the Church likely to do to check this disintegration? Theoretically she was bound to work only along spiritual lines; this, however, was obviously not practicable. For, deeply embedded in her spiritual doctrine, was the material doctrine that the rich should give their substance to the poor. This generous precept many of the rich wished to follow. Yet how should they proceed? The great wealth of those days was in land, and the marketability of land, never conspicuously good, was now at its worst. Anything like a forced sale, therefore, must be at a great sacrifice, and the loss would fall, not on the generous donor, but on the poor he was so eager to enrich. The Church here offered the only practicable solution: she would accept conveyance of the land from the donor, undertaking to administer it and distribute the proceeds as she saw fit. The proportions were later fixed at three quarters for the Church and one quarter for the poor;[1] at this time the determination of the poor's share was left to the bishop's free discretion. A forced sale at half the true value, with all the proceeds going to the poor, would have provided the poor with twice as much, but it must be remembered that the Church was, as an administrative as well as a charitable or-

---

[142] Aristotle, although born in Chalcidice, was of pure Greek stock: Fuller 1931 III 2.

[1] See pp. 253–54, & 299 n. 74.

ganization, rightfully entitled to some share in the donor's generosity. Furthermore it was then already understood that if the poor were to be permanently benefited they must not be allowed to squander their capital. Therefore the Church's share, while excessive according to modern standards, was analogous to a trustee's fee for management. This solution may not have been the best even under the circumstances, but at least no one seems to have complained; its chief effect, nevertheless, was not a radical re-distribution of wealth but the transformation of the Church into a powerful economic machine.

These gifts of land were made in various ways: [2] besides the immediate conveyance in fee during the donor's life, there was the conveyance of the remainder, the donor reserving a life interest, or — which amounted to much the same thing — outright conveyance by testament. These would be unconditional gifts; but there were also gifts with conditions attached and which therefore had a business as well as a charitable purpose. Here the transaction, as we might expect, became analogous to that already described between the rich landlord and the impoverished freeman, the more so since the economic position of the Church was fast approximating that of the landed plutocracy. Bishop Paulinus of Nola, for instance, transferred many of his *fundi* [3] from himself as Senator of the Empire to himself as bishop of the Church of Nola. The impoverished freeman now had the choice of becoming the serf of either a lay landlord or the Church — in each case conveying legal title in return for the guarantee of protection of both his possession and his person. Exactly what considerations governed his choice must have depended on many ephemeral factors: conveyance to the Church satisfied his conscience if he were a good Catholic; it must often have promised a more considerate treatment. On the other hand, where the needs of physical protection rather than financial difficulties were prompting him, he might prefer the lay protection offered because of the Church's unwillingness to resort to force. Yet even this would depend on the conditions of the moment: where the marauders were physically powerful yet well disposed towards the Church,

[2] Cf. Onory 1932 279–80.   [3] See p. 236 n. 61.

spiritual protection would be the more effective. In this way the feudal system developed along two parallel lines, lay lord and bishop vying with each other for the ownership and control of the soil.

Besides these gifts of land the Church had other sources of income. The pious donor might occasionally be able to sell to advantage, or at any rate might prefer to sell, even at a disadvantage, in order to make the whole principal available at once. In other cases he would have substantial liquid assets that he could dispose of, or well secured debts that he could assign. His gift of these would be unconditional or else for a specific purpose — as for the repair or construction of a church. If unconditional, the Church could spend the whole, treating it as income if the immediate need suggested this; otherwise she might invest it, by the purchase of more land, in order to increase her capital, or by the repair or construction of buildings.

A second source of income was from contributions for current expenses. There was not yet any obligation to contribute a stated percentage of one's income [4] — like the later ten per cent tithe — so that the amounts received must have been variable. The labourer was in this way encouraged to contribute his mite.

A third source of income came from conveyances of land by the *civitas* or imperial *fisc*.[5] Here the Church undertook to manage the property and, out of the proceeds, to help in the maintenance of roads, bridges, levees, aqueducts, and even city fortifications.[6] The civil authorities were apparently authorized to do this in order to take the administration of the properties out of politics — in order to prevent graft, squandering, or waste — and in this way save the revenue.[7] The Church was willing to accept the conveyances on these conditions because she was concerned for the public welfare. This not only increased her temporal power, it also put her

[4] Marignan 1899 I 296–97.

[5] Much of this was property of the pagan Churches, confiscated from 363 on: Jullian 1926 VIII 153–54. Much more came from forfeitures or confiscations at the expense of individuals: ibid. 49–50. This does not mean, however, that the domain of the *fisc* was always increasing, for parcels of it were constantly being turned back into private ownership, by sale or otherwise: Fustel de Coulanges 1891 II 76.

[6] Onory 1932 108–09.

[7] Ibid. 109–10.

under certain obligations to the civil power that might later prove awkward. Her acceptance, therefore, was prompted by a sense rather of public duty than of private advantage.

That the authorized public officials, because of their confidence in the integrity of the Church, often abused this right to alienate the public property is indicated by the decrees not only of the pagan Emperor Julian but also of the Catholic Emperor Theodosius which demanded the restoration to the State of all properties illegally conveyed.[8] But the tide was running so strongly against the State and towards the Church that these decrees accomplished little. Fate had decreed that the Roman Church should supplant the Roman State; against this, the decrees of Emperors rebounded like rubber balls.

In those days land — with its appurtenances of buildings, equipment, and slaves — was almost the only kind of capital wealth;[9] what it produced was income. The lands held by the Church had therefore become one of the important reservoirs of capital on which the Romans could still draw, and it was to everybody's interest that they remain intact. In the deeds of conveyance from State or *civitas* alienation was probably expressly forbidden; in the deeds of individuals, however, there must often have been no such clause. Here lay a danger. An unscrupulous — or an over-generous — bishop might be tempted to gain an immediate financial advantage — for himself or his flock — at the expense of the income to accrue to later generations. This risk was so great that, already before 400, various Councils had forbidden any such alienations; at the Council held at Carthage in 398 the only exception allowed was where three co-provincial bishops agreed that the contemplated sale was a necessity.[10] Similar restrictions were repeated at various later times,[11] and the State enacted concurrent legislation. In general the State did not seriously object to illegal conveyances of the public lands to the Church; but it did object to conveyances by the Church, because if land got into the hands of either the rich or the impecunious, it was likely to escape taxation.[12] The Church alone was both honest and solvent.

---

[8] Ibid. 110.

[9] Fustel de Coulanges 1891 II 150–51 & 192–93; Bloch 1922 255 & 262.

[10] Dill 1926 441.

[11] In 447 by Pope Leo, see *Letter* # 17; in 483: Hodgkin 1896 III 2 143; in 506: Dill 1926 441.

[12] On the efforts to check the dissi-

By the year 406, therefore, the bishop was already bur-
dened with enormous temporal responsibilities: he became,
in addition to much else, a great landlord, with a large part
of Rome's wealth, and a large part of Rome's population, in
his charge.   In an earlier day the bishop was chosen, by pious
laity and professional clergy, because of his spiritual qualifications.   How should such a person effectively manage huge
estates and revenues, govern large communities of men?   The
difficulty was partially solved by the assistance of laymen to
do the things that they could do as well as, or better than, a
priest.

There already existed a lay officer with the title of *defensor
ecclesiae,* appointed by and under the orders of the bishop.[13]
At first his chief function had been to see that religious factions did not too seriously disturb the public peace; [14] later he
was also charged to hear complaints of the poor against exploitation by the rich.[15]   This latter function may have suggested the imperial law of 364 or 368 which authorized the
appointment, by the *curia's* election, of a *defensor civitatis*
' in order that the people . . . may be protected against injuries done by the *potentiores.*' [16]   As the temporal responsibilities of the Church increased so did the powers of the
defensor ecclesiae: as he was charged with the enforcement of
the canon law,[17] so he initiated the prosecution of heretics
before the civil courts.[18]   It was therefore natural that, as the
landed properties of the Church increased, it should be the
defensor ecclesiae who was charged with their administration.[19]   Occasionally this lay office was held by a priest; [20] in
such a case Church and lay administration seemed indistinguishable.   The bishop could of course dismiss his agent —
as he had appointed him — at his pleasure; but so long as he
kept his place his authority was wide.   Where the bishop was
not worldly-wise and where the *defensor ecclesiae* was honest,
the arrangement served its purpose admirably.

---

pation of the *curiales'* property see
p. 243 n. 115.
   13 Onory 1932 146.
   14 Ibid. 142–43.
   15 Ibid. 143.
   16 Quoted by Onory 1931 326 n. 31.
Cf. Fustel de Coulanges 1891 II 39.
And see Jullian 1926 VII 65 n. 5 & 69

n. 5 on the veto power over the election reserved to the praetorian
prefect.
   17 Onory 1932 153–54.
   18 Ibid. 142–43.
   19 Ibid. 150–51.
   20 Ibid. 146.

A good illustration of how the Church became more and more involved in the temporal activity of the *civitas* is furnished by the Church of Piacenza which, not long before 400, was building levees along the Po in order to protect her lands from floods.[21] If these lands were among those conveyed by *civitas* or State, she was obliged to do this; but even if they were hers unconditionally she was under a moral obligation to do it because she received her revenue as a public trust. And as Church she was not unconcerned with the protection of the peasants' lands equally exposed to floods. The time was soon to come when, if the Church did not build levees, they simply were not built.

Besides the laws putting restraints on the alienation of land and the appointment of a *defensor ecclesiae,* there was another factor conducive to the maintenance of a maximum revenue: the Church secured certain exemptions from taxation. Until 360 these exemptions had been considerable; [22] thereafter they were confined to the tax *munera sordida,* imposed to defray certain expenses in the upkeep of roads and bridges.[23] Intrinsically such an exemption was negligible; it was valuable, however, because it established a most fruitful precedent for the future.

The Church was so rich and prosperous in these years [24] that it has often been supposed that she received more substantial exemptions. But there is no evidence of this. She was rich rather because she was receiving gifts in ever increasing quantity and because she administered what she was given with a skill and integrity hardly now to be equalled within the Empire. In an age when everyone not only wanted to cheat everyone else but was too often able to do it, an organization which did not itself try to cheat and whom few therefore wished to cheat was by far the fittest to survive.

It is not clear how much freedom the bishop had in the spending of the income. There was apparently no machinery whereby clergy or people could restrain him. The fact that his discretion long remained so wide indicates that cases of abuse or even of alleged abuse were rare. Jerome and John

---

[21] Ibid. 107–08.
[22] Lot 1927 113.
[23] Onory 1932 100. Jullian 1926 VIII 41 n. 4 thinks that Church property was also exempted from the land tax, but he admits that this is problematical.
[24] Onory 1931 254.

Chrysostom believed that the current contributions should go to the support of the clergy; [25] Augustine thought that these should go exclusively to the poor.[26] Doubtless a conventional division of the revenue for the various needs of the diocese took shape at an early time, but until after 470 [27] no decree made any such division obligatory. Until then the bishop had to be trusted, and he rarely betrayed this trust.

Although in the fourth century the bishop of Rome was already a conspicuous figure, the recognized governing authority of the Church was the Ecumenical or General Council, composed of all the bishops; and its recognized leader — if any — was, following the precedent set by Constantine at Nicæa in 325, the Roman Emperor, who alone had the power to summon such a Council and to dissolve it.[28] This Council was, however, only a legislative — perhaps only a judicial [29] — body; the executive power lay with each bishop of the many hundred dioceses.[30] The bishops of those dioceses which were also, as *civitates,* the provincial capitals of the civil government, came to be known as archbishops, and they had a certain ill-defined precedence over the other, suffragan, bishops within that province. But their superiority depended rather on the importance of their *civitas* than on any traditional or legal distinction.[31] Thus in the East the greatest were those of Alexandria, Antioch, Jerusalem, and Constantinople; in the West those of Rome, Milan,[32] Carthage, Trier,[33] Lyons,[34] and Arles — the largest cities respectively of Italy, Africa, and Gaul. Ambrose, bishop of Milan from 373 to 397, overshadowed his contemporaries, bishops Damasus and Siricius of Rome, partly because he was the greater man, but partly also because it was the Milanese — whose city was

---

25 Robinson 1914 64.
26 Ibid.
27 See p. 248 n. 1, & 299 n. 74.
28 Caspar 1930 I 119.
29 See p. 231.
30 See Duchesne 1911 III 4 25–31.
31 Turner 1911 153; Bayet 1911 22.
32 Milan had been the western capital since 286, and the Cæsars and other military commanders made it their headquarters: Lot 1927 24, 41, 234 & 241–42. Ricimer, the real

ruler of Italy after 455, resided in Milan, whereas the Emperors of his time resided in Rome: ibid. 242. During the fifth century Milan was almost as populous as Rome: Hartmann 1923 I 2 7.
33 Salvian *D.G.D.* VI § 75 says that when Trier was sacked in the early fifth century it was ‘ the richest city in Gaul ’.
34 Jullian 1920 VI 515–27.

then the Western capital [35] — and not the Romans, who chose him.

Since the ecclesiastical provinces and dioceses corresponded to the civil provinces and *civitates,* the apportionment was fore-ordained. In Africa the number of dioceses was enormous — 466; [36] in Italy there were 250; [37] in Gaul only 112. In Gaul the number of provinces was large in proportion — 17 — averaging less than six suffragans for each archbishop.[38] Had there been Western Councils with anything like a full attendance of bishops, Africa would have had an overwhelming numerical advantage. Such a Council was never held, however; consequently the African Councils, huge as they were, bound Africa alone. In the development of canon law Africa led the Latin West; one reason may have been her need to exercise a close supervision over so numerous an episcopate.

From a temporal standpoint the Church's most daring and successful experiment was the popular election of her bishops by the combined vote of clergy and populace.[39] This of course meant the Catholic populace, and as this was at first a small group the system was natural and practicable. The marvel is that when this group expanded to include a huge city population the principle was never altered and rarely disregarded — an extraordinary indication of the solidarity of the faithful. The classic Latin election is that of Ambrose in Milan in 373. The Arian bishop, Auxentius, having died, it became the duty of Ambrose, as governor of the province of Æmilia-Liguria, to maintain order and see that the election of the new bishop be fairly conducted.[40] Our description is by Paulinus of Milan, a disciple of Ambrose writing more than a generation after the event:

When, now that the see was vacant, the populace began to riot, since it was his duty to suppress the sedition lest the people be endangered, he proceeded to the church; and there, as he was

---

[35] So often as Theodosius resided at Milan, Ambrose was his personal bishop. On the prestige of Milan see Dudden 1935 64.

[36] Onory 1931 592.

[37] Or at least in the year 600: ibid. 249.

[38] This figure is also for the year 600: Pfister 1911 208.

[39] Bayet 1911 22 & 24; Onory 1931 252.

[40] As Milan was the capital of the province (Dudden 1935 62), Ambrose was already well known to her citizens.

haranguing the people, suddenly the voice of an infant in the crowd is said to have piped up that Ambrose was bishop. At the sound of this voice the shouts of the whole people changed, crying out that Ambrose was bishop; so that those who before were violently disagreeing because both the Arians and the Catholics desired, upon overcoming the other, the ordination of a bishop of their own party, now suddenly, with marvellous and unbelievable accord, agreed on this one man.[41]

At this time Ambrose was not only a civil official, he was, technically, a catechumen and therefore a pagan, for he had not been baptized. Taken aback by this unexpected manifestation he slipped out of the city, probably rather to collect his thoughts than because he wanted to dodge the responsibility. But he was pursued, captured, and finally persuaded:

> Thus discovered and brought to Milan, when he learned what God willed of him and that he could not longer resist, he asked only that he should not be baptized except by a Catholic bishop; for he was wary of the perfidy of the Arians. And, having been thus baptized, it is said that he filled [in turn] each of the ecclesiastical offices, and on the eighth day was ordained bishop to the great relief and delight of all.[42]

Whatever may be the inaccuracies of this account two matters are clear. Ambrose, being a layman, was a far more acceptable candidate than any priest could have been. Had he at that time been a priest, even the more lukewarm Arians would have opposed him. It is also clear that the tradition of a popular election was still vigorous — *vox populi, vox Dei* — a current running directly counter to the absolutism of the State. The Church here offered a welcome outlet for democratic instincts that the Empire had repressed.

Of course in the majority of cases the nomination was made by a small group: the local clergy, the adjacent bishops, the archbishop — even the State officials.[43] Often too, as did Augustine just before his death in 430, the dying bishop named his successor.[44] In a good many cases the nomination was arbitrary and was even foisted on a reluctant electorate. Yet, so rare were the flagrant abuses, that the people ever regarded their bishop as their own representative acting

41 Paulinus of Milan *Vita S. Ambrosii* § 6.
42 Ibid. § 9.

43 Onory 1931 262. Cf. Sidonius *Letters* IV # 25, & VII # # 5 & 9.
44 Augustine *Letter* # 213.

in their interest, as the man through whom they were able to play a real if modest part, not only in their city but also in the whole Church and the whole world. To be sure, the archbishop could refuse to consecrate as bishop one who was unqualified — he must be a priest, must be orthodox in doctrine, must have a clean record. To this extent, unavoidably, the archbishop retained a veto power; [45] but such a restriction was so natural and proper that it was rather cherished than resented. Strictly speaking, then, the people were not wholly free to choose their bishop, but, if they felt they were free, and if they treated him as their own man, the restriction was incidental.

Certainly in the West, perhaps in the East too, it was Ambrose above all who set the example of what a bishop could be. For he was not only a great spiritual leader; he was also a great temporal leader. His philosophy, as we have seen,[46] was tinged with the excessive other-worldliness of Neoplatonism. Perhaps, man of action that he naturally was, he needed such a slant in his philosophy in order to keep the proper equilibrium between the soul and the body: since he must act, let the body follow the most intangible instincts of the soul. In Ambrose the justice of God was first concretely applied to human affairs; he made justice as apparent to the hardened worldling as to the sensitive dreamer; he did not merely talk about it, he imposed it on all who crossed his path.

In his fierce desire to see justice done Ambrose championed the cause of all who suffered injustice. Theoretically justice was obtainable in the civil courts, but practically the judges were so corrupt that the poor or helpless got none — for they could not pay for it. Ambrose, being a trained lawyer,[47] chose to champion such persons in the courts. They might not be heard; he would be.

Nor was such action a novelty to the Romans. The conception of patronage and protection was a familiar one in a society swarming with slaves, serfs, freedmen, and other de-

---

[45] Milan being an archbishopric, not only the suffragan bishops of that province but also neighbouring archbishops would have a voice. These evidently consented only with the proviso that Ambrose should first qualify by baptism, ordination, etc.
[46] See pp. 67–69.
[47] Dudden 1935 58.

pendents. It had also been a pagan habit to commend oneself to some god or to the priest of that god.[48] Ambrose could
therefore present himself not only as the popular representative of his city but also as the priest of the new God. Apart
from the poor in general, who were of course his first concern,[49] Ambrose particularly chose to champion the cause of
widows; [50] and not so much because of the life of chastity that
they now presumably led as because they were the favourite
victims of the unscrupulous. The pauper was not easily
cheated because there was nothing to cheat him out of; the
widow on the other hand very often inherited a competence
and the game of the scoundrel was to get it away from her,
often no doubt by promising the judge a share of the spoils.
Her inheritance being usually in the custody of others, if
these should refuse to make delivery, she might have a hard
time in raising the money to pay the lawyer's fee and the
judge's bribe. The many analogous cases that called for the
bishop's intervention may be easily imagined: in one category
would be the freeman who was claimed as a serf, in another
the victim of a tax-collector who was trying to extract more
than he should.[51] Here would be a case of bureaucratic
collusion between tax-collector and judge,[52] with the bishop
champion of the people against the tyranny of the State.

In this the bishop acted merely as counsel for the aggrieved
party, whether plaintiff or defendant.[53] This accomplished
something, but not enough. Therefore the bishops, and Ambrose in particular, went a step further: they offered themselves as arbitrators in civil disputes.[54] In such a case the
judgment had no legal validity and could not be enforced,
but, unless the defeated litigant repudiated the judgment, he
must make a legal settlement in accordance with it which
could be enforced. At first the services of the bishop were
sought chiefly by honourable litigants who wanted no more
than justice and wished to save the costs of fees and bribes;
but, as the practice gained popularity, it may be that litigants

---

[48] Bloch 1911 442; Onory 1932 293
& 306.
[49] Cf. Onory 1931 277–83.
[50] Onory 1932 298–99.
[51] Cf. Onory 1931 317.
[52] Bloch 1922 249–50.
[53] Onory 1931 310.

[54] Having served as governor
of Æmilia-Liguria, Ambrose was
trained as a judge and was therefore
all the more sought after as an arbitrator: cf. Onory 1931 260–61 & 303–
04; & Dudden 1935 61.

dared not refuse the bishop's offer — particularly if they were Catholics who wanted to keep a good name.

By an imperial decree of the year 408 the bishop was formally empowered — still, however, only if both litigants consented — to adjudicate in civil cases.[55]   His judgments now had the force of law.   The bishop already had this power in civil cases where the defendant was a priest; [56] the machinery was therefore at hand.   This added power probably had little concrete effect, because litigants who had consented to arbitrate would usually abide by the decision; but it had considerable psychological effect because it made the bishop an integral part of the civil judiciary.   The consent of both parties was still requisite, but every day there were fewer and fewer litigants who dared to withhold that consent — for to do so was to confess that they sought an unjust advantage.

A sufficient — although not the only — reason for the increasing popularity of the episcopal courts was their impartiality.   The corruption in the lay courts had come to be appalling.   Even if we make allowance for the bitterness with which Ambrose or Augustine flayed them, it remains certain that conditions were unbearable.   To the torture of many of the accused and the cruel punishments — which at least were legal — were added great cruelty in the prisons and shameless perjury, bribery, and intimidation — which were quite illegal.   In theory — if we allow for differences in status — there was substantial equality before the law; in practice there was none.

That is why the bishop, representing the common opinion of all decent Romans, Christian or pagan, welcomed the chance to intervene.   And that is why, having assumed the duties, first of arbitrator later of judge, his court was so greatly preferred — often no doubt even by pagans — to the lay courts.[57]   For the high standard set much of the credit is due to Ambrose, he who, although devoted only to God, insisted that a Roman judge should heed no other law than that of Rome.   On the bench sentiment, even love, have no place:

---

[55] Onory 1931 302–07. This right had before been momentarily conferred by Constantine: Lot 1927 38 n. 2.

[56] Caspar 1930 I 206–07.

[57] Dalton 1927 I 303. Litigation was incidentally much cheaper, as bribery was eliminated: Bayet 1911 25.

He who judges is bound to follow not his own will but the law.[58]

And it was precisely because the lay courts did not execute that law that he consented to arbitrate out of court. Exasperated no doubt by the popularity which the decisions of Ambrose quickly acquired, the pagan Symmachus on one occasion sarcastically reminded him that

there are laws, there are tribunals, there are magistrates of which, saving your conscience, the litigant may avail himself.[59]

But it was precisely because the magistrates of the lay tribunals did not administer those laws honestly that Ambrose undertook to do this himself.

In the time of Ambrose, certainly, and probably too for a good many years after the law of 408 allowing episcopal adjudication, the Church fought for justice rather indirectly than directly — trusted rather to spiritual than to temporal weapons. In the many cases involving hereditary status it was only where a feudal relationship had been established that the State occupied an outside position as a third party. Moreover in cases involving the non-payment of taxes the creditor-plaintiff was the State, as the State was also plaintiff in all criminal suits. In all such litigation the bishop must act in a purely private capacity, for it was inconceivable that the State should ever consent to episcopal adjudication of suits brought by the sovereign power. Nor, if one of the private litigants were a pagan or a scoundrel, would there be consent to episcopal jurisdiction by both parties even in a civil suit. In the great majority of cases, therefore, the bishop must be content openly to espouse the cause of the aggrieved plaintiff or defendant, seeking either to touch the judge's conscience or — if he were a Christian — to rouse his fear of God's wrath.[60] And, as the taxpayer or alleged criminal was defended against the rigour of the law, so was the slave defended, and the serf, widow, orphan, bastard, and stranger.[61] Where men like Ambrose fought, at least justice would be done, and not infrequently equity too.

Bishops like Ambrose championed a strict enforcement of

[58] Quoted by Onory 1931 310.
[59] Quoted by ibid. 314.
[60] The threat of excommunication was their most effective weapon.

[61] Onory 1931 290–91.

the Roman law.[62]   But this was not because they respected its sanctity as they did the law of the Gospels.   Christian respect for Roman law could begin only with the reign of Constantine, and the approbation which it was now receiving from such men as Ambrose [63] became possible only as Roman legislation began to favour not only the Church as an institution but Christian ethics as the basis for a new legal equity.   To the State, therefore, the Church was under a deep obligation.

Nevertheless, even by the year 390, Roman law had not become synonymous with Christian ethics, and, as the bishop felt his prestige and authority grow, he was tempted, by a very liberal interpretation,[64] unobtrusively to correct certain discrepancies still subsisting.   To what degree the fifth century bishops actually undertook to legislate for the *civitates* we cannot say, but, as even criminal law came more and more under their influence, it must have been a temptation to plead emergency as a pretext for a less literal interpretation of the laws than Ambrose, for instance, could logically have approved.   The law regarding slaves was a case in point.   Christianity recognized the status, but resented the brutality which that status implicitly countenanced.[65]   If the Old Law demanded a strict justice, the New Law demanded also a discriminating mercy.   That the New was now often substituted for the Old we cannot doubt.   For one thing tax abatements must, in one way or another, have been often secured.   Even the unwritten law of war was criticized.   This had apparently not been affected by Christian influence, so that crimes committed by soldiers remained, if not technically legal, at least effectively excusable.   Against this soldier's privilege Ambrose thundered: of killing in a just war he tacitly approved, but he denied that acts of violence incidental to war — robbery, rape, the killing of prisoners — were any less criminal because committed by soldiers in the field.[66] And so even of the oath: because made to an enemy it was no less made to God, and if, therefore, a commander promised the enemy that he would attack only at a given time or place,

---

[62] Ibid. 271–76, 310, & 321.
[63] See Dudden 1935 524 & 537–38.
[64] Onory 1931 315.
[65] The Church, for instance, maintained the validity and sanctity of

a marriage between slaves: Marignan 1899 I 119; & see ibid. 305.
[66] Onory 1931 319.   Cf. Synesius of Cyrene *On Kingship* ch. 18.

he was bound to keep his word.[67]   Although a Christian might serve as a soldier and hence kill men in battle, he must never imagine himself to be an ordinary soldier.

It was in criminal law, of course, that the Christian doctrine chiefly differed from the pagan Roman.   And this was because, strictly speaking, the Christian did not believe in taking life except in self-defence.   The reason given was that in case the victim were in a state of sin he would have no time properly to repent, do penance, receive absolution.[68]   But the underlying reason was that the Christians recoiled at cruelty — however traditional the form it might take.   A condemned criminal might have ample time to make his peace with God — more time than if spared in order later to die as nature decreed; yet the Church would have no hand in bloodshed even of this kind, favouring a maximum of thirty-nine stripes as the extreme penalty consonant with her principles.[69]   And, since all capital punishments were unjust, it was the task of the bishop to prevent them, and therefore to resort to specious arguments and moral pressure which pagans thought both tactless and demoralizing.[70]

The protection of all fugitives and other strangers was another task new to the Romans which the bishops undertook. Under the pagan Empire such persons had not been welcome,[71] partly because slavery, and later the laws imposing hereditary occupations, raised a presumption that the newcomer was a fugitive from justice — to be treated accordingly.   This heartless system the bishops, supported by the humane precedent of certain lay landlords, resisted vigorously and, in order to emphasize their disapproval, took pains to receive all newcomers with an almost ostentatious hospitality.[72]   To this end

[67] Onory 1931 320.
[68] As Ambrose argued: Dudden 1935 121.
[69] Cf. Cyprian *Vitae Cæsarii* (of Arles) I § 25; & Grisar 1912 II 348. This was certainly a wholesome reaction against such laws as that of the loyal Catholic Emperor Valentinian I (364–375) which made insolvency a crime punishable by death: Bloch 1922 274.
[70] Germanus of Auxerre — faithful to *Psalm* # 146 7: 'the Lord looseth the prisoners' — set prisoners free in Ravenna in about 440, by a miracle after his effort to obtain their pardon had failed: Constantius *Vita Germani* § 36.   How many of these were poor debtors condemned to death?   Geneviève is said to have done likewise in Paris in about 470: anonymous *Vita Genovefae* § 26. See Dalton 1927 I 309 for sixth century instances.   The eastern hermits were acting on this principle as early as 387: Dudden 1935 365.
[71] Onory 1931 296.
[72] Ibid. 292 ff.

Ambrose [73] was among the first to provide accommodation for such persons, usually in a building adjoining the episcopal residence. No charge was exacted, no questions were asked, but if a more positive help were requested the bishop put himself at their disposal. Ambrose said a bishop must so act because Christianity taught the brotherhood of man; [74] actually there were more tangible reasons: for the stranger was as often a fugitive from injustice as from justice — and, in these last years of the fourth century, was often fleeing from the cruelty of a Roman usurper.[75]

Closely associated with this practice of hospitality was the Church's recognition of the right of asylum or sanctuary: when any fugitive — from justice or injustice — was able to reach the altar of a church, the bishop took him under his protection, refusing to surrender him until his pursuers had given certain assurances. It happened that this was a pagan Greek [76] and Roman,[77] and even a pagan Germanic,[78] custom — originally conceived in order to prevent the sacrilege of bloodshed in the temple — and it was, therefore, instinctively respected even by the pagans and barbarians.[79] Pursuers who hoped to carry off the fugitive by violence were in this way effectively [80] foiled. The bishop could not of course refuse to turn him over to the civil authorities should they demand this; but such a demand was not likely to be made unless apparently a valid one, for these civil officers knew that the bishop would follow up the case in order to see justice done.[81] And, in certain cases where the law itself offended Christian sensibilities, he was likely to resort to tactics that made prosecution and conviction inexpedient. For behind the bishop were the people, whereas behind the prosecution there was no one but an Emperor.

---

[73] Ibid. 285. Paulinus of Nola founded a hostel for pilgrims to the tomb of the martyr Felix of Nola when he was still a layman — perhaps as early as 385: Lagrange 1877 34 & 216; & Krüger 1923 191. Fabiola founded a convalescent home in Rome and another in the country: Jerome *Letter* # 77 § 6. On the precedent set by the East in this respect see ibid. # 66 § 11.

[74] Onory 1931 295.

[75] And Emperor, perhaps; for a season or several seasons.

[76] Dill 1926 452.

[77] See Carlyle 1927 I [2] 49 n. 5, quoting *Digest* I 6 § 2.

[78] Brunner 1928 II [2] 756 & 791.

[79] Onory 1931 297–98.

[80] For a case of divine vengeance for an Arian flouting of this right in 396, see Dudden 1935 486–87.

[81] Cf. Dalton 1927 I 312, for the later period.

We have already mentioned a law of Constantine which forbad any of the unfortunate *curiales* from taking Orders.[82] Should such a person slip away in order to join the clergy, yet be discovered before he had qualified for ordination, doubtless he must go back, and pay a penalty to boot. But if he had been ordained before he was discovered the matter was not so simple: would the Church be willing to recognize the ordination as invalid, or proceed to annul the ordination because in conflict with the civil law? Such delicate questions must not infrequently have arisen, and it is safe to suppose that the Church usually got her own way.[83] Particularly would this be so where the fugitive had escaped from one of the humbler of the hereditary occupations: in this case the ordination was sustained. Nevertheless in all these cases the priest was obliged to make such reparation as he could, handing over so much of his property as was necessary to indemnify the aggrieved party.

In regard to the fugitive in general we know much more of the law than of the reality. How effectively were the laws enforced and what were the loopholes discovered, enabling men to evade their apparent intent? We at least know that many of the laws of this time were very poorly enforced; we know that even before the invasions the country-side was already dotted with fugitives from the new Roman justice,[84] and we may safely assume that only a small proportion of these were ever recaptured. How, in the late fourth century, was any fugitive from Sicily to be recaptured in Gaul? How was an obscure runaway serf to be apprehended even in the next province? We know too that the Church was in constant need of more priests, of many, many more recruits to serve in the lower orders. In a day of regimentation, hereditary occupations, and a stationary if not declining population, the problem of supply was a serious one. There was perhaps a second reason, therefore, why the Church chose to welcome all strangers with open arms, asking no questions. According

---

[82] See p. 243 n. 113.

[83] Cf. Onory 1931 251.

[84] Lot 1927 115 says: ' Chacun se trouve mal dans sa condition et cherche à y échapper. Le paysan déserte la campagne, l'ouvrier abandonne son métier, le décurion fuit le sénat municipal. A ces maux le pouvoir ne trouve qu'un remède: river chacun à sa condition, boucher les issues par lesquelles il pourrait s'évader.' Enforcement was doubtless irksome without being effective.

to Severus, Martin obtained his discharge by the personal intervention of the pagan Emperor Julian.[85] This is a rather surprising statement.[86] But even if Martin himself was not a fugitive from justice, many another soldier certainly was, and surveillance would be stricter in the army than elsewhere. We are here in the realm rather of surmise than of certainty, but to the extent that the clergy of this time were recruited from the fugitives — whether of the middle or lower classes — their attitude towards the State must have been rather resentful than grateful, one of rivalry rather than co-operation.

But did not the Church offer merely another kind of serfdom? Were not the priests bound, like so many lay Romans, to a life service of obedience? A large proportion joined because of a sincere wish the better in this way to serve God, but many, too, joined for more worldly reasons. In many cases the priests had children, born before their ordination. How were these now to be provided for? This problem entails so many ramifications that it cannot be effectively resolved; but we may fairly observe that, as a career, the Church offered the solid advantage of quick promotions — for she was still elastic and growing fast. And she also offered novelty: escape from a hated present bondage to a new one that could not prove more irksome and might prove light. If serfdom it must be, let it by all means be a privileged serfdom, serving not man but God.

How much direct good the Church did by these various interferences with the orderly — or rather disorderly — processes of civil administration, is hard to say. Certainly she did much to popularize the ideals of honesty, decency, and humanity; at the same time, by contrast, she tended to discredit the State at the moment of crisis, and to draw the best men away from civil life. Economically and politically she probably did as much harm as good; her most substantial contribution of a temporal kind was in the domain of justice. Yet even here the immediate benefit is questionable: certainly capital punishment did not become discredited, nor even torture, mutilation, oppression, and slavery. On the other hand the worst evils of Roman criminal law were laid mercilessly

---

[85] Severus *Life of Martin* 8 & 9.   [86] Cf. Monceaux 1926 20 & 25.

bare, and, had the barbarians not come so fast to topple Latin civilization, a substantial humanitarian reform might gradually have been effected. The Church gave the Roman world its first glimpse of a regime where justice was generously tempered with mercy; [87] but the move was ill-timed: for as the Roman heart grew kinder it grew also humbler. The Church was willing to fight for temporal justice but not for temporal rule — Ambrose preferred intercession and arbitration to adjudication — and to go half-way was not enough. Supported by an iron-clad political rule, the new justice might have prevailed — as within the Church it did — but in a regime of mounting chaos it was doomed. Eschewing direct political control, the justice of Ambrose, too sheltered from the circle of reality, was likely to degenerate into the promiscuous mercy of the doctrinaire. For salutary mercy is a refinement of justice and can therefore flourish only when justice is itself secure. Where, instead, violence rules, mercy is premature and sterile.[88]

To the bishop's temporal undertakings, as landlord, as lawyer and judge, as the host of strangers, may be added a few others in which he served quite directly as an agent of the State. On many occasions, for instance, he served as ambassador or negotiator, Ambrose undertaking such missions for the Emperor himself.[89] In such cases the bishop was of course free to decline, he was therefore an official of the State only if he chose; but in other matters he was a permanent cog in the civil machinery: as where he must serve, *ex officio,* as a member of the municipal *curia,*[90] or where he must take a leading part in the election of the *defensor civitatis.*[91] If such tasks were willingly undertaken for the sake of spiritual ends, where was the line to be drawn? If the general welfare were a spiritual end, might not the Church take over the State itself?

Shall we rather say that the Church was willing to assume temporal tasks so long as these involved persuasion only, and

[87] Cf. Salvian *Letter* # 4 §§ 15 & 24–25, written in about 440.

[88] For a late fifth century instance see Hodgkin 1896 III [2] 331.

[89] Duchesne 1910 II [4] 551 & 554; Dudden 1935 223–24 & 346–50.

[90] Gouilloud 1881 244.

[91] Onory 1931 326 n. 31: together with clergy, *honorati, possessores,* and *curiales.*

not force? Even this was only half true, for the bishop had become, whether he liked it or not, the virtual ruler of the city, the man to whom the citizens turned for help. How could he refuse this help on the plea that the service asked was temporal? Consequently there were cases, even before the invasions, when a city, besieged in the course of civil war, took orders from its bishop.[92] One reason was that the *curator*, technically in charge, was usually an outsider who felt no loyalty to the city and who was, as likely as not, in collusion with the besieging faction. The bishop might not relish the responsibility, but he must relish the trust that the people put in him. Consequently, however diffidently, he took the lead.

Had a bishop who acted in this capacity been accused of embarking on a military venture he would have been profoundly shocked: he would have protested that he was a man of peace, even a pacifist, preaching the doctrine of non-resistance, that he was encouraging resistance only in the name of justice and in order to protect his flock from annihilation — ultimately defending, not even the lives of individuals as such, but only the faith — because a part of that faith was in them and would die if they died. By a canon of the Council of Rome held in 386 no one who had served in the army after baptism was qualified for ordination as a priest.[93] How then might a consecrated bishop undertake to lead an armed citizenry? The explanation is that such a citizenry was wholly distinguishable from the army as then understood. It had long been the law that no citizen could bear arms. This meant that no citizen might bear arms unless regularly enrolled in the imperial army. The law was intended to prevent insurrections by the civilian population, it did not aim to punish citizens who, within their own walls, armed to defend their city from a siege,[94] especially if the besiegers were acting against the Emperor. Therefore an imperial army and an armed citizenry were two quite different things, and this a bishop, being a Roman as well as a priest, understood instinctively. The citizenry were fighting in a cause undeniably just; the imperial army was fighting in a cause often

[92] Onory 1932 250.
[93] Hefele 1908 II 2 69–70.
[94] Onory 1932 264 & 267 n. 65.

unjust and, if also often just, for a kind of justice that only a farsighted patriot can appreciate.

This bishop was thus unwittingly encouraging a tendency which was typical of the times: to fight for one's country was a folly; to fight for one's city was a merit. Patriotism was already shifting from the invisible, impersonal State,[95] to the visible and personal city. Temporal civilization was beginning to shrink.[96]

Was the character of the bishop and priest of this time quite as high as our knowledge of the great leaders like Martin, Ambrose, Jerome, and Augustine might lead us to believe? Not if we may trust the records which they themselves have left us, for their picture is of a general corruption so rife that every honest man constituted an oasis in a desert, and, if this be so of the laity, it cannot have been quite untrue of the clergy. That the clergy as an institution were honourable, even noble, we may well believe; but in our admiration for the great men and for the deeds wrought by the Church as a whole, we must not forget that she had enemies not only outside but inside — enemies, not of society perhaps, but of holiness.

Conversion, from a worldly handicap, became after Constantine a worldly advantage.[97] It was inevitable that many, although actuated chiefly by worldly considerations, should seek not only baptism but also ordination and even consecration. The fashion changes more quickly than the heart. This is how Jerome describes a certain type of priest all too prevalent in the later fourth century:

Hastily, at sun-rise, he gets up, lays out the order of his visits, picks the shortest routes, indeed the importunate old man all but intrudes into the [lady's] bedroom. When he sees a cushion, a fine cloth or some other object of this kind, he praises it, pats it, gazes admiringly at it, complains that he has nothing of such quality at home and so manages that he is made a present of it. . . .

---

95 Orosius, born in 384 and therefore ten or fifteen years older than Salvian or Leo, had already condemned the brutality and injustice of the original Roman conquests of Carthage and Spain (his own land): *H.A.P.* V 1 §§ 5 & 6.

96 Cf. Lot 1927 403; & Onory 1931 270–71, 556–57, & 570–71. On the effect of a more restricted area for marketing and trade, see Jullian 1926 VIII 202–03.

97 See pp. 61, 337, & 536; & Labriolle 1934 438.

Wherever you go, he is always the first person you meet; he knows all the latest news; runs in order to be the first to repeat it; if necessary he invents or at any rate embellishes it each time, with new details.[98]

This, even if not an exaggeration, is innocent enough; even if the cushion or cloth had been the more easily acquired because he was a Christian priest, the fact would have raised smiles rather than accusations. But the picture given to Severus a few years later by Postumianus [99] is of rather a different kind:

We shall suppose a man remarkable neither for his wisdom nor his virtue, and that this man takes Orders. At once his borders are enlarged. He delights in being saluted in the streets, he swells with pride at his many visitors, and he himself parades in public whenever it is possible to do so. Formerly he travelled on foot or astride an ass; but now he is a personage and is whirled along by foaming steeds. In the days of old he was content to dwell in a small, poor cell, but now his abode is beneath high-panelled roofs; many fine apartments are planned for him; his doorways are carved and his cabinets inlaid. He despises rough, coarse garments, and clothes himself in soft raiment. Accordingly he makes good use of his well-beloved widows and of the holy virgins who are his friends; some will weave for him a warm, soft overcoat, and others will furnish a beautiful flowing mantle.[100]

And, as if to prove that this picture is not a caricature, Gallus tells Severus something of the career of the priest Brictio before he succeeded Martin as bishop of Tours on the latter's death in 397:

Brictio, who before he became a priest had possessed nothing of his own, who had even been maintained at the monastery by Martin's charity, this very Brictio now kept horses and purchased slaves. And it was even said that, not content with buying youths of alien races, he also dealt in young and pretty girls.[101]

If many Romans, by becoming Christian priests, could not change their spots, we cannot suppose that a Roman who, though converted to Christianity, still chose to live in the lay world, underwent any more radical transformation. In

[98] *Letter #* 22 § 28.
[99] See pp. 180, & 190.
[100] *Dialogue* I 21.
[101] Ibid. III 15; partly quoted p.

195. For the bias of Postumianus and his friend Gallus, see pp. 194 & 196 n. 16.

many, no doubt, the change effected by conversion was revolutionary, but in many too it was perfunctory.[102]

By the year 406, therefore, Christianity had already become a respectable, conventional, and even fashionable religion whose priests and laymen were hardly distinguishable from the pagan population. It had cut deep only into the hearts of a few sensitive and imaginative persons; the rest admired rather its prestige than its creed, found it more picturesque than engrossing. There was now, to be sure, a new philosophy of life; but the Roman world was still the same world, irresistibly tempting men to live in it much as they always had. Life might now seem better explained, but it was still the same life that was being explained. Viewed teleologically, therefore — and even historically — the invasions and the fall of the State were probably essential in order that the Christian revelation might be complete. Ambrose, Jerome, and Augustine did not require this final disclosure, but the bulk of Romans did. For, without imagination, instruction must fail; only acute personal experience will serve; only as the Earthly City melted before men's eyes did the City of God take shape; only as the Roman body was wracked could its soul be heard. Before 406 Christianity's popular appeal was rather to curiosity or disgust; after 406 rather to conviction or despair. Among the ungifted but honest believers Christianity passed in the course of a generation from an enticing theory to a stern fact. There may have been more real doubt, but there was also infinitely more terror of doubting. As a great historical force Christianity now passed on from speculative adolescence to practical maturity. Leaving the schools, it entered the seat of government.

C. Role of the Bishops, 406–454

It was in the year 400 that Alaric and his Visigoths crossed the Alps into Italy. Although stoutly resisted by the Romans in the Po valley, Alaric held out so tenaciously that in course of time the Emperor Honorius became uneasy and recalled

102 Babut 1912 126–30.

to Italy the legions guarding the Rhine frontier.   It was this
which precipitated the first major invasion: hordes of Vandals, Alani, and Sueves poured across the Rhine in 406 to
inundate Gaul, and then, when Gaul had been thoroughly
pillaged, passed over the Pyrenees three years later to do the
same in Spain.[1]   And whatever the legions of the Rhine may
have achieved as reinforcements against Alaric, it was not
enough: in 410 he and his Visigoths sacked Rome.[2]

Alaric died soon after, but the Visigoths stayed on in southern Italy.   Thereupon Honorius resorted to a second device
at the expense of Gaul, allowing, perhaps encouraging, the
Visigoths to leave Italy for Aquitaine.   A few years later they
overflowed into Spain; finally in 419 Honorius, in the hope
of quieting them, granted them legal possession of *Aquitania
Secunda* — or western [3] Aquitaine north of the Garonne —
on condition that they should serve as allies of the Empire.
Here, with their wives, their children and their booty, they
settled.[4]

This occupation of Gaul by the Visigoths, coming as it did
immediately after the destruction wrought by Vandal, Alan,
and Sueve, was to the Romans an unforgettable nightmare.
Prosper of Aquitaine, writing in 416,[5] gives this lurid account:

> He who before tilled his land with a hundred plows
> Now longs to be able to have a single yoke of oxen.
> Habitually borne through the great cities in coaches
> Painfully now he plods on foot to his desolate farm.
> He who before had ten lofty galleys sailing the sea
> Now boards a small cutter and sails it himself.
> Nothing is any longer as it was, on farm or in city,
> Everything runs precipitately to its destruction.
> With sword, plague, hunger, chains, cold, heat,
> In a thousand ways one death seizes every wretch.
> Everywhere wars rage, madness has seized all men,
> Everywhere with arms kings rush at kings.[6]

[1] Although many of the fortified
cities held out, at least for a time:
Altamira 1913 I 168–69.

[2] On the fifth century invasions of
Italy the account of Hodgkin 1892–
96 is very complete.

[3] The territory west of Poitiers
and Périgueux from the Garonne to
the Loire: Shepherd 1924, map 42–43,
district # 11.

[4] Bayet 1911 70–72.

[5] Ibid. 78.

[6] *Poema Conjugis ad Uxorem*,
lines 17–28. And cf. the *Epigramma*
of Paulinus, bishop of Béziers, lines
10–29, describing conditions south of
the city of Narbonne in about 408.

And, somewhat later,[7] another Aquitanian, Orientius, echoes the plaint:

Observe how suddenly death has overwhelmed the whole world,
How the violence of war has shattered great nations.

. . . .

For many treachery, for others perjury, for others
Civil treason was the cause of death.
Open violence no less than secret attacks were the cause.
Those not overcome by force died of starvation.
The unfortunate mother died with child and husband,
Together with his servants the master was enslaved.
Here lay bodies as food for dogs; glowing pyres
Consuming life were the homes of many.
Throughout villages and estates, country-side and cross-road,
Throughout every district and along every road, was only
Death, grief, destruction, slaughter, fire and lamentation.
All Gaul smoked like a single funeral pyre.[8]

The same sort of destruction was wrought in Spain, whence Vandal had followed Alan and Sueve seeking new lands to pillage. By 428 the Vandals found Spain in its turn too wasted;[9] therefore they set sail — in ships supplied by a disloyal Roman governor[10] — to pillage Africa as well. Within two years they were besieging Hippo just as Augustine was dying there; then for a time, as they came to denser populations, resistance increased. But even Proconsular Africa could not long withstand them: independent Berber tribes attacked from the desert;[11] Roman Berbers, numerous and still pagan,[12] did not fight too loyally; in the year 439 Carthage fell and with it most of Africa.

Eastern Spain, evacuated by the Vandals, reverted for a time to Rome;[13] by continual warfare Roman armies kept back the hordes of Franks and Burgundians who now occupied the whole Rhine valley;[14] by a treaty of 442 Rome re-

---

[7] Migne *P.L.* 61 976A.

[8] *Commonitorium* II lines 165–66 & 173–84. Orientius was bishop of Auch and wrote between 430 and 440: Bayet 1911 77.

[9] An uncomfortable pressure was also being exercised against them by the Visigoths, acting as the alleged allies of the Empire: Lot 1927 238, 284 & 301.

[10] Boniface, military Count of Af-

rica, who was at odds with the Emperor: Hodgkin 1892 II 2 225–26 & 246.

[11] Mesnage 1915 II 37.

[12] Cf. Monceaux 1894 466–68 on the prevalence of Punic paganism up to 439. The chief rivals of their god Tanit were Baal, Eschmoun and Christ.

[13] Cf. Lot 1927 246.

[14] Bayet 1911 72. By a treaty in

gained Africa west of Cirta — a region too poor and extensive
for the Vandal to covet.[15]   Yet for all this by the year 445 half
of southern Gaul had been lost, western Spain and all that
was best of Africa.   And Britain too had crumbled — before
attacks from three sides by Scot, Pict, and Saxon.[16]   Italy for
the time being was safe, but a fair half of the Latin provinces
had become barbarian kingdoms.

These barbarians were ruthless fighters, ruthless pillagers,
but they were not wholly savage, knew enough to appreciate
Roman civilization.   Consequently, if unmolested, they were
ready to behave themselves.   Thus it was only eight [17] years
after the first barbarian eruption into Spain that **Orosius of
Tarragona**, after describing that eruption, goes on to say:

Yet, almost immediately after this, these same accursed barbarians turned their swords into ploughshares and began to treat the
Romans as companions and even as friends, with the result that
certain Romans are to be found among them who prefer an impoverished freedom among these barbarians to the nightmare of
taxation among the Romans.[18]

Writing thirty years later, Salvian said much the same of the
Romans in Aquitaine.   Speaking of the cruel oppression of
the poor in the Roman parts of Gaul, he contrasts this with
conditions in Aquitaine:

For in the Gothic country the barbarians are so far from tolerating this sort of oppression that not even Romans who live among
them have to bear it.   Hence all the Romans in that region have
but one desire, that they may never have to return to the Roman
jurisdiction.   It is the unanimous prayer of the Roman people
in that district that they may be permitted to continue their present lives among the barbarians.

Yet we are surprised that the Goths are not conquered by our
resistance.[19]

And in another passage Salvian reports a condition in the
Gaul of 445 that Orosius, speaking of Spain in 417, does not
mention: even the Roman who lived in territory that was still
Roman longed to live instead under a barbarian regime:

---

443 the Burgundians were allowed to
settle peaceably in Savoy: Lot 1927
240–41.
   [15] Mesnage 1915 II 5.

[16] Hodgkin 1935 I 53–73.
[17] Bayet 1911 72.
[18] *H.A.P.* VII 41 § 7.
[19] *D.G.D.* V §§ 36–37.

Meanwhile the poor are robbed, widows lament, orphans are trampled upon, to such a degree that many of them, including persons well born and educated, are fleeing to the enemy lest they die under the afflictions of the State's persecution, actually seeking Roman kindliness at the hand of the barbarians because they cannot endure barbarous cruelty at the hand of the Romans. And, however much they differ from those to whom they have fled, both in customs and language, and however much they are tried by the odour of the bodies and clothes of the barbarians, they nevertheless prefer to endure an unfamiliar life among the barbarians to an unjust harshness among the Romans.

Everywhere, therefore, men are going over to either the Goths, the Bagaudes, or some other of the barbarian rules, and they are not sorry to have done so; for they prefer to live free in technical captivity than as captives in technical freedom. Consequently the name of Roman citizen, which was formerly not only much prized but bought at a high price, is now gladly repudiated and shunned, and is held not only cheaply but almost in abomination.[20]

The first phase of the barbarian invasions ended with the two great raids into Gaul and Italy by the Huns under Attila. Crossing the Rhine early in 451, they swept unresisted to the walls of Orleans, to which they laid siege. Here it was her bishop, Anianus, who conducted the defence and who sent messengers to the Roman general Aetius, informing him of the city's plight. In the nick of time Aetius and his Romans arrived, reinforced by the Visigoths and other barbarian detachments. Attila thereupon raised the siege, was overtaken in his retreat near Troyes, where the memorable battle occurred on the Mauriac Plain, ending in the definite defeat of the invaders. The destruction had been terrific: almost every city wiped out in the Moselle valley and on the upper Seine and Marne. But most of Burgundy, from the Saône southward, was untouched: Rome, although only with Visigothic help, had triumphed. It was well that she could then rejoice for a moment, for it was to be her last victory.

In the next year Attila and his Huns, revived in strength and self-confidence, poured over the Rhætian Alps, razed the great city of Aquileia to the ground and occupied every city of the Po valley as far as Milan. Thereupon occurred the

[20] *D.G.D.* V §§ 21–22. And Bloch 1922 270 says 'Le probe historien Ammian Marcellin ne dit pas autre chose que le déclamateur Salvien.'

famous parley on the banks of the Mincio, between bishop
Leo of Rome and the Hun leader.   What occurred there we
are not told, but, shortly after, the barbarian army withdrew
out of Italy, never to return.[21]   Was Attila overawed, and,
if so, by whom or what?   The enigma leaves it none the less
certain that in 453 Aetius still held most of Gaul and that
Valentinian still ruled over Italy.   The final and decisive
blows were yet to fall.

Already before these invasions the Romans were thoroughly
demoralized; afterwards they became infinitely more so.
Even during the civil wars armed marauders followed in the
wake of the armies like carrion, and thieves followed these to
gather the crumbs.   Yet taxes moved stolidly along as if nothing had happened, levelling first the layer just above destitution, then the layer next above that.   Under such conditions
even the prudent lost all sense of security, learned the futility
of obedience to the law, became indifferent to their Roman
citizenship.   Needing protection, yet receiving harm rather
than help from the State, the Roman instinctively turned to
whatever other power or agency could offer it.   Fortunately,
as law and order broke down, flight from his State-imposed
serfdom became the easier: unless he were disposed to join
some outlaw band, three courses were open to him: flight to
the barbarians, or to the domains of either the *potentiores* or
the Church.

So powerful and well entrenched were the *potentiores* that
even after 383 — when imperial, in place of municipal, officials were charged to collect the taxes they owed [22] — they do
not seem to have been harmed.   Probably even then they only
paid as much as they had a mind to.[23]   This precedent of independence the bishops now adapted to good purpose, substituting the no less effective threat of moral, in place of
physical, resistance.   How often the exorbitant sums which
the tax-collectors demanded were legal yet out of all proportion to real value, and how often they included an illegal
commission, we cannot be sure.   But that the commission
was a common practice appears from the diatribes of certain

21 For an account of the Hun in-   22 Lot 1927 148.
vasions see Hodgkin 1892 II 2 100–60.   23 Bloch 1911 448.

bishops of the time.   In a Sermon of about 440 Peter Chrysologus of Ravenna thus expounds *Luke* iii 12–13:

The publicans also came, saying: what shall we do?   These publicans heard the words: *Demand no more than you are authorized.*   He makes known what makes a publican guilty in order
that you publicans may not ask for more.   He who asks for more
is a collector not of tribute but of fraud.   Let them reflect how
guilty is he before God who exacts from the weak and weary;
more and more does he weigh down and exhaust them by his
fraud and, on top of the almost unbearable amount owed, im-
poses rising sums not owed.[24]

And bishop Maximus of Turin echoes these sentiments:

It is no crime to administer the public property, but so to deal
with it that you increase your own property is damnable. . . .
Before God it is not the imposition itself, but the unjust imposition that is condemned. . . .   What Cæsar prescribes must be accepted, what the Emperor decrees must be borne, but it becomes
unbearable when exaction for the sake of booty is added to it.[25]

Nor, according to the priest Salvian, of Marseilles, were these
conditions then one whit better in Gaul.   Speaking of the
poor he says:

They must endure the frequent, even continuous, ruin of State
requisitions, always menaced by severe and unremitting proscription; they desert their homes to avoid being tortured in them,
and go into voluntary exile to escape heavy punishment.[26]

And he describes a further outrage often perpetrated:

Frequently there come from the highest imperial officials new
envoys, new bearers of dispatches, sent under recommendation to
a few men of note, for the ruin of the many.   In their honour
new contributions and tax levies are decreed.   The mighty determine what sums the poor shall pay; the favour of the rich decrees what the masses of the lowly shall lose; for they themselves
are not at all involved in these exactions.[27]

The landlords and officials were, it is fair to assume, good men
as well as bad.   The best ones — like Paulinus of Nola,
the princely squire, and like Ambrose, the governor — were

[24] *Sermon* # 137.
[25] *Homily* # 114.
[26] *D.G.D.* V § 28.   And see the
anonymous *S. Hilarii Arelatensis Vita*

20.   This *Life* was written in about
470; Hilary was bishop of Arles from
429 to 449: see pp. 521–22.
[27] *D.G.D.* V § 30.

likely soon to find themselves bishops. Therefore when Salvian was writing — in about 445 — the great landlords and
officials, precisely because the Church had not chosen them,
were more often bad than good. The Church, by monopolizing the virtuous, left the lay world an easier prey to the
scoundrels.

In 440 — the year after the Vandal capture of Carthage —
a law was passed authorizing all Romans to bear arms as often
as the need arose.[28] The immediate aim was to allow the
Italians to arm against expected coastal raids by the triumphant Vandals; its wider effect was to legalize a practice that had
long since become general. It was one thing to forbid Romans to arm when the danger was support of a civil war; it
was quite another thing to forbid this when barbarian hordes
were overrunning the country-side and besieging the cities
What better proof of the impotence of the imperial govern
ment than this law, which, in the year 440, still decreed no
universal drafting of the citizens, which did not even call for
volunteers, but which merely allowed the citizens who were
so minded and in peril to take up arms in their own defence!

The few remaining detachments of the regular imperial
army in the West were still commanded by professionals, as
the careers of Aetius [29] and others indicate. If the ranks were
largely composed of barbarians and serfs, at least many of
their leaders were Romans well trained in the art of war.
But who was there to take command of the newly recognized
militia of the cities which recruited itself in self-defence and
might prove the more effective force of the two? The landlords had long ago formed their own militia,[30] often into a
capable if small body, and well led, whether by the landlord
himself or by one especially chosen to serve him well. The
Church had her domains to protect, just as had the lay landlords; and, in addition, she had the city to protect. If the
bishop did not build the levees they were not built; if he did
not repair the fortifications they were not repaired. Was it

---

[28] Onory 1931 263.
[29] ' Aetius, the brave captain, but
also the shifty intriguer, Roman by
birth, but half barbarian by long
residence at the Hunnish court ':
Hodgkin 1892 I 2 872. There were

also Litorius, lieutenant under Aetius,
Boniface Count of Africa, Ecdicius,
Syagrius, etc.
[30] Bloch 1922 264; Jullian 1926
VIII 142–43.

not equally likely that if he did not also assume command of
the city militia no one would — or at least no one whom
bishop and citizens could trust?

Technically the *defensor civitatis*,[31] provided that office
had not been vacated, was, in default of a trained soldier, the
logical leader of this militia. But technically he was an imperial official, and easily suspected, therefore, of subordinating municipal to imperial interests.[32] So long as he was
effectively backed by the imperial organization his powers
might remain intact, but the need for an active militia only
arose at the moment when a city was cut off from the larger
imperial centres. Thus isolated, the *defensor civitatis,* representative of the central despotism, even if he had ingrati-
ated himself with the citizens, could no longer dispose of any
organization or revenue other than what the city could itself
supply.

The most powerful layman of the *civitas* was the large
landowner. Why, then, might he not be prevailed upon to
lead? This too was impracticable because his organization
was not only exclusively rural but was rather the envied rival
than the admired benefactor of the city.[33] Moreover, as we
have seen, many of the most honourable of this class had already joined the hierarchy of the Church and conveyed their
lands to her.[34] Before the middle of the fifth century the
largest landowner of the *civitas* was very often the Church.
Thus, in place of the *defensor civitatis* and the lay landlord, the prominent figure of the *civitas* in both town and
country-side was the bishop.

If then, after the first invasions, the Church still had to
face moral and economic crises, she had now also to face the
much more acute crisis of war. No longer could she afford
merely to theorize and preach about it, she must deal with
it. What attitude did she actually take? Evidently Germanus, the famous bishop of Auxerre, believed that the policy
of non-resistance might at times be subordinated to the dic-
tates of justice. For when he was in Britain in 429 on a
mission to check the Pelagian heresy there, a Saxon raid oc-

---

[31] Who had virtually superseded
the *curator* as the Emperor's municipal representative: Bloch 1922 283.

[32] See pp. 252 n. 16, & 266 n. 91.
[33] Lot 1927 147–49.
[34] See pp. 276–77.

curred, and Germanus had no hesitation in accepting command of the Roman soldiers.   It is true that his victory was
a bloodless one — for he brought it about not by the use of
arms but by a great shout which he caused his men to make in
such terrifying unison that the raiders fled.[35]   Yet I think we
may fairly assume that, since he had been a Roman general [36]
before becoming a priest, he would, if necessary, have urged
and even ordered resistance with the sword.   For why should
the instinct to fight in a good cause be extinguished by enlisting in the priesthood?   Salvian, to be sure, writing in Gaul
about fifteen years later, preached the doctrine of invariable
non-resistance; [37] but we must remember that he wrote more
than thirty years after the first great invasions, and before the
coming of Attila.   When the Huns were besieging Orleans in
451, bishop Anianus implored the military aid of both Roman and Visigoth that the siege might be raised.[38]   He cannot either have expected or wished that this aid be rendered
only if without bloodshed.   How, indeed, could any true
Roman, steeped now in the lore of the Old Testament, have
felt otherwise?

The next year, in 452, it was Italy's turn to meditate on
the treatment to be accorded the Huns.   Already masters of
Milan and Pavia, their outriders could be seen from the walls
of Turin.   Such was the situation when Maximus, the bishop
of that city, delivered his 87th *Homily*:

You remember that last Sunday we preached on how by good actions, by assiduous prayers, we could open the gates of justice to
ourselves, and on how by constant donations we could fortify ourselves as in a fort of mercy.   Resisting the foe with works of charity, fighting him with fasting, constitutes as it were an impreg-
nable defence.   However strong the foe's weapons may be, the
armour of the Saviour is stronger: he who is so armed, although
he may appear defenceless in the eyes of men, is nevertheless
adequately armed because God on high defends him.   When in
trouble, therefore, it is best to pray, fast, sing hymns, do deeds of
mercy.   With such weapons, just as we have shown in the case of
David against Goliath, Christians have been conquering their
enemies; these weapons guard the State's battlements.   For the
holy prophet says: *Unless God guards the city vain are the pre-
cautions of those who watch over it* (Psalm 126).   In vain, there

---

[35] Constantius *Vita Germani* § 18.   [37] See pp. 367–70.
[36] Ibid. § 1.   [38] Hodgkin 1892 II 2 119–21.

fore, does the man stand guard who thinks that he has garrisoned the city, when he lacks the arms of faith.   In vain, evidently, does he labour who imagines that he can furnish protection for another, when he himself lacks the grace of God.   Says the Lord in the Gospels: *Physician, heal thyself* (*Luke* iv 23).   Which is as much as to say, ' First of all, O man, provide for thine own salvation, in order to provide for the salvation of the many.'   When, moreover, I see you feeble and weak, and without the help of the Divinity, I not only have no confidence in the defence of the city which you have prepared for resistance, I even fear lest your foolhardiness should actually throw the city into confusion.   The city is truly fortified, then, rather when God Himself defends it; moreover God then defends it, as it is written, when the inhabitants of it are all gentle, serious, Christian and Catholic.   For it is inevitable that God should take care of a city in which He finds a part of His own commandments to save.   Where, moreover, there is dissipation, perfidy and blasphemy, that city the Lord does not defend, lest not so much the city, as the sins in it, be saved. Therefore he who undertakes the defence of the city in the name of the Lord, he it is who truly furnishes security to the citizens. For he who, lacking the grace of God, tries to organize the defence of the city, seems, as is customary in the case of foxes, to be preparing himself a hole as a hiding-place.   For is not this man like the fox in that hole, who is constantly burrowing the earth and never contemplates the heavens?   For the Lord says, as we have just heard it read: *The foxes have holes and the birds of the sky have nests, where they may rest; the son of man, however, has nowhere to lay His head* (*Matt.* viii 20).   Let us carefully attend to the meaning of this utterance.   For the Lord was not speaking particularly of the animal itself; but of those men who, ever crafty and sly, ever seek in their ways to imitate the foxes; while they are fraudulently despoiling others, they are digging the pits of their own damnation; wherefore the head of Christ, which is God, cannot find a hut among those who live in pit-holes.   Moreover the reason why heretics are especially compared to foxes need not cause us hesitation.   For they are, like foxes, deceitful, troublesome, and cowardly; where they find peace, there they practise their slippery madness; where they find vigilance, by some fraudulent trick they disperse. . . .   Therefore, brothers, let us arm ourselves throughout this week with fastings, prayers, and vigils in order that, with the help of God's mercy, we may repulse the fierceness of the barbarians and beat back the plots of the heretics.[39]

This *Homily* — characteristic of several others — might be taken as a microcosm of this history: the state of mind of the

[39] Migne *P.L.* 57 451–54.

Roman of 452 is here vividly yet simply revealed.   Even the balance between Christ's divine and human natures appears in a symbol.   All lies in God's power; yet all too lies in man's. The grace of God is essential; but no less so the co-operation of man's feeble will.   Here too is revealed one certain cause of the fall of Rome: an excess of perfidy, of selfishness, of shortsightedness.   If men will not love and trust each other, if they will not co-operate for the common good, no ingenuity, no craft or cunning, can save them from the powers of evil.   Maximus speaks particularly of the heretic.   Whom does he have in mind?   Surely not the Arian only, nor the Pelagian or Manichee, but rather all those who are not good Catholics at heart; not the heretics and unbelievers only, but also the orthodox who are lukewarm.   And since evil is folly and it was this folly that brought the barbarian in, who shall say that Maximus was wrong?   The cultivation of piety and virtue will rarely prove the most expedient tactics when a hostile force is already surrounding a city, but it may prove very good strategy provided that force is still a contingency. The bishop of 452 had acquired solid knowledge of the extraordinary temporal power of moral and spiritual energy, and of the surprising weakness of mere physical energy. Maximus did not perhaps gauge the situation with complete accuracy, but we shall not be wrong in supposing that he gauged it quite as accurately as we can, even with our hindsight and our science.

Direct contact with war conditions made Maximus a realist in another respect.   For whereas Ambrose had said that all fugitives must be hospitably received as a matter of Christian principle,[40] without inquiry into how much or little they deserved to be, we find that Maximus recommended a more discriminating mercy.   Expounding the duties of a Christian host, he says that

although he may have committed crimes shortly before, however offensive he may have been, if he receive an innocent man he is transformed by the merits of that innocence.[41]

From which we may infer that to receive a guilty man was rather a waste of time.

The reason why Maximus made such an apparently un-

[40] See p. 263 n. 74.   [41] *Sermon # 96.*

Christian restriction appears from his castigation of the man who deserts his city in time of stress. In *Homily* 91 he says:

Stop sinning, therefore, and the State will not perish. Why do you desert your country? If you want security, flee rather from your sins. If you stop sinning the enemy is conquered. Divine Scripture says to Abraham that through ten just men the country can be saved. If, therefore, those are just who keep their country safe, surely those are unjust who desert it; and if the former obtain grace on account of their loyalty, it must follow that the latter deserve misery on account of their flight. Manifestly unjust and wicked is the son who deserts his imperilled mother. For in a sense your country is your sweet mother; she has borne you, reared you, even made you rich so that you can flee to safety. If your abundant wealth were not at hand you would not have the protection of flight; and for that reason, led on by avarice because you fear to lose your riches, you do not hesitate to be wicked to your mother. This proves that you look more to your riches than to your salvation. Why do you abandon your country? Do you by chance fear captivity; do you not know what generosity is? Do you not know that not seeing one's country is the worst captivity, and that the bitterest of all evils is a sojourn among the enemy? He who admits his guilt is usually condemned by such a punishment — exile and isolation in an unknown land. You are thus imposing on yourself of your own free will the very evil which the condemned man is usually made to receive as a punishment.[42]

There is in this passage a new cry, a new appeal, a call to a new patriotism. Fifty years of civil wars and barbarian invasions, fifty years of isolation and disintegration, had destroyed the spiritual solidarity of the Roman Empire. Many, as we have seen,[43] preferred to seek a new life among the barbarians; those who did not choose, or were unable, to go to such an extreme, transferred their instinctive territorial loyalty from the Roman Empire to a Roman city. Civilization, as we have said,[44] was shrinking: men could believe only in what they could themselves see and know. The larger molecules were breaking up into atoms: around the fortified walls dominating the *fundus* grew up the countryman's loyalty to his overlord and this overlord's domain; behind the fortified walls of the city grew up the townsman's loyalty. This latter loyalty was not even to the whole *civitas,* but only to the

---

[42] Migne *P.L.* 57 462–63.   [44] See p. 268 n. 96.
[43] See p. 274 n. 20.

city itself and to the land which, being owned by its bishop, seemed a part of the city. As the leadership of the Emperors waned, as the prefects and other civil officials melted into the obscurity, the bishop, lord of his city, became the true and only lord of the Roman.[45]

Another factor encouraged this concentration of loyalty within the city walls: the cities had been the first to go over to the Christian religion — even the heretic had often found it wise to retire elsewhere — whereas the farmer-peasant had been the least affected, often clinging to a pagan faith that was not even Roman. The cities were therefore the centres of Catholic power. And besides there were still many cities which had never been captured by the barbarians, or, if captured, had been evacuated. The city population, therefore, was peculiarly Catholic in religion and peculiarly Roman in blood; so that loyalty to it could satisfy the religious as well as the racial craving. Within the city there might be heretics of many kinds, but at least there were in it few pagans, and fewer barbarians.[46] Within the cities were concentrated the seeds laid bare as the luscious fruit had rotted, those seeds which kept alive the memory of ancient Rome down the long years that led to the Middle Ages. It was, for instance, in one of the northern Italian cities that the *Digest* of Justinian, tucked obscurely away under the weight of the Lombard occupation, survived till its discovery in the eleventh century.

So violent did the impetus of episcopal power become under the pressure of the invasions that we find certain laws of this time re-enacting earlier restrictions which in the interval had fallen into disuse. So feeble, evidently, had been the effective power of the civil authority that the Church had been chronically acting beyond the authority delegated to her. In 443 were re-enacted the provisions of Julian and Theodosius that all lands illegally conveyed to the Church in the last thirty years must be restored to their former owners.[47] Such lands may have come from the *civitas* or from the imperial *fisc*, or they may have come from individuals; that the illegality was technical [48] and not fraudulent we may fairly believe — at least in the majority of cases — but the State

[45] Onory 1931 246, 268, 581–82, etc.

[46] Onory 1932 246–48.

[47] Ibid. 110.

[48] Cf. Bloch 1911 443, 445 & 447.

resented the practice because the resources of the Church were beginning to rival her own. That the Church administered these resources far more effectively than the State could have, was beside the point; the real issue was that of the State's survival.

Another law re-enacted in 443 provided that the bishop be responsible for the proper maintenance of the city's aqueducts and fortifications.[49]   On this matter we may sympathize with the State: bishops, however concerned for military defence and public health, were even more concerned with other less material considerations: the Church buildings, the standard of living of the clergy, above all the care of the fugitives, the sick, the old, and the poor. The Church, true to the divine precept, gave little consideration for the morrow. The real task was today's task — of saving life and inculcating virtue. To prepare for the plague of next year or for the invasion of the year after was rather a matter for God to attend to, as He, in His unfathomable wisdom, might see fit. That the Church, however well-intentioned and efficient, too often would not see beyond her own nose, caused the civil authorities no little exasperation. Wealth involved corresponding civic responsibilities which the Church was reluctant to assume. And she felt so sure of herself that she would brook no worldly though friendly counsel.

Finally, by a law of 452, the bishop was forbidden to adjudicate in any civil case unless with the consent of both parties.[50]   This was simply a re-enactment of the law of 408 which allowed the bishop to adjudicate any case provided there was such consent.[51]   This restriction did not apply where, in a civil suit, the defendant was a cleric, nor to a criminal suit against a cleric,[52] for here only the Church could now prosecute. The trouble evidently was that the Church had in one way or another been bringing an undue pressure on laymen to give such consent. The old law was therefore re-enacted in order to check this abuse. A layman, even if he were a Catholic in good standing, might not be browbeaten by an over-zealous clergy. The civil courts might be more

49 Onory 1931 597.
50 Ibid. 301 & 308–09.
51 See p. 259 n. 55.

52 This privilege was obtained at some time between 412 and 452: Lot 1927 56 n. 1.

corrupt and expensive than was right; still, if the litigant preferred to take his chance before them, he must feel free to
exercise that preference. In a good many of these cases the
interests of the Church would be in conflict with those of
the layman; and the layman could suspect that the episcopal
court might sacrifice individual rights for the sake of an apparent public need. The most honourable court may not be
free from bias, especially when an appealing cause is at stake.

In the West these were the last flourishes of the dying State,
the last acts of composure before the agony.

D. ROLE OF THE BISHOPS, 455–486

In 454 the great general Aetius, having been summoned to
Ravenna by the Emperor, was there assassinated, and the
henchmen of Aetius quickly reciprocated by murdering Valentinian.[1] The dynasty of the Spaniard Theodosius, which
had ruled the Empire for the last seventy-five years, was now
extinct. What, henceforth, should an Emperor mean to a
Roman? For whom, now, should a Roman fight?

In the following year the Ostrogoths crossed the Danube
to occupy the large province of Pannonia;[2] and the Franks
moved southwestward to the Somme and the upper Moselle.[3]
And in this same year 455 the Vandals set sail from Africa to
sack the city of Rome. It was due to Pope Leo's intervention
that their leader Genseric[4] agreed to take no life, to do no violence to persons, to destroy no buildings.[5] As Genseric was
above all seeking such plunder as could be transported in
his ships,[6] these conditions hardly cramped him — they even
assured him that in his search for gold and other treasure the
inhabitants would not molest him. Rome was ransacked for
fourteen days; the Vandal ships being by that time full to
overflowing, Genseric and his men departed.[7]

[1] Hodgkin 1892 II² 196–97. And
cf. Bayet 1911 77.
[2] Lot 1927 243.
[3] Ibid. 248–49.
[4] For the spelling see Hodgkin
1892 II² 227 n. 1.
[5] Ibid. 283.
[6] Ibid. 283–84.
[7] Also carrying off certain members of the imperial family for ransom: ibid. 286–87.

Psychologically the importance of this sack of Rome cannot be over-estimated; physically, however, its importance is due not to the actual loss suffered but to its being the most startling of a series of victories by which the Vandals gained undisputed naval command of the western Mediterranean. For it was at this same time that they conquered the Balearics, Sardinia, Corsica, and even Sicily.[8] Thus consolidated by sea they also overran and occupied that western part of the African coast which Rome had retained by the treaty of 443.[9] One immediate result of this barbarian control of the sea was to deprive Rome of the grain supplies of Africa;[10] another was the conquest by the Visigoths of all eastern Spain.[11]

Following the death of Valentinian in 455 the Gallo-Roman nobility of the territory around Lyons, chose a candidate of their own as Emperor, and at the same time invited the Burgundians to share their lands. The scheme had the double advantage of relieving the district of the imperial taxes, and of gaining an ally against other barbarians. By 465 this mongrel kingdom of the Burgundians stretched from Langres on the north, to the upper Loire, to the Durance and the Alps.[12] And in these same years an analogous change occurred in Italy, the Suevic[13] barbarian Ricimer became virtual ruler,[14] bound, however, to maintain armed forces to defend the peninsula from further invasions like those of Alaric, Attila, and Genseric.[15]

It was the turn of the Visigoths to make the next move. In 466 the energetic young Euric became king. Casting aside all further pretence of a Visigothic alliance with Rome, Euric set out to conquer what he could, moving steadily eastward

---

[8] Victor of Vita *H.P.A.P.* I § 13. And cf. Hodgkin 1892 II [2] 251, 435 & 503-04.

[9] Mesnage 1915 II 5-6.

[10] Lot 1927 240.

[11] Hodgkin 1892 II [2] 388-89. The Suevi had held Galicia, Lusitania and Baetica throughout. Tarragona and Carthagena had reverted to Rome when the Vandals evacuated these provinces in 428, but fell to the Visigoths in 456: Lot 1927 246. Cf. Kiepert, map XII.

[12] Bayet 1911 86-87; Lot 1927 247-48.

[13] Hodgkin 1892 II [2] 398-99.

[14] At least the Emperors Majorian (457-61), Anthemius (467-72) and Julian Nepos (474-75) showed ability, especially Majorian; but as the barbarian leaders, with the title Patrician, had the army, they were virtually the masters so long as the Eastern Emperor did not interfere: Lot 1927 241-42.

[15] Cf. Hodgkin 1892 II [2] 389 & 446-49.

from Poitou, Périgord, and Guyenne, into Berry, Limousin, and Velay. Only in Auvergne did he encounter stubborn resistance: with the help of the Burgundians Roman forces held out for the three years 471 to 474, and even then succumbed only because of Roman treachery.[16]   The leading spirit of this resistance was Ecdicius, brother-in-law of the literary bishop Apollinaris Sidonius of Clermont.   In a later letter to Ecdicius, Sidonius recalls an episode of the siege of Clermont in 474:

At midday, and right across the middle of the plain, you brought your little company of eighteen safe through some thousands of Goths, a feat which posterity will surely deem incredible. At the sight of you, nay, at the very rumour of your name, those seasoned troops were smitten with stupefaction; their captains were so amazed that they never stopped to note how great their numbers were and how small yours. They drew off their whole force to the brow of a steep hill; they had been besiegers before, but when you appeared they dared not even deploy for action.[17]

Even allowing for rhetorical exaggeration, a fifth century Roman, when he chose, could still strike the barbarians with awe.[18]   But how few, apparently, troubled to.   Auvergne having succumbed, and the eastern line of the upper Loire being already in the hands of the Burgundians, Euric now turned south.   Within a few years he had taken Arles, Marseilles, and all Provence below the Durance.[19]

What little remained of the Western Empire now fell fast: in 471 the Ostrogoths began their sweep over the whole vast territory from the Danube to Thessaly on the south and the Alps on the West; [20] in 476 Odoacer, the new barbarian ruler in Italy, deposed the child Emperor Romulus Augustulus and neglected to nominate another; at Soissons in 486 the Franks under their young king, Clovis, defeated the last Roman army of the West under Syagrius.   Every inch of the Latin speaking half of the Empire was now under the rule of barbarians, and, of these many races, not one was of the orthodox or Catholic faith.   The Franks were still pagans; the rest were

[16] Bayet 1911 83–84. As further evidence of the energy of Euric, in 469 he also drove the Suevi out of Lusitania into Galicia: Lot 1927 284.

[17] *Letters* III # 3 §§ 3 & 4.

[18] Aegidius in 463, for instance —

also fighting against the Visigoths: see Hodgkin 1892 II ² 436 n. 2, citing Priscus.

[19] Duchesne 1911 III ⁴ 613. Cf. Malnory 1894 45; & Lot 1927 284–85.

[20] Lot 1927 243.

Arian heretics — alien to Rome, therefore, in religion as well as in race and culture. A Roman of 486 did not need to be a congenital pessimist in order to fear that neither Roman Empire nor Roman Church could long survive.

So long as history was treated as an art the violence of the change thus wrought was exaggerated, but as, in the later nineteenth century, history tried to become a science — searching for deep, impersonal causes and effects — at least the abruptness of the change was denied. Consequently, the selection of any specific date — such as 400 or 476 — to mark the end of the ancient world and the beginning of the Dark or Middle Ages, began to be frowned upon, and, instead, a period of twilight was conceived, lasting from the third till the eighth century.[21] During the third century, undeniably, Roman government became disorganized and economic depression set in,[22] the native population declined and barbarian infiltration began; it was then, too, that the oriental religions first fired the Roman imagination.[23] Already by the year 300, therefore, the West had fallen heir to incipient feudalism, barbarian influence, and the religions of other-worldliness. It is equally true that in the eighth century Roman blood at last lost all self-conscious identity, the papacy rose to political power, the Merovingian dynasty collapsed, and the Mohammedan Arabs gained control of the Mediterranean Sea and of Africa and Spain. The greatness of these changes must certainly not be overlooked, yet the fact remains that if there really was an ancient and a medieval civilization there is little evidence of any third one between. Now, to the extent that we are willing to recognize in Augustine the most brilliant, profound, and enlightened Greek or Roman since Aristotle, we must also admit that Roman intelligence did not begin to decline until after the year 406. And, if this be so, it can hardly be pure chance that, while that last great work of antiquity — the *City of God* — was being written, the barbarians were already overrunning Gaul, Spain, Britain, and Africa. Natural scientists tell us that while change normally

[21] For a bibliography of Pirenne's theory of relative continuity until after 650, see Onory 1931 560 n. 12.

[22] See, for instance, Lot 1927 1-2, 67, 144-47 & 150.

[23] Cf. Renan 1881 595 & 603.

proceeds imperceptibly, it occasionally proceeds violently.
Why is not the contemporaneity of Augustine and the invasions corroborative of this?. Are not scales supporting heavy
objects reversible by an imperceptible shift of weight? I like
to think the Western Empire fell on that day of the year 430
when, in Hippo, besieged by the Vandals, her bishop Augustine died.

Certainly the most obvious change brought about by the
fifth century invasions was racial: new men mean new civilizations. The Romans of most of Gaul and northern Italy
were Celts. Were the Germans of a radically different stock?
Strabo, writing in 16 B.C., described the Celts of Gaul as very
like the Germans,[24] and in the country-side they doubtless so
remained for several generations. But Romanization of the
Gaul inexorably proceeded, with such effect that the difference between the two peoples is today more obvious than it
was to Strabo. The progress of Celtic transformation may
be roughly gauged by the linguistic change: in Cæsar's day
every Gaul, unless he was a German, spoke some form of
Celtic; in 450 when the young Sidonius and Ecdicius ' resolved to forsake the barbarous Celtic dialect ',[25] they probably merely meant a Latin tainted with Celtic remnants.
After the fall, the Gauls again changed their language; but
their French was no reversion, because in it there is barely a
trace of Celtic words [26] — its foundation is wholly Latin and
so Roman.

The persistence of the German dialects in Gaul is quite a
different matter. Beyond the Roman frontier only the Picts
and Scots spoke Celtic, but almost every tribe and people beyond the Rhine and Danube spoke German, so that the Ger-
man-Roman of this whole long frontier was constantly hearing his ancestral tongue. Consequently in Roman cities like
Cologne and Mainz German was always a familiar vernacu-
lar.[27] A Persian or Syrian soldier quartered in one of these
cities must take his orders in Latin, but many of his pleasures
in German.

The number of un-Romanized Germans who, in 406, were

[24] Steinhausen 1913 I [2] 33.   [26] See p. 5 n. 36.
[25] Sidonius *Letters* III # 3.   [27] Bloch 1911 382.

living in Noricum, Pannonia, Gaul, and Italy can be only very vaguely estimated. There were first the Germans living just inside the frontier who, though legally Romans, had only acquired a Roman veneer. In addition there were the active soldiers, the veterans who had received land as a pension,[28] and the prisoners of war who had been sold into slavery. The raids of the third century too, which extended not only to Paris, Autun, and Lyons, but to Bordeaux and even into Spain,[29] must have left a residue of German blood in certain territories. And during the third and fourth centuries, especially in Italy,[30] there had been peaceful immigration, with the acquiescence and even the encouragement of the State; to these farmers must be added house servants,[31] squatters, hawkers, entertainers, and vagabonds. Some of these doubtless often re-emigrated, but others must have settled down with wives and children. Shall we suppose that these various German elements constituted, in the year 406, between five and ten per cent of the Latin-European population?

We are less, but only a little less helpless to estimate the number of Germans who came in with the fifth century invasions. In 406 the Gallo-Romans may have numbered four million;[32] in contrast, the Vandals who crossed to Africa in 428 were not over 80,000.[33] If, on this basis, we estimate the Visigoths at 130,000,[34] the Franks at 60,000 and the Burgundians at 60,000,[35] their total is 250,000, or about six per cent of the Gallo-Roman population. If we may at all trust these figures, we must suppose that in the year 480, the Germans constituted only fifteen per cent of the inhabitants of Gaul, and that, as this proportion was greater near the Rhine, it was less elsewhere.

If we may further assume that a disproportionate number of these Germans were men of military age, the fifteen per

---

[28] Steinhausen 1913 I² 70.
[29] Jullian 1913 IV 601 n. 7.
[30] Speck 1906 III 554.
[31] Dopsch 1923 I² 103 & 197.
[32] This four millions is based on the estimate of fifteen millions for the western half of the Empire: see Lot 1927 75–76; & p. 247 n. 137.
[33] Including women and children: ibid. 267 & 301.
[34] Yet Ziegler 1930 14 says the

Visigoths, if we include Roman slaves, deserters, etc., might have mustered 100,000 warriors in Gaul alone.
[35] Lot 1927 418 says that the Burgundians were not at all numerous; & cf. Dill 1906² 299. Orosius *H.A.P.* VII 32 § 11 says there were 80,000 of them, but this figure may be safely reduced.

cent becomes a really powerful minority. There is, however, no reason to suppose that these Germans acted as a hostile or even as an organized unit. On the contrary, the tradition of all those living on Roman territory before 406 was to defend Rome against her assailants, and, even among those entering later by force, the Visigoths had been granted western Aquitaine on the understanding that they were to defend the Roman name there, while the Burgundians had been thoroughly trounced by the Roman Aetius before being allowed to settle in Savoy. It was with Hunnish mercenaries that Aetius had trounced the Burgundians; [36] it was with the help of the Visigoths that he defeated the Huns near Châlons. The Franks, too, fought on the Roman side from time to time, both as mercenaries and as allies.[37] Even much later, in the time of Clovis and Theodoric, it rarely occurred to any of the Germans that they might be fighting against rather than for Rome.[38]

A kindred problem concerns the extent and nature of the changes in the ownership of buildings and land.[39] It might be supposed that, since the available lands were enormous and the barbarians not only few but rather hunters and herdsmen than farmers, little arable land changed hands. It might also be supposed that, since the invaders must conceive of cities merely as places of refuge and defence, city property was rather looted than appropriated and utilized.[40] On the other

[36] The Burgundians had crossed the Rhine in 413 — it was their stay at Worms that the *Niebelungenlied* recalls. Their defeat by Aetius was in 435. See Lot 1927 240–41; and Prosper of Aquitaine's *Chronicum* for the year 443.

[37] Tradition had it that Merovech fought on the side of Aetius against Attila in 451: Dalton 1927 I 90, citing Fredegaire, who gave the year as 431. Also the Frank Childeric fought as an ally of the Roman Aegidius against the Visigoths in about 463: Bayet 1911 95; Kurth 1919 II 66; & Duchesne 1925 IV 488.

[38] Lavisse 1885 402 pictures the relation of Visigoth and Gallo-Roman at this time in the following way:

'Figurons-nous la France déshabituée à la guerre, des tribus d'Arabes employées à la défense de notre sol, les chefs comblés d'honneurs, faits généraux et maréchaux, les hommes soldés et nourris, tout un petit peuple étranger, d'humeur indépendante, incapable de discipline, mais incapable aussi de faire autre chose que servir, toujours en quête de cantonnements meilleurs, traînant leurs smalas de province en province, les chefs réclamant de plus grands honneurs, la tribu de plus amples distributions de vivres et d'or: tels étaient les Wisigoths. Souvent révoltés, ils retombaient toujours dans l'obéissance.'

[39] On the change in Gaul see Bayet 1911 79; on the change in Italy see Lot 1927 278–79.

[40] Steinhausen 1913 I 2 57.

hand, the invasions of the fifth century were migrations, and
it is therefore likely that the women and children were eager
to make use of all the available buildings, fields, and slaves.
Nothing will make a people agricultural so quickly as the
possession of fertile, cultivated land.[41] And so of the cities —
until the barbarian had cities to live in how could he tell if he
liked them or not?[42] That the changes were neither wholesale nor violent was not because the barbarians were too primitive but because they were few and the available land enormous.

There was, in addition, a religious change brought about
by the invasions. By a curious chance, of all the invading
peoples, only a very few, and these the least influential for
the time being, were pagan. Such were the Huns, Saxons,
and Franks. The rest — who occupied all southern Gaul,
Spain, the Balkans, and Africa — were already converted to
the Arian faith, an earlier and, since 378,[43] an heretical form
of Christianity which denied the equality and so the identical Nature of the three Persons of the Trinity.[44] Yet because
it was, after 381, exclusively a Germanic, in contrast to a
Latin faith, we may not infer that it was more primitive; on
the contrary, from the year 341 — when the Goth Ulfilas first
carried that doctrine to his people — until the death of Valens
in 378, it had been the official Roman faith,[45] and a hardly
less intricate and metaphysical affair than the now dominant
Athanasian view. This is the confession of faith of Ulfilas,
made on his death-bed in 381:

[41] See Orosius *H.A.P.* VII 40 § 10,
& 41 § 7; in Sidonius *Letters* IX # 3
there is a brief reference to the loss,
presumably by confiscation, of his
estates. In certain districts, at any
rate, there was systematic confiscation: Marignan 1899 I 97. Ziegler
1930 14 says that in certain districts
in which they settled they confiscated
two-thirds of the arable land.

[42] Cf. Marignan 1899 I 61; & Ziegler 1930 23. Malnory 1894 21 says
that the Germans settled in large
numbers in the cities.

[43] Arianism had been condemned
at the Council of Nicæa in 325, the
Emperor Constantine having supported the proceedings. But Arian-

ism remained, if in a somewhat attenuated form, the majority view of
Roman Christians for another fifty
years: see pp. 544–45.

[44] Duchesne 1911 III [4] 321.

[45] Valens, the Greek Emperor,
who was a strong Arian, died in 378.
The western Emperor until 375 was
Valentinian I, who resisted the Arians, but with discretion. His successor Gratian, much influenced by
Pope Damasus and Ambrose, turned
squarely to the Athanasian or Catholic side, and, when Valens died, appointed the Athanasian Theodosius
to succeed Valens in the East: Lot
1927 51. Cf. Hodgkin 1892 I [2] 90;
& Steinhausen 1913 I [2] 87.

' I believe in one God the Father, alone, unbegotten and invisible; and in His only-begotten Son our Lord and our God, artificer and maker of every creature, having none like unto Himself . . . and in one Holy Spirit, an illuminating and sanctifying power . . . neither God nor Lord, but the faithful minister of Christ, not equal but subject and obedient in all things to the Son, as the Son is subject and obedient in all things to God the Father.' [46]

And his admirer Auxentius said of him:

By his sermons and his tracts he showed that there is a difference between the divinity of the Father and of the Son, of the God unbegotten and of the God only-begotten; and that the Father is the Creator of the Creator, but the Son the Creator of the whole creation; that the Father is God of the Lord, whereas the Son is God of every creature.[47]

In this doctrine Christ resembles the Neoplatonic Mind or νοῦς and the Holy Spirit the Neoplatonic Soul or ψυχή, and such a hierarchy of divinities therefore betrays the belief that God can only control the material world indirectly and so imperfectly. From this it was only a step to acquitting God of real responsibility for earthly evil. To the monotheist Augustine, therefore, Arian theodicy was as pagan as that of Manichee or Neoplatonist.

But the German invaders could not be expected to appreciate this Arian implication. As Salvian, writing in about 445, observes,

The barbarians, indeed, lacking the Roman training or any other sort of civilized education, knowing nothing whatever unless they have heard it from their teachers, follow blindly what they hear. Such men, completely ignorant of literature and wisdom, are sure to learn the mysteries of the divine law through instruction rather than reading, and to retain their masters' doctrines rather than the law itself.[48]

To them, therefore, the Athanasian or Catholic doctrine of a Trinity of Persons with a single, identical Nature, seemed a distinction without a difference. For, they could well argue, if this Arian creed which the Roman had himself taught them

[46] Kaufmann 1899 76 lines 6–18.
[47] Ibid. 73 lines 40–46. Cf. the passages on barbarian Arianism in sixth century Spain in Gregory of Tours *History* V 43 & VI 40. Auxen-tius was the Arian rival of Ambrose during the cabal at the Milanese court in 382–386: Duchesne 1910 II 4 552–54; & Dudden 1935 280.
[48] *D.G.D.* V § 8.

was good enough for the Roman of a generation or two before, why was it so damnable a creed for the Goth now? It was one thing for professional theologians to bend to every wind of doctrine, but warriors, having other concerns, preferred to rely on an authoritative tradition. Because of some such reasoning, it followed that, whereas the pagan barbarian who wanted to become a Roman could soon be persuaded to adopt the Catholic faith, the Arian barbarian could regard himself as the repository of true Roman tradition — all of which intensified rather than allayed the racial antagonism.[49] If often there was outward respect, more often there was inner distrust.

To extirpate Catholicism was of course beyond the power, as it was probably beyond the ambition, of most of the barbarians; but to humiliate it when it had the temerity to reproach them was a natural temptation. To do even this, however, was not easy, for the Catholic Church not only evaded pretexts for a quarrel but was so powerfully entrenched as an institution that government without her co-operation was impracticable. Searching for an alternative to martial law, there was no other responsible Roman body with whom the barbarian could deal. Some of the barbarians, therefore, notably the Burgundians[50] and the Ostrogoths, were extraordinarily tolerant. Such a policy was, however, one of calculation and self-control; it was not an instinctive attitude, and, as we shall see, it was adopted neither by the Visigoths in Gaul[51] and Spain, nor by the Vandals in Africa. Indeed the Vandal persecution, from 480 to 494, was an open effort at annihilation.[52]

The war powers assumed by the bishops as a result of this second wave of disasters were certainly not less than before; yet curiously enough the great military churchman of this age was not a bishop but a monk — the holy Severinus who, speaking perfect Latin[53] but coming from the East, had settled

---

[49] Cf. the *Letter* of bishop Avitus of Vienne to Clovis in 496 where he contrasts the Arians with the innocence of 'those other people whom, being in a state of natural ignorance, no germ of depraved dogmas has yet corrupted.'

[50] Bayet 1911 89–90.
[51] See pp. 301–02.
[52] See pp. 302–03, & 627–28.
[53] Eugippius *Letter to Paschasius*.

in Noricum — modern Bavaria — soon after 453, just as the barbarians were beginning to overrun it. Not many years later he was urged to accept a bishopric,[54] but he steadfastly refused. Not only did he prefer the independence of the monk on account of personal spiritual reasons but also on account of public temporal reasons. For one thing — being uncloistered — he could travel freely, in this way helping where help was most needed,[55] and establishing friendly relations with certain barbarian tribes which, like the Rugian, had already settled down within the province.[56] And this freedom gave him an added power: being known and beloved throughout the province as a bishop confined to a single diocese could not be, he became, if quite informally, the leader of the bishops. On one occasion, for instance, we find him communicating with Constantius, bishop of Lauriacum, the largest city of the province,[57] in these peremptory terms:

' Set the customary guards at the walls tonight, and keep a stricter watch; and beware of a sudden and treacherous assault by the foe.'

adding,

' If I be proved a liar, stone me.' [58]

This Severinus had an extraordinary gift of prophecy; [59] it was this uncanny talent, added to his holiness, that made him the virtual commander of the Romans in Noricum. His disciple and biographer Eugippius naturally attributed this gift to divine revelation — the reward of his holiness; but it is also conceivable that, through his intimacy with the Rugians, he may have received confidential information of the intentions of the more hostile tribes — he may, in other words, have been a good diplomat. Often it happened that the Roman cause was also the Rugian; [60] because the Rugians did not trust the Romans they would have no official dealings with them; but because they did trust Severinus, and because they knew that the Romans also trusted him, he became the inter-

---

[54] Eugippius *Vita S. Severini* 9.
[55] Ibid. 11.
[56] Ibid. 5.
[57] Ibid. 21.
[58] Ibid. 30 §§ 2 & 3.
[59] A good instance is ch. 24 where Severinus warns the citizens of a certain town to evacuate it at once. But they demur, with the result that the town is surprised and the bishop and many others massacred.
[60] Ibid. 5.

mediary between them.[61]   It does not follow that Severinus
imposed on anyone's credulity: he very intelligently inferred
far more than the Rugians explicitly told him; why should he
not further infer that the uncanny correctness of his inferences
pre-supposed divine guidance?   If Emperors and Popes could
conscientiously ascribe their infallibility to such guidance
why should not a saint?

To say that the bishops — or, as in the case of Severinus,
the monks — assumed a military command is of course not
technically correct: they took over a political command [62]
which often involved them in the direction of military operations — as it did Abraham Lincoln.   They ought to be described, therefore, rather as military governors than as field
generals; nevertheless they directed [63] in much the same spirit
as did the patriarchs and prophets of whom they read every
day in their Old Testament.   All encouraged sound prayer
rather than sound military strategy,[64] did more to foretell than
to forestall disasters.   Yet they also did what they could to
rouse the citizens to a fighting pitch.[65]   That they won few
victories and small reputations as commanders, that they depended too much on fervour and too little on preparation, we
may not doubt.   Since, however, the imperial professional
armies fared little or no better, the strategy of the bishops
may not have been wholly outlandish.   Where failure is invariable blame should be withheld.

In these times one of the more important duties of a bishop
was the ransoming of prisoners of war.   Occasionally he could
redeem these prisoners wholesale,[66] but more often it was the
rich who benefited.   Thus when the Vandals returned to
Africa with their Roman booty, a large part of it consisted of
women of imperial or senatorial rank.   On this occasion it
was the bishop of Carthage, Deogratias, who himself undertook to ransom them.   In order to raise the necessary funds

61 Eugippius *Vita S. Severini* 31.

62 In ch. 4 is Eugippius' only mention of a lay official — a military
tribune who afterwards became a
bishop.

63 Onory 1931 581–85 & 600.

64 Even the more energetic Severinus is at times imbued with a
fatalistic quietism, as where, faced
with a plague of locusts, he advises

prayer exclusively: ' Let no one go
out to his field, as if concerned to
oppose the locusts by human effort;
lest the divine wrath be yet more
provoked ': Eugippius *Vita Severini*
12.   Contrast Augustine, see p. 147 n.
31; & cf. pp. 77 n. 24, & 401 n. 67.

65 Onory 1931 319.

66 Ennodius   *Vita . . . Epiphani*
(*C.S.E.L.* VI 360–61 & 375–76).

he sold all the gold and silver vessels of his Church,[67] follow-ing a precedent already set by Ambrose and Augustine.[68] Of course it was natural enough that this duty fall on the bishop, for no other authority or agency had the funds — to say nothing of the heart — which the task required. So exclu-sively did the bishop become associated with the ransoming of prisoners that by a law of 468 it was provided that where a testator willed money for the redemption of prisoners of war, but named no executor of the fund, the bishop of the testa-tor's diocese automatically became its administrator.[69]

Again because of the bishop's material resources, he came also to be relied upon to furnish grain to the people in times of famine. Whether provident bishops were already storing grain with possible future emergencies in mind is not sure, but such a practice was gradually inaugurated, following the dramatic distribution made by bishop Patiens of Lyons in about the year 473. In that instance the grain was shipped from an undevastated to a devastated area; but, even if both had been overrun, the barbarians who would pillage a private or government granary with impunity must often have hesi-tated to pillage an episcopal granary, the more so since it lay within the stout walls of the episcopal edifice, which itself lay within the walls of the city. The grain of the Church was protected by three walls, one spiritual, the other two material. Here are two passages from the letter of thanks written to bishop Patiens in 474 by bishop Sidonius of Cler-mont. After a recital of bishop Patiens' many marvellous good deeds, Sidonius says,

It may be true that some of these good deeds are not peculiar to you, and are shared by colleagues; but there is one which is yours, as a first charge as lawyers say, and which even your modesty cannot deny; it is this, that when the Gothic ravages were over, and the crops were all destroyed by fire, you distributed wheat to the destitute throughout all the ruined land of Gaul at your own expense, though it would have been relief enough to our starving peoples if the wheat had come to them, not as a free gift, but by the usual paths of commerce. We saw the roads encumbered by your grain-carts. Along the Saône and Rhone we saw more than

---

[67] Victor of Vita *H.P.A.P.* I § 25. And cf. Hodgkin 1892 II 2 287–88.
[68] Dudden 1935 118–19.
[69] Onory 1931 288. And cf. ibid. 284–87.

one granary which you had entirely filled. . . . I cannot exactly tell the sum of gratitude which all the people owe you — inhabitants of Arles and Riez, Avignon, Orange, Viviers, Valence, and Trois Châteaux. It is beyond my power to count the total thanks of men who were fed without having to pay out a penny. But for the city of Clermont I can speak, and in its name I give you endless thanks; and all the more because your help had no obvious inducement: we did not belong to your province, no convenient waterway led to us, we had no money to offer. Measureless gratitude I give you on their behalf; they owe it to the abundant largess of your grain that they have now their own sufficiency once more.[70]

Observe the wide extent of the Gothic sweep, from the Saône to Arles. The fortified cities might hold out for a time, but if the surrounding crops were destroyed their ultimate fall was sure. Such strategy was therefore successful. Patiens evidently did not try to intervene until ' the Gothic ravages were over ' — for his grain-carts would then have been intercepted. This very helplessness must often have added to the prestige which the bishops were now acquiring: their economic powers were enormous, their physical powers insignificant; consequently in time of war they could pose as the champions both of plenty and of peace. So happy a combination explains why the Church could go on — as Salvian had — preaching the virtue of weakness and non-resistance: [71] the bishop alone never fights, the bishop alone grows every day richer.

The generosity of bishop Patiens teaches still another lesson: that the universality of the Empire — now in ruins — was to be succeeded by the universality of the Church. To the fifth century Roman the *civitas* was the unit of loyalty, to this same man as a Catholic the unit of loyalty had no territorial or racial bounds.[72] Patiens was the bishop of Lyons, capital of the Roman-Burgundian federation; but he was, even more, bishop of the Catholic Church. He therefore deliberately impoverished his own diocese and province in order to relieve distress in a land now conquered by the enemy Visigoths. Here was a practical and concrete demonstration of the spirit of universality within the Church which

[70] *Letters* VI # 12 §§ 5 & 8–9.   [72] Onory 1932 246.
[71] See pp. 367–70.

was to hold the Latin West together throughout the centuries of anarchy to follow.

It may be objected that Patiens, according to Sidonius, distributed this grain out of his own private possessions, not out of the episcopal revenues; he was therefore acting, not as bishop, but as landlord. This is true, and it may be that he chose to retain title to his vast properties rather than convey them to his Church precisely for this reason: he wanted to be free to expend his revenues at discretion. And it may be that he in this way set a precedent of the utmost importance: he, a bishop, had given generously to persons living beyond not only his diocese but beyond his province. Henceforth a bishop must seem more than a local official; he was also the representative of a Church designed to embrace all mankind. His constituents chose him to serve not themselves only but all others — as Christ had served.[73]

Almost in this same year 473, when Patiens distributed his grain, the Pope, Simplicius, decreed that the episcopal revenues be divided, not less than one quarter going to the bishop to be spent at his discretion, not less than another quarter going to the support of the clergy. The third quarter was to be spent on the poor; the fourth on the maintenance and construction of Church buildings.[74] Probably some such division had long been customary, but there had seemed no need of codifying the practice so long as normal conditions prevailed. With the greatly increased violence and distress which began after 454, however, new and extraordinary demands were made on the Church revenues: besides the tributes and ransoms imposed and the grain distributed to the starving, there would often be an imperative need to rebuild the walls of a captured city. Generous bishops must have been too inclined to satisfy these emergency demands, with the result that if the poor still got their quarter, the clergy, and especially the buildings, did not. Yet it would not do to impoverish the clergy and allow the buildings to fall in. Most of the bishops must have welcomed the decree that prevented this: it would serve conveniently to mollify the im-

[73] Cf. Sidonius *Letters* VII # 5 §§ 3 & 5.
[74] *Letter* # 1 § 2. Pope Gelasius confirmed this decree twenty years later: Dalton 1927 I 314.

portunate beggar and to reinforce the bishop's own cooler judgment.   An expedient was probably employed which softened the rigour of this quarterly division: donors, instead of giving to the episcopal Church outright, gave for a specific purpose — as for the ransoming of prisoners of war.[75] Others no doubt left funds specifically to care for widows, or to buy stores of grain for future emergencies. Certainly if the bishop were willing to accept gifts on such conditions no one was in a position to object. In this way elasticity in expenditure might be maintained within the rigid framework.

The chronic warfare since 454 also retarded the growth of canon law, leaving the bishops with a discretion in many matters where standardization was desirable. This canon law had grown up organically for the most part. The General Councils of the East, those of Nicæa, Constantinople, Ephesus, and Chalcedon,[76] had issued some disciplinary and administrative decrees, but had chiefly concerned themselves with dogma. The Pope at Rome, too, had issued many decrees, and these had been well enough observed. But the bulk of canon law existing in 454 had issued from the local or provincial Councils, and particularly from the many African Councils which represented the clergy of all the African provinces and dioceses with their 466 bishoprics. After 439, however, for many years there were no African Councils. Pope Leo, writing in 443, refers to the impracticability of holding any Councils in Spain.[77]   In Gaul there were no Councils from 450 until after 500; [78] in Italy only the local Roman.[79]   In a sense, therefore, the bishop was never so independently powerful as in this later fifth century.

Yet there is a dark side to the picture: every year a larger number of dioceses was falling into the hands of barbarians professing the heretical Arian faith. These had Arian bishops of their own, who must be tolerated and who often vied with the Catholic bishop for recognition. So elementary was the faith of the barbarian, and so overwhelming was the majority of Romans, that in most instances the barbarian authorities left the Catholic bishops alone. They were un-

---

[75] See pp. 296–97.
[76] In 325, 381, 431 & 451 respectively.
[77] *Letter* # 15 § 1.

[78] Marignan 1899 I 169.
[79] For the list of these see Chapman 1913 198, 199 ñ. 1, & 320.

willing to jeopardize their political control for the sake of a
rather technical point of theology. Where they courted the
friendship of the Roman population they therefore chiefly
courted the Roman bishop.

When, on the other hand, the barbarians chose to embark
on a policy of open hostility to the Roman population, the
bishops were their first victims. Rarely were they killed except as a last expedient, but they were very generally exiled
and their places taken by Arians. Just such a reversal of
policy [80] was undertaken by the Visigoth Euric on his accession to the throne in 466. Not only did he aim to conquer
the Roman population eastward from his own *Aquitania
Secunda* to the Rhone and even the Alps; he aimed also to
extinguish the spirit of Roman civilization within his *Aquitania Secunda*.[81] In a letter of about 473 bishop Sidonius of
Clermont describes the consequence:

Bordeaux, Périgueux, Rodez, Limoges, Javols, Eauze, Bazas, Com-
minges, Auch, and many another city are all like bodies which
have lost their heads through the death of their respective bishops. No successors have been appointed to fill their places and
maintain the ministry in the lower Orders of the Church; the
boundaries of spiritual desolation are extended far and wide.
Every day the ruin spreads by the death of more fathers in God;
so pitiful is her state that the very heresiarchs of former times, to
say nothing of contemporary heretics, might well have looked
with pity on peoples orphaned of their pontiffs and oppressed by
desperation at this catastrophe of their faith. Diocese and parish
lie waste without ministers. You may see the rotten roofs of
churches fallen in, the doors unhinged and blocked by growing
brambles. More grievous still, you may see the cattle not only
lying in the half-ruined porticoes, but grazing beside altars green
with weeds. And this desolation is not found in country parishes
alone; even the congregations of urban churches begin to fall
away. What comfort remains to the faithful, when not only the
teaching of the clergy perishes, but their very memory is lost out
of mind? When a priest departs this life, not merely the holder
of the sacred office dies, but the office itself dies with him, unless
with his failing breath he gives his blessing to a successor. What
hope remains when the term of a man's life implies the end of
religion in his parish? If you examine more closely the ills of the
body spiritual, you will soon perceive that for every bishop

[80] Writing in about 445 Salvian
D.G.D. III § 21 says: ' Since even our
princes are Christians, there is no
persecution and religion is not disturbed.'
[81] Bayet 1911 83.

snatched from our midst, the faith of a population is imperilled. I need not mention your colleagues Crocus and Simplicius, removed alike from their thrones and suffering a common exile, if different punishments. For one of them laments that he cannot see whither he is to return, the other that he sees only too clearly where he is to return no more.[82]

The conduct of the Vandals in Africa was even more destructive. For nearly fifty years their persecution of Romans and Catholics had been rather sporadic than systematic.[83] But in 477 king Huneric succeeded to the throne. Whether he felt that Vandal policy up to then had failed to demoralize the Roman population, or whether that policy seemed now so far advanced that a *coup de grâce* could safely be given, we cannot tell. More probably the natural impatience of youth precipitated that most terrible persecution which aimed to convert every African to the Arian faith or let him die.[84] Africa had ever been a mass of heterogeneous racial elements; the Vandals had merely added a modest measure to the racial confusion.[85] They therefore could not rule as Vandals; their best hope was to rule as Arians, for men could be made Arians — if necessary by violence. The issue thus joined was religiously false, but it was diplomatically sound: by conversion to Arianism an African virtually took the oath of allegiance to the Vandal State; by rejecting the oath he branded himself a public enemy.

The very oddity of the situation is important. The bishops — and many of the clergy and laity — regarded themselves as Catholics exclusively; that they happened also to be Romans mattered hardly at all. It happened, however, that because Catholicism was the one distinctively Roman manifestation that survived the fall of the State, this Catholicism became the State, not in the eyes of the Roman himself, but in everyone else's eyes, including the barbarian's, and ours. The Vandals felt no bitterness towards the Catholic faith, but because they did feel bitterness towards the Roman State they vented their spleen on that faith which alone kept the

[82] *Letters* VII # 6 §§ 7–9.
[83] Hodgkin 1892 II² 269–79; Duchesne 1911 III⁴ 634.
[84] Victor of Vita *H.P.A.P. passim;* & Duchesne 1911 III⁴ 638–45.
[85] Duchesne ibid. 640. Cf. Grisar 1912 II 211; & Mesnage 1915 II 49.

Roman State alive.   Therefore Huneric resorted to every
brutal expedient except the actual death penalty, in order
to induce conversions.   How many recanted in this extremity
we cannot tell: a good many of the laity, not a few of the
clergy, but hardly a single bishop.   Accordingly these bishops
were herded into the desert, usually to die there, or put to
forced labour in the fields or in Corsica cutting timber for
ships,[86] and the clergy and laity who stood by them shared
their fate.   For every see lying vacant in *Aquitania Secunda*
there were a dozen in Africa.[87]   Many of the exiles survived;
some even returned for a time to their dioceses during later
lulls in the persecution.[88]   But the African Church never
really recovered from Huneric's *coup de grâce*.   Unlike that
of Gaul and Italy, the African episcopate went down with the
ship of State.   Should we be inclined, therefore, to regard
most of the fifth century bishops as men who, however honourable, took good care to feather their own nests, we shall
do well to call to mind the African bishops, most of whom
suffered and many of whom died, as true martyrs to their
faith.   Whatever else these Latin bishops may be accused of,
they were never content to be insignificant, never lay back
or took the easier way: they either led men or died for them.[89]

Wherever the barbarians rose in their wrath and sought
to exterminate the episcopate, no *modus vivendi,* no division
of labour between civil government and Church was possible.
But over most of the West, and during much of the time even
in Aquitaine and Africa, compromises were sought and effected.   In such cases there gradually evolved an arrangement whereby the Church, on the one hand, left foreign
relations, military affairs, and general control over the non-
Catholic elements to the civil authority, but on the other
obtained a surprisingly complete control over all Catholics.
Here was a further cause for the material growth of the
Church: Catholic Romans sought to place themselves under

---

[86] Duchesne ibid.; Victor of Vita
H.P.A.P. III § 20.

[87] Already before 484 the number
of bishoprics in the Proconsular,
Byzacene and Numidia had shrunk
from 517 to 300: Mesnage 1915 II
12–13.

[88] Duchesne 1911 III [4] 644.

[89] On the devotion to duty of the
Italian bishops see Onory 1931 570–
75.

Church rather than civil jurisdiction. Any transaction which would effect this result found favour. Already after 454 the Church was presuming to claim patronage rights over all Catholics; [90] but this might not suffice; before the end of the century, therefore, we find the Church claiming jurisdiction over all her dependents — that is, over all the laymen who worked on the Church lands or whose living depended on the Church revenues.[91] To become such a dependent was a privilege of importance because it gave the right to live under Roman-canon instead of under barbarian-civil law, and to be judged by a bishop instead of by some barbarian appointee. To be sure this civil law and its judges were still Roman. The judges were, however, servants of a barbarian, and bound to please him or resign; even if not so personally corrupt as their predecessors whom Ambrose had resisted, their souls were not their own. By this division of labour the bishop here and there lost ground: by a law of Odoacer in 476, for instance, bishops were forbidden to take part in the election of the *defensor civitatis*,[92] a right they had had since the creation of that office long before 400.[93] The reason no doubt was that the barbarian king wanted to put in his own man, not the bishop's, desiring, not unnaturally, that in each city there be at least one man on whom he could rely. This office, originally created in order that the poor be protected from exploitation by the rich and powerful, now served rather in order that the citizen who was a heretic — especially if he were an Arian — be protected from persecution by a militant Catholicism.

Thus in an unpredictable and yet not unaccountable fashion the Earthly City and the City of God came to live, and often quite amicably, side by side. If, of the two, the Roman City of God was the more spiritual, it was hardly the less material: each was equally a kingdom of this world. Already in the course of her short history, the Church had been many things; during this later fifth century she was chiefly one: the old Roman State, shrunk into many isolated atoms; and, if this were the Church, the State was the new barbarism, struggling for self-confidence in a baffling and uncomfortable posi-

---

90 Onory 1932 297. Cf. pp. 641–42.   92 Ibid. 227.
91 Onory 1933 202–04 & 210–11.   93 See p. 266 n. 91.

tion. The task of shifting the old load to young shoulders required many centuries of darkness and misery.

E. The Nobles as Bishops

Since in the fifth century the bishops became not only the spiritual but also the temporal leaders of the Roman population, it is doubly important to determine from what class they were drawn. In earlier times they had been recruited chiefly from the middle and lower classes; had this continued it is unlikely that they could have discharged such varied and heavy responsibilities as they in fact did. In the later fourth century, however, Christianity began to win many converts among the upper classes: Ambrose, chosen bishop of Milan in 373, is one of the earlier and more conspicuous instances of a Latin noble assuming the episcopal office.

When elected, Ambrose was serving as governor of Aemilia-Liguria. It was these higher civil offices — long a monopoly of the nobles [1] — which, apart from literature and agriculture, chiefly engrossed them. The encumbents, being appointed by the Emperor and serving as his deputies in the name of the Empire, enjoyed a prestige, and even a power,[2] which no other officials could rival. But the very fact that the bishop was, by contrast, locally elected, while it added to the obscurity of his office, also added to its strength. For, as the imperial power faded — passing gradually into the control of barbarian military captains whose policies were as vague as their capacities [3] — the civil machinery which depended on a highly centralized authority gradually faded too.[4] Throughout the fifth century the noble continued to monopolize the higher civil offices as hitherto,[5] but every year such service became more vain and irksome, less agreeable and honourable. For more and more often now his appointment as well as his orders came from a barbarian clumsily posing as a Roman, and too often ruling to suit rather his own than imperial or even local

---

[1] Coster 1935 4, 10 & 24–25.
[2] Ibid. 4, 10 & 13.
[3] Notably in Italy after the advent of Ricimer in 456.

[4] Duchesne 1911 III⁴ 605; Lot 1927 445.
[5] Dalton 1915 I xc.

Roman interests. A bishop, on the other hand, however little the people had actually dictated his election, had usually been approved by them. He was, moreover, serving an organization which was not only essentially Roman but — for the time being — highly decentralized. There were, of course, rules of canon law, occasional meetings of Councils,[6] and sporadic interferences by archbishop [7] or Roman Pope,[8] but during the years 440 to 460 the decline of even this modest supervision set in. Unless the bishop's title to his office was disputed, or unless he entered the lists of speculative theology, his liberty of action was wide.[9] Except during the periods of brazen barbarian persecution only the great landed proprietors could afford to defy him. Under such circumstances a noble, unless he was a pagan, must prefer to rule a *civitas* rather as bishop than as *defensor civitatis,* to rule a province rather as archbishop than as governor, so that, as if by a law of inverse ratio, the appointee of a single city became mightier than the appointee of an Empire. And incidentally, in a day when security turned into insecurity over-night, the bishop's life estate in his office seemed preferable to the civil officer's tenancy at will.

We have already indicated how, by about 455, Catholicism had conquered not only the Roman religion but also what was left of the Latin-Roman State.[10] This, it seems, would not have been possible had not Catholicism conquered the Roman noble.[11] As we shall see,[12] philosophical speculation,

---

6 See p. 300.

7 Dalton 1927 I 268–69 says of the fifth century in Gaul: ' Had the imperial system endured, the nominal authority conceded to the metropolitan might have become effectual.'

8 Until after 430 the African Church either frightened or defied the Roman. Of Gaul Dill 1926 480 says: ' The see of S. Peter had sometimes asserted an authority in Gaul in the fourth and fifth centuries, although in the end of the fifth Popes Gelasius and Symmachus had found themselves paralysed by the invasions in deciding between Arles and Vienne for the primacy of Gaul.' Cf. p. 597.

9 Marignan 1899 I 168; Dalton 1927 I 389; Onory 1931–33 *passim.*

10 See p. 282. Dalton 1915 lxxiii says: ' The bishops of the expiring fifth century were powers in the land and powers for good, mitigating the hardships of a dangerous epoch, and standing forth in the public eyes as the true representatives of national life. They were indeed almost the only conspicuous figures who were visibly doing national work, and the fact was widely recognized.'

11 Until after about 382 (Jerome) and 386 (Martin: Jullian 1926 VII 271 n. 3) the Latin Christians were bourgeois artisans rather than aristocrats: Jullian 1926 VII 139 & 265. Labriolle 1934 340 picks the earlier date of 355.

12 See pp. 339 n. 12, & 344 n. 62.

whether by Manichee, Neoplatonist, Epicurean, or Christian, was now a monopoly of the upper classes; so, evidently, was political authority, whether exercised by pagan or Christian, by State or Church. New Causes and movements, as in this case, are first bruited among the humbler classes; but they are doomed to failure unless some part of the upper class comes to their support.

From the letters of Jerome and from other miscellaneous sources we learn that it was especially to the Latin women of rank that Christianity first appealed; [13] and it was through them that the husbands, sons, and brothers were in their turn won over. The women's part was inevitably a modest one: to take a vow of chastity, to found a convent or a hospital for the poor and diseased; the man, on the other hand, could aspire to offices wielding an ever wider influence. In the course of the fifth century so many of the aristocrats chose the ecclesiastical career that the *potentior, defensor civitatis,* or governor of an earlier day was often now a bishop.

How universal this transformation was is hard to say. In both Africa [14] and Spain [15] the social origin of most of the fifth century bishops is wholly unknown. In Italy a very large number were recruited from the nobility; a fair number, however, came from the middle and lower classes.[16] Two of her most distinguished bishops, Ambrose of Milan and Epiphanius of Pavia,[17] were nobles; of the bishops of Rome, on the other hand, only Felix III was of the highest rank.[18] Evidently the Church of Rome had already acquired a hierarchical tradition before the noble became Christian: a long apprenticeship in the lower Orders was required, consolidating an exclusive middle class bureaucracy. Being so large, the city's populace could not act as the electorate; therefore con-

[13] See Dill 1906 [2] 13–14; & Dudden 1935 4.

[14] Augustine was of good family but not of the aristocracy. His friend Alypius belonged to the first family of Tagaste and later became bishop of that city: *Confessions* VI 7; *The Book of Saints* 1921 15. The father of Nebridius, Augustine's other most intimate friend in youth, was very rich in lands: *Confessions* VI 10. But the origins of most of the African bishops are unknown: Mesnage 1915 70.

[15] Priscillian, bishop of Avila, who was executed as a heretic in 385, was a man of wealth.

[16] Onory 1931 263.

[17] Hodgkin 1892 II [2] 468.

[18] The origins of most of the other fifth century Popes are not known. Leo was probably of middle class Tuscan stock.

trol fell to a close corporation of professionals. There were many occasions of controversy and bloodshed when appeals were made for public support; but the popular choice was always between nominees of rival factions within the hierarchy.[19]   If a noble aspired to be bishop of Rome he must serve a long apprenticeship in the hierarchy, rising to prominence only as fast and as far as its members saw fit.[20]   Had Ambrose in 373 been prefect in Rome instead of governor in Milan the populace would not have dared to nominate him as their bishop.

In Gaul, on the other hand, the noble acquired virtual control over the Church: every one of the twelve most famous Gallic bishops of the fifth century was a noble.   Beginning [21] with Paulinus,[22] who came from Bordeaux and became bishop of Nola in Italy in 395, there were Germanus of Auxerre,[23] Lupus of Troyes,[24] Honoratus of Arles,[25] Hilary of Arles,[26] Eucherius of Lyons,[27] Constantius of Lyons,[28] Patiens of Lyons,[29] Remi of Rheims,[30] Sidonius of Clermont,[31] Ruric of Limoges,[32] and Avitus of Vienne.[33]   And among the most famous Gallic priests of this time who, although also nobles, never reached the episcopate, were Sulpicius Severus of Toulouse,[34] Vincent of Lerins,[35] Salvian of Cologne,[36] and Claudi-

---

[19] As in the disputed elections of 364 and 500.

[20] In *Letters* ## 12 & 19 Leo urged promotions according to seniority.

[21] For two fourth century cases in Gaul see Gregory of Tours *History* I §§ 44 & 47.

[22] 'Paulinus belonged to one of the richest and noblest families in the Roman world': Dill 1906 [2] 396.

[23] Germanus, according to Constantius *Vita Germani* § 1, was 'parentibus splendidissimis procreatus.'

[24] Lupus married Pimeniola, a sister of Hilary of Arles: see the anonymous *Vita Lupi* § 1. Cf. Sidonius *Letters* VIII # 11 § 1.

[25] Honoratus' family was of the highest rank: Hilary *Vita S. Honorati* § 4. Cf. Duchesne 1911 III [4] 271.

[26] Hilary was a kinsman of Honoratus: *The Book of Saints* 1921 136.

[27] Duchesne 1911 III [4] 273; & see

pp. 344–46, & 490–93 for the career of Eucherius.

[28] Sidonius *Letters* III # 2 § 3 says to Constantius 'despite your noble birth.'

[29] See pp. 297–99.

[30] Of Remi Dill 1926 30 says that 'he and Principius, bishop of Soissons, were probably brothers, sprung from a family of rank in the district of Laon.'

[31] Sidonius' own *Letters* are ample evidence.

[32] Engelbrecht 1891 lxiv.

[33] Arnold 1897 II 318 lines 22–26.

[34] Monceaux 1926 14.

[35] *Encycl. Brit.* 1911 28 [11] 92 says he was 'possibly a brother of' Lupus. Gennadius *De Script. Eccles.* ch. 64 says he was a Gaul who held important civil offices before he retired to the monastery of Lerins.

[36] Sanford 1930 9 says that 'his parents were clearly of the Gallo-Roman aristocracy.'

anus Mamertus of Vienne.[37] The most prominent priest who
was not of the nobility was the sceptical Vigilantius.[38] Of his
own predecessors, bishop Gregory of Tours, writing just after
590, lists four who were consecrated during the fifth century,
Eustochius, Perpetuus, Volusianus and Verus; and each of
these was not only of senatorial family but was related to
Gregory himself.[39] He says, indeed, that of the eighteen bishops of Tours before his own consecration in 573 only five were
not related to him![40] Now what was true of this see must have
been more or less true of the others — especially as we know
that it was generally true for some time after 500.[41] Gene-
alogies of the fifth century are scarce: but we do know that
both of the sons of bishop Eucherius of Lyons became bishops
in their turn;[42] we know that bishop Lupus occupied the see
of Troyes for fifty-two years[43] — which suggests a suspiciously quick promotion; and we know that Remi of Rheims
was consecrated at the age of twenty-two.[44] Nevertheless, that
the bishopric could long have persisted as an hereditary vocation of the nobility is unlikely — neither Church nor barbarian ruler would have tolerated it — but the rule, now generally operative, of clerical celibacy,[45] was itself enough to
undermine the practice. Lupus and Remi, for instance, had
small time for generation. So long as conversions in middle

---

[37] Claudianus Mamertus the phi-
losopher-theologian (see pp. 528–
30), was a friend of Sidonius: Sidonius *Letters* III # # 2 & 3. He was
also a friend of Salvian's and his
brother was bishop of Vienne: Dalton 1915 I clxxiii.

[38] Jülicher 1908 XX 630 lines 51–
54 describes Vigilantius as 'ein
begüterte Mann in einer vornehm-
lich von Weinbau lebenden Gegend
gewesen, hat also gewiss auch Wein-
berge besessen.'

[39] *History* X 31. Gregory does not
say explicitly, as he does in the case
of the other three, whether Verus
was of senatorial family; but he must,
according to Kurth 1919 I 251, have
been related to Gregory's own family.

[40] In *History* V 49 Gregory says
that 'praeter quinque episcopos
reliqui omnes, qui sacerdotium
Turonicum susceperunt, nostrorum
prosapiae sunt conjuncti.' As to

Gregory's parents' own rank he says:
'Pater eius nomine Georgius, mater
vero Leocadia a stirpe Vectii Epagati
descendens . . . qui ita de primori-
bus senatoribus fuerunt ut in Galliis
nihil inveniatur esse generosius atque
nobilius': *Vitae Patrum* VI § 1.

[41] See Kurth 1919 I 183–200.

[42] See p. 484 n. 9.

[43] In 472 he had been bishop for
45 years: Sidonius *Letters* VI # 1 § 3.
And he died in 479: Dalton 1915 I
clxxii.

[44] This was in 461: *The Book of
Saints* 1921 229. He lived until 533:
Dill 1926 30. Yet twenty years
earlier, in 441, a Council held at
Orange had decreed in canon # 24
that no one might be a deacon until
he was twenty-five, or be a priest
until he was thirty: Marignan 1899
I 194. Cf. Siricius *Letter* # 1 § 13.

[45] Lot 1927 444; Dudden 1935 124.

life were frequent there would be sons available for the succession, but the second Christian generation usually took Orders at a tender age. Nephews might still succeed, and did, but this tie was a loose one.

Therefore the young bishop rarely succeeded as the direct heir of his predecessor; on the other hand he sat very often as the heir of his *gens* or clan — in fifth century Gaul, indeed, almost invariably. And, as we shall see, after 430 the abbots of the Gallic monasteries were likely to be nobles too.[46] Nor is it surprising that the class which held a dominating position in the organism of the now dying Roman Empire should maintain it in the growing Roman Church. In histories of the Church this fact has rarely been emphasized, perhaps because pious Christians have felt squeamish to admit that so many of their greatest heroes and saints were recruited from the rich nobility — the inference might be drawn that such persons were peculiarly susceptible to enlightenment. Yet who, after all, is the rich man but one who has had the full advantage of civilization — who has received leisure, instruction, refinement, tradition? In our Utopias are these not the very boons guaranteed to all?

If there were many good reasons why a noble should covet a bishopric, there were just as many why he should be coveted as a bishop. Certainly many instances are recorded where the diocese wanted him more than he wanted it.[47] Among those who showed an extreme reluctance to serve were — besides Ambrose [48] — Germanus,[49] Eucherius,[50] Hilary,[51] Severinus,[52] Sidonius,[53] Remi,[54] and Ruric.[55] Modesty played its part here, and so did the wish for a life of contemplation rather than of action; to a great noble, nevertheless, who could hope to be promoted to the highest offices of the Empire, a life term as

---

[46] See pp. 488–89. Severus *Life of Martin* 10 says that of the eighty who followed Martin's monastic regime near Tours in about 375 many ' were, it is said, of noble birth.' And in ch. 23 Severus speaks of ' a young man of the name of Clair who was a great noble, who in later years became a priest.'

[47] Hence the familiar *Nolo episcopari.*

[48] See p. 256.

[49] Constantius *Vita Germani* § 2.

[50] Dufourcq *L'Av.* 1911 V³ 35.

[51] Anonymous *S. Hilarii . . . Vita* 6.

[52] Eugippius *Vita S. Severini* 9.

[53] Dalton 1915 I xxxv & lxiii.

[54] If we may rely on Hincmar's ninth century biography: ' Raptus potius quam electus ': Dalton 1915 I clxxvii.

[55] Dufourcq *L'Av.* 1911 V³ 35.

head of a single *civitas* was no great enticement. From the standpoint of the citizens, on the other hand, the advantage of an aristocratic bishop was obvious. If among the nobility there were many undesirables there were also many of high quality. The citizens had no need to choose any but the best. The noble, moreover, would be trained to speak and write, would have a wide acquaintance and influence,[56] would be experienced in public affairs. He would not be tempted to use of the office for personal profit or glory, he would not easily be tricked or bribed, or be treated with contempt — even by the barbarian. And, even if he did not convey many of his properties to the Church,[57] the income from these, as in the case of bishop Patiens,[58] could safely be counted on in time of need. Not that the citizens craved wealth above all else: in most cases the diocese was already wealthy.[59] The need was above all for an honest and efficient administration, and only the noble, because of his experience in administering large properties employing thousands of men,[60] could assure the diocese not of honesty only but of efficiency too.[61]

I do not wish to eulogize unduly either the Roman noble or the Catholic bishop of this time — too much of our information comes from their admirers. Still, we do know that a

[56] Dill 1906 [2] 216–17.

[57] Several bishops of Ravenna before 400 gave liberally of their own property to their sees: Onory 1931 280. So, of course, did Paulinus of Nola. But it is hard to say how far this was the general practice. Salvian, writing about 445, says that in his diatribe against the ungenerous clergy ' I do not mean to include all the saints but only those who, although they have adopted the true religious life, nevertheless do not give away their property ': *Ad Ecclesiam* II § 12.

[58] See p. 297. And cf. Dill 1906 [2] 191 & 218.

[59] Bayet 1911 24; Dalton 1915 I lxxiv.

[60] Cf. Malnory 1894 121–23.

[61] Dalton 1915 I lxxiii–lxxv says: ' Good men of wealth and standing, condemned to inaction by the absence of any secular career, must have cast envious eyes upon this episcopal office which enabled its holders to serve their country so well; the hierarchy and the people, equally alive to the importance of strengthening the Church by the admission of such valuable recruits, did not discourage their aspirations. . . . The aristocratic bishops could serve her best not only in her relations with imperial officials, whose day was almost gone, but also with the barbarian princes, whose favour grew more important every year. As the empire was ever further dismembered, and the Church provided the one bond of union between the subjects of isolated kingdoms, the diplomatic bishop continually proved his worth. The Visigoth and the Burgundian were impressed by his culture and his experience of the world; moreover, they were by tradition disposed to favour high birth.'

very large proportion of the fifth century bishops — in Gaul
especially — were recruited from the Roman nobility — evidently from the cream of it — and we have hardly a record of
a bishop who notoriously failed.[62]   Granted that the good
bishop has been extravagantly glorified, it is probable that a
bad bishop would have been just as violently reviled. Salvian
was a fanatic whom almost no one could please. To him
urbanity was synonymous with villainy. Yet, though he tells
us that the clergy were not all they should have been,[63] he
makes hardly a disparaging remark about bishops.[64]

The advocate of popular sovereignty is in this case vindicated: for fifth century Gaul, at least, offers good evidence that
a city or people, when in dire straits, is likely to choose as
leader the best man that can be found; nor need he invariably
be, as Ambrose was, a great man. So long as Romans of the
highest type could be prevailed upon to serve — as, during
the emergency, they could be — there was no reason for select-
ing other men less conspicuously qualified. Technically the
bishop had, by his ordination and consecration, renounced
the temporal world, but the layman turned suddenly priest
could not be expected to take this renunciation too literally;
even the priest who, as in Rome, rose slowly up through the
hierarchy to this episcopal summit could not renounce. The
bishop, indeed, found himself almost the only Roman left
with a plain duty to face the world squarely, exchanging
blow for blow: for the more he came to be looked upon by
others as their temporal leader, the more he must so look
upon himself.

Theorists find it comparatively easy to segregate the functions of priest from those of ruler, but many of the most con-

[62] Patroclus of Arles, who held
that see from 417 to 426, was a poli-
tician with an unsavoury reputation:
Caspar 1930 I 344–45 & 382–85. He
was a political appointee of the Patrician Constantius: Malnory 1894 39.
And there was danger of an unfortunate choice at Chalon-sur-Saône in
470: Sidonius *Letters* IV # 25.

[63] Salvian *D.G.D.* V § 52 speaks of
the clergy in general in these terms:
'They have altered in their profession but not in their actual way of
life, and, thinking that the service of

God depends on costume more than
on action, have changed their garments but not their hearts.' And on
the African clergy before the Vandal
invasion he says only this: 'The
Church was, to be sure, completely
under the care of the priests and
clergy, whom I do not discuss, because I owe reverence to the ministry
of my Lord ': *D.G.D.* VII § 74. Naturally the clergy as a whole did not
behave as he would have liked.

[64] See p. 372.

scientious and able who have tried to put this theory into
practice have failed. The problem which Gregory the Great,
Bernard, and Calvin each vainly tried to resolve was never
more acute than in this fifth century. The difficulty is very
simple: for salvation presupposes virtue, and virtue presupposes acts as well as states of mind. The act, however, is a
civic affair and active virtue is therefore civic virtue. That is
why Ambrose, in his treatise *De Officiis* — *On Duty* — could
find no better model than Cicero.[65] Every elementary Christian virtue is equally a civic and a pagan virtue. And for the
higher and specifically Christian virtues — of mercy, humility, and love — these others are an indispensable foundation.[66] What are the vices of self-indulgence, sloth, cupidity,
envy, or cruelty?[67] Are they not equally spiritual and temporal, Christian and pagan? No good priest will ignore murder on the pretext that it is exclusively Cæsar's concern. If
Cæsar will not act, he will.

This interference of the bishops in temporal and even in
military affairs was, in later centuries, to be greatly, and justly,
decried; but we are bound to conclude that its inception in
this fifth century was dictated by motives worthy of all that
is noblest in man.[68] The precedent it set later proved an awkward one and the abuses it engendered proved beyond the
power even of the monastic Orders to counteract. But in
times of emergency even the wisest men cannot afford to be
seers.

[65] Duchesne 1910 II 4 557.

[66] Only these latter, however, are
saving virtues, and therefore dependent on the receipt of grace: see pp.
137, & 476.

[67] Cf. pp. 279–83, on Maximus of
Turin.

[68] Cf. Gouilloud 1881 232–33.

CHAPTER V

JUSTICE ON EARTH

A. Denial of Justice on Earth

Man's religious dilemma — of whether to believe or not to believe — is very old; Christianity merely revived the issue in a new disguise. Augustine describes how he supposed the problem had presented itself eight hundred years earlier:

> Among the Athenians did there not flourish both the Epicureans, who alleged that human affairs did not have the care of the gods, and the Stoics who, holding contrary opinions, maintained that these affairs are controlled and supported by assisting and tutelary gods? [1]

And the pagan poet Claudian shows how the Roman of 396 [2] was still confronted by the problem:

> My mind has often wavered between two opinions: have the gods a care for the world or is there no ruler therein and do mortal things drift as dubious chance dictates? For when I investigated the laws and the ordinances of heaven and observed the sea's appointed limits, the year's fixed cycle and the alternation of light and darkness, then I thought everything was ordained according to the direction of a God who had bidden the stars move by fixed laws, plants grow at different seasons, the changing moon fulfil her circle with borrowed light and the sun shine by his own, who spread the shore before the waves and balanced the world in the centre of the firmament. But when I saw the impenetrable mist that surrounds human affairs, the wicked happy and long prosperous and the good discomforted, then in turn my belief in God was weakened and failed, and even against mine own will I embraced the tenets of that other philosophy which teaches that atoms drift in purposeless motion and that new forms throughout the vast void are shaped by chance and not design — that philosophy which believes in God in an ambiguous sense, or holds that there be no gods, or that they are careless of our doings. [3]

This passage reveals the weakness of Stoicism: for it apparently argued the existence of a Providence from the fact that there was justice on earth. [4] Consequently it tacitly admitted

[1] *D.C.D.* XVIII 41.
[2] Platenauer 1922 I xiv.
[3] *In Rufinum* I lines 1–19.
[4] Cf. Nock 1933 100.

314

the corollary that if there were no justice on earth there could be no Providence.

Now it was particularly obvious to the fourth century Romans that there was no such justice; at the same time it was becoming almost as obvious to them that the world was ruled by something more than chance. A doctrine that could reconcile these two apparently contradictory convictions was therefore becoming every day more indispensable. The Manichees failed because they conceived of a God who, though ruling in heaven, could not enforce His will on earth. He was not therefore that Providence whose existence men so strongly suspected. Nor was Neoplatonism more satisfactory, for, though it offered a compromise, it was a negative one — the operation of earthly government being unjust precisely to the extent that God fell short of being a Providence. A doctrine which could plausibly explain how a complete absence of justice on earth was compatible with a complete control over human affairs by a good God, was what the fourth century Roman was looking for; and what is zealously sought is likely to be found.

The first Christian reaction had been against the Jews; and, because the heavenly rewards of the New Testament contrasted with the earthly rewards of the Old, to these early Christians the idea of justice on earth had been abhorrent.[5] And to this they added an almost equal abhorrence for the whole world of matter and flesh. Ignatius, the famous bishop of Antioch at the close of the first century, had said:

I no longer have any zeal for matter . . . I no longer take pleasure in corruptible food or in the joys of this life. . . . I no longer care to live as do men.[6]

And fifty years later Marcion, leader of the Gnostics in their prime, preached that matter was evil and the antithesis of God.[7] The spiritual descendants of such men were the Manichees who continued the repudiation of the Old Testament.

There was, however, another kind of Christian who had the good sense to accept the Old Testament as prophetic of and therefore reconcilable with the New. It was this that gave Christianity its balance-wheel. For it was obvious from

---

[5] See Tixeront 1924 I⁹ 163 on Clement, Hermes, and Polycarp.

[6] *Epistola ad Romanos* §§ 7 & 8.

[7] Dufourcq *L'Av.* 1909 III³ 154.

the Old Testament that God had created the world for the express purpose of serving man,[8] and, if made by God for man, how could man conscientiously repudiate it? How could God have created matter if it were, as Marcion had alleged, His complete antithesis?

Out of this need to reconcile injustice on earth with God's Providence grew up the purgatorial idea of mortal life. God had put man into the flesh for a specific and intelligible purpose: to try his mettle, to test his endurance and faith in the good, to qualify him for immortality. On this hypothesis justice during this transitory period was impracticable: for if justice should operate automatically, so that reward would come simultaneously with the effort, there could be no sacrifice and so no test of character. The wicked, having the same incentive to act virtuously as any saint, would, as a matter of expediency, act as virtuously. But could not justice be postponed a while and still be enforced before death? Perhaps, theoretically, it could be, but manifestly it in fact was not, and it could only be inferred that mortal life was so short that the postponement, though it might seem interminable, was in fact only for an instant.

The conviction that God did, indeed, will injustice on earth and willed, therefore, that virtue and suffering should go hand in hand, was further consolidated by the persecutions and martyrdoms of the third century. Occasionally, perhaps, God had condescended to reveal His presence by a miraculous Sign, but He never raised a finger to relieve the physical agonies of the tortured or to save them from a humiliating death.

Then came Constantine and first toleration, then dominion, throughout the Roman world. Was God now changing His tactics? A few were doubtless tempted secretly to suspect so; but the illusion was short-lived. There were now Christian Emperors and Christian bishops, wielding between them a sovereign authority. The heresies, however, did not stop: Arians fought with Orthodox, Manichees arose to challenge the foundations of Christian dogma. Paganism too remained a serious threat. And, throughout all this, the State

---

[8] *Genesis* i 26 & 28. **Cf.** Jerome
Contra Jovinianum II §§ 5 & 6.

was unmistakably crumbling under pressure of forces both within and without. Even a mild degree of justice on earth was evidently not to be expected; [9] therefore even the new Christian regime seemed rather for the perfection of the purgatorial machinery.

There is, however, a curious passage in which Jerome reviles the heretical monk Jovinian:

But you, perversely and deceitfully, make the life of this world illustrate that of the life to come.[10]

Good Catholics doubtless believed themselves free of any such delusions; yet it is possible that, to outsiders, many of them unwittingly betrayed hopes that they dared not formulate. The Manichee, Faustus, at any rate, hurled this reproach:

The god of the Hebrews in his stone tablets promises you gold and silver, an abundance of food and the land of Canaan. Such low rewards have tempted you to be unfaithful to Christ.[11]

Ostensibly this thrust was merely at the Catholic belief in the divine inspiration of the Old Testament, but, knowing as we do something of the Catholic priesthood of that day, and something too, as we shall see in a moment, of the self-assurance of many of the monks, it may well be that the thrust was designed to cut deeper.

In his enthusiasm at the elevation of the young Gratian to the imperial power, Ambrose, writing in 379,[12] allows himself to say:

You know that victory is to be sought rather by the faith of the prince than by the capacity of the soldiers.[13]

A few years later, however, chastened and disillusioned by the assassination of Gratian and the return of the Arians to power,[14] he asserts that it is a peculiarity of the pagans that

they have believed victory to be a goddess, whereas in fact it is not a power but a gift, does not rule but is bestowed, comes not by the power of religion but by the aid of the legions.[15]

---

[9] Cf. Firmicus Maternus *Matheseos* I ch. 7 §§ 19–30, of about 355.

[10] Jerome *Contra Jovinianum* II § 24.

[11] Acc. to Augustine *Contra Faustum Manichæum* XV § 1.

[12] Uberweg 1915 II [10] 148 line 3.

[13] *De Fide* I § 3.

[14] Batiffol 1924 [2] 53–56 & 60–61.

[15] *Letter # 18* § 30.

The grief and disillusionment of Ambrose seem to have taught him a permanent lesson,[16] for in his *De Officiis* of 386 [17] he adopts the pessimistic view with sound theological deliberation, arguing indeed rather as a Manichee might, in full reliance on the authority of the New Testament:

There is laid up for us a crown of righteousness which the Lord, the righteous Judge, shall give us on that day.

Commenting on this text from 2 *Timothy* iv 8, he says,

on that day he [Paul] says He will give it — not here.[18]

And he asks further:

Is the palm ever given or the crown granted before the course is finished? . . .
A reward future, not present, in heaven, not on earth, has He promised shall be given.[19]

Earthly delights and sin, indeed, go hand in hand, for

No victory is glorious unless the contest has been difficult.[20]

And conversely, as in *Matthew* v 10:

Blessed are they which are persecuted for righteousness' sake.[21]

Or in *Luke* xvi 25:

Those worldly persons seek profit in good things, we actually seek it in injurious things; since he who, like that rich man, here receives good things, is there tormented, and Lazarus, who here suffered evil things, there finds consolation.[22]

The Spanish poet Prudentius also adopts this pessimistic conception. He describes how the martyr Laurentius, having been ordered to produce the hidden treasures of his Church, assembles all the blind, halt, and lame, and then boldly offers them as that treasure:

' These are the disciples of light whom a feeble body contracts lest through the good health of the flesh the mind should swell to insolence. When sickness destroys the limbs the soul thrives

---

16 See Dudden 1935 518.
17 Uberweg 1915 II [10] 148 line 27.
18 *De Officiis* I § 58.
19 Ibid. §§ 58 & 59. Cf. on the view of the Greek Pseudo-Justin, Labriolle 1934 502 & 504.

20 Ibid. § 58.
21 Ibid. § 59.
22 Ibid. § 29.

more vigorously; by strong limbs, on the other hand, sensitiveness is impaired. . . . These whom you proudly despise, whom you judge execrable, will soon lay aside their ulcerous limbs and be whole; when at length relieved and free of their most corrupt flesh, in the most beautiful condition of life they will shine in the citadel of the Father.' [23]

Here is manifested a peculiar kind of justice — akin to that to which modern communism aspires: everyone is to get an equal share of joy and misery regardless of merit. At the Last Judgment a man's virtue will be gauged, not by his heart, but by his past misery; if only he has been more miserable than wicked he has earned an eternal reward. And woe to the good man who has had the misfortune of earthly happiness! This seems a doctrine unworthy of Christianity because it subordinates merit to a contractual right — to just so much happiness and no more. Of course the doctrine was based on the assumption that earthly happiness was in inverse proportion to virtue, earthly misery in inverse proportion to sin. This might be correct, but it was also Manichæan, doctrine. If the good God created this world for man's sake, why should man be punished for enjoying what God in His infinite goodness gave him? Again, as in so many other cases, correction of error was reserved for the genius of Augustine.

Ambrose and Prudentius had both spoken before the great invasions of 406 had begun. Augustine's discussion of justice on earth, on the other hand, is largely to be found in his *De Civitate Dei,* a work begun in 413 and finished only in 426,[24] and written, therefore, not only after these invasions but specifically in order to explain why they had occurred. When the others were writing,[25] the complete victory of orthodoxy throughout the Roman world seemed more complete and secure than ever before; whereas when Augustine wrote, this great fabric was already crumbling, with the Catholic sovereignty, both temporal and spiritual, apparently doomed to share the fate of the State. Moreover Augustine was a somewhat younger man: fifteen years younger than Ambrose, six years younger than Prudentius.

---

[23] *Peristephanon* II lines 205–12 & 265–76, partly quoted pp. 150–151.
[24] Lacey 1929 683.

[25] Ambrose died in 397. Jerome, see p. 330, changed his opinion in that very year.

These things being so, common sense might suggest to us that Augustine would take an even more pessimistic view than they had; and yet, curiously enough, the reverse is true. He was younger and wrote later: this might account for the difference, paradoxical as this may seem. But there may be other reasons too: having been himself a Manichee he had reacted more violently against their pessimism; being an empiricist who was tireless in his scrutiny of man and his dilemma, he observed that the pessimistic hypothesis did not fit the observed facts.

He does make one concession — that any of us would make:

To be quite free from pain while we are in this place of misery is only purchased, as one of this world's literati perceived and remarked, at the price of blunted sensibilities of both mind and body.[26]

And he also says that

the Stoics maintain, not that the fool, but that the wise man, cannot be sorrowful,[27]

by which he means to imply that the wise man must and should be often sorrowful — not at all that he must chronically remain so.

In the first Book of the *De Civitate Dei* he is still rather consciously resisting pagan and Manichæan doctrine:

If no sin received now a plainly divine punishment, it would be concluded that there is no divine Providence at all. And so of the good things of this life: if God did not by a very visible liberality confer these on some of those persons who ask for them, we should say that these good things were not at His disposal.[28]

The intimation here is that if there were not far more justice on earth than could possibly be accounted for by blind chance, men could not be blamed if they doubted the Christian God's existence. But writing about ten years later, in 423, either the bogey of the Manichee has faded or his doctrine has matured; for he then feels safe to say that if only

none but wicked men won the transitory prosperity of earth, while only the good suffered its ills, this could be referred to the just

---

[26] *D.C.D.* XIV 9. The man of letters is Crantor, an Academic philosopher quoted by Cicero in *Tusc. Quaest.* iii 6: Schaff 1887 270 n. 3.

[27] *D.C.D.* XIV 8.
[28] Ibid. I 8.

and even benign judgment of God. We might then suppose that they who were not destined to obtain those everlasting benefits which constitute human blessedness were either deluded by transitory blessings as the just reward of their wickedness,[29] or were, in God's mercy, consoled by them, and that they who were not destined to suffer eternal torments were afflicted with temporal chastisement for their sins, or were stimulated to greater attainment in virtue.[30]

Here Augustine agrees with Ambrose and Prudentius that a systematic injustice on earth was an admirable proof of the reality of a Providence. But there is here the important difference that Augustine denied free will, denied merit: the virtuous man having received this virtue as an undeserved gift, God could justly subject him to every earthly misery and, although he qualified for eternal life, he did so because of God's mercy and not because this was justly due.

And if complete injustice would be proof of Christian truth, conversely, Augustine argued, an equally unvarying justice would be proof of its falsity. If in the one case future rewards and punishments must be in store, in the other case they cannot be:

For if every sin were now visited with manifest punishment, nothing would seem to be reserved for final judgment. . . . And so of the good things of life . . . if He gave them to all who sought them, we should suppose that such were the only rewards of His service.[31]

In such a case men would be back in the pre-Redemption world described in the Old Testament.[32]

To Augustine, however, both of these regimes seemed purely hypothetical: he was too devout an empiricist not to see that on earth there was actually no complete justice or injustice but rather a delicate balance of the two:

But now, as it is, since we see not only good men involved in the ills of life and bad men enjoying the good of it, which seems

---

[29] That is, in order that they may be furnished with no occasion which would tend to induce repentance?
[30] *D.C.D.* XX 2.
[31] Ibid. I 8.
[32] Faustus of Riez, writing in about 473, argued that God's indulgence or patience is a *sine qua non* of human sin, for it is His determination to postpone a deserved punishment which gives man his false sense of security and impunity: *De Gratia* I ch. 17 (*C.S.E.L.* XXI 54 lines 24-5 & 54 line 30 — 55 line 19), & II ch. 1 (58 line 26 — 59 line 26). Cf. pp. 315-16.

unjust, but also that evil often overtakes evil men and good surprises the good, rather on this account are God's judgments unsearchable and His ways past finding out.[33]

His observation and experience, therefore, not only discredited the optimism of Jew and Stoic, and the pessimism of
the Manichees, Ambrose and Prudentius; they also actually
corroborated the Catholic reconciliation of the Old Testament with the New: life on earth was to be faced, was to be
lived as God when He created the earth intended that it
should be — even though it must ever be regarded merely as
a means to an end. Why is Augustine not arguing here
as the devil's advocate, proposing a regime of blind chance?
Because he is not proposing such a regime; he is merely acknowledging the existence of a regime which bears a superficial resemblance to one of chance — that is why God's judgments are unsearchable.

When Augustine says that on account of the mixture of
justice and injustice on earth ' God's judgments are unsearchable and His ways past finding out ', he is merely politely
deferential: he does not for a moment think he cannot search
and find them out, for already in earlier passages he had
largely done so.[34] Here as elsewhere he uses the inductive
method, analyzing particular cases and generalizing from
them. Here is a case of manifest justice, there one of manifest injustice: he must consider what, in each case, God's motive might be, and what to infer, from a methodical classi-
fication of these cases, in regard to God's general policy. The
cases fall naturally into two classes: those where the individual
is dealt with according to his own behaviour, and those where
his lot is dictated, not by his own behaviour, but by considerations of the general welfare. In the latter case there is a close
analogy to the subordination of the individual to the State.

In the first category the purgatorial idea is prominent.[35]
In this group are those cases where a limited justice on earth
seems to have been administered. Referring to the rape of
holy virgins by Alaric during the sack of Rome in 410, he says:

---

[33] *D.C.D.* XX 2.
[34] All but one of the passages now
to be quoted are from the earlier
books.

[35] Augustine *Enchiridion* 69 said
that a Purgatory after death was a
mere possibility. There is no hint
of any such reformatory in ibid. 109.

Moreover it is possible that those Christian women, who are un-conscious of any undue pride on account of their virtuous chas-tity, whereby they sinlessly suffered the violence of their captors, had yet some lurking infirmity which might have betrayed them into a proud and contemptuous bearing had they not been sub-jected to the humiliation that befell them in the taking of the city.[36]

Or again the absence of righteous indignation towards pagans and other sinners may be the occasion of misfortunes that seem to be merely bad luck:

For often we wickedly blind ourselves to the occasions of teach-ing and admonishing them, sometimes even of reprimanding and chiding them, either because we shrink from the labour or are ashamed to offend them, or because we fear to lose good friend-ships, lest this should stand in the way of our advancement, or injure us in some worldly matter which either our covetous dis-position desires to obtain or our weakness shrinks from losing.[37]

In these cases venial sins are punished with severity because the victims are destined for the infinite reward of salvation. But what of the pagans who, although ineligible for salva-tion unless converted before death, live as virtuously as their ignorance permits?

Now, therefore, with regard to those to whom God did not pur-pose to give eternal life . . . if He had also withheld from them the terrestrial glory of that most excellent empire, a reward would not have been rendered to their good arts — that is, their virtues — by which they sought to attain so great glory. For as to those who seem to do some good that they may receive glory from men, the Lord also says, *Verily I say unto you, they have received their reward*.[38]

In neither of these cases is there complete justice on earth, for in both that justice is subordinated to future rewards and punishments. Yet in both there is a tendency towards it, for the venial sin of the Christian is punished, and the feeble virtue of the pagan is rewarded. In each such case there is swift judgment according to behaviour. The difference is that the New Law applies to Christians on earth and to pagans in hell, while the Old applies to Christians in heaven and to pagans on earth.

In another class of purgatorial cases — and they are by

[36] *D.C.D.* I 28.
[37] Ibid. 9.
[38] Ibid. V 15, quoting *Matt.* vi 2.

far the most common — men as yet committed to neither virtue nor sin, are forced to undergo trials, not as punishments or chastisements, but as tests of their true mettle, for

the same violence of affliction proves, purges, and clarifies the good, but damns, ruins, and exterminates the wicked.[39]

Job's was of course the classic case — there was no need for Augustine to enlarge on it — but it is as well that we should never forget this cardinal point of the doctrine: at birth man was a potentiality, a kind of raw material. Earthly life, with all the vicissitudes ingeniously provided by God, was designed to actualize that potentiality, to shape it into a finished product.[40] Technically it was the Fall that explained why man must suffer in order to realize his full nature; actually the Fall was merely a plausible explanation of a truth that no amount of optimism could gainsay. No man was to be trusted until he had been tried; his nature could only be tempered by suffering. Failure to acknowledge and courageously face this disagreeable fact is one reason why Stoicism died.

In all these cases the individual is dealt with on the merits of his own case: the judgment is not affected by extrinsic considerations. Many things could be explained in this way, but not all. Just as it was easy to see that God created horses in order to ease man's physical tasks but not so easy to see why He created ants, so it was easier to see why He tried Job than to see why He rewarded Marius. And so, just as it was concluded that the ant was created to teach men the virtue of industry, Augustine concluded that Marius was rewarded in order to teach pagans that injustice could not be allayed by worshipping demons. In the course of his demonstration that the pagan gods did not promote justice on earth Augustine says,

If in temporal matters they have power either for good or for evil, why did they stand by Marius, the worst of Rome's citizens, and abandon Regulus, the best? Does this not prove them to be most unjust and wicked?[41]

[39] *D.C.D.* I 8.
[40] The phenomenon of infant mortality of course embarrassed this, as it did every other theory.

[41] *D.C.D.* II 23.

Of course the pagan demons could do no more evil than God allowed; He therefore allowed them to deal so unjustly with these men for the express purpose of teaching the Romans the absurdity of their faith. Justice towards Marius, whether on earth and so ephemeral or in heaven and so eternal, was clearly not done, for he deserved not even the smallest and briefest reward. Clearly, therefore, God cannot have intended to deal justly with him, but rather to reward him unjustly in order to teach the pagans the folly of their religion. And, as Marius was the undeserving beneficiary, so Regulus was the undeserving victim, of God's need to teach men the folly of their ways. Like the ant they had merely an extrinsic, vicarious, and, as it were, a symbolic importance.

Moreover this explanation might occasionally be tacked on to the other:

It was not only for the sake of recompensing the citizens of Rome that her empire and glory were so signally extended, but also that the citizens of that eternal city, during their pilgrimage here, might diligently and soberly contemplate these examples, and see what a love they owe to the supernal country on account of life eternal, if the terrestrial country was so much beloved by its citizens on account of human glory.[42]

No better illustration can be found of how closely Augustine sought to dog the footsteps of divine ingenuity: God extended the Empire and glory of the Romans not only in order to prepare the world for the diffusion of the Gospel,[43] not only in order to reward those Romans who sacrificed their leisure and lives for an ideal they thought noble,[44] but also in order that later Christians might learn what infinitely greater rewards awaited those who similarly sacrificed their leisure and lives, not for noble error, but for noble truth.

Marius suffered less, even in this life, than he deserved; Regulus, on the other hand, suffered more. The latter's fate was by far the more usual, as if God found harsh methods more effective than gentle. Two such victims were the Emperors Jovian and Gratian:

Lest any Emperor should become a Christian in order to merit the happiness of Constantine, when everyone should be a Chris-

---

42 Ibid. V 16.   44 See p. 126.
43 See p. 124 n. 25.

tian only for the sake of eternal life, God took away Jovian far
sooner than Julian, and permitted Gratian to be slain by the
sword of a tyrant.[45]

And there are even harsher cases:

Even baptized infants, who are certainly unsurpassed in innocence, are sometimes so tormented in order that God, who permits
it, may thereby teach us to bewail the calamities of this life and to
desire the felicity of the life to come.[46]

A final case has almost a primitive and pagan grimness: the
persecutions were engineered by God

in order that the number of martyrs or witnesses for the truth
might be completed.[47]

Truly the God of Augustine was omnificent; but the devices
He resorted to in order to give effect to His will were occasionally more those of a fiend than a Father. His omnificence
evidently exceeded His mercy.

We must admire the ingenuity and profundity of Augustine's argument, but we cannot see how, even then, it could
have seemed unanswerable. The events of 406–410 had already dramatically shown the plausibility of the pagan explanations: that incarnated man was being buffeted by either
an angry Jupiter, an insensitive and inexorable matter, or a
malicious demon. The most that Augustine could do was to
show that these events were equally consistent with earthly
control by a benevolent and omnificent God. He had exposed the tenets of the various rival creeds to exhaustive ridicule, he had argued a brilliant case for the credibility of his
own, but he had rather defied than confuted his opponents,
had rather unsettled than unhorsed them. For was not he
too adding his voice to the swelling chorus of those who had
cursed the world and seen that curse fulfilled?

The next work of Christian apologetics however — the
anonymous *De Providentia Divina* [48] — does nothing to ab-
jure the curse. The pagan could admit that the Christian

[45] *D.C.D.* V 25.
[46] Ibid. XXII 22.
[47] Ibid. X 32.
[48] I think it should be considered
as following Augustine in chronology

because, although written in 415 or
a few years later, Augustine was
already sixty-one years old in that
year, whereas the anonymous poet
was probably younger.

God, being omnificent, caused every event and so every horror. But, even granting further that He was a jealous God,
could it nevertheless be exclusively for man's own good that
these new horrors were now being perpetrated? Such was the
troubled query of the pagan not yet convinced:

But the innocent boys and girls, what have they done, their short
life allowing them no time for evil deeds? . . .
  If the Providence of God looked down from the high heavens
and held our affairs under its sovereign sway, then either crime
would not escape its avenging retribution or virtue would be
found to hold exclusive sway on earth.[49]

In the year 415 [50] this was evidently the most prevalent and
serious objection to the Christian explanation of things. It
was this difficulty that must be satisfactorily resolved if Christianity was to conquer the heart as well as the obedience of
the Romans. Yet this *De Providentia Divina* does no more
than reiterate the unpalatable explanation of Augustine:

What place on earth would there be for a holy virtue which, with
present rewards being showered on it, should nevertheless await
those stored up in heaven? . . .
  But with the punishment of many sinners thus delayed, some
will surely be called back to the practice of virtue. . . .
  Those, however, who persist in their long-standing error,
though they may live unpunished to a hoary age, heaping sin
upon sin, will nevertheless come to a terrible end where there
will be no hope of pardon, where the smallest fraction of evil will
call for its just retribution.[51]

The punishment is sure. Justice will ultimately be done.
But the reckoning will come only after death. Until then evil
need not fear the divine retribution.
  Now, knowing Augustine as we do, the ingenuity and even
cogency of the argument is impressive; but, knowing as we
also do the horrors of that time and the state of mind they engendered, we can also see how distasteful the hypothesis
might become. Familiar horrors can be borne and so ac-

---

[49] *D.P.D.* Prologue lines 43–44 &
83–86.
  [50] In the Prologue lines 33–34 the
author says ' caede decenni vandalicis
gladiis sternitur et geticis '. Hodgkin 1892 I 2 99 says that *geticis* means
Goths. From the entry of the Van-

dals into Gaul in 406 Ebert 1889 I 2
317 n. 4 adopts the date of composition as 415; but as the Visigoths
entered Gaul from Italy only in 412
the date might almost as well be 422.
  [51] *D.P.D.* lines 753–54 & 791–94.

cepted, but strange new horrors cannot be. For there is a limit to the injustice which can be recognized as injustice; beyond that limit it can be borne only by being denied.

B. JUSTICE ON EARTH FOR MONKS

It was in about the year 402 that the monk Rufinus of Aquileia, a close friend of Jerome's, translated into Latin, with the title of *Historia Monachorum,* a Greek text which gave a detailed account of the lives of the Egyptian monks.[1] Through this translation the Latin speaking world was furnished abundant evidence that these monks thought they were receiving justice on earth as their reward for a voluntary exile in those desert solitudes. A typical passage tells of how, in the case of the hermit John,

God, wishing even in this life to reward his faithful intentions, out of the solicitude of His Providence, took over the task of providing him with his daily bread.[2]

And it was there related how, on other occasions, a hermit's prayer for food would be instantly and abundantly answered.[3] One of the hermits even boasted that every one of his prayers was answered.[4] Another story tells of how a certain Apollonius, seeing his brother monks sorrowing,

admonished them, saying that there ought to be no sorrow whatsoever in those whose salvation is in God and whose hope is in the kingdom of heaven. Let the Gentiles be sad and the Jews wail; let sinners constantly grieve, but the just be joyful.[5]

In one case so charming a description was given of an oasis [6] where a group of hermits lived that a doubter expressed the fear that it might have been devised by the devil in order to ensnare them:

For if, truly, as they say, it is a delicious and fruitful spot, what are we to hope for in a future life if we may enjoy such delights here? [7]

[1] See pp. 184–185.
[2] Migne *P.L.* 21 401B.
[3] Ibid. 416–17.
[4] Ibid. 428D. Cf. p. 185 n. 64.
[5] Ibid. 418C.
[6] Another idyllic picture is on pp. 439B–440B.
[7] Ibid. 453B.

This rather crude streak of optimism offers a striking contrast to the pessimism of Ambrose, Prudentius, Augustine, and the *De Providentia Divina;* we are at once led to wonder what was Jerome's view on this vital question. For if Jerome was a theologian — of reputation if not of distinction — forming with Ambrose and Augustine the renowned triumvirate of Latin Fathers, he was also a monk who, renouncing the world, had retired to Palestine on the Egyptian frontier. Did Latin speculation lose some of its charm for him in his new environment of Oriental contemplation?

His views of justice on earth, at any rate, appear to conform to such a gradual evolution: from the passages which he wrote before he was fifty years old it is clear that he was even satisfied with the excessively pessimistic view of Ambrose and Prudentius — which imagined a calculated regime of injustice where the wicked are rewarded and the good punished. He says, for instance,

Do we not see numbers of heathens, Jews, heretics, and men of various opinions rolling in the mire of lust, bathed in blood, surpassing wolves in ferocity and kites in rapacity, and for all this the plague does not come near their dwellings? . . . We know, on the other hand, that holy men are afflicted with sicknesses, misery, and want.[8]

And further:

How comes it, I ask, that godless men live to old age in the enjoyment of this world's riches? How comes it that untutored youth and innocent childhood are cut down while still in the bud? Why is it that children three years old and two, and even unweaned infants, are possessed with devils, covered with leprosy, and eaten up with jaundice, while godless men and profane, adulterers and murderers, have health and strength to blaspheme God?[9]

He concludes with the exclamation, ' Truly the judgments of God are a great deep ', but elsewhere he makes it clear that he understands the divine purpose — which is to punish, try, and correct:

To us men this life is a race-course; we contend here, we are crowned elsewhere.[10]

---

[8] *Letter* # 68 § 1 (of 397).   [10] *Letter* # 22 § 3 (of 384).
[9] Ibid. # 39 § 2 (of 384). Cf. his
Contra Jovinianum II § 24 (of 393).

Therefore joy in this life is to be avoided at all costs, for in determining who shall be saved, the pleasures and pains suffered here below will be meticulously weighed:

You fancy those blessed who enjoy in this world happiness and pleasure? . . . When once a doctor gives over caring for a patient it is a sign that he despairs.[11]

These passages were all written by Jerome in his earlier years, when we may suppose that the ardour of his enthusiasm was still untempered: he had renounced the world because it was a wicked place in which God's justice was conspicuous only by its absence. The monk, however, whether Jerome realized it or not, could not renounce the world: he could merely substitute one kind of worldly existence for another. We must bear in mind, moreover, that Jerome was not born, as so many of the aristocrats were, to fame; by becoming a monk, therefore, he actually came to win a worldly renown which he knew he could hardly have won in any other way. As a man best wins happiness by shunning it, so it must be with that most poignant happiness which is fame. And because renunciation had so richly rewarded him, it was natural that he should recommend this course to others.

Here, for example, is what he wrote to Pammachius:

This is what the Lord promised: *Those who glorify me, I shall glorify.* Some may think that this refers to the future, when grief is turned into rejoicing and, the world having died, the circle of saints survives; but I understand by it that the promises are to be fulfilled during the present life of the saints.

Then, speaking of Pammachius in the third person, he adds:

Him whom the whole world admires as a pauper, it was ignorant of so long as he was rich.[12]

A few years later, in his eulogy of Paula, he tells of how she, ' fleeing fame, won fame ',[13] and in 414 he encourages the nun Demetriades to persevere in her way of life by describing her as one

[11] *Letter* # 68 § 1 (of 397). Cf. ibid. # 14 § 10 (of 373), # 22 § 39 (of 384), & # 48 § 21 (of 393).

[12] Ibid. # 66 § 7 (of 397).
[13] Ibid. # 108 § 3 (of 404).

whom as bride of a man one province would have heard of, as virgin of Christ the whole world hears of.[14]

Now it is of course true that if the examples the monks set should pass unnoticed in the Roman world they would win few converts; some minimum of renown was therefore unavoidably desirable. Jerome, however, does not bother to remind his correspondents of this advantage — to the faith — his point is invariably the advantage accruing to the monk himself, and in this present life. When we recall that most of Jerome's correspondents were persons who had given, and were still giving, money away on a lavish scale, we easily see the cogency of his argument: whether they liked it or not, these persons were buying an abundance of fame — just as Paulinus of Nola had bought it. Even to this day it is the cause of their earthly fame. Not that any of them courted publicity: the sacrifice in physical well-being is proof enough that their passion for the faith was both real and deep. Yet we cannot help picturing the wry smile on Augustine's face as he read one of these widely circulated letter-treatises of Jerome's — a smile none the less wry because Augustine must have realized how right Jerome actually was, how, for this once, at any rate, it was Jerome who was the better empiricist of the two.

It was while Jerome was writing these very cheering words to his aristocratic disciples that Cassian, a Scythian monk, after spending many years in the Egyptian desert, came to Marseilles to found the first important monastery in the West. Born in about 360,[15] Cassian was thirteen years younger than Jerome and six years younger than Augustine. His opinions, therefore, although not published until about 425,[16] are still those of the earlier generation which had matured before the great invasions.

That injustice abounds on earth Cassian is quite sure: there are many instances of it even in the Old Testament.[17] His explanations are Augustine's: some receive rewards in

[14] Ibid. # 130 § 6 (of 414). Cf. ibid. # 77 § 11 (of 399), & # 118 §§ 3 & 5 (of 406).
[15] See p. 474 n. 28.

[16] See p. 474 ns. 30 & 31.
[17] *Conlationes* VI 10–11; & VII ch. 31, citing *Psalms* lxxii 2–5 & *Jeremiah* xii 1–2.

this life only because already marked for damnation; [18] others suffer here that they may be prepared for the kingdom of heaven.[19]   To these latter the present life is a purgatory, and those possessed by demons should rejoice that God troubles to chastise them — that He has not despaired of them is reason enough that they should not despair of themselves.[20] Moreover the glory of God requires certain ephemeral injustices,[21] which will, of course, be amply rectified in eternity.

To Augustine happiness was compatible with suffering: this is one of those profound paradoxes that particularly appealed to the Roman imagination.   This elusive conception, too, is emphasized by Cassian.   But his recommendation that we ought so to act that

we gain one and the same advantage out of good and bad fortune [22]

has a ring of Stoic contraction; and certainly the word *fortune* is not one that Augustine would have chosen.[23]   The Stoic, however, merely steeled himself to indifference in the face of injustice on earth, whereas the Christian monk positively rejoices in it:

By what wrongs also, by what persecutions, will he be frightened, nay what punishments can fail to be even delightful to him who . . . longs to be counted worthy to suffer shame for the sake of Christ? [24]

Madness this may be, yet there is method in it too: after quoting *Matthew* xix 29,

And everyone that has left house, or brethren, or sisters, or father, or mother, or wife, or children, or lands, for my name's sake, shall receive an hundredfold in the present time and shall inherit eternal life,

he goes on to tell of how the mutual love of the monks brings far more happiness than any other human loves.   This may well be, but how is it compatible with the monks' renunciation of ' all delights in things present '? [25]   Clearly these delights refer to purely physical or sensuous delights; the ' hundredfold ' is therefore in super-sensuous or spiritual delights.

18 *Conlationes* VII 31.
19 Ibid. 28.
20 Ibid. 31.
21 Ibid. VI 11.
22 Ibid. 10 § 10.

23 See Augustine *Retractationum* I 1 § 2, 2 § 3, & 3 § 2.
24 *Conl.* XXIV 23 § 4.   Cf. ibid. XVI 6, & *De Institutis* XII 33.
25 *Conl.* XXIV 26 §§ 12 & 13.

There is a difficulty here, however, for to the Christian, far more than to the Stoic, there were spiritual as well as physical sins and the chief of these was pride. Now if God granted spiritual delights by the hundredfold was there not a danger that He might seem at times to be granting the delights not only of spiritual love but also of spiritual pride? Elsewhere Cassian discourses judiciously on the peculiar susceptibility of even the best of monks to this most insidious and obstinate sin, yet he chooses to wind up his longest and most famous treatise — the *Conferences* — with the astounding statement that it is surely to receive a hundredfold

when for His name's sake they [the monks] are honoured by the greatest princes, and, although they do not look for the praise of men, yet become venerated in the trials of persecution whose humble condition would perhaps have been looked down upon even by common folk, either because of their obscure birth, or because of their condition as slaves, if they had continued in their life in the world. But because of the service of Christ no one will venture to raise a calumny against their state of nobility, or to fling in their teeth the obscurity of their origin. Nay rather, through the very opprobrium of a humble condition by which others are shamed and confounded, the servants of Christ are more splendidly ennobled, as we can clearly show by the case of Abbot John who lives in the desert which borders on the town of Lycus. For he sprang from obscure parents, but, owing to the name of Christ, has become so well known to almost all mankind that the very lords of the temporal world who hold the reins of empire and are a terror to all powers and kings, venerate him as their lord, and from distant countries seek his advice, and entrust to his prayers and merits the crown of their empire, and the state of safety, and the fortunes of war.[26]

It is true that Cassian is here addressing not the well-disciplined monk but the hesitant layman; he is therefore making concessions which are inconsistent with his general doctrine. But may not this concession be rather more honest than he would himself have admitted? When Cassian wrote this he was already famous; if he was — as he may well have been — of obscure birth, by what other vocation could he have so completely broken down the barriers of the Roman caste system? What shorter cut could he have taken to fame? None of this was premeditated — the good priests and monks

[26] *Ibid.* §§ 15–17.

had no ulterior motives — but they were obliged to take the realities substantially as they came. And it was becoming more and more evident that the religious vocation of the early fifth century was closely analogous to that of the industrialist of 1800 or of the scientist of 1900: it was fast becoming the career that to the obscure but ambitious youth promised the most dazzling future. However unpalatable, it was becoming undeniable that Christianity offered the ideal worldly as well as unworldly career.[27]   If there were no justice on earth in a material sense, a man of discretion was bound to suspect a good deal of it in a spiritual sense. As the reward of virtue no animal cravings were satisfied, but certain very human cravings were.

In Jerome and Cassian there were not, as in the *Historia Monachorum,* any suggestions of sensuous delights as the reward of renunciation; but there were suggestions of earthly fame and hence of temporal prestige and power. Monks, after all, were human — they were the first to admit it. In their honest efforts to renounce the world and the flesh it was to be expected that they should fail to renounce as much as they professed to. If we are to detect a doctrine suggesting a present reward for virtue, where should we be so likely to find it as among those who most hungered for the eternal reward? For the distinction is merely the incidental one of time.

About twelve years younger than Cassian was the Gallic aristocrat Eucherius, probably born in Provence,[28] for some time a monk in the neighbouring monastery of Lerins, and, in his later years, archbishop of Lyons. Only a few years after Cassian had written his *Conferences,* Eucherius wrote his *De Laude Eremi:* [29] to glorify life in the desert, or rather, since the island of Lerins was included, to glorify retirement from the ordinary habitations of men. To the advantages of such a life as they had been expounded by Cassian, Eucherius offered others — more concrete — of his own. *Exodus* sup-

---

[27] And Cassian was conscientiously sincere where, as in ibid. IV 12 § 1, he speaks disparagingly of those Christians who are ' anxious to pursue future blessings in such a way as not to lose present ones.'

[28] Gouilloud 1881 50–53.

[29] Hennecke 1898 V 573 line 17, says 426–429.

plies him with his first proof: how could Moses have regretted his choice to live in the desert when, by doing so, he saw, heard, and conversed with God?   Whereas

he entered the desert as shepherd of flocks, he returned from it shepherd of the people.[30]

And all who followed him there were rewarded, first by rations of *manna,* later by entry into the Promised Land.[31] Thus

he who wishes to see the good things of God while in the land of the living, must live in an uninhabited land.[32]

Even as Eucherius writes, the Egyptian monks are reaping an analogous reward:

In olden times the care of the Divine Providence was at its peak towards those of the desert, but even now it is not small.   For now when divine food comes to the inhabitants of the desert with unexpected abundance, how otherwise does it pour down unless from heaven? [33]

Eucherius had not been in Egypt himself,[34] but he had eagerly read of all these wonders.   It was only natural that God should be as solicitous of the monks who retired to Lerins, and it need surprise no one to learn, therefore, that at Lerins the monks enjoyed the most complete felicity:

Through the infinite mercy of Christ, they earn many things in the present life that they merely hoped for in the future life. Indeed they are already in possession of the thing itself while they are still pursuing the hope of it.   They obtain not a little, by the very labour itself, of the reward of that labour, because the reward that shall be is already almost in operation.[35]

We may make due allowance for the fact that this work is special pleading, skilfully conceived in order to attract men to the monastic life.   Nevertheless the utilitarian note is unbecoming; for monks should not — even if they too often did — retire in order to advance their selfish interests.   Eucherius was in danger of forgetting the words of Augustine:

[30] *Epistula De Laude Eremi* § 7.
[31] Ibid. §§ 12 & 16.
[32] Ibid. § 16.
[33] Ibid. § 29.
[34] Gouilloud 1881 83–84.
[35] *Ep. De Laude Eremi* § 43.

The Stoics maintain, not that the fool, but that the wise man, cannot be sorrowful.[36]

Certainly there were delicate distinctions to be made between the possible rewards for virtue: from the grosser pleasures of the senses to the more refined — as from food to music or from sexual passion to sexual love; and further from fame during life [37] to fame thereafter, or from this earthly fame in heaven to eternal fame in the eyes of God. At the summit of the rewards was the grace-given love of God, that which made Augustine happy. No Christian cultivated virtue except in order to increase his own happiness; in that sense, therefore, no Christian ever denied justice on earth. The issue was rather in regard to the form of the reward God was willing to bestow. Ambrose and Augustine had said only the love of God, Jerome and Cassian had added earthly fame, but Eucherius now, perhaps unduly influenced by the marvels related in the *Historia Monachorum,* goes much further, alleging that the hermit at any rate, and perhaps any monk even if living in a community, will receive present rewards which, if more innocent, are also more carnal; rewards which, unlike those assumed by Augustine, Jerome, and Cassian, could be recognized as such by any unimaginative layman. The rewards, although frugal enough, could offer a worldly temptation to many a lay outcast who asked for no more than to live in security and die in peace.

C. MANICHEE AND EPICUREAN IN 445

Cassian and Eucherius were monks, but they were also the youngest of what we may term the earlier generation. In the year 406, when Gaul was first invaded, Augustine was already fifty-two years old, but Cassian was only about forty-six and Eucherius, at thirty-four, had not yet reached Dante's 'mezzo del cammin'.

Whether the speculative doctrines of these younger men

---

[36] *D.C.D.* XIV 8 (see p. 320 n. 27).

[37] Hilary of Arles born in about 400, wrote shortly after 429 of Honoratus and his brother: ' The more their lives were secluded, the more fame sparkled ': *Serm. de Vita S. Honorati* II § 10.

were decisively affected by such outward events is, of course, a matter of opinion — though certainly they cannot have been wholly unaffected by the enormity of the miseries then inaugurated. Another thing, moreover, cannot have escaped their notice: henceforth the Church must tend more and more to supplant the State. Until these invasions the Church had grown up under the indulgent if unwieldy tutelage of the civil Empire, had been fostered and guided by a temporal discipline having the momentum and self-confidence of a thousand year old tradition. Only because the State was so incontrovertible a fact could the Church afford to treat it with condescension; only because the State was already regulating temporal affairs did it seem sensible to preach their insignificance. Before the year 406 the Church had only to prove herself a way of life within the State; after 430 she was obliged to prove her fitness as a way of life without it. Augustine was the last great Christian to live wholly within the State. His doctrine, as we shall now see, proved unfit to survive it.[1]

As, at the turn of the century, pagan worship and belief became illegal and all pagans soon after became disqualified from holding public office, conversions to Catholicism were artificially induced, with the result that many became nominal and superficial believers without inner conviction. They professed a new faith but still harboured the old.[2] They might even believe that the faith they held was Catholic and orthodox; yet it was in fact more often heterodox and not infrequently barely Christian at all.[3]

Of the pagan and pseudo-pagan doctrines prevalent in the Roman world just before the invasions we have much knowledge — Augustine's evidence of itself is abundant. Particularly in his *De Civitate Dei,* finished only in 426, is every pagan belief of any importance carefully presented and refuted.[4] From it we may easily infer what beliefs lay hidden

---

[1] Augustinian theology was revived for a time under Charlemagne, but its greatest vogue occurred between 1530 and 1680.

[2] Cf. Salvian *D.G.D.* III § 5, IV § 86, & VIII § 10. Nock 1933 159 thinks that even Augustine's *D.C.D.* was aimed at incipient apostates as well as at professed pagans.

[3] The professed pagans alone outnumbered the Christians as late as 400: Lot 1927 47.

[4] And we also have Macrobius' works written soon after 400: see p. 205 n. 49.

under the crust of a Catholic orthodoxy imposed by the arm
of the law.   For the next seventeen years evidence is lacking.
In the meanwhile the new generation, hardly grown up in the
years before 406, had come to maturity.   Then, in the fifth
decade, with a world of new men and new conditions of life,
comes new evidence, particularly on the Manichees by Pope
Leo [5] and on the Epicureans by the Gallic priest Salvian.[6]

The geographical distribution of these Manichees is not
well known.   Africa was certainly more affected than other
parts of the West, and Rome, as Augustine has told us, held
a nucleus of these dissidents.   But it is not likely that in his
day the rest of the West was much infected.   In 429, however,
the Vandals invaded Africa and it is precisely in that year
that Cassian,[7] then living in Marseilles, denounced the sect.
No European port was more accessible from Carthage, so we
may imagine a descent of Manichæan refugees there in that
very year.   Again in 434 these Manichees were denounced,
by Vincent of Lerins,[8] and from that time on, even into the
early sixth century,[9] we hear of them, in this region and elsewhere.   A larger exodus from Africa followed the capture of
Carthage by the Vandals in 439.[10]   It was four years after this,
in 443, that Pope Leo discovered their presence in Rome in
large numbers and heard of the damage they were doing to
the Church in Spain.[11]   He at once denounced them [12] and in

[5] Leo's *Letter* # 15 was written in
443. The authenticity of this famous
letter was questioned by Künstle
Antipriscilliana 1905 117–26. But
Dufourcq *G.M.R.* 1910 IV 14 n. 2
refutes Künstle's arguments, and, in
my opinion, successfully. Duchesne
1911 III [4] 587 treats the letter as
genuine, and so does even the can-
tankerous Turmel in 1931 I 224 n. 1.

[6] Salvian wrote his *D.G.D.* between
439 and 451: Sanford 1930 7.

[7] *Conlationes* VIII 6 & 24. Batiffol 1924 [2] 434 says that the Manichæan heresy spread particularly
after the Vandal invasion of Africa
in 429–39.

[8] Stoop 1909 90.

[9] Julius Pomerius argued against
them in Arles in 480: Stoop 1909 90,
& Dufourcq *G.M.R.* 1910 IV 52–54.

Cæsarius of Arles did likewise in the
earlier sixth century: Dufourcq ibid.
49. A certain Prosper abjured Manichæism at Carpentras in 526: Stoop
1909 90.   On their prevalence in
Rome see Duchesne 1911 III [4] 663
n. 3. Priscillianism was still cor-
rupting Spanish priests as well as
laymen in 527: Hefele 1908 II [2] 1084.

[10] Duchesne 1911 III [4] 661–62.

[11] Leo in *Letter* # 15 introduction,
said that the spread of Spanish Priscillianism — which he declared to be
virtually Manichæism — had been fostered by the collapse of the civil
authority there.

[12] See Leo *Letter* # 15 introduction; Prosper of Aquitaine *Chronicum* for the year 443 (600A & B);
Dufourcq *G.M.R.* 1910 IV 1–30;
Duchesne 1911 III [4] 661–63.

445 procured civil legislation prescribing confiscation of their property and exile.[13]

It was not, however, their numbers which caused the authorities anxiety — for outside of Africa they were never numerous [14] — rather it was their influence,[15] their methods, and their doctrine. Most of the converts, apparently, were recruited from the nobility and professional classes — that is, from the intelligentsia [16] — and so from the very layer of society which formed and guided public opinion and which the Catholics were above all anxious to monopolize. As a religion Manichæism sought to appeal to reason rather than emotion, to convince the mind rather than to overcome the heart.[17] As, by its cold plausibility, it had once enticed Augustine, so now, according to Leo, it was seducing even the Catholic priest.[18] Thus the wound it inflicted, though not extensive, was deep.

Nor were the methods employed by the Manichees less disquieting than their social importance; for in order to facilitate secret propaganda [19] and forestall persecution they might conscientiously pass themselves off as Catholics.[20] At least Leo so declared:

[13] Duchesne ibid. 663.

[14] Stoop 1909 47–48 & 142–43 thinks they were never numerous anywhere.

[15] Dufourcq G.M.R. 1910 IV 393 says: ' On peut affirmer à tout le moins que, du début du cinquième à la fin du dixième siècle, le Christianisme Catholique a été aux prises, en Occident, avec un adversaire dangereux: au cinquième et sixième siècles surtout, la bataille est chaude entre les deux frères ennemis: elle semble s'assoupir ensuite, comme ils s'assoupissent eux-mêmes au milieu de l'anarchie seigneuriale, sans cesser tout à fait; elle reprendra de plus belle, durant la période féodale, lorsque l'un et l'autre auront repris des forces.'
Stoop 1909 45–50, etc. will not go so far, but he does think that the Manichees might well, on account of the cogency and plausibility of their doctrine, have been regarded by the Catholics as a serious menace.

[16] Stoop 1909 10, 42, 47, 49–50, 84 & 122.

[17] Ibid. 6–7.

[18] Letter # 15 introduction. The Council of Nimes of 394, canon # 2, says that the Priscillianists ordained women as deaconesses: Hefele 1908 II 2 93 n. 9. The Nestorians gave analogous powers to women: ibid. 448. It would be interesting to know what part women played in the Manichæan Church, and whether their collaboration enhanced or detracted from the popularity of the cult.

[19] Stoop 1909 46.

[20] They must have been fond of quoting Ephesians vi 12: ' For we wrestle not against flesh and blood, but against principalities, against powers, against the rulers of darkness of this world, against spiritual wickedness in high places.' The Catholic Church held baptisms performed according to Manichæan rites to be valid: Duchesne 1911 III 4 663 n. 5.

They attach themselves to the catholic Church with all this difference of opinion in their hearts, with the object of both making such converts as they can, and escaping the rigour of the law by passing themselves off as ours.[21]

Other heretics openly declared their doctrine and argued its orthodoxy — these were enemies who waged their warfare honourably; but the Manichees hid their doctrine. They were the enemy within the walls, the false friends, the spies and traitors.

Their doctrine, towards which that of the Spanish Priscillianists was now gravitating,[22] appears to have remained, in 445, virtually as it was when divulged to Augustine in 373.[23] It was still Satan, for instance, and not God, who was the creator and ruler of the world.[24] Man found himself here in the flesh because Satan had been able to catch errant [25] divine souls and encase them as prisoners in material bodies.[26] Matter and the flesh were therefore intrinsically evil, and it fol-

---

[21] *Letter* # 15 § 16. Cf. Stoop 1909 27–28.

[22] Leo ibid. § 16 says of the Priscillianists and Manichees that 'there is such a close bond of union between the two that they are distinct only in name.' And he goes into some detail in the earlier sections of this letter. Doubtless he is exaggerating somewhat: he knows that if he can get the Priscillianists identified with the Manichees he can get them condemned by the civil law, and this is one of the purposes of his letter. Stoop 1909 90–102 & 130–31 thinks this alleged affinity untrue. On the other hand Duchesne 1910 II⁴ 548, and Dufourcq *G.M.R.* 1910 IV 93–101 both think that the Priscillianists really did conceive of a dualism with the devil as an autonomous power, and so, presumably, that the devil was the prime cause of the evil in the world. Jerome *Letter* # 133 § 3, written in 415, says that Priscillian's infamy made him as bad as any Manichee. One difficulty is that Manichæism was the rallying point of the defeated pagans: Dufourcq ibid. 43 & 117–19. Certainly Leo's description of the Priscillianists is very close to the descriptions of the Manichees of fifty years earlier.

But whether Leo was accurately describing the Spanish Priscillianists or not, he was certainly describing a cult approximating that of the Manichee of 443 — a cult which he knew very accurately from its activities in Rome.

[23] Dufourcq *G.M.R.* 1910 IV 97–102.

[24] Ibid. 102. Cf. the Council of Toledo of 446 or 447, canon # 9: Hefele 1908 II² 486.

[25] According to Augustine *Contra duas Epist. Pelag.* IV § 6 the Manichees believed that the soul 'comes into the flesh of man with the merits of its own defilements, with which it was polluted before the flesh.' Leo *Letter* # 15 § 10 found this belief subsisting: 'They are reported as asserting that the souls which are placed in men's bodies have previously sinned in their heavenly habitation, and for this reason, having fallen from this higher estate to a lower one . . . are enclosed in bodies of different sorts and conditions, so that whatever variety and inequality is meted out to us in this life, seems the result of previous causes.'

[26] Leo *Letter* # 15 § 10; Dufourcq *G.M.R.* 1910 IV 102.

lowed that so long as these souls were obliged to stay in the
flesh they did not think themselves morally responsible for
any sin their flesh might induce them to commit; [27] they therefore

accuse nature of their own spontaneous delinquencies.[28]

Before they could win release from the lower regions, however, they believed that they had to achieve a complete purification [29] — if they died impure the souls passed on, either
into other bodies [30] or into a purgatorial [31] or infernal [32] region
where their ultimate fate would be determined. This puri-
fied state, involving as it did complete chastity,[33] abstinence
from meat [34] and much more, even when attained could not
be long maintained: consequently suicide was then commendable.[35] Nor were many of their doctrines less eccentric: for
their destiny lay with the stars,[36] Christ was to be worshipped
in the sun,[37] and the Holy Ghost was their founder Mani.[38]
And, since matter was evil, the idea of a divine incarnation
was a sacrilege [39] and any resurrection of the flesh an im-
possibility.[40] Necessarily, therefore, the Passion was a pious
fraud, a tactical feint designed to delude Satan and his mortal
captives — for it was some other, and not the real Christ,
whom the Jews crucified.[41] Furthermore the Jehovah of the
Old Testament was Satan posing as the true God, and its text
was written at Satan's inspiration.[42] That is why Faustus had
said [43] that the Old Testament falsely teaches temporal justice
and an earthly reward: it is a snare laid by Satan to wean the
imprisoned souls of men from their allegiance to God.

---

[27] Dufourcq ibid. 49, citing Cæsarius of Arles (born in 469).

[28] Leo *Letter* # 15 § 6.

[29] Ibid. § 13. Cf. introduction.

[30] Augustine *Contra Faustum
Manichæum* V § 10.

[31] Wesendonk 1922 35.

[32] Ibid. 36-37.

[33] Leo *Letter* # 15 § 7. Cf. Dufourcq *G.M.R.* 1910 IV 97.

[34] Dufourcq ibid. 98.

[35] Ibid. 102.

[36] Leo *Letter* # 15 introduction &
§§ 11-12.

[37] Ibid. § 4. Cf. Dufourcq ibid. 6
& 100.

[38] Dufourcq ibid. 100. Cf. Leo
Sermon # 34 § 4, & Augustine *Contra Faustum Manichæum* VI § 8.

[39] Dufourcq ibid. 97-98.

[40] Ibid. 102-03.

[41] Leo *Letter* # 15 § 4. Cf. Dufourcq ibid. 97 & 104.

[42] The Priscillianists refused to
admit this, but, in order to make the
Old Testament text conform to their
ideas of what God must have revealed, they doctored it freely: Leo
Letter # 15 §§ 15 & 16, & *Sermon*
34 § 4. Cf. Dufourcq ibid. 97.

[43] See p. 317 n. 11.

The Manichæan conception of the devil's independent power so vividly recalls the Catholic conception of the pre-Redemption era, especially as it was imagined by Ambrose,[44] that it is worth considering for a moment how Leo's own views differed from those of his opponents. One difference was his insistence that God had the physical power to dispossess the devil by violence; [45] but, since he was equally insistent that such violence would have been unjust to the devil, such power was academic — for God has no real power to act unjustly.[46]

Leo evidently believed that the devil had enjoyed a just, and therefore a legal, possession of men's souls which was irrevocable so long as the terms of the compact were respected.[47] But God had given him no authority to hold an innocent man; therefore when he laid hold on the innocent Christ he acted beyond his authority [48] and thereby automatically forfeited his rights.[49] To be sure the device of the Virgin birth and of clothing a divinity in human form was resorted to with the specific purpose of deceiving the devil — of enticing him to act beyond his authority.[50] But was it not proper to trick him where the consequence of freeing men from his clutches was to enable God to dispense His grace on a more lavish scale? [51]

If Leo, however, accepted the compact theory he also explained many aspects of the Redemption in Augustinian fashion: as designed to produce a salutary psychological effect.[52] Presumably this must facilitate a desire to be baptized — which was of course accentuated by grace — with the result that many submitted themselves to this ritual and came out

---

[44] See pp. 55–56.
[45] *Sermons* # 22 § 3, # 63 § 1, & # 68 § 1.
[46] So that in *Sermons* # 27 § 2, & # 28 § 3 he says that God had no alternative than to redeem man as He in fact did.
[47] In *Sermon* # 22 § 4 he speaks of 'the malevolent terms of the deadly compact.'
[48] Ibid.: 'through the injustice of an overcharge' the devil 'went beyond the bond on which he rested'.
[49] *Sermon* # 49 § 3: the devil thereupon 'sees himself robbed of all

his tyrannic power'. Cf. Sidonius *Carmen* XVI (*L.C.L.* I 246–47).
[50] *Sermon* # 62 § 3: if the devil 'could have known the counsel of God's mercy he would have aimed at soothing the Jews' minds into gentleness, rather than at firing them with unrighteous hatred, lest he should lose the thraldom of all his captives in assailing the liberty of One who owed him nothing.'
[51] See p. 57.
[52] *Sermons* # 24 §§ 1 & 2, # 55 §§ 4 & 5, # 58 § 5, # 67 § 7, & # 73 § 1.

of it not only pardoned but innocent. This extraordinary ritual — in which the grace of God was loosed in all its might [53] — constituted the great achievement of the Redemption; yet it was rendered effective only by tricking the devil out of his legal rights. Extrinsically and psychologically the Redemption could — and did — induce an incipient contrition; but not such a full contrition as to produce complete innocence. Yet short of such innocence the devil's legal rights remained unimpaired, since no merciful reward for an incomplete contrition could be bestowed. By inducing the devil to act beyond his authority, however, God was able to vest baptism with the magical power of momentarily transfusing the person of the baptized with all the innocence of Christ's no less human person.[54] By this newly acquired divine power to dispense mercy, man's innocence — and therefore his freedom — were restored.

In one of Leo's Sermons we read that

The mercy of the Trinity divided for Itself the work of our restoration in such a way that the Father should be propitiated, the Son propitiate, and the Holy Ghost enkindle.[55]

Evidently the Son, by His sacrifice, made it possible for the Holy Ghost psychologically to infuse an incipient contrition, and for the Father to reward this small beginning with a physiological infusion of His merciful grace.[56] Hitherto the degree of contrition requisite for pardon had been a matter of fact; henceforth it became a matter of divine discretion.[57] Therefore, in contrast to Augustine, Leo saw the Redemption primarily as an intrinsic act which restored man from the just regime of the devil to the merciful regime of God.

We see, therefore, that Leo, in spite of his stress on the psychological effect of the Redemption, relied more on his

[53] *Sermons* # 23 § 4, & # 24 § 1.

[54] *Sermon* # 23 § 5 says 'As the Lord Jesus became our flesh by being born, so we also become His body by being reborn'. And cf. *Sermon* # 63 § 6. This was of course the traditional conception in the Church; but the complication was that it explained the Incarnation only, and not the Passion. So Leo must have supposed that this divinization could take effect only after Christ had, by His Passion, restored man to the jurisdiction of God. Cf. p. 87.

[55] *Sermon* # 77 § 2. This is Leo's only suggestion of a difference between Father and Son.

[56] Leo emphasizes the unity of will between Father and Son in *Sermons* # 67 § 7 & # 68 § 1.

[57] Leo *Sermon* # 49 § 3 says that henceforth 'justification is not paid for deserts, but is simply given as a free gift.'

fellow-Italian Ambrose than on the African Augustine; for he believed, as Augustine did not, that Christ's triumph over the devil was cosmologically as well as psychologically necessary. It was this literal elimination of the devil's powers that enabled God to produce the magical effects of baptism, whereby man received not only pardon for his past sins, both original and personal, but also the free will accorded the innocent Adam.[58] Leo, indeed, in contrast to Augustine, thought man now even better off than the innocent Adam had been: [59] for he had the same free will and, in addition, the precious instruction afforded by the Redemption.

Augustine thought that God had always ruled both earthly and eternal life; but both the Manichees and Leo denied that He had done so during the pre-Redemption era. The Manichees thought He had always ruled eternal, but had never ruled earthly, life. That was why they supposed the Old Testament description of a divine bestowal of earthly rewards to be a satanic falsification. Leo, on the other hand, supposed the precise opposite, believing that God had then conferred the earthly rewards because He could not confer the eternal.

If Leo in Rome attacks the Manichees as the great menace to the triumph of Catholic orthodoxy, Salvian, of Cologne, who had long been a priest at Marseilles,[60] centres his attack rather on those whom he terms ' Epicureans and certain of their imitators '.[61] In the Gaul of 445 these were evidently the most numerous category of dissidents, and it is interesting to observe that this school of thought too, like that of the Manichees, flourished particularly among the nobles and the highly educated.[62] The truth is that the philosophical ferment was largely confined to this upper layer of Roman society — the middle classes had been dispersed, almost annihilated,[63] while the lower had neither the education nor the leisure to indulge in these intricate speculations. Abstract as well as concrete expediency obliged most of them to take their cues from their betters. Any faith which could reconcile men

[58] See pp. 390–91.
[59] *Sermons* # 72 § 2, & # 73 § 4.
[60] Sanford 1930 6, 8 & 12.
[61] *D.G.D.* I § 5.

[62] Ibid. III § 52, & IV §§ 13–31. Cf. p. 339 n. 16.
[63] Cf. Jullian 1926 VII 123, & VIII 242–46 & 265–66.

to misery and humble obedience suited the serf practically as
well as it suited his master.   In this sense, therefore, not only
Catholicism, but also Manichæism and Epicureanism, spread
because each appealed to the cultivated.

As a sect the Epicurean was purely amorphous.   It was not
a positive religion, but merely a point of view.   Unlike the
earlier sect of that name it was now a vaguely Christian conception, its votaries passively receptive to everything the
Church demanded,[64] and, in contrast to the Manichees, not
only reluctant to resist, but wholly indifferent to, the pressure
being constantly applied by the Church militant.   For their
first tenet was a doubt of the efficacy of their own or any other
faith.   Thus Salvian cannot flay them for what they do believe,
but only for what they don't.   Before their dull eyes he flaunts
the text of the *Apocalypse:*

I would thou wert hot or cold; so then, because thou art lukewarm, I will spew thee out of my mouth.[65]

Salvian, no doubt quite sincerely, believes it is their sins which
have invited his wrath; actually it is rather their apathy.   It is
likely, moreover, that Neoplatonism was producing this same
negativity, for some years later bishop Sidonius reminds his
friend Eutropius of an earlier year, when

You were deep in the tenets of Plotinus, and the Platonic school
had seduced you into a quietism unsuited to your age.[66]

The difficulty in dealing with these later pagans — the true
descendants of the old — was not in persuading them of the

[64] *D.G.D.* I § 1, & III § 5.
[65] Ibid. IV § 91 — from *Revelations* iii 15–16.
[66] *Letters* III # 6 § 2, written in
about 470. And in *Letters* I # 6 § 5,
written in about 467, he chides this
same Eutropius for his undue inclination to 'the tenets of Epicurus.'
Salvian *D.G.D.* I § 3 carefully distinguishes the Platonists from the
Epicureans: ' Plato and all the Platonic school confess that God is the
controller of all things.   The Stoics
testify that He remains always as
steersman within that which He
guides.'   Evidently there was now an
overlapping of creeds and philosophies, and the names no longer

corresponded very closely to the real
beliefs.   Roughly, however, the categories were: (1) the Manichees who
thought that the devil ruled on
earth; (2) the Epicureans who
thought that either destiny or man's
own efforts controlled; (3) the Neoplatonists who thought that God
ruled on earth, but only ineffectively,
on account of the resistance of matter; (4) the Stoics — to the extent that
they still existed — who were not sure
whether to blame God's forgetful-
ness, or His need of evil in order to
produce good by contrast (Seneca);
(5) Augustine, who inclined to this
latter view.

error of their faith — for they believed only in a vague destiny or chance — but rather in persuading them to have a faith in Providence. For they were sceptics. Surveying and ruminating on man and the events of this world, they failed to recognize a guiding Hand.

They did not deny that God might well have been the creator of man and of this visible world,[67] but they did deny that God any longer ruled.[68] It is to these same Epicureans, no doubt, that the *De Providentia Divina* of 415 had referred:

For they who attribute to God an idle leisure are afraid, I suppose, that watchful care and difficult toil will tire an attentive God, and that a single God cannot regulate so many matters at one and the same time.[69]

According to Salvian, the Epicureans of his day ' have associated God with carelessness and sloth ',[70] believing that

after He had formed and perfected the whole scheme of things He abdicated, and renounced the administration of earthly matters.[71]

And truly

they who declare that nothing is seen by God are very near to denying His actual substance.[72]

The danger of such scepticism also lay at the root of Neoplatonism, for a pantheistic tendency which identifies God with all Being tends necessarily to identify Him with the concrete and tangible, and so with Nature. But the moment God becomes Nature, Nature becomes God — and Providence vanishes.

Why did the Epicureans so imagine God? Very simply, says Salvian,

---

[67] ' Quid enim tam furiosum est quam ut aliquis, cum deum creatorem rerum omnium non neget, gubernatorem neget ': Salvian *D.G.D.* IV § 41.

[68] A phrase in Victor of Vita *H.P.A.P.* II § 78 who wrote in about 485 suggests why the Epicurean conception did not survive: ' nam ubi virtus ibi necesse est persona subsistens.' This argument was unanswerable until in the seventeenth century it was learned that motion, and therefore energy, is as much a product of inertia as is rest: Pickman 1932 219.

[69] *De Providentia Divina* lines 156–58.

[70] *D.G.D.* I § 5.

[71] Ibid. § 20. Cf. p. 215 n. 23.

[72] Ibid. IV § 41.

on the ground that He neither protects good men nor restrains the wicked; and they claim that this is why at the present time the good are generally wretched and the wicked happy.[73]

And in the last book, Salvian adds that

this is not all the abuse given Him . . . men even brand Him as unjust.[74]

This last allegation is serious.   Augustine had said

we see not only good men involved in the ills of life and bad men enjoying the good of it, which seems unjust, but also that evil often overtakes evil men and good surprises the good.[75]

Such was a judicious opinion of an earlier year; and even in Salvian's day there were still many Catholics who would not believe that temporal good and evil were in equal proportion, but clung tenaciously to the older view that temporal evil predominated — that this life was not even a neutral purgatory but an iniquitous hell.

Yet any longer to preach such doctrines was suicidal.   For the false but plausible assumption of injustice was bound to suggest God's impotence to thwart malice rather than His thoughtless negligence, and this was precisely the dualistic creed of the Manichees.   And, as practical proof of this sad truth, here, within the Church — and even among her priests — were these Manichees insidiously plying their trade of seducing souls from their timid faith in the governance of God.[76]   If God did not rule then probably He could not, and, if He could not, the obstacle, though it might be unwieldy matter, was more probably the rebellious devil.   Leo believed that only by the recent Redemption had the devil been quelled, and the events since the year 400 could easily suggest that the spirit of evil was loose again.   Between the ruthless justice of God and the tempered dualism of Leo there seemed no middle ground.   Scepticism might hold its own for a time, but sooner or later the Epicurean, unless he could be persuaded of God's temporal justice, was likely to fall a victim to Manichæan logic.   For the Augustinian argument, that the more temporal injustice the better the proof of eternal justice,

---

[73] Ibid. I § 1.
[74] Ibid. VIII § 5.

[75] See p. 322 n. 33.
[76] See p. 339 n. 18.

was both too subtle and too unpalatable to suit the ordinary
man: he might persuade himself that he believed, but he
could not possibly comprehend or welcome, such perverted
ingenuity.

The situation of the Catholics was, therefore, still critical,
and, had their successes since 325 been less remarkable, they
might not have prevailed.   By 440 they were, however, in a
worldly sense, already firmly entrenched: they alone had an
organization well evolved, the civil law behind them, and
more than a century's tradition as the religion of the Empire.
Since, moreover, the basis of their philosophy was a judicious
compromise with the world and the flesh, clearly they had a
duty, still unfulfilled, to defend the world against all those
who still so drastically cursed it.

The propinquity of the Manichæan and Epicurean to the
Catholic view can hardly be overlooked: the Manichee said
God was helpless to resist Satan's will on earth; the Epicurean
said God was either negligent, slothful, indifferent, or helpless; the Catholic said that at best God dispensed justice and
injustice in about equal proportions.   Thus all three, each in
his own way, denied the operation of retributive justice on
earth at the very moment when faith in that operation was the
paramount need and so the paramount desire.   But how was
such a faith to be defended, how demonstrated?   Christ had
said ' My kingdom is not of this world ' [77] and every event of
the last forty years had tended to substantiate Him.   The God
of the Old Testament, moreover, had conferred temporal
benefits, had administered a meticulous justice on earth, so
that it must clearly appear that the New Law introduced by
the Redemption had reversed this condition, transforming
temporal justice into eternal.[78]   It was, indeed, because of the
antinomy of the two laws that the Manichees rejected the Old
Testament as the work of Satan, and that the Christians were
led to read that text symbolically.   Augustine has made this
clear:

For first of all the things began to appear unto me as possible to
be defended: and the Catholic faith, in defence of which I thought

---

[77] John xviii 36.

[78] Augustine *D.C.D.* X 25 says that

Psalm # 73 is a prophecy of the New
Testament regime.

nothing could be answered to the Manichees' arguments, I now
concluded with myself might well be maintained without absurdity: especially after I had heard one or two hard places of
the Old Testament resolved now and then — which, when I understood literally, I was slain.   Many places therefore of those
books having been spiritually expounded I blamed my own
desperate conceit, whereby I had believed that the Law and
the Prophets could no way be upheld against those that hated
and scorned them.[79]

Thus it was precisely because the Old Testament promised
earthly rewards according to merit that the Manichee rejected
it, and it became acceptable to Augustine only as he learned
to read it as something preparatory and subordinate to the
New.   Thus to both, the New Testament was divinely inspired for the very reason that it not only affirmed eternal justice but also denied temporal justice.   Probably no doctrine
or religion which, in the Latin fourth century, alleged justice
on earth could possibly have spread and prospered. The only
rivalry was between a variety of pessimistic hypotheses.

Then, between 406 and 445, the Roman disposition
changed.   Just as anarchy will temper pessimism, so will it
temper bland indifference to the present.   It is not surprising,
therefore, that whereas in 406 the chief concern of the Catholic was with his personal dilemma, in 445 it was rather with
the survival of his civilization: his own salvation, although
still vital, was now somehow bound up with the salvation of
the Catholic faith and this in turn was partly because his
Church was now also the bulwark supporting his civilization.
But these wholesome changes were induced only at great sacrifice: during these forty years the mental fibre of the Roman
deteriorated, sinking from the heights of the New Testament
to the rolling plains of the Old.

Whatever the causes, the fact is undeniable: by 445 temporal optimism was again raising its head.   To distinguish
this from the traditional Christian optimism is not easy,
for here the minds themselves were muddled — the tem-

---

[79] *Confessions* V 14. In such passages as *D.C.D.* XIII 21, & XIV 22
Augustine says the literal meaning is
not to be denied merely because the
text also has other meanings.   He
says this partly no doubt because the
literal meaning is often illuminating
and corroborates the faith, but it
seems likely that wherever the literal
meaning conflicted with one or more
of the others he sacrificed it.

poral triumph of the Church, the pleasant dreams of the saints, the cult of virtue, all these indications of justice on earth are acknowledged by the pessimists, by Ambrose and Prudentius as well as by Augustine. Yet, because these earlier generations admitted the existence of a spiritual justice on earth which was none the less real because hidden from vulgar eyes, it is untrue to say that they were rendering a mere lip service to the New Testament. Theirs was nothing more nor less than the familiar psychology of heroism, where happiness is achieved by suffering for the sake of another. But the paradox was that the spiritual triumph of the Church involved a temporal triumph also: for the Church had been organized for the specific purpose of furthering God's will on earth. Unless God somehow willed that there be justice on earth, how was she to co-operate? How could she undertake to further the injustice conceived by the earlier generation? This pragmatic truth they had none of them, apparently, envisaged.

Apart from the suggestions of a weird justice on earth to be found, as we have seen, in the stories of the monks — suggestions not yet broached by orthodox teaching — the earliest indication of a shift in Catholic sentiment is to be found in the *History* of Orosius, a Spaniard born in about 384 [80] and so precisely a generation younger than his master Augustine. Written when Orosius was still a young man,[81] the work was designed as an empirical demonstration of Augustine's philosophy of history; [82] yet what does he try to prove if not that the more wicked pagans have suffered greater woes than the less wicked Christians! [83] Let us take as an instance his account of Alaric's sack of Rome. Having duly recited the manifold sins of her citizens, he proceeds:

And so after these ever-increasing iniquities and still no repentance, that final and too long postponed chastisement of the city now followed. Alaric appeared, besieged, upset, and broke into terror-stricken Rome, having previously given orders, however, first that those who took refuge in holy places — and especially in

---

[80] Augustine *Letter* # 169 says that Orosius was a young man when they first met in 414.

[81] His work was completed by about 418: Ebert 1889 I² 337 n. 3.

[82] *Historiarum Adversum Paganos* I prologue § 9.

[83] Cf. Boissier 1906 II⁶ 401–02.

the basilicas of the blessed Apostles Peter and Paul — must be left
inviolate and safe, and secondly that his men, in their greed for
plunder, must nevertheless, as far as possible, abstain from bloodshed.   It happened also — in order that this sack of the city might
be shown to have been due rather to the wrath of God than to the
strength of the enemy — that the blessed Innocent, bishop of the
city of Rome, like that virtuous Lot who was borne out of Sodom,
was by God's secret counsel at that moment staying in Ravenna
in order that he might not be obliged to witness the destruction of
the sinful people.[84]

The story of Lot is here understood literally — as evidence
that God applies His retributive justice to earthly affairs.
Pope Innocent is spared not only all personal violence but
even the sight of the just sufferings of others.   Such is the
earthly reward of virtue.   The punishment of the wicked, in
contrast to that inflicted according to the *De Providentia
Divina* of 415,[85] overwhelmed the citizens during their
earthly lives and not merely after death.   Yet even so it was
too long postponed — as if Orosius still suspected that God's
justice, although temporal as well as eternal, was not always
as prompt as it ought to be.   At least the patience of Orosius
would have been exhausted long before!   Where the chastisement occurs just before instead of just after death the
discrepancy in time is of course slight, but it is, nevertheless,
ample to re-establish that very principle of justice on earth
which most Romans, both pagan and Christian, had for many
years past denied.   Evidently Orosius, while keeping one eye
on Christ and Augustine, had kept the other on Jehovah and
that multitude of unregenerate Romans who, as the price of
their conversion, demanded some assurance that the rewards
of virtue and the wages of sin were being distributed in this
present life.

On the problem of this justice Pope Leo, born in about
395, does not commit himself because he wrote no systematic
work involving this problem.   His Sermons, nevertheless, are
definitely optimistic: for, speaking of the effect of the Redemption, he says

[84] *H.A.P.* VII 38 § 7 — 39 § 2. Many
other passages might be cited, as for
example VII 28 §§ 2–4; 32 § 3; 33
§§ 15 & 19; 35 §§ 15 & 17, etc.

[85] See p. 327.

Sinfulness returns to guiltlessness and the old nature becomes new; strangers receive adoption and outsiders enter upon an inheritance. The ungodly begin to be righteous, the miserly benevolent, the incontinent chaste, the earthly heavenly.[86]

And later he speaks of

these days, in which war is proclaimed against vices and progress is made in all virtues.[87]

This implies only an increase of virtue, and not an increase of temporal rewards for virtue; yet it is hardly conceivable that if men grow in virtue their earthly lot will not be ameliorated, and this not because God must intervene for this purpose but simply because men will then deal more gently with each other and thereby add to the joy of living.

Referring, however, to the recent sack of Rome by the Vandal Genseric in 455, Leo exclaims

Who was it that restored this city to safety? That rescued it from captivity? The games of the circus-goers or the care of the saints? Surely it was by the saints' prayers that the sentence of divine displeasure was diverted, so that we who deserved wrath were reserved for pardon.[88]

What else is this but an effort to demonstrate the regime of justice on earth? If the wicked are spared by the appeal of the saints to God's mercy, surely the virtuous will be spared — without the necessity of intercession — by the routine power of the divine justice.

It is not surprising that whereas Augustine denied both the pre-Redemption pact and justice on earth, Leo believed in both: for the two doctrines have an affinity. To Augustine Christ's sacrifice had merely made men less benighted, more susceptible to grace; because it had given them no capacity to acquire merit, had therefore given them no rights, God could not treat them with less justice than they appeared to deserve. But Leo, having adopted the theory whereby certain rights of the devil had been forfeited, naturally inferred that the right originally conferred upon Adam, having been wiped out by the pact, revived with its termination. Thus, in another form, the theory survived the Redemption:

---

[86] *Sermon* # 27 § 2.   [88] Ibid. # 84 § 1.
[87] Ibid. # 40 § 2.

God's generosity to the innocent Adam now bound Him again in His dealings with Adam's baptized descendants. To Augustine God's government was still a despotism; to Leo man now, like the devil before him, had rights God was bound to respect. Leo might still have argued that eternal felicity was ample reward for any merit a man might now acquire, that no one need complain, therefore, because no earthly reward was conferred. But it was impractible to preach that man, although he had rights, had none so long as he remained in the flesh: for it was too well known that real justice is swift and that justice ' too long postponed ' is to that extent injustice. It was natural, therefore, that Leo should say: since man now has rights, among these is the right to reasonably swift, and hence to temporal, justice.

These conceptions, however, of Orosius and Leo, are really only straws in the wind — indicating inclination rather than conviction.[89] The first categorical demonstration of the operation of justice on earth was reserved for Leo's contemporary, Salvian of Cologne.[90]

D. Salvian: Justice on Earth

Salvian was a Gallic noble, born at Cologne in about the year 400. It was in 418 that the prefect of the Gauls transferred his capital from Trier to Arles, and it is likely that Salvian's father, holding some important civil office, moved himself and his family south at this time.[1] When Salvian grew up he became a priest at Marseilles, and he was evidently in close touch with the neighbouring monastery at Lerins, for when Eucherius came to Lerins, bringing along his two sons, it was to Salvian that he entrusted their education.[2] Both of these sons later became bishops[3] — this is one reason why Gennadius, writing much later, chose to describe Salvian as ' master of bishops.'[4] He was evidently an important link con-

---

[89] Cf. Orientius, a Gallic poet of about 440: *Commonitorium* I lines 21–24 & 111–34, & II lines 173–74.

[90] Leo was born in about 395, Salvian in about 400.

[1] Sanford 1930 11.
[2] Ibid. 6.
[3] Ibid. See p. 309 n. 42.
[4] *De Script. Eccles.* ch. 67.

necting the monastery with the episcopate. And if we have
this direct evidence of Eucherius' confidence in Salvian, we
also have circumstantial evidence of Salvian's admiration for
Eucherius. Both were Gallic aristocrats who had chosen to
renounce the world to which they had been bred; an intellectual affinity was therefore to be expected. It need not surprise us to learn, as we now shall, that Salvian, a good deal
younger than Eucherius, derived as much from him as Eucherius had derived from Cassian.

But although these monks of Lerins, whom Salvian knew
so well and admired so much, certainly gave him his theory,
the task he undertook in his *De Gubernatione Dei* was none
the less a bold and original one. Where they had hinted and
suggested, he must assert and demonstrate. His metaphysical
proof must demolish the theodicy of Manichee and Epicurean which denied the premise of God's omnipotence. His
textual proof must interpret Christ's ' My kingdom is not of
this world ' [5] in the light of that same Old Testament which
the Manichee — and with some reason — considered un-
Christian. Finally he must prove empirically that justice on
earth actually had been and still was fully operative — a fact
which not only the Manichee, the Epicurean, the New Testament, and Ambrose and Augustine, but also the events themselves, seemed clearly to deny.

His metaphysical argument is inadequate because he does
not pretend to refute the dualism of the Manichee, but only
to convince him who, like the Epicurean, ' does not deny that
God is the Creator of all things.' [6] Even with the advantage
of this premise, indeed — which is philosophically an arbitrary one — he shows no dialectical ability. Here is a sample
of his arguments:

Are we to believe that Christ listens or denies His attention according to the diverse nature of our prayers, that He closes His
ears when we ask for present boons, and opens them when we ask
for blessings to come? [7]

Yet, if the present boon asked be frivolous, worldly or otherwise injudicious, Salvian must admit that Christ will deny
it. The intensity of Salvian's emotion numbs his thought.

---

[5] *John* xviii 36.   [7] Ibid. I § 24.
[6] *D.G.D.* IV § 41 (see p. 346 n. 67) .

His textual argument is at least more elaborated. After a feeble effort to show that both Cicero and Virgil shared his conception,[8] he launches into an extended quotation of Old Testament passages, unhesitatingly taking them in a wholly literal sense. The demonstration, as we can easily foresee, is here effective. For although he sidesteps the alleged incompatibility of the Old Law with the New, he is able to avoid the embarrassments of symbolic explanations, and able at the same time to show the hesitant Christian that, by trusting to the literal meaning, he could not only confound the Manichee but also trust in God's help here and now. Thus, having quoted from the *Psalms,* ' Deliver me from the deceitful and unjust man ',[9] he proceeds

Certainly it is the immediate judgment of God that he demands who begs to be freed from the hands of the persecutor.[10]

And so from the Psalmist he cites

Judge, O Lord, them that injure me; fight against them that fight against me; seize arms and shield and stand up for mine help.[11]

Or again

Thou sittest on the throne and judgest.[12]

And Salvian contrasts the use of the present tense ' deliver ' and ' judge ', with other passages where the future tense is used, as

He shall judge the world in righteousness [13]

concluding that

By these words surely he made a clear distinction in time between the present and future judgments of God. For to indicate the present he wrote, ' thou judgest ', and to distinguish the future from the present he added, ' he shall judge '.[14]

Again he cites *Leviticus:*

And the Lord spake unto Moses, saying: ' bring forth him that hath cursed without the camp; and let all that heard him lay

[8] Ibid. § 4.
[9] *Psalm* # 43 1.
[10] *D.G.D.* II § 26.
[11] Ibid. § 27 — from *Psalm* # 35 1–2.
[12] *Psalm* # 9 4.
[13] Ibid. # 96 13.
[14] *D.G.D.* II § 28.

their hands upon his head, and let all the congregation stone him.' [15]

He then adds:

Was not God's judgment immediate and manifest and His sentence pronounced as if the heavenly decision followed the forms of our legal procedure?   First the man who had sinned was arrested, then he was led, so to speak, before the judge's seat, thirdly accused and then sent to prison, lastly punished by the authority of the divine judgment; furthermore he was not only punished but punished in accordance with the evidence given, so that God's justice and not merely His power was seen to condemn his guilt. [16]

Salvian's greatest difficulty is to explain why, for a single sin, David was so afflicted, but after arguing this point at some length he confidently concludes:

Condemnation followed close on the heels of the fault, a condemnation punishing immediately without reservations and arresting the wrongdoer on the spot, not putting off the charge to a later time.   Therefore He did not say: ' Because you have done this, know that the judgment of the Lord shall come and you shall be tortured hereafter by the flames of Gehenna.'   No; He said: ' You shall suffer torture at once, and shall feel the sword of divine justice already at your throat.' [17]

Salvian, however, was obliged to show not only how God punished, but also how He rewarded, in this world.   It is not surprising, therefore, that he did not discuss, or even mention, the trials of Job, but chose instead to cite the fortunes of Noah.   After summarizing that story he observes:

Now at this point I wish to ask those who call God indifferent to human affairs whether they believe that at that time He either attended to or judged human affairs?   For I think that He not only judged but rendered a twofold judgment; for in saving the good He rendered a retributive justice and in condemning the wicked He rendered a strict justice.

Since these things happened before the Flood — that is, as if in another age — they may seem to stupid persons to have small authority: as if, indeed, some other God existed then, or as if He did not afterwards wish to give the world the same attention.   To be sure I am able with divine help to prove what I say for each generation since the Flood.   But the great number of such instances forbids. [18]

15 xxiv 14.
16 D.G.D. I § 50.

17 Ibid. II § 18.
18 Ibid. I §§ 33–34.

Thus by the year 445 the status of the Old Testament had become curiously anomalous. Forty years earlier the tendency had been for Catholics to accept it only on the assumption that the truth it contained was chiefly symbolic and only incidentally literal; the Manichæan view was then unacceptable. But now the Catholics are taking a leaf from the book of the Manichees: Pope Leo readily reverts to their dualistic hypothesis in order to explain the eccentricities of the Old Law, acknowledging that God's omnipotence was at that time not complete; and Salvian too follows the Manichees in thinking the Old Text literally true.[19]   Just as Augustine was accused of compounding with the Manichees because he did not think the Redemption decided God to grant a contingent salvation to all; just as, in the East also, as we shall see,[20] the heretic Eutyches was similarly accused because he declared the Incarnation a sham; so now Leo and Salvian might also be so accused, Leo because of his pre-Redemption dualism, Salvian because of his literal acceptance of the pre-Redemption text.   The symbolic view, everywhere prevalent in the later fourth century and consolidated in the West by the glamour of Ambrose and Augustine, was less scientific than ingenious, but it was also less dishonest than sophisticated.   The effort to read the Old Text in the light of the New was one which might well be thought possible only with the help of divine inspiration; the effort to read and comprehend it merely as it was written required no more than literacy.   A more fundamental distinction underlies this difference: in the year 406 the anomaly of the Old Law was unmistakable — it was a primitive law which civilization had outgrown in contrast to a divine law to which civilization aspired; but by 445 the distinction had already become blurred because civilization had itself reverted — because anarchy is itself primitive it demands a primitive law.   There was still need of Christ, but the need for Jehovah was far greater.   Mercy — the need of forty years before — was now a luxury, for even the most rigorously merciless justice, since it was lacking, became the object of human longing.   Where there is at least some enforcement of civil law, men can wait

[19] But the Manichees alone supposed that the devil was tempting men, then as now, with the lure of fleshly rewards in return for obedience to his will.

[20] See p. 604 n. 79.

patiently for the justice of God; but where, as now, even that
had broken down, men lose all patience. That Christ might
rule in heaven gave little consolation so long as Jehovah —
in the guise of civil justice — did not also rule on earth.

That Jehovah did rule on earth Salvian had tried to prove,
both theoretically and by resort to authority. But these
proofs were surely not conclusive: for the acid test was
whether His justice, as it had been revealed to men, continued to operate after the Redemption as it evidently had
before. Was it just, first of all, that Christ should die on the
Cross? Having eschewed the problem of God's treatment of
Job, it is natural that he eschew too the problem of the Passion. Next comes the problem of the martyrs: guiltless like
Christ they certainly were not; yet was their punishment
quite what even Jehovah would have chosen for them? Here
again Salvian is silent. Nor does he mention the triumph of
the Christians under Constantine, although this argument
would have proved effective. The truth is that Salvian was
arguing with men concerned only with present, not with past,
justice: if he could show that justice, though it had in past
times been ineffective, was now, and would continue to be,
effective, this would amply suffice. As Salvian well knew,
the empirical attack not only had to be made, it must be
made boldly at the centre. Yet to prove that God was in complete control of the Roman world of 445 and that every man
was therefore receiving a temporal reward in exact proportion to his merit, must have seemed, to anyone less courageous, a hopeless effort. For every day events seemed more
and more to belie such a possibility.

His first problem concerned the barbarians: why should
they, who were either Arian heretics or benighted heathens,
be the ones to gain the Promised Land? One reason was
that, not being true believers, they were probably doomed to
damnation. And in such a case, as Augustine had explained,[21] whatever rewards unbelievers might deserve must
be bestowed, if at all, in this present world.[22] The merits of
the barbarians did not seem to Salvian conspicuous,[23] but

---

21 See p. 323 n. 38.
22 Although Salvian puts it rather
on the ground of mercy: 'quia ig-
nosci aliquatenus ignorantiae po-
test': *D.G.D.* V § 11.
23 Ibid. IV §§ 67–70.

they did worship and honour God according to their lights.[24]
They, for instance,

believed that victory depended on God, we that it depended on
ourselves.[25]

They are, therefore, the unredeemed victims of the Fall —
the innocently guilty. But although God's mercy gives them
victory His justice makes it hollow. There is, however, another reason for their victories: God's need of pawns or instruments in order to compass His stern ends. The Vandals,
Salvian says, had no good reason for crossing to Spain,

but surely the heavenly hand that had dragged them thither in
order to punish the vices of the Spaniards, compelled them also
to cross the straits to devastate Africa. In fact they themselves
confessed that they did not act of their own volition, for they were
driven and urged on by a divine command.[26]

Like the tyrant of Augustine,[27] whom God inflicts on a people
for their sins, the earthly reward bestowed on the Vandals
was a by-product — for heathen and heretic possess a merely
extrinsic significance.

So far, then, the empirical argument of Salvian is purely
Augustinian. But the real problem, of the Catholic Roman's vicissitudes, had still to be grappled with — and a more
ungrateful one is hard to imagine. Here Salvian was not
always — and we can hardly blame him — wholly consistent:
there is one passage where he frankly despairs:

The question is raised why, if everything in this world is controlled by the care and governance and judgment of God, the
condition of the barbarians is so much better than ours, why
among us the fortune of good men is harder than that of the
wicked. Why should upright men fall ill and reprobates recover? Why does the whole world fall prey to powers for the
most part unjust? Perhaps a rational and fairly consistent answer would be: I do not know. For I do not know the secrets of
God.[28]

And in another passage he says,

Surely we are not to wonder that holy men are now suffering certain hardships, since we see that God even at that time permitted

---

[24] Ibid. V §§ 8–11.   [27] Ibid. II § 23, & V §§ 16 & 23.
[25] Ibid. VII § 44.   [28] Ibid. III § 2.
[26] Ibid. § 54.

the first of his saints [Abel] to be most wickedly slain. As to the reasons why He permits such actions, it is not within the power of human weakness to discover fully.[29]

These statements oblige us to suspect that when the facts are against him Salvian takes refuge in that very intellectual humility which he so despises in his Epicurean friends; but that when the facts suit his thesis he regains full confidence in his capacity to fathom the divine ways.

Salvian's easiest case is where a notoriously bad man comes to a miserable end. This was almost the only cheerful kind of thing that happened in the fifth century, and that God's wrath might be the cause of this required no ingenious demonstration. The case of the saints was a harder one. Abel's, like that of the martyr, involving as it did an ignominious death, was not clear. But the contemporary saints, the saints who had lived since Constantine, had suffered less brutally — so that a case might be made out for them:

Far less should we lament in the case of the saints, for however unhappy they may seem to men who do not understand their condition, it is impossible for them to be otherwise than happy. Moreover, it is superfluous to think them wretched because of sickness or poverty or any like misfortune in the midst of which they count themselves happy; for no man is wretched because of other men's judgment, but only in his own.[30]

This is hardly more than Stoic doctrine turned Christian. Nevertheless the Passion and martyrdom were not yet so interpreted, and it was not until Pope Gregory 150 years later that a saint's death, however it should occur, was pictured as a pleasant, even as a rapturous, experience.

But the fate of neither notorious villain nor notorious saint presented the decisive problem: the vast majority of men are, and always have been, no more of the one sort than of the other. If, as Salvian insists, ' I assuredly suffer in the proportion that I deserve ',[31] how can it be that a mean man will often prosper to a hearty old age while a kindly or innocuous man is subjected to every humiliation and horror? In the passage already quoted Salvian confesses he does not understand; yet his faith in the truth of his hypothesis is so solid that his whole work is an attempt to prove that he vir-

---

[29] *D.G.D.* I § 30.   [31] Ibid. IV § 10.
[30] Ibid. § 8.

tually does understand. To be quite fair we must acknowledge that he does not profess to have proved beyond cavil that events allow of no other interpretation, but he does allege that his hypothesis, firmly founded as it is on the Revelation of God's omnipotence and on the historical truth as related in the Old Testament, is not incompatible with contemporary actuality. Some, even many, incidents, to be sure, remain obscure, but there are none which actually contradict the hypothesis and there are innumerable instances tending directly to corroborate it. His arguments in the main are two: first, that those who are guilty even of venial sins must be chastised by God in order that they may recognize that they have displeased God and so mend their ways before it is too late:

> Yet they ought to be most wretched in order that they may cease to be wicked, that they may cease to apply the name of religion to their most evil gains and to bestow the title of sanctity on their most sordid traffickings; in such a case, indeed, a comparison of the misfortunes of sinners with their misdeeds shows that they are less unfortunate than they deserve, for the utmost misfortunes they can suffer leave them still less wretched than they are wicked.[32]

And this argument itself includes the other: that the majority of the Catholics are far more wicked than is commonly supposed: they have been told what God expects of them, they have made solemn profession to imitate Christ's ways, yet they have done literally nothing beyond that empty profession; the revelation of evil has resulted only in a more deliberate cultivation of it, the Passion has taught them nothing that the apple had not already taught.

Still, these persons had chosen to profess the faith and receive baptism: it might casually be assumed that they ought to be given preferential treatment. Otherwise would they not have earned more merit and so deserved greater mercy by rejecting even the rather idle gesture of conversion? But no; this would have availed them nothing. For the Roman was not a barbarian: the Catholic faith had for so long now been the Roman faith that no one could possibly plead an innocent ignorance of Christ as an excuse for his misdeeds.[33]

[32] Ibid. I § 7. Cf. ibid. III § 6.   [33] Ibid. III §§ 6 & 25.

It was precisely because he was a Roman, and not because he was a Catholic, that he incurred special responsibilities. The only good Roman now was a Catholic Roman, and the only good Catholic Roman was one who genuinely strove to follow Christ. As there had once been a pagan Roman justice, so there was now a Catholic Roman justice. The canon law was no less Roman because it was also Catholic.

At this point in his argument Salvian's rhetoric swells. If he is to prove that immediate justice is being meted out here and now, he must make men's vices appear to equal their misfortunes, and, since misfortunes cannot be minimized, the vices must be exaggerated: for otherwise it cannot be maintained that ' I assuredly suffer in the proportion that I deserve.' Above all — since it is particularly to them that Salvian addresses himself — the rich and noble are singled out for condemnation:

Who can find words to describe the enormity of our present situation? Now that the Roman commonwealth — already extinct or at least drawing its last breath in that one corner where it still seems to retain some life — is dying, strangled by the cords of taxation as if by the hands of brigands, a great number of wealthy men are still found, the burden of whose taxes is borne by the poor; that is, very many rich men are found whose taxes are murdering the poor.[34]

They are, indeed, far more guilty than any slave — the best proof being, perhaps, that God has punished them more —

Take for example this crime, a very great one indeed, of which almost the whole mass of slaves is guiltless. Has any slave throngs of concubines, is any one of them defiled by the stain of polygamy or do they think they can live like dogs or swine with as many wives as they have been able to subject to their lust? The answer, I suppose, is obvious, that slaves have no such opportunities, for they surely would take them if they had. I believe this, but I cannot consider actions I do not see performed as having taken place. However dishonourable his intentions are, however evil his desires, no one is punishable for the crimes he does not commit.[35]

Nor have misfortunes chastened these rich:

Even in my own country, in the Gallic states, almost all men of high degree have been made worse by their misfortunes. I myself

have seen men of lofty birth and honour, though already de-
spoiled and plundered, less ruined, nevertheless, in fortune than
in morality; for, ravaged and stripped though they were, something still remained to them of their property, but nothing of
their character. . . .

The chief men of the *civitas* were reclining at feasts, forgetful
of their honour, age, faith, and rank, gorged with food, dissolute
from wine-bibbing, wild with shouting, giddy with revelry.[36]

Most of them, doubtless, were merely trying to forget their
troubles by a conventional and perhaps even innocent gaiety;
but Salvian, taking his Catholicism too rigidly, was secretly
pleased to find a telling reason for condemning such indulgences. For if these men were overwhelmed by disaster, and
if this was surely a divine judgment, then they had griev-
ously sinned, and since they were men honourable in other
respects this grievous sin must have been their irresponsible
and frivolous feasting. By Salvian, as by many other reformers, no distinction is seen between the thoughtless fool
and the villain.[37]

The vices of the rich were the most conspicuous and in-
excusable; nevertheless the whole Roman population had to
assume almost its full share of the guilt. Take, for instance,
the recent disasters in Africa:

While the barbarian armies were clashing about the walls of
Cirta and Carthage, the Christian congregation of the city raved
in the circuses and wantoned in their hearts. Some had their
throats cut without the walls while others were still fornicating
within.[38]

Most heart-rending is his description of the capture of Trier:

For some died lingering deaths from deep wounds, others were
burned by the enemy's fires and suffered tortures even thereafter.
Some perished of hunger, others of nakedness, some died limp,
others rigid, and thus, though dying in different ways, they tum-
bled together into the common outlet of death.

What more is there to say? By the fall of this one city other
cities were also afflicted. Scattered all around there lay — as I myself saw and endured — the torn and naked bodies of both sexes;
lacerated by dogs and birds, they were an eyesore to the whole city.
The deadly stench of the dead was a pestilence to the living: death
was breathed out by death. And thus even those who had not

---

[36] Ibid. VI §§ 72 & 74.   [38] *D.G.D.* VI § 69.
[37] Cf. Dill 1906 2 180.

died in the fall of the aforesaid city, suffered the evils of another kind of death.

And what more is to be said after all these things, I ask, what more after all these things? Who is able to realize the enormity of the madness that followed? A few of the nobles who survived the catastrophe — as if this were the best possible medicine for the ruined city — petitioned the emperors for circuses. . . .[39]

Do you then seek public shows, O citizen of Trier? Where, pray, are they to be given? Over the pyres and ashes, the body and blood, of the dead? . . . The remains of a most unhappy people lie on the graves of their dead, yet you ask for circuses; the city is blackened by fire, yet you put on a festive countenance; all things mourn, but you rejoice.[40]

Salvian chooses to forget that, just as the rich needed the solace of a pleasant feast, so the poor needed their circuses. If such indulgences were sufficient cause for the destruction of cities, it is hard to imagine how any cities had ever grown up — or endured. But, since Salvian was searching for empirical arguments to support his thesis, the folly of men was argument enough. So it had been under the Old Law; so it was still under the New.

What was the effect of Salvian's philosophical diatribe? That the biographer Gennadius chooses to call him 'master of bishops'[41] is some indication of his influence; that his work has come down to us is perhaps another. But rarely, if we except the works of great men like Ambrose, Jerome, and Augustine, can we know what were the things most read in those agitated days. It is fair to assume that the work, though a mere annoyance to laymen, was not without real influence on the clergy, and that, through these rather than directly, the work lived and bore fruit. But apart from this the view of Salvian deserves our most serious attention, for it was written by a cultivated Gallic noble of the middle of the fifth century, and thus indicates what must have been a characteristic disposition of the men among whom he lived. To the Roman who at heart was still rather a Stoic, Neoplatonist, or Epicurean, the world seemed still, as it had to Augustine, as well disposed to injustice as to justice. Whispering in this man's ear was the ubiquitous Manichee, striving to convince

---

[39] D.G.D. §§ 83–85.   [41] See p. 353 n. 4.
[40] Ibid. § 89.

him that the world was wholly unjust. How was the Catholic to refute the Manichee? To the minds of that day, grown sluggish with misery, neither the relentless subtlety of Augustine nor the intangible subtlety of Christ would any longer serve. A simpler, grosser fare was requisite, and the Old Testament offered that very blundering optimism which the average Catholic Roman now craved.

Therefore this vicious blow of Salvian's, although it must have been felt alike by pagan, heretic, and Augustinian, hit none so hard as the Manichee — he who believed that man was wholly the slave of evil. For to the Epicurean, as to the Stoic and Neoplatonist, evil was due merely to dead matter, and so to blind destiny or chance rather than to malice; and to Augustine there was, quite apart from future life, no more injustice than justice. But, to the Manichee, the world of the flesh, since it was being actively ruled by Satan, could never witness anything but a regime of systematic and violent injustice.[42] And, since the smallest evidence of true justice on earth contradicted their doctrine, so every such demonstration by Salvian was a blow in the Manichees' face.

On an extremely important if not fundamental point, therefore, Salvian's treatise is an introduction to the Middle Ages. The philosophies of late antiquity — as well as Christian Stoic, Neoplatonic, Manichæan, — had each supposed the world rather a distortion or contradiction, than an image, of the real world of the spirit. Whether because of a hyper-sensitiveness or an inherited exhaustion, each had become peculiarly conscious of the misery and injustice of the present life, and from this each drew the inference that these were themselves presumptive evidence of the joy and justice to prevail in heaven. But to Salvian, born in a new generation grown more callous, temporal events could appear rather a replica in miniature of eternal justice — the more prophetic of, precisely because analogous to, the world invisible to come.

A minor historical cycle is thus completed. The earlier Roman paganism had believed in temporal justice and its present rewards, but under the later Empire this optimistic

[42] Stoop 1909 10 says that Mani's religion is a most complete expression of pessimism and disgust with the world.

view had been successively denied by Stoic and Epicurean, by Neoplatonist, Manichee, and Catholic. The work of Salvian [43] heralds a return to the earlier view, challenging Catholicism, whether officially or substantially, to make its choice.[44]

E. Salvian on Virtue

That Salvian championed the hypothesis of justice on earth was undeniably of great significance. At the same time his idea of that justice was hardly what an earlier Roman, or we, might imagine it. His temporal justice does mean temporal welfare for the virtuous and so an indiscriminate happiness, for his happiness is still that rather of the saint than of the layman, that rather of Augustine than of Alaric. Recall that Augustine had said

For a happy life is a rejoicing in the truth; for this is a joying in Thee Who art the Truth.[1]

And, taken in this sense, Augustine must himself admit that there was a real, if a weird, justice on earth. But Augustine was far too worldly-wise to argue, even to himself, that, using words in their ordinary sense, it could be alleged that such justice existed. Too often had he seen the weak but innocent, the ignorant and uninspired but kindly, carried mercilessly to misery, anguish, and physical torture. He would not confound his own happiness with that demanded by a workaday world. Now Salvian will, on occasion, follow Augustine: as where he says of the saints that

It is impossible for them to be otherwise than happy.[2]

But as soon as he undertakes to apply a standard of happiness to the world at large he becomes confused. Now it is precisely this confusion which is so enlightening — he does not

---

[43] Not forgetting the earlier intimations of the monks and Orosius, and the contemporary intimation of Leo, to which may be added that of Maximus of Turin in the passage quoted p. 280.

[44] See pp. 525–28.

[1] See p. 78.

[2] See p. 360 n. 30.

quite know which is his real skin, the old one he is shedding
or the new one being bared to view.

If the virtuous are to receive temporal blessings, one of
these — and in the fifth century the most prized of all — was
immunity from the horrors of a disastrous war. For conquest
by an alien foe brought with it almost every conceivable
human misery — if not death, then poverty, disease, exploitation, and persecution. Now Salvian, by his insistence that
the current Roman defeats were to be interpreted as divine
punishments for vicious living, made it clear that he believed
a prime reward of virtuous living would be immunity from
such trials. And here he makes a judicious inference: since
the Romans have hitherto tried to avert military disasters by
resort to armed resistance yet without making any effort to
mend their vicious habits, it is quite evident that the opposite
policy — of non-resistance and a life of virtue, as recommended by Christ — must prove a success:

[God] handed the people of Spain over to the weakest of the
enemy expressly in order to show that it was not the strength but
the merit of the Vandals that conquered. . . .
    This should serve to confound and punish us, that we were
given into the power of the weakest, and must recognize the correction of God's hand in the fact that not the bravest but the most
despised of our enemies overcame us.[3]

Nor, as the past had already shown and as the future would
show, was this opinion so foolish as it may appear. Of Christianity's earlier triumphs Pope Leo said:

But against the threatened attacks of persecutors, against the terrifying shouts of the ungodly, they [the disciples] could not fight
with bodily strength or pampered flesh, since that which delights
the outer does most harm to the inner man.[4]

And this was hardly less true in 445. In the interval, to be
sure, after Constantine and before the invasions, physical
force had seemed advantageous to the Christian cause: we
therefore find neither Ambrose nor Augustine protesting
against the use of it. Until 406 the Roman State seemed still
secure, and the Church not responsible, therefore, for the
maintenance of law and order; but by 445 it had become evi-

[3] *D.G.D.* VII §§ 28–29.   [4] *Sermon* # 78 § 1.

dent that the earthly destinies of Rome and so, perhaps, of
Catholicism, lay at the mercy of the Church — the responsibility, whether she liked it or not, had now shifted to her
shoulders. But how could she promote the temporal welfare?
Not, surely, by recruiting and leading armies, not by physical strength. Her power was moral and psychological; her
weapons were fasting and prayer. The rewards of the flesh
were to be won by a denial of them. It was only by seeking
to deprive himself of those rewards that man could induce
God to confer them! We cannot therefore blame Salvian:
the physical way of procuring immunity from invasion was
not only theoretically wrong — because it was the antithesis
of the spiritual; it was also empirically wrong — because it
had, during the past forty years, produced only a succession of
hideous defeats. Thus, after describing the capture of the
Roman Litorius when seeking to retake Toulouse from the
Visigoths in 439, Salvian concludes,

Why did these things happen? Surely because . . . the enemy
were humble before God, whereas we were rebellious; they believed that the victory lay in His hand, we that it lay in our own —
a sacrilegious and wicked conception which makes our sin so much
the worse and more injurious to us.[5]

The idea that physical weakness somehow produced spiritual strength is much more a pagan than a Christian conception. It is not to be confused with the doctrine of non-
resistance which merely forbids the exercise of physical force
to the injury of another. This latter is a doctrine of love,
whereas the other is a doctrine of magic. Even Jerome, extreme as his asceticism was, could not accept the cruder
hypothesis:

Now, although in my fear of hell I had consigned myself to this
prison where I had no companions but scorpions and wild beasts,
I often seemed to be surrounded by a bevy of young girls. My
cheeks were pale and my body chilled with fasting; so that in front
of this man, already almost dead in the flesh, only the flames of passion remained hot.[6]

That the way to strengthen the spirit was to weaken the flesh
must have been a very early conviction — a case of primitive
dialectic — the trouble was that in practice it too often did

5 *D.G.D.* VII § 44. Cf. p. 359 n. 25.   § 7, & # 125 § 7. Cassian *Conlationes*
6 *Letter* # 22 § 7. Cf. ibid. # 107   XXI 35 subscribes to this conclusion.

not work. The idea was, however, so deeply ingrained in the
Roman mind that even had the Church tried to eradicate it
she must have been unsuccessful,[7] and particularly at a time
like this when the physical world had become so disordered
that the only refuge from chaos was in the mind. Pope Leo's
statement — just quoted [8] — that

that which delights the outer does most harm to the inner man

is conventionally rather than insistently presented; but Salvian reverts whole-heartedly to the pagan and Stoic conception. In his Letters he speaks of the human body

whose strength, as you know, is always inimical to the mind.[9]

and he thus enlarges on this idea:

For weakness of the body sharpens the vigour of the mind. For,
the limbs being weakened, the vigours of the body are transferred
to the vigours of the mind, so that to me there seems to be a certain kind of health where the man himself is not healthy. For
there is absolutely no struggle then between the soul and the body
— that is, between the divine propensity and the earthly enemy.
The bones do not burn with evil flames, secret desires do not
wrongly inflame the healthy mind, the wandering senses do not
wanton among a variety of delights, but the soul alone exults, rejoicing in the body's weakness almost as if in the subjugation of
the adversary.[10]

Here, bobbing up again, is that very contraction and repression, elimination and impoverishment, against which Augustine had so constantly protested.[11] To Augustine above
all was Catholicism indebted for the momentous discovery
that the flesh was not sinful, and that only by a judicious use
of the flesh, therefore, could men earn spiritual rewards. Yet
within a generation the discovery is already being forgotten.
Reverting to the age of dialectical magic, Salvian presumes
that in order to make the spirit strong the flesh must be made
weak; and from this he draws the further inference that by
a repudiation of the flesh there will come not only the eternal
rewards of the spirit but also the temporal rewards of at least
the chastened flesh. Because, in Augustine's day, the fleshly

---

[7] Prudentius *Peristephanon* II
lines 205–16 gives the conventional
view. See pp. 318–19.
[8] See p. 367 n. 4.

[9] *Letter* # 5 § 3.
[10] Ibid. § 4.
[11] See p. 65, 96 n. 68, & 100.

rewards were too often to be had for the asking, it seemed un-
wise to court them; but because, in Salvian's, these rewards
were no longer available, it seemed vital to regain them.
Who, then, was the Manichee: Augustine, who declared that
there was no possibility of evil in material flesh, or Salvian,
who believed that virtue would be infallibly induced by its
repudiation? To Augustine the cardinal sin was spiritual
pride; to Salvian it was a compounding with matter. Yet in
both there was a certain logic: as the soul must be battered in
order to be worthy of its reward, so must the flesh. Each
sought ways and means to strengthen the will, but because
each sought this for a different reward so each sought it by a
different technique: the one by love, the other by magic.

Immunity from invasion was obviously the first requisite
of temporal welfare, but this could only be a negative good.
There can be miseries even when there is no war — drought,
disease, murder, persecution and much more. How was the
Catholic to ward off these evils? How promote positive
blessings? Chiefly, no doubt, by piety — by alms-giving, fasting, and prayer. But has Salvian not some more concrete
suggestions? Repudiation of the theatre and the circus is
one requirement on which he insists; chastity is another.[12]
He follows the conventional Christian precepts in these matters. There remained, however, one thorny question not so
easily resolved: that of the use and disposal of wealth.

Christ — or so it seemed to Salvian [13] — had enjoined the
rejection of all riches, of all property over and above the bare
necessities of life. Now this conception was sensible, even
logical, so long as temporal welfare was not a consideration.[14]
But Salvian had committed himself to the Old Testament,
which offered wealth as the chief reward of virtue. Salvian
dwells continually on the miseries of the poor and on the
virtue of charity, making it clear that many of man's worst
miseries are due to the absence of wealth. On this point
Pope Leo supports the best Catholic tradition where he declares that

---

12 Cf. *D.G.D.* IV §§ 24–28.
13 Cf. *Ad. Ecclesiam* I §§ 6, 8 & 20,
II §§ 39, 40, 51, 65, etc.
14 Cassian *Conlationes* VII 16 says

the text 'it is more blessed to give
than to receive' is no excuse for
holding on to one's property.

wealth, after its kind and regarded as a means, is good, and is of the greatest advantage to human society when it is in the hands of the benevolent and open-handed.[15]

And this is, without a doubt, no less the view of Salvian, the only difference being that Salvian chose to write a special tract [16] — the *Ad Ecclesiam* — on the problem and therefore gives us a concrete picture of the Catholic attitude of that time.

To Salvian the problem is, of course, one not of economics but of ethics: if everyone deals with his wealth as Christ has enjoined, prosperity will be automatically conferred; [17] if only we see to it that we are virtuous, God will see to it that we prosper. The disposal of wealth cannot, therefore, be either injudicious or judicious, but only vicious or virtuous.[18]

Christ's precept, undoubtedly, is to give up all that we possess. But to Salvian it seemed that this injunction was not, like those of the Old Testament, to be taken quite literally.[19] In applying the teaching of the New Law, allowance must be made for the frailty of even the Catholic Roman. And so, in the best manner of the later casuist, he laid down the order of sinfulness — the degrees of imperfection from the venial to the mortal sin.

The mildest offence was for a layman to keep the bulk of his property during his life,[20] thus maintaining himself and his family and dependents substantially in the style to which they were accustomed; and it was only slightly more serious to leave such persons a moderate property by testament.[21] It was, however, a mortal sin not to leave to the Church any sur-

---

[15] *Sermon* # 10 § 1.

[16] Pauly 1883 xii says the *Ad Ecclesiam* was written a good while before the *D.G.D.* This latter was written at some time between 439 and 451. The former work has often been called, though inaccurately, the *Adversus Avaritiam.*

[17] Although of course Salvian denies that poverty is the sole virtue requisite for salvation, or that man can, by giving away his property, buy salvation. For a real contrition and change of heart must accompany this outward sacrifice: *Ad Ecclesiam* I § 43.

[18] Nor has this view become quite obsolete today.

[19] The Council of Antioch of 341 canon # 24 provided against appropriation by the Church of the private property of a deceased bishop: Hefele 1907 I 2 721. Cf. the Council of Sardica of 343 canon # 12: ibid. 742 & 793–94.

[20] *Ad Ecclesiam* III § 5.

[21] Ibid. § 19. For Faustus of Riez's view of the degrees for a monk, see *Letter* # 8.

plus beyond the reasonable needs of the heirs.[22] A practice
that particularly goaded Salvian was that of discriminating
against those children who had adopted a religious vocation.
In some cases they were left a reduced share outright,[23] in
others their inheritance was left only in trust and so for
life [24] — manifestly in order to prevent their leaving it to the
Church.[25] But the culminating and most contemptible outrage was committed by those who left their property to some
man of rank, alleging that he was the true heir and in this
way buying not only a posthumous but a false title of nobility. For some, he says,

suddenly introduce into their wills persons whom they have never
introduced into their hearts, and these are chiefly, as I have said,
either millionaires, nobles, or men who have held public office;
and, were these not men of influence, they would hardly have
found themselves relatives. Ridiculous is the ambition of so
wretched a testator, who pays out of his very resources for a fraudulent kinship; who buys a legatee's name at the cost of a legacy;
who employs the whole of his inheritance in order that the man
whom he has written down as his heir may not deny kinship, and
in order that this unfortunate testator, having with stupid and
miserable vanity made the noble his heir, may after his death be
looked up to, who during his life was looked down on. O what
blindness and insanity.[26]

And in a letter Salvian says that even certain bishops, being

without loved ones, without relatives, having neither families nor
children, leave their riches and property, not to the poor, not to
the Churches . . . but to laymen, and chiefly to rich persons and
to strangers.[27]

In the case of some Romans, evidently, not baptism, not even
the episcopal consecration, could temper their vanity. We
cannot wonder, therefore, that to the pious, real Christianity
was so welcome that the excesses which it incidentally countenanced were readily forgiven. Nor can we wonder that

[22] *Ad Ecclesiam* I § 34, II § 22, &
III §§ 5–6 & 19. Augustine was far
more moderate in his views: Possidius *S. Augustini Vita* 24; & cf. Montalembert 1863 I 2 213.
[23] *Ad Ecclesiam* III §§ 21–22.
Jerome *Letter* # 130 § 6 records such
a case in 414.

[24] *Ad Ecclesiam* III §§ 28–29.
[25] Ibid. § 29.
[26] Ibid. § 60. Cf. ibid. § 10.
[27] *Letter* # 9 § 11. Cf. *Ad Ecclesiam* II § 41.

Salvian deemed it excusable to coax the obstinate rather by the Old than by the New Revelation.

So long as such practices as these could, even if infrequently, occur, there was small likelihood that Salvian's injunctions of perfection would be carried out on a large enough scale to upset the economic equilibrium. The Church, as we know, was constantly growing richer as individuals grew poorer; but private property was never in danger of extinction. It is interesting, nevertheless, to consider for a moment what sort of an economic Utopia Salvian envisaged. It was immaterial to him, apparently, that the rich man or any other give his property to the poor rather than to the Church [28] — for charity was the object and this virtue was not complicated by any exigencies of a calculated political economy.[29] But if one man distributes all his worldly goods among the poor, these poor thereby become property owners and hence obliged, in their turn, to divest themselves of this worldly encumbrance. The game must therefore resolve itself into a race to see who can get rid of his property first. Of course it might be conceived that if all wealth were distributed meticulously according to bare need there would be no surplus of wealth anywhere. But there is no intimation that Salvian envisaged this possibility; he merely hoped that at least all surplus wealth would find its way into the hands of the Church. In that case the bishops and clergy would hold the legal title to all the landed wealth and every layman would be a pauper [30] dependent for his living on his wage plus the alms which the Church saw fit to dispense. Not that Salvian had any such concrete picture of the ideal Catholic Commonwealth. That his argument in fact aimed at a sort of theocratic communism is a matter of chance, not of design. He merely exhorted men to rid themselves of dangerous encumbrances and thereby, if rather incidentally, do what they could to alleviate the miseries of the poor.

[28] *Ad Ecclesiam* IV § 35.

[29] Vigilantius, in contrast, had reflected on the consequences of indiscriminate giving, advocating measure and discretion, and asking who, if all should give everything away, would then be able to support the monks by alms: Jerome *Contra Vigilantium* §§ 13–14.

[30] As land, which in the fifth century was the source of virtually all wealth, must, sooner or later, pass to the Church by testament or otherwise; and this land the Church was forbidden to alienate except in special cases.

That a communistic, or capitalistic, or any other system would in this way emerge was a matter of indifference to him, for if only men were virtuous they need not worry; all the rest was not their responsibility but God's.

There is only one distasteful element in this work of Salvian's: his constant emphasis on the value of virtue rather to the individual who cultivates it than to his fellow men. Such an appeal to fear and to man's selfish instincts was no doubt the most effective one at that time. Nevertheless it is regrettable that he shows no disposition to see virtue in a less egoistical light. In his appeals to prospective testators we find such arguments as these:

You think how well others will live after you; you do not think how miserably you yourself will die.[31]

For it is an imprudent and stupid love which is mindful of another and not mindful of itself.[32]

Behold, He Himself calls to you at the moment of your death, He who, as your judge, will judge you that you may not, in perpetuating [the private ownership of] your goods and resources, love any other person more than yourself, that, in regard to your property, you may not, in dying, consider any other more than yourself, that you may judge no one to be nearer or dearer to you than your own soul.[33]

Perhaps this view was orthodox then — as it still is today. To many, however, it must seem as if the conception of the Stoic who loved virtue for its own sake, or that of Loyola [34] and Bérulle [35] who loved it for God's sake, or that of the school of Paray-le-Monial which ' honoured the love of Jesus for men ',[36] was a nobler one. We have only to contrast Salvian's view with the intangible mysticism of Augustine:

Thus man himself, consecrated in the name of God and vowed to God, is a sacrifice in so far as he dies to the world that he may live to God. For this is a part of that mercy which each man owes to himself; as it is written, *Have mercy on thy soul by pleasing God.* . . .

Therefore true sacrifices are works of mercy to ourselves or others, done with reference to God, and . . . works of mercy have

---

31 *Ad Ecclesiam* III § 14.
32 Ibid. § 44.
33 Ibid. § 83. Cf. ibid. II § 46, &
III §§ 12 & 15.

34 Bremont 1921 III 29 n. 1.
35 Ibid. 23–43.
36 Ibid. 668.

no other object than the relief of distress or the conferring of
happiness, and . . . there is no happiness apart from that good of
which it is said, *It is good for me to be very near to God.*[37]

Here in Augustine, as in Cassian,[38] the love of self, of good,
of God, of man, was all one. But there was a new world now,
with new men, and Salvian was not formed to rise above the
level of his age, even by clutching at great memories.

Yet let us not fail to do honour to this righteous and practical Gaul. If he is among the weaker links in the evolution of
Catholic theology, he is a vital one. For he had come fearlessly to the defence of this earth at a time when it was the
fashion to libel her, and this deed was not only courageous
but opportune. Augustine, racked as he was by the prodigal-
ity of temporal evil, had persuaded himself that the world
was, if not a caricature, at least a radical contrast to the real
world of the spirit; he persisted — almost Platonically — in
considering the visible world as something incidental, fragmentary, and distorted. Out of the ruck of Manichæan
pessimism Augustine had managed to contrive a ticklish
equilibrium between spirit and matter; but it required the
humdrum mind of a Salvian to give that equilibrium a
homely solidity which was comprehensible and palatable to
the ordinary man. Logically, of course, Salvian was right:
if God is able and willing to dispense eternal justice He must
be equally able and willing to dispense temporal justice: for,
unless He do so, there must, inevitably, be ephemeral injustice — that is, an appreciable interval of time during which
justice remains in default. Augustine could of course see the
logic of this as well as Salvian — so elementary a deduction
cannot have escaped him — but, unlike Salvian, his perceptions obliged him to acknowledge that justice on earth, however likely in theory, did not in fact obtain. Both invented
reasons: but whereas those of Augustine were dictated by observed facts, those of Salvian were dictated by his own wishes.
Augustine having declared the temporal world to be innocent, Salvian capitalized the discovery by declaring that this
temporal world was also just. Each view was, though in a

<hr>

[37] *D.C.D.* X 6. Although Bremont
ibid. 25 thinks that Augustine had
leanings towards Salvian's view.

[38] See p. 475–76.

different way, psychologically judicious; each was characteristic of, and suited to, the age which produced it. Salvian's
view prevailed only because his world was fast approaching
the Dark Age that was to come.

F. Survival of the Fittest

And yet, even thus attenuated, that Christianity triumphed
so magnificently is a great wonder — even to us who can see
the story in perspective. How, in competition with the rival
philosophies of a cosmic destiny or a cunning malice, was it
possible for Christianity, cast now into the physical convul-
sions of the fifth century, to survive? To the Romans of that
day who had become convinced of man's evil nature only the
miracle of Christ explained the triumph — the miracle of the
divine mercy, sacrifice, and dispensations of grace. Love,
humility, non-resistance, prayers instead of deeds, how is the
complacent biologist of today to explain such a miracle —
he who, after the manner of Nietzsche and Spengler,[1] bases
man's fitness to survive on his willingness to trample weaker
creatures underfoot? How is he to explain the triumph of
Christianity not only over the Roman Manichees and Neoplatonists, but also, in due course, over the rough barbarians?
If Christian ethics was so unfit to survive, why did it?

Since man was once an animal, doubtless he then behaved
like one; but, having ceased to be one, why assume that he
is bound still to behave as before? Is it not more sensible to
suppose, on the contrary, the very early discovery of a survival value in winning the confidence and love of other men?
Survival would then still depend on power — but it would
now be the new power of confidence and love. It would still
depend too on physical power — but this would now no
longer be only induced by fear.[2] To be sure no one in the
fourth or fifth century could clearly contemplate so radical a
temporal transformation, but the Catholics, with their faith
in the power of mercy, humility, and love, missed it only with

[1] See, for instance, Spengler 1931
14–25.

[2] Did the Germans who have written about their defeat in 1918 take
this fully into consideration?

their heads, not with their hearts. Much earlier, the Greeks had had a premonition, had therefore identified the essence of man's soul with the divine.[3] But, as these over-estimated, so other schools belittled,[4] man's nobility; the true man, therefore, they never found. It was the Christians, indeed, who — through Adam's fault and Christ's Redemption — first found him. That the evil was inherited, the good infused, may seem to us a mere hypothesis of the intangible How; but at least the nature of the tangible What was now gauged with a wholly new precision.

Since Catholic ethics did survive, it was therefore fit to — that no one can deny. But can we see why? Since the Manichee taught that the good man must abandon the earth and his own body to the evil creator, we can see why his cult died. But why was that cult more fit to survive which eschewed not only such worldly arts as flattery, self-advancement, boasting, or the exploitation of one's riches or one's friends, but also such an innocent art as that of physical well-being? Or which exhorted mothers to abandon their children [5] and men to 'take no thought for the morrow'?[6] How can it be alleged that such a cult survived because it precisely gauged the essence of human nature? For, if this in fact be true, why this excess?

It was the excess of reaction, of revolution, of intoxication breeding rash idealism. But hand in hand with this excess went a paradoxical realism that made the idealism tangible as well as unattainable, as human in its imperfection as it was inhuman in its perfection. Take the case of the warrior, fighting in defence of the Catholic cause: we do not have to wait till the Crusades in order to find a Christian glorification of heroism in battle, for Constantine's defeat of Licinius, Stilicho's of Rhadagasius,[7] Aetius' of Attila, had seemed as admirable as any saint's defeat of the eternal adversary. Yet the military victories were manifestly won by men who, instead of weakening the flesh, had strengthened it.[8] Why did

3 See p. 27.
4 Of course only while man was encumbered with flesh. And the Hedonists and Epicureans had emphasized man's animal traits.
5 As in Jerome *Letters* # 14 §§ 2 & 3, & # 108 § 6.

6 Cf. Salvian *D.G.D.* III § 10.
7 Cf. Paulinus of Nola: Lagrange 1877 540.
8 See a curious passage in Jerome *Contra Jovinianum* II § 6, on why pigs were created.

God choose to reward such men as these? And why, by good Christians, should they not rather have been reproved than acclaimed? The Church's solution here was as practical as it was illogical, as simple as it was wise.

For it was obvious that the soldier, though imperfect, must, if otherwise virtuous, be saved; in the fifth century particularly, fighting was almost as indispensable a vocation as motherhood, and any sect, Manichee or other, which denied this was doomed. And besides, who could deny that the soldier was obeying the divine injunction: ' Render therefore unto Cæsar the things which are Cæsar's '? [9] Or deny that although his soul belonged to God his body belonged to the State as does the slave's to his master? For we must not forget that, in contrast to modern times, even the chaotic fifth century was an age of bondage; when the father did not dictate his son's vocation the State or another did. Not slaves only, and soldiers, but almost everybody else, including Emperors,[10] became what they were much less from natural inclination than from necessity.[11] Thus upon Catholic Romans a career of imperfection was usually imposed, and the Church could therefore conscientiously declare that he who lived perfectly in imperfection sinned not and would be saved. It was in this way that the lay Catholic could give not only children,[12] riches,[13] military victories [14] to the Church, but also judicial and administrative services to the State,[15] and yet be holy.[16]

Surely it was largely due to this felicitous compromise that the faith and the Church survived. For in Catholicism not only was perfection recognized as indispensable, but imperfection too. In the Church it is, even today as it always has been, an imperfection to live in the world, and it is this very extra dimension that produces its incalculable stability.

Then was none of it folly? No, certainly, in comparison

---

[9] *Matt.* xxii 21.

[10] Recall the cases where generals were acclaimed Emperor by their troops so that it may have been hard for them to refuse. The imperial dynasty was also revered so that some were already being born to the purple: Jullian 1926 VIII 10–11.

[11] See pp. 241–42.

[12] Cf. Leo *Letter* # 167 § 12.

[13] Ibid. # 159 § 11.

[14] Ibid. # 167 § 12. Cf. Jerome *Letters* # 79 § 2, & # 107 § 13.

[15] See Caspar 1930 I 305–06 on Pope Innocent I (402–417).

[16] Although it was of course far more difficult to be so: see Leo *Letters* # 159 § 11, & # 167 § 12.

with the folly of the Manichees, who found no mean between a repudiation of matter and collusion with evil demons. Certainly in Catholicism there was much folly, because there is much in men; but their folly was not specifically Catholic,[17] whereas their wisdom was.

In one of Leo's Sermons is this passage:

Use visible creatures as they should be used, as thou usest earth, sea, sky, air, springs, and rivers; and whatever in them is fair and wondrous, ascribe to the praise and glory of the Maker. . . .
We do not bid or advise you to despise God's works or to think there is anything opposed to your faith in what the good God has made good, but to use every kind of creature and the whole furniture of this world reasonably and moderately.[18]

And in a letter of the year 472 bishop Sidonius thus describes a friend:

I recently visited the illustrious Vectius, and was able to study his way of life at close quarters. . . . In the first place — and this may rightly be regarded as the highest praise of all — the whole household emulates the master's flawless purity of life. . . . It is of less moment that the man of whom we speak is without a rival in training a horse, judging a dog, or bearing a hawk afield; that his dress is always exquisite and his girdle to match; that all his accoutrements are splendid. . . . With all this he is a regular reader of the Scriptures; even at meal times he enjoys this nutriment of the soul. He studies the *Psalms,* and yet more frequently chants them, setting a new precedent by living after this fashion in martial dress, the complete monk in all but the monastic habit.[19]

Catholicism evidently did not conquer pagan or heretic, Neoplatonist or Manichee, primarily because of any superior subtlety of dogma or temporal organization; rather it conquered because, alone of all the later Roman creeds, it could reconcile, and so face, both a wise God and foolish Matter. It was because of the faith that evil did not abide in his flesh that the Catholic could abide in it.

[17] I mean this very sense of an inherent imperfection in living a normal life in the world, which was certainly a more pronounced characteristic of the Stoics, Neoplatonists and Manichees than of the Jews. The Manichees did recognize a double standard, but apparently only the 'elect' were thought able to achieve any sort of perfection. The rest, known as 'hearers', were rather like the Catholic catechumen.

[18] *Sermon* # 27 § 6.

[19] *Letter* IV # 9 §§ 1–3.

CHAPTER VI

FREE WILL

A. EARLY THEORIES OF FREE WILL

FOR several centuries the evolution of Catholic theology was guided wholly by the Eastern theologians writing in Greek; the Latin writers assumed importance only after 373 when Ambrose, having been chosen bishop of Milan, lent his powerful support to enhance the prestige of the Roman See under Damasus.

The earliest articulated doctrine of free will was that of the Greek Apologists before 200,[1] and in the East their view prevailed without question until after 400.[2] Starting with the assumption, never thereafter challenged, that Adam, having the free will not to sin, had been given as good a chance as the angels, many of whom actually did not sin, the Greeks recognized the justice of Adam's penalty. And they also accepted, if with more reluctance, the justice of imposing that penalty on all Adam's descendants. They recognized that it included not only suffering and death of the body but also a loss of the knowledge of God; they even recognized a loss of Adam's power to avoid sin, but they believed that there subsisted enough free will to make the acquisition of merit still possible, and that this merit could, if only in exceptional cases, earn as its reward the grace which saves. For the Old Testament seemed to show that, although every man had sinned, a few had so piously repented that God pardoned

[1] Tixeront 1924 I [9] 258–60. On Irenæus see also Dufourcq 1904 [3] 139–40 & 164–67.
[2] A rough list follows, the dates being about 50 years after birth:
200 Clement of Alexandria: Tixeront 1924 I [9] 288.
235 Origen: ibid. 311 & 317.
250 Denis of Alexandria: ibid. 492–93.
250 Adamantius: ibid.
264 Gregory Thaumaturge: ibid.
325 Eustathius of Antioch: ibid. II [6] 8.

346 Athanasius: ibid. 137–38.
363 Cyril of Jerusalem: Turmel 1931 I 56.
371 Diodorus of Tarsus: Tixeront 1921 II [6] 8.
375 Gregory of Nazianzus: ibid. 145–46.
384 Gregory of Nyssa: ibid. 145.
397 John Chrysostom: ibid. 8 & 146–47.
400 Theodore of Mopsuestia: ibid. 8.

their sins, enhanced their merit, and in this way rendered them worthy of Him.

Then came Christ, with His Revelation that regeneration could come only through baptism. To be sure many of the Patriarchs and Prophets had died unbaptized and yet won salvation, but there was then the extenuating circumstance that the rite of baptism was not yet known. Those dying since Christ, however, could offer no such excuse: they had had the power to acquire the merit of wishing to be baptized; therefore their failure to exercise that power was wholly their own.

Since the descendants of Adam were each left a minimum of free will, each must technically have an equal, if slight, chance of effecting his own salvation. The Revelation of Christ's coming had been made, however, only to the Chosen People, so that the distant heathen actually had no more than the proverbial Chinaman's chance.[3] Already in the Old Revelation, therefore, lay the germ of a predestination doctrine — the suspicion of a congenital inequality of opportunity: no descendant of Adam could be called lucky, but the Jew could certainly be called the least unlucky. And the Redemption had done nothing substantial to alleviate the Chinaman's lot.

This dilemma the resourceful Origen sought to explain by the help of Greek philosophy: here, conveniently at hand, was the theory of the pre-existence of souls.[4] Man, with his myopic vision, sees injustice; God, with His telescopic vision, sees justice. The trials of man on earth are therefore most surely just penalties for misdemeanours committed by the soul before its incarnation on earth. That is why the lot of some is heavy and that of others light. No pagan argument was acceptable to Christians unless it was superlatively good. This one was so good that it was adopted not only by the Greeks but also by many Latins, until the condemnation of Origen's doctrines just before 400.[5] Yet it was never wholly satisfactory because, apart from the injustice of handicapping men on account of sins they had committed in a previous ex-

---

[3] On the Romans' knowledge of Chinamen, see Yule 1910 VI [11] 189.

[4] Turmel 1931 I 45–46.

[5] Among the Greeks were Didymus, Eusebius of Cæsarea, Pamphilius, and Gregory of Nyssa: Tixeront 1921 II [6] 5–8 & 136. Among the Latins were Victorinus: Tixeront 1921 II [6] 276, Jerome, until after 396: ibid., and Prudentius: Turmel 1931 I 73.

istence, there were no biblical texts suggesting any previous existence and no memories of it in men's minds.

In early times, when only a devout few chose to be baptized, this rite was thought virtually a guarantee of salvation: for even if it did not lead to martyrdom it expressed a willingness to face martyrdom if God so willed. Therefore only an apostate forfeited the guarantee. The unbaptized, accordingly, had free will; while the baptized, unless successfully intimidated by threats, were virtually predestined to be saved. But when, after 324, many chose to be baptized for worldly reasons, the theologians naturally preferred to restrict the baptismal guarantee to a mere fair chance of being saved.[6] This was certainly a better chance than anyone had had under the Law; the advantage, nevertheless, was in degree rather than in kind: for instead of bringing the proverbial life in place of death it simply added somewhat to man's own capacity to earn salvation. This view — of the full free will of both unbaptized and baptized — continued to be held in the West as in the East [7] until about 370, notably by Hilary of Poitiers and Optatus of Mileve.[8] But it was not destined to last, for if the advantages to be secured by baptism must now be curtailed, the disadvantages of remaining unbaptized must be accentuated; if the Redemption had raised men less high than had formerly been supposed, then the Fall must have precipitated them farther.

The plight of the Chinaman facilitated the new solution: if he was practically doomed to damnation it must seem probable that he was also theoretically doomed; if, as a matter of fact, no Chinaman ever had been saved, this was probably because God had thus predestined him. And if this were true of the unbaptized Chinaman it was probably equally true of the unbaptized Roman. The explanation must then be that Adam and his descendants had forfeited not merely the innocent Adam's power invariably to avoid sin but also the power ever to avoid it: they must sin invariably and exclusively, and the few who were saved must have obtained that boon

---

[6] See pp. 61, 268 & 337.

[7] Gregory of Nazianzus, Gregory of Nyssa, and John Chrysostom, among others, insisted on this: Tixeront 1921 II [6] 142–49.

[8] Ibid. 147 & 282. Following Tertullian: Tixeront 1924 I [9] 410.

not as an earned but as an unearned grace. Only by the baptism which the Redemption had made possible was the free will to acquire merit restored. Instead of free will changed by baptism into sure salvation, there would then be sure damnation changed by baptism into free will.

The first Latin to hold this view was apparently the African Victorinus.[9] It was an easy matter for him because, as a convert from Neoplatonism in about 355,[10] he could explain that the unbaptized had been justly condemned at birth on account of sins they had committed before. The second step — only slightly less awkward than the first — was taken by the author, known as Ambrosiaster, who in about 373 wrote his *Commentary on the Epistle to the Romans*. To him, likewise, the baptized were the undeserving recipients of a wholly gratuitous grace, while those who died unbaptized were damned through no real fault of their own.[11] But Ambrosiaster does not explain the justice of this according to any theory of past misdeeds; quite the contrary, he explains it according to a theory of future misdeeds:

These, therefore, are designedly called who, as God foreknew, would, as believers, be worthy, so that they might be known before they believed.[12]

The baptized are called because their propensities are such that, if given free will, they are likely to make good use of it; whereas the unbaptized are not called because their propensities are such that, even if they should be given free will, they would make no good use of it. To draw such men as these to baptism would be not only useless but deceitful.

The objections to this theory were serious: God can know the future as He knows the past because He is outside of time, but it is not so certain that He can also know all that might happen yet in fact does not. The justice underlying this theory is also questionable: according to it the baptized are damned, not for sins they in fact did, if involuntarily, commit, but rather for sins they might voluntarily have committed yet in fact did not. It was fundamental Christian doctrine, moreover, that not only the devil but also the world

9 Tixeront 1921 II 6 281.
10 Labriolle 1934 340.
11 *Commentaria* VIII §§ 28–29 &
IX § 28. And see Tixeront 1921 II 6 282 & 284–85.
12 *Commentaria* VIII § 28.

and man's flesh were expressly created in order to force man to actualize his propensities before being judged. Whereas according to Ambrosiaster those who died unbaptized must have been equally damned had there been no devil, world, or flesh.

Observe, however, that Victorinus and Ambrosiaster have one point in common: both suppose that, already at birth, some men were more crippled than others. Thus, if their conclusion was welcome, their reasons were unwelcome, and not only as dogma but also as morals. The task which Ambrose undertook between 386 and 390 [13] was to reach this new conclusion by a process of reasoning that must command respect.

If infants who died unbaptized were damned, and yet not because of sins which they had committed in a previous life [14] or might have come to commit in this life, it must be because of some sin common to all the descendants of Adam. And did not the Bible say that all shared his guilt and punishment? But how could this justly be? At this point Ambrose rejected the traducianist theory,[15] according to which every soul actually existed in Adam and therefore sinned as so many parts of his soul. But he was not squeamish about adopting the alternative creationist theory:

Before our birth we are tainted with contagion, and before we enjoy the light we receive injury in our very origin and are conceived in wickedness. . . . The mother generates each human being in transgressions. . . . Conception is not free from wickedness, since the parents are not without concupiscence. And, if the babe of a single day is not without sin, much more are those days of the mother's conception not without sin. So we are conceived in the sin of our parents, and in their transgressions we are born.[16]

Having explained why it is reasonable to believe that every man is born equally guilty, Ambrose proceeds to show how it happens that, although many are damned, a few are saved. And first he shows that those who die unbaptized are damned, not because they freely choose not to be baptized, but be-

---

[13] See Dudden 1935 688, 692–94, & 701–02. The *De Mysteriis*, however, cannot be dated: ibid. 698.

[14] Dudden 1935 507. Although Turmel 1931 I 63 seems to think that

Ambrose's use of the word *revolans* indicates otherwise.

[15] Dudden 1935 507.

[16] *De Apologia Prophetae David* § 56.

cause they have been deprived of even that free will which might have enabled them to choose: God

separates the Christian from the Law. Lest the unwilling might seem to succumb to the Law He calls him to the Gospel which the willing both preach and abide by.[17]

The only cleverness of the contracted soul is its power to mislead.[18]

Man cannot take any direction unless he has God going before him.[19]

In fact the unbaptized is not even entered in the competition:

No one is admitted to the contest of virtue unless, having previously been cleansed of every spot of sin, he shall be consecrated with the gift of heavenly grace.[20]

According to what principle God chooses whom He shall grace and whom He shall not, Ambrose does not profess to know:

For him whom He has mercy on He calls.[21]

God calls those whom He deigns to call, and makes religious whom He chooses.[22]

But Ambrose is very careful to avoid any suggestion that the divine choice is determined by human merit — for in that case grace would not be a gift but a reward.

The grace thus arbitrarily and gratuitously given takes the form of a will to be baptized. He next explains the effect produced by this rite:

Peter was clean, yet He was obliged to wash his heel; for he was guilty by his inheritance from the first man when the serpent tripped him up and seduced him into error. For that reason his heel was washed: in order that our hereditary sins might be removed — for our own are washed away by baptism.[23]

Thus baptism by immersion[24] served only one purpose: to pardon the personal sins committed during life. It did nothing to make it easier to avoid future sin. But the baptism by a washing of the feet, which at that time accompanied the

---

[17] *Letter # 37 § 22.*
[18] Ibid. # 41 § 6.
[19] *Expos. Ev. sec. Lucam* II § 84.
[20] Ibid. IV § 4.
[21] Ibid. I § 10.

[22] Ibid. VII § 27.
[23] *De Mysteriis* § 32. And cf. *In Psalm. 48 enarr.* 9.
[24] See p. 455 n. 5.

other, removed the inherited guilt, removed a part, at least, of the penalty imposed on account of that guilt. That penalty comprised a variety of punishments: mortality, bodily pain, and toil, and also ignorance of God's ways and incapacity to serve Him. It was not the bodily penalties which were removed by the foot-washing — for these manifestly subsisted — but the spiritual penalties: by this rite man again became aware of God and thereby re-acquired so much of the free will of the innocent Adam as enabled him to choose some good in addition to much evil:

Jew under the Law, Christian through the Gospel; under the Law servitude, in the Gospel that freedom which comes from an understanding of true wisdom.[25]

The double rite of baptism having been performed, man can now, if he chooses, acquire merit, and this merit in turn induces God to bestow further grace:

It suits God that those whom He shall have invited through grace, He should carry forward with increases of His grace. To this end He bestows a gift on us even before — through baptism — and afterwards more liberally to those who serve Him well. In this way the benefactions of Christ are both incentives to and rewards of virtue.[26]

Only the Christian has free will. The heathen must passively wait for the chance that God will grace him with the desire to be baptized. Unless this comes — and he cannot raise a finger to invite it — he must die damned.[27]

The desire to be, and the act of being, baptized, was therefore purely a matter of good luck. Many of the baptized were, like the unbaptized, being damned for their sins, but, unlike the unbaptized, they had no one to blame but themselves. And the baptized who were saved, while they could attribute this in part to their own merit, must attribute it no

[25] *Letter* # 37 § 22.
[26] Ibid. # 41 § 6.
[27] See Tixeront 1921 II[6] 282. Dudden 1935 632–33 cites certain passages of Ambrose indicating that none lose free will. But the quotations on p. 633 notes 2, 4, & 5 are addressed in the first or second persons and therefore to Christians; that of n. 3 suggests that grace is resistible, but is not specific; that of n. 1 says that the Israelites received a resistible grace, but this must have seemed to Ambrose to correspond to the Christian grace of baptism. At most Ambrose may have thought that the grace to wish to be baptized was also resistible, although how an unbaptized had any capacity not to resist would be hard to explain.

less to the lucky chance that God chose to give them the free
will with which to acquire that merit.

Here, in Ambrosiaster and especially in Ambrose, is the
germ of predestination grown to adolescence. That the
Chinaman, in spite of his free will, had no chance, did not
seem fair; but that the hopelessly sinful Chinaman had no
chance, seemed wholly fair. To be sure the Christian had got
something for nothing; but that was no just reason why all
Chinamen should also get something for nothing. To give
one beggar a penny is no injustice to the other beggars. True
the Chinaman was unlucky, but that was all he deserved.
Moreover it was salutary for the lucky man to know that he
was lucky, for this must serve to chasten his pride, inducing
that sense of gratitude and humility which even the baptized
must cherish if his luck were to last.

By this doctrine too is the germ of original sin grown to adolescence. Everyone not born as Adam was — in the Garden
of Eden, immortal, with the capacity, if he chose, never to
sin — must be in some degree the victim of original sin,
predestined to suffering and death, to ignorance, to the commission of many sins. But according to the old Greek theory
no man was ever predestined to hell; every man could win
salvation if only he would. The new Latin theory, on the
other hand, extended the penalty of original sin to include,
for some, an inevitable hell; in the words of Ambrosiaster
mankind, as Adam had left it, ' sinned virtually in a lump.' [28]
Out of it God chose a man here and there as a vessel of grace;
as a beast, marked for slaughter, is let loose to be the sport of
the huntsmen and to escape if he can.

In the course of this evolution of ideas from the earlier
Greek to the later Latin the unbaptized lost all chance to save
themselves, while the baptized lost all assurance of being
saved. By the same token the jurisdiction of the devil was
enlarged. At first it had been thought that he only controlled
as many heathens as wished to serve him, and that he lost almost all Christians. But it was now thought that he had maintained his control over all heathens, whether they liked it or
not, and also over many of the Christians. This may have

[28] ' Manifestum   itaque   est   in   massa ': *Commentaria* V § 12. See p.
Adam   omnes   peccasse   quasi   in   75.

been one reason why in the later fourth century many returned to Origen's theory that most, if not all, would eventually be saved. Gregory of Nyssa actually believed that all
would be; [29] Ambrosiaster excluded only those idolaters who
had actually spurned baptism; [30] Ambrose,[31] Rufinus,[32] and
Jerome [33] thought that all who had been baptized, but no
others, would in time be purged and saved. It is Ambrose
who marks the culmination of Christian self-satisfaction: all
the unbaptized are predestined to damnation; all the baptized are predestined to be saved.

To such a point had the doctrine of free will proceeded
when the fourth century closed. Steps of vital importance
had been taken, but there had been little or no open controversy, with the result that the deep and elusive issues
involved had not been sharply defined. The theologians,
indeed, were here still groping in a fog of uncertainty, favouring those views which at any given time seemed the
most expedient or salutary, without much regard for consistency. Their doctrines seem rather emanations than creations,
rather instruments of nature than of art. Then, shortly after
410, the Briton Pelagius took up the problem in earnest, and
a controversy arose in the West which subjected every aspect
and consequence of the doctrines to the eye of the theological
microscope. Within a generation blind tendencies and inclinations gave way to highly co-ordinated systems each of
which cut to the core of Christian doctrine.

B. Augustine on Free Will

This controversy over free will was the first in which Latin
Christianity played a leading part. Precipitated by Pelagius

---

29 Tixeront 1921 II [6] 199–200.
30 Ibid. 340.
31 Dudden 1935 658 & 663.
32 Tixeront 1921 II [6] 335–36.
33 But only so long as he stood by
Origen and Rufinus, or until 396.
On the question of free will Jerome
was confused: in *Letter* # 122, § 3
(*C.S.E.L.* 56 68 line 13) he says ' for

we do not what we would but what
we would not '; & cf. # 132 § 6. And
in *Dialogus adversus Pelagianos* I
§ 24 he says that grace may even be
irresistible: ' God, if He chooses, can
keep a man free from sin.' But he
seems to favour free will in *Letter*
130 § 12, and in *Dialogus adv.
Pelag.* I § 13, & III §§ 1, 10, & 12.

of Britain, raised to philosophic heights by Augustine of
Africa, it became the most perplexing and engrossing problem of the fifth century Latin Church. That at a time when
civilization was crumbling, the best minds should have concentrated on this most abstruse of questions, is the best
possible explanation of why civilization fell. Perhaps the
spiritual and material are equally essential human preoccupations; if either one acquires a preponderance, sooner or later
a compensating reaction must set in, and, as this reaction
gathers momentum, the preponderance is not only eliminated
but reversed. Thus the excess of materialism during Rome's
political prime led, in the third century, to a reversal of the
current, which, gathering headway, swept by the neutral
point of equilibrium to a preponderance of the spiritual.
This book is a general history of Latin thought in the fifth
century. That the Latins dwelt hardly at all on political,
economic, or scientific matters, but almost exclusively on
theology, is a fact which the historian cannot ignore. Thus
elementary honesty must lead us to the centre of that thought,
where we find Augustine; and from there to the centre of his
thought as distinguished from that of the Church tradition,
where we find his doctrine of predestination.

This doctrine, which he evolved in order to determine
precisely in what sense God was everything and man nothing,
is as elusive as it is lucid. It is exceptionally hard for us to
understand, chiefly because we have never made the effort.
In the sixteenth century, when the Calvinists revived his
doctrine, and in the seventeenth when the Jansenists also accepted it, the problem was understood because it tortured
the minds of many of the greatest men of that time. Today
it is academic history, but, since it was not such in the fifth
and sixth centuries, nor in the sixteenth and seventeenth,
its future recrudescence is still a contingency — the more so
because it raises — quite apart from formal religion — not
only a fundamental, but also an unsolved, issue. Are we
guided by some force outside ourselves, are we wholly free,
are we limited by inheritance or environment and, if so, in
what ways and to what degree? The problem still smoulders
in each of us. We have not resolved it; we merely shy at it,

just as Augustine shied at other problems — as of science —
which we face without a qualm.

Of course Augustine was neither a discoverer nor a pioneer
in this study: the mystery of Fate is as old as the mystery of
man's consciousness. But the Fate of the early Greek, of the
Manichee and Neoplatonist, was now discredited, discarded
in favour of a living God. The old Fate had been dead and
blind, indifferent to right and wrong; the new Fate was alive
and omniscient, indifferent to all else but right and wrong.
The earlier Christian theologians had, as we have seen, attacked the hoary problem in the light of Revelation; they
had struggled to raise God to the pinnacle of power; but because they divided Him into at least two parts and recognized
the devil as an independent power, they did not dethrone
Fate. Instead, in the guise of a Justice which knew too little
of mercy, they left Fate shaken but intact.[1]

But with polytheism, even in this most attenuated and sub-
limated form, Augustine had no patience. God, Christ, Justice, and Mercy, were one and omnipotent; the devil was
nothing and Fate in the old sense a delusion. For the only
Fate was the divine love. Surely the whole world, with its
men and its events, could have no other cause. Dead matter
could initiate no cause; nor could man — slave to his evil
desires. God loved man because his soul could still conceive
of the good, conceive of loving and of the pleasure such love
must bring. Yet man, although he might wish to try to
love virtue, could not try; he must instead, without trying,
love himself and his carnal life. What fool, then, would put
his faith in man? Could Divinity have been so foolish as to
create such a being? From the pessimism of the worldly-wise,
Augustine was saved, as if miraculously, by the story of Adam,
by whom man came into this plight, and of Christ, by whom
man might be extricated from it.

Augustine's first assumption is that Adam was given the divine gift or grace [2] of a really free will:

For he could persevere if he would, but that he would not was the
result of free will, which at that time was in such wise free that he
was capable of willing well and ill.[3]

[1] See pp. 61–62.   [3] Ibid. § 32. Cf. ibid. §§ 31 & 33.
[2] *De Correptione et Gratia* §§ 29 &
31.

And since God was outside of time, and yet Adam was really free, God

foreknew what he [Adam] would do in unrighteousness; foreknew, however, but did not compel him to this.[4]

By his sin Adam incurred not only guilt but its penalty:

In original sin there are two things, sin and punishment.[5]

It followed, however, out of the penalty which was justly due for such a defect, that henceforth it became difficult to be obedient unto righteousness; and, unless this defect were overcome by assisting grace, no one would turn to righteousness.[6]

And this guilt arising from a past sin and the weakness of will imposed as its penalty, were both transmitted to all the descendants of Adam.[7] It is true that Augustine insisted that man's will was still free, but in a very different sense now:

Who of us will say that by the sin of the first man free will perished from the human race? Through sin freedom indeed perished, but it was that freedom . . . to live well and righteously.[8]

Since Adam man's will has been

free, but not freed — free from righteousness, but enslaved to sin.[9]

Man has therefore been deprived of the capacity to choose either good or evil; his only choice now is between alternative evils. He can sin merely from weakness and with a bad conscience,[10] or by adopting an heretical faith,[11] or by acting, even beneficently, from fear rather than from love of God,[12] or again

either by ignorance of the truth or by delight in iniquity, or by both evils — as well of blindness as of weakness.[13]

---

[4] Ibid. § 37. Cf. *Enchiridion* 104, & *D.C.D.* XIV 11.

[5] *D.C.D.* XXII 24 (*D. & K.* II 610 lines 8–9).

[6] *De Pecc. Meritis* II § 33. Cf. ibid. § 36.

[7] Ibid. I § 33.

[8] *Contra duas Epist. Pelag.* I § 5.

[9] *De Corr. et Gratia* § 42. Cf. *De Spiritu et Littera* § 5; *De Pecc. Meritis* II § 5; *Contra duas Epist.*

Pelag. I § 6, & III § 24; & *De Natura et Gratia* § 79. Ambrose *De Joseph Patriarcha* ch. IV § 20 says: ' Servile est omne peccatum, libera est innocentia.'

[10] *De Gratia Christi* I § 13.

[11] *Contra duas Epist. Pelag.* III § 14.

[12] Ibid. II § 21, & III §§ 9 & 11.

[13] Ibid. I § 7. Cf. ibid. § 5.

Yet it cannot be said that a man is prevented from doing a truly righteous deed by any other power or agency than himself. Not only is he his own worst enemy, he is his only enemy. For the devil, if he can accentuate a proclivity, cannot initiate one. It is not true, therefore, as the pagan faiths had alleged, that

' all are forced into sin by the necessity of their own flesh ', rather . . . they are both retained in sin by their own will, and by their own will are hurried along from sin to sin.[14]

One of his analogies seems particularly apt:

What, then, if another should say: ' inasmuch as not to wish for unhappiness is ours, we are able both to wish for it and not to wish for it '? And yet we are positively unable to wish for it. For who could possibly wish to be unhappy? [15]

Therefore just as a man never really tries to be unhappy and consequently never seriously wishes to try, so man never really tries to be righteous and consequently never seriously wishes to try. To say that he can try but can never succeed is another way of saying the same thing: for the fact is that the will, because of the penalty of weakness it incurred, somehow or other invariably fails.[16]

Without grace, therefore, no man can act righteously in the sight of God, can do any slightest thing to please Him. Augustine, however, often uses the word grace more loosely: to mean any gift of God. Since to him there was no real distinction between the natural and supernatural,[17] everything, from Creation onward, was a gift, and so a grace, of God. Such, for instance, was Adam's free will.[18] So is our human reason:

Let the grace, therefore, whereby we are living and reasonable creatures, and are distinguished from cattle, be attributed to nature.[19]

[14] *Contra duas Epist. Pelag.* I § 7.
[15] *De Natura et Gratia* § 57. Cf. *Contra duas Epist. Pelag.* I § 10. Salvian *D.G.D.* III § 11 says: ' Even if a man compels himself to do so [love his enemies], still it is his lips alone that act, and not his mind; he lends the service of his voice to the action without changing the feeling of his heart. Therefore even if he forces himself to say a prayer for his adversary, his lips move, but he does not really pray.'
[16] Cf. Nicole (born in 1625) *Des Manières dont on tente Dieu* chs. 5 & 6; & *De la Charité et de l'Amour-propre* ch. 1.
[17] See pp. 123 & 216.
[18] See p. 129.
[19] *De Predest. Sanctorum* § 10. Cf. *Letter # 177* § 7.

Besides this purely natural grace is another, namely

that grace whereby God points out and reveals to us what we are bound to do, but not that whereby He endows and assists us to act.[20]

This grace is the Law of the Old Testament:

The man, however, who has learned what ought to be done, but does it not, has not yet been ' taught by God ' according to [true] grace, but only according to the Law.[21]

Thus a man may have received the grace of nature and the grace of Law — may therefore distinguish right and wrong and understand what the Law asks of him — but unless he also has the grace of the Holy Ghost made available to man through Christ, he can work no righteousness and cannot be saved.

Just as the preliminary grace of reason makes the second grace of learning more likely to follow, so the grace of learning in its turn makes the third grace, of contrition, more likely to follow. This latter includes a capacity as well as a wish to be baptized, but it includes only a wish, not a capacity, to be righteous. Baptism is not, therefore, a fourth grace, because once the third grace, of contrition, has been received, baptism is no longer a contingency but an inevitable and invariable consequence. If a man, contrite and therefore intending to be baptized at the earliest opportunity, dies before this is possible, he is deemed a Christian; [22] if, on the other hand, he dies while not so intending he is deemed not to have been contrite. Furthermore if a man who is not contrite chooses nevertheless to be baptized, such baptism is inoperative until he repent.[23] A baptized person may die with all his inherited and pre-baptismal personal sin still unexpiated; an unbaptized person may die pardoned of these sins and hence in that state of grace which saves. Therefore

---

[20] *De Gratia Christi* I § 9. See, however, that part of *Letter* # 186 § 11 which was incorporated as canon # 9 of the Second Council of Orange in 529.

[21] *De Gratia Christi* I § 14.

[22] Tixeront 1921 II [6] 410.

[23] Ibid. 404–05. Tertullian had said no less two hundred years earlier: Tixeront 1924 I [9] 431, and on this account disapproved of infant baptism: ibid. 432, since he of course regarded original sin merely as a weakness and not also as a guilt: ibid. 408. Cf. pp. 86–87.

baptism proves nothing, adds nothing to what the grace of contritely wishing to be baptized has already conferred.

The predecessors of Augustine thought that this third grace which induces contrition conferred not only pardon for all past sins, both inherited and personal, but also that free will which, if it could not avoid all sin, could at least acquire a real merit and thus earn further grace.[24] Augustine agreed that it pardoned,[25] but he denied that it in any way revived the free will occasionally to be righteous and so to acquire merit: for

it does not remove the weakness.[26]

That is, the weakness which prevents man from ever having a good thought or acting from a righteous motive.   So, although it is

the grace of forgiveness of sins,[27]

neither the knowledge of God's Law, nor nature, nor the mere remission of sins is that grace which is given us through our Lord Jesus Christ,[28]

which is that of the Holy Ghost made available by the Redemption.

By its capacity to pardon, however, the third grace of contrition can save in the rare case of those adults who

quit this life immediately after baptism [29]

---

24 See pp. 60, & 386–88.

25 De Pecc. Meritis I § 23, & II §§ 4 & 44; & Contra duas Epist. Pelag. III § 5.   According to Hefele 1908 II² 110, the Council of Carthage of 398 contained in canon # 1 the words ' tam illud originale contractum, quam illa quae voluntarie admissa sunt.'

26 Contra duas Epist. Pelag. III § 5.   Cf. De Pecc. Meritis II §§ 4, 44 & 46.

Tixeront 1921 II⁶ 496, while admitting that, according to Augustine, man cannot earn either the first or the last grace, maintains that he ' can, if he has faith, in a certain sense earn both the grace to act virtuously and also justification.' And in support of this view he quotes a passage in Augustine Letter # 194 § 9, written to Sixtus III — who was then a deacon — in 419: ' But the re-

mission of sins itself is not without some merit, if faith brings this to pass; for the merit of faith is not a nothing.' But even if faith is meritorious it does not remove the weakness or incapacity to act virtuously, nor does it do anything to attract true grace. I cannot see, therefore, in what ' certain sense ' this faith could, according to Augustine, ' earn both the grace to act virtuously and also justification '. Since Sixtus had so recently been a Pelagian, Augustine did not want to bear down too hard; therefore he says in effect: undeniably faith ' is not a nothing '; and since it is certainly not a demerit it ' is not without some merit '. But this merit, being itself unearned, earns nothing.

27 De Pecc. Meritis I § 55.

28 De Gratia et Lib. Arb. I § 27.

29 De Pecc. Meritis II § 46.

— or so long as their state of desire to be righteous subsists —
for, having no time to sin again,

there would be nothing at all left to hold him liable.[30]

In one case, moreover, baptism invariably does constitute
grace, and often saving grace: where it is administered to an
infant too young ever to have been guilty of personal sin.
Here baptism is valid as forgiveness of original sin apart from
any contrition: whereas the infant who dies unbaptized is
damned, he who dies baptized is saved.[31]   In this exceptional
case only is baptism, rather than contrition, itself the grace.

The ground is now prepared for the planting of the fourth
grace and the first bestowed by the Holy Ghost.   This is the
gift of strength to love, and to resist weakness.   For the mere
third grace of contrition — to wish to love — although it
must rouse a man to be baptized, confers no power to achieve
that wish:

By such grace is it effected, not only that we discover what ought
to be done, but also that we do what we have discovered; not only
that we believe what ought to be loved, but also that we love what
we have believed.[32]

This true belief is not merely a change of conviction but a
change of heart:

If this grace be called ' teaching ', let it at any rate be so called in
such wise that God may be believed to infuse it . . . in such a way
that He not only exhibits truth but imparts love. . . .

    [For] the surest sign that you have been taught by God is that
you put into practice what you have been taught.[33]

---

[30] Ibid. Cf. *De Spiritu et Littera*
§ 58, written in 412: ' When it happens that infidels act contrary to the
will of God — as when they will not
believe in His Gospel — they do not
on that account conquer it, rather
they deprive themselves of the great
and highest good and get entangled
in evil ways and punishments,
thereby making trial of His power in
punishments whose mercy, in the
form of gifts, they spurn.' Does this
passage suggest a real free will? The
gift of faith, like that of teaching, is
not true grace; its acceptance, even if
there be contrition and hence a valid
baptism, is not effectively meritorious because it involves no act of vir-

tue or love, but merely feeble good
intentions. Yet he who is baptized
and dies immediately thereafter, is
saved, just as would be the infant
whose parents manifested a similar
feeble good intention in his behalf.
If even such persons are saved by free
will there is no invariable predestination to salvation or damnation. Yet
if these inconsequential decisions are
not free, no human decisions are free.
  [31] Cf. *De Pecc. Meritis* I § 70.
  [32] *De Gratia Christi* I § 13. Cf.
Ibid. I § 10: ' And the love of God is
not shed abroad in our hearts by the
Law, but by the Holy Ghost, which is
given to us.'
  [33] *De Pecc. Meritis* I § 14.

To Augustine this grace to love — and so to feel and act as a true lover must — is irresistible. It does not, as did the grace of free will bestowed on Adam, allow a rejection of the gift:

This first is the grace which was given to the first Adam, but more powerful is that in the second [or redeemed descendant of] Adam. For the first is that whereby it is effected that a man may have righteousness *if* he will; the second, therefore, can do more than this, since it is thereby further effected *that* he will.[34]

This grace does not impose or even permit a perfect virtue and righteousness — this state is reserved for the blessed in heaven.[35]   On earth there must still be passion and desire, but there is no longer a capacity to give in to these.   There will still be evil thoughts and temptations — imperfection — but, so long as the grace persists, no voluntary yielding to them.[36]

The grace, however, may not persist; though it be irresistible while it does, it may well lapse.   For men may

receive the grace of God, but only for a season, so that they do not persevere.[37]

And,

were that [grace] only to withdraw itself, man falls, not raised up, but precipitated, by free will.[38]

It is, indeed, to be wondered at . . . that to some . . . to whom He has given faith, hope, and love, God does not give perseverance also, when to the children of another He forgives so much wickedness, and, by the bestowal of His grace, makes them His own children.[39]

So the fourth grace of strength to love, because it is ephemeral, is not enough; to it must be added the fifth grace of perseverance which alone can save.[40]   How is this to be procured? Usually, we are told, it follows the fourth grace — because

---

34 *De Corr. et Gratia* § 31.   Cf. ibid. §§ 33, 34, 38 & 42; *De Gratia et Lib. Arb.* § 31; & *De Predest. Sanctorum* § 30.

35 *De Perfectione Justiciae* § 8; *Contra duas Epist. Pelag.* III § 17.

36 *De Natura et Gratia* § 72; *De Gestis Pelagi* § 36; *Contra duas Epist. Pelag.* I §§ 18, 24 & 28.

37 *De Corr. et Gratia* § 42.

38 *De Gratia et Lib. Arb.* § 13.

39 *De Corr. et Gratia* § 18.   Cf. *De Dono Persev.* § 1, & *De Corr. et Gratia* § 16.

40 *De Corr. et Gratia* § 38; & *De Dono Persev.* § 10.

the virtue engendered by it attracts this fifth.[41] But since, although a usual consequence of good behaviour, it is not a consequence of merit, the man who has received this grace of love is as helpless to procure that of perseverance as is the most ungodly. He is more likely to receive it,[42] but he can do nothing to encourage its coming. Why must this be?

Because Augustine relied on the truth of this passage in 1 *Corinthians* iv 7:

For who maketh thee to differ from another? And what hast thou that thou didst not receive? Now if thou didst receive it, why dost thou glory, as if thou hadst not received it?

For to Augustine [43] as to Paul it was clear enough that men did differ, but no less clear that it was not the men themselves who were the cause of this. Therefore it was God who was the cause, of all virtue as of all grace, and man no cause of anything good:

And what is more ungrateful than to deny the grace of God itself, by saying that it is given to us according to our merits? [44] The enemy of grace presses on and urges in all ways to make us believe that grace is given according to our deservings, and thus grace is no more grace.[45]

Nor is this true merely of the preliminary graces; it is true of all grace including the saving grace of perseverance:

God does not, for any merits of our own, but from His own divine compassion, prolong our existence to everlasting life.[46]

---

[41] Cf. pp. 416–17 on Cassian, and p. 441 n. 27 on Faustus of Riez.

[42] Cassian *Conlationes* XXIII 10 explains the passages of Paul on which Augustine relies, as referring to Paul himself and so to the obstacles confronting a saint approaching perfection, and as not referring to the obstacles confronting the average sinner.

[43] In *De Gratia et Lib. Arb.* § 4 Augustine says: ' When, wishing, a man acts, then it must be called a good act, then the reward of the good work must be hoped for from Him of whom it was said: *Who renders unto each according to his works.*' *Matt.* xvi 27). Now virtuous acts are an invariable result of the receipt of grace; these acts deserve their reward. But as the man did not earn the reward — since his power was a gift — although he could hope for the reward he could not claim that he was in any way fairly entitled to it. He could hope for persevering grace, but he could not complain if it did not come. If it did not come the past good acts would quickly be more than cancelled by the inevitable bad acts, so that, when he died and was damned, it would still have been rendered to him according to his works.

[44] *De Dono Persev.* § 56.

[45] Ibid. § 40.

[46] *De Gratia et Lib. Arb.* § 21.

It follows then, dearly beloved, that, since your good life is nothing else than God's grace, so is the eternal life — which is the reward of a good life — also the grace of God; moreover it is given gratuitously, even as that [grace to lead a good life] is given gratuitously on account of which it [the grace of eternal life] is given. . . . Grace is for grace.[47]

The good angels, to be sure, but only they — because they were able to sin and yet did not — received the grace of eternal life as a reward of merit.[48] Could living men acquire merit they could properly boast of it; and, were this so, pride, the most insidious of sins, must cease to be such.[49] If it be merit which draws grace to itself, why do we pray for the salvation of evil men,[50] why do we pray ourselves — if we can earn the desired reward as of right? Not even the man-Christ acquired any merit; [51] nor the thief on the cross.[52]

And yet, in spite of this, man's will is never forced. All grace must remain ineffectual unless his will co-operates:

Nobody can be helped who does not make some effort of his own.[53]

No one is forced by God's power unwillingly into either evil or good, but . . . when God assists, without deserving he is converted to good.[54]

In fact the will is actually freed by grace:

Do we then by grace make void free will? God forbid. We rather establish that faculty. . . . Free will is not made void by grace, rather it is thereby established. . . . Through grace comes a cleansing of the soul from the vice of sin; through this cleansing of the soul comes freedom of will.[55]

But it is a queer kind of freedom: unlike that bestowed on Adam and the very antithesis of the will to sin; for whereas

the first liberty of the will was to be able not to sin, the last will be much greater, not to be able to sin.[56]

47 *De Gratia et Lib. Arb.* § 20.
48 *De Corr. et Gratia* § 32.
49 *De Natura et Gratia* §§ 33–36, & 38 & 42.
50 *Contra duas Epist. Pelag.* I § 37; *De Dono Persev.* § 65.
51 *De Pecc. Meritis* II § 38; *De Predest. Sanctorum* § 30. Being incapable of sin because of the irresistibility of the grace he had.

52 *De Pecc. Meritis* I § 31; *De Anima et eius Origine* II 14.
53 *De Pecc. Meritis* II § 6. Cf. *Letter # 214* § 7; & *De Spiritu et Littera* § 53.
54 *Contra duas Epist. Pelag.* I § 36.
55 *De Spiritu et Littera* § 52. Cf. *De Gratia Christi* I § 14, quoting *Psalm # 119 68.*
56 *De Corr. et Gratia* § 33.

Through grace man is given the free will of God, who cannot sin.

Yet it is still man's will, and man's will only, that wills:

The soul cannot receive and possess these gifts . . . except by yielding its own consent. So that whatever it possesses and whatever it receives, is from God and belongs to God, and yet the act of receiving and having belongs, of course, to the receiver and possessor.[57]

For

though it is He who makes us act by applying efficacious powers to our will, it is certain that it is we who act when we act.[58]

A strange kind of co-operation and obedience this, by human wills incapable of righteousness, incapable of a single meritorious thought or act.   Remember that to Augustine man was ethically nothing. He was merely so much raw material out of which God, by His grace and mercy, could fashion virtue.   There is a Platonic remnant here — of evil as non-being, but the solution is not Platonic for the real is not Virtue but virtuous individuals, it is not a unity but a multiplicity.   Yet if the only source of virtue is God's grace, how can there be a multiplicity of virtue and so of virtuous men? Augustine did not, as did the medieval scholastics, try to evolve a physics of individuality. He would have preferred an image to an analysis. Let man without grace be sound, and let God write the music. God here needs sound as much as sound needs God. Because God writes the music must He ever re-write the same piece? Are the Fugues of Bach identical because he wrote them all? Would it have been better had he written only one, leaving the rest to others? God is Himself virtue. Who shall write so well of it as He? Who is fitter than He to vary the themes? Because each piece betrays the hand of the master, is it therefore without individuality? Because each saint will be virtuous must he on that account cease to be himself? No. That was the pagan conception.[59]   In Christianity, on the contrary, there is a great va-

---

[57] *De Spiritu et Littera* § 60.
[58] *De Gratia et Lib. Arb.* § 32.
[59] This seems to me just as conceivable, and far more spiritual, a doctrine than that of Aquinas, who argued that form by itself was identical in all men until differentiated by its junction with variegated matter (See Gilson 1927 [3] 183 n. 1). For if God can create variety in matter, He

riety in virtue, and therefore — although Catholic biographers too often forget the fact — saints differ from one another in many more essential ways than in the accidents of time and place. Let Augustine's own earthly pilgrimage bear witness!

But if, without grace, man's will is merely an automatic force or propensity equal in all men — a substance inflammable but incapable of spontaneous combustion — of what use in that case is human effort? Technically it is of no use, but it is infinitely consoling because effort is itself evidence of an incipient grace.[60] For it is a gift of God even to ask for faith, and a true grace to live by it:

The surest sign that you have been taught by God is that you put into practice what you have been taught.[61]

Yet even apparently good thoughts and acts are not sure signs of true grace because that which is thought or done either from fear of God [62] or in the hope of earthly reward,[63] however virtuous it may appear even to the man himself, is not virtue.

Is it not, however, most dangerous to preach this doctrine of man's helplessness? Many of Augustine's Sermons seem so explicitly to teach that man possesses the free will of the first Adam, that some have supposed either a real inconsistency or an evolution in his conception of the problem. Yet Augustine has fearlessly given his own explanation. He says, to be sure,

The enemy of grace presses on and urges in all ways to make us believe that grace is given according to our deservings, and thus grace is no more grace; and are we unwilling to say what we can say by the testimony of Scripture? [64]

Yet he also says

---

may also create variety in virtue. Contrasted with Aquinas' Platonic conception of the simplicity of perfection and divinity, is this conception of Augustine's of an increasing complexity in the higher essences, which accords far better with modern conceptions. Certainly to Augustine God seemed infinitely complex!

[60] *De Pecc. Meritis* II § 33; *De Perfectione Justiciae* § 20. Cf. *Letter* # 215 § 8.

[61] *De Gratia Christi* I § 14.

[62] Ibid. II 29; *Contra duas Epist. Pelag.* II § 21.

[63] *Contra duas Epist. Pelag.* III §§ 9 & 11.

[64] See p. 397 n. 45.

It is easy, nay, and it is useful, that some truth should be kept back because of those who are incapable of apprehending it.[65]

And a few moments later he says,

For it is not . . . desirable, but abominable, and it is excessively harsh and hateful, to fly as it were into the face of an audience with abuse, when he who speaks to them says, ' and if there are any of you who obey, and yet are predestined to be rejected, the power of obedience shall be withdrawn from you, that you may cease to obey '. . . . Doubtless this is very true, assuredly it is; but it is very monstrous, very inconsiderate, and very unsuitable, not by its false declaration, but by its declaration not wholesomely applied to the health of human infirmity.[66]

Finally, in order to show that it is not the doctrine of predestination alone which must be preached with circumspection, he observes how

even the foreknowledge of God, which certainly men cannot deny, seems to be refuted if it be said to them, ' whether you run or sleep you shall be that which He who cannot be deceived has foreknown you to be '. . . . But it must be said ' So run that you may lay hold '.[67]

Truly Adam has put not only his descendants but God Himself in a dilemma:

God no doubt wishes all to be saved . . . yet not so as to take away from them their liberty of will.[68]

And the consequence is that, contrary to God's hope,[69]

in comparison with those that perish *few*, but in their absolute number *many*, are delivered.[70]

Therefore

what is written, that *He wills all men to be saved* [1 *Tim.* ii 4], while yet all men are not saved, may be understood in many ways, some of which I have mentioned in other writings [71] of mine; but here I will say one thing: *He wills all men to be saved* is so said that all the predestined may be understood by it, because every kind of man is among them.[72]

[65] *Contra duas Epist. Pelag.* III §§ 9 & 11.
[66] Ibid. § 61.
[67] Ibid. § 57.
[68] *De Spiritu et Littera* § 58.
[69] See *Enchiridion* 97 & 103.

[70] *De Corr. et Gratia* § 28.
[71] *Enchiridion* 97 & 103; *D.C.D.* XXII 1 & 2; *Contra Sec. Juliani Resp.* IV § 8.
[72] *De Corr. et Gratia* § 44.

How much better then is it that I should . . . simply hold what I
see the Apostle has most plainly taught us: that . . . to those
whom He has predestined to eternal death, He is also the most
righteous awarder of punishment, not only on account of the sins
which they add in the indulgence of their own will, but also because of their original sin, even if, as in the case of infants, they
add nothing thereto.[73]

Now it might be, in fact had been,[74] maintained that God
predestined certain men to eternal death as a punishment for
the sins which His foreknowledge told Him must be committed. The punishment would then be foreordained only
because the sin was foreseen. This may properly be said of
Adam's sin, because Adam was free to choose good or evil;
but in the case of Adam's descendants God foreordained that,
without grace, they could not choose other than evil. And
grace too was foreordained, so that those who did not in fact
receive it were foreordained both not to receive it and not to
will righteousness.[75] Except in the case of Adam, therefore,
God's foreknowledge was superfluous.

How could Augustine, with his enlightened perceptions,
accept so harsh a doctrine? Partly because it tallied with his

[73] *De Anima et eius Origine* IV
16.
[74] By Ambrosiaster, see p. 383; and
cf. p. 414 ns. 55 & 56.
[75] Duchesne 1925 IV 515 n. 1
says ' Saint Augustin n'enseignait pas
la prédestination au mal, *ad culpam*,
mais seulement la prédestination au
châtiment, *ad poenam*, en ce sens que
ceux que la miséricorde de Dieu
n'avait pas prédestinés au salut éter-
nel, tombaient comme toute la *massa
perditionis* sous le coup des peines
par lesquelles la justice divine ven-
geait la faute originelle.' That is,
since Adam was not predestined to
sin, neither were any of his descendants. Only after Adam had sinned
could God know apart from foreknowledge that every man who was
not given persevering grace must be
damned. If not a specious, it is certainly an academic distinction. So
we may say, especially in view of
Duchesne's statement in 1911 III 4
274–75, that he recognizes Augus-

tine's doctrine as one of predestination.
    Gilson, on the other hand, in 1929
195, says ' la grâce augustinienne
peut donc être irrésistible sans être
contraignante ' because it is still
man's will that makes the choice
And on 196 he concludes: ' La
prédestination divine n'est donc que
la prévision infaillible de ses oeuvres
futures, par laquelle Dieu pré
pare les circonstances et les grâce
salutaires à ses élus.' It is true tha
without foreknowledge of what He
Himself will do, God cannot fore
know whom He will save and whom
He will not. But without foreknowl
edge of what any man may will –
knowing only what He shall will –
God can foreknow who will be saved
and who not. I should therefore say
that the distinction between grace
that is *irrésistible* and grace that i
contraignante is also, if not specious
at least academic.

observation of human nature, for he saw that many of those who were born mean and vicious were unable, of their own wills, to change their evil ways. And he saw too that some men were born with such gentle and humane instincts that they really enjoyed the practice of righteousness.. Since neither the evil man seemed responsible for his sins, nor the good man for his virtues, the human will or ego failed adequately to explain matters. This discovery is no more original in Augustine than it is in modern criminology; the recognition of inherited sin, indeed, is common to primitive people.[76] If a modern State nevertheless punishes a wrong-doer and calls this justice, so does the God of Augustine. Is the punishment not in both cases based rather on public expediency than on private equity? Is not the good of the individual subordinated to that of the community? Of Augustine it had been queried why, since God was good and so must wish all to be saved, He carefully refrained from bestowing His grace on all. Note Augustine's answer:

Were every man to be freed it must inevitably remain obscure what was the just penalty of sin; if no one, what grace was being bestowed.[77]

By not giving to all He has shown what all deserve.[78]

For remember that without the co-operation of the human will the grace of God is ineffectual; yet, unless this will be given an incentive to achieve righteousness, it must remain largely inert. Therefore, should God try to save all by bestowing grace on all, the co-operating human will, becoming apprised of this, would cease to strive as it must, and God, instead of saving all, would save none.[79]

As with the Redemption, the miracle, and baptism, so in the matter of free will God had, according to Augustine, resorted to a pious fraud. Augustine never openly argued that the Redemption [80] or the miracle [81] was only to impress, or

---

[76] The Neoplatonic and Manichæan theories of a previous existence of the soul presumably arose out of this realization. On the former see pp. 34–35, & 38 n. 57, on the latter see p. 340 n. 25.

[77] *Letter # 194 § 5.*

[78] *De Dono Persev.* § 28.

[79] Wesendonk 1922 34 says that the Manichees held this view, but his statement is not clear and he cites no authority.

[80] See pp. 82 n. 17, & 93 n. 58.

[81] See p. 219.

baptism only to console [82] — he would not openly betray God; but he was, under the pressure exerted by the Pelagians, driven in the last years of his life to argue that God gave man the mere illusion of a free will. For God knew that man would exert his full energy only if he believed his salvation depended on it. And in a sense, but only in a sense, man's salvation did depend on this: for, though it was true that such exertion was fruitless if not strengthened by a free grace, it was also true that without such exertion even the free grace would not strengthen. The most high-minded and judicious father habitually practises analogous deceits on his wayward children. Augustine is like the eldest of the children, who thinks he detects the fraud yet is so convinced that the motive is honourable and the effect salutary, that he is embarrassed to admit his suspicions. He blurts them out only in an extremity.

Is the punishment, however, quite consonant with the character of even a Roman father? Granted that it is not only civically salutary but also individually equitable, is it also socially impartial? This certainly, on Augustine's own admission, it is not: for, while the elect receive a reward which they do not deserve, the unelect, though no more undeserving, receive nothing. Because he conceived of justice as being solely between man and God, he insisted that the bestowal of grace on a few did not constitute ' acceptance of persons '; [83] such a discrimination was possible only if justice could be assumed as a relationship between man and man. Augustine's justice was, therefore, rather mystical and practical than sentimental and theoretical. It is the antithesis of the current doctrine that no one has a fair, unless he has an equal, chance.[84]

To Augustine the human will is a real force: not only is its co-operation indispensable to the operation of grace, it is also still, in a sense, free — free to sin, and free, therefore, to

---

82 See p. 393 ns. 22 & 23.
83 *Contra duas Epist. Pelag.* II § 11. Cf. ibid. § 13; *De Pecc. Meritis* I § 29, & II §§ 43 & 45; *De Corr. et Gratia* § 28; *De Dono Persev.* § 16. Cf. *Ephesians* vi 9, & *Coloss.* iii 25.
84 See Wörter 1898 124. Yet Augustine was in favour of equality as contrasted with domination or oppression, arguing that men, in so far as they were equal, should be so treated: see Carlyle 1927 I [2] 126 & 130. The explanation may be found in Augustine's sense of expediency, desiring the greatest good to the greatest number.

choose between two or more evil courses. Man cannot choose to love God, but he can, for instance, choose to love drink, or, as Regulus did, to love his country. Both are sinful loves, both, therefore, deserve punishment — but in varying degree. Augustine's classic example is that of the infants who, though inheriting a guilt, die too young to have indulged their inherited propensity to sin:

It may . . . be correctly affirmed that such infants as quit the body without being baptized will be involved in the mildest condemnation of all.[85]

This, obviously, is only fair. But Augustine goes on to differentiate even between adults:

The punishment of each will be more tolerable in the next world, according as his iniquity has been less in this world.[86]

And he offers a specific consolation to the Chinaman:

But even the ignorance which is not theirs who refuse to learn knowledge, but is theirs who are, as it were, simply ignorant, does not so far excuse a man as to exempt him from the punishment of eternal fire, even if his failure to believe in Christ has been the result of his not having at all heard what it is that he should believe; though probably his punishment will be a milder one.[87]

The decisive text proving degrees of punishment is *Matthew* xi 21–22 — which Augustine quotes —

Woe unto thee, Chorazin and Bethsaida. . . . I say unto you it shall be more tolerable for Tyre and Sidon in the Day of Judgment than for you.[88]

Within the circle of those predestined to be damned there is therefore a certain free will — to earn a milder or harsher punishment. In the realm of Satan a regime of rough and ready justice exists where the punishment fits the crime. Heaven, however, is won only by men who are all equally undeserving, for these are as incapable of acquiring any good merit as the damned are capable of acquiring evil merit. Yet what is this that we read in the *Enchiridion*? Speaking of

---

[85] *De Pecc. Meritis* I § 21. Cf.
Enchiridion 93.
[86] *Enchiridion* 93.

[87] *De Gratia et Lib. Arb.* § 5.
[88] *De Dono Persev.* § 23. Cf.
Enchiridion 95.

the two kingdoms, of Christ and the devil, which will subsist after the Last Judgment, he says,

Among the former there shall be degrees of happiness, one being more pre-eminently happy than another.[89]

How is this to be consistently explained unless the highest reward be arbitrary: according to the amount of grace each of the elect happens to have received?   There is another possible explanation: men are predestined to fall into one of two classes, the elect or the damned — personal merit is here irrelevant.   But, if among the damned personal merit determines the degree of punishment, may not Augustine have conceived that among the elect personal merit also determined the degree of reward?   No amount of merit can invite election but, should election by any chance come, rewards will be dispensed according to the extent or iniquity of each man's evil disposition.[90]   There would be no choice of the category but free choice within each category.

C. PELAGIUS AND CASSIAN

In those very years 397–405 [1] when Augustine was evolving his mature doctrine, another — diametrically opposed to his — was being aired by a Briton [2] living in Rome.   This was Pelagius, a monk with strong ascetic inclinations, already a close friend of Paulinus of Nola,[3] Rufinus,[4] and other influential Christians.   Although Pelagius was probably not younger than Augustine, the controversy between them nevertheless broke out only in the year 415,[5] when both men were already about sixty years old.   Which of the two precipitated the argument cannot be determined.   Probably both had

[89] *Enchiridion* 111.
[90] Cf. p. 434 n. 77.

[1] See pp. 73–75 & 78; Tixeront 1921 II [6] 457; & Turmel 1931 I 107–08.
[2] Loofs 1904 XV 749 lines 30–60; Duchesne 1911 III [4] 207–11, who says he was in Rome by about 400. Cas-

par 1930 I 387 says that Pelagius was Irish.
[3] Duchesne 1911 III [4] 234 & 240.
[4] Turmel 1931 I 107 note. But Tillemont and Tixeront 1921 II [6] 437 doubt that this Rufinus is to be identified with Rufinus of Aquileia.
[5] Loofs 1904 XV 758 lines 57–58, & 754 lines 20–21.

previously had Ambrose in mind as a rival rather than each other: Augustine seeking to carry the idea of prevenient grace to its logical conclusion, Pelagius reacting against what seemed to him an unwarrantable innovation. It has been said that in his commentary on the *Epistles* Pelagius was chiefly concerned to reconcile them with the Stoic doctrines of Seneca.[6] That man can acquire a state of perfect virtue while on earth is undoubtedly a Stoic rather than a Christian doctrine;[7] on the other hand his denial that the flesh was the cause of evil[8] and his belief that the Redemption was merely a teaching[9] marked Pelagius as not only a Catholic but an Augustinian. His doctrine of free will, moreover, was quite as natural an evolution out of Christian tradition as was Augustine's doctrine of predestination; in the emancipation of Christianity from the cosmology of antiquity, Pelagius played a real if modest part.

His doctrine was really based on a faith in human nature. Adam had not differed radically from his descendants, and the apparent deterioration was due to a habit of slackness acquired after the Fall had left men to shift blindly for themselves.[10] If Adam had not had a streak of perversity before the Fall he could not have brought it on. There was no real Fall, therefore, since Adam transmitted to posterity no more

[6] Ibid. 758 lines 17–18; & cf. ibid. 754 lines 40–44, Caspar 1930 I 332, & Nock 1933 249. Jerome *Letter* # 133 § 1 says that the Pelagian heresy was Stoic.

[7] Whether Pelagius believed in this capacity because he accepted the Neoplatonic and Manichæan belief in the divine nature of the human soul, is not certain. Celestius, however (Augustine *De Gestis Pelagii* § 65), and Vincentius Victor (Augustine *De Anima et eius Origine* II 5) both believed this. And so did the Priscillianists (Leo *Letter* # 15, 5th and 14th errors).

[8] Cf. Loofs 1904 XV 752 lines 18 & 28. Since Pelagius denied any Fall, the flesh was as undefiled as that of the created Adam; and since he supposed that man can, of his own strength, become perfect in the flesh, that flesh cannot be in any way blamed for man's evil behaviour.

Yet, if he did believe in the divine nature of the soul, it is not clear how he would explain its corruptibility. By analogy to the pride of Satan, most logically.

[9] *Pelagii ad Demetriadem Epistola* ch. 8, where the Redemption is described as an illustration, an instruction, an example. Cf. Loofs 1904 XV 753 lines 15–17 & 39–41, 754 lines 38–39, 755 line 56; Tixeront 1921 II 6 444–45; Plinval 1934 13; & Augustine *Contra duas Epist. Pelag.* § 39, *De Gestis Pelagii* § 65, & *De Gratia et Lib. Arb.* § 40 where he says: 'And the Pelagians even say that they possess God Himself, not from Him but from themselves: and whereas they admit that knowledge of the Law comes to us from God, they think that love emanates from ourselves.'

[10] *Pelagii ad Demetriadem Epistola* ch. 8.

than he had been born with,[11] and this fact seemed evident from the high character of such descendants of his as Abraham, Isaac, and Jacob, who were most certainly saved.[12] When God perceived that in spite of these few the majority of men could not resist temptation so long as they remained in ignorance of true virtue, He revealed His Law to Moses. But the prospect, of earthly felicity in the Promised Land,[13] only aggravated the evil; for not only were all who did not live under that Law the more surely damned for failure to observe it [14] but even those who did live under it now sinned with a guiltier conscience.[15] No provision having been made, moreover, for pardoning sins,[16] this experiment of the Law, however well intentioned, had miserably failed.

The second Revelation, of Christ, was then undertaken; and His success had been as conspicuous as the previous failure. Through the deep impression He had made on men by His precepts and example a large proportion of mankind had been induced to seek a life of virtue, and every day His saints were spreading His Gospel farther. To supplement Revelation, baptism was added: by it the infant earned heaven instead of an eternal life in a neutral limbo; [17] by it the adult was not only cleansed of his past sins but heartened to resist the temptations to come. Yet human nature had not in any way been changed; it had merely been touched by the beauty of Christ's teaching. Sins could now be properly forgiven as they could not be before, because the contrition induced was so abject that it wiped away all guilt. As to Augustine, therefore, so to Pelagius, it was the impression produced by the Redemption that made baptism practicable because just.

By Pelagius, therefore, no less than by Augustine was the Redemption cleared of all magical encumbrances, of all cosmological fancies. In this newly conceived world there was no Fate, no hierarchy or oligarchy of gods, no heavenly war-

---

11 Loofs 1904 XV 751 lines 51–59, 752 lines 11, 15–16, 38–39 & 49–60, 753 lines 14–15; Tixeront 1921 II⁶ 442; Augustine *De Natura et Gratia* § 59.

12 *Pelagii ad Demetriadem Epistola* ch. 5.

13 *Commentarii in Epist. S. Pauli.* ch. VII (675C). Tixeront 1921 II⁶

437–38 says, however, that if this work is by Pelagius, it has been corrupted.

14 Loofs 1904 XV 753 lines 1 & 15–17.

15 Ibid. line 6.

16 *Commentarii* ch. VII (677B).

17 Tixeront 1921 II⁶ 445.

fare between spirits of good and evil, and no divine wrestling with a degraded and obstinate matter. The victory of the Hebrew God over Greek Fate was at last complete. For the first time disputants agreed to ignore the traditional premises of antiquity, to take the revelation of the Bible at its face value, to assume nothing but the bare appeal of one heart to all other hearts. The clear issue between predestination and free will arose through the realization that man faced only one reality — the Almighty God.

Pelagius is known today, and justly, as the great champion of human free will. This Briton from the northern fogs had a faith in the capacity of man to live nobly which the African could never feel. He had the courage born of simplicity. No more than Augustine did he deny the reality of divine grace, the need of man to be supported by God in his quest for virtue; but to him this grace was bestowed rather through outer revelation than through inner infusion — as a light rather than as a force.[18] Augustine, we will remember, believed that man's regeneration required both the inner infusion of grace and the outer inspiration of revelation. Pelagius, perhaps because he could not grasp the true meaning of this inner grace, denied its existence. Augustine had been so impressed with the apparent capacity of a few men to rise above the mean level of the rest that he assumed an infusion of some spirit no longer innate and congenital in human nature; Pelagius, no less impressed by these rare evidences of human capacity, drew the opposite inference that every man possessed latent capacities far beyond those commonly attributed to his nature. The marvel of Christ's Redemption was that it had in so many cases actualized this hidden potentiality.

According to Pelagius the Redemption had so stirred these potentialities in man that many were roused to seek baptism. This was not, therefore, induced by any infusion within of a strength transmitted from without, but by the free acceptance of an outer revelation. The will was not forced involuntarily — there was no duress or undue influence; rather it acted on its own spontaneous initiative. God does not impose virtue; He merely solicits it. Baptism, therefore, with

[18] See p. 91 n. 54 end.

its forgiveness of sins, is to Pelagius the first reward of merit.[19] Cleansed of all guilt the baptized is now less encumbered, freer to follow virtue; [20] and, as he gains in virtue through his own free will, he becomes more susceptible to the teachings of Revelation. Through this susceptibility his original merit is rewarded by this further illumination,[21] and this in turn facilitates the acquisition of further merit. By this reciprocation a sort of geometrical progression is induced, whereby the momentum may be infinitely accelerated. This natural deduction, from the two premises of full free will [22] and the Revelation of love, led Pelagius on beyond even the Greek tradition to the startling conclusion that man could, of his own initiative and guided only by the divine teaching, achieve, while still alive, the full purity and sinlessness of the saints in glory.[23]

Adam had certainly been endowed with this capacity; so had a few of the Old Testament saints. Who, then, would dare to say that the divine Christ, loving man and concerned for his regeneration, was either unwilling or unable to repair the injury done by the wholly human Adam? That the reparation had been complete was certainly a doctrine long believed and still freely alleged. Rather than derogate from the prestige of the Redemption Pelagius preferred to hold to it, be the consequences what they might. He therefore alleged further that Adam's flesh had been created mortal,[24] thus restoring man's present status to a full equality with that of Adam.

The temperament of Pelagius was the antithesis of Augustine's. The African, disgusted with human nature, thought God was devising ways and means of keeping man's courage up. He saw man helpless, and saw God trying to make man think he was not so. The Briton, on the other hand, enchanted with human nature, thought God was devising ways

---

[19] Loofs ibid. 753 lines 20–21 & 27–41, 757 lines 58–60, & 766 lines 47–48. Cf. Augustine *De Natura et Gratia* § 39, *Contra duas Epist. Pelag.* § 39, & *De Gestis Pelagii* § 65.

[20] Loofs ibid. 754 lines 30–32.

[21] Loofs ibid. 758 lines 9–10. Cf. Augustine *De Gestis Pelagii* § 65, *Contra duas Epist. Pelag.* § 8, & *De Dono Persev.* § 2.

[22] *Libellus Fidei Pelagii ad Innocentiam* § 13.

[23] Loofs ibid. 755 line 12, & 764 lines 17–30. Cf. Augustine *Contra duas Epist. Pelag.* § 8, & *De Dono Persev.* § 2.

[24] Tixeront 1921 II 6 441.

and means rather to dampen man's self-confidence — lest knowledge of the truth invite an ugly pride:

So long as we are in this body we may never believe that we have it in our power to become perfect: for it is in this state of mind that we can best achieve perfection.[25]

Is it not curious that these two theologians should agree regarding the superficial appearance of man as neither wholly helpless nor wholly free; yet should draw such different conclusions? For Augustine thought he saw through this appearance to the underlying reality of man's impotence, while Pelagius thought he saw through this identical disguise to the truth of man's unconditioned freedom. Both were willing to believe that God must stoop to deceit in order to advance man's chances of salvation, that God was somehow the victim of expediency. And both were willing — up to a certain point — to reveal this divine deceit. For Augustine is eager to make man realize how helpless he is, yet urges him never to relax his efforts in the despairing belief that they are vain. Whereas Pelagius is eager to give man confidence in his free will, yet not to such a degree that he fall into pride.[26]

Associated with Pelagius in the propagation of this doctrine was a certain Celestius, of whose origins we know nothing.[27] Besides making the crude allegation that no rich man could possibly be saved,[28] he insisted that grace was not indispensable to salvation.[29] Since he cannot have meant by this that a man could save himself apart from Revelation, he must merely have meant that Revelation was not a grace. To this, curiously enough, Augustine must heartily have subscribed. This fact, however, hardly made the view of Celestius appear less heretical, for he was in fact fully revealing the extent of the Pelagian heresy. For to the Pelagians God can influence men only as men can influence each other: through the natural medium of the five senses.

[25] *Pelagii ad Demetriadem Epistola* ch. 27.

[26] Ibid. chs. 2 & 8. Various other texts attributed to Pelagius do not vary his doctrine: see Plinval 1934 13.

[27] Although Haller 1934 I 109 says he was of a 'good Roman family.' Our only records of him are between 410 and 430: Loofs ibid. 773 line 29, & 774 line 57.

[28] Loofs ibid. 764 lines 16–30. To which Pelagius probably subscribed: Plinval 1934 21–22.

[29] Loofs ibid.; Tixeront 1921 II⁶ 444.

The controversy did not break out until 411. In that year the doctrine of Celestius was denounced in Africa.[30] A lull of four years followed; then, in 415, Pelagius procured himself an acquittal before an Eastern Council.[31] Thoroughly roused by this, the Africans, led by Augustine, in 416 condemned the doctrines of both men and prevailed on Pope Innocent to ratify their verdict.[32] The next Pope, however, the Greek Zosimus, having proposed a revision of this verdict,[33] an African Council of over two hundred bishops met at Carthage in 418 and repeated the earlier condemnation.[34] At the same time an imperial decree was extracted — probably by Augustine's influence [35] — which declared all Pelagians subject to confiscation of property and exile.[36] As a result Zosimus was forced to convoke a Roman Council, and this Council ratified the decree.[37] Eighteen of the Italian bishops refused to subscribe — among them Julian, bishop of Eclanum in Apulia — they denied original sin and affirmed the sinlessness of the saints of the Old Testament. They were deposed and exiled.[38]

No more is heard of either Pelagius or Celestius. Julian [39] now became the Pelagian leader. Shortly before 430 he also was honoured by an attack from the great Augustine.[40] He was at that time enjoying the protection of Nestorius,[41] bishop of Constantinople, and on that account a dangerous man. The Roman Popes, however, first Boniface and then Celestine, remained devoted to Augustine; [42] therefore, when in 430 Nestorius began to lose favour at Court, he was either unwilling or unable to stay the decree of banishment from Constantinople which overtook the Pelagians in that year.[43] Two years after the death of Augustine Pope Celestine also died and was succeeded by Sixtus III. This Sixtus had shown certain Pelagian proclivities,[44] was for a time inclined to heed

---

30 Loofs ibid. 759 lines 10–17.

31 Loofs ibid. 763 lines 42–47, & 764 lines 16–23; Hefele 1908 II [2] 182.

32 Loofs ibid. 765 lines 15–22 & 38–40; Duchesne 1911 III [4] 225.

33 Loofs ibid. 766 lines 19–48; Duchesne 1911 III [4] 234.

34 Duchesne 1911 III [4] 236–37.

35 See Turmel 1931 I 119–20.

36 Duchesne 1911 III [4] 238–39.

37 Ibid. 239.

38 Tixeront 1921 II [6] 458.

39 Julian was born in about 383: Loofs ibid. 769 line 19; Duchesne 1911 III [4] 260. He died in about 448: Loofs ibid. 774 lines 50–52.

40 His Contra Secundam Juliani Responsionem.

41 Loofs ibid. 773 lines 29–32.

42 Ibid. 774 lines 12–20.

43 Ibid. 773 lines 38–45.

44 Augustine Letter # 191 writes

the plea of Julian that he be reinstated in his See of Eclanum;[45] but opinion was too hostile, and, although the heresy smouldered on in Italy throughout the fifth century, notably in Illyria and Campania,[46] its back had been broken.

Only Britain really succumbed to Pelagianism. Probably the general view had always been orthodox there; probably Pelagius, while in Rome just after 400, was preaching rather a doctrine he had been taught than a doctrine he had invented. At all events a Briton, bishop Fastidius, was writing Pelagian treatises between 420 and 430,[47] and it was during these same years that bishop Germanus of Auxerre undertook two missions into Britain to win over the Christians there to the Catholic faith.[48] Great as were the reputed achievements of Germanus, his second mission suggests that the first was not a complete success. Probably we should have heard considerably more of the heresy of Britain in the decades to follow had not the Saxon invasions beginning in about 440 wiped out all records of Christianity there for the next one hundred and fifty years.[49]

The early eclipse of the Pelagian heresy is partly to be explained by the introduction into the West of the traditional Greek doctrine, by Cassian,[50] a monk probably from Scythia,[51] who, after extensive travel in the East, founded a monastery at Marseilles in about 415.[52] Whether or not Cassian had been stirred by Augustine's apparent indifference to this tradition, he incorporated in his instructions to his monks an exposition of a current Greek view. This was pub-

---

to 'deacon Sixtus' to congratulate him that he has turned against Pelagianism.

[45] Leo, when a deacon, was instrumental in dissuading Pope Sixtus from acceding: Prosper of Aquitaine *Chronicum* for the year 439 (*P.L.* 51 598B).

[46] Under Popes Boniface and Leo respectively. Nests of this heresy persisted under Gelasius in 495: see his *Tract* V in which he directs his attack against the belief that man is able to attain a sinless state on earth.

[47] Tixeront 1921 II [6] 438.

[48] Duchesne 1911 III [4] 284–85. The authority apparently came from

a Council held at Troyes, and on one of these occasions bishop Lupus of Troyes accompanied Germanus: Hefele 1908 II [2] 216–17.

[49] In Wales, for example, which was not soon invaded, Pelagianism was still being resisted by the Church in 519: Hefele 1908 II [2] 1053.

[50] Cassian was born in about 360 and died in about 433: Grützmacher 1897 III 746.

[51] Duchesne 1911 III [4] 272, relying on the authority of Gennadius. But Grützmacher ibid. says he was a native of Provence.

[52] Batiffol 1924 [2] 224.

lished in about 428, and Augustine heard of it just in time
to write, in his *De Predestinatione Sanctorum* and *De Dono
Perseverantiae,* a most categorical and uncompromising refutation.[53]   For the next one hundred years it was a burning
issue in the Latin West.

Cassian published this work ten years after the formal condemnation of Pelagianism by Pope Zosimus.   It was therefore
only natural that he should ignore those doctrines which had
precipitated that condemnation, and should insist instead on
the necessity of infant baptism and on a grace which strength-
ens rather than instructs.[54]

And he does so insist, but for reasons very different from
those Augustine had advanced.   The unbaptized who die in
infancy are, he admits, doomed to damnation, but this, he
says, following Ambrosiaster,[55] is because God, foreknowing
that if they had lived they would have sinned, on that account
purposely withheld the grace of baptism.[56]   It was not to wipe
out original sin that infant baptism was necessary, for there
was none to wipe out.   In the same way, while recognizing
the necessity of an inner [57] or strengthening grace, Cassian
insists that it is usually induced, not by the divine will, but
by human merit.[58]   Augustine, as well as Pelagius, is therefore flatly contradicted.

Can a man acquire merit before baptism?   It would seem
so, because it is not

denied to us naturally to think or imagine anything good.[59]

And often God

sees in us some beginnings of a good will . . . sees us inclined to
will what is good.[60]

These very slight indications, moreover, are enough to attract the vital preliminary grace of ' good thoughts ': [61]

[53] Wörter 1898 23–30.
[54] Leporius, a monk of Marseilles
and therefore probably a disciple of
Cassian, was condemned as a Pelagian at Carthage in 426 and was induced to retract: Hefele 1908 II [2]
215–16.
[55] See p. 383 n. 12.
[56] At least according to Augustine

De Predest. Sanctorum § 24, and to
Prosper of Aquitaine: see p. 423 n. 18.
[57] *Conlationes* XIII 13.
[58] Ibid. 8, 9 & 15.
[59] Ibid. 12 § 6.
[60] Ibid. 8 § 4 & 11 § 5.   Cf. ibid. 9
& 17, & Augustine *De Predest. Sanctorum* § 38.
[61] *Conlationes* XIII 3 § 5.

The first stage in the divine gift is for each man to be enflamed with the desire of everything that is good.[62]

So, by a mere thought of or inclination towards good, a man may acquire, through this answering grace, an actual, realized desire for good. And baptism is the best evidence that this grace has been bestowed, because it proves that desire has passed beyond the stage of mere inclination. It is indeed precisely this step which the Redemption made possible, for until then good inclinations could not attract grace and so could never evolve into good thoughts. Before the Redemption there had been a virtual predestination to evil, but now, through baptism, man virtually received again the free will of the first Adam.[63]

Ordinarily, to be sure, this grace of Cassian's is withheld until a man evinces some slight meritorious inclination,[64] but occasonally God chooses to confer it before there is even this small merit.[65] Yet, however the grace may have come, baptism gives assurance that, for the moment at least, it has been offered and accepted. Thereafter the only concern need be how a man may keep it. Like Augustine's grace of love, this grace enables its possessor to have good thoughts and desires. But here the resemblance stops. For whereas Augustine's grace cannot be earned, Cassian's can be. And no man can reject the grace of Augustine, while any man can reject that of

[62] Ibid. 18 § 4.

[63] A statement of Augustine's supports this inference: in *De Predest. Sanctorum* § 2 he says that the ' Massilians ' — that is, those whose doctrines emanated from Marseilles and Cassian — have at least, in contrast of course to the outright Pelagians, ' attained with Christ's Church to the belief that the human race is born obnoxious to the sin of the first man, and that none can be delivered from that evil save by the righteousness of the Second Man.' Now Augustine evidently thought that Cassian, in contrast to Pelagius, denied salvation to all, whether they lived before or after the Redemption, unless they had been baptized — and I see no reason for doubting the correctness of this assumption. That Augustine thought salvation came only through baptism because it remitted past guilt, whether inherited or acquired, whereas Cassian thought it necessary only in order to remit acquired guilt and to restore the free will of the first Adam, is not here the issue. On Cassian's evasion of the problem of original sin, see Augustine *De Predest. Sanctorum* § 24. Augustine was momentarily gratified by Cassian's view because it at least declared baptism indispensable to salvation. For, were the doctrine of Pelagius accepted, he who was baptized merely facilitated his salvation: it was still possible for him to achieve salvation merely by leading a blameless life.

[64] *Conlationes* XIII 8, 9 & 15. It is only on the authority of Augustine *De Predest. Sanctorum* §12 that we may believe that Cassian thought merit followed by grace was the more usual sequence.

[65] *Conlationes* XIII 7, 11 & 17.

Cassian. Augustine's grace of love, since it does nothing to confer the power of perseverance to the end, may, sooner or later, lapse of its own nature; but, so long as it does not lapse, it is irresistible. Cassian's grace, on the other hand, lay in man's power either to reject or to keep — and to keep either for a time or for ever:

For the reception of grace was of no profit to Simon, doubtless because he had received it in vain, for he would not obey the Commandment of the blessed Peter.[66]

And contrariwise of the Apostles:

Certainly the divine righteousness would not have permitted them to be tempted, unless it knew that there was within them an equal power of resistance.[67]

Consequently Paul declares that

the grace of God does not co-operate with the idle and careless, but only with him who labours and exerts himself.[68]

Yet this grace, although it repays a thousandfold the small merit which induced it,[69] is still quite inadequate for salvation. To the ' good thoughts ' or faith which it brings, must be added ' good deeds ' or works, and this capacity is bestowed or not according to how well the will has co-operated with the first grace.

The second stage of the divine grace is to make possible the practice of virtue.[70]

And this grace, like the first, is usually bestowed in proportion to past performance:

[God] imparts to each one according to his capacity the grace of His bounty, so that He wills to grant His healing, not according to the uniform power of His Majesty, but according to the measure of the faith in which He finds each one, or as He Himself has imparted to each one.[71]

Or, to use Augustine's terms, either as ' grace for grace ' or as ' grace for grace and merit '. Yet occasionally this second grace, too, is a gratuity:

[66] *Conlationes* XIII 12 § 9.
[67] Ibid. 14 § 6.
[68] Ibid. 13 § 5.

[69] Ibid. 13, 16 & 18.
[70] Ibid. 18 § 4.
[71] Ibid. 15 § 2.

the grace [72] of God is superabounding and sometimes overflows the narrow limits of man's lack of faith.[73]

This second grace is no less indispensable than the first and far more powerful, yet it is still both inadequate and resistible, so that, only if the will choose to co-operate with it, can the final grace come which saves:

The third stage also belongs to the gift of God, so that it may be held by perseverance in the goodness already acquired, and in such a way that the liberty may not be surrendered and bondage experienced.[74]

And thus it is even of this last grace that saves: as it can be won, so it can be kept, only by human merit. God no doubt wishes to save all; [75] but He is not willing to save any who do not use their free will to save themselves.

It is apparent, therefore, that although Cassian gives his doctrine an Augustinian tinge, it contradicts that theory at every vital point. To Augustine the only need of infant baptism was in order to wipe away original sin; yet in the case of infants Cassian denies that sin's existence. To Augustine grace must precede any good inclination because without it there can be no good inclination; yet Cassian alleges that grace only precedes occasionally and exceptionally. To Augustine this grace of perseverance is necessary for salvation because man, even with the help of the grace of love, cannot continue to do good of his own will; yet Cassian thinks it necessary only because man cannot of his own will continue to do good enough. To Augustine man can neither reject grace nor keep it; yet Cassian believes he can do either.

If the average Christian of the year 429 was anything like a modern Christian there was only one thing in all this controversy that interested him: did it, or did it not, lie within his own power to be saved? Augustine said No; but Cassian, like Pelagius, said Yes. The details of what a man must do in order to be saved and of how this salvation was mechanically

---

[72] Cassian must here, of course, have the second grace in mind, for no faith, but only inclination, can precede the first grace.

[73] *Conlationes* XIII 16 § 1. Cassian must here have had Paul in mind: Grützmacher 1897 III 747.

[74] *Conlationes* XIII 18 § 4. Cf. Augustine *De Dono Persev.* § 43. Cassian's last two words are evidently directed at Augustine.

[75] For quotations see Grützmacher 1897 III 748, & Loofs 1906 XVIII 196.

brought about — questions of baptism and grace — were, after all, relatively incidental. And this Cassian knew quite as well as Augustine. There was not, therefore, in 429, a new issue: it was still the old case of Augustine vs. Pelagius. But Pelagius, having pleaded rashly, had been convicted on his plea. So Cassian raised the issue again and filed a more judicious answer. Would it have a happier fate than the first?

D. PROSPER; THE ANONYMOUS TEXTS

Barely a year [1] before Augustine's death he received a letter from an admirer of his, Prosper, a layman of Aquitaine, informing him of the opposition his doctrine of predestination was encountering in certain parts of Gaul:

Many of the servants of Christ who live in the city of Marseilles think that the works which your Holiness has written in order to refute the Pelagian heretics are contrary both to the opinion of the Fathers and to the understanding of the Church in so far as you argue in these how the elect are called according to the divine plan. . . .[2] And when we show them the writings of your Beatitude, enriched by the most certain and abundant testimonies of the divine Scriptures and, following the line of your arguments, add some decisive argument of our own, they defend their obstinacy by appealing to tradition; and those things which, in writing about the Epistle of the Apostle Paul to the Romans you adduce in order to explain the merits of the elect as a manifestation of divine prevenient grace, these they affirm never to have been so understood as now explained, by any of the clergy. And when we request that they should themselves explain those things according to whatever conceptions they may choose, they confess that they have found no satisfactory solution, and they insist that there be silence concerning those things to whose height no one can attain. In fact so utter is their obstinacy that they say our faith is injurious to the edification of the people, on which account, even if it be true, it ought not to be adduced, because it not only harmfully teaches what ought not to be taught but also deals with a dangerous subject which they cannot grasp.[3]

After explaining at some length how the clergy of Marseilles denied the indispensability of prevenient grace, Prosper says,

---

[1] § 9 of the *Letter* refers to Hilary as bishop. His election was in 429.
[2] *Letter* # 225 § 2 of Augustine's

correspondence (*C.S.E.L.* 57 455).
The *servi Christi* are the monks.
[3] Ibid. § 3.

For one of them, a man of great authority and devoted to spiritual
things, holy Hilary, bishop of Arles, your Blessedness knows to be
an admirer and follower of your doctrine in all other respects,
and, regarding this matter which is in dispute, also knows that
for a long time now he has wished to present his view to your Holiness by letter. But since it is uncertain whether this will be done,
or how, the anxiety of all of us . . . feels the need of the support
of your love and learning.[4]

Now this Hilary had, in that very year 429, just been elected
to the see of Arles and had thereby become the acknowledged
leader of the Gallic clergy.[5] He had come, not from Cassian's
monastery or from Marseilles, but from the neighbouring
monastery of Lerins.[6] Evidently this Semi-Pelagian doctrine
was not the phenomenon of an isolated monastery but the prevailing doctrine in Gaul, and the Gauls were alleging that
their view was the traditional one in the whole Church.

The next year Augustine died, and very shortly after this
Pope Celestine wrote a letter ' To the bishops of the Gauls '
in which, after describing the disquieting reports he had received, he says:

If these things are as reported, let novelty cease to assail tradition,
let restlessness cease to disturb the peace of the Churches.[7]

And the next paragraph begins:

Augustine, man of blessed memory, on account of his life and
merits we have always held in our communion, nor has even a
rumour of evil suspicion ever bespattered him whom we remember to have long since been of such learning that he was ever held
even by my predecessors as among the greatest masters. Therefore
everyone in general thought well of him since he was everywhere
loved and honoured by all.[8]

Had Augustine been younger, or at any rate lived longer,
or had Celestine lived longer, it is conceivable that the Semi-
Pelagians of Gaul might have shared the fate of the Pelagians.
But by the death of Augustine and the Vandal invasion the
African Church was submerged, and two years later, in 432,
Celestine died and was succeeded by Sixtus III, who began

[4] Ibid. § 9.
[5] The primacy of the see of Arles
for the Gauls was generally admitted,
although what this primacy should
amount to was much disputed.

[6] See p. 488.
[7] Letter # 21 § 1.
[8] Ibid. §2.

his pontificate inauspiciously by opening negotiations with
the exiled Pelagian leader, Julian of Eclanum. Thus, in a very
few years, the theological complexion of things was reversed.
To this there was added a further complication. Celestine
was apparently not a profound theologian; in defending Augustine was he quite sure what Augustine's doctrine really
was? The Semi-Pelagians were denying prevenient grace;
Augustine not only championed it, but alleged in addition
that even baptism did not emancipate man's will. Ambrose
had preached that only those who died unbaptized had been
predestined to damnation; Augustine preached that many
even of those baptized had also been predestined. The Semi-
Pelagians were challenging the doctrine not only of Augustine but of Ambrose. Was it certain that Celestine, in championing Augustine, knew he was condemning the doctrine
not of Cassian only but of Ambrose as well? And, even if he
did know this, did the Italian clergy know it, and did they
approve?

In 428 the doctrine of Augustine appeared to be unchallenged in the West; in 433 the only Augustinian we can clearly
identify is this Prosper, the layman of Aquitaine, whose distress at the turn of affairs in Gaul had led him to write to Augustine, four years earlier, for moral support. Now Augustine was no longer alive to help him; he, a mere layman, must
fight alone. It was under these circumstances that he wrote,
in about this year 433, his *Responsiones ad Capitula Objectionum Gallorum* and *Liber contra Collatorem*. It was
no easy task to fight, almost alone, against the might of the
Gallic Church. Its leaders now were being more and more
frequently recruited from the monasteries at Marseilles and
Lerins,[9] and monks naturally stress the ascetic effort — the
need of works in addition to love. Such men are suspicious
of a patient, because a perhaps too passive, waiting for grace
to come. They are naturally hostile to the layman who, resisting renunciation and persisting in his temporal life, finds
consolation in the Augustinian belief that the initiative to
holiness is exclusively with God.

Although Prosper was not so trained that he could follow

9 See pp. 488–89.

Augustine's intricate speculations in all their details, he cannot be said to have misrepresented them in any essential
respects. Yet he does offer certain variations in emphasis and
in doing so perhaps betrays more than he intends.

For one thing he insists repeatedly that it was Adam, and
not God, who put man into so evil a plight.[10]   Adam is the
culprit. But who made it likely that Adam become the culprit, and who so arranged things that all Adam's descendants
must share his fate? Prosper, wisely no doubt, avoids any
discussion of these matters; he is either too unaware or too
timid to repeat the Augustinian explanation of a Creation in
which man's soul is tested and tried as in a crucible to satisfy
the demands of a God who will make no smallest compromise with imperfection. But in stressing the responsibility of
Adam and the irresponsibility of God, Prosper does his master no service: for, if it was not God who imposed the penalties on Adam and his descendants, then it was some other
power. And this power, unless responsible to God, was that
very Fate or demon whose capacity Augustine had taken
such pains to disprove.

Prosper further insists that the fate of the damned is rather
foreknown than predestined by God, because God does not
oblige, but merely allows, man to sin.[11] The fact that man,
in spite of his subsisting free will, can use it only in order to
sin, is the work of Adam alone. Prosper is here up to the
old trick of juggling the meaning of a word. It is true that
God can foreknow the fate of a man — because He is endowed with foreknowledge by being outside of time. But
if no man can be saved unless he receive grace,[12] and if this
grace is arbitrarily bestowed by God regardless of behaviour,[13] God does not need to be outside of time in order to
know who will surely be saved or damned. He has only to
know His own will, to bestow grace here and withhold it else-

---

[10] *Pro Augustino Responsiones ad
Capitula Objectionum Gallorum* chs.
1 & 2.

[11] Ibid. 3.

[12] Ibid. 6 & 8; *Liber contra Collatorem* 10 § 2; *Epist. ad Rufinum* §§ 7,
8 & 10.

[13] *Pro Augustino Resp. ad Capit.
Gall.* 8; and including all the neces-

sary graces, as of perseverance: *Liber
contra Coll.* 16 § 2. Prosper's standard of virtue which could qualify as
merit was, of course, very high: beyond mere faith, learning, piety, and
effort, to love: *Epist. ad Rufinum* § 8.
Cf. ibid. § 17 on death-bed repentance.

where. Prosper admits, moreover, that the elect are predestined to be saved; [14] surely, then, it was not difficult for
God to know the fate of those not so predestined! He may
quite legitimately insist on the distinction between a salvation imposed by God and a damnation merely permitted by
God. But here again Prosper is doing his master no service,
for the suggestion is that man may be the victim, not only of
God's justice, but of Nature or Fate. Augustine was more
jealous of God's omnipotence.

A third variation is suggested by Prosper's declaration that

He who denies that one who, after baptism, relapses into infidelity
and evil ways has been purged of original sin, holds as false a
view as he who alleges that such a person should not be damned
for eternity.[15]

So rash a statement was calculated to make not only Augustine but also Ambrose and Cassian, turn in their graves. For
if the baptized were wholly purged of the original sin inherited from Adam they must regain the free will of the first
Adam and hence the capacity — if they chose — never to sin,
which was precisely the view of the Pelagians! Of course
what Prosper meant to say was that baptism wiped away the
guilt, leaving only the weakness. But whether this weakness
was the comparative weakness of Ambrose, which, if it still
obliged man to sin, allowed him to acquire some small merit,
or whether it was the complete weakness of Augustine, in either case it was a defect caused by Adam and saddled on
his descendants. Prosper's statement, therefore, gets him nowhere. For if it does not allege the Pelagian view it becomes
equally consistent with Augustine's rigidity and the mildness
of Ambrose and Cassian.

One of Augustine's arguments in favour of predestination
had been based on the doctrine of infant damnation: [16] if
infants who die unbaptized may be justly damned on account of their inheritance, why may adults not also be justly
damned? Cassian had tried to evade this difficulty by arguing
that such infants were justly damned only because God fore-

---

[14] *Pro Augustino Resp. ad Capit.
Gall.* 14; *Epist. ad Rufinum* § 15; *Pro
Augustino Resp. ad Excerpta Gen-
uens.* § 8.

[15] *Pro Augustino Resp. ad Capit.
Gall.* 2.
[16] See p. 72 n. 8.

knew what evil deeds they would have committed had they lived.[17]   But it is absurd, says Prosper, to suppose that

both the things that do not happen should be foreknown, and that the things foreknown should not happen.[18]

Although Prosper's instinct is sound he misses the real objection which was, as we have said,[19] that the devil's and even the world's only licence to exist was that they might actualize the evil potentialities of men.   If men could be justly punished for sins they must yet in fact never did commit, both devil and world were theologically superfluous.

Prosper's effort is the first, and perhaps the clumsiest, of the many thousand that have been made to contrive a compromise between the two doctrines of free will and predestination.   If, as Cassian had insisted,[20] it was unjust to condemn adults for sins they cannot avoid, how could it be argued that it was just to condemn infants who died unbaptized?   And if, as Augustine alleged, it was just to condemn these infants, how could it be argued that it was unjust to condemn the adults?   Did, or did not, the sons of Adam have rights that God was bound to respect?   Out of this dilemma Prosper was utterly unable to extricate himself, and we must conclude that although he was inclined towards Cassian as a matter of tact, and towards Ambrose as a matter of taste,[21] he clung loyally to Augustine as a matter of logic.

It is of course easy to see why Prosper, as a layman and a Gaul, was led to commit these indiscretions.   His emphasis on the responsibility of Adam and man's dependence on the laws of nature, on God's knowledge as a substitute for His power, and on the extinction of original sin through baptism, are ample evidence that he hoped to sugar the pill of Augustinian theology.   His work, nevertheless, to the extent that it

---

[17] See p. 414 n. 56.

[18] *Letter* # 225 § 5 of Augustine's correspondence (See p. 418 ns. 2 & 3).   Cf. the view of Ambrosiaster, see pp. 383–84.

[19] Cf. pp. 383–84.   And cf. p. 362 on Salvian.   God could hardly punish men because they *might* have renounced their faith rather than suffer martyrdom.

[20] Cf. *Liber contra Coll.* 9 § 4.

[21] In *Pro Augustino Resp. ad Capit. Gall.* 3 & 7, he stresses the free will acquired by baptism — which is a gesture of approval of the view of Ambrose; but as it is merely a grace freeing man from the necessity of sinning, and not a greater power to choose the better course — cf. *Liber contra Coll.* 12 § 4, & 18 § 3 — it is not a greater freedom or capacity to earn merit: see pp. 396 n. 38, & 398 n. 55.

produced any effect at all, can only have been to weaken the
Augustinian structure at its foundation. For to Augustine
the peculiarly rigorous justice of God was the direct cause
of every event, with nature, man, and all the rest merely so
much putty in His hands.

There is no slightest indication, however, that Prosper
was, either secretly or subconsciously, inclined to prefer the
Semi-Pelagian view. His variations were merely so many de-
ceptive baits, set to lure the Gauls from their delusions. And
in at least one instance he develops an argument beyond the
point at which Augustine had left it. Cassian, we will remember,[22] had inferred from his purely human conception of
justice, that every man, Chinaman or other, had an equal
chance to save himself if he chose. But how was this to be
possible if no word of Christian teaching had ever reached
him? Since mere good inclinations sufficed to attract grace
the Chinaman must occasionally have received grace and
been baptized. Yet this had very evidently not been the case.
Now Prosper well shows how, according to Ambrose or Augustine, no man at birth deserved anything better than damnation.[23] Consequently the millions of Chinamen who had
died unbaptized without exception were quite justly damned.
And Prosper shows further how a Chinaman really had a
better chance according to Ambrose and Augustine than according to Cassian: because if he were obliged to wait for instruction in order to capitalize his own good inclinations he
was virtually without hope, whereas initiating grace was inwardly infused independently of any teaching.[24] Experience
no doubt indicated that the Chinaman was at a disadvantage,
but there was no theological explanation of this. In the one
case it was his bad luck that he was born in China; in the other
it was merely his bad luck that he received no grace. For
according to Ambrose and Augustine the arbitrariness of
God's choice was so unconditioned that it was, in a certain
sense, peculiarly fair.

One other point made by Prosper is interesting because
it is so natural a product of the lay mind. In the course of

22 See pp. 414-15, & 417 n. 75.   24 Ibid. 5. Cf. p. 415 ns. 62 & 63.
23 *Pro Augustino Resp. ad Capit.*
Gall. 11.

his effort to explain why the doom of so many was consonant with justice — why God had not chosen to save all [25] — he offers a reason which I do not find in Augustine. How could the temporal world survive, Prosper asks, if God should choose to give grace to all? Does not a temporal world require an abundance of temporal vocations?

Who does not see that the variety of this world is embellished by the creation of such men — if he only observe how many conveniences of the present life have been taught by the efforts and activities of certain unbelievers, as in the invention of the arts, in the building of cities, in the drafting of laws, and in international agreements? [26]

We must not forget that Roman civilization rested on a substructure of human slavery, where the labours of the many were necessary in order to gratify even the most honourable desires of the few. The pragmatic significance of Augustine's doctrine becomes quite clear only with this passage of Prosper's: that a chosen few might be saved, many must be sacrificed. Ambrose, Augustine, and now Prosper, mark the stages in the Empire's evolution from a physical reality to a theological **image**.

At some time between 432 and 440 [27] appeared a papal document declaring its position on the now burning issue. It was entitled ' Decisions of past bishops of the Apostolic See in regard to the Grace of God and Free Will.' [28] It is generally known as the *Præteritorum*. The earlier chapters contain quotations from Popes Innocent [29] and Zosimus [30] declaring the grace of God indispensable to any good thought or deed, and an extract from the proceedings of a Council of Carthage [31] specifying that this grace was just as indispensable after as before baptism. Although these decisions, having been rendered before Cassian published his *Conferences,* were specifically aimed at the Pelagian view, their insistence that grace must invariably precede merit made them equally

---

[25] Ibid. 8.
[26] Ibid. 13.
[27] Duchesne 1911 III 4 285, says it was written before 441.
[28] The full title in *P.L.* 51 205 ff. is *Præteritorum Sedis Apostolicae Epis-* *coporum Auctoritates, de Gratia et Libero Voluntatis Arbitrio.*
[29] Chs. 1–4.
[30] Chs. 5 & 6.
[31] Ch. 7.

effective against the Semi-Pelagians. That is why they are here repeated.

The author next expounds the current papal position:

> Let us confess God to be the author of all the virtues by which, from the beginning of faith, we strive towards God, and let us not doubt that all the merits of men are preceded by His grace, by means of which we begin both to wish and to do anything good. By this gift of God's help free will is by no means taken away, rather it is emancipated so that it changes from confused to clear, from depraved to righteous, from sick to healthy, from unforeseeing to foreseeing. For such is the goodness of God towards all men that He wishes us to have, as merits of our own, things that are but gifts of His own, and He will grant eternal rewards in return for what He has Himself bestowed on us.[32]

Taken by itself this passage appears to be a mere restatement of the Augustinian position. But, if it is that, how are we to explain the passage that immediately follows it?

> Nevertheless, just as we do not presume to disparage, so we have no need to add to, those deeper and subtler parts of the questions involved which those who have combated the heretics have dealt with at greater length. And this is because, in regard to our faith in the grace of God — from whose operation and dignity nothing must be subtracted — we believe that the above decisions of the Apostolic See can, of themselves, teach us to regard as utterly un-Catholic any view that appears to be contrary to them.[33]

The heretics referred to are certainly the Semi-Pelagians as well as the Pelagians. Those who have, in combating them, gone into the deeper and subtler aspects of the doctrine, can only be Augustine and such disciples of his as Prosper. The papacy does not wish to disparage their work; at the same time she makes it very clear that in order to be a good Catholic no one is obliged first to be a good Augustinian. Though polite, the rebuff is explicit.

Pope Celestine had declared that the view of Augustine was identical with that of the Church. But on his death in 432 Sixtus III became Pope and his willingness to listen to the Pelagian Julian, who was intriguing to win back his See of Eclanum,[34] suggests that Sixtus was elected as a reaction against the papal tendency to take its cue from Africa. This

---

[32] Ch. 9.
[33] Ch. 10.
[34] Loofs 1904 XV 774 lines 21–29; Duchesne 1911 III⁴ 282. Prosper, in

his *Chronicum* for 439 (*P.L.* 51 598B), said that Pope Sixtus resisted these intrigues ' urged on by the deacon Leo ', the inference being that Sixtus

Præteritorum, therefore, represents the opinion of Rome under Sixtus or during the period 432 to 440. Being apparently hostile to the Semi-Pelagians, yet politely suspicious of the Augustinians, it left the way deftly open for some other doctrine which should temper the violence of the Augustinian. Was it possible that the view vaguely outlined by Ambrose more than forty years earlier had not been wholly forgotten?

To the years 432–440 [35] also belongs an anonymous treatise, the *De Vocatione Omnium Gentium,* which is thought to be of Italian [36] origin. Here the doctrine of the necessity of a prevenient grace, as alleged by Ambrose, Augustine, and Prosper, was again stoutly defended,[37] chiefly on the ground that man's capacity to be truly [38] virtuous was a gift brought by the Redeemer and therefore conferred only by baptism.[39] The author insists, moreover, that this baptism is the key to regeneration [40] and that it restores man to the full status originally conferred on the innocent Adam.[41]

Augustine had said that baptism, while it wiped away the guilt, left the weakness intact. He was therefore obliged to conclude that it did not restore man to the full status of the innocent Adam. Furthermore only the Pelagians had dared to argue that the Redemption had, through baptism, so completely restored that status as to leave man free never to sin at all. What, then, did the author of the *De Vocatione* really mean in saying that baptism restored the original status? A few passages defining the status of the baptized will show us:

He so bestows the desire to be obedient to Him that even from those who will in fact persevere He does not remove the power not to desire.[42]

---

might otherwise have been persuaded. This inference is the more plausible because we know that, when a deacon, Sixtus was congratulated by Augustine in *Letter # 191* because he had bowed to the decision of the Roman Council of 418 which condemned the Pelagians. Evidently in 439, twenty-one years later, he was still inclined to sympathize with them.

35 *De Vocatione Omnium Gentium*

I § 1 (*P.L.* 51 648–49. And cf. ibid. 647–48 bottom, where 440 is conjectured to be the date).

36 See Migne *P.L.* 51 643–44 last paragraph.

37 *De Vocatione* I §§ 4, 24 & 25.

38 Ibid. I § 8.

39 Ibid. I § 17.

40 Ibid. I § 18.

41 Ibid. I § 8.

42 Ibid. II § 28.

Although it is by God's help that they stood, nevertheless, because they retained the capacity to fall, it must be because of their merit that they stood.[43]

We know most certainly that no one of the faithful who does not withdraw from God is abandoned, and that no one's ruin has been determined by divine decree; but, to the many who can now use their reason, freedom to withdraw is given precisely in order that there be merit in not withdrawing, and in order that what cannot be done without the help of the Spirit of God may nevertheless be attributed to the merit of him by whose will it might possibly not have been done.[44]

It is certainly not the Pelagian status that is here attributed to the baptized, for the author is careful to explain that no man can will to be virtuous unless supported by God's grace. Might it possibly be the Augustinian status? It would have to be argued that man's power to fall from grace was merely the exercise of that hopelessly vicious free will imagined by Augustine, and that the merits so-called were merely the free gifts of grace. Yet this is clearly just what the author does not mean, because in each of the passages quoted grace is described as resistible,[45] whereas Augustine had declared it irresistible. This is why Augustine had said that there was no merit in submitting to grace, and why the author of the De Vocatione now declares that such submission is the criterion of merit. Cassian had said that merit could be acquired before the bestowal of grace and could induce that grace as its reward. To him, therefore, even the unbaptized could save themselves. Augustine had said that merit could not be acquired even after the bestowal of grace, and that even the baptized, therefore, could do nothing to save themselves. Ambrose, on the other hand, had previously intimated that although the unbaptized could do nothing, the baptized could do everything, to save themselves, and it is this view which is expounded in the De Vocatione. According to it the pagan remained helplessly at God's mercy; but the Christian could effectively force God's hand. The pagan still had no rights that God was bound to respect, but the Christian was no longer a slave at the mercy of his master: he was a free citizen with rights guaranteed by the law.

---

[43] De Vocatione II § 28 (P.L. 51 714C).

[44] Ibid. II § 12.

[45] Final saving, or persevering, grace is, however, irresistible: ibid. II § 11. Cf. p. 417 n. 74 on Cassian.

One mystery the author confesses he cannot explain: [46]
Christ came to save all men,[47] that is, to give every man a fair
chance to save himself if he will. Now the baptized very evidently receive this chance. But the unbaptized apparently
do not. In his anxiety to contrive some explanation the author reminds his readers that grace may be conferred by many
other devices than knowledge of the Redemption — as by an
infusion of a virtuous desire to seek an unknown Messiah; [48]
and he also observes how often God may purposely withhold
grace until just before a man's death.[49] This, however, does
not at all explain how God allowed heathens actually to die
unbaptized: for to say that the indirect infusion proved inadequate, or that the direct infusion came too late, is merely to
accuse God of incompetence.

This dilemma reveals the fundamental weakness of the Ambrosian view. The doctrine of Cassian was consonant with
justice because every man had a chance to save himself; the
doctrine of Augustine was also consonant with justice because
no man had this chance. But, according to the Ambrosian
view expounded in the *De Vocatione,* the heathens had no
chance and the Christians every chance. Now Augustine imagined that the infants who died unbaptized got the lightest
of all punishments because they had not personally sinned;
should not the heathens similarly get a light punishment, because, although they had personally sinned, they had had no
alternative? Should they not at least get a lighter punishment than the Christians who, having received grace, repudiated it? Yet, if this were so, there was considerable risk in
becoming a Christian, for, should the grace thereby received
be resisted, God's resentment must lead to punishments that
no heathen ever deserved.[50]

That the snub administered to the Augustinians in the
Præteritorum was induced by papal unwillingness to abandon the view of Ambrose, is corroborated by the doctrine expounded in the *De Vocatione.* Evidently the Ambrosian
tradition of forty years earlier had been overshadowed, but

---

[46] Ibid. I § 13.
[47] Whence the title of the work.
[48] Ibid. II §§ 4 & 9. This would be the Chinaman.
[49] Ibid. II § 3.

[50] Consider the severity of Adam's punishment: taken by itself his sin was slight, but his excuse for sinning was even slighter.

not destroyed, by the Augustinian. To be sure we do not
know who wrote this *De Vocatione,* but scholars agree that
its author was an Italian and there is the further evidence
furnished by Pope Gelasius or one of his immediate successors in about 500 that its author was then regarded as a doctor of the Church.[51] Sixtus III, as a Pope, might conceivably
have been so described; but it is far more likely that the
doctor referred to was the one famous Catholic of Italy during this period, his successor Pope Leo.[52]

Certainly such an attribution is far from improbable, and
scholars are today somewhat inclined to it. Leo was a Tuscan
and had therefore been thoroughly exposed to the influences
emanating from Milan; furthermore he became an archdeacon in Rome during the pontificate of Sixtus III, employed Prosper of Aquitaine there as his secretary,[53] and, because of his dominating personality, may very well have
guided the policy of the papacy during those years.[54] Can
it be said with any degree of certainty, however, that he either
wrote or inspired the *Præteritorum* and the *De Vocatione*?

Unfortunately his authentic texts are indecisive: we are
obliged to read between the lines. It is not a case, however,
of conjecturing what a writer would have thought about a
question if he had thought about it, for the controversy over
grace and free will had been raging violently in the West
ever since 428 so that Leo must have given serious attention
to it and his failure to commit himself as Pope must have
been deliberate. Leo most certainly had an opinion; the
problem, therefore, is to see whether he has, or has not, in
some passage inadvertently said more than he meant to.

One passage betrays his impatience with a view propounded

[51] See Migne *P.L.* 51 647–48 lines
13–14.

[52] Duchesne 1911 III [4] 285 says of
the *Præteritorum* that it is a 'document . . . romain d'origine et que
l'on a toute raison d'attribuer au
diacre Léon.' And on page 286 n.
2 he says of the *De Vocatione* that it
has been 'souvent attribué au diacre
Léon.' Cf. *P.L.* 51 644–48; & Loofs
1906 XVIII 198.

[53] Loofs ibid. 126. Cappuyns 1927
passim argues that Prosper actually

wrote the *De Vocatione,* but he recognizes (p. 225) that Leo strongly influenced the composition.

[54] Leo commissioned Cassian to
write against the Nestorians, and Cassian probably died in 433: Caspar
1930 I 393. In his preface to that
work Cassian spoke of Leo as 'an
ornament to the Roman Church and
the divine priesthood': *De Incarnatione* (*C.S.E.L.* 17 235). And cf. Bonwetsch 1902 XI 367 line 60 — 368 line
4.

by Prosper. In the *Responsiones ad Capit. Gall.*[55] Prosper said that God had, for the fulfilment of His divine purpose, predestined the Jews to attack Christ; for in no other way could the effects produced by the Crucifixion be secured. Leo, however, declared that God, merely through His foreknowledge, had utilized the malice of the Jews. He had not obliged, but merely permitted, them to act so.[56] It may be argued that the difference here is one of words and that Augustine might, had he been alive, have sided with Leo, for Augustine invariably maintained that human nature, even if it could never in fact avoid sin, acted of its own free will and not under compulsion. Nevertheless, the fact that Leo chose to challenge the view of Prosper indicates a determination not to be bound by Augustine according to Prosper, and may, in view of his emphasis on foreknowledge, indicate an impatience with Augustinianism itself. This suspicion is fortified by his eagerness to reproach the Priscillianists for denying man's moral responsibility for good or evil acts.[57]

Another passage is more decisive: speaking of Christ's victory over Satan, he says,

When the prince of the world is bound all that he held in captivity is released. Our nature, cleansed of its old contagions, regains its honourable estate; death is destroyed by death, nativity is restored by nativity: since at one and the same time redemption does away with slavery, regeneration changes our origin, and faith justifies the sinner.[58]

The first clause reminds us [59] that Leo accepted the traditional doctrine, rejected by Augustine, that before the Redemption the devil had a power which frustrated God's merciful will. From this he inferred — just as did those of his predecessors who shared his view — that, the devil being now bound, man almost automatically re-assumed the full status of the innocent Adam. But by what process does Leo imagine that this restoration is achieved? Observe that by the phrase ' regeneration changes our origin ' he can only mean that by bap-

---

[55] Ch. 13. And cf. ibid. ch. 11 on God ' hardening their hearts ' etc.
[56] *Sermon* # 67 §§ 2 & 3.
[57] *Letter* # 15 introduction. In *Sermon* # 42 § 3 Leo speaks of ' those good desires to which we are confi-dent that you are prompted of your own selves.'
[58] *Sermon* # 22 § 4: ' quoniam simul et . . . et . . . et . . .'
[59] See pp. 55–56.

tism man is cleansed of the inherited guilt,[60] and that by the phrase 'faith justifies the sinner' he can only mean that by baptism all past sins are forgiven.[61]   But there is also the phrase that 'redemption does away with slavery'.   Now since all these effects are produced 'at one and the same time' this redemption is also the result of baptism, and since it can refer neither to inherited guilt nor to past personal sin it can only refer to an incapacity to do other than sin.   The emancipation from slavery is from predestination to damnation.   Furthermore Leo cannot have meant that baptism conferred an irresistible, saving grace, for in that case every baptized person would be saved.   He can only have meant, therefore, the resistible grace which is described in the *De Vocatione*.

That this is Leo's real understanding appears further from a letter in which he speaks of 'Christ's sacrament of baptism, in which there are no distinctions between the reborn.' And he adds:

Behold how the grace of God makes all these unequals [in worldly condition] equal, who, whatever their labours in this life, if they abide faithful, cannot be wretched.[62]

According to Augustine and Prosper baptism created no equality because, among these, some were predestined to be saved, others to be damned.   But what else can Leo mean by the phrase 'if they abide faithful' except 'if they do not choose to resist the grace thus conferred'?

The problem remains, however, why, if Leo really held this opinion, he was unwilling to speak out.   He was defending the middle ground between Nestorius and Eutyches with penetrating and interminable arguments.[63]   Why, then, was he unwilling to defend the middle ground between Cassian and Augustine?   Why, if he were actuated by political expediency, was he so categorical in the one case and so non-committal in the other?   It may, of course, be conjectured that Leo was so implicated in the East that he could

---

60 See Ambrose *De Mysteriis* § 32. See pp. 385–86 on how carefully this distinction was observed.

61 See, for instance, *Sermon* # 49 § 3, where Leo says of the baptized that after justification 'no one is debarred by sin either of his own or original.'   And in the same way Prosper *Pro Augustino Resp. ad Capit. Gall.* 3 speaks of how men 'may have been reborn and justified, and yet they were not predestined.'

62 *Letter* # 15 § 10.

63 See p. 601 n. 66.

not afford to risk dissension in the West. But, granted that expediency was a plausible motive, principle offers a motive infinitely more plausible: for the Gospels and Paul revealed no clear doctrine; neither Nicæa nor any other Council had broached the problem; and, except for Celestine's eulogy of Augustine's orthodoxy, no previous Pope had committed himself. In default of more official authority the doctrine propounded by Augustine deserved the greatest consideration. To Leo, still an impressionable young man when Augustine died,[64] the African giant must have appeared as the recipient of a special grace of understanding. Augustine was now dead and Leo was now Pope — he to whom Peter communicated his instructions for the government of Christendom. But to Leo it was not at all clear that on this vital subject Peter had yet enlightened him. Deep in his heart Leo doubted the doctrine of Augustine, and yet, awed by its logic, consistency and force, he still more doubted his own doubt.

To this period must be ascribed still another anonymous treatise, the so-called *Hypomnesticon*.[65] Some scholars have thought it Gallic in origin; [66] others have suggested that Pope Sixtus III might be the author.[67] Such opinions, however, seem to be pure conjecture; and certainly its Gallic origin is unlikely because it refutes the Pelagians [68] and, in refuting them, also refutes the Semi-Pelagians.

That grace must invariably precede and be the cause of a meritorious will is many times reiterated.[69] This grace, moreover, is no natural grace, as of reason, which is conferred universally on all men: for the author admits that grace does not come to all and justifies this apparently arbitrary discrimination by resort to the argument of Augustine, according to which all men deserve to be damned and cannot complain, therefore, if some are given a mercy that is not deserved.[70]

But, if the author shows a certain sympathy with the hea-

[64] Leo was probably in his early thirties in the year 430.

[65] The text is in *P.L.* 45 1611–1664.

[66] Loofs 1906 XVIII 199 lines 16–21.

[67] Migne *P.L.* 45 1611–12 lines 41–42.

[68] The full title is *Hypomnesticon contra Pelagianos et Coelestinos*. *Hypomnesticon* means memorandum.

[69] *Hypomnesticon* III 4–6, 9 & 10, & VI 5.

[70] Ibid. III 7.

then who are denied grace, and a certain embarrassment to explain how this is consonant with God's justice and Christ's sacrifice, he has no patience with the baptized who fall from grace:

When one already redeemed through the grace of baptism by his own will sins and, while persisting in his evil ways, dies, a vessel of wood is constructed which is easily consumed by the fires of hell.[71]

For a man acquires evil merit when by his own vice, being already baptized, he rejects virtue and does evil: that is, when he abandons God and takes delight in the world.[72]

And, as the natural corollary:

He acquires a good merit when in all things he does not resist the benefits of the grace of God operating in him, but rises instead as a co-operator and puts all his hope in that grace.[73]

This is certainly not the language that we should expect an Augustinian to use, for grace does not here abandon man; it is rather man who abandons grace — which is the doctrine of the *De Vocatione*.[74]

We notice, however, that, according to Ambrose, God

bestows a gift on us . . . through baptism — and afterwards more liberally to those who serve Him well.[75]

This can only mean that grace may be conferred on the baptized as a reward of merit, a supposition which Augustine had insistently denied but which Cassian affirmed. Evidently the authors of the *De Vocatione* and the *Hypomnesticon* were contriving to effect a compromise which should save both Augustine's ' grace only for grace ' and the free will of the baptized. They therefore conceived of the baptismal grace as itself a saving grace although given gratuitously, and supposed merit to consist merely in not resisting that grace. Thus merit did not invite further grace; it merely clung to the grace originally conferred.[76] Eternal rewards would then presumably be graded according to the amount of baptismal grace still subsisting at death.[77]

The theory is ingenious, but its merit is wholly dialectical.

---

71 *Hypomnesticon* 9 § 17.
72 Ibid. 13 § 30.
73 Ibid.
74 See pp. 427–28.

75 See p. 386 n. 26.
76 *Hypomnesticon* 10.
77 Ibid. 13 § 30.

For Augustine's 'grace only for grace' aimed to show that man had no cause, and should therefore be allowed no pretext, for pride. Yet according to the *De Vocatione* and *Hypomnesticon* no less than according to Ambrose and Cassian, man could properly boast of his virtue because it proved that he was still successfully clinging to his baptismal grace.

Whether a good man had any pretext for pride was, therefore, the crux of the controversy. In order to deny this Augustine was driven to his theory of predestination; in order to deny predestination the other theologians were driven to a theory which allowed a just pretext for pride. The Pelagians had been condemned because they preached that men were saved or damned, not by God's will, but by the good or bad use they made of their own. The Semi-Pelagians avoided condemnation by resorting to the subterfuge that merit was adequate only because it attracted a grace proportionate to that merit. The authors of the *De Vocatione* and *Hypomnesticon*, since they affirmed that a baptized person could save himself without need of further grace, were actually reverting, however innocently, to the brazen conception of the Pelagians.

For the Pelagians admitted that grace was indispensable, provided that grace be taken to mean those natural endowments with which all men are equipped — such as reason and a sense of good and evil. The Church had decided, however, that a natural grace given to all men was not grace, for this, by definition, was a special mercy bestowed or withheld at God's discretion. What, then, would the Church say of the divine power conferred automatically on all men through baptism? Was this not, according to these treatises, the power of a free will tantamount to that conferred on the innocent Adam? Yet, if this were so, was not the baptized able to save himself wholly by the aid of this free will and without the help of any special graces — a doctrine which differed from that of the Pelagians only because it was applied exclusively to the baptized? The jump was out of the frying-pan into the fire.

By the examination of these texts we perceive how the aspect of the controversy had changed between the death of

Augustine in 430 and the death of Leo in 461. In the earlier year the doctrine of Augustine, apparently championed by Innocent, Zosimus, Celestine, and the African Church, was securely holding the citadel of Catholic orthodoxy against the assaults of the Semi-Pelagians. Yet already by 435 that doctrine no longer had any active defenders — Prosper being by that time in Rome in the service of the papacy. The attitude taken by Sixtus III remains a mystery; even the attitude of Leo is not as plain as we should like. None the less the *Præteritorum* and the *De Vocatione* were certainly published under their auspices; the *Hypomnesticon,* whatever its origin, ably defends a doctrine that closely resembles theirs. It is therefore safe to say that at the death of Leo the papacy and Italy possessed a well formulated doctrine of their own with which effectively to combat the Semi-Pelagians without resorting to the excesses that the Augustinians insisted on. Rome, with her customary political instinct, had allowed others to take the initiative, had allowed others to commit themselves; biding her time she put into circulation certain anonymous papers, as trial balloons, to see how the wind blew. Not until Peter spoke to her would she speak in his name.

E. FAUSTUS OF RIEZ ON FREE WILL

Pope Leo had been dead twelve years when, in 473, appeared the treatise *De Gratia,* the work of Faustus, a fellow countryman of the Briton Pelagius. Born in about 408,[1] he had entered the monastery of Lerins at an early age and had there shown such promise that in 433,[2] when only twenty-five years old, he was elected its abbot, serving in that honourable capacity for the next twenty-six years. We shall speak of Lerins at length in the next chapter; it is enough to say here that this monastery lay close to that of Cassian at Marseilles and that the influence of Cassian's doctrine on these

---

1 Engelbrecht 1891 vi. Cf. Sidonius *Letters* IX # 9 § 10 which may or may not refer to the *De Gratia:* Dalton 1915 II 250–51.

2 Engelbrecht 1891 vi.

other monks at Lerins was deep and lasting. The monastery at Marseilles did not prosper, but that at Lerins did. It is not too much to say that from 430 on the Lerins monks assumed control of the Gallic Church. It is probable, therefore, that this Church became the citadel of Semi-Pelagianism because Lerins championed that doctrine. Furthermore Faustus must from the beginning have been a Semi-Pelagian, for, had he not been, how would he have been elected abbot at twenty-five years old, and how would he have retained that most influential office in the Gallic Church for the twenty-six years following?

In 459 Faustus resigned his abbacy in order to become bishop of Riez;[3] yet he wrote nothing on the burning question of grace and free will until fourteen years later.[4] Why did he wait so long? Was he waiting for the Augustinian prestige to fade,[5] or did he choose to strike only in the face of an Augustinian recrudescence? Whatever his reasons, when he did choose to strike it was done boldly,[6] not anonymously but under his own name, with no slightest effort to find a way out of the dilemma by ingenious compromise. It is the work of a man who is confident not only that he is right but also that the Church will declare him so.

According to this *De Gratia,* Adam, at his creation, was gratuitously endowed with the three natural[7] graces of reason, free will, and virtue;[8] by abusing his free will he sinned, and by this sin copulation, which might otherwise have been practised without voluptuous passion, was henceforth tainted with lust.[9] Consequently Adam's descendants were doomed to be the fruit of sin and therefore to be born in a state of sin.[10] If they died young, before they were old enough to

---

[3] Ibid. ix inclines to the year 452, but Gouilloud 1881 212 prefers 455, and Seeberg 1898 V 783 says between 456 & 462.

[4] Engelbrecht 1891 vii.

[5] Loofs 1906 XVIII 198.

[6] In spite of the fact that Faustus cites Augustine by name only twice: *De Gratia* I § 5, & II § 9. He probably wanted to give the impression that he was only refuting a doctrine exaggerated by Augustine's followers, but it is likely that he was intending to attack Augustine, although he did

not dare to do this openly. See p. 531 n. 29.

[7] In addition to the very special grace of immortality: *De Gratia* I § 1 (*C.S.E.L.* XXI 9 line 4 — 10 line 2).

[8] Ibid. II § 8 (76 line 7) & § 9 (78 line 30 — 79 line 18).

[9] Ibid. I § 2 (12 line 26 — 13 line 9). Cf. pp. 81 & 384 n. 16. Faustus follows Cassian's theory that incontinence is born of pride: ibid. I § 2 (13 lines 24–27).

[10] Marriage is licit because it is not the act of generation but the passion

exercise their reason and free will, they were doomed to damnation,[11] but if they lived and made good use of the reason and free will which neither Adam nor they had forfeited,[12] they might acquire such merit that God must confer on them — as a special grace [13] now — that virtue with which Adam had been naturally endowed at birth. It was in this way that such men as Abel and Abraham were saved.[14]

Such a doctrine was hard on those who died in infancy, but the punishment thereby inflicted on adults was not as severe as might be supposed. For Adam's innocence, being unearned, was precarious, and he was eternally damned for a sin that was rather venial than capital; Abel's guilt, on the other hand, not being merited in equity, was equally precarious, so that a little prudence resulted in his eternal salvation. Thus it might plausibly be argued that the innocent Adam, the sword of Damocles hanging, without his full knowledge, continually over his head, held the more unenviable position of the two. Moreover this Pelagian tendency to minimize the injury done by the Fall presented a further embarrassment: since no one had ever alleged — or could allege — that Christ raised anyone above the status of the innocent Adam, the less far Adam fell the less high Christ raised Adam's descendants. The changes wrought were rather in degree than in kind.[15]

The Father's teaching having already revealed much, that of the Son could not do more than amplify it. The chief advantage accruing from the Redemption was the sacrament of baptism, by which man was infused with the Holy Ghost and hence with a natural disposition to virtue withdrawn since the Fall. But Faustus is emphatic that this special disposition conferred by baptism comes only as the reward of a

---

now accompanying it that is sinful: ibid. I § 2 (14 lines 4–6).

11 Ibid. I § 13 (46 lines 10–12).

12 Ibid. I § 7 (23 – 24 line 16), & II § 8 (76 lines 6–10).

13 Free will (libertas arbitrii) and resemblance (imago) to God are described as natural graces. These are given to all men at birth and are irresistible. But freedom (liberatio) and likeness (similitudo) to God are special graces and are therefore resistible: ibid. II § 10 (88 lines 28–30). And cf. ibid. II § 9 ff. on imago and similitudo. Adam's case was unique because he also received these latter as natural graces — because he was all men — and yet learned, to his cost, that they were resistible.

14 Ibid. II § 9 (80 line 5 – 81 line 18).

15 Ibid. II § 10 (83 lines 14–28).

pre-existing merit,[16] and that this merit is induced, not by grace, but merely by an innate capacity stirred by divine teaching: [17]

But, even at baptism, the will of him who assents is inquired into, so that the grace of regeneration may ensue.[18]

And, generally speaking, without specifying whether he has the baptized or the unbaptized in mind, he says:

Nor shall I seem overbold if I should admit that frequently — not in infancy, of course, but in maturity — our will, God having so ordained, precedes those graces which are special and supplied out of the abundance of Another.[19]

In speaking thus Faustus must have been well aware that not only the African, but the Roman Church too, in the *Præteritorum,* had declared itself categorically in favour of prevenient grace. Yet he chooses here categorically to deny it. Why? Because he is unable to believe that those who die unbaptized were born, in spite of Christ's Redemption, predestined to be damned:

If God, as the impious blasphemously assert, disposes of man's estate not by justice but by might, it may be that he who knocks is kept out while he who does not seek is let in; and thus He will neither seem merciful towards those saved since He did not allow them to earn His mercy as a matter of right, nor will He seem just towards those damned who, although innocent of any crime of their own, are refused mercy. Because, if both are by nature guilty, not only is justice jeopardized in this man who, being unworthy, is chosen regardless of merit, but mercy also in that man who, without trial to determine his sin, is condemned to damnation.[20]

Here Faustus, in spite of his paradoxical intimation that one ' by nature guilty ' requires a ' trial to determine his sin ', is

---

[16] Faustus *Letter* # 1 (*C.S.E.L* XXI 163 lines 11–13) argues, however, that the reward is really a gift because the merit is only a duty.

[17] Man's reason of itself gives man an intuitive knowledge of God: ibid. II § 9 (82 lines 15–23), & § 10 (87 line 7). This is a natural grace which can, but with difficulty, rouse the will to virtue. But of course the Old and New Revelations make this much easier: ibid. I § 16 (52 lines 11–14 &

28–30), & § 18 (57 lines 27–28), & II § 9 (82 line 26 — 83 line 10).

[18] Ibid. II § 10 (84 lines 6–8).

[19] Ibid. (83 line 29 — 84 line 3). Turmel 1931 I 408–09 thinks Faustus held the magical infusion theory of the Redemption (see pp. 87 & 343 n. 54. But Faustus was anything but categorical. It is consistent, however, with free will for the unbaptized.

[20] Ibid. II § 4 (65 lines 15–23).

getting uncomfortably close to the essential weakness of the Augustinian doctrine. For on the one hand Augustine had said that the measure and degree of punishment in hell was based on the degree of evil that men freely willed,[21] while on the other hand he declared that grace was conferred irrespective of these degrees. Man was therefore subject to two kinds of law: the human, which operated to punish according to deserts, and the divine, which rewarded irrespective of deserts. But what can be said for a justice so capricious that it deals with men partly according to civil law and partly almost according to Fate? Had Augustine been satisfied to believe that God's judgments were invariably and inevitably inscrutable he would have been impervious to attack, but, by saying that they were scrutable yet inconsistent, he laid himself open to legitimate criticism.

But Faustus, although able enough as the world goes, lacked the penetration to expose this defect in the Augustinian argument. He was satisfied instead to expound a system of a much more elementary kind in which none of the real difficulties, empirical or dialectical, were clarified. For according to him God's justice required that He reward and punish strictly according to human merit and without the smallest discretion. His God is no more than an automaton whose every act is determined by the free will of His creatures. Man is invariably the initiating cause and God the servile effect.[22]

Apparently Faustus was unable to conceive of any standard of virtue higher than the currently conventional. Thus, striking at Augustine's doctrine of a grace arbitrarily dispensed, he says:

Righteousness in man is not a personal, but a general and public, gift of God.[23]

He seems unaware that to Augustine's ruthless idealism there were, below the moral level of love of God, innumerable degrees of evil behaviour which, although to the human eye only

---

[21] See p. 405.

[22] 'And for this reason the Creator and guardian of man delegated to man the use of a good will, but kept control of the effect it produced': ibid. I § 9 (30 lines 4–6).

[23] Ibid. I § 9 (30 lines 9–10). And cf. ibid. I § 12 (43 lines 8–17 & 44 lines 3–17). *Justitia* is sometimes used in the technical sense of justification: perhaps the translation should be ' the opportunity to obtain justification '.

relatively evil, to God seemed equally undeserving of the real reward. That a man might be less sinful than other men was to Augustine no criterion of virtue: a man deserved reward, not according to his virtue as compared with that of other men, but only according to the absolute quality of his virtue as measured by divine standards. God could have no interest in saving the least guilty, but only in saving the truly guiltless; [24] otherwise the criterion of virtue would be set, not by God, but by the behaviour of the average man.

The view of Faustus, on the other hand, although more humane, was also more thoughtless; for he relied on the analogy of civil or man-made law precisely where such reliance must prove fatal. For the essence of divine law is its contrast to human law,[25] is its capacity to set an absolute standard above the comprehension of a lay jurist or lawgiver — a standard set not by expediency but by principle. It was because Faustus failed to recognize this difference that he rejected not only the universal predestination [26] imagined by Augustine but also that partial predestination — of those who died unbaptized — assumed in the doctrine of prevenient grace.[27] Since, said Faustus, a man can, by his own efforts, acquire merit in the eyes of men, he can also acquire merit in the eyes of God. But Augustine would have countered that this merit in the eyes of other men God was not in the least concerned to reward, and he would have added that the Revelation taught something more than a sociological justice, more than the true relation between one man and another: for it revealed the true relation existing between man and his God.

In few other theological controversies has geography appeared so significant. From the Greek East came an amor-

---

[24] Cf. Salvian *Ad Ecclesiam* II § 9.

[25] Cf. Augustine *Contra Secundam Juliani Responsionem Imperfectum Opus* III 24.

[26] Faustus admits predestination only in the sense that God's foreknowledge informs Him of how men will in fact use their free wills and therefore what treatment they will receive according to the divine justice: *De Gratia* II § 2 (61 lines 24–25), & § 3 (63 lines 11–19).

[27] When he says ' I attribute both the inchoate beginnings and the final consummation to the work of grace ' — ibid. II § 10 (84 lines 13–14) — he has in mind for the beginnings those natural graces of reason and free will which were universally and irresistibly bestowed: ibid. I § 9 (36 lines 15–23). For the final consummation, the grace is of course that which is given as the reward of merit.

phous Pelagianism that secured a foothold in eastern and southern Italy — in Aquileia, Picenum, and Apulia — and which took deep root in Britain. To Pelagius may be added the names of Fastidius[28] and Agricola:[29] by 429 the whole island was rife with that heresy. Faustus — also a Briton — was a Semi-Pelagian only because in his day Pelagianism was utterly discredited.[30] The innate and organic conception of the Italians was outlined at an early date by Ambrose; the southern temper was so well represented by Augustine that his only opponents there were the Priscillianists and Manichees, who deemed his fatalism too qualified. Only in Gaul does the instinctive disposition seem hesitant. In the northerly circle that formed round Martin Pelagianism was in favour; this spread into Aquitaine touching Severus and Paulinus,[31] and by Paulinus was carried into Campania. Prosper of Aquitaine, on the other hand, and later Lucidus of Riez,[32] preferred to follow Augustine. The first Semi-Pelagian, Cassian, brought his conception from the East; of the monks of Lerins who appropriated and diffused that doctrine, a fair proportion came from the northerly region of Burgundy.[33] Thus, very securely, one may move north, from Manichæan and Augustinian fatalism, to Italy and prevenient grace, to Gaul and grace for merit, to Britain and merit without grace. Was the cause racial instinct, intellectual disposition, maturity of civilization, climate, or mere chance? We do not know.

---

[28] Fastidius wrote in about 425: Migne *P.L.* 6 1043.

[29] Agricola is mentioned in Prosper *Chronicum* for the year 429 (*P.L.* 51 594C).

[30] Although Faustus followed Cassian very closely, his doctrine deserves a full exposition because it was not, like Cassian's, something of a restatement of the views of others — as of the abbot Chæremon — but was the organic product of fifty years of Gallic meditation. He differs from Cassian, moreover, in regard to the pre-Redemption era. Cassian saw only a general doom; Faustus thought that the Patriarchs, and hence some others, were quite able, even then, to take care of themselves. This may mark a return to favour of the Old Testament, now that the gibes of Manichee and sophisticated pagan could be safely ignored. Salvian shows this same inclination. Yet in doing this the degree of change wrought by the Redemption was inevitably minimized.

[31] The Pelagians had secured a foothold in southwestern Gaul before 400. Severus of Toulouse was one for a time: Duchesne 1911 III[4] 268, citing Gennadius *De Script. Eccles.* ch. 19; and Paulinus of Nola, who was from Bordeaux, was a close friend not only of Severus but also of Pelagius: Duchesne ibid. 234.

[32] Faustus *Letters* # 1; Hefele 1908 II[2] 909–10.

[33] Gennadius the Marseilles biographer of about 490, was a Semi-Pelagian: Migne *P.L.* 58, 979–80.

F. Astrology and Theurgy

This conflict within the Church between grace and free will was merely one of the many ways of representing a conflict that concerned every Roman, were he a Syrian or a Spaniard, were he an Epicurean or a Stoic, a Neoplatonist or a Manichee. If fatalism is a disease and free will an illusion, at least both are endemic in man and are constantly colouring his behaviour. Anyone who claims that he does not think about this question is really boasting that he hardly thinks at all.

Early Christians were so optimistic that we are tempted to exaggerate their faith in free will. Yet the paradox could not be more glaring than we see it in the *Epistles* of Paul. Origen's insistence on free will is all but contradicted by his theory that souls enter human bodies with the handicap of sins committed in a previous existence. The pagan Plotinus, being purely a philosopher, reduced the role of free will almost to nothing;[1] and it was perhaps only because his disciple Porphyry had a more human disposition that he made room in his system for the still innocent mischief of dead souls.[2] It was soon after this[3] that Manichæan dualism began to spread through the Empire, and, according to that belief, the lost souls, far from being the sport of accident, were the authorized agents of that Evil Deity who not only ruled matter but ensnared into that matter the errant particles of the Divine Light. If only man could devise a way of harnessing some of these evil powers he too might share in the temporal rule. If inclined to evil he might gratify his malice; if inclined to good he might, by flattery or bribery of the demons, avert catastrophes impending.[4] Remember that to the Manichee the prize for which God and the devil fought was the soul of man. Thus, although theoretically at the mercy of two inexorable fates, practically man held the balance of power: for he who wanted man's soul must pay for it. The stars

---

[1] See pp. 35 n. 44 & 121 n. 14.
[2] See p. 36 n. 50.
[3] Cumont 1929[4] 131 says that the transmogrification of Mithraism into pseudo-Christian Manichæism fol-

lowed Constantine's support of Christianity.

[4] Ibid. 141. On the Priscillianist propitiation of demons in 443 see Leo *Letter* # 15 introduction.

might rule; yet might not the forces that ruled these stars be tampered with or circumvented? [5]

It was with Iamblichus, who lived in about 335, that this Manichæan theory of the exploitation of demons entered Neoplatonism too; [6] and with Julian, the Emperor, the use of demons in order to compass worldly ends became a highly technical and exacting art. [7] The Christian contemporaries of Julian were the Greek Fathers, Basil and the two Gregories, and the Latins, Ambrosiaster, Ambrose, and Jerome. It was the moment when Origen was again in favour, [8] and it was out of his theory of inequality of opportunity, based on sins committed before incarnation, that the Latins evolved their theory that the unbaptized had had no opportunity at all. The Christian magic which corresponded to the Neoplatonic was the rite of baptism, by proper use of which sinful man might circumvent the doom that a cosmological justice had decreed. By means of this rite man believed he could extricate himself from the net which Fate had spread. Both by Greek Neoplatonism and by Latin Christianity the rule of Fate was acknowledged, but each carefully left a loophole by which it might be dodged.

The harder the late Roman fought against Fate with his wits the more he succumbed to it with his disposition. He was tired, and his philosophies were picked to match. Again the greatest man is the most complete exponent of his age: Augustine symbolizes the dying State. The Roman had failed, and only Augustine perceived the whole import of that failure. Man was still man — he would not perish — but the Roman was no longer a Roman. Earlier philosophies had included both otherworldliness and fatalism, [9] but Augustine was the first not only to teach these doctrines but also to impose them on the State.

Yet the ancient world had never before been so intellectu-

[5] Cumont 1929 [4] 167–68.

[6] See p. 326 of the *L.C.L.* ed. of *Philostratus and Eunapius;* & cf. Fitzgerald 1930 I 48–49.

[7] Bidez 1930 78–79 & 253–54, etc. Gibbon 1776 ff. ch. 24 records that Julian had foretold the date of his own death. If he tried to avert this doom he must have failed!

[8] See p. 98 n. 74.

[9] For Augustine's answer to the Pelagian allegation that his view did not differ from that of the Manichees, see *Contra duas Epist. Pelag.* I §§ 4 & 7, & II § 9.

ally alive as at this moment; never before had such diversely brilliant philosophies clashed in mortal combat. As men debated what the world was, how made, and why, that world fell suddenly about their ears. So long as they had it they declared who wanted it could have it; then, having lost it, they complained and mourned. Was this too, then, another paradox of life that the Christian must face? Must man be a political animal as well as a holy soul? However that may be, it is clear that this late Roman mentality, while showing extraordinary intellectual vigour, also betrayed a biological lassitude. At least to the sensitive Roman, even though outwardly prosperous, life in the year 400 no longer seemed good: in answer to his summons the three great cults had presented themselves, each expounding its reasons why.

It was a full generation later that we find the first signs of a change. That the duration of this state of mind was so short is due, no doubt, to the way mankind is made. For pessimism and fatalism are both luxuries — to be afforded only so long as inaction can seem plausible, only so long as discontent can outweigh discomfort, disgust outweigh despair. When, in 410, Alaric sacked Rome, both Jerome and Augustine were mortified as well as shocked; [10] but in that year Jerome was already sixty-three years old and Augustine fifty-six. How, at such ages, could they adjust themselves to a new conception of life? How could they adjust their faith to a world bereft of that very State they thought they despised? Men of the new generation, on the other hand — Orosius, Maximus, Leo, Salvian, Faustus, and presumably the authors of the anonymous treatises on free will — were all born near the end of the century and had therefore been still young when Rome fell. These adjusted themselves quite naturally to the new situation. That is why, after 430, we see Latin opinion gradually shaking itself free from the iron grip of Augustinian philosophy, raising, very timidly, first a doubt here, then a doubt there, until at last it became expedient to doubt not only Augustine's infallibility but even his orthodoxy. A world without a State needed a philosophy that could produce one.

[10] See p. 147.

Inextricably bound up with the question of free will was that of justice on earth. If there were no free will no such justice need be expected; but if there were free will, if real merit could be acquired, it was almost unthinkable that there could be adequate reward if this were wholly confined to advantages bestowed hereafter. Already among the unorthodox, like the Pelagians and the disciples of Martin, the inference drawn from an unbridled free will had suggested justice on earth.[11] According to Severus the merits of Martin were so conspicuous that he was, as in the case of the hailstorms on the estate of Auspicius,[12] able to ameliorate the earthly evils that an inexorable justice had decreed for his friends. The innumerable cures which Martin effected had no other meaning.[13] We have already quoted the passage in Orosius [14] where the merits of Pope Innocent are rewarded by his fortuitous absence in Ravenna during the capture of Rome by Alaric. Salvian, however, is careful to explain, in contradiction to Severus, that no saint, while still alive, has the power to ameliorate the earthly lot of his fellow creatures. He takes a passage in *Ezekiel* as his text:

God spoke thus of a certain land and a sinful people: *though these three men, Noah, Daniel, and Job, were in it, they shall deliver neither sons nor daughters; they only shall be delivered.*[15] . . . Thus is destroyed our confidence in the false notion that an innumerable host of sinners can be saved from the evils that threaten them by the intercession of a few good men.[16]

That Salvian, in speaking of ' the false notion ', had partly in mind the followers of Martin seems certain. He wrote before 451 at the latest, barely a decade before the memory of Martin became everywhere rehabilitated.[17]

While still alive even the holiest men were sinners, however. Even the Pelagians did not deny this; they only alleged that it was theoretically possible for them to be sinless, not that they ever had been, or would ever be so. The Church must therefore deny to the living, powers which arose only out of a perfect virtue. Saints who had died and been saved, on the other hand, were, by very definition, free from sin.

---

11 See especially Severus, *passim*.
12 See p. 191 n. 97.
13 See Severus, *passim*.
14 See pp. 350–51.

15 *Ezekiel* xiv 14 & 16.
16 *D.G.D.* III § 58.
17 See pp. 517–18.

It was logical, therefore, that the Church should ascribe to the dead, powers analogous to those the Pelagians theoretically ascribed to the living. During life the saint was naturally solicitous of both the earthly and the eternal welfare of other men, and, since this saint's personality survived intact in the after-life, it must be assumed that his solicitude would also survive. This saint was now free from sin and deserving of the reward of happiness. Yet how could he be happy if, by death, even his small efforts to alleviate man's lot must cease? When still a living sinner he could console, counsel, chastise, exhort; being cleansed of sin should he now lose his power to cleanse the sins of others?

In answer to the high hopes entertained by such enthusiasts, Pope Leo administered these words of caution:

Although in the sight of the Lord the death of many of His saints has been precious, yet no innocent's death was the propitiation of the world. The righteous have received, not given, crowns; and from the endurance of the faithful have arisen examples of patience, not the gift of justification. For their deaths affected themselves alone, and no one has paid off another's debt by his own death.[18]

And if the most renowned martyrs were not given this power, surely no confessor will obtain them. Leo is speaking here, however, only of the dead saint's power to facilitate another's salvation; of his power, at least when acting in concert with other saints, to alleviate man's earthly lot, Leo speaks in a very different way. Recall[19] his comment on the evacuation of Rome by the Vandals after their sack of that city in 455:

Surely it was by the saints' prayers that the sentence of divine displeasure was diverted, so that we who deserved wrath were reserved for pardon.[20]

Leo does not explain how it happened that the saints prayed, but in every cited case of intercession they acted in response to the prayers of the living: evidently it was not thought that they could act unless requested.[21] They could exercise a

[18] *Letter* # 124 § 4. Cf. Tertullian *De Pudicitia* ch. 22 (*P.L.* 2 1027).
[19] See p. 352 n. 88.
[20] *Sermon* # 84 § 1, quoted p. 352. It is unlikely that Leo here has living as well as dead saints in mind, for no

one is technically a saint until death. Moreover it is also unlikely that he would contradict the authority of *Ezekiel* already quoted by Salvian.
[21] See pp. 157 n. 36 & 184.

discretion but no initiative.   It is here that the theurgic element is introduced: God had decreed that for their sins the
Romans be pillaged and enslaved; but, because of the prayers
addressed to the saints by these miserable Romans, the saints
in their turn interceded by prayer to God that the prayers of
the Romans be heard and His decree withdrawn.   Thus,
through an appeal to spirits, the Romans were able partially
to ward off that fate which justice had imposed.   Had these
Romans, ignoring the saints, instead prayed directly to God,
the saints, even had they been able to intercede, might well
have refrained from doing so — out of pique.   Under Leo
we are already far from the government of God as conceived
by Augustine.

Until after the death of Augustine in 430 the Church had
no alternative but to stand by him: it was only after this that
certain practical and embarrassing problems fully revealed
themselves.   Predestination was an admirable way of championing God's omnificence and man's impotence, of recon-
ciling Providence and fatalism; but, if God in fact dictated
every thought and act of man, was it not natural to infer
that His power, and hence all earthly energy both physical
and psychological, was somehow communicated to the earth
via the planets and stars?   And, if this were so, was the astrology of Neoplatonist and Manichee quite the vain superstition that the Church declared it?   If man were helpless to
carve his own destiny, did it matter so much that the power
which moved him like a pawn was a Hebrew, rather than a
Greek or a Persian, Deity?   And, if man were in fact helpless, why was it nevertheless his duty to be ever impotently
striving?

A passage in one of Leo's Sermons shows how deeply rooted
was the Romans' respect for the sun.   After describing some
of the still prevalent astrological conceits, he says:

By such practices impiety so flourishes that by some of the more
foolish the sun is worshipped from the tops of the hills as it rises
daily at dawn; and there are even some Christians who think this
so much a part of piety that, before they enter the basilica of the
Apostle Peter — which is dedicated to the true and living God —
on the upper steps by which one ascends to the elevation of the
upper platform they turn round to face the rising sun and with
bent necks bow down in honour of that brilliant disk.   We mourn

and grieve much that — partly through the vice of ignorance, partly in a heathen spirit — this should be done; because even though some of these persons are perhaps really worshipping the Creator of this beautiful light and not that light itself — which is a mere created thing — nevertheless, even the semblance of this act must be avoided, for when he who has forsaken the cult of the gods finds this rite a part of our cult, will he not then cherish within him, as if still probable, a remnant of his old faith, observing that the rite, at least, is common to both cults? [22]

This worship of the heavenly bodies as the agencies through which earthly events were contrived from on high was a thorn in the side of the Church throughout the fifth century. At first such trust in astrology was confined to pagans — the remnants of whom in Leo's day still ' worshipped from the tops of the hills . . . at dawn '; others, less isolated and innocent, took refuge either in Neoplatonism or among the heretical Manichees.[23] But there were also sincere converts — including even priests [24] — who, while they now put all their trust in Christ, still harboured a lingering faith in the intermediary guidance of the stars. Nor was this conceit merely a passing phase of the transition from paganism to Christianity: for in the later Middle Ages it revived with even more intensity, in the fourteenth and fifteenth centuries rivalling in popularity that utterly disparate intermediary, the Blessed Virgin.[25]

And as in that later age astrology and demonology went hand in hand, so did they in the time of Leo. The devil, he says, has many men

whom he has bound still more tightly because they are suited for his designs — that he may use their abilities and tongues to deceive others. Through them are guaranteed the healing of sicknesses, the prognostication of future events, the appeasing of demons and the driving away of apparitions. They also are to be added who falsely allege that the entire condition of human life depends on the influence of the stars, and that that which is either the divine will or ours rests with the unchangeable fates. And yet, in order

---

[22] *Sermon* # 27 § 4. The present church also faces east.

[23] Leo *Letter* # 15, introduction, says that according to the Priscillianists and Manichees ' a fatal necessity drives the impulses of the mind to either side, and all that men do is through the agency not of men but of stars.'

[24] Leo ibid.

[25] Pickman 1932 220–21 & 227–28.

to do still greater harm, they promise that they can be changed if supplication is made to those constellations which are adverse.[26]

A serious weakness of this theurgy was, however, that the demons could not be trusted: too often they promised what they were either unwilling or unable to perform. If to many Catholics God seemed to promise far too little, to the pagans and Manichees [27] the grievance rather was that the demons promised far too much. In a letter of Sidonius to Lupus of Troyes in 480 we are not told to what shifts a certain victim resorted in the hope of averting his doom, but we may presume that the demons had made him glib promises:

Unfortunately he had the indefensible, I might say the fatal, fault of superstition. He was curious as to the manner of his death, and consulted those African astrologers whose nature is as fiery as their native clime. They considered the position of the stars when he was born, and told him his climacteric year, month, and day — I use astrological terms — as men to whom the scheme of his nativity was revealed in all its sinister conditions. It seemed that in the year of his birth all the planets which rose favourably in the zodiac sank with blood-red fires; whether it was that Mercury made them baleful, asyndetic upon the diameter, Saturn retrograde upon the tetragon, or Mars returning to his old position upon the centre. Beliefs like these, whatever their precise form, are false, and cannot but delude. . . . [Yet] it must be admitted that in the present case there was neither appearance of mere conjecture nor deliberate ambiguity; death enmeshed our reckless inquirer into the future exactly when and as it had been foretold; all his shifts to evade it were in vain. He was strangled in his own house by his own slaves.[28]

Theurgy and astrology, then, had their deceptions. Nevertheless, against the small chance of performance must be weighed the wide scope of the promise. And promises have always proved alluring, no matter in what field they have been made. Of course tampering with magic for selfish or evil ends is an unholy practice, and always has been. Leo, however, speaks of pacts with the demons whereby ' are guaranteed the healing of sicknesses ' — which recalls the cures

---

[26] *Sermon* # 27 § 3.

[27] For some of the weird conceptions concocted by the Priscillianists out of Christianity and astrology, see Leo *Letter* # 15 §§ 12 & 13.

[28] *Letters* VIII # 11 §§ 9–11. Before his consecration Sidonius had himself been under the spell of astrology: see *Carmen* XXII (*L.C.L.* I 258–61).

that had already enhanced the reputations of many Christian saints. What policy should the Church adopt on this pressing issue? If God's will were just and therefore satisfactory to man, and if it were His will that mortal man be afflicted with disease and suffering on account of his sins, did it not imply a distrust of that justice to capitalize one's merit in order to circumvent that will?

For a moment, in the time of Augustine, it might have seemed a sacrilege to try to impose on God's very merciful justice: for man could seem to be deserving, even with the added mercy, every bit of misery he got. For such a disposition of mind the doctrine of predestination was appropriate, for it denied the existence of human merit and hence of any power which could soften the will of God. The dead saint, even the living saint, might have that precious virtue which gives power, but, since that virtue came freely from God, so did the power; wherefore man, alive or dead, still deserved nothing.

How long could man remain thus hypnotized, deprived of his fond illusion of power? If the pagan could not stand this strain was it possible for even the stoutest Christian to hold out? If paganism should make way for human foibles how long could the Church afford to scorn them? Here was the pragmatic, as distinguished from the philosophical, import of the great controversy. Philosophically man is a fool, pragmatically he must live. With this ramification of the doctrine also, Leo had to concern himself. What would be the result if the Church should give way, not only to political, but also to psychological, expediency? It was futile to champion free will and justice on earth if these doctrines were not in fact true. But might they not be true? These doctrines were not appropriately designed to appeal to an Augustine; but why assume that God designed the world to suit this one man's fancy? Did He not rather design it to suit the fancy of the average man?

By embracing the doctrines of free will and of some small measure of justice on earth the path of theology seemed enormously facilitated. The holy man will accumulate a merit which deserves reward, and this reward may, not unreasonably, begin to be bestowed in the present life. For a reward, if it be real, must satisfy some holy wish, and, among the more common, was the wish that the lot of sinful man be lightened in this world as well as in the next. A true saint might suspect an affront were his reward on earth not shared in some degree by others, and this suspicion, however unfounded, would be a cross he did not deserve to bear.

Yet there was the reverse of the medal: if the wishes of the saints were to be respected, the wishes of God may at times be overruled. Not that a thing may happen against God's will, but a thing may happen because He wills to defer to the will of another. Theoretically, of course, no one would be a saint if his will conflicted with the will of God; practically, however, there has never been a saint who has not wished to see the lot of man alleviated, and, if it had been God's will to alleviate it, the fulfilment of that will must have already occurred. Even if a saint can conscientiously say 'Thy will be done', he can hardly view with full complacency what God's will has up to now achieved.[29] This statement is theologically incorrect, but psychologically it is undeniable.

Leo's dilemma was, therefore, the most momentous that confronted Christianity: for, if the Church were to admit that merit could be earned, she must also admit that it was rewarded, and, since this reward would not be just unless real, such a doctrine put God's whole system of justice, both on earth and in heaven, in jeopardy. Moreover, gloomy as the prospect was when viewed through the eye of Augustinian theology, Leo cannot have been for a moment unmindful of Augustine's warning: that once a man — even if a saint — is allowed to think he is something before long he will think he is everything.[30]

As Leo chose to play a waiting game, so did his successors; and the century ended without any official pronouncement. Free will still ruled in Gaul under Faustus, predestination still ruled among the persecuted Roman Catholics in Africa. In Italy the doctrine of Ambrose was being prepared as a

---

[29] See for example in Victor of Vita *H.P.A.P.* II § 54 where in 484 the persecuted Catholic bishop Eugenius cries, 'May God see the violence we are suffering, may He learn the afflictions to which we are being subjected by our persecutors.' Cf. ibid. III §§ 69–70.

[30] See pp. 75–76 & 129–130.

third conception. And everywhere, as embarrassing allies of
Augustine, the astrologers subsisted, Christian and even Catholic in name but unregenerate still, who taught that God's
will might be foreknown by a reading of the heavens.   Indeed thirty years after Leo's death Pope Gelasius is complain-
ing — much as Salvian had — of those who

are neither Christians nor pagans, who are ever perfidious and
never faithful, everywhere corrupt and nowhere honest, who are
as unable to hold to either faith as these two faiths are unable to
be reconciled with each other.[31]

That a large proportion of these were the believers in astrology is evident from a later passage in this Tract of Gelasius
where, speaking of the disasters that afflict mankind, he observes how

It is not surprising that men should wish to believe that these
things happen, not by divine judgment, but rather by the intervention of an empty superstition; for, in order to cover up their
infamies and crimes with the dictation of the heavens, they choose
to suppose that the stars are active and cause fatal error even to
the necessity of sinning, and thus that their infamies do not proceed from the perversity of their own hearts but depend on the
dictation of heaven.[32]

In the light of this passage it is inconceivable that Gelasius
did not clearly perceive the danger of sanctioning the doctrine of Augustine.   The good Sidonius cannot have been
the only bishop — and certainly not the only pious Catholic
— to talk loosely of how ' the real cause lies in mere earthly
fortune '.[33]   If the Roman was ever to be broken of his habit
of never blaming himself, some other doctrine than Augustine's was imperative.   The paradox that for his incapacities
man has only himself to blame may be the truth, but it is
only the sublime sophistry of genius that can steadily see
things so.[34]   And this genius, when Gelasius wrote, was now
over sixty years dead.

[31] *Tract* VI § 9 (on the Lupercalia).
[32] Ibid. § 22.

[33] *Letters* VII # 6 § 6.
[34] See pp. 77 n. 24 & 158–159.

CHAPTER VII

MONASTICISM

A. MONASTICISM BEFORE 406

So LONG as the persecutions lasted the layman could be as perfect as any other Christian — he had only to bear witness to his faith and thus, if need be, to die for it. But with the coming of Constantine his worldly position soon came to be as enviable as it had before been unenviable. The Christian religion, however, like almost any other, cries for self-sacrifice; above all, perhaps, as a mark of gratitude for divine favours already bestowed, but also in order to invite further favours. Yet how, now that the risk of martyrdom had passed, was a devout suppliant to prove the sincerity of his gratitude, how prove himself worthy of those further favours which, if he were to be saved, must also be bestowed? Prayer merely expressed intent; in order to prove that intent, even in the eyes of God, there must therefore also be works.[1] What was a work of self-sacrifice? It must be manifest and consequently physical, at least in part. This meant asceticism, a primitive practice which above all included chastity [2] because it was a sacrifice of the highest form of physical pleasure. Next came abstinence from food and drink, from comfortable and becoming dress, even from cleanliness and sleep. Not that this ascetic life was itself thought perfect, but it was thought to facilitate perfection — even to induce it automatically.

This ascetic life was first practised in the Egyptian deserts; soon after in Palestine and elsewhere in the East. First-hand knowledge of it reached the West only with the advent in Rome in 339 [3] of the great bishop Athanasius, in exile from his see of Alexandria. He had talked with the Egyptian hermits and now told tales of their wonders, of their mortifi-

---

[1] Cf. Faustus, according to Wörter 1899 80.
[2] See p. 175 n. 72.

[3] Spreitzenhofer 1894 9–10; Duchesne 1910 II [4] 449.

454

cations and miracles unapproached since the days of the Apostles.

The earliest recorded monastery in the West was a private nunnery in Rome, founded in 353 by Marcellina, elder sister of the great Ambrose.[4] The need was palpable, for women as well as men desired to lead the perfect Christian life and since the priesthood was closed to them [5] the nunnery in some form became imperative. Chastity, moreover, was a virtue particularly appropriate to women and it is probable that these first nuns in Rome took a vow of perpetual chastity in the presence of the bishop. At about the same time Eusebius of Vercelli, then the most imposing bishop in Italy, founded a monastery for men, one of its purposes, perhaps the decisive one, being to train boys for the priesthood.[6] Here the need was hardly less than for the nunnery. In an earlier day when every Christian was an enthusiast the priesthood could draw at will from the laity, but since the temporal triumphs of the preceding generation a more artificial apprenticeship was needed. We do not know what was the destiny of these first foundations; the monastic idea grew, however, from that time, though for another generation it was the Greek rather than the Latin element that predominated.[7]

The growing importance of the ascetic vocations is reflected in three civil laws of the year 370. One exempted the community property of nunneries from taxation: [8] the State evidently wished to encourage so worthy and innocent a vocation. Another law forbad monks as well as priests to accept legacies or gifts from widows or minors,[9] which indicates that monks had become numerous enough to include unscrupulous elements. Vowed to chastity, but uncloistered and undisciplined, the profession offered unfortunate opportunities for preying on the innocent. A third law declared that the taking of the monastic vow exempted no one from his hereditary obligations: neither *decurio* nor soldier could evade his duties by so simple an expedient.[10] These

---

4 Spreitzenhofer 1894 30; Dudden 1935 4.

5 See Dudden 1935 146. Until baptism in the nude was abolished in 440, however, decency required that women be delegated to baptize other women: Hefele 1908 II² 451.

6 Spreitzenhofer 1894 13–16.

7 See pp. 461 n. 51, & 486 n. 6.

8 Spreitzenhofer 1894 133.

9 Ibid. 78–79; Babut 1912 191.

10 Spreitzenhofer 1894 128. The date of the law was either 365, 372 or 373.

laws indicate that monasticism owed its first successes to worldly as well as unworldly considerations.[11]

In Gaul the first monk was Martin. Born in Pannonia, educated in Italy, he saw long service in the army, leaving it as an officer, but probably before the full legal enlistment of twenty years. Fired by ascetic Christian zeal, he moved, following his discharge at Worms in about 356, over much of Gaul, practising mortifications and working miracles.[12] For a time an exorcist under Hilary, bishop of Poitiers,[13] after a visit to his parents in Pannonia and a stay in Italy, he resumed his vocation as an itinerant miracle-worker in Gaul. Possibly his success in Tours was no greater than elsewhere; in the year 370, however, that see became vacant and the populace, in defiance, apparently, of the local clergy, elected Martin bishop by acclamation.[14] A miniature social revolution was thus effected: in place of the customary worldly and urbane priest the new bishop was a fanatical monk, virtually ignorant of theology and perhaps of letters, a miracle-man, who spent his time in fasting and prayer, who was clad in rags, dirty,[15] uncouth in behaviour,[16] scornful of rank and hierarchy,[17] incapable as an administrator,[18] humble only before God. But the still Celtic populace of Tours had insisted on him because he offered the kind of leadership they had faith in: because he was ascetic he was holy, because he was holy he possessed that magic ' virtue ' which made him a master of destiny: he could control the weather, control animals, control even men.[19] That the God to whom he so constantly prayed was the Christian God seemed to many of the people to be incidental; the important thing was that his prayers were answered, and they supposed that this was because his life was without a blemish, because he had disentangled himself from the coils of a hostile matter, from that Nature which

[11] The Council of Saragossa of 379 or 380 declared excommunicable all priests who took the monastic vow out of pride, as where they alleged that the New Law was better observed in that status: Hefele 1907 I 2 987.

[12] Babut 1912 197–98.

[13] Although ibid. 65–73, 184 &

187–89 doubts the truth of the whole episode.

[14] Ibid. 119–21.

[15] Ibid. 121.

[16] Ibid. 204–06.

[17] Ibid. 246.

[18] Ibid. 119–21.

[19] Ibid. 258–59; & cf. pp. 191 n. 97, 187 n. 78, & 189 n. 90.

so battered and broke them.   In this faith there was nothing
specifically Christian: pagan priests and philosophers [20] had
held their prestige by similar methods, and even the physicians of that day were expected to be chaste and abstinent
during a stated period before administering their cure.[21]   A
canon of the Council of Tours held much later, in 461, shows
that this conception was never eradicated:

Priests and deacons are urged to be always chaste: for at any moment they may be called upon to perform some holy office, as to
say mass, baptize, etc.[22]

Evidently asceticism's popular appeal in those days was less
on account of its psychological effect on the ascetic himself,
than of its physical effect on those to whom he ministered.
It was the chosen weapon of the humanitarian.   That is why
before long a physician who did not become a monk lost
his practice.

Not long after Martin became bishop of Tours he established an informal community of monks outside the city at
Marmoutier, imposing — rather by his prestige than by his
authority — an ascetic regime of the severest kind.[23]   One of
its chief aims was to train men for the priesthood.[24]   To the
customary austerities of chastity, fasting, and ragged poverty,
he probably added a minimum of sleep.[25]   Above all he
forbad manual labour of any kind — except the copying of
manuscripts by adolescents [26] — and filled the long hours thus
left at the monk's disposal with interminable prayers.   This
is interesting, because manual labour was favoured by the
Egyptian monks and was soon prescribed in the various monastic *Rules*.   Martin's objection to it may be inferred: asceticism involved a complete repudiation not only of women,[27]
but of all physical matter even in its most innocent forms.
Now of all activities prayer in silence was the least physical.

In 385, the sixteenth year of Martin's episcopate, Priscillian, the Spanish heretic, was tried as a Manichee before a

---

[20] Ibid. 89–91, & 254–55.
[21] Ibid. 256.
[22] Canon # 1: Hefele 1908 II 2
899.
[23] Babut 1912 134–35, 238 & 241–
42.
[24] Ibid. 245.

[25] Ibid. 238.
[26] Ibid. 243.
[27] Martin decried marriage: Babut
1912 152; and he avoided the smallest
physical proximity to women: ibid.
204–06 & 244.

civil court at Trier and was condemned and executed with several of his followers. This Priscillian was a highly educated person, bishop at Avila and the head of a powerful minority of the Spanish clergy. The affair caused a great stir. Priscillian was probably not a Manichee,[28] but he was an ascetic and so a declared enemy of matter; in addition he was a dualist who did not believe that the good God had created the material world and the material body of man.[29] Incidentally he had unorthodox views on the nature of the Trinity.[30] Ambrose, the Pope, and other important churchmen had at first encouraged proceedings against the sect; [31] later, when they saw that Priscillian was to be accused as a Manichee and was therefore in danger of execution, they tried, though in vain, to stay the proceedings.[32]

It was probably the next year, in 386, that Martin appeared in Trier.[33] His biographer Severus says he went of his own initiative to protest against further violence against Priscillian's sect; it is likely, however, that he was summoned.[34] At any rate he was, on his arrival, accused of being a Priscillianist.[35] He was acquitted, but perhaps only after a formal recantation of certain views — which he may or may not have held — and was allowed to retain his bishopric only after receiving communion with the other bishops, many of whom had been the ring-leaders against Priscillian. Martin later said this act was a shame he could never forget, and he never thereafter, during the eleven remaining years of his episcopal life, attended a Synod. Thus he returned to Tours in disgrace; scorned now by many of the populace as well as by the clergy, he admitted that from that time forth his miraculous powers diminished.[36] As his people lost faith in him, he lost faith in himself. In his old age he talked more freely than ever with angels and devils, but over men his spell was broken.

[28] Babut 1912 152.
[29] Fourth Council of Carthage of 398, canon # 1: Hefele 1908 II [2] 110 & n. 1; Duchesne 1910 II [4] 548.
[30] Duchesne 1910 II [4] 548.
[31] Ibid. 533 & 535–36.
[32] Ibid. 538. In the interval Pope Siricius had succeeded Pope Damasus, in 384.

[33] Babut 1912 149.
[34] Ibid.
[35] Severus *Chronica* II ch. 50. And cf. Babut 1912 140–42, citing *Dialogue* III 12 & 13.
[36] Babut 1912 140–50 & 154–55. Cf. p. 191 n. 96.

That Martin was accused of Priscillian's heresy is clear, but that he was in any sense a member of that sect is most unlikely. That heresy had spread into Aquitaine; [37] it may have reached Tours, but it was, in so far as we know it, an intellectual conception, like the Manichæan, whose tenets appealed primarily to philosophically-minded men. Martin was not a theologian; he was merely a saint. Probably he did show sympathy for Priscillian — but so, in the last phase, did Ambrose and Pope Siricius — and his sympathy was based not only on horror of cruelty but also on admiration for what he had heard of Priscillian's holy abstinence. And precisely because Martin espoused the same principles of living, berating the worldly clerical standard and even decrying marriage, he was suspected of complicity with the Priscillianist sect.[38] The affinity, indeed, went deeper than he or anyone else probably realized: it is hardly a coincidence that both Priscillian and Martin's disciple and biographer Severus quoted freely from the Apocryphal Acts.[39] Now these were a tissue of miracles and the Catholic clergy were not yet reconciled to such fantasies. The association of ideas is a natural one: the extreme ascetic seeks to free himself from the taint of matter; he does this because he believes that matter and spirit are incompatible, that unless evil matter is overcome by spiritual virtue the soul is impotent, but that if this evil matter is overcome the soul will acquire a potency that will enable it to conquer matter. Priscillian, in so far as he was a Manichee,[40] hoped to free the soul from matter in order that it might re-assume its pristine divinity; Martin, as an ascetic Catholic, hoped that by freeing himself from matter he could not only circumvent and escape but manipulate and tame it. To the Priscillianist matter was an enemy; to Martin it was merely a slave. Certainly no Manichee would have described a demon, even though he were Jupiter, as ' heavy, stupid, and dull '.[41] For Martin had faith not only in God's goodness but in His omnipotence. He differed from

[37] Duchesne 1910 II 4 536; & Dudden 1935 228.

[38] Babut 1912 138–39.

[39] For Priscillian, see Duchesne 1910 II 4 530; for Severus, see Babut 1912 226–29 & 234–36 — & 89–91 for the Neopythagorean influence on Severus.

[40] Babut 1912 152 says Priscillian was not one.

[41] See p. 191 n. 99.

the clergy of his day and from Augustine only in his conception of the purpose for which God created matter: to them
God intended it, by its use or abuse, to actualize the potentialities of the soul for good or evil; to Martin God intended
it, by its rejection or use — for any use was an abuse — to
become either man's slave or his master. Augustine sought
a happy marriage with matter; Martin sought a tyrannical
mastery over it. To Augustine man's mastery of himself was
an end; to Martin it was a means to a physical control over
a physical world. This does not mean that Martin was inferior in holiness; but it does mean that he was inferior in
imagination.

Damasus, who was Pope from 366 to 384, was partial to
monasticism: two of his sisters were nuns [42] and he befriended
Jerome during the latter's stay in Rome.[43]   But to him succeeded Pope Siricius, who proceeded to make Rome so uncomfortable for Jerome that he and his disciples left almost
at once for Palestine [44] — never to return.   Siricius also disliked [45] that other famous Italian ascetic, Paulinus, who came
to Nola in 392 in a blaze of publicity.   Siricius had no objection to monasticism in principle.   He recognized the validity of the vow of chastity by penalizing its breach with life
penance; [46] he was also ready to accept as an aspirant for the
priesthood any monk who could prove himself qualified.[47]
On the other hand an official letter of his, written in about
386, shows clearly why he viewed this novel profession with
misgiving:

Here, however, which is most contrary to the laws, are itinerants
— monks they call themselves whether they really are such or not
— men whose past and manner of baptism we cannot verify, whose
real faith is unknown and unproved; bishops are unwilling to
give them alms, but they show haste to make them deacons or to
ordain them priests, or — what is worse — do not hesitate to install
them even as bishops.   It seems to them cheaper to give itinerants
holy orders than alms.   The monks are not tried out; hence they

42 Spreitzenhofer 1894 30–31.
43 Duchesne 1910 II [4] 478–82.
44 Ibid. 483–84; & see Jerome Letters # # 22–25, 39 & 127.
45 Lagrange 1877 196–97; & Caspar
1930 I 260.

46 Spreitzenhofer 1894 99–100.
47 By the prescribed periods of apprenticeship in the lower offices of
the clerical hierarchy: Letter # 1
§§ 13 & 18. Cf. pp. 309 n. 44, & 641
n. 22.

become puffed up with pride and — what is worse — soon fall into heresy. For it is matter of common knowledge that strangers are more than likely to hold unorthodox views.[48]

Surely in issuing this warning Siricius had bishop Martin in mind. For Martin had been baptized, no one knew how, in Pannonia, had clung to monkish ways after assuming the episcopal office, and had been accused, and barely acquitted, of heresy. Siricius may have had other bishops in mind too — Victricius of Rouen who was a friend of Martin's, and Delphinus of Bordeaux.[49] And Paulinus of Bordeaux was soon to assume the see of Nola in a similar state of ascetic exaltation. Siricius may also have had in mind [50] the Priscillianist bishops, who before 385 controlled much of Spain, and who had also persisted in their ascetic life after election. An added reason for the prejudice of Siricius was the oriental character of the ascetic movement. In Rome, at any rate, most of the monks were either Greeks or else, like Jerome, Latins under the oriental spell. It was a popular pastime in the streets of the city to greet the passing monk with a Greek epithet.[51] How Siricius the priest rated the monastic vocation is further indicated by his decree that the penance for Manichees who recanted [52] and for priests who had obtained a fraudulent ordination [53] was to spend the rest of their days in a monastery. Under the Merovingians this use of the monastery as an involuntary penitentiary became habitual.

Officially, then, and among the intelligentsia, monasticism at the end of the fourth century was still under suspicion. It was regarded as a foreign importation, a breeding-ground for heresy and social unrest, to exist only on sufferance and under strict surveillance. A civil law of 390 had actually banished all monks from the cities.[54] In the West it was the severely ascetic Ambrose who [55] first effectively espoused their cause. In 392 he secured the repeal of the law of banishment,[56] and throughout his episcopate he lent the monks a generous hand. When he died in 397 the fame of Paulinus was already abroad. He, not only an enormously rich Gallic aristocrat

---

[48] *Letter # 6 § 4.*
[49] Cf. Babut 1912 195–96 & 260–62.
[50] Cf. ibid. 194 n. 3.
[51] Ibid. 191–92.
[52] Spreitzenhofer 1894 10–11.
[53] Ibid. 98.
[54] Ibid. 128.
[55] Dudden 1935 513.
[56] Spreitzenhofer 1894 128.

but also a man of real force and talent, stamped the ascetic life with a prestige it had hitherto lacked. Paulinus was the first Latin to become a monk without losing caste; he, more than any other, helped to make the vocation respectable as well as alluring. At the same time the growing reputation of Jerome as translator of the Bible — out of the Hebrew as well as out of the Greek — and as a learned commentator on its divinely revealed obscurities, served to teach many that asceticism and learning were compatible.

Augustine's attitude, on the other hand, was non-committal: he loved the wise monks, despised the foolish ones; [57] he encouraged the nunneries — actually drafted a *Rule* for them [58] — avoided a conflict with the tempestuous Jerome, even longed himself for the quiet of the contemplative life. His relations with Paulinus also were invariably friendly. It was otherwise, however, with those two close friends of Paulinus, with the priest-monk Severus, biographer of Martin, and with Pelagius the itinerant monk of Britain. Augustine's disapproval of Pelagius was open and vociferous; his disapproval of Martin and Severus is to be inferred by his utter silence in regard to both of them during the 33 years between the publication of the *Life* of Martin and his own death in 430. Why was this? Since Augustine carefully refrained from telling why, it would be presumptuous of us to speak for him. At the same time it is safe to assume that the unremitting emphasis on the miracle [59] was most offensive to him. Augustine was too honest to discredit the stories without investigation; at the same time he did not believe them. Silence was in such a case the only prudent course. Another thing in the *Life* too, must have repelled Augustine. Over and over again he had emphasized that the apparent miracle, when it occurred, did so not by any positive act of virtue by any man but wholly by the arbitrary will of God. God's hand was not to be forced, even by a show of virtue. Yet he must have been aware that the constant emphasis in the *Life* on Martin's virtue as the cause of the miracle was insidious. For the human power to work miracles must inevitably seem a delegation of superhuman and so divine power. In the recipient this must lead

[57] Montalembert 1863 I 2 216–17.   [59] See pp. 188 ff.
[58] See *Letters* # # 210–11.

to pride and so to that very sin which precipitated the devil into hell. What was this pride if not that of the Stoic, Neoplatonist, Manichee, Priscillianist, and Pelagian, each of whom harboured a faith in the essential divinity of the human soul? If a human soul could, by emancipating itself from matter, escape the fate which that matter held in store, it was no longer a human but a divine soul. Matter would then be the source of evil and the soul what many pagans had always imagined it: a particle of the divinity. Augustine clung desperately to his extreme doctrines because he believed that only by doing so could the kernel of Christianity be kept intact. Once the essential principle had been lost sight of, it must only be a matter of time before the relapse into paganism became complete. All these things Augustine did not specifically prophesy, but a predilection for prophecy is not a characteristic of the humble and wise.

It was just at the turn of the century that monasticism was first widely advertised in the West: in 396 appeared the *Life of Martin;* the *Letters* and *Dialogues* followed by 404. Not long before this [60] the monk Rufinus of Aquileia had offered the Latin world a translation from the Greek of Basil's monastic *Rule,* the first demonstration to the Latin West that monasteries might have an aim, a discipline, a consistent order of living. Then in about 402 Rufinus made his translation of the *Historia Monachorum,* a forerunner of Palladius' more famous *Lausiac History* [61] from which Palladius was to draw much of his material. Here the great panorama of Egyptian monasticism in all its variety and eccentricity was spread before the eyes of the Latins. Here were revealed the lives of many thousands of Christians leading, at that very moment, a life hitherto associated with a miraculous past age. Here the marvellous experiences described in the *Acts* were being re-lived by ordinary men in ordinary human flesh. What the Egyptians were doing any man might also do; if he cared sincerely to save his soul, here and now was his opportunity.

[60] Rufinus, in his continuation of Eusebius' *Ecclesiastical History* II 9, refers to his Latin translation of Basil's *Instituta Monachorum.* This continuation was written in about 401: Migne *P.L.* 21 222.

[61] Which was written in about 420: Zöckler 1904 XIV 610 lines 44–48. But the first Latin translation of it was made in Africa only shortly before 500: Butler 1898–1904 I 63–64.

For obvious reasons nunneries had won official favour much sooner than monasteries — in the closing years of the fourth century a great number of canons are devoted to the protection and regulation of nuns.[62]   But up to this time the laws and canons which concerned monks had betrayed rather resentment than good will.   Now, however, there were signs of a change of attitude towards the monks.   In 398 a civil law saddled the bishop with responsibility for the crimes of monks as well as of priests.[63]   That the bishop accepted this burden with some misgivings we may well believe; at the same time it offered him a pretext for exercising a control over their vagaries.   In one sense still repressive legislation, in another sense it was a tacit recognition by the authorities that the monk was an integral part of the ecclesiastical hierarchy. No longer, as in 390, was he a public nuisance; properly disciplined he might prove a beneficent element in the community.   A canon of the Council of Toledo of 400 now conferred on the monks their first concrete privilege: it declared that where an unclaimed slave, freedman, or serf fled to a monastery he could not take his vow for three years, but if, having taken it, the master thereafter came to claim him, though his property might be taken he himself could not be.[64] Such a canon would hardly have been promulgated unless with the consent of the State, and it therefore appears that the monkish vocation was winning a new respect.   Furthermore a law which thus favoured the serf presupposes an analogous privilege accorded to freemen bound, like soldiers or *decuriones,* by the law of hereditary occupations.   With this canon of Toledo, therefore, monasticism began its thoughtless work of undermining the civic fabric.   The monks had challenged the sovereignty of the State, and the State here shows a first sign of debility.

Pope Siricius had forbidden monks to accept clerical offices until they had served the apprenticeship, and reached the age that canon law prescribed.[65]   After a three year pontificate

---

[62] Council of Hippo of 393, canons 5 & 35; Council of Carthage of 398, canon 12; Council of Toledo of 400, canons 6, 9, 16, & 19; Council of Rome of 402, canons 1 & 2: Hefele 1908 II 2 82–107.

[63] Spreitzenhofer 1894 122–23.
[64] Ibid. 52 n. 3.
[65] See p. 460 n. 47.

Pope Anastasius had died in 401, and he was succeeded by Innocent I. This Innocent now decreed that no monk might evade his vows by ordination.[66] May this not imply that Siricius had intimated the contrary? For a clerical career was very different from a monastic, especially in such matters as fasting and poverty: the abstinence imposed on a priest was relatively mild, the degree of poverty expected of him was vague, he was allowed, even expected, to keep a decent table, to dress well, to maintain an impressive retinue — outwardly, indeed, to live much like his civilian counterpart, according to his exalted station. It is likely that Siricius conceived of the priesthood as a clear promotion to a higher status than the monastic and therefore wished the vow to be conditional and so automatically invalidated by such promotion. Perhaps the view of Siricius did not go so far; but at least he was non-committal, whereas Innocent — and Pope Zosimus after him [67] — spoke out categorically. Further evidence of a growing respect for the monastic vow is Innocent's decree that monks or nuns who fornicate shall undergo first a public penance and thereafter a life penance in a monastery, being qualified to receive the sacrament only on their deathbeds.[68] Moreover Innocent [69] was the first Pope to distinguish the regular nun from the laywoman who has merely made a vow of chastity: [70] either kind commits a sin in marrying, but the penance imposed on the latter is milder and her marriage is validated. Thus under Innocent both monks and nuns are becoming disassociated from laymen and are becoming an integral part of the ecclesiastical hierarchy.

It was early in the pontificate of Innocent that the priest Vigilantius of Narbonne, once associated with the priest-monks Paulinus and Severus, turned against the whole monastic conception of life. In his quarrel with Jerome he had argued that the marriage, at least of deacons, was wholesome, that it was folly for a rich man to strip himself of his wealth and so of his civic responsibilities, that the monastic vocation

---

[66] Spreitzenhofer 1894 94–95 & 101 n. 1.

[67] Ibid. 95. But Celestine revived the old prejudice: see p. 490.

[68] Ibid. 101. Pope Leo repeated his decree: ibid.

[69] Ibid. 1894 100.

[70] As understood by Ambrose: Dudden 1935 152–57.

was too often a pretext for the evasion of irksome duties, and that miracles which furthered other objects than conversions were likely to be fraudulent.[71]   Unlike Augustine, who was incomparable, Vigilantius was merely the representative of a fast-dying type; an enlightened but uninspired Roman-Christian who could see all the sides of a problem, he counselled discretion at a moment when the average man had lost all patience.   In the conflict now going on between the two Cities, he stands out as the eternal neutral, inviting only the contempt of both the belligerents.   In the jaws of a cataclysm he spoke impotently for an orderly evolution.   To both his Roman urbanity and his Christian devotion men turned only a deaf ear.

Jerome's controversy with Vigilantius occurred in 406, the very year in which the barbarians broke the Rhine frontier and poured over Gaul and into Spain.   A physical convulsion was now superimposed to accelerate and accentuate the spiritual convulsion.   Up to that year monasticism had hardly been a factor in the Roman world; it had been chiefly a subject of irritation or derision.   At Rome itself it had secured a foothold chiefly among the Greek-speaking residents; elsewhere in Italy it had won respect only in a few regions, notably at Vercelli,[72] Milan, [73] Naples,[74] and Aquileia.[75]   By the year 450 there were also foundations at Ravenna, Pavia,[76] Novara, Cremona, Bologna,[77] and Terracina [78] for men, as well as others for women,[79] and some of these date from before 406. On the whole, however, the monk of 406 was still regarded as a freak.   To most Romans, even if Christians, the name monk called to mind chiefly the hermits who lived almost like beasts on the islands off the coast — a friend of Jerome's lived on an island in the Adriatic; others lived on islands off the Tuscan

[71] See p. 198. And cf. Babut 1912 49.

[72] See p. 197 n. 6 on Eusebius of Vercelli.

[73] Ambrose founded two monasteries and a convent: Spreitzenhofer 1894 18–19.

[74] Paulinus of Nola was instrumental in starting two monasteries there before 412: ibid. 22.

[75] Where Rufinus and Jerome were trained in about 370: ibid. 19.

[76] Dudden 1935 145.

[77] Soon after 400: Spreitzenhofer 1894 19.

[78] By 400: ibid. 23.

[79] Ibid. 32–34.   Convents were more numerous, especially in Rome: ibid. 30–31. And see Dudden 1935 146.

or Ligurian coast.[80]   What Christians thought of these folk must have depended chiefly on their own disposition of mind; what at least one pagan thought of them is made plain by a passage of the Gallic poet Rutilius Namatianus, written as he sailed past one of these islands on his way home from Rome in the year 416:

Now, by our advance over the sea, Capraria rises.
This island swarms with men who shun the light.
They call themselves monks after the Greek name
Because they want to live alone without witnesses.
They fear the gifts of chance because they fear its injuries.
Why should anyone make himself voluntarily miserable
In order that he may be unable later to become so?
What madness of a perverse mind was ever so stupid
As to reject good things from dread of evil things?
Such men either seek prisons as if punishments imposed by Fate
Or else their gloomy viscera swell with black gall.

I shun those rocks, monuments of a recent catastrophe:
Here a fellow-citizen was lost in a living tomb.
Until lately he was one of us, a youth of distinguished family,
Not lacking in money and happily married.
But, driven by the furies, he abandoned both men and gods,
So that now, a credulous exile, he seeks a base concealment.
This wretch thinks that in his filth he is feeding on heavenly
      things,
Yet actually the offended gods are not oppressing him as he op-
      presses himself.
I ask whether this sect is not worse than the poison of Circe:
For in that case only the body was transformed; now it is the
      soul.[81]

The venom of Rutilius betrays the consciousness of a lost cause.

The decrees and canons of this time show that there were monasteries in Spain and Africa as well as in Italy, but there is no record of specific foundations.   Of Gaul we know more. Besides Martin's Marmoutier he may have instituted something of the sort at Ligugé, near Poitiers, though the evidence of it is vague.[82]   Severus also tried to carry on the tradition of Martin at his estate of Prémillac, in Périgord.[83]   Apart from

[80] Gouilloud 1881 35.
[81] De Reditu Suo I lines 439–48 & 517–26.
[82] Babut 1912 185–89.
[83] Ibid. 39–42.

these the only indications are of foundations by Martin's friend Victricius, bishop of Rouen,[84] and of hermits on the Stoechades islands off Hyères.[85]

B. Cassian's Monasticism

The Christian monks sought to cultivate perfection of the soul; since this had been an instinct with good men from the earliest times, the monastic movement was partly a recrudescence of an ancient phenomenon. As antiquity had matured, its imperfections had matured with it, had crystallized and hardened, grown ineradicable short of some cataclysm of nature. The spiritual energy unloosed by the Christian Revelation had little effect so long as antiquity was content, but as the old world gradually lost faith in itself the Christian pressure increased. As the temporal life became more unlovely it became the easier to forsake. In an earlier chapter [1] we spoke of the growing impatience with cruelty, obscenity, gluttony, riches, and pride, and of the natural recourse to their ascetic opposites, to mercy, chastity, fasting, poverty, and humility. Of this Christianity was perhaps rather the happy occasion than the original cause. Yet it has been too often alleged that Christianity's triumph should be ascribed, not to the peculiarities of its doctrine, but to its opportune promise of a Utopian salvation at a moment when hope of an earthly Utopia had gone. In a sense, of course, this is true, for the Christian heaven undeniably offered an alluring consolation to the broken and battered. A certain discrimination, however, must here be exercised. It is true that many, perhaps most, Christians of this time were much influenced by both the fear of hell and the hope of future delights; it is true that these delights included not only things to charm the senses — rich fabrics, a profusion of gold, music, a healthy body, and much more [2] — but also a healing of the wounds of the soul — if

---

[84] Dalton 1927 I 348–74 — at Boulogne and Thérouanne.
[85] Gouilloud 1881 35.

[1] See pp. 140 ff.
[2] Cf. Prudentius *Peristephanon* II 275–76; & anonymous *S. Hilarii Arelat. Vita* 19.

not actual pride at least a sense of achievement, coupled with the assurance that no further effort would be demanded. But these things merely substantiate our suspicion that man is human and will long remain so; it proves nothing as to the peculiar quality of the Christian ideal. For the truth is that the qualifications required for admittance to this heaven and the standard set for the life there after admittance were novelties of a very high order. The old pagan gods had carried on a life of petty scandal and intrigue, wielding wide powers without conscience or even decency. Nor were the gods of many of the oriental cults always more dignified. Such gods could not require of men a higher standard of virtue. Of all the pagan conceptions of an after-life the least uninspiring was that of the Neoplatonist or Manichee who conceived of a re-absorption of the human soul into the immensity of the perfectly virtuous One.[3] Yet this, although noble and flattering, presupposed an annihilation of the soul's individuality.[4] In complete contrast was the Christian conception of a reality ordered only for the furtherance and glorification of virtue in its purest and yet wholly individual forms. That few Christians could grasp the essence of this virtue without debasing it with gold ornament and the prospect of a safe indulgence in self-respect, merely proves what we already knew: Romans in becoming Christians, even in becoming saints, did not wholly cease to be Romans and men.

To say, then, that Christianity triumphed because the misery of its hell was matched only by the delights of its heaven is merely to repeat a platitude about human nature; it tells us virtually nothing about that Christianity which, while it appealed to men, also transformed them. For it was above all a revelation of a new kind of human virtue, hitherto envisaged by a few heathens only, and by these vaguely and ineffectually. For the decisive conception, both intrinsically and pragmatically, was of a Being, divine in His power and perfection, human in His understanding and mercy. Christ's

[3] To be sure Plato had had a conception of individual immortality in a state of pure virtue and bliss: see for instance von Hügel 1909 II 203–11. But the popular appeal of this doctrine was always slight, and this was probably because it offered no real human contacts, either with a personal God or with others. Instead it offered a rather forbidding isolation, each soul having its own separate star.

[4] See pp. 36 n. 48, & 65 n. 14.

importance was not only as the historical Saviour but also as
the eternal Demigod, a living proof of the compatibility of
complete virtue and complete manhood.   The problem of
maintaining the concept of God's perfection and of man's
corruption, and at the same time the compatibility of the two,
was the most unremitting task of an Augustine and a Leo.[5]
It was their faith in the apparently and logically impossible
that brought antiquity to their feet.

It is odd, therefore, that monasticism, which was to prove
the reality of this incredible revelation, started its career on
the tangent of chastity — as if divine and human love offered the vital antithesis.   And — as if chastity were only a
symbol of all human or carnal love — not only was the love of
man and woman belittled but even that of mother and child.[6]
Lest this carnal love of man for man should raise its ugly
head, monasticism at first demanded that holiness be ugly:
a coarse raiment, a foul skin, and an emaciated body were
thought appropriate to virtue not only because of the discomfort it caused the person himself but also because of the
sensuous repulsion it induced in the beholder.[7]   Even Ambrose and Augustine, though they could thank God for the
beauty of His sky and air and light, thought His last and
supreme creation, of the young woman, had beauty less to
regale and console than to seduce and destroy.   And to
monks like Martin [8] and Jerome marriage was offensive, not
only because it sanctified the love of man and woman but
because it might lead to child-birth and so to the equally
carnal seduction of mother-love.

Today the familiar monastic vow of ' chastity, poverty and
obedience ' betrays an historical rather than a logical origin:
for if these virtues should be realized there would be no children, no creature comforts, no mental activity.   The vow
sounds fortuitous, moreover, for the good reason that it was
so: a hermit who was not chaste would be a satyr; a hermit
who was served by slaves would be a contradiction in terms.
On the other hand a hermit who obeyed would be no less
of an anomaly.   Thus the idea of obedience arose only as the

[5] See pp. 50 n. 46, & 604–05.

[6] Cf. Jerome Letter # 108 § 6; & cf.
on Cassian, p. 482 n. 80.

[7] Cf. Martin, see p. 456 n. 15; &
Jerome Letter # 45 §§ 3 & 5.

[8] Babut 1912 152.

hermits ceased to be anchorites and, banding together into a community, became cenobites. The monastery having thus been formed, the older conceptions, of chastity and poverty, subsisted, although the latter soon underwent the happy transformation from misanthropy to charity. As the cenobitic community evolved it solicited riches and obtained them; it even embarked on a systematic cultivation of the soil and built hospitals [9] as well as churches, thereby accumulating a surplus for distribution in charity. This was a gradual change, more characteristic of a later age than of this one, for in the year 400 few Latin [10] monasteries had anything to spare. Among the first foundations which could afford the luxury of effective charity were those fathered by bishop Cæsarius of Arles in the early sixth century.

Monastic charity did, indeed, have its beginnings at this time; but only because of a few very rich persons who adopted the monastic way of life. Paulinus of Nola was doubtless a great saint, but his fame could hardly have arisen without the sensational sale of his great estates in order that the proceeds might go to the poor.[11] Furthermore, Paulinus even long after his definite renunciation, was still a rich man: whether he found it hard to find purchasers willing to pay a fair price or whether he held on to the proceeds with future needs or emergencies in mind, the fact remains that even ten years after his determination to adopt a life of poverty he was spending money lavishly on his foundations at Nola.[12] The same is true of the noble men and women whom Jerome was at this same time enticing from Rome to a monastic life in the East. Their income was no doubt spent on the poor rather than on themselves; at the same time it is not always clear that they relinquished control over the disposal of their principal. On the contrary their resources seem to have remained unimpaired even after many years of holy living in the East.[13] Willingly or unwillingly, then, they clung to the power and prestige which ownership confers. To be obsequi-

[9] See pp. 263 n. 73, & 638 n. 14.

[10] Cassian De Institutis X 22 describes it as an Egyptian practice; but in Conlationes IX 5–6 he suggests that its desirability was questionable.

[11] On Melania see Goyau 1921 [9] 56.

[12] Lagrange 1877 480. On Melania see Goyau 1921 [9] 130.

[13] Spreitzenhofer 1894 80–81. Observe that Jerome Letter # 79 § 1 says that 'wealth need not stand in the way of the rich man, if he makes good use of it.' And cf. ibid. § 3. On

ous to a Pammachius, to flatter his vanity, was still profitable: it might lead to the most unexpected largesses and endowments. To insinuate that Jerome so demeaned himself is gratuitous; yet the fact remains that his correspondence — and so his flattery — was confined largely to persons not only noble and prominent but still very rich. That Jerome wanted no money for himself does not mean that he was wholly indifferent to it.

Variations in standard of living among monks living in a single community would naturally have been intolerable; nevertheless it must be obvious that some communities, because of the wealth still at the disposal of their members, enjoyed advantages impossible in others. It was only in 466 that the civil law, prompted by a growing public opinion, declared monks incapable of devising their property except to their own monasteries.[14] Henceforth, so long as they remained monks, their ownership became a mere life tenancy, their monastery holding the reversionary right to the principal. A monk might, of course, still inherit property, for if rich parents could not legally devise property to their own son they might be reluctant to devise instead to his monastery. But until after 450 when monasticism began to be popular it was dangerous to restrict the monk's rights — because the chief effect would have been to divert the prospective inheritance into alien hands.

It is unfortunate that we do not know more about the nature of the monastic vow: that chastity was invariably involved, and that the vow was solemnly taken in the presence of a bishop, seems clear. It is safe to assume, too, that it included an acknowledgment of episcopal authority — although this may simply have been implied from the nature of the ceremony itself. The bishop could then properly instruct the monk to regard himself as subject to a given community and its abbot. Since the monk was offensive to the Church, and so to the bishops who received the vow, until after 386,[15] the additional vow of poverty was perhaps not at first included. And, even if and when included, this must have been with the

---

Ambrose's disposition of his property when he became bishop in 373, see Dudden 1935 107.

[14] Spreitzenhofer 1894 82–83.
[15] Babut 1912 156.

tacit understanding that it meant, not legal poverty, but a life of poverty. That after 401, however, the monastic vow included more than chastity is clear from the distinction first made by Pope Innocent between the woman who merely makes a vow of chastity and one who takes the regular monastic vow.[16]

The turning point was the shift from the irresponsibility of the hermit to the organization of the cenobite — from independence to obedience. Technically no other vow than that of obedience was necessary: for chastity, poverty, fasting, physical trials, and labours, could all be then imposed at the abbot's discretion. But it was also necessary to set a limit to the abbot's authority; before taking the vow a man must know the extent of his submission, and what guarantees, if any, he might rely on against a tyrannical regime. Some *Rule* was therefore needed which should bind not only the community but abbot and bishop also — a *Rule* of laws and not of men.

The first *Rule* known in the West was Basil's, through Rufinus' Latin translation made shortly before 400.[17] It had a considerable vogue in Italy,[18] although rather as a guide to abbots in making their own than as a law imposed from outside. It was designed independently of Egyptian models,[19] yet borrowed much from their wider experience; it differed chiefly in mitigating the harshness of their asceticism.[20] In place of excessive fasting and physical discomfort the requirement was rather of hard work with both hand and brain — including instruction of the young.[21] Designed for the climate of temperate Asia Minor instead of tropical Egypt, it allowed more food[22] but also demanded more work.[23] Essentially, however, there was no contrast; and if individual weaknesses were taken into account in the allotment of work,[24] individual tastes were mercilessly trampled upon.[25] Rabelais' motto *Fay ce que vouldras* died as the hermit life did: the taming of lions or a sojourn on pillars was giving way to a

---

16 Spreitzenhofer 1894 101.
17 Ibid. 41; and Migne *P.L.* 21 222B & 520C.
18 Spreitzenhofer 1894 42–43.
19 Ibid. 89.
20 Ibid. 87–89.

21 Ibid. 93.
22 Ibid. 84–85.
23 Montalembert 1863 I 2 111.
24 Spreitzenhofer 1894 87–88.
25 Montalembert 1863 I 2 111.

methodical and impersonal routine. Man's individuality was henceforth the old Adam in him which must be crushed.[26]

About a generation after Basil's *Rule* had appeared in Italy another and more impressive one became generally known: this was the *Rule* of Cassian, the monk of Provence whom we have already mentioned as the initiator of the doctrine called Semi-Pelagianism. Cassian was born in Scythia[27] in about 360[28] and much of his earlier life was spent in visiting and studying the monks of Egypt.[29] Following this thorough apprenticeship he appeared in Provence at some date not long after 405 and there, with the consent of the bishop of Marseilles, founded a monastery in or close to that city. It was in about 417 that, upon the request of another bishop, Castor of Apt,[30] he drafted his famous *Institutions,* in which he incorporated his views of a proper monastic law. His source was Egypt, the modifications were his own. It was the first systematic exposition on this subject and, as such, had so great a success that in subsequent years, between 423 and 429,[31] he was induced to elaborate on the same theme in three Books of *Conferences,* in which the various leaders of Egyptian monasticism appear to give their views on a variety of pertinent matters. It was in Book II, for instance, that the famous *Conference* XIII occurs, where Cassian chooses above any others the doctrine of abbot Chæremon on merit and grace. Perhaps other abbots and holy men held other views on this delicate subject, but Cassian reproduces this one of the abbot Chæremon because it seemed to him the most orthodox and convincing. Whatever may have been his models, therefore, it is safe to assume that the doctrines and rules contained in these two works were, if only by adoption, his own.

Now the very interesting thing to be observed about these

---

[26] Which was in line with the tendency to regimentation and standardization so characteristic of the times: see p. 265.

[27] See Duchesne 1911 III⁴ 272 n. 2 on Gennadius' description of Cassian — *De Scriptoribus Eccles.* ch. 61 — as ' natione Scytha '. Since his Latin is excellent he must have come from a Latin speaking part of Scythia.

[28] ' mit einiger Sicherheit ', says Grützmacher 1897 III 746.

[29] 383 says Grützmacher ibid.; 390 says Spreitzenhofer 1894 43, as the earliest date.

[30] Gouilloud 1881 169; Spreitzenhofer 1894 43.

[31] Gouilloud 1881 172.

works is a clear indication that chastity and poverty, that fasting, mortification, and prayer, that obedience even — though
stressed above all [32] — are each merely means to an end, and
that this end is not renunciation of the world and the flesh
but rather the pure love of God.   Already well evolved is that
conception of the ladder of perfection which is the mystic
way; already is here revealed to us the immensity of the scale
— the width of the sweep, the depth of exploration below the
surface.   Combining four passages in these works we can
piece together an already ordered sequence whereby, rung by
rung, corrupt man may rise to that ' experimental conception
of the presence of God in the soul '.[33]   That the conception
of such a ladder was specifically Christian, Augustine himself
would not have alleged; but already here in Cassian there is
both a concreteness and a subtlety which no Neoplatonist or
other pagan had matched.

Very roughly, the rungs follow this order: faith leads to that
fear of hell — or of God's wrath — which breaks the devil's
pride and induces a servile obedience.[34]   This first involves
salutary compunction [35] or remorse, and so confession [36] and
penitence.   Next come the concrete renunciations or mortifications of desire [37] — of property, of women, of relations and
friends, of the whole sensuous and physical world.[38]   The
carnal sins having thus been shackled,[39] the time is ripe for
active discipline, for the performance of menial and even repulsive tasks,[40] for the effort to obey impossible commands.[41]
These acts induce the first step in humility by eliminating all
excuse for pride.[42]

At this point the fear of hell is replaced by a mercenary
hope of salvation; [43] there ensues a violent effort to acquire a
real virtue because of the selfish advantage that this promises.[44]
The simpler spiritual virtues which lie easily within the reach
of all who try hard — as of patience, gentleness, forebearance,
silence,[45] etc. — are first acquired, and from these arise the

[32] Montalembert 1863 I 2 111;
Spreitzenhofer 1894 55.
[33] See p. 47 n. 40.
[34] *Conlationes* XI 6–8.
[35] *De Institutis* IV 43.
[36] Ibid. 39.
[37] Ibid.
[38] *Conl.* III 6.
[39] *De Inst.* IV 34.
[40] Ibid. 39.
[41] Ibid. 10.
[42] Ibid. 39.
[43] *Conl.* XI 6–8.
[44] Ibid. 8–9.
[45] *De Inst.* IV 39.

capacity to live in consciousness of nothing except the super-sensuous world.[46]

So far paganism had, in a sense, already gone: the cultivation of an utter indifference to earthly things as a way to be free of them and so to move on into the realm of spirit leading to a final reunion with Divinity — all this had a Stoic and Neoplatonic precedent. Yet even in this intermediate or mercenary stage there was an emphasis on gentleness and humility which is fresh. We shall now see why.

For the third and final stage leading up the last rungs of the ladder is no longer egotistical; the calculation of one's own advantage is now submerged and extinguished by the joy of a positive love, of a charitable love, not for oneself but for another. Self-interest having been controlled by disciplining the character, it is now for the first time effaced by a love which is preferable, not any longer for what it may bestow in the way of future reward, but for what it here and now bestows as a present delight.[47] It is the love for the God who died out of love for man, for the God with an overflowing heart, for the God whose virtue is divine precisely because it is also human.[48] This is neither servile respect nor mercenary loyalty, but honourable and filial love.[49] At this point there is only one anxiety: the fear that, out of human frailty, this love — and so the joy of it — may some day cool and be lost,[50] for want — as both Augustine and Cassian said — of the grace of perseverance.[51]

This ladder roughly reproduces that chronological way by which Augustine climbed: the lower third — with its repudiation of matter and the flesh — is Manichæan; the middle third — with its hope that, through virtuous living and a concentration on the super-sensuous, man can resume his spiritual nature — is Neoplatonic; the last third — with its indifference to both matter and spirit provided the joy comes of loving a God whose might is only equalled by His mercy — is Christian. It is this love and joy that is the gift of grace. To the Latins, therefore, it was through Cassian and the monks that Christianity first became widely known, not merely as

---

[46] *Conl.* III 6.
[47] Ibid. XI 6–8. Cf. pp. 360, & 366.
[48] See pp. 604, & 606.
[49] *Conl.* XI 7.
[50] Ibid. 13.
[51] See pp. 396–98, & 417 n. 74.

another and deeper philosophy, but as a novel yet simple way of life.[52]

The ancients had not been unmindful of morals. It was indeed one of their most constant preoccupations, so that in a sense Christianity reaped where others had sown. The analysis of right and wrong, however, of good and bad behaviour and intention, had never been woven into the popular faith: philosophy had remained the luxury of a few and no concerted effort had been made to unify the discordant speculations into a system which could be popularly diffused. Consequently public opinion in regard to moral questions had remained always a matter of circumstance and chance. The civil law — that is, concern with practical justice — had grown into an impressive and enlightened system, but its precepts never received the popular acceptance they deserved because no higher, theoretical standard co-existed. Roman law was, like that of the Old Testament, largely a series of ' Thou shalt nots ', and the reasons given were political or social expediency; no effort was made to show that certain acts or thoughts were intrinsically wrong apart from time, place, and circumstance. This is the weakness of any purely temporal civilization: it inevitably encourages men to suppose that rights and wrongs can be created by legislation. Not until the Middle Ages did it become clear that in matters of right and wrong civil law is intrinsically impotent.[53]

We cannot be sure that Christianity disclosed ultimate right and wrong, discovered the key which unlocked the whole mystery. But what it certainly did do was to convince first itself and then the rest of the Roman world that right and wrong were intrinsic and absolute realities, of vital importance and capable of reliable analysis. The Gospels furnished a revelation of certain facts which thousands of quiet individuals had long suspected: that there was an intrinsic good modestly lying far below the surface of things, which could be probed deeper and deeper without any likelihood of reaching bottom. That is why they spoke of the infinite goodness of God, of a goodness far beyond any human conception.

---

[52] Naturally there were other precursors, notably the Greeks Basil, Gregory of Nazianzus and Gregory of Nyssa: von Hügel 1909 II 166.

[53] Cf. John of Salisbury *Policraticus* IV chs. 2–7, written in 1159.

In a very real sense, therefore, the monks were the scientists of this age: the only men who, as a class, disinterestedly sought to widen the bounds of human knowledge. That they sought the dissection of the human soul rather than of the human body, the study of psychology rather than of physiology, was a matter of circumstance; they were scientists none the less. For the wise scientist follows the line of least resistance, seeking the light where he believes it may best be found. Where a certain line of research promises nothing a good scientist will forsake it for another that promises more. The Bible, and particularly the text of the Gospels, was the microscope or telescope of the fourth century, heartening men to renew the assault against the wall of ignorance that encompassed them. Nor were the monks distinguishable from other scientists because they were tempted to exaggerate the importance of their discoveries.

That chastity is the beginning of virtue seems doubtful to us today. We should prefer not to stress that phase of their doctrine; yet to pass it over would be to distort the picture, for the more they repressed sexual desire the more their minds were haunted by it. Cassian relates how the famous hermit Paphnutius, being once angry that a flame had had the audacity to scald him, in a dream heard a voice which sarcastically told him he might expect exemption from the hostility of fire only when

you can hold a beautiful and naked virgin in your arms and yet find that the peace of your heart remains steadfast.[54]

Some of the monks' early experiments recall those of the alchemists: they betrayed more daring than technique.

Cassian's mind, however, was not lubricious: he was more interested in fasting than in chastity, perhaps because only fasting can be practised to excess. The Egyptian monks had fasted excessively; yet even so several of the more famous had lived over a hundred years. Cassian, however, had particular reasons for urging moderation: even when fasting did not produce delusions [55] it often numbed the mind and senses into a weary negativity.[56] One excess, indeed, leads to another;

[54] *Conl.* XV 10 § 3.   [56] *De Inst.* V 9.
[55] Ibid. II 5–8.

often the monk who fasts too much actually stimulates his
carnal desire,[57] and this in turn is a symptom of pride [58] —
of self-satisfied over-confidence:

If a man fasts openly he is attacked by the sin of vanity; if he conceals it for the sake of despising the glory of it he is assailed by the
sin of pride.[59]

Such excess is the complement of the sin of gluttony:

We ought then with all our might to strive for the virtue of discretion by the power of humility, as it will keep us uninjured by
either extreme, for there is an old saying . . . that extremes
meet.[60]

And as in fasting so in the general routine of living; there
must be measure.[61]   To Cassian one of the supreme advantages of the monastic life was the elimination of worry over
details, over plans for the future: true contemplation can
come only with peace of mind, with a serene unconcern for
the morrow.[62] It is also in order to promote this disposition
that relief from prayer or other effort must be provided, and
by manual labour rather than by idleness [63] — the particular
tasks being varied by a weekly rotation.[64] No less important
was distraction, for

unless the strain and tension of their mind is lessened by the re-
laxation of some changes, they fall either into a coldness of spirit
or at any rate into a most dangerous state of bodily health.[65]

A favourite story was of a philosopher who visited the hermit
John in order to study his holy way of life and chanced to
come upon him while he was stroking a partridge.[66]
    These admonitions, however, concerned only physical acts
— against fornication, against gluttony or excessive fasting,
against undue strain on the mind — and were on that account
preparatory.   For Cassian was no Manichee:

It is not an external enemy whom we have to dread.   Our foe is
shut up within ourselves: an internal warfare is daily waged by

---

[57] *Conl.* XXI 35. Cf. p. 368 n. 6.
[58] *De Inst.* XII 22.
[59] Ibid. XI 4.
[60] *Conl.* II 16 § 1.
[61] Cf. ibid. 5–8 & 10.
[62] Ibid. XIX 8.

[63] *De Inst.* X 7 & 22; *Conl.* IX 5–6,
XIV 13, XXIII 5, & XXIV 12.
[64] *De Inst.* IV 22.
[65] *Conl.* XXIV 20 § 2.
[66] Ibid. 21.

us. Once he has been conquered, all external things will become impotent.[67]

All these measures were but so many preparations for the decisive assault on the only really dangerous enemy, an assault no pagan had ever thought to undertake: against pride.

There was first the foolish pride of the beginners, which Cassian describes as carnal. They are puffed up

because they can sing well, or because their bodies are emaciated, or because they are of a good figure, or because they have rich and noble kinsfolk, or because they have despised a military life and honours.[68]

Or they will perhaps

go round in mind and imagination to the dwellings and monasteries of others and make many conversions — under the inducement of an imaginary exhortation.[69]

All of this is natural and innocent enough and not troublesome to overcome. The real danger comes when this carnal pride takes a spiritual form. This

generally attacks those only who have conquered the former faults and have already almost arrived at the top of the tree in virtue. And because our most crafty enemy has not been able to destroy them through a carnal fall, he endeavours to cast them down and overthrow them by a spiritual catastrophe.[70]

Nor does this malady endeavour to wound a man except through his virtues. . . . And so it results that those of us who could not be vanquished in the conflict with the foe are overcome by the very greatness of our triumph. . . . The more thoroughly it has been resisted the more vigorously does it attack the man who is elated by his victory over it.[71]

By this obstacle the fifth century scientist finds his way blocked. His desperate efforts to get over, or round, or under it are the key to many of the noblest and most extravagant conceptions of the time. Witness Augustine, who could see no way of killing pride but by killing all excuse for pride, and so by killing all freedom of will, all merit, all human capacity. Cassian was not willing to go so far, but, because he was not willing, he fell into another dilemma: rather than seek a

[67] *De Inst.* V 21 § 1. [70] Ibid. XII 24.
[68] Ibid. XI 13. [71] Ibid. XI 6–7.
[69] Ibid. 14.

truth that was palatable and yet consistent with humility, he preferred to tamper with truth. At least he seems to quote with approval a remark of the hermit John:

I think that some instruction may be given you if I lay aside my humility and simply lay bare the whole truth about my aim.[72]

To pit humility against truth was rash, for humility must surely be worsted and a pious hypocrisy bred in the process. Cassian, however, in his effort to circumvent the obstacle of pride, showed a willingness to sacrifice everything if need be — even truth itself. Nor was he the first — or last [73] — seeker after truth who had to be unfaithful to it. For the noble Cassian is best known to posterity as the father of the noble lie, of the unholy but seductive precept that the end justifies the means:

Some have arrived by means of acts in themselves reprehensible at the height of righteousness.[74]

And after justifying the conduct not only of Jacob [75] but also of Rahab — the whore who betrayed her own citizens because she 'could only escape death by means of this remedy' [76] — he glibly concludes that

Since we read that even those men who were holy and most honourable in the eyes of God took advantage of a lie, so that in doing this they not only committed no sin but actually attained to the highest justice, since upon these a lie could confer glory, what, contrariwise, should the truth have imposed except a condemnation? [77]

In moralizing about veracity it would have been better had Cassian eschewed the tempting revelation of the Old Testament.[78]

---

[72] *Conl.* XIX 3 § 3; & cf. ibid. XVII 23 & 24.

[73] Cf. Hilary on Honoratus: *Sermo de Vita S. Honorati* § 37. And see pp. 577-78, 607-08, & 629.

[74] *Conl.* XVII 11.

[75] Ibid. 12.

[76] Ibid. 17 § 4.

[77] Ibid. § 1.

[78] The ascetic heretics like the Manichees (see pp. 64-65) and the Priscillianists (Duchesne 1910 II⁴ 547) also championed this doctrine.

Can it be wholly by chance that whereas Cassian advocated free will, frequent communion (*Conl.* XXIII 21), and holy dissimulation, the Jesuits of the 17th century did likewise; and that whereas Augustine (see *Enchiridion* 22, & *De Mendacio passim*) and Prosper of Aquitaine disapproved of free will and of holy dissimulation (Dufourcq *G.M.R.* 1907 II 82 n. 1), the Jansenists did likewise? And may not this coincidence betray two natural dispositions of

Nor is this doctrine, of 'holy dissimulation' [79] as Cassian calls it, the only by-product of his quest for virtue which is unpleasant: the effort to dissipate man's natural affections because these are carnal occasionally led to really offensive experiments. In one place Cassian relates, with evident approval, the ordeal imposed on a man whose dogged persistence finally induced the monks

to receive him together with his little boy who was about eight years old. [The two were separated] . . . and that it might be more thoroughly tested whether he would make affection and love for his own flesh and blood of more account than obedience and Christian mortification — which all who renounce the world ought out of love for Christ to prefer — the child was on purpose neglected and dressed in rags instead of in proper clothes; and so covered and disfigured with dirt that he would rather disgust than delight the eyes of his father whenever he saw him. And further the boy was exposed to blows and slaps from different people, which the father often saw inflicted without the slightest reason on his innocent child under his very eyes, so that he never saw his cheeks without their being stained with the dirty marks of tears. And though the child was treated thus day after day before his eyes, yet still out of love for Christ and the virtue of obedience the father's heart stood firm and unmoved. For he no longer regarded him as his own son, as he had offered him equally with himself to Christ.[80]

Although this Christ had asked men to love Him, to love Him above all, He never asked men to love nothing else. But to the early monks this love for Christ was a new love, an intoxicating passion; and, just as men sought a short cut to the spirit by shunning matter, so they sought a short cut to the love of God by shunning man [81] and even life itself. The only

mind rather than mere attachment to two traditional schools of thought?

[79] *Conl.* XVII 19.

[80] *De Inst.* IV 27 §§ 1–3; & cf. ibid. V 38, & *Conl.* XXIV 9. Cf. Jerome's description of Paula's abandonment of her children: *Letter* # 108 § 6.

[81] In *Conl.* XXIV 26 Cassian declares that the monks' mutual love should come to outweigh any love for wife or family. Presumably the love is real and therefore presumably based on the other monks' virtues. Yet a wife can apparently only be loved for the passion she arouses, not

for the sake of her virtues. As there is a paradox in the doctrine of humility, so does there seem to be one in the doctrine of love. To love nothing that is of this world and yet to love one's fellow monk because he professes not to be of this world, is holy sham. Augustine knew better: just as he did not allow his quest of humility to blind him to the truth, so he did not allow his quest of divine love to blind him to the true nature of profane love. No greater picture of the love of mother for son and of son for mother has ever been

other burning love the monks applauded was of suffering [82] and death.[83]

It was with these grandeurs and absurdities that Cassian triumphantly inaugurated Latin monasticism. Whatever his sources — whether the Bible, the Egyptian monks, the Greek Fathers, Jerome and Augustine — whatever his originality or unoriginality, it was these *Institutions* and *Conferences* that set the ideal moral standard in Western Europe for the next thousand years. It was out of Cassian even more than out of Augustine, that the future grew. For the future lay with the monks; and the rule of life for the Middle Ages was, through Benedict, Cassiodorus, and Pope Gregory, the *Rule* of Cassian.[84]

C. The Monastery of Lerins

Cassian's second series of the *Conferences*, which happened to include the famous Books XIII on free will and XVII on dissimulation, were written at the request of two monks of the neighbouring monastery situated on the island of Lerins just off the coast at Cannes. The one was Honoratus, its founder, the other, Eucherius, of whose *De Laude Eremi* we have already spoken.[1] This was in 425.[2] Both of them were Gallic aristocrats who had renounced their patrimony and worldly career in order, following Cassian, to seek perfection of the soul.

Honoratus, the elder of the two, was born ten years later than Cassian — or in about 370 [3] — of a noble family established on the Moselle.[4] Leaving home when still a young

---

drawn than his picture. His love for his friends, too, was deep and human. But because Cassian feared matter he also feared sex. Cf. ibid. V 18, & XXIV 19.

[82] *Conl.* XXIV 23-24.

[83] Ibid. XVI 6. Sorrow was distinguished from suffering: only the former must be expelled: *De Inst.* IX 12; & cf. Rufinus *Hist. Monachorum* 7 (*P.L.* 21 418C). Suffering must of course be courted.

[84] Cf. Gouilloud 1881 179.

[1] See p. 334 n. 29.
[2] Gouilloud 1881 172.
[3] This date is an approximation. He would in such a case have been thirty-five when he founded Lerins in 405, and fifty-nine when he died: ten years younger than Cassian, three older than Eucherius and thirty older than Hilary.
[4] *The Book of Saints* 1921 137

man he set out for the East, intending no doubt to visit the monastic communities whose fame was just then becoming known. In Greece his brother, who had accompanied him, died; whereupon he abandoned his design, returned through Italy and then, at a date quite uncertain but probably in about 405, obtained episcopal permission to found a monastery on this small and deserted island of Lerins.[5] His monastery prospered in a way that Cassian's at Marseilles did not. One reason may have been that Cassian, himself a Scythian, drew too largely on the Greek population of Marseilles,[6] thereby incurring something of the distrust that hampered the earlier foundations in Rome. Another reason may lie in the rank and prestige of Honoratus, a Gallic noble and therefore likely to attract other Gallic nobles.[7] At any rate this nobility was attracted to Lerins, among the first being Hilary, a kinsman of Honoratus, Lupus of Périgueux [8] — the famous Saint Loup — and above all Eucherius,[9] a great noble, probably of Provence, who came to Lerins with his two sons, dedicating them as well as himself to the new life. Eucherius was about three years younger than Honoratus; Lupus was about twenty-eight years younger; [10] Hilary was about thirty-one years younger and perhaps his nephew.

Lerins had a *Rule* of some kind; even though Honoratus felt at liberty to amend it at his pleasure it was not likely that his *Rule* deviated much from the conventional models. Unfortunately, however, there is no record of it, possibly it was

says Lorraine; Grützmacher 1902 XI 400 line 36 says in northern Gaul or Belgium.

[5] Hilary *Sermo de Vita S. Honorati* 2 & 3.

[6] Dufourcq *G.M.R.* 1907 II 96 properly reminds us that Lerins too must have been subject to the influence of the Greek-speaking East. For Provence had Greeks all along the coast, Cassian's influence was Scythian and Egyptian, and Basil's added that of Asia Minor. Honoratus, moreover, had himself been in Greece.

[7] Germanus of Auxerre, born in 378, was of course an exception, for, after a military career, he was elected bishop in 418. Thereafter he did,

however, live as disciplined a life as any monk: see Constantius *Vita Germani* §§ 3 & 4. In about 470 Claudianus Mamertus *De Statu Animae* II § 9 — who was a priest of Vienne — spoke of Germanus as 'by far the greatest of the bishops of his day.'

[8] Sidonius *Letters* VIII # 11 § 1. Although *The Book of Saints* 1921 171 says he came from Toul.

[9] On Eucherius see the too diffuse biography by Gouilloud 1881.

[10] Sidonius *Letters* IX # 11 § 8, written in about 478, says that Lupus had then been bishop of Troyes for fifty years. Having been a monk at Lerins he would hardly have been elected a bishop until he was about thirty.

never put in writing,[11] and the few facts we glean of the life
there tell us nothing specific or original.[12]   This is why Cassian's composite [13] *Rule* has a double importance: apart from
its later influence on the *Rule* of Benedict, it must have had
an immediate influence on the *Rule* under which Lerins
throve.   No doubt Honoratus and his successors deviated from
Cassian in many particulars — just as each abbot deviated
somewhat from his predecessor — but if there had been any
contrasts of importance it is probable that some record of these
would have survived.   To be sure the two monasteries were
nearly one hundred miles apart; there is every reason to think,
however, that their relations were close and harmonious.
Honoratus, for instance, then a famous abbot, so admired the
Institutions of 417 and the first ten Books of the *Conferences*
of 423, that in 425 he requested Cassian to write a second series
of *Conferences*.   Furthermore this second series contained the
notorious Semi-Pelagian Book, and, although that view was
castigated a year or two later by Augustine, the abbot elected
by the community of Lerins shortly after this — in 433 [14] —
was Faustus, still a young man, but soon destined to become
the arch Semi-Pelagian of this century.   Cassian was by then
an old man; [15] evidently Lerins wanted an abbot who would
remain true to the tradition of the *Conferences*.

Lerins was at this moment about to embark on its great
career.   When, in 425, Cassian began his second series of
Conferences, monasticism was still being eyed by the Latins
with some distrust.   In Gaul there were remnants of monastic
foundations, as at Marmoutier near Tours,[16] and on the lower
Seine near Rouen,[17] but we can do no more than assume a
survival.   The two monasteries at Marseilles and Lerins are
the only ones of which we know anything certain.   No doubt
the invasions, which grew serious in 406, and thereafter became every year more destructive, were accelerating the disposition of sensitive men and women to retire from the world;
but whatever new foundations these changes provoked their

[11] Grützmacher 1902 XI 401 lines
6–19.
[12] Cf. Goux 1856 43–59.
[13] Comprising both the *De Institutis* and the *Conlationes*.
[14] Seeberg 1898 V 782–83.
[15] About 73 years old, if he lived

so long: Grützmacher 1897 III 746
says he died after 431 and before 436.
[16] Although we hear no more of it
after 397.
[17] Founded by bishop Victricius of
Rouen, who died in about 407: Migne
P.L. 20 437.

beginnings were obscure.[18] At Rome the Pope since 422 was
Celestine who, although devoted to Augustine,[19] was a dim
figure, without force or originality.[20] Apparently he was no
more favourable to monasticism than Siricius and Innocent
had been,[21] and there is no indication that in Italy the monk
was more highly regarded in 425 than he had been in 385.
The African probably took about the same attitude: Augustine judged the monks rather on their individual merits than
on any general principle, and he did much to discredit monastic vagaries and to promote organizatioŉ and discipline.
But that he much helped the Africans to become reconciled to
the monks before his death in 430 is improbable, for Salvian's
description of the Africans' attitude, however embittered and
exaggerated, cannot be lightly dismissed. Now Salvian was
born at Trier in about 400; in the eighth book of his *De Gubernatione Dei*, written in about 445, he speaks with venom
of the Africans' attitude, and with a concreteness that suggests
first hand knowledge.[22] Since, moreover, his literary sources
are largely African, it is probable that he lived there for a time
and, if this be so, his stay must have occurred between 420 and
440. Harping as usual on the un-Christian lives led by most
professed Christians, he compares them to the Jews in their
hatred of Christ. He then goes on,

Thus, therefore, is the hatred of the Africans for the monks proved
— that is, for the holy of God — because they mocked and cursed
them, attacked and execrated them, because they did virtually
every one of those things that the impious Jews did to our Saviour
— up to the shedding of His divine blood. But these, you say, did
not kill the holy men as we read that the Jews did. Whether they
actually did kill I do not know, I do not say, yet it is indeed a fine
defence that they stopped short of the extreme of the pagan persecution.

Let us admit, therefore, that the saints there were not actually
killed: what does this prove, since those who hate with a murderer's heart are not very different from murderers, especially
since the Lord Himself has said, *Whosoever hateth his brother
without cause is a murderer* (I *John* iii 15) . Therefore there is
ample reason why they persecuted the servants of God. For who
can say that it was without reason that they saw, in men who

18 See p. 489.   21 See pp. 461, & 464–65.
19 See p. 419.   22 Sanford 1930 8 n. 11.
20 See p. 585 n. 63.

differed from themselves in every inclination and habit of life, nothing of themselves, since everything of them that they saw was of God? Diversity of wills, indeed, is the prime cause of discord, because it is almost — if not wholly — impossible for anyone to love that quality in another of which he himself disapproves.

And thus not without reason, as I have said, did they hate those in whom they perceived everything to be antagonistic and hostile to themselves, for those lived in perpetual sin, these in innocence, those in lust, these in chastity, those in brothels, these in monasteries, those almost uninterruptedly with the devil, these uninterruptedly with Christ. Therefore it was not without reason that in the cities of Africa and especially in Carthage a people that was as unhappy as it was faithless could hardly look without abuse and execration at a man wearing a cloak, pale, and with the hair of his flowing locks razed to the skin.

And whenever any servant of God came to that city, either from the monasteries of Egypt, the holy places of Jerusalem, or the sacred and honourable retreats of the desert, no sooner had he appeared than he would become the object of scorn, sacrilege and curses. Nor was this all: for he became the object of the foul jests of evil men, and of the detestable hissing and almost whipping of the scoffers; so that in truth if an uninformed man saw these things he would not imagine that a human being was being mocked but rather that some new and unheard-of monster was being chased and expelled.[23]

Finally it was the Vandal invasion of 429–439 that furnished Salvian with the clinching empirical argument for justice on earth:

So God is just and His judgments righteous. . . . Shall we then be surprised and angry that they now endure some few trials at the hands of men?[24]

Salvian had probably not been a monk at Lerins, but he was certainly closely associated with the community, teaching there for some time and a friend of their abbots and great alumni.[25] If, when he witnessed these things in Africa, he was not yet a monk at heart it may be that it was his sight of the treatment the monks received there which finally won him to their cause.

The monk had been unpopular in Rome in 385, in Trier in 386, in Tours in 397, in Périgord in 404.[26] Since he was no

[23] *D.G.D.* VIII §§ 19–22.
[24] Ibid. § 25.
[25] See Sanford 1930 11–13.

[26] Where Severus wrote his *Dialogues.*

more popular in Carthage in 425 it is likely that what was true in Carthage was somewhat true all over the West. As the second quarter of the fifth century opened, therefore, the monk still had his way to make — the burden of proof was still on the saint. Then, in 426, occurred a decisive event: Honoratus, for twenty years abbot of Lerins, a great noble by birth and the most conspicuous monk in Gaul, was elected archbishop of Arles. Now Arles was the greatest city of Gaul and her bishop outranked every other Gallic bishop — he was often, in fact, the recognized representative of the papacy there.[27] Presumably this was a popular rather than a clerical choice; presumably the clergy would have preferred the selection of one of their own number. But the case is not parallel with Martin's, for whereas Martin was an obscure miracle-worker Honoratus was not only a great noble but also an important abbot who had made Lerins known and respected throughout Provence. Nor was this selection made by a small border city, but rather by the largest and most enlightened city beyond the Alps. Presumably Arles had had enough of worldly bishops who ruled the diocese and province as might any civil official; instead she wanted a really Christian bishop who preferred his religion to his career.

The experiment was evidently a success, for in 428 a certain James, of Lerins, was elected bishop of Moutier in Savoy,[28] and on the death of Honoratus in the next year the people of Arles chose as his successor another monk of Lerins, his younger kinsman Hilary. And Hilary was destined to hold Arles — and therefore much of Gaul — to the ideals of Lerins for the next twenty years. This, moreover, was only the beginning: for in 428 Lupus — of Périgueux and Lerins — was elected bishop of Troyes;[29] in 433 Maximus, then abbot of Lerins, was elected bishop of Riez;[30] in this same year Vincent, perhaps a brother of Lupus, became bishop of Saintes;[31] it was at about this time that Antiolus, a contemporary of Lupus and Maximus at Lerins, became a bishop — of what

[27] The efforts of the papacy to bestow, and then withdraw, the Gallic primacy, so that Arles should not imagine that she had any vested right to it, is a long story and well known.

[28] Gouilloud 1881 204–05.

[29] Goux 1856 34 says that Lupus was a kinsman of Honoratus and that he married Pimeniola, a sister of Hilary.

[30] Gouilloud 1881 205–06.

[31] Goux 1856 35–36; & Gouilloud 1881 207.

see we are not told; [32] then in 434 Eucherius, second in honour
at Lerins to Honoratus only, assumed the archbishopric of
Lyons; [33] Valerian became bishop of Cimiez in about 440; [34]
we know that Salonius and Veranus, sons of Eucherius, soon
after became bishops of Geneva [35] and of Vence; [36] and finally,
a vacancy occurring at Riez in about 459, Faustus, the already
famous abbot of Lerins, took over that see.[37]   Lerins-trained
bishops in this way controlled the whole region between the
Rhone and the Alps, with outposts at Saintes and Troyes.
Since the records are sparse they doubtless controlled much
more than this.   Now when we recall that by 430 to 440 much
of Aquitaine was in the hands of the Arian Visigoths and that
the north and east were overrun by Franks, Alamanni, and
Burgundians, it becomes clear that the Lerins monks had acquired ecclesiastical control over the most important territories left to the Romans in Gaul.   Spain and Britain had
been lost and now Africa was going too.   If we except Italy,
therefore, it can be said that in a single decade the Lerins
monks assumed control of the Latin Church.   And although
our records of monastic foundations in this period are scanty,
it is probable that these Lerins bishops not only fostered existing, but founded many new, monasteries.   Yet only four foundations are sure: that of Castor at Apt in 420,[38] that at Condat
in the Jura in 425,[39] that founded by Hilary at Arles soon after
429,[40] and that at Clermont in about 440.[41]

It was a curious device that was employed to save Roman
civilization, this alliance of the worldly Gallic noble with the
oriental hermit.   Yet there is an unconscious distillation here
of the miscellany of antiquity which lay shattered at the feet
of this youngest Roman generation.   As in a blazing house
where time is short, the things to save are the smallest and
most precious.   Nor did the Roman's instinct play him false:
he saved the thing he had never used but which he now needed
most.

[32] Sidonius *Letters* VIII # 14 § 2.
[33] Gouilloud 1881 228.
[34] Dufourcq *G.M.R.* 1907 II 81.
[35] Or perhaps Vienne: Cooper-
Marsdin 1913 234.
[36] Veranus was consecrated in 442:
ibid.
[37] Gouilloud 1881 212 says in 455;

Seeberg 1898 V 783 says between 456
and 462.
[38] Gouilloud 1881 172 thinks it
existed before 417; Seeberg 1898 III
746 says before 423.
[39] Montalembert 1863 I 2 257.
[40] Goux 1856 156.
[41] Besse 1906 39.

Yet for a moment even now the old-fashioned clergy remained ungracious, and it is Pope Celestine who utters the last clerical snarl. Writing to the bishops of Narbonne and Vienne he insists that bishops must be chosen from among the lower clergy and not among strangers.[42] Surely this letter was prompted by the consecration of Honoratus at Arles in 426,[43] for he goes on to say that

We must be distinguished from the people or from others by our doctrine, not by our clothes; by our speech, not by our costume; by the purity of our mind, not by the peculiarity of our dress. . . . Therefore we ought not to stir the simple minds of the faithful by such methods. . . . Their eyes ought not to be imposed upon; rather ought their minds to be instructed.[44]

There should not be vainglory for those wearing the pallium of the monk. Those who are bishops must observe the ecclesiastical custom.[45]

This passage must serve as an epitaph for the old Roman clergy; for actually it was this old clergy which relied on outward display and it was the new monastic clergy which relied instead on a mere show of piety.

With the death of Augustine and the Vandal invasion the Latin centre of gravity moved from Africa to the Rhone; the monks, still so despised and reviled at Carthage, were at that very moment taking over the helm in Gaul. Strangely enough it was to Jerome's rather than to Augustine's philosophy of life that the Roman aristocrat turned. Jerome's disciples were aristocrats; Ambrose, Paulinus of Nola, and Severus were aristocrats too; so were Honoratus, founder of Lerins, and one of his first disciples, Eucherius. One of the famous tracts of the day was the *De Contemptu Mundi* of this Eucherius, written in 432 [46] in order to convert a powerful noble, Valerian,[47] to the true Christian life. The picture it paints of the outer world is as dark as any by Jerome; it was, in effect, a funeral oration memorializing the death of the State. To Eucherius the temporal world is incurable; its honours are

42 *Letter* # 4 §4.
43 Cf. Migne *P.L.* 50 433 end of n. C.
44 *Letter* # 4 §2.
45 Ibid. § 8.
46 Gouilloud 1881 153.

47 Should this be, as Dufourcq *G.M.R.* 1907 II 79–80 conjectures, the same Valerian who became bishop of Cimiez in about 440, this tract of Eucherius certainly effected its purpose.

now shared equally by good and bad; [48] the prodigies which once foretold progress now foretell only disasters. [49] To him the reason was obvious enough, for the temporal State has now clearly served its humble purpose of diffusing the Christian revelation. Its work having been done it is now superfluous and obsolescent; any effort to revive it is vain and even sinful — because God has doomed it to fade. [50]

And, as it faded, this temporality retained only its anxieties and cares [51] — its charm was gone:

Up to this point I have been speaking of the inextricable allurements of the treacherous life, of its honours and riches, just as if the world were still flourishing and delightful in its enticements. Whatever the surface of the world was, once polished with a deceitful glitter, it has now grown old and its every painted splendour is dead. No longer has the world this power to deceive. That illusion is gone. . . . Formerly it thought to seduce us by a real brilliance, but it could not; now, with its false brilliance, it is virtually powerless to corrupt us. Even then it lacked solid merit; behold it is now losing even its perishable merit. Neither momentary brilliance can adorn this world, nor permanent brilliance affirm it to be real. Unless we deceive ourselves the world is now almost powerless to deceive us. [52]

This tract is not a dispassionate judgment, it is an impassioned argument. After contrasting the old temporal life with the new monastic — which offers, in addition to the prospect of eternal felicity, [53] a present peace and security [54] — Eucherius reaches a climax:

If anything formerly impressed you as seemingly suited and appropriate to glory, nothing is more glorious than He. If you were led by your eye to the splendour of brilliant things, nothing is more splendid than He. If you were attracted by the sight of beautiful things, nothing is more beautiful than He. If in some matter you thought you understood the truth, nothing is truer than He. If you believed that in some case generosity should be shown, no one is more generous than He. Do you admire anything pure and simple? Nothing is more genuine than His goodness. Are you tempted by an abundance of wealth? Nothing is richer than His bounty. Are you fond of anything because of its

---

48 Migne *P.L.* 50 716D, 725A & 726B.
49 Ibid. 722D.
50 Ibid. 721C–722A & 723A.

51 Ibid. 715C & D.
52 Ibid. 722B & C.
53 Ibid. 714D.
54 Ibid. 715C & D.

loyalty to you? Nothing is firmer than His loyalty. Do you love anything because it is suitable? Nothing is more suitable than His love. Is there anything that attracts you because of its severity or pleasantness? Nothing is more awe-inspiring than that grandeur of His, or gentler than His regard for us. Sympathy is needed in adversity, courtesy in prosperity; from Him alone comes joy in happy times, solace in time of sorrow. And so it is most appropriate that you should love Him — in whom you possess all things — above all things. Riches, and whatever those other things are which now hold you by their loveliness, are not only found in Him but are also held by Him. . . . For so great is He that those who do not love Him, while acting wrongly, can nevertheless love nothing except what is His.[55]

The realm of the spirit now supplies all that the world at its best once offered in the realm of matter. Through it human life may, in a new way, become as intensely dramatic, as replete with sensations and experiences, as any temporal life had been or ever could be.

This *De Contemptu Mundi,* however, was not a judicial analysis of evidence and motive but rather a plausible argument designed to upset a lukewarm scepticism. In his earlier [56] *De Laude Eremi* Eucherius probably gives a more honest argument for a renunciation of the world: it allows a man to meet himself face to face. Here the decks are cleared, here all extraneous elements are eliminated. Here a man can strip himself for the real combat — alone with his own flesh and his own sin.[57]

Now when these Lerins monks one by one reluctantly accepted bishoprics, they were abandoning pure research for general practice, were jeopardizing their own perfection in order to heal the gaping wounds of other men. They were sincerely [58] reluctant to teach perfection while their own imperfection remained. They persisted in retaining the monkish garb and routine, not only that others might be reminded of the frailty of their teacher, but also that they might constantly be reminded of this themselves.[59] This *De Laude*

[55] Migne *P.L.* 50 720C–D.

[56] Written in 426 to 429 says Hennecke 1898 V 573 line 17.

[57] *De Laude Eremi* § 27.

[58] Maximus refused the see of Fréjus in about 430: Cooper-Marsdin 1913 229.

[59] Cassian *Conlationes* I 20 tells of how the devil ' incites a man to desire the holy office of the clergy under pretext of edifying many people.' And cf. ibid. XXIV 16.

Eremi was written in 428 to congratulate Hilary for abandoning service under Honoratus at Arles, for spurning the new *cursus honorum* which would probably lead to a bishopric. Little did Eucherius — or even Hilary perhaps — imagine, that within a year Hilary would have the see of Arles thrust on him by the death of Honoratus, and that within six years he would himself be installed at Lyons.

These monk-bishops aimed primarily to popularize a new way of life; their concern was with moral and not with intellectual truth and error.   Since, however, the two problems were entwined and interdependent, they were obliged, if perhaps unconsciously, also to popularize certain theological and dogmatic ideas which had grown up round and encrusted themselves upon the moral idea.   What might these most naturally be?

According to the Lerinian doctrine the monk's life was likely to be a far happier one than the layman's or even the priest's.   Outwardly it might appear difficult and wearing, but actually it offered welcome relief — from anxieties, ambitions, responsibilities, and temptations.   Here there was love in place of envy, serenity instead of remorse.   By merely doing what he was told a monk was reasonably assured of adequate food, shelter, books, medical care, and kindly treatment — every virtuous felicity in fact.[60]   Generous endowments and honest and efficient administration may have deserved much of the credit, but only God was given any.   Because the monks loved God He loved them, and therefore provided for them.   It is not by chance, then, that — apart from certain unconscious intimations in Orosius [61] — the earliest text alleging justice on earth should be the closing paragraph of Cassian's *Conferences* in which the monastic vow is pictured as the royal road to posthumous fame.[62]   It is Eucherius, moreover, who takes the next step, alleging that God may be trusted to take care — if necessary by a miracle — of the simple daily needs of His true disciples.[63]   And it is to Salvian — at least a

[60] *De Laude Eremi* § 42.
[61] Orosius wrote his *History* ten years earlier than Cassian wrote, but he was born about 24 years later. Cf. p. 351 n. 84.

[62] Cf. Cassian as quoted p. 333; & *Conlationes* XXIV 16.
[63] See p. 335 n. 35.

teacher if not also a monk at Lerins — that we owe the first systematic exposition of the doctrine.[64]

This doctrine was certainly an ingenious one: since there was obviously no temporal justice in the lay world the inference had to be drawn that this was because the lay world did not deserve any. Where there is no virtue not even God can dispense rewards. Renunciation of the world is, therefore, the indispensable prerequisite to a virtuous life, and those who renounce are the only ones to reap the present advantage of God's Providence. The temporal world, on the other hand, is governed by chance — which is all it deserves. The miseries of fickle chance are the just punishment of sin. As a curious corollary Cassian pointed out that to be possessed of a devil was a propitious symptom because it showed that God was concerned enough over the victim's possible salvation to set the devil on him![65]

It is easy for us to see that some exception to the traditional pessimistic doctrine was inevitable; for no Council, Pope, or bishop could seriously promote justice on earth without the faith that God Himself willed it. Otherwise their efforts would thwart His will. This is of course true: the monks were moving with the current; but the fact remains that they were the first to move. Even great men cannot do more.

In his *De Contemptu Mundi* Eucherius argued[66] that the monastic life was not only the wiser in the long run but also the pleasanter at the time. Yet, should this fact come to be generally recognized, that life would particularly attract the weak and self-indulgent and there would then be no merit in the renunciation. Eucherius clearly had allowed his enthusiasm to get the better of him, for if this renunciation is a first act of virtue and so of merit, it necessarily involves a sacrifice, and any sacrifice involves a rejection of the more pleasant. For if every sin were immediately punished and every virtue rewarded there would be no sacrifice possible: as Augustine had said:

---

[64] See pp. 353 ff. Dufourcq *G.M.R.* 1907 II 100 argues that Salvian wrote, or helped to write, the text of the martyrdom of Sebastian — see p. 511, which raises this very problem.

[65] *Conlationes* II 11.

[66] See pp. 490–92.

If every sin were now visited with manifest punishment, nothing would seem to be reserved for final judgment. . . . And so of the good things of life . . . if He gave them to all who sought them, we should suppose that such were the only rewards of His service.[67]

Consequently Eucherius can only have really meant that the renunciation offered certain present consolations in addition to the future reward, in consideration of a real sacrifice and so a real act of merit. For the idea of sacrifice and merit lay at the very root of the monastic conception.

It is not surprising, furthermore, that the first Latin Christian to emphasize [68] the importance of merit was a monk, the notorious Briton, Pelagius. His fellow-heretic Celestius was perhaps also one.[69] These had maintained that man could, by his own merit and without the help of grace, acquire enough virtue to be saved.[70] The monks, however, had seen this doctrine formally condemned in favour of the opposite doctrine which declared grace not only indispensable but gratuitous: for Augustine had denied that fallen man was capable of acquiring any merit adequate to advance his chances of salvation. But in that case the renunciation was not proof of merit but only of a gratuitous grace; he who renounced deserved no more consideration than any other and was therefore no more likely to receive the final grace of perseverance and so be saved. Strictly conceived, therefore, the Augustinian doctrine made the monastic renunciation paradoxical, so that, to those who had renounced, a denial of it was imperative. Therefore, the monks, whether Egyptians, Dalmatians, or Britons, whether followers of Cassian or of Honoratus, had really no alternative but to defend free will and the reality of human merit. They could retreat from outright Pelagianism to Semi-Pelagianism, they might retreat further if this were practicable, but they could never accept a doctrine which seemed to make a mockery of their renunciation. For if their progress in holiness was a gift and not a reward, creating no innate strength and hence no divine obligation to reciprocate, it was in fact no progress at all and their apparent holiness was an empty semblance.

[67] See p. 321 n. 31.
[68] On his contemporary Severus see p. 446.
[69] Duchesne 1911 III 4 210–11.
[70] See p. 410 n. 23.

Cassian too — as well as Augustine — had observed how often a monk, after a long life of holiness, fell into sin when on the brink of a death which promised salvation: in Book II of the *Conferences* such cases are cited.[71]   He too admitted, therefore, that the grace of perseverance was indispensable and that in certain cases it was mysteriously and distressingly withheld.   Yet these facts were not enough to shake his conviction that there had once been merit, and that this, with the help of the grace it induced, had created a reservoir of strength which, if it did not eliminate, at least greatly reduced the chance of an eleventh hour collapse.[72]   He did not claim that the renunciation in any way guaranteed consolations in this life or salvation thereafter, but he did claim that without this renunciation neither consolations nor salvation were likely. The monks of Lerins merely elaborated this conception: a rich man, so long as he chose to remain rich, lost the prospect of both peace on earth and joy in heaven.[73]   And, if it were hard for the rich man, it was almost as hard for any layman, hard even for any priest who was not also a monk.   Eucherius' plea, and Salvian's, really amount to this: become a monk and play safe.

Since Cassian was not connected with Lerins, it has been argued [74] that the monks of that monastery were never contaminated by him.   It may be that Honoratus held views that were less extreme [75] — for Hilary says he always insisted that his merit was not his own — but there is no evidence that any of them clung to the Augustinian doctrine after the publication of the *Conferences* in 425.[76]   Quite apart from Cassian's significant dedication of his second series of *Conferences* to Honoratus and Eucherius, there is this casual passage in Eucherius' *De Contemptu Mundi:*

If He is so generous in gifts, how generous will He be in rewards.[77]

Now a reward, even if merely heavenly, is distinguishable from a gift by being earned or deserved, and this presupposes

---

71 Chs. 5–8.
72 See p. 417 n. 74.
73 See pp. 370–74 on Salvian's *Ad Ecclesiam.*
74 By Montalembert 1863 I 2 249; and by Gouilloud 1881 180–86.

75 Cf. Hilary *Sermo de Vita S. Honorati* § 37.
76 Honoratus died in 429.
77 Migne *P.L.* 50 726B.

merit. That the irresistible receipt of a gratuitous and undeserved grace was an act that could be rewarded is inconceivable. It is clear, therefore, that Eucherius believed a man
could acquire merit and so earn a reward. Furthermore
Eucherius gives a list of great Christians: we find the names of
Ambrose and Paulinus of Nola, but the name of Augustine
is absent.[78]

That Hilary, ardent disciple of Honoratus and close friend
of Eucherius, did not subscribe to Augustine's doctrine on
predestination is known by a passage in a letter to Augustine by the layman Prosper of Aquitaine, which we have
quoted: [79]

For . . . Hilary, bishop of Arles, your Blessedness knows to be
an admirer and follower of your doctrine in all other respects,
and, regarding this matter which is in dispute, also knows that
for a long time now he has wished to present his view to your
Holiness by letter.

That is why Hilary could say that the merit of Honoratus is
proved by his conviction that he had none.[80]

But if the disapproval manifested by Eucherius and Hilary [81] is not enough to implicate Lerins in the doctrine of
Cassian, at least the career of Faustus must be held conclusive.
Now Faustus, who was born in Britain in about the year 408,[82]
was elected abbot of Lerins in 433. This office he held, presumably with the general approval of the monks, for the next
twenty-six years. In about 459 [83] he was elected bishop of Riez,
and it was soon after this that he launched a public defence of
Cassian's doctrine, with such increasing success that during
this episcopate of thirty-four years he became the dominating
intellectual figure in Gaul.[84] Now, if Faustus was elected
abbot in 433, at the age of about twenty-five, it is certain that
he had already served a full apprenticeship at Lerins. From
what other source, then, than the Lerinian might he have im-

---

[78] Ibid. 719A.
[79] See p. 419 n. 4.
[80] Hilary *Sermo de Vita S. Honorati* § 37.
[81] Dufourcq *G.M.R.* 1907 II 80
characterizes Valerian, of Lerins and
Cimiez, as a Semi-Pelagian. So does
Cooper-Marsdin 1913 226.
[82] At least he died either in 493:

Seeberg 1898 V 784; or in 490: Dalton
1915 I clxviii. He was already a very
old man in 485: Duchesne 1911 III⁴
614.
[83] See p. 437 n. 3.
[84] He was exiled to Limoges from
477 to 485 by the Visigoth Euric for
writing against Arianism: Duchesne
1911 III⁴ 613–14.

bibed the Semi-Pelagian view? If he had found it in neighbouring Marseilles because there was another doctrine in vogue at Lerins it seems unlikely that he would have been chosen abbot. Monks do not elect an abbot of twenty-five years old unless they have confidence in his orthodoxy as well as in his capacity. It is much more likely that he was chosen abbot because in 433, when the controversy was at its height, the monks felt the need of some vigorous young mind to withstand the assaults of the Augustinians. Cassian was old, was perhaps already dead; a new champion had to be found. Faustus was probably elected because he had already shown unusual ability as an apologist for the view which seemed to them fundamental and essential.[85]

Augustine marks the highest point which both Rome and Christianity reached. But he himself, dying only in 430 at the age of seventy-six, outlived his own time. Through his prestige he had fostered the illusion that the ideas of 400 were still the ideas of 430; it is because they were not that the last years of his life witnessed that growing opposition to his domination which forced him to assume a defensive role. In the year 400 the Church needed only to teach; she now needed to govern. The turmoil of 430 to 435 is that of water spilling over a dam. The inarticulate noise was a mixture of the mature cry of a Eucherius with the youthful cry of a Salvian, a Hilary, or a Faustus. Augustine had pleaded for the impotence of man and so for the absence of human justice, and for the neutrality of nature; Cassian and Lerins harked back to the old faith in man, in merit and so in human justice, and to the old fear of nature. In Augustine antiquity had repudiated and so destroyed itself; in Cassian and Lerins there was a return to the old, for a strength with which to create the new. On Augustine blew the dying air of antiquity; on Cassian and Lerins blew the first faint breeze of the Middle Ages. And if, as is now thought, time and space are only one thing and not two, a change in time will bring a change in space and the Vandal may seem the blind instrument of a deep and organic process. For by destroying Augustinian Africa he raised Cassian and Lerins to the rank that the new time demanded. The bold African was willing to condemn man, to condemn

[85] See p. 437.

his abuse of nature, but he was reluctant to condemn the innate loveliness of that nature — it had too much light, too soft an air, too much colour and vibration. If there were evil it was in active, living minds. The Gaul,[86] on the other hand — or the Briton [87] — was more bewildered by nature and less seduced; he saw man antagonistic to rather than unworthy of nature; and he saw that man must be stronger than nature if he were not to perish.[88] In some such way, at any rate, even if time and space are not one, they here played prettily into each other's hands.

Gaul had not awaited the death of Augustine in order to launch her own Catholicism. Italy, which had been more deeply under his spell, took no corresponding initiative until after the death of Augustine's admirer, Pope Celestine, in 432. To his successor Sixtus III, however, who lived until the year after the fall of Carthage in 439, Augustine and Africa were more convincingly dead, and a change now occurred, in Rome at least, analogous to that already largely achieved in Gaul.

For one thing Sixtus showed an inclination to heed the claims of Julian, the deposed bishop of Eclanum, who had been removed for persisting in Pelagianism and was now trying to regain his see.[89] For another thing at a Council held in Rome in 433 he allowed monks to be present; we do not know whether they were allowed to vote but we do know that it is the first recorded case of monks taking any part at all in Latin Church affairs.[90] Furthermore Sixtus is the first Pope who himself founded a monastery; his precedent was followed henceforth, by Leo and by Leo's successor Hilary.[91]

At the same time the civil law took a more favourable attitude towards the monks, and this was presumably done with the approval, if not at the instigation, of Pope and Church. A law of 434 allowed the monks in certain kinds of cases to be tried in the ecclesiastical courts,[92] a privilege hitherto enjoyed by the secular clergy only. Another law of that year provided

---

[86] Honoratus, Vincent, Hilary, Salvian, and perhaps Lupus all came from the Moselle district.

[87] Pelagius and Faustus were Britons, and Cassian, as a Scythian, was hardly a Mediterranean product.

[88] Cf. pp. 459–60.

[89] Prosper of Aquitaine *Chronicum* for 439 (Migne *P.L.* 51 598B).

[90] Spreitzenhofer 1894 126–27.

[91] Ibid. 11–12.

[92] Ibid. 123.

that the property of an intestate monk should go to his monastery unless he left heirs of very near degree.[93]   A third law of that year exempted monks from all obligations incurred before taking their vow, unless they had been slaves, freedmen, or serfs.[94]   This not only wiped out their debts but also their hereditary civic duties: the son of a *decurio* or other freeman could henceforth become a monk and remain one.

The early history of monasticism may be said to close with the enactment of canon 4 of the General Council held at Chalcedon in 451:

Those who live a truly monastic life ought to be esteemed as they deserve to be.   But since some, for whom the monastic life is only a pretext, make trouble in the Church and in the State, move indiscriminately from one city to another and even wish to build monasteries for their own private use, the Council has decided that no one may anywhere build or found a monastery or church except with the consent of the bishop of that *civitas;* also that the monks of the locality and of the city shall be subject to the bishop, that they shall love peace, devote themselves to fasting and prayer and settle in the places assigned to them; also that they shall keep clear of the Church and of temporal affairs, that they shall not concern themselves with these or leave their monasteries unless the bishop of the *civitas* asks this of them in a case of necessity; also that the monasteries accept no slave as a monk except with the permission of his master.   Whoever disobeys this order is to be excommunicated in order that the name of the Lord may not be blasphemed.   The bishop of the *civitas* must superintend the monasteries very closely.[95]

But surely the bishop's control over the monasteries was not to be a wholly despotic one: a new bishop could hardly amend the various *Rules* of the monasteries in his diocese at his own pleasure.   There had of course long been a custom regarding such matters, but Chalcedon had not made all the points clear and the Council of Arles of 453 now undertook to make them so.   The case that was brought before it concerned the rights of the bishop of Fréjus over Lerins and her able but quarrelsome abbot Faustus.   This Council determined as follows:

93 *Theodosian Code* Fasc. I 1923 164–65.

94 Spreitzenhofer 1894 134.   Presumably the three year interval was still necessary.   See p. 464 n. 64.

95 Hefele 1908 II² 779.   This canon was, of course, a codification — by General Council — of current practice: see Spreitzenhofer 1894 123–24.

that the abbot should be freely elected by the monks themselves — without interference from the bishop; that the
monks be under his orders exclusively; that the abbot have
control over the property of the monastery, including gifts;
that the bishop should not ordain a monk as priest without
the abbot's consent; that the bishop alone, however, may ordain and confirm.[96]   That canon 4 of Chalcedon had gone to
the heads of some of the Gallic bishops is probable; that within
two years the monks nevertheless got adequate recognition at
Arles was surely due to the prestige of Lerins.[97]   Hilary of
Arles was then dead; his successor Ravennius may not have
been a former Lerinian.   Faustus as abbot of Lerins was therefore the natural leader of the Lerinians and, as such, the virtual leader of the Gallic Church.   For why, otherwise, should
the bishops assembled at Arles have upheld the monks' claims
at the expense of their own?

Although we have no definite texts it is probable that the
great Leo, who was Pope from 440 to 461, was well enough
disposed towards the monks.   He was certainly deeply sympathetic with their striving for inner perfection; on the other
hand he was almost as sympathetic as Augustine had been
with those who defended the innocence of Nature.[98]   He
probably believed in free will after baptism;[99] he urged a
wider veneration of the saints and intimated that their cult
might serve to promote justice on earth [100] as well as piety and
hence salvation.   On the other hand he showed no inclination
to encourage a belief in the miraculous, in fact on one occasion
declared that the miracles wrought by Christ were proof that
He was more than a man.[101]   Leo's real opinions on most of
these matters are undeniably obscure: having no leisure to
study and reflect on them he wisely chose not to commit himself.   But from the little we can glean it seems probable that
his views were close to those of Lerins.   He trusted matter
more than they; he doubted the possibility of free will before

[96] Grützmacher 1902 XI 401 lines
45–58; Hefele 1908 II ² 886–87.

[97] Goux 1856 178–79 thinks that
Faustus was vindicated at Arles.
Hefel 1908 II ² 886 thinks that bishop
Theodore of Fréjus came out best.
But this all depends on who was the
aggressor, that is, on who would have

come out best had there been no
decision.

[98] See p. 613 n. 119.

[99] See pp. 431–32.

[100] See p. 352; & cf. Dufourcq
G.M.R. 1907 II 270–71.

[101] Letter # 28 (the famous Tome
— see p. 605 n. 85) §4.

baptism; [102] but if on these points he preferred the Augustinian solutions on all the rest he was a virtual Lerinian.

The civil laws of the years 455 to 469 gave monasticism final and complete recognition as an integral part of the new Christendom. A law of 455 qualified monks to receive and retain as individuals any gift or legacy made in their favour.[103] To be sure this was followed by a law of 466 which forbad a monk to will his property except to his own monastery; [104] but here we must distinguish between canon and civil law. By the former no monk could renounce or evade his vows, the penalty for a serious breach of these was excommunication and a life penance, this sentence being served in a monastery. The recalcitrant thus remained a monk till his death. Theoretically he might, by remaining openly impenitent, escape the sentence, but practically this was not so easily accomplished. Furthermore, if exiled or a fugitive, his heirs would not have an easy time in validating his will. Yet there was evidently some conflict here between the canon and civil law, for a civil law of 466 provided that if a monk left his monastery and returned to the world his personal property devolved on the monastery whereas his real property remained his own.[105] Evidently the State was not willing to recognize the monastic vow as irrevocable: if the wrong-doer chose to accept penance and the canon law penalties that this entailed, well and good; but if he rejected penance and chose instead to resume his lay status the State was unwilling to grant the Church more than this peculiar compromise.

Finally, by a law of 469, monks were exempted from civil jurisdiction in all — and not merely in specified — cases; [106] and in this same year canon 4 of the Council of Chalcedon was incorporated into the civil law; the abbot was made legally responsible for the acts of his monks, and the bishop for the acts of his abbots.[107]

---

102 Which was alleged by Cassian and Faustus. On the other hand, if not Hilary of Arles (see p. 497) at least the author of the *S. Hilarii Arelat. Vita* (see p. 531) seems to have agreed with Leo on the necessity of the prevenient grace of Ambrose.

103 Spreitzenhofer 1894 131 n. 8.
104 Ibid. 82–83.
105 Ibid. 132.
106 Ibid. 116.
107 Ibid. 117.

D. The Miracle after 406

One of the many peculiarities of Augustinian doctrine was its conception of a single kind of event.[1] That Cassian and Lerins should differ with him on this point too is not surprising, for the conception of two kinds of events runs back far beyond the beginnings of Christianity, probably to the point where men first perceived that some events occurred automatically — as if by natural law. Such a belief does not mean, therefore, that these monks were unduly credulous; it simply shows that they were less imaginative than Augustine — which signifies nothing, for so was everybody else. Our problem is, therefore, not why the monks were credulous, but rather what determined the degree of their credulity.

It was certainly a propensity of the early monks to report a generous number of miracles. Even the stolid Athanasius, in writing of Anthony, told of wonders, and Jerome followed his cue. In the West Severus in his *Life* of Martin followed that precedent. Consequently the public which read those various accounts must have associated the monk with the miracle. And if this was an incentive to the credulous to admire the monks and even to follow in their footsteps, to the incredulous it was a reason for distrusting them: for if they seemed to lie about one thing they probably lied about much else. Now from what we can judge of the temper of the educated classes in the early fifth century it is probable that credulity was associated with ignorance and so with inferiority, and it is more than likely that the contempt with which the monk was then regarded arose as much from his apparent credulity as from his even more apparent ugliness.[2] His humility only confirmed the suspicion that he was a poor specimen of a man.

A very different reason why monks were expected to be credulous lies in the fact of their renunciation. For renunciation involves a sacrifice to which men are not naturally inclined unless they have an expectation of reward. They must suppose that this sacrifice was their own, initiated by their own will and not by any gratuitous grace — for otherwise

---

[1] See pp. 216–18.   [2] See pp. 456, & 470 n. 7.

they could claim no merit and so deserve no reward. And, although the real reward was expectant, even contingent, they must also suppose that an incidental, ephemeral reward might be bestowed during the present life. For God was just, and justice too long postponed is not complete. Now on the theory of predestination there was not only no need of justice; there was no need of any miracle except the didactic.[3] That is, God might need to startle the beholders, which was a wholesale bestowal of one of Augustine's preliminary graces; but, since He was the sole cause, He had no need to re-adjust the course of events. With free will, on the other hand, the conception was introduced of an infinite number of new original causes.[4] The world would then no longer be operated by a single will but by an infinite number of wills. To be sure God's foreknowledge allowed Him to know how these free wills would act and know what the consequences would be. Theoretically, therefore, He might have designed the operation of things so cunningly that every contingency could be provided for in advance. Theoretically God could do this because He was assumed to be infinitely clever; practically, however, it was impossible for the human mind fully to believe this, and it was therefore inevitable that believers in free will believe also that God must periodically re-adjust matters by some amendment or suspension of His laws. Let us take a concrete example. A certain man, having been baptized and having thereby received free will, chooses to renounce the world, and in due course becomes so holy that he chooses to wander off into a desert. Now how, as a practical matter, was God to prevent his starving? Perhaps He ought not to have created a desert. And if He did He ought to have foreseen that this holy man would come there on a certain day badly in need of food and drink. If, however, He left food and drink there at the Creation this must either have grown stale and rank or have been appropriated by some earlier passer-by. Having created a desert and permitted a saint to wander over it, God could only save his life by some juggling with the laws of nature.[5] A man could think he believed that God designed

---

[3] See p. 219.
[4] See pp. 128–29.
[5] This was a frequent situation and God almost invariably intervened:

see Rufinus *Hist. Monachorum* (*P.L.* 21 401D, 406C, 416–17, 423B & C, & 431C). And see Eucherius *De Laude Eremi* § 29. But Cassian *De Insti-*

nature so cunningly as to render such intervention unnecessary, but no man really could believe this — particularly at
a moment when the occurrence of miraculous cures was an
already well established fact.

A peculiarity of the miracle is, however, that it can be believed without being experienced.   For many a believer in
miracles has been doubtful that he ever saw one.   Now this
was the situation at Lerins: the monks had heard of many
miracles and believed what they heard, but they seem to have
had few personal experiences of such events.   Lerins undoubtedly held many monks who were uneducated or stupid, but
her leaders were highly educated nobles whose natural credulity was feeble.   Cassian, moreover, as we shall soon see,
frankly belittled the miracle; Eucherius, Hilary, and the rest
laid little emphasis on it.   May not this attitude have been induced by the fact that for the most part they observed none?
It has been argued, to be sure, that Lerins is responsible for
the miraculous elaborations [6] woven around the bare records
of the martyrs — a phenomenon which becomes marked soon
after the year 450.   I think, however, that these miraculous
elaborations have another cause.

Our chapter on the miracles ended in 406 — with Vigilantius, Claudian, and Augustine.   At that time Martin was
dead and he and Severus discredited, and Jerome in the East
was otherwise occupied; of the earlier proponents of the
miracle only Paulinus of Nola kept his prestige after 406.
About ten years after this, however, there was a feeble recrudescence of credulity at Milan.

At some time between 412 and 422 [7] another Paulinus, of
Africa [8] and Milan and a disciple of Ambrose, wrote, at the
request of Augustine, a *Life* of his beloved master.   In it occurs a famous passage:

When he, as an infant, placed in a cradle within the courtyard of
the Governor's residence [at Trier], was sleeping with his mouth

tutis V 40 tells of a case where two
pious youths died in the desert in
spite of their prayers.

[6] By Dufourcq *G.M.R.* 1907 II 87–
159.   The monks of Lerins no doubt
did their share of natural inventions
— their activity was quite equal to
their zeal.   But Dufourcq should

have perceived that they were loath to
introduce miracles other than cures;
Cassian's *Conlationes* XV should have
warned him of this distinction.

[7] Hefele 1908 II [2] 171 n. 1.

[8] In 411 he was a deacon in Carthage: Turmel 1931 I 109.

open, suddenly a swarm of bees came and covered his face and lips in such a way that they kept entering and coming forth from his mouth alternately. . . . And, sometime later flying out, they rose to such a height into the air that they could not be seen. . . . For already at that time the Lord . . . was working for the fulfilment of what has been written: *good words are as a honeycomb*.[9]

Paulinus of Milan clearly hoped that this would be thought a miracle, although it could only seem such in retrospect — when Ambrose later became so renowned for his eloquence. Another alleged miracle may also have been a mere coincidence: Ambrose prays when the Arians are throwing a victim to the leopards, with the result that the leopards jump the barrier and lacerate their masters.[10]

A case of hypnotic control has a conventional ring which calls to mind certain of the more credible episodes told of Martin by Severus:

Another man came even to his bedchamber, carrying a sword to kill the bishop; but when he [the Bishop] raised his hand the man became motionless with drawn sword in his stiffened right hand.[11]

And the rest of the alleged miracles are medical cures, of paralysis, blindness, possession, and one revival of the dead.[12] A case of possession has a special interest:

At the same time when a certain Probus, a man of high rank, had sent to the bishop his servant, a secretary, who was being seriously troubled by an unclean spirit, the devil left him as he departed from the city [of Rome], fearing to be brought to the holy man. And so long as the boy was with the bishop in Milan no power of the devil appeared in him; but when he left Milan and came near the city, the same spirit which had possessed him before began to torment him. And when the devil was questioned by the exorcists, why he had not appeared in him so long as he had been in Milan, he confessed that he had feared Ambrose, and therefore had withdrawn for a time and had waited in that place where he had withdrawn from the boy, until he should return, and when he did return he had sought again the vessel which he had deserted.[13]

This story has a ring of authenticity; modern psychiatrists will recognize it. Even the confession of the devil is credible,

---

9 *Vita Sancti Ambrosii* § 3, quoting *Prov.* xvi 24.
10 Ibid. § 34.
11 Ibid. § 20.

12 Ibid. §§ 10, 52, 43, & 28 respectively.
13 Ibid. § 21.

since he presumably spoke from the mouth of the boy who believed he was possessed.

Evidently Paulinus was anxious to show that as a wonder-worker Ambrose was comparable to Martin or any Oriental. But he was too conscientious not to be clumsy. It may be suspected that there was a popular demand for a biography of this kind and that Paulinus acquitted himself of the novel task as adroitly as he knew how. A time had now come when the local and popular fame of Ambrose could no longer be maintained unless supernatural powers were attributed to him. Human merit was not enough, because it was coming to be supposed that absence of supernatural powers implied a corresponding absence of merit.

Belonging to this second decade of the fifth century are two other Milanese texts: both of them elaborations of martyrs' records. Shameless invention of facts and episodes is characteristic of both, but these additions are hardly if at all miraculous; they show no historical, but considerable scientific conscience. One account is of the martyrdom of Gervasius and Protasius,[14] whose relics Ambrose believed he had unearthed. Here the only miracle is the executioner's complaint that one of the dead martyrs is burning him. This may be unlikely; at the same time a remorseful man would very naturally imagine that his victim was torturing him. The other Milanese invention is of the martyrdoms of Cantius, Cantianus, and Cantianilla; here too, although the account is again glibly circumstantial, the only incredible wonder described is of how:

they kneel, they are decapitated; their blood flows, as white as milk.[15]

It cannot be said that even Milan had yet succumbed in any serious degree to the glamour of the miraculous.

Nola, at the death of Paulinus in 431, must have been in much the same state of mind as Milan: there was an eagerness to detect the miraculous, but few experiences of it, and there was still an unwillingness to invent. Likely facts are given a miraculous interpretation but there is no intent to deceive. At least this is the impression left by the story a certain Ura-

---

[14] Dufourcq *G.M.R.* 1907 II 37–39.   [15] Ibid. 213.

nius tells of the death of Paulinus. Here three episodes are told as if miraculous — they were evidently the best that Uranius could conscientiously use. First it is related that as Paulinus died those at his bed-side felt an earthquake, although no one outside the sick room noticed it.[16] How much more impressive would have been an earthquake which was felt throughout the countryside. Since the account was doubtless written soon after the event such an invention would not have been easily believed; nevertheless Uranius certainly showed an honest restraint. The second wonder, that at death the body of Paulinus turned white, is equally modest.[17] The third is the appearance of Paulinus to the bishop of Naples three days after the saint's death.[18] Since a vision is not to be clearly distinguished from a dream, there is no reason to question its reality.

Yet mild as these wonders were which Paulinus of Milan tells of Ambrose, and Uranius of Paulinus of Nola, there was nothing of the sort elsewhere at this time, in either Africa or Gaul. In Africa a certain Possidius wrote a memoir of Augustine shortly after the great bishop's death in 430.[19] Two cures [20] are credited to him, but not another achievement of a supernatural kind.[21] And the same can still be said of Gaul.

It was Cassian who here set the wholesome precedent. At the very beginning of his *Institutions* designed to describe the ways of the Egyptian monks, he says:

Nor certainly shall I try to weave a tale of God's miracles and signs, although we have not only heard of many such among our elders — and those past belief — but have also seen them fulfilled under our very eyes; yet, leaving out all these things which only cause the reader astonishment and give him no instruction in the perfect life, I shall try . . . only faithfully to explain their institutions.[22]

It is likely indeed that Cassian wrote of the oriental monks partly in order to dispel the false idea of them which the ac-

---

16 *Epistola* § 4.
17 Ibid. § 10.
18 Ibid. § 11.
19 Babut 1912 7 n. 7 says 430; Weiskotten 1919 12 says 432 or soon after.
20 *Sancti Aug. Vita* 19.
21 The miracles described by Orosius in 417 as having happened since

the year 300 are all explicable as coincidences and are often not even that. The cases are chiefly either of premature death or else of military victories against superior numbers: cf. *H.A.P.* VII 36 § 12. Orosius was born in about 384.

22 *Conlationes* Preface § 7.

counts of Rufinus and others had disseminated: the true monk, said Cassian, though he might work miracles at times, was anything but a professional magician; his aim was not to control nature but to control himself:

The height of perfection and blessedness does not consist in the performance of those wonderful works but rather in the purity of love.[23]

The miracle, moreover, being a physical and therefore a despicable act, may be performed by demons as well as by saints: as the Lord has Himself said:

For there shall arise false Christs and false prophets, and shall show great signs and wonders.[24]

And for this reason the power to exorcize demons may be a low and contemptible one: [25]

For in truth it is a greater miracle to root out from one's own flesh the incentives to wantonness than to cast out unclean spirits from the bodies of others, and it is a grander sign to restrain the fierce passions of anger by the virtue of patience than to command the powers of the air, and it is a greater thing to have shut out the devouring pangs of gloominess from one's own heart than to have expelled the sickness of another and the fever of his body. Finally it is in many ways a grander virtue and a more splendid achievement to cure the weakness of one's own soul than those of the body of another. For just as the soul is higher than the flesh, so is its salvation of more importance, and as its nature is more precious and excellent so is its destruction more grievous and dangerous.[26]

This passage is not unworthy of Augustine, and the one that follows tells us why:

Rejoice not that the devils are subject to you.[27] For this was wrought, not by their own power, but by the might of the Name invoked. And therefore they are warned not to claim for themselves any blessedness or glory on this account as it was done purely by the power and might of God.[28]

Convinced as Cassian was that man could acquire merit, he was no less convinced that man's cardinal sin was pride. For

[23] *Conl.* XV 2 § 3.
[24] *Matt.* xxiv 24, as quoted in *Conl.* XV 1 § 6.
[25] *Conl.* XV 7.
[26] Ibid. 8.
[27] *Luke* x 20.
[28] *Conl.* XV 9.

this reason his fifteenth *Conference* was devoted to a denial of the popular notion that the saint was primarily a miracle-worker or the miracle-worker necessarily a saint. That demons as well as saints were granted miraculous powers was sufficient proof that holiness was quite another matter. Before a man might be thought holy he must become far more than a kindly magician.

Turning next to Lerins we observe that in neither of the important texts of Eucherius is there any suggestion of a miracle, even though in the *De Laude Eremi* the eulogy is of the desert. There is abundant reference to miracles, beginning with those of *Exodus;* [29] there is the intimation that the holy man may expect miraculous help in time of need; [30] but no contemporaneous miracle is cited and there is no suggestion that the initiative can come from any source but God. Eucherius also wrote an account of the massacre of the Theban Legion, a wholesale martyrdom alleged to have occurred under Diocletian at Agaune, on the Rhine just above the lake of Geneva. Here the account, although apparently legendary, is very detailed, yet no miracle occurs until after the martyrs have suffered and died. There is then a paralysis cure [31] and an apparition of the martyrs before a pagan peasant.[32] Thus Eucherius deliberately leaves the impression that God did nothing, either to extricate the martyrs, to console and fortify them by a Sign, or to punish the perpetrators. He also makes it clear that the martyrs did not try to save themselves or to terrify or humiliate their enemies. The account, indeed, is unusually dramatic, and for the very reason that the martyrs, although soldiers under arms, submitted with complete humility; to Eucherius their faith in God not only required no Sign, it would have resented one.

Shortly after the death, in 429, of his beloved master and kinsman Honoratus, Hilary wrote his *Life*. Here, as in the case of the Theban Legion, a miracle or two are inserted, probably in order to show that Honoratus did have the power, but he makes it clear that the glory of Honoratus depends on other very different considerations. Incidentally this passage refers sarcastically to Martin and Severus; Hilary

---

names no names but he intends to leave no doubt in the reader's mind.[33]   The two miracles, moreover, were conscientiously related: before the advent of Honoratus the island of Lerins had teemed with poisonous snakes and provided no fresh water, but Honoratus found no such snakes [34] and did find a pure spring.[35]   Since the island had long been uninhabited there was probably little reliable information to be had about it when Honoratus made his preliminary inquiries. Venturing there he was doubtless not wholly surprised to find the stories current about it to be unfounded.

A third Lerinian of prominence who has left us texts is Salvian.   In neither of his extant works is there any suggestion of miracles.   It is true that they were not pertinent to his themes, which were justice on earth and charity.   Nevertheless a time was fast approaching when the miracle was to be the central factor of every theme.

There are also three stories of martyrdoms which were concocted in about the year 450.   One of these, on Sebastian,[36] was written either by Salvian himself or by someone closely associated with him.[37]   It contains no miracle.   The second account, of the martyrdom of Pontius,[38] was probably written by Valerian,[39] formerly of Lerins, by this time bishop of Cimiez which is twenty miles from Lerins.   There is only a vague suggestion of miraculous occurrences at the moment of the martyrdom.[40]   Of similar provenance is the text of the martyrdom of Victor of Marseilles.[41]   The only miracle referred to is the appearance to Victor of Jesus accompanied by angels.   The evidence of these and other texts clearly emanating from Lerins shows a great readiness to introduce episodes for which there was, at most, an unauthenticated local and oral tradition, but also shows an unwillingness to introduce miraculous episodes.   Here, as at Milan, there was a disposition to embroider the tradition if not to fabricate one

---

[33] Sermo de Vita S. Honorati § 37.
[34] Ibid. § 15.
[35] Ibid. § 17.
[36] Dufourcq G.M.R. 1900 I 186–87. This martyr was from Narbonne, was brought up in Milan, and suffered under Diocletian.
[37] Dufourcq G.M.R. 1907 II 97–107.

[38] Ibid. 73–75.
[39] Ibid. 75–81.
[40] Ibid. 75: 'in vain they expose him in the amphitheatre to the bears of Dalmatia, in vain they place him on a pyre, in vain they try to seduce him.'
[41] Ibid. 107–08.

out of nothing; there was, however, a disinclination to give the episodes a supernatural character.

Our history would have more symmetry if it could show that Lerins reversed Augustine on asceticism and miracles as well as on justice on earth and predestination. The truth rather is, however, that Lerins did much to temper the monastic predilection for both. For it was precisely in regard to these matters that Lerins diverged from the monastic tradition and accepted instead the Augustinian; and it was largely because Lerins did so that the Gauls chose to entrust these Lerinians with the destinies of their Church. Lerins whittled away the excesses of both the monks and the Augustinians, producing a composite doctrine that was at once deeply Christian and discreetly practical. She won the confidence of the Gauls — and later of the Latin West [42] — because she was both idealistic and reasonable, and because she frowned on violence of any kind, either speculative and abstract or active and concrete. Apparently these nobles, from Britain and the banks of Moselle and Rhone, had never, in becoming monks, ceased to be men of the world.

The years 451 to 455 marked the peak of the barbarian onslaught: it was in 451 that the pagan Huns laid Gaul waste from the Rhine to Orleans, clearing the way, after their withdrawal, for the advance of the Franks and Alamanni to the Somme and Meuse; it was perhaps the Huns' exposure of Italy's weakness in 452 that suggested to the Arian Vandals a raid on the city of Rome itself. Since these invaders were as hostile to Catholicism as to the Roman State, the one seemed as much imperilled as the other. Most of the educated Romans were now enlightened Catholics, but many of the less educated held views which, although technically Catholic, still contained many superstitious and even pagan excrescences. And the rural population were in many places not yet Catholic at all.[43] Therefore should the barbarian invasions lead to a general levelling and subordination of the Roman population, the faith, although it would presumably survive, might suffer a dreadful degeneration.

[42] Dufourcq, *G.M.R.* 1907 II 88.   [43] See pp. 229 n. 1, & 514.

Canon 23 of the Council of Arles of 453 gives us a glimpse of the situation in southern Gaul in that year:

A bishop shall not tolerate that within his diocese, infidels should either light torches or venerate trees, springs or rocks. If he neglects to eradicate these customs he is guilty of sacrilege. If the owner or overseer of the place, having been given warning, does not correct the condition he should be excommunicated.[44]

These pagans might be weaned of their devotion to specific local deities but they could hardly be weaned of their innate polytheism. They could not be asked to abandon their devotion to deities who lived in the neighbourhood and were familiar with each individual inhabitant, and to pray instead to a single God whose flock comprised all the peoples of the earth. Already the simpler-minded Christians were bestowing some of their devotion on local martyrs, and it was in order to encourage this inclination that the monks concocted appropriate episodes of heroism. The embroideries made by the Lerins group of texts were clearly intended to foster this devotion of the humbler Roman-Christian. Such persons demanded an edifying story but did not demand a succession of miracles; they were satisfied to be assured that their martyr could, if need be, call forth a miracle and that his present holiness gave him a virtue capable of inducing simple cures. But the rest of the population, whether Arian barbarian invaders or still pagan peasants, would require a cruder and more violent pressure, for to such persons the Christian religion must seem a delusion if it did not provide local deities whose supernatural powers at least equalled those ascribed to the pagan gods.[45]

We have shown how the doctrines of free will and of justice on earth might easily encourage a faith in the miracle, and how Lerins held nevertheless aloof. On this point, however, if on no other, the judgment of Lerins was overruled. From 420 to 440 the task of the Catholic leaders was to win the allegiance of the educated Roman to the vital tenets of the faith; after 450 their task was quite as much to win at least the nominal allegiance of the pagan and barbarian multitude. In-

[44] Hefele 1908 II 2 472.
[45] Cf. *De Sancto Marcellino* § 7 bis, see p. 516.

deed Martin's strange story suggests that so soon as a Catholic leader found himself confronted with a missionary problem he must become more resourceful and less scrupulous, wielding any weapon that lay conveniently at hand. During the early fifth century the Church's diplomacy was concentrated on the government and aristocracy; after 450 it had to be concentrated rather on the barbarians and the populace. True the Church was concerned with the spirit only, but her concern with this spirit was henceforth with the power of spirit to govern matter. Leo might awe Attila by his dignity,[46] but this psychological control was not invariably to be relied on and in case it should fail another kind of awe must be held in reserve. This could only be the awe induced by a power which, although remaining itself spiritual, could produce a physical effect. This marks a further step in the Church's gradual resort to force: from the purely spiritual force exerted during the persecutions, by 380 she had enlisted the physical force of the Roman State; now, in 450, she took the next step by enlisting the help of the magician; in due course she was to take the final steps leading to the institution of the military Orders of Hospitaller and Templar, and of the Holy Inquisition.

In one of his Sermons of about this time bishop Valerian of Cimiez enlarges on the advantages which must accrue to those who render faithful devotion to the martyrs of that city; [47] and under the weight of discouragement imposed by the Vandal sack of Rome in 455 Pope Leo is driven to express an analogous view: the extract, which has already been quoted,[48] must be repeated,

Surely it was by the saints' prayers that the sentence of divine displeasure was diverted, so that we who deserved wrath were reserved for pardon.

[46] Prosper of Aquitaine, born in about 395, is our only contemporary authority for this famous episode: 'Relying on the help of God who never, he knew, failed in works of piety, the most blessed Pope Leo undertook this negotiation with the ex-Consul Avienus and the ex-Prefect Trigetius. Nor did it turn out otherwise than faith had expected. The king received the whole delega-tion courteously, and he was so flattered by the presence of the highest priest that he ordered his men to stop the hostilities and, promising peace, retired beyond the Danube.' *Chronicum* for the year 452 (*P.L.* 51 603B & C). This was the extent of the miracle.

[47] Dufourcq *G.M.R.* 1907 II 77 n. 2.

[48] See pp. 352, 447, & 614.

By saints he must have meant the local Roman martyrs, for who, so much as they, would cherish the welfare of the city? And observe that the just God is thought to want the permanent enslavement of the citizens; to the local saints, by contrast, is attributed the quality of mercy. In the year 456 it evidently appeared even to a great Pope that the mercy of God, even the mercy of Christ, was not of much account. Appeal had been made to the mercy of the supreme God; this appeal had failed, and the only hope was now an appeal to a local deity. The cult of the martyr was not, then, wholly a missionary device by which to catch the ignorant, it was also a reaction against that extreme monotheism on which Augustine had so insisted, caused by the very disappointing effects produced by that form of worship during the preceding fifty years. There could be no better illustration of the strain under which the Romans had now been labouring for nearly two generations than this pathological outburst of the greatest Roman of that day. It may well be, indeed, that from this time on it was those very Christians who felt and cared most deeply who were the readiest to succumb.

The Church's surrender to the miracle may be said to have begun in 450, for it was in about this year that two accounts of martyrdoms were drafted in which for the first time in almost fifty years, the miracle again plays the leading role. The first is of the passion of Nazairus, emanating from Milan: [49] there is a series of apparitions and revelations as well as of cures; [50] a guard conducting the martyr falls and puts out his eye; the martyr prays and an earthquake ensues which upsets the pagan idols; as he is being cast into the sea a bright light appears and an angel descends to console him; he and his fellow martyr Celsus

walk on the quieted waves, glorifying God. The ship that had carried them, on the other hand, is about to be swamped, when, at the sailors' cry for help, he saves her by climbing on board again.[51]

Barring a few stories in Prudentius there had been nothing like this written in the West since the accounts in Severus of Martin's miracles at Tours.[52]

---

[49] Dufourcq ibid. 83–84.
[50] Ibid. 65–66.
[51] Ibid. 65.
[52] See pp. 188–92.

The other account is of the martyrdom of Marcellinus, first bishop of Embrun in the Alps of Dauphiné. The author begins with the statement that Marcellinus

was performing such extraordinary miracles by his virtues that as often as his devoted faith petitioned they would do the thing he wished.[53]

The account which then follows is a succession of miracles: in his lifetime Marcellinus punishes his enemies by burning them with a ball of fire [54] or by possessing them with a devil; [55] he causes the arrows of his enemies to fall back on them; [56] he easily carries a load that is too heavy for a mule; [57] he makes a broken plate whole again; [58] confronted once by a swollen stream his prayers divert it behind him. In this last case Marcellinus exclaims

How can that renowned right hand of God assert itself without miraculous powers when we know that all power resides in it? [59]

The circle of theories of the miracle is here almost completed: we are, as the crudeness increases, returning towards Augustine's single kind of event. But we are not entirely back, for the assumption is not that every event is a miracle but only that every event caused by God is a miracle and that every event not a miracle is not caused by God. What a fall, in less than fifty years, from the sublime to the ridiculous! The whole of the third and last Book [60] is devoted to the cures effected by the virtue of Marcellinus after his death. Now these all occurred at Embrun, where the saint was buried, and the aim of the work is clearly one of salesmanship — to draw sick persons to Embrun with their offerings for the financial and worldly advantage of that place. This is the first case of a new kind of pious fraud that was to become universal; for it aimed not only to promote conversions and a warmer faith but even more to serve a local need and ambition.[61] Jerome, Prudentius, and Severus had each written in order to glorify a man whom they admired as holy;

---

[53] *De Sancto Marcellino* Preface § 1.
[54] Ibid. § 10.
[55] Ibid. § 11.
[56] Ibid. § 17.
[57] Ibid. § 9.

[58] Ibid. § 8.
[59] Ibid. § 13.
[60] Ibid. §§ 16–24.
[61] Cf. Dufourcq *G.M.R.* 1907 II 90–91 and notes.

this *Life* glorified a man because if he could be made to seem holy his city would gain a material advantage.

Of the five Passions presumably written in about the year 450, two emanated respectively from Milan and Embrun and abound in miracles. The other three, which emanated from Lerins, contain barely a single one.[62] These Lerins monks did their fair share of fabrication where natural events were concerned, but they showed no liking for supernatural inventions. That a change of attitude occurred during these years 445 to 455 is indirectly corroborated by the curious history of Martin's posthumous fame. We have said that Paulinus of Nola admired him; so also did Uranius [63] and Paulinus of Milan.[64] The Greek writer Sozomen praised him in about 443.[65] But we have also said that Jerome and Augustine were curiously silent about him, and this silence becomes ominous when we note that there is also no mention of him in any Lerinian text — of Eucherius, Hilary, or Salvian.[66] In fact the only Gaul to speak of him between 404 and 450 is the lay chronicler Prosper who, in 433, inserts this item under the year 381:

Martin, bishop of Tours, is regarded as illustrious by many Gauls.[67]

Then soon after 450 the tide turned at last in Martin's favour. That the earliest [68] Gallic praise of Martin is to be found in the story of Marcellinus [69] makes it plain that his only admirers were those who were partial to the miracle, and that it was only by about 450 that such views again became respectable enough to be safely put in writing. That the revival of Martin's fame should therefore coincide so precisely with the revival of a miraculous disposition of mind, need not surprise us. The first dated eulogy of Martin written in Gaul is in the Chronicle of Marseilles for the year 452,[70] and his first mention by a Council was at Tours in 461.[71]

---

[62] Those of Sebastian, Pontius, and Victor: see p. 511.

[63] Babut 1912 15. Bishop Severus of Naples, an admirer of Paulinus of Nola, founded a monastery there in honour of Martin before 412: Spreitzenhofer 1894 22.

[64] Babut 1912 15.

[65] Ibid.

[66] Or in the work of their master, Cassian of Marseilles.

[67] *Chronicum* (*P.L.* 51 585 line 10).

[68] That is, after Severus' *Dialogues* of 404.

[69] In the Preface § 1.

[70] Babut 1912 14.

[71] Ibid.

This latter mention was the consequence of a memorable event: in that year the *civitas* of Tours elected as its new bishop a certain Perpetuus, who was an enthusiastic admirer of Martin. It is most probable that the partisans of Martin, defeated by Brictio's election in 397, never wholly died out, remaining as a minority faction for sixty-four years.[72] Finally, in 461, they achieved their long-deferred triumph. Perpetuus quickly made up for lost time: he built a new church, very large for that impoverished age, in honour of the saint; [73] he delegated to a poet, Paulinus of Périgueux, the task of rendering Severus' *Life* and its appendages into verse [74] — in order that it might be read aloud to the illiterate populace; he added a Book of the *Miracles of Saint Martin* in which were included those attributed to him since 404; [75] he invited the neighbouring bishops to Tours on November 14th to celebrate Saint Martin's Day; [76] he persuaded bishop Sidonius of Clermont to write a poetic inscription to be placed in the church; [77] and, to cap the climax, he solemnly declared Brictio to be a saint — still familiar today as Saint Brice — obviously as a way of placating the opposition party and so of securing the unanimous support of the people.[78] With Martin thus revealed in all his glory the progress of the miracle in Gaul was from this moment rapid; probably no one even tried any longer to check its irresistible momentum.

This rehabilitation of Martin belongs to the years 461 to 465. In 466 the young Euric became king of the Visigoths. Boldly repudiating the fiction of an alliance with Rome he set out at once to conquer, first northward towards the Loire and Brittany, then in 468 eastward, seizing Bourges in 469, Clermont in 475, and finally Arles in 485.[79] At the same time

---

[72] According to Gregory of Tours *Hist. Francorum* II § 1 Brictio was ousted in 430 — on a charge of adultery — but regained his office in 437 and died only in 444. As Gregory was born only in 538 and did not become bishop of Tours until 573 his first-hand knowledge of the history of his see did not go so far back. If he is accurate, however, we may suppose that the accusation, whether true or not, was a symptom of the re-

vival of Martin's ascetic party, which tried to overthrow Brictio and was successful, although only for seven years: cf. Babut 1912 289–92.

[73] Babut 1912 294.

[74] Ibid.

[75] Ibid.

[76] Ibid. 293–94.

[77] Ibid. 294–95.

[78] Ibid. 298.

[79] Bayet 1911 83–84.

the Burgundians, moving westward and southward to resist him,[80] completed the barbarian conquest of the whole Rhone valley, over which the Lerinian bishops held sway.

It was at about this time [81] that Constantius, a priest of Lyons, then advanced in age, wrote a *Life* of the famous bishop Germanus of Auxerre who had died long before, in 448, at the age of about 70.[82] This Germanus had been born in Auxerre, of noble parents, had studied rhetoric and law in Rome, had held high military office, and in 418 had been elected bishop of his native city by popular acclamation. Germanus had been a conspicuous figure in his day, had been twice sent to Britain — on one of these occasions with Lupus of Troyes — to suppress the Pelagian heresy which was raging there, and he died at Ravenna while on a mission to negotiate a settlement between the Empire and the Bretons.

Most of these facts are known only through this *Life* written so long after the events by Constantius, but they have never been doubted because the account has the ring of authenticity and because other texts corroborate many of his statements and contradict none of them. Constantius had evidently known Germanus well during the last years of his episcopate and wrote the *Life* because he was at that late date the man alive best qualified to write it. Nevertheless it is to be observed that the writing of the *Life* was deferred for about twenty-seven years after Germanus' death — which leads us to suspect that it was not written exclusively in order to keep green the great man's memory. The abundance of alleged miracles the *Life* contains surely gives us the clue. Roused by the success of Martin's rehabilitation and by the renown this had brought to the city of Tours, Constantius had a twinge of jealousy. If Martin deserved such glory, did not others deserve it too? To Constantius his master Germanus was the holiest [83] and greatest of bishops; if Gaul were to have saints as her national heroes Germanus must have his full share of repute. Germanus himself had craved obscurity during his life and might still crave it; his sensibilities need

[80] Ibid. 87.

[81] Levison 1919 230–31 thinks the date was about 480. I should incline rather to 475.

[82] Ibid. 225–26.

[83] In *Vita Germani* §§ 3–5 Constantius enlarges on the rigidly ascetic life that Germanus led as bishop. And cf. p. 484 n. 7.

not, however, be too much respected. Gaul needed him now, and especially that part of Gaul extending from Auxerre to Lyons. The blessed Germanus must swallow his humility and cheerfully lend his name to the greater glory of the Gallic Church.

This *Life* by Constantius is really an admirable one, the best that was written in the fifth century. It is the equal of Severus' late fourth century *Life* of Martin. In both the portrait is lifelike, in both the love of the writer for his hero is communicated to the reader, in both the real events are convincingly told, in both the abundance of miracles not only adds a leaven of charm but also gives the portraits a higher relief.

It is unnecessary to describe the miracles in detail; the strong impression they leave is due more to their abundance than to their novelty or fancy. In addition to the many cures [84] there are six cases of telepathy,[85] but the most impressive wonders are those which show the psychological power of Germanus over the barbarian — a power which Constantius cannot be blamed for thinking miraculous. One of these episodes recalls the more famous account of the meeting, ten years later, between Pope Leo and Attila. For it was in 442 that Germanus, acceding to the prayer of the Bretons that he ask Goaris, chief of a band of Alani, to desist from his incursions, hastened after Goaris, and,

catching up with the armed chieftain who had already advanced on his way, faced him amid the bands of his men. First, through an interpreter, he addressed him a fervent appeal; then rebuked him; and finally with a thrust of his arm he seized the bridle of the chieftain's horse and in doing so halted the whole army. At this, by God's help, the anger of the ferocious chieftain was turned into admiration; he was astounded by his firmness, awed by his venerable presence, and profoundly impressed by his authoritative insistence. The warlike preparation and commotion of arms and all the haughtiness gave way to the courtesies of a conference and they negotiated how to carry out, not what the king had planned, but what the priest had asked for.[86]

---

[84] §§ 26–27 & 30 of paralysis, § 45 of dumbness (a relic is here used), §§ 24, 29 & 39 of epilepsy, § 38 of fever, & § 8 of a tumor.

[85] In §§ 20 & 33 he receives information; in §§ 9, 13, 26 & 32 he transmits it.

[86] § 28.

Martin had been able to overawe the peasants in this way, but it required one who had been born to rule, both as land-lord and as general, to overawe and mollify a rough barbarian chief at the head of his troops. Let us not cavil, therefore, at the story Constantius tells of Germanus at Ravenna. Walk-ing the streets one day he came upon a prison filled with those awaiting torture and death. Whereupon they, recognizing the bishop, set up a shout.

He asked, and was told, the reason for this; he then called the guards but they withdrew.

Germanus then went to the court and was granted an inter-view with the Empress Galla Placidia herself. But of no avail.

Returning then to the prison he there prostrated himself in prayer. Then indeed did our Lord show to the throngs of by-standers what mercy He had imparted to His servant. The chain and the tight bolt were loosened; the iron bars burst apart; divine piety opened that which human cruelty had closed. The crowd came out freed from the weight of their chains, holding the fetters by which they had a moment before been bound. Now at length was the prison innocent because empty and, with faith leading triumphantly, the crowd of wretches was received into the bosom of the rejoicing Church.[87]

Without wishing to doubt the sincerity of Constantius, it is hard not to suspect that Germanus here dealt with the gaolers as he had previously dealt with Goaris.

If all the saints were of the stature of Germanus, and all their biographers as gifted as Constantius, every saint would richly deserve the veneration he was now about to receive. With these two men — after Martin and Severus — begins the spell which French history has ever since cast.

In comparison with this *Life* the contemporaneous [88] *Life* of Hilary of Arles, by an unnamed hand, is somewhat staid and drab. Hilary accepts the bishopric of Arles only after a dove has alighted on his head; [89] he has a dream of heaven in which the richness of his apparel seems a guarantee of the greatness of his coming reward; [90] he prophesies his death

---

[87] § 36. And cf. *Acts* xii 7 & 10, & xvi 26.

[88] *S. Hilarii Arelat. Vita.* In ch. 24 the author says he is writing 'tot annorum spatiis evolutis' after Hil-ary's death, which was in 449: so 475 seems a fair date for the text.

[89] Ch. 6.

[90] Ch. 19.

eleven days hence and this prophecy is exactly fulfilled.[91]　For so famous a bishop as Hilary was, these are feeble miracles.[92] Apparently the biographer felt he must cater to the contemporary taste and tried his best to do so; but the tradition of Lerins obstructed him and his efforts proved lame — for he could not bring himself to tell lies.　A typical episode is that in which Hilary admonishes his congregation for leaving church after the reading of the Gospel, saying peevishly, ' Go out, go out, for you will have no chance of doing this when you are in hell.'　Soon after a fire breaks out which burns a large section of the city, and the people, recalling Hilary's words as if they must have been a prophecy, ran to him to implore his mercy.[93]　There is no reason to doubt this account — certainly as a miracle it is quite unconvincing.　We must note too that Hilary did not pray or even wish that the fire break out, so that the miracle, if any, was initiated entirely by God.　With such a miracle even Augustine could have had no quarrel.　It is further related how, on another occasion, a deacon hurt his foot as he was tearing down a pagan building in order to use the stones in the construction of a church.　Hilary was greatly upset by this and in a dream a noble figure appeared to him and promised to cure the deacon's foot if Hilary would allow him to cut his foot off instead. Hilary having consented the figure starts to do so but the pain wakes Hilary and he thereupon learns that the deacon's foot is well.　The point the author brings out is not the miraculous power of Hilary but his mercy, for, not satisfied to obey the divine injunction that he must love his neighbour as himself, he chose actually to love his deacon more than he loved himself.[94]　Even as Arles and Lerins were being irresistibly drawn into the maelstrom of the miraculous the essential part of Christianity is never lost sight of: there is a poor display of miracles because miracles were themselves a poor display; Hilary's glory rested on the really essential qualities of humility and love.　With this *Life* the old Lerins, of Honoratus, Eucherius, Hilary, and Salvian, is submerged, but it goes down with colours flying.

---

[91] Ch. 21.

[92] There are, to be sure, some cures: chs. 13 & 14.

[93] Ch. 14.

[94] Ch. 15.

As the last quarter of the fifth century opened there was no longer any real resistance to the idea of the miracle as the instrument by which God rules the earth. Even the aristocrat Sidonius of Clermont, when he was still a layman, took it for granted that cures of bodily ills must come, not from physicians, but from the direct intervention of God and His saints. In 467 he writes from Rome that a high fever which he had had on his arrival was at once dispelled by a visit to the ' threshold of the Apostles.' [95] Sidonius had no pretensions to being a saint and so a wonder-worker, yet he believed that even the prayer of a sinner was more efficacious than any natural skill of the doctor. And after he became bishop of Clermont his faith in the miracle grew. Recalling how a fellow-bishop had once stayed the advancing flames by prayer, he declares,

It was a miracle, a formidable thing, unseen before and unexampled: the element which naturally shrinks from nothing retired in awe at your approach.[96]

In an address of the year 472 recommending a certain candidate for the vacant see of Bourges, he says,

Lastly let us not forget, beloved brethren, that this is he whom the barbarians held in darkness and duress, and for whom God flung wide the prison gates with all their bolts and bars.[97]

This is a companion-piece to the miracle told by Constantius of Germanus at Ravenna, and the family likeness is less surprising if we recall that Sidonius was a close friend of Constantius and even dedicated his collection of *Letters* to him. These *Letters* do not, as does the *Life of Germanus*, describe a miraculous world — a rich aristocrat devoted to rhetoric and poetry could not be expected wholly to transform his outlook on life. But if he does not picture a miraculous world he nevertheless believes that at bottom the world is miraculous. Even the enlightened Roman had always been bored by science; it required no very violent wrench, therefore, in order to destroy his respect for it. Yet sixty years earlier lay nobles like Sidonius had been inclined to revile the monks because they sought to impose on men by miraculous fables and tricks; it was during this interval between 415 and

[95] *Letters* I # 5 § 9.   [97] *Letters* VII # 9 § 20.
[96] *Letters* VII # 1 § 4.

475 that the miracle first became respectable and later fashionable. For it is obvious that in the Roman world of 475 Sidonius represented all that seemed admirable.

True to the tradition of Augustine, in contrast to that of Martin and Severus in Gaul, Africa resisted the spell of a miraculous world more obstinately. So it seems, at least, judging by the history of the Vandal persecution there in 484 which Victor, bishop of Vita, wrote in order to honour its victims. In this extensive account only twelve miracles are alleged. Coincidences adequately explain four of them; [98] three are cures; [99] two concern the absence of any marks of violence on the bodies of martyrs.[100] Of the three remaining one describes how a wooden spear rotted,[101] another how the bonds of a victim snapped.[102] The third is the most puzzling: where the tongues of certain persons having been cut out they were able to speak as distinctly as before.[103]

Taking into account the seriousness of these Vandal persecutions and the emotional strain which they induced, it is surprising that the supernatural plays such a minor role in Victor's story. The explanation must be that the African, even after over fifty years of Vandal domination, still remained less credulous than his Gallic contemporaries. Not that Victor was made uncomfortable by miracles; on the contrary he longed for them, rejoiced at them, and prayed most fervently for more. But they came very rarely. Crying to the Apostles he reminds them that although they were fishermen and sinners Christ in His mercy gave them fame and holiness; let them, therefore, deal with the Africans as Christ dealt with them! [104] The justice of God had become unendurable; let the saints in heaven bestir themselves! Yet the only sign that they had bestirred themselves in order to affect the course of events was the coming of a severe drought which killed Arians and Catholics indiscriminately.[105] Was this, Victor complained, the best the saints could do?

[98] *Historia Persecutionis Africanae Provinciae* I § 46, II §§ 17–22 & 37, III §§ 55–60.
[99] Ibid. I § 38, & II §§ 11 & 50.
[100] Ibid. I § 34, & III § 28.
[101] Ibid. I § 34.
[102] Ibid. I § 43.
[103] Ibid. III § 30.
[104] Ibid. III § 70.
[105] Ibid. III §§ 55–60.

E. Justice, Matter, Will: 470 on

How easy was the transition from the worldly and almost pagan, to the now prevalent Christian, conception of life is revealed in an early letter of Sidonius to his brother-in-law Agricola — son of the Emperor Avitus. Speaking of the illness of his daughter Severiana he says:

Under Christ's guidance we are determined to fly the languor and heat of the town with all our household, and incidentally escape the doctors also, who disagree across the bed and by their ignorance and endless visits conscientiously kill off their patients. . . . Let us then with all the more diligence entreat and beseech the Lord that the cure which our efforts fail to effect may come down to our invalid from above.[1]

Here there is not only a confidence again in the miracle instead of in science; there is, in addition, a confidence in justice on earth. Successful cures, indeed, were inevitably regarded as adequate proof of it. According to Augustine — as to Vigilantius and Cassian — prayer cannot influence God's will to ameliorate present misery. God will deal justly with our future destiny, but He remains capricious in regard to our earthly vicissitudes. Unless, therefore, God sees a didactic reason for intervention, man's sole reliance must lie in the science of the physician. But, in so far as Salvian's theory — which the experience of the miraculous cure corroborates — is sound, God also deals justly with men here and now. Therefore if Severiana does not deserve to suffer and die, and if those who love her do not deserve to lose her, God will see to it that she is saved. Theoretically, since God knows all, He will save her irrespective of human prayers; practically, however, prayers might serve to call the matter more forcibly to His attention, and above all they must serve as evidence of the faith, humility, and piety of those who make them, thereby increasing their merit and so their rightful claim to God's mercy. Any enlightened pagan could see the logic of that.

The author of the *Life of Hilary* seems to cling still to the Lerins idea of justice on earth as operative almost exclusively

[1] *Letters* II # 12 § 2.

within the monastic world. He has Honoratus say, when seeking to convert the young Hilary to the monastic vocation:

I promise that from thee I shall reap great things and higher than can be conceived of, and that there will be provided to you in the present life things you cannot estimate, and, in the future, things which cannot now be imagined.[2]

And later the author tells how Hilary 'enters the terrestrial paradise of Lerins.'[3] It naturally follows too, in contrast to the age of Jerome and Severus, that the cult of ugliness passes: for the author says that Hilary

proved the merits of the interior man by the beauty of the outer.[4]

Moreover if the miraculous cure seemed a proof of the operation of justice on earth, how much more forcibly the physical miracle proved it. When Constantius tells of how Germanus set the Ravenna prisoners free,[5] he wishes us to understand not only that God was rewarding Germanus' good intentions but also that He was freeing men who were being unjustly constrained. The degree, indeed, to which justice on earth might operate for the benefit of saints is shown in another of Constantius' stories of Germanus:

He had left the city and was making his journey with happy delays when he came upon beggars who asked for alms. Germanus asked his deacon how much money they had. On being informed that there were just three pieces of gold, he instructed that they all be given away. Upon which the deacon said, ' With what, then, shall we get anything to eat?' Answering, Germanus said, ' God feeds His poor; therefore hand over all that you have to the needy.' But the deacon, as if out of prudence, handed out only two of the pieces, retaining the third. When they had resumed their journey they shortly perceived horsemen riding up behind at great speed. These quickly came up, dismounted, and, clasping them by the knees, entreated them as follows: ' Our master, the very eminent Leporius, lives not far from here; he and his family are so enmeshed in disconcerting trouble that he is borne down by both his own and his family's illness. We convey his tears to you; if you think this invalid worthy, visit him. And, if the pressing business of your office outweighs our plea, will you not make a

---

2 *S. Hilarii Arelat. Vita* ch. 2.   5 See p. 521.
3 Ch. 5.
4 Ch. 7. On Jerome see p. 470 n.
7; on Severus see Babut 1912 121.

prayer of intercession; for if he does not deserve to be seen by you let him at least deserve your blessing.' Filled with mercy at these words, the most saintly man desisted from his journey, and judged that road the better one which leads to the reward of a good deed. In spite of the protests of his men he turned about and made the visit his petitioners had begged for, saying to the former: ' I let nothing interfere with the fulfilment of the Lord's commands.' Thereupon the latter were exultant with joy and presented him with the sum of two hundred *solidi* with which they had been furnished. Whereupon, turning to the deacon, Germanus said: ' Take what is offered and know that you defrauded the poor; had you handed over the whole sum to the beggars, our benefactor would today have requited us with three hundred.' [6]

The earthly felicity of monks and holy men is one thing, however; that of casual Christian laymen quite another. Yet Sidonius, being intimate not only with the saints but also with his old lay friends, is quite ready to extend the idea in order to include the latter too. Writing to a kinsman of his who had previously endowed the Church of Clermont with his estate of Cutiacum, he says that, as a consequence,

God has picked you out to be exalted by unusual good fortune in inheritances. He did not long delay to reward your devotion a hundredfold, and it is our sure belief that these earthly gifts will be followed by heavenly gifts hereafter. I may tell you . . . that the Nicetan succession is heaven's repayment for Cutiacum surrendered.[7]

True piety, then, was doubly worthwhile; Sidonius nevertheless set a limit to the operation of this justice. If it prevailed among pious laymen as well as among monks, it did not prevail among the heretics. For, speaking of the Visigothic Euric, he observes how:

he attributes his success in his designs and enterprises to the orthodoxy of his belief, whereas the real cause lies in mere earthly fortune.[8]

As the State recedes and the Church advances, the area in which chance operates is reduced: to Cassian it seemed to be universally operative; [9] to Lerins it still operated through-

[6] *Vita Germani* § 33.

[7] *Letters* III # 1 § 3.

[8] *Letters* VII # 6 § 6, quoted p. 453 n. 33.

[9] See pp. 331–32.

out the lay world; [10] but to Salvian, and above all to bishop Sidonius, it operated only among heretics — perhaps only among barbarians. Throughout the Roman-Christian world not Providence only, but also justice on earth, everywhere prevailed.[11]

Almost at the end of the fifth century the Roman Pope was the African Gelasius, a highly intelligent theologian who might well, we should suppose, retain a certain loyalty for the tradition which Augustine had inculcated in Africa. Yet he too seems inclined to adopt the hypothesis of justice on earth. Answering the allegations that the miseries of his day were caused by the recent abolition of the pagan festival of the *Lupercalia,* he says,

Is it the *Lupercalia* that have done this, or rather our conduct: stealing, homicide, adultery, injustice, iniquity, ambition, cupidity, perjury, false witness, oppression of the unfortunate, the discrediting of good causes and the defence of evil causes, and an unheard of perversity in all things; and finally, and above all, hypocrisy towards God and sacrilege and magic that even the pagans must abhor? [12]

The implication is clear. If the Romans had behaved the way decent Christians should, God would not have visited these miseries on their city. If sin invites present punishment then surely virtue will invite present reward.[13] Gelasius accepts the communal justice that was operative at Sodom; [14] Augustine's idea of a teaching is here eclipsed by the primitive theory of peremptory and wholesale vengeance.

In about 470 [15] a controversy took place between Faustus, then bishop of Riez, and Claudianus Mamertus, a priest of Vienne. Both of them were highly educated — as learned in

---

10 See p. 335.

11 Writing shortly after 500, Eugippius records words of bishop Severinus, a contemporary of Constantius: ' had you offered tithes for the poor, not only would you enjoy an everlasting reward, you would also be able to abound in earthly comforts ': *Vita S. Severini* 18 § 2.

12 *Tract* # VI § 15.

13 Pope Gelasius *Letter* # 12 § 4 says to the Emperor ' you who desire not only the present but also the future rewards of Christ ' had better heed Rome's counsel. The intimation is that while good intentions invite earthly rewards orthodoxy alone invites heavenly.

14 See pp. 85–86.

15 Arnold 1898 IV 133 line 9 says that Mamertus wrote his *De Statu Animae* in 470. Uberweg 1915 II [10] 189–90 says 468 or 469. Wörter 1899 51 says that Faustus wrote his *De Gratia* in 474.

pagan philosophy as in Christian theology.[16] The issue was in regard to the nature of the soul. It is quite clear [17] that Augustine, influenced by Neoplatonism and even by Manichæism, had denied the presence of any matter in the soul. Cassian, however, had thought the soul a compound of matter as well as spirit.[18] There was a danger lurking in both conceptions; for if the soul were pure spirit it might easily be treated the way the Manichee and Neoplatonist did treat it: as a particle of divinity. While if there were matter in it the suspicion must arise that the evil in man was caused by this matter, and man would come to blame his sins rather on this alien substance within his soul than on his whole soul and so on his whole self.[19] Now Faustus had followed the Lerinian tradition of Cassian, and one of his arguments was that since the soul was confined in space it must have quantity and if it had quantity it must be material.[20] He therefore pictures the soul, in so far as it is spirit, as imprisoned by matter, which is closer to the Manichæan conception than he perhaps realized. Faustus is thus a lineal descendant of the whole ascetic movement based on the conception of matter as the real cause of sin and misery. Very roughly it would be from Stoic [21] to Manichee to Priscillianist to Martin [22] to Cassian to Lerins.

Now Faustus was at this time the leader of the Gallic Church; his sway, however, seems to have been fitfully disputed. The attempt of Claudianus Mamertus to refute him in this matter is one such case. Mamertus has justly been described as among the earliest specimens of the scholastic.[23] In a general way this seems to mean that he applied Aristotelian methods and language in the elucidation of his problems. His task was to show that the soul had nothing in it that was

---

[16] On Faustus see Dalton 1915 I clxviii; on Mamertus see Arnold 1898 IV 132–33.

[17] See pp. 64–65, 67 & 97.

[18] As had also Tertullian and Jerome: Dill 1906 2 219–20.

[19] Probably it was the spiritual part of the soul that was deemed capable of acquiring merit, and grace was probably needed in order to make up the deficiency in divinity caused by the base alloy of matter in the soul. To Faustus a soul wholly spiritual would have been too Pelagian a conception.

[20] Ueberweg 1915 II 10 189.

[21] May Tertullian be classed as a Stoic in this regard?

[22] Arnold 1898 IV 132 includes Hilary of Poitiers, which suggests the disputed link between him and the Priscillianists on the one hand and Martin on the other: see pp. 456–59.

[23] Arnold ibid. 133.

either material or divine, and he accomplished it by the
time-honoured device of declaring it to be a third element,
which resembled divine spirit in some ways and resembled
matter in other ways. Faustus had said that it had quantity
because it existed in space, Mamertus admitted that it had
quality — as of virtue and understanding — but denied
that it had quantity on the theory that although it was confined within the human body it existed throughout the body
and not at any particular point in it. One could not argue
that God was quantitative because He existed only within the
confines of reality; yet the soul existed in the body in precisely that way. On the other hand the soul was like matter
because it existed in time; it was a thing created in time,
which divinity was not. The soul was therefore a counterfeit
of God: eternal yet created in time, ubiquitous yet confined
within the space of a body.[24]

In spite of the fact that the argument of Mamertus won
favour, was used and admired by Cassiodorus, Berengar of
Tours, Bernard, Aquinas, and Descartes, it leaves us with
the uncomfortable feeling that it was a little too simple to be
sound. Yet this was in fact its virtue, for it gave a simple
explanation of a distinction which men wanted to make but
had not before found how to. If the soul must not be God
or matter, it must, inevitably, be something else. Mamertus
was defending, whether consciously or unconsciously, a vital
hypothesis of Augustine's: man's soul was the source of evil,
and matter as well as God was guiltless. Consequently neither matter nor God abode in the soul, for if either could be
implicated in the slightest degree man would certainly take
advantage of the fact in order to excuse himself. Mamertus,
the priest and scholastic, was in fact defending Augustine
from the ascetism of the monks: matter was as helpful to a
virtuous soul as it was harmful to a sinful one; and virtue did
not come in as matter went out, it came in only when man
came to love it enough to seek it.

This boldness of Mamertus in defying Faustus suggests the
possibility that Augustine was not yet wholly forgotten in
Gaul. And how, so long as intelligence remained active,

24 Uberweg 1915 II 10 189-90.

could he be? There was still, for instance, the problem of
free will, acute and not yet resolved. The last Gallic champion of Augustine, Prosper of Aquitaine, had retired from
the field in about 434,[25] leaving Faustus in possession. Faustus had not succeeded, however, in winning the papacy to
his views, and so long as the papacy remained non-committal
the issue must remain alive.

The author of the *Life of Hilary,* who wrote in about 470,
carefully slips this clause into his account of Hilary's conversion:

just as prevenient divine grace, for instance, transforms the
human will for the better.[26]

Now Faustus had maintained that merit might precede grace;
was it not with a certain malice, therefore, that the author
took pains to show how in Hilary's case grace quite obviously
preceded merit? This was as much as to say, the papacy is
right and you, Faustus, are wrong.

Moreover there were still at this time some few who dared
to go further and defend the propositions of Augustine. At
a Council of Arles, held in about 475,[27] Faustus forced a priest
named Lucidus to retract certain doctrines: that Christ did
not die to save all; that man was invariably helpless to attract grace; that a baptized person who sinned and was
damned was a victim of the sin of Adam.[28] Augustine was
here clearly being condemned,[29] yet there is no indication
that the papacy protested or even suggested greater prudence.
To be sure the Popes of this time had other things to worry
them: the Arian barbarians were acquiring a strangle hold
on Italy, and the Eastern Church and State were defying
Nicæa and Leo. Yet the papacy, even so, would have acted
had there been a real reason. It did not move because the

---

[25] See p. 430 n. 53.
[26] S. *Hilarii Arelat. Vita* ch. 4.
[27] Hefele 1908 II 2 909–10.
[28] Ibid.
[29] At least Lucidus was not a Predestinarian of the kind described by
Vincent of Lerins — *Commonitorium*
§ 69 — for that sect believed that *all*
its adherents were predestined to salvation: ' quicumque illi ad numerum
suum pertinent.' For, if so, would

not this tenet have been specifically
condemned? Lucidus admitted he
had previously believed that Christ
came to save only those whom He
foreknew would exercise their free
will in order to help save themselves:
Hefele 1908 II 2 911. Now this is
rather Cassian's view; it falls far
short of Augustine, and still farther
short of the Predestinarian views as
described by Vincent.

Council had not openly raised the issue of prevenient grace, condemning only those doctrines of Augustine which the papacy had not yet chosen either to affirm or deny. If Faustus were denounced Augustine might have to be accepted, and it seemed safer to abandon Augustine than to champion him. As for Faustus, it was clear to Rome that he did not want to precipitate the issue of prevenient grace; and, so long as he did not, the papacy preferred to let the matter drift. Since in 475 Faustus was nearly seventy, the papacy was perhaps trusting that his doctrine would soon die with him.

Faustus lived on for some time, but in about 493 [30] he died, and it was in this very year that Pope Gelasius, in an official letter to the bishops of Picenum in Ancona, declared

that this will of natural freedom does not earn grace, but rather receives, through grace, a merciful deliverance from the bondage which it deserved on account of its sins. [31]

This is a reiteration of the doctrine of the *Præteritorum* which insisted on prevenient grace. With Faustus dead the papacy dares speak its mind again. [32] Yet it remained suspiciously obscure what man's status might be when grace had once loosed him from servitude. If it was no longer slavery might it by any chance be freedom?

With Faustus died the last chance of overthrowing the doctrine of prevenient grace, for here Africa was clearly supported by Rome. The unbaptized had, therefore, been predestined to remain so, and hence predestined to be damned. At this point, for the next thirty-six years, the matter was left. But this crystallized only half the doctrine of grace and free will, for the problem of whether this wholly unmerited grace, once received, could be resisted, was left in abeyance. Augustinian Africa still maintained that it could not be resisted, but the Vandal persecutions of 484–494 so distracted and disorganized Catholicism there that this influence was fast waning. When the issue should be raised again — as,

[30] Seeberg 1898 V 784 line 7.
[31] *Letter* # 6 § 8.
[32] Chapman 1913 195 maintains that chapter V of the *Decretum Gelasianum* is a product of Gelasius, and in this chapter V the writings of Faustus as well as of Cassian are declared to be apocryphal, that is, unorthodox: Dobschütz 1912 13.

sooner or later, it must — Rome could hardly again evade a decision.   So far she had intimated that baptism conferred free will and therefore the capacity to act meritoriously, yet she had said nothing to suggest that this capacity could do anything to attract grace.   But, since grace was essential to salvation, unless the merit earned could attract that grace, of what use was the free will thus bestowed?   The point was no less vital than delicate, for, now that virtually every Roman of consequence had been baptized, the issue of whether the baptized were or were not predestined overshadowed every other.   A definite settlement had long been postponed; it might be deferred for a time longer; but, sooner or later, the momentous problem which Augustine had raised must be faced, and either accepted or rejected.

CHAPTER VIII

THE PAPACY

A. NICÆA TO DAMASUS, 325–373

HARDLY had the Emperor Constantine granted toleration to the Christians when a bitter controversy arose among them over the definition of Christ. It was then [1] that Arius, a priest of Alexandria, revived that metaphysical view which may be traced through Philo the Jew, the Gnostics, Origen, Plotinus, and Lucian of Antioch. According to it Christ was merely the first thing created by God out of nothing; like Adam he had free will, and God, because He foreknew that Christ would persevere in virtue, adopted him as His Son and empowered him to create all subsequent creatures and things — the first of which was the Holy Ghost. [2]

Thereupon Constantine, distressed by the storm of violence which followed the diffusion of this Arian doctrine, pleaded for a compromise, and, when this failed, he summoned the first Christian General Council, that of Nicæa, to settle the matter. [3] Bishops came from all over the Eastern half of the Empire and a few also from the West; the bishop of Rome did not come, but he sent two bishops as his representatives. This Council condemned the doctrine of Arius, and in the following terms:

We believe in one God, the almighty Father, creator of all things visible and invisible; and in one Lord, Jesus Christ, born of the Father, only-begotten — that is, of the substance of the Father, true God from the true God, born, not made, *homoousion* — that is, with the substance of the same Father, through whom all things were made which are in heaven and on earth; who, for the sake of us men and for the sake of our salvation, descended, and was incarnated, and was made man, suffered, and arose again on the third day, ascended to heaven, whence he will come to judge the living and the dead; and [we believe] in the Holy Ghost.

However there are those who say: there was a time when he was not, and before he was born he was not, and that he was not created out of any substance, or who say that he was transformed

---

[1] In 318: Duchesne 1910 II [4] 126.   [3] Ibid. 140.
[2] Ibid. 128.

from some other substance or essence — that is, that the Son of God is changeable or mutable — these the Catholic and Apostolic Church anathematizes.[4]

It is strange how each of the rival doctrines contains a Neoplatonic element: that of Arius a hierarchy of created beings, that of Nicæa a multiplication by emanation. It is this perennial interweaving of metaphysical elements that made — and still makes — the issue so elusive. But one thing is clear: the Christ of Arius was merely adopted as a God, the Christ of Nicæa was a God, although He temporarily played a human role; the substance of one was created out of nothing and in terms of time, that of the other was uncreated and eternal. Thus whereas the one view left the completeness of Christ's divinity in doubt the other made His weak humanity seem unauthentic.

Constantine and many others believed that this Nicene Creed would settle the dispute for ever. In fact, however, it settled nothing.[5] Instead, the issue continued for centuries — especially in the East — to be the most disputed problem of Christianity, and indeed it has ever remained so.[6] As, a few years after Nicæa, the controversy blazed up again with all its earlier fury, it became clear that Christianity might not long survive and prosper unless it would create and acknowledge some sovereign authority. But where was such a power to be sought, and lodged?

Technically, of course, there was no need of a legislative sovereignty, because all Christians acknowledged that the Bible text had been divinely revealed and contained all that need be known.[7] As nothing could be taken from it, so nothing could be added to it. The text was fundamental and therefore unamendable.[8] Yet the fact that there was no need of a sovereign legislative power made the need of a sovereign judicial power so much the greater: for the more unalterable the law the greater must be the need for judicious — and the

[4] Galante 1906 69; & cf. 67.
[5] Duchesne 1910 II 4 156–57.
[6] Today especially in the Protestant sects.
[7] In the time of Irenæus, shortly before 200, and for some time after that, custom and tradition vied with the Bible as the authority, but in the fourth century reliance seems to have been much more on the Bible text, especially in matters of dogma, but also in any other matters where a text could seem pertinent.
[8] This was certainly Augustine's view: De Baptismo II § 4. Cf. Caspar 1930 I 341 line 30.

greater must be the danger of injudicious — interpretations. Heresy and adultery, for instance, were both sins — there was no doubt of that and no authority could ever declare them otherwise — but there must be some authority to decide what thoughts and acts constituted those sins, and what should be the penalty imposed on those committing them.

In the early days the episcopal organizations,[9] functioning as an informal federation, had sufficed; but they were now beginning to prove ineffectual. So long as persecution held all Christians in a common misery, incipient disputes were nipped in the bud. But the Christians were now triumphant, not only dominating the spiritual world but affecting the temporal. Pride, ascetic and worldly, began to raise its ugly head, and conversions were no longer confined to men seeking a spiritual vocation; instead, as we have said,[10] there was now a whole world of ordinary men to be governed. Suppose a bishop had preached a doctrine that seemed heretical; suppose he had assumed an authority in defiance of tradition; suppose even that his election had raised unsavoury rumours of undue influence, bribery, or a threat of violence. Who, in such cases, might judge and so, if need be, depose this bishop? Surely the archbishop or his provincial Council. But suppose that here, too, there was complaint of irregularity: to whom might the appeal go then?

It was just such questions as these that were being raised as resistance to the Nicene Creed grew in intensity. If a Nicene archbishop deposed an Arian bishop, an Arian archbishop would be quick to retaliate by deposing a Nicene bishop. The situation soon became intolerable. Why, then, should not such matters be left to the Emperor's decision? It is true that the Emperors were often eager to assume this responsibility, and they at least had the advantage of an armed force at their command with which to execute their decisions. No one, however, except an Emperor could take such a proposition seriously: for one thing he was likely to be grossly ignorant of the real issues involved;[11] secondly he must be unduly tempted to put political above spiritual ex-

9 Indeed a bishop acquired civil power over his clergy only in 408: Fustel de Coulanges 1891 II 70.

10 See pp. 268 n. 97, & 337 n. 2.

11 On Constantine, see Duchesne 1910 II⁴ 138-39. On Ambrose's defiance of Valentinian II in 386, see Batiffol 1924² 61-64.

pediency; [12] and thirdly he might well be a heretic and even, as Julian was to be, a pagan. The Emperor had already appropriated the prerogative of summoning General Councils [13] — this power was quite enough.

Why, then, were not the General Councils — provided the Emperor did in fact call them — the very authority needed? Chiefly because it was impracticable to call these except rarely and in emergencies; for how could bishops rule their own dioceses if they spent many months each year or two attending far-off Councils? [14]   Basil, the great bishop of Cæsarea in Cappadocia who died in 379, had conceived of Church sovereignty as the majority opinion of all the bishops, even if not in Council.[15]   But this left unsolved the question of who should draft the questions they should vote on, and of who should count the ballots and announce the result.

The need for a provincial organization with the bishop of the metropolitan city outranking the other or suffragan bishops had been quickly felt: unless the individual bishop were in some degree made responsible to one or more of his fellow-bishops he could indulge his whims — theological, moral, or other — with impunity. Canon 5 of Nicæa recognized this need in the case of a sentence of excommunication rendered by an individual bishop against one of his own clergy or laity by providing for a review of the sentence by a Council 'composed of all the bishops of that province' with power 'at their discretion to mitigate the sentence.' [16]   The conduct of the bishop in many other important matters was subject to review by this provincial Council, although what, precisely, constituted an important matter is not always clear to us and was probably not always clear to them. This canon 5 merely declared one of these matters — of excommunication — to be of such importance. Encroachment on the pristine autonomy of the individual bishop was here approved in principle; the question now was how far this encroachment should be allowed to proceed.

[12] The trial of Pope Damasus in 371 before a civil court on a charge of murder (see p. 545) must have scandalized every good Catholic, including those who were civil officials.
[13] Batiffol 1924 [2] 286–87; Caspar 1930 I 403.

[14] See the Emperor's letter of 381, quoted in Hefele 1908 II [2] 50 n. 1; & Jullian 1926 VIII 209.
[15] Batiffol 1924 [2] 91–92 & 102–03.
[16] Hefele 1907 I [2] 548–50. Cf. p. 573 n. 13.

The principle of provincial autonomy, on the other hand, was at this time still being upheld — at least it was thought subject only to the declarations of a General Council such as this one now being held for the first time at Nicæa. And the spirit of Nicæa was itself distinctly judicial rather than legislative: to declare what the law was and always had been, rather than what it should be henceforth. Thus its famous sixth canon acknowledges certain exceptions to the principle of provincial autonomy:

Ancient custom shall be preserved in Egypt, Libya, and Pentapolis, so that the bishop of Alexandria shall have authority over all of these. And this because there is a similar custom in the case of the city of Rome. And so, too, in the case of Antioch and the other provinces shall the privileges of their Churches be preserved.[17]

The city of Rome had set the precedent for such anomalies because Italy, not having been divided by Diocletian into civil provinces, was administered by the State as a unit. Consequently, when the Church adopted the civil as ecclesiastical divisions, the bishop of Rome automatically became the archbishop of all Italy.[18] A later, or at least a more organic, centralization had developed in Egypt and Asia, whereby the cities of Alexandria and Antioch had subjected the provinces surrounding them to their overlordship. Legal or illegal, desirable or undesirable, it was an established fact — a right acquired, one might say, by prescription — which Nicæa had no discreet alternative but to recognize. Whether or not this ought to be, it was so. But if the bishops of Nicæa explicitly approved this anomaly they implicitly disapproved of it in principle: no other cities than those already exercising super-metropolitan rights could claim them, and even these privileged cities had no other rights than those they were already exercising — Rome no rights beyond Italy, Alexandria none beyond Egypt, Antioch none beyond Asia proper.

Yet precisely because the object was merely to clarify and define the status quo these canons of Nicæa were virtually obsolete before they were decreed. A few years later, with the Arian heresy and its infinite variations overrunning the

17 Galante 1906 62–63.   18 Batiffol 1924 2 151.

East like a plague, not only laymen, priests, and bishops but
even archbishops and their provincial Councils began to
champion unorthodox views and to excommunicate the orthodox. Undoubtedly another General Council, like Nicæa,
whose bishops represented all Christendom, was thought authorized to pass on the validity of these excommunications;
but unless such a Council were held every year or two its decisions were doomed to prove ineffective, as bishops were ex-
communicating each other every month and consecrating
others of their own party in their stead. It was vital, therefore, that there be some central authority wielding the powers
of a General Council to whom the excommunicated could
have prompt recourse. Unless this authority be the Emperor
himself it must be some other individual or compact body
that could sit as a court of appeal almost continuously.[19]

The rise of the Roman papacy in order to supply this need
is one of the most dramatic events in history, and for the very
reason that it is so dramatic, and proved so decisive, the explanations suggested have been as multiple as they have been
diverse. Whether or not this rise was caused by divine guidance, it was certainly also, if more immediately, caused by
human expediency — for no more and no less than any other
human institution, could the Church long survive without
some acknowledged sovereign power. Since theocracy under
the Emperor was repugnant to Christians and since the General Council was repugnant to nature, some other authority
must arise which was less repugnant on both counts. Theoretically it is conceivable that no sovereignty should arise.
In that case all hope of enduring unity would have fled and
Roman Christianity in the fifth century would have become
like German Christianity in the sixteenth. Christians like
Augustine were emphatic that God had willed the expansion
of the Roman Empire in order that Christianity might be the
more effectively diffused; they might have added — for certainly they perceived, although darkly perhaps — that God
also willed this in order that Christianity might, in spite of its
wide diffusion, remain unified, in faith and purpose — as sixteenth century Germany, with her *cuius regio, eius religio*

[19] Cf. ibid. 34.

did not. And what was the centre of the Empire — certainly
until the death of Constantine in 337 and probably for many
years thereafter — if not the city of Rome?[20] That city
started with an incalculable advantage in the blind, organic
race for Christian sovereignty.

One serious handicap, and only one, did Rome have: because Christianity came out of the East, spreading westward,
the centre of the Christian passion and turmoil remained in
the East.[21] But for certain fortuitous circumstances Rome
might never have prevailed: one was that the three largest
cities of the East effectively counterbalanced each other, creating jealousies, and jealousies with teeth in them. The
mere fact that one of them tried to lead disinclined the others
to follow. Another circumstance fortunate for Rome was
geographical: observe that the geometrical centre of the
Greek-speaking Roman East was far out in the Mediterranean
Sea, at a point almost equidistant from each of the three
rival cities of Constantinople, Alexandria, and Antioch.

What a contrast was the position of Rome! Wholly dis-
regarding her prestige as the real heart and soul of the Empire, her position, geographically speaking, was strategically
ideal. She was not only the largest city, she was at the very
centre, of the Empire, and she was also at the gateway leading from east to west and from west to east. She was near
enough to the East to make the Greeks feel they knew her
ways and wishes, yet far enough from it to keep clear of their
private quarrels. To them she seemed at once always present and always aloof.[22] Thus portrayed, Rome was outwardly
the ideal arbitrator of disputes between the rival Greek cities.
Looking at our map we may imagine that we see Rome seated
on the Bench, facing various members of the Bar as each
pleads his cause.

Moreover the one apparent advantage that the East possessed over Rome actually turned out to her disadvantage:
being the centre of the passion and turmoil, controversies
arose more frequently and acutely, to intensify the natural
local rivalries. Alexandria would side at one time with the

[20] On the glamour of the city in
357 see Dudden 1935 22–25; & see
pp. 239–40.

[21] Haller 1934 I 34.

[22] Ibid. 91–92.

Arians while Antioch championed the orthodox, a few years later there would be a reversal of alliances — just as the Seven Years' War followed the War of the Austrian Succession.[23] The West, on the other hand, including Italy and Rome, had neither the geographical nor the theological rivalries. When the Nicene Creed was declared, the West accepted it at its face value; glad to have the matter determined decisively whatever subtle implications might be extracted from it, the Latin bishops were disgusted when the whole controversy burst out again.[24] Perhaps the Latins were not as fond of metaphysics as the Greeks; certainly they were much more fond of politics, and politics, translated now into Christian terms, meant a deep concern for the historical success of their religion. Instinctively they felt that, because their religion was destined to triumph, whatever did triumph must be the true religion. Not that they were over-ready to compromise their faith for the sake of that temporal triumph — for they were neither opportunists nor time-servers; rather they felt that God was quite as capable of revealing the truth to them as He was of procuring its temporal triumph, and that, as humble cooperators with God in His immense task, they too must concern themselves with both, encouraging not only the triumph of the truth within the Church but also the triumph of the Church.[25] Logically — and the Greeks respected this logic — action should only follow thought. The action of teaching should come only after the knowledge of what to teach. But the Latin knew that things do not in fact happen that way: man is somehow doomed to teach while still learning.[26] That is why the Latin resented heresies on principle and by instinct, and why he was gradually induced to rest all the Church's authority in the bishop of his capital city of Rome.

In 335 Athanasius, bishop of Alexandria and staunchest supporter of the Nicene Creed, was deposed by a packed [27] Council held at Tyre in Phoenicia, whereupon the Emperor,

---

[23] Cf. Carré 1911 254 ff.

[24] Hilary of Poitiers, then one of the leading Latin theologians, was ignorant of the exact language of the Nicene Creed until he was exiled from his see in 357 for adhering to it; Batiffol 1924 [2] 5.

[25] Cf. pp. 570, 600, & 653–54.

[26] As Ambrose confessed: De Officiis I § 4.

[27] Duchesne 1910 II [4] 175–76.

in order to render that decree effective, banished him to Trier in Gaul.[28]   What authority had this Council of Tyre thus to depose the bishop of Alexandria, and, if it had no authority to do this, what other person or body short of a General Council did have this authority?   After several years of argument and violence the Emperor resorted again to a General Council, to meet at Sardica on the frontier between East and West.   The Eastern [29] contingent of bishops, who were for the most part hostile to Athanasius, as soon as they perceived that the majority of the Council would be favourable to him, refused to take part in the deliberations,[30] thereby depriving the Council of any authority as a General Council.   The Western bishops met nevertheless, proceeded to reinstate Athanasius, and to decree the following:

Whenever a condemned bishop continues to believe in the justice of his cause, so that a second trial is required, out of respect for the memory of the apostle Peter, Pope Julius may be written to in Rome, and he shall, if he chooses, create another tribunal composed of bishops of adjoining provinces whom he shall name.[31]

A later canon [32] added that the condemned bishop might, if he chose and the Pope chose, obtain a representative of the Pope as presiding officer of this tribunal.   It was further provided [33] that the sentence of deposition should not become effective until the appeal had been heard and judgment rendered.

Because these canons appear to be an acknowledgment by the Latin episcopate that the Pope was the ruling power of the Church, some scholars [34] have supposed — and not wholly without reason — that they must be later interpolations. Yet surely their language reveals desperation rather than premeditation.   Recent experience had shown that Emperors acted only as the political expediency of each moment suggested; the defection of the Eastern bishops now proved not only the clumsiness of the General Council but its impotence to organize in time of crisis.   Someone had to decide, if not what was right, at least who should be authorized to decide

28 Duchesne 1910 II 4 181–82.
29 Cf. ibid. 219.
30 Hefele 1907 I 2 750–52.
31 Canon # 3 § 3: Hefele ibid. 762–65.

32 Canon # 5: ibid. 769–70.
33 Canon # 4: ibid. 766–67.
34 See the bibliography in Caspar 1930 I 587–88. Cf. Turmel 1933 III 125–69.

what was right. The analogy to the American form of government comes to mind. The United States Supreme Court may determine how both the Constitution and the Statutes are to be understood; like the Pope according to Sardica, it has no legislative power. The States may amend the Constitution, Congress may amend the Statutes, but so long as these are not amended only such and such things, and no others, are permissible. If we may visualize the Nicene text as a Constitution and local provincial practice as a series of Statutes not inconsistent with that Constitution, we can see something of the real intent of the canons of Sardica. Some say that the Supreme Court, notably under John Marshall, arrogated this right to itself. Perhaps it did, and perhaps Rome did likewise. The strict legality and morality of such action may be open to question; the fact remains, nevertheless, that in each case the law of nature operated to supply a demand. And, where nature takes matters into her own hands, man-made law and man-made ethics will quickly succumb.

These canons of Sardica, moreover, were not brazen innovations, much more were they codifications of a practice already familiar. The theory of Rome's supremacy had been outlined before the year 200 by the greatest Christian authority of the early period, Irenæus, who was born a Greek! [35] Cyprian of Carthage, although he spoke ambiguously,[36] had not hesitated to request Pope Stephen to depose Marcion, bishop of Arles.[37] And Cyprian, too, like Irenæus two generations earlier, was the most distinguished Christian of his day. In the year 254 Pope Stephen restored to their sees two Spanish bishops who had been deposed by their colleagues, and a year before Sardica Julius had, at the request of the Nicene party, restored Athanasius to the great Eastern see of Alexandria.[38] These precedents established no legal rights but they did establish a practice, and practice is the mother of legal right, as the law itself recognizes. It is true that an aggrieved bishop did not appeal to Rome unless he thought that Rome would choose to reinstate him. But at least he

---

[35] Caspar 1930 I 17 & 78.
[36] Ibid. 78–79; & Koch 1930 esp. 154–70.
[37] Duchesne 1902 143.
[38] Ibid.

rarely appealed to any other bishop; if he appealed at all it was to the Emperor — which was the one practice that all bishops, when in their right minds, wanted to stop. The canons of Sardica may therefore be said to constitute a challenge to the Greeks: if they wanted a chaos of separatism and heresy they could leave matters as they legally were; if they wanted a theocracy they could appeal to the Emperor; if they wanted a Church they must leave the final judicial determination, however this might be circumscribed, to some one of the great sees. And the Latin candidate for this honour was the see of Rome.

Nothing came of this effort for a good many years more. Instead the anti-Nicene party, predominant in the East, began, with the help of the Emperor Constantius, to impose itself on the West. In 355 Pope Liberius was exiled; [39] in 356 the bishop of Milan was also exiled and an anti-Nicene, Auxentius from Cappadocia, was installed in his place; [40] in 357 Liberius, under pressure, succumbed, rejecting communion with Athanasius.[41] Finally, in 359, the bishops of a Western Council summoned at Rimini were held virtual prisoners until almost all of them followed Liberius' example.[42] Among the few who held out were the leading Latin bishops Hilary of Poitiers [43] and Eusebius of Vercelli.[44] But, naturally enough, they took their stand by the authority of the Nicene Creed and not by that of the bishop of Rome.

The short pagan interlude under Julian followed. Then, two years later, in 365, the new Emperor was Valentinian I, a lukewarm supporter of the Nicene party.[45] A year later Liberius died; a disputed and bloody election followed, with the rivals, Damasus, supporter of Nicæa, and Ursinus, inclined toward the Arians,[46] both helplessly pleading their cause before the Emperor. Concerned above all for law and order, Valentinian exiled both from Rome, but Ursinus having proved himself untrustworthy, Damasus gained the Emperor's precarious support.[47] The party of Ursinus remained

---

[39] Duchesne 1910 II [4] 259–60.
[40] Caspar 1930 I 174 & 188.
[41] Duchesne 1910 II [4] 281.
[42] Ibid. 299.
[43] Batiffol 1924 [2] 34.
[44] Caspar 1930 I 192; & cf. ibid.

[45] Ibid. 199.
[46] Ambrose *Letter* # 11 § 3; & cf. Batiffol 1924 [2] 24. Haller 1934 I 76, says that Ambrose's characterization was biased and groundless.
[47] Duchesne 1910 II [4] 455 ff.

active, however, and in 371 even managed to have Damasus haled before a civil court on a charge of murder, of which, mercifully, he was acquitted.[48]

It was during this time so mortifying to friends of the papacy that certain theories were advanced by Latins which indicate a wide-spread readiness to recognize the Roman Emperor as the sovereign authority of the Church. The General Council had proved impracticable, even a single see like that of Rome seemed incapable of self-government. That any spiritual authority could be physically effective was in any case doubtful; if there were to be any unity at all it must come from the will of the Emperor, who was already posing as a being more than human. We therefore find Optatus, bishop of Mileve in Africa, writing in about 367 [49] that

the State is not within the Church, but the Church within the State, that is, within the Roman Empire.[50]

And he bases one of his arguments on the premise that

there is no one superior to the Emperor except God, who made the Emperor.[51]

Similarly it was in about 372 [52] that Ambrosiaster, speaking of David's deference to Saul, made the cryptic remark that

the king bears the image of God just as the bishop bears the image of Christ,[53]

adding, after using the word *vicar* to describe the relation of the incarnated Christ to God, that

the king is honoured on earth virtually as the vicar of God.[54]

These were not Asiatic but Latin priests who were talking. Observing that the Church must be governed and that the bishops, whether individually or collectively, seemed unequal to the task, it was not unnatural to turn for relief to the traditional head of the Roman's religion which was the State.[55]

[48] Caspar 1930 I 203–05.
[49] Batiffol 1924 2 36.
[50] *De Schismate Donatistarum* III ch. 3 (74 lines 3–5).
[51] Ibid. (75 lines 10–11).
[52] Batiffol 1924 2 35.
[53] *Quaestiones Veteris et Novi Testamenti* ch. 35.
[54] Ibid. ch. 91 § 8.

[55] The Roman of the fourth century never thought of a separation of Church and State as a possibility: Fustel de Coulanges 1891 II 61. Nor did he conceive of the Roman State as in any way less universal and eternal than the Roman Church: Jullian 1926 VIII 351–52.

B. Damasus and Ambrose, 373–397

Then, in 373, occurred the momentous circumstance of the death of the Arian bishop Auxentius and the miraculous election of Ambrose as his successor; [1] and in the very next year Valentinian died, leaving Gratian, now seventeen, as sole Emperor of the West. When elected, Ambrose was a Roman layman of thirty-four,[2] and Damasus, then sixty-eight [3] years old, was his bishop. How, on his election, could Ambrose not look to Damasus as his guide and master? Similarly when, in 375, Gratian succeeded to the Western Empire, the most inspiring of the Latin bishops was the thirty-six-year-old Ambrose. How should Gratian not look to Ambrose for guidance [4] as Ambrose looked to Damasus? Only four years earlier Damasus had been tried for murder before an imperial court and, although he was acquitted, the papal prestige had been left at a low ebb.[5] But after 373 Damasus had the support of Ambrose, and after 377 Ambrose had that of Gratian.[6]

Because a private institution which fails to govern itself is a nuisance and may prove a threat to law and order, the State hopes it may succeed. It had therefore been a routine law by which Constantine in 314 had authorized the clergy, in matters concerning faith and discipline, to judge each other.[7] It was the misfortune of the Church, however, that, having been until recently persecuted, she had had to remain decentralized, with each bishop virtually his own master. Canons 5 and 6 of Nicæa had sanctioned a certain degree of centralization within each province, with Rome, Alexandria, Antioch, and a few other sees enjoying an even more extended jurisdiction; but the inadequacy of even the enlarged unit of the province was indicated by the decrees of Sardica in 343 which authorized the bishop of Rome to review the provincial judgments and provide for a new trial at his discretion. This effort to give Rome final authority was far-sighted, but

---

1 See pp. 255–56.
2 Dudden 1935 2 & 68.
3 Caspar 1930 I 196.
4 Batiffol 1924 [2] 23. Gratian was also favourably predisposed to the aristocrats: Coster 1935 22–25.

5 Caspar 1930 I 205.
6 Dudden 1935 189.
7 Caspar 1930 I 116 & 207.

because far-sighted it was premature and therefore a failure; neither Church nor State seems to have paid any attention to it. Appeals continued to come to the Pope as often as his attitude was thought favourable, but since only one party appealed, and only when he chose to, the Pope's judgment was something of a farce.

In an effort to wash his hands of the quarrel between Damasus and Ursinus, the Emperor Valentinian I had re-enacted the law of Constantine requiring ecclesiastical courts alone to judge the clergy in matters of faith and discipline.[8] He might well have saved himself that trouble, because the clergy could not agree among themselves as to who could judge whom.[9] It was here that the momentous entente between Damasus, Ambrose, and Gratian stepped into action: Damasus called a Council of Rome in 378 and induced it to request Gratian to enact a law giving the bishop of Rome direct jurisdiction over all the Latin archbishops and the right to hear appeals from the judgments of Latin provincial courts.[10] Gratian, eagerly exhorted no doubt by Ambrose, complied, instructing the prefects of Italy and Gaul and the proconsuls of Africa and Spain to execute Rome's judgments.[11] Actually these papal judgments were wretchedly enforced,[12] but this was somewhat true of enforcement in general in this late fourth century. Far more important than the immediate power gained was the precedent it set. By the Church no such authority had been conferred; nevertheless Rome had formally declared her candidacy for Latin sovereignty and had further dared to enlist the support of the temporal State in her behalf. Rome was no longer satisfied to bask in the enjoyment of a vague primacy which was never defined; she now sought sovereignty, with the imperial authority standing guard to proclaim and defend it.

Evidently the majority of the Latin episcopate — certainly if we except the Africans — had now come to realize the dire need of further centralization and were not unready to sub-

[8] Ambrose *Letter* # 21 § 2.
[9] Haller 1934 I 85.
[10] Caspar 1930 I 210.
[11] Ibid. 213. Batiffol 1924 2 40 thinks that the Emperor meant to transfer to the Pope a power previously claimed as his own. But who,

then, could judge the Pope? Koeniger 1919 21 says that the Council of Rome of 378 admitted the Emperor's competence in this special case.
[12] Batiffol 1924 2 41 & 47–50; Seppelt 1931 I 122.

ordinate themselves if it could be shown that this was their
duty. But they could hardly believe it their duty to submit
to Roman overlordship merely because a Roman Council
wished this and had prevailed on a young Emperor to support
its wish with the temporal sword. If Rome wished to rule the
Latin Church she must find reasons more plausible than those
furnished by the events of 378.

It was in this same year that Gratian, having a premonition
of the imminent defeat at Adrianople, transferred eastern
Illyria to the control of the Eastern Emperor Valens;[13] and
it was shortly after this[14] that two Arian bishops of that region, being threatened with deposition, asked Gratian to
submit their cause to a General Council. What they wanted
was the support of the many Eastern bishops who were inclined to Arianism, and they could now plausibly argue, not
only that as Greeks they should have some Greeks among
their judges, but also that their sees were now politically
within Greek jurisdiction. But Ambrose, seeing the danger,[15]
was technically within his rights in persuading Gratian that
their sees, being in *Moesia Superior,* were still, ecclesiasti-
cally,[16] under Latin jurisdiction, and Gratian accordingly
summoned a Council at Aquileia which met in May 381. Of
the mere thirty-two bishops who attended — although all, including the Greeks, had been invited — a large majority
came from either the province of Milan or southeastern
Gaul.[17] The deposition of the two Moesian bishops thereby
became a foregone conclusion.[18] Had Pope Damasus no part
in the affair then? From a letter inspired, if not written,[19]
by one of the deposed bishops, Palladius, to Ambrose, we
learn, on the contrary, that Damasus wrote three letters[20]
to the Council, and that Ambrose read them in order to give
the key-note. It is clear that Ambrose was posing as the representative of Damasus; for Palladius complained that

the see of the most blessed Peter, with the acquiescence of your
friends and clients, arrogates to itself a prerogative.[21]

---

13 Caspar 1930 I 293.
14 Dudden 1935 199.
15 Caspar 1930 I 293.
16 Dudden 1935 200.
17 Hefele 1908 II 2 50. And two
from Africa: Batiffol 1924 2 25.

18 Caspar 1930 I 237.
19 Batiffol 1924 2 27. But Caspar
says the actual writer was a certain
Maximin: 1930 I 244.
20 Caspar 1930 I 237 n. 4.
21 Quoted in Batiffol 1924 2 28.

What was this prerogative? Palladius proceeds:

Why do not both he [Damasus] and you realize that the see of Peter is common to and shared by all the bishops, because the memorable and holy apostle, by divine dispensation, consecrated this same see not only to the bishop of the city of Rome but also to all others? [22]

In his letters to the Council Damasus had evidently claimed for the bishop of Rome the exclusive inheritance of the powers conferred by Christ on Peter in the famous passage in *Matthew* xvi 18–19:

Et ego dico tibi, quia tu es Petrus, et super hanc petram aedificabo ecclesiam meam, et portae inferi non praevalebunt adversus eam.

How could this text be interpreted as a transfer of the Church sovereignty to the bishop of Rome? How was it possible that any argument based on this text should satisfy Ambrose, the lordly bishop of Milan, and thirty-one other bishops? Everything depended on whether they could be convinced that Peter had been the first bishop of Rome, which was likely only if they believed that he had suffered martyrdom there. It happened, however, that these were both already generally accredited traditions; had they not been, Damasus would not have dared to adopt the line of argument that he did. But it was also accredited tradition that Peter transmitted his episcopal powers indiscriminately to all bishops, through successive consecrations. This is what was known as the apostolic succession. The bishop of Rome occupied a unique position of honour because of Peter, but the early Church had so emphasized equality and popular sovereignty that even this vague honour was often grudgingly acknowledged.[23] In testimony of the fundamental equality of the episcopate, Cyprian of Carthage was commonly quoted,[24] and it was to this tradition that Palladius referred.

The strategy of Damasus and Ambrose, however daring, proved successful for a simple and practical reason: the bishops assembled at Aquileia wanted to rid the West of every bishop who opposed the Nicene Creed. In order to do this

---

[22] Ibid.
[23] Cf. the medieval recognition of a king as first among the barons.

[24] Ibid. 26; Koch 1930 *passim*.

they must depose them, first by canon law, secondly by physical violence. It was here that the decree of Gratian of 378 played its part: unless the deposition decree were executed it would be futile, and the only way to get it executed was by obtaining that ratification from Rome which the civil authorities were bound by. Yet in order to get Rome's ratification the bishops had to acquiesce in the Petrine claim of Damasus. I do not say that the Latin bishops much resented this papal claim — many of them, Ambrose among them certainly, applauded its ingenuity. Quite apart from any decree of Gratian these Latin bishops must soon have had to acknowledge the leadership of Rome. The fact is, nevertheless, that through the alliance of Damasus, Ambrose, and Gratian, the Latin episcopate was already in 381 more than half committed to papal sovereignty.

In that very month of May 381 [25] when the bishops were assembling in Aquileia, a much larger Eastern [26] Council was assembling in Constantinople, ostensibly only in order to reaffirm the Creed of Nicæa,[27] but also, very evidently, for other reasons. Canon 1 reads:

The profession of faith of the 318 Fathers assembled at Nicæa in Bithynia is not to be abrogated but is rather to remain in full force.[28]

The canon following, however, declared that the East be divided into five patriarchates. Nicæa had already created two of these: Alexandria over all Egypt and Antioch over all the Orient. To these were now added patriarchates for the rest of the East, for Asia, Pontus, and Thrace.[29] The names of the ruling sees of these three territories were omitted, however, namely Ephesus, Cæsarea in Cappadocia, and Heraclea; and this was probably because Constantinople intended to supplant Heraclea but preferred not to do so openly.[30] Canon 3 following betrays the full intent:

The bishop of Constantinople shall have the primacy of honour after the bishop of Rome because that city is the new Rome.[31]

25 Hefele 1908 II ² 3.
26 Ibid. 4.
27 And especially to make more explicit the definition of the Holy Ghost: Hefele 1908 II ² 16.
28 Ibid. 20. Cf. Ambrose De Fide I Prologue § 5.
29 Hefele 1908 II ² 21–23.
30 Caspar 1930 I 294.
31 Hefele 1908 II ² 24.

Quite openly this canon declares that Constantinople shall outrank the other patriarchal capitals; cautiously it intimates that the ecclesiastical jurisdiction and authority must conform to the political. To be sure it admits Rome's superiority to the new Rome; nevertheless every Latin knew that Constantinople was now the real political capital. This capital was taking over all Thrace and was surely planning to add eastern Illyria. Not content with this she was claiming primacy over the whole East, a claim which, if successful, would upset that Eastern balance of power which the prestige of Alexandria and Antioch had so far preserved.[32] Once she had gained full control of the East all chance for Rome's claim to universal sovereignty must vanish.

This third canon of the Council of Constantinople was therefore a challenge, but it was a challenge in the form of a bribe: in return for Constantinople's admission of Rome's superiority Rome was being asked to abandon Alexandria and Antioch to their fate. But Damasus was not to be tempted: at a Council of Rome held in the following year 382,[33] at which both Ambrose and Jerome were present, it was decreed that

surely all Catholics must be aware that the holy Roman Church is not superior because of any decrees of Councils but rather because she has received the primacy by the angelic voice of our Lord and Saviour, where he said to the blessed apostle Peter: *Thou art Peter and on this rock I will build my Church.*[34]

And this decree goes on to say that the second see is Alexandria because it was consecrated by Peter's disciple Mark, and the third see Antioch because Peter lived there before proceeding to Rome.

The authenticity of this decree has been doubted by some modern scholars,[35] although the majority have believed it to

[32] Rome's eastern might be compared with England's continental policy.

[33] Hefele 1908 II² 57–59; Caspar 1930 I 246–47.

[34] Since the text of the decree as it has come down to us through incorporation in the *Decretum* of Gelasius has been casually edited and interpolated, I have preferred to quote the text as it appeared in the Preface to

the Nicene Council, which is in Dobschütz 1912 88–89, since this version is thought by many to date back almost to 419: see Chapman 1928 20 n. 2; and cf. Caspar 1930 I 598 lines 27–30. The Gelasian text is given in Dobschütz 1912 7.

[35] Dobschütz 1912 vi, 251–60, etc.; whose elaborate arguments have convinced Morin 1913 340, & Batiffol 1924² 146–50.

be genuine.[36]   Our extant texts have certainly been corrupted and have even suffered from interpolations; [37] nevertheless the oldest manuscripts attribute it to Damasus,[38] and certainly it is just the kind of answer — indirect and polite, but quite firm — which the situation called for.   Constantinople wished Damasus to confirm this canon 3; he must either comply or give his reasons.   We know that he did not comply, and it is surely in this decree that he was giving his reasons. It was of course not the bishop of Constantinople whom Damasus feared; it was the Emperor.   In the year 382 theocracy still loomed as a serious possibility — that is an additional reason why Ambrose was so ready to play into the hands of Damasus, at both Aquileia in 381 and Rome in 382.   The issue was narrowing down to the rival candidacies of Greek Emperor and Roman bishop for Church leadership, and all those who did not want the Emperor were obliged, however reluctantly, to stand by Damasus.   The favour of Gratian, the Western Emperor, offered a happy occasion for a defiance of the East, but it offered no permanent solution.   It happened, indeed, that Gratian was assassinated the very next year.

Why was Damasus at such pains to declare that Rome was ' not superior because of any decrees of Councils '?   Because the Council of Constantinople claimed to be a General Council whose decrees bound the whole Church, Latin as well as Greek.   And if, as such a Council, it could set Alexandria and Antioch down, why could it not set Rome down too?   The belief was then prevalent that Rome derived her unique authority from canon 6 of Nicæa as well as from the glory of her first bishop Peter.   Damasus wished to disabuse people of this.   Her authority, he says, derives wholly from Peter and therefore from Christ, and Nicæa simply made a passing acknowledgment of this fact.[39]   Since Nicæa did not in any

---

[36] Maassen 1870 239 & 463; Hefele 1908 II² 55 n. 2; Dufourcq *L'Av.* 1910 IV⁵ 114 n. 2; Turner 1913 (according to Chapman 1928 20 n. 2); Chapman 1913 187-207 & 315-33; Caspar 1930 I 247-50 & 598-99.
I might add that, if it is a later fabrication, it must have been done after 485 as papal fabrications are otherwise unknown before that date: see p. 629. And it is not likely that

so good a fabrication could have been made over one hundred years after 382.

[37] See Dobschütz 1912 *passim;* Chapman 1913 *passim;* & Caspar 1930 I 598 bottom — 599.

[38] Chapman 1913 188.

[39] As we shall later see, reliance on Nicæa by Popes Zosimus, Celestine and Leo was actually on a canon of Sardica: see pp. 575 n. 24, 582

sense create, but merely acknowledged, Rome's unique authority, it was clear that no subsequent General Council could do more. It was a bold and a useful argument, because it declared that the right to interpret a biblical passage lay, not with any General Council, but with Rome.

On the death of Damasus in 384 Siricius became Pope. In his very first letter he says, speaking in the first person plural,

We bear the burdens of all those who are overloaded, or rather the blessed Peter bears them, in us who are the heirs of his rule, and whom in all matters, as we firmly believe, he protects and watches over.[40]

This was his inheritance from Damasus. Now that sovereignty had been claimed over both East and West and had been acknowledged in the West, the task devolving on Siricius was to play the role of a sovereign. To this end Siricius adopted a new style of letter-writing. Hitherto the Popes had written chiefly in answer to letters to them, and the tone had been modest, furnishing opinions and recommendations as these were asked for; but Siricius wrote letters which imitated the tone of the imperial rescripts, sending them out unasked and embodying commands.[41] Although they might technically be addressed to a single bishop, copies must have been systematically distributed wholesale — at least we must hope so, for Siricius, in one of these letters, declared that no bishop could plead ignorance of either the Conciliar canons or the papal decrees.[42]

When in 356 the Emperor Constantius set up the Arian Auxentius as bishop of Milan, he transferred to that see the patriarchal rights over northern Italy which then belonged to Rome.[43] But the exceptional power which Ambrose wielded was not because of this; rather it grew out of the fortuitous coincidence that Milan was the residence of the Western Em-

---

n. 49, & 607 n. 95. And by Pope Leo was on the revised Roman version of canon # 6 of Nicæa in addition: see p. 629 n. 62. In 382 reliance on Nicæa would have been folly.

[40] *Letter # 1 § 1.*

[41] Caspar 1930 I 262–64; Seppelt 1931 I 138–39; Haller 1934 I 92–93.

And this practice was repeated thereafter: by Innocent: Batiffol 1924[2] 163 & 237; by Boniface: ibid. 260; by Celestine: Caspar 1930 I 387.

[42] Caspar 1930 I 297.

[43] Duchesne 1911 III[4] 184–85; Batiffol 1924[2] 153–54; & cf. Jolowicz 1932 435.

perors and that Ambrose was more masterful than those Emperors.   Both Gratian and Theodosius became members of the Church of Milan during their official residences there,[44] and it became the duty of the bishop of Milan to see that they remained good Catholics and earned salvation.[45]   Moreover as good Catholic laymen they were bound to obey his instructions and the fact that they were also Emperors did not alter this elementary and undisputed principle.   That the bishop's instructions might be unreasonable or unwarranted was for the whole Church, not for the individual layman, to determine.   Somewhere, be it in Milan or elsewhere, the Emperor was an ordinary Catholic layman like any other Roman.   It was against this Achilles' heel of incipient theocracy that Ambrose launched his attack.   For how could any layman profess to pass judgment in spiritual matters, and was not the Emperor, as temporal chief, the incarnation of the layman? [46] In the face of so simple a fact the absurdity of such arguments as those of Optatus and Ambrosiaster became apparent: not God only, but also His bishop, was superior to the Emperor, and, if the king was vicar of God under the Old Law, the bishop is vicar of Christ under the New.   In order to prove that he could act as well as argue, Ambrose on one occasion actually imposed a public penance on the Emperor Theodosius; and Theodosius deemed it prudent to acquiesce.[47]

From this premise of the bishop's authority over every Catholic layman of his diocese the argument of Ambrose moved irresistibly forward: this imperial but untrained and undisciplined layman, since he was bound to obey his bishop, must all the more obey the whole Church.   Therefore he could enact no laws which conflicted with canon law — or, if he did, such laws were of no effect.   Ambrose admitted two jurisdictions: no more than the State could interfere in Church matters could the Church interfere in State matters. But the Church, and only the Church, had the right to decide whether a matter concerned Church or State.

One or two cases suggest where he thought the line should be drawn: he admitted the State's authority over land owned

---

44 That is, they communicated there: see Dudden 1935 386–90.
45 Cf. Batiffol 1924 2 62 & 69.
46 Ibid. 61–64 & 69.

47 Duchesne 1910 II 4 556; Dudden 1935 381–92, & cf. on Eugenius, 425.

by the Church, but made an exception of buildings used for ecclesiastical purposes; [48] he also protested vigorously when it was suggested that the pagan Altar of Victory in Rome be raised again.[49] His guiding principle is revealed in a letter to Theodosius, where he says reproachfully:

But, O Emperor, it is concern for order that determines thee. Yet which is the more inclusive, the appearance of order or the cause of religion? Surely repression ought to yield to piety.[50]

In this appeal is the key to the Christian revolution: expediency must give way to principle — for God has willed it so.[51] Moreover this was the Christian teaching as specifically applied to politics, and the Church — exponent and champion of that teaching — existed in order to impose it. The world was to be subjected to a new law, that of justice. Man was tired of rule by expediency; the time had now come for rule by conscience. Man no doubt had, for a long time, been a political animal; but he was now a Christian soul, and he insisted on conducting his politics accordingly.

The victory under Constantine had been won by Christianity; the victory under Ambrose was the first won by the Church. It was not a complete victory; for the East, lacking an Ambrose, soon became a virtual theocracy.[52] But for the West these years 375 to 395 mark the decisive struggle for control over a new force which all knew was destined to rule the future. It was clear too that this force, precisely because it would prove irresistible, must create its own centre, as a nationalistic force produces a dictator, or an astronomical force a sun. For a force, in preparing for action, tends to concentrate, as a beast will crouch or a snake coil. It is thanks to Ambrose that this centripetal force, which until 375 was gravitating towards the Emperor as its centre, was diverted to seek its centre within the Church.

Where within the Church that centre should be lodged was of less concern to Ambrose. This would be something for his successors to determine. To him the Nicene or orthodox party was a band of brothers fighting in a common cause.

[48] Batiffol 1924 2 64; Carlyle 1927 I 2 183–84.

[49] *Relatio Symmachi* & *Letter* # 18 (*P.L.* 16 966–82).

[50] *Letter* # 40 § 11.   And cf. ibid. # 10 § 12.

[51] Cf. Ambrose *De Officiis* III § 37.

[52] Cf. Batiffol 1924 2 287–88.

If for the time being Rome seemed the most effective leader, then let her lead. No more than a soldier worries about the next battle did Ambrose consider whether Rome's present leadership of the West set a dangerous precedent. A leader was now vital; so long as one did lead, and well, let him give the orders and let the rest obey. Whether he should on that account be for ever after obeyed did not yet need to be decided. Therefore Ambrose invariably worked in the closest harmony with Popes Damasus and Siricius; [53] just as he capitalized his own prestige as bishop of the Latin political capital, so he capitalized their prestige as the successors of Peter — in each case in order to promote Catholic unity according to the Nicene Creed. The letter that he addressed to the Emperor in 381 on behalf of the Council of Aquileia says:

> Your clemency ought to have been beseeched not to allow both the Roman Church, head of the Roman world, and that most holy faith of the apostles, to be disturbed; for from these the laws of holy communion flow forth into all.[54]

This 'most holy faith of the apostles' can hardly refer to anything else than the Nicene Creed.[55] Since the Roman Church is in accord with it, he argues that both authorities must be respected. He gives no hint of which, in case the two were not in accord, was to be followed. From another letter, however, written by Ambrose to the Emperor a year later, we perceive that his conception of Rome's authority is distinctly one of leadership among equals. The gist of his argument is that when any bishop is deposed and appeals against that deposition to a Western Council, no one should be consecrated in his place until and unless such Council has rejected the appeal:

> It is both law and tradition that they should take care — as did both Athanasius of holy memory and more lately Peter, bishop of the Church of Alexandria, and many other Eastern bishops — to conform to the judgment of the Church of Rome, of Italy and of

[53] Batiffol 1924 [2] 171-72.
[54] *Letter* # 11 § 4.
[55] Batiffol 1924 [2] 25 & 31 argues that this passage refers to Romans i 8: 'First I thank my God through Jesus Christ for you all, that your faith is spoken of throughout the whole world.' Jerome *Letter* # 15 § 1 probably does refer to this text, but Jerome says 'fidem apostolico ore laudatam', whereas Ambrose speaks in the plural: of the 'sacrosanctam apostolorum fidem'.

the whole West. . . . We do not claim the prerogative of making the examination; nevertheless there ought to be the fellowship of a common will.[56]

It might be argued that Ambrose actually believed in the divine sovereignty of the Church of Rome, yet in his letters to the Emperor did not think it diplomatic to insist on this. But surely he was not the person to waive a principle for the sake of expediency. And unless we are willing to brand him as something of a hypocrite we must suppose that he still clung to the belief in the sovereignty of a General Council which, precisely because it truly represented the 'common will', could claim 'the prerogative of making the examination.' In a letter of this same period he recommended that the Emperor summon a General Council at Alexandria in order to determine who was the rightful bishop of Antioch.[57] Did he believe, and yet omit to add, that its decision was nevertheless valid only if and when the Pope should ratify it? There is only one intelligible conclusion: Ambrose utilized the papal prestige and claims merely as a means of strengthening the cause of the Nicene Creed; had the Arian Ursinus obtained control of the Church of Rome,[58] ousting Damasus, Ambrose's professed loyalty to Rome would have melted overnight. We can too easily forget that in men like Ambrose the faith was the only burning reality, so that even the General Council was merely a means of securing it.[59] Short of the doctrine of infallibility — whether of papacy or General Council — there was really no alternative position.

Ambrose, moreover, was a bishop and a native of the city of Rome.[60] If he were willing to go only so far and no farther, it was natural that many others would not go even so far as he. Jerome, for instance, was neither a bishop nor a native of Rome, but an Illyrian monk. Nevertheless, when Jerome was a young monk living in Rome Pope Damasus had befriended him. A letter written by him to Damasus from the

---

[56] *Letter* # 13 § 4.
[57] *Letter* # 12 § 5.
[58] Cf. Batiffol 1924 [2] 24.
[59] Cf. Zeiller 1933 844, citing Ambrose's *Explanatio Psalmorum XII* # 38 § 37. Compare also Carlyle 1927 I [2] 162 on Ambrose's doctrine that a temporal ruler's authority depends on the justice of his rule. The analogy between the temporal and ecclesiastical basis of authority may have an affinity to the analogy between civil divorce and Catholic annulment.

[60] Dudden 1935 2 n. 3.

East in 377 reveals not only his admiration for Damasus but also the fact that the Petrine claim had been aired by Damasus in Rome several years before the Council of Aquileia. Jerome says, for instance:

I thought that the see of Peter ought to be respected, and the faith that was praised by the apostolic word.[61]

I address myself to the successor of the fisherman . . . I join the communion of thy beatitude, that is, of the see of Peter. I know that the Church has been erected on that rock. He who shall have eaten the lamb outside this house is impious.[62]

Of one in Jerome's position — an obscure monk only thirty years old — common politeness to the august Damasus required some measure of flattery, and in 377 this flattery could evidently take no more appropriate form than a reference to the Petrine claim. But this does not mean that in saying this Jerome was insincere.

It happened, however, that the new Pope in 384 was Siricius, who was hostile to the monks.[63] Would Jerome be so eager now to conform himself to the will of the see of Peter? Apparently not. For in about the year 390 he wrote to an antagonist:

You allege that the Church is founded upon Peter. The truth is that all the apostles received the same powers.[64]

And in a letter of uncertain date but probably before 402 [65] he says, referring to a discrepancy between Roman practice and that familiar elsewhere,

If the matter be considered from the point of view of authority, the world is larger than the City. And all the bishops, whether they are at Rome or at Eugubium, at Constantinople or at Rhegium, at Alexandria or at Tanis, have the same dignity, the same priesthood. Neither the power of riches nor the meekness of poverty makes any bishop superior or inferior. After all, they are all of them successors of the Apostles.[66]

When in 397 Jerome joined in the struggle to get a condemnation of the doctrine of Origen, he wrote to congratulate

---

[61] *Letter #* 15 § 1.
[62] Ibid. § 2.
[63] See pp. 460-61.

[64] *Contra Jovinianum* I § 26.
[65] See Migne *P.L.* 22 1192 n. (h).
[66] *Letter #* 146 § 1.

bishop Theophilus of Alexandria that he had supported the faith of Rome; [67] but when in 404 Theophilus brought about the deposition of John Chrysostom as bishop of Constantinople and Pope Innocent protested, Jerome stood by Theophilus.[68]

He who alternately flatters and flouts an authority — at his own theological convenience — cannot be said to hold that authority in very deep respect. To the Roman papacy Jerome — unlike Ambrose — proved a false friend.

Jerome, to be sure, although familiar with Rome, was an Illyrian monk who spent most of his life in the East. This may help to explain why his ardour for the cause of Roman sovereignty waxed and waned according to circumstances. We might suppose, however, that most of the Latin bishops, following the example of Ambrose, would do what they conscientiously could to back the papal claims which had been presented and accepted at Aquileia. Such was the case so long as Damasus lived: there are several cases of appeals to his judgment shortly before 384.[69] But with the advent of Siricius this practice became much less frequent. Already at the time of the Priscillianist affair of 385 Severus speaks of Ambrose as one of

the two bishops whose authority was at that time the highest.[70]

And, especially from 390 on, appeals, coming from East as well as West, were more often addressed to Milan than to Rome. Such, for instance, was the appeal in 390 of the monk Jovinian,[71] advocate of free love and denier of Mary's permanent virginity. Such too was the appeal of a certain bishop Bonosus a year later.[72] In 390 also a group of Gallic bishops appealed to Ambrose,[73] in 395 a group of Spanish bishops did likewise,[74] and in 397 the African bishops appealed to Rome and Milan jointly.[75]

In 397 Ambrose died, but so great a prestige had he gained for the see of Milan that appeals to it continued for several

[67] Ibid. # 63 § 2.
[68] Duchesne 1911 III 4 105–06, & cf. 222.
[69] Batiffol 1924 2 181–83.
[70] Chronica II § 48.

[71] Caspar 1930 I 284.
[72] Ibid. 283.
[73] Ibid. 280.
[74] Ibid. 280–81.
[75] Duchesne 1911 III 4 125.

more years.   In 400 the Spaniards asked for a joint ratification from Rome and Milan; [76] in 401 the Africans appealed
in like manner; [77] in 401 the Gallicans appealed to the Council of the Milanese province held at Turin; [78] in 404 John
Chrysostom asked the bishops of Rome, Milan, and Aquileia
to protest against his deposition and to request that he be
tried within his own patriarchate as the Council of Constantinople had prescribed.[79]   It was at about this time that
the pendulum swung back towards Rome.   In 402 the energetic Pope Innocent succeeded the feeble Anastasius, and
very soon after this the Western capital was withdrawn — before the Visigothic advance — from Milan to Ravenna.[80]
Already in 404 we find the Gallicans appealing to Innocent
alone.[81]

Actually these were not appeals in the legal sense; [82] for,
if the State recognized such a right by its decree of 378, the
Church did not.   At Sardica in 343 the Western bishops had
authorized the Pope to review episcopal judgments and, at
his discretion, to order a new trial, but this practice was never
— or rarely — adopted.   The real inducement was the wide
reputation won by Ambrose as an arbitrator, and in civil as
well as in ecclesiastical disputes.   Popular local pressure was
doubtless brought to bear on both disputants to let Ambrose
arbitrate their case.   So unimpeachable was his reputation for
wisdom and impartiality that a disputant who refused virtually impugned the justice of his cause.

Ambrose therefore did much to set the precedent for such
a recourse to a central authority.   But the Emperors must have
aided and abetted.   At this moment it was not a strongly centralized Church that they feared: rather it was a decentralized
Church, with its attendant quarrels and disorders.   The Emperors were the last persons in the world to have any love for
popular sovereignty,[83] and the primitive Church theory of a
popular election of bishops governing through General Coun-

---

[76] Batiffol 1924 [2] 193; Caspar 1930
I 280–81.

[77] Duchesne 1911 III [4] 126; Caspar 1930 I 291–92.

[78] Batiffol 1924 [2] 211; Caspar 1930
I 308.

[79] Duchesne 1911 III [4] 101; Caspar
1930 I 316.

[80] In about 404: Duchesne 1911
III [4] 184.

[81] Innocent *Letter* # 2 §5.

[82] Cf. Batiffol 1924 [2] 47–50; Caspar 1930 I 306–07.

[83] Cf. Carlyle 1927 I [2] 63–69 & 159.

cils was by now as alien to the tastes of the people as it was to that of their responsible leaders. The Emperors did not really covet theological leadership; they had no fond dreams of imposing a theocracy. But they did long for law and order within the Church as well as without it, and were prepared, in case the Church could not govern herself, to govern for her. Gratian and Theodosius withdrew when they saw Ambrose step up; and their successors held back because they saw Innocent [84] continuing where Ambrose had left off.

C. AUGUSTINE AND THE PAPACY

Judging by his age Augustine belongs to the years before the invasions, as he was already fifty-two when the barbarians first swept over Gaul, Spain, and Italy. And he was seventy-five when the Vandals first invaded his own Africa. On the other hand his development, hampered as it was by the enticements of Manichee and Neoplatonist, came late: first a Christian at thirty-three, he did not evolve his mature doctrine until he was forty-five, and this in its turn grew without interruption till the closing years of his life when he wrote his final conclusions on grace and free will. Naturally enough, his influence throughout Christendom proceeded at the same deliberate pace. He became the acknowledged embodiment of Catholic wisdom only in the years following the outbreak of the Pelagian heresy in 411. Most of his other more important works, too, were written only after the first invasions. He was therefore something of a Janus, looking both ways at once, the presiding genius over past, present, and future. He was apparently destined, chronologically as in almost every other way, to be in a class by himself.

Since politics has for a long time now been the spoilt child of historians, every phrase, every suggestion of Augustine's on that subject has been minutely investigated.[1] Nor has so much labour been in vain. For what Augustine has to say about politics — as we find it, scattered here and there hap-

---

[84] Cf. Seppelt 1931 I 147.   [1] Cf. Troeltsch 1915 *passim*.

hazardly — cuts deep into the anatomy of human society.
And as we shall see, somewhat to our surprise, he was, in our
modern terminology, both a democrat and a progressive.

What was Augustine's theory of Church sovereignty? In
a letter of 408 he recalls Christ's prophecy that his doctrine
would be preached to all nations.[2] Now such a prophecy
must have come true; therefore the doctrine that in fact had
been and was still being generally preached must be Christ's
doctrine, and that is also why the Catholic or universal doctrine must, by the mere fact of its universality, be the true
doctrine. This argument, however, although irrefutable as
far as it went, left quite unsettled the question of whether past
universality bound present universality, the question of what,
precisely, these past and present universal doctrines were,
and the further question of whether the destiny of future universal doctrine was to be concentrated in the hands of leaders
or be left at the mercy of undirected public opinion. Evidently there must also be a Catholic doctrine in regard to
where the power to decide these questions was lodged.

On one point — the very one that most concerned the Roman papacy — Augustine was categorical enough: no opinion
of an individual had the slightest binding authority, nor
even the opinion of any one Church. For the judgment of
individuals is fallible, as the career of Peter, prince of the
apostles, clearly teaches. Writing in the year 400 to a Donatist heretic who cited the authority of Cyprian, bishop of
Carthage in the year 250, Augustine answered:

If, contrary to the rule of truth to which the whole Church later
adhered, Peter compelled the gentiles to be circumcised, why,
contrary to the rule of truth to which the whole Church later adhered, was it not possible for Cyprian [mistakenly] to compel the
heretics and schismatics to be baptized anew?[3]

It was Peter's destiny — for didactic reasons no doubt — to
live to see his error and to acknowledge it. Why assume, then,
that Cyprian was infallible simply because, unlike Peter, he
died before recognizing his error?

Peter's alternating phases of faith and doubt, of understanding and misunderstanding, teach us the infirmity of all

---

2 *Letter* # 93 § 23.   3 *De Baptismo* II § 2.

human judgments and the need for humility in order that
we may recognize our own infirmities and fight them. But
they also teach us, symbolically, the infirmity of collective
human judgments:

In that single apostle Peter, in rank the first and chief of the apostles, in whom the Church was prefigured, both aspects are intended
to be emphasized, that is, both the firm and the infirm: because
without both of these there is no Church.[4]

This passage is not aimed specifically at Rome; but a passage
of 415 rather appears to be. He there goes far afield for his
text — to *Deuteronomy* xxv 5:

If brethren dwell together and one of them die having no child,
the wife shall not marry without unto a stranger: her husband's
brother shall go in unto her and take her to him to wife, and perform the duty of an husband's brother unto her. And it shall be
that the first born which she beareth shall succeed in the name of
his brother who is dead, that his name be not put out of Israel.

Augustine's commentary follows:

Christ died, arose, ascended, divested Himself of His body: His
brothers have taken His wife [the Church] in order to generate
sons by preaching the Gospel . . . for the sake of their brother's
name. *For in Jesus Christ,* says Paul, *I begat you through the
Gospel* (1 *Cor.* iv 15). And thus stirring up seed for their
brother, those whom they have begotten they have not called
Paulians or Petrians, but Christians. . . .
Who is honoured in Peter unless it be He who died for us? For
we are Christians, not Petrians. Although we were born of the
brother of the deceased, nevertheless we were given the name of
the deceased.[5]

Is this not a clear warning to Rome that Peter, on whose authority she relies, is, like any of the other disciples of Christ,
to serve the Church in all humility for Christ's sake and not
for his own? Peter's authority is as nothing compared to that
of Christ, and the heirs of his authority, though they be the
Romans, are as fallible as he or any other.
Augustine concluded that consensus of Christian opinion
was the least fallible criterion of truth and orthodoxy, and
that there was no better machinery for determining this con-

---

[4] *Sermon # 76 § 4.*
[5] *Enarrationes in Psalmos # 44*   § 23. Cf. *Retractationum* I 20 § 2;
   & Haller 1934 I 102.

sensus than the General Council, in which the majority judgment, being the most universal, should bind all. Counting noses, even though they be episcopal noses, may not seem to us a reliable way of arriving at the truth. Augustine did not think it wholly reliable either, but he was more sanguine than we might have been because he believed that God arranged matters in such a way that His prophecy must come true. Furthermore, because it was the least defective method, he had every reason to suppose that God would wisely choose to avail Himself of it.

Speaking of the ancient controversy [6] in 250 between Cyprian of Carthage and Stephen, bishop of Rome, he says:

Nor should we ourselves have dared to assert anything of the sort had it not been confirmed by the unanimous authority of the universal Church; to which he [Cyprian] himself would certainly have bowed if already at that time the truth of this question, clarified and declared by a plenary Council, had been confirmed. For if Peter praises and preaches that he was patiently and sympathetically corrected by a later colleague [Paul], how much the more quickly would he [Cyprian] himself, together with the Council of his province, have yielded — the truth having become clear — to the authority of the whole world? [7]

Granted that the General Council was supreme, was it also sovereign? Clearly in the ordinary sense of that word it was not because it could not, even by a unanimous vote, declare, as did the Manichees, that the Old Testament was a work of the devil. Could it claim, however, that the Gnostics taught the true doctrine? There was a time, just before Irenæus, when theirs was perhaps the prevailing Christian doctrine. Although it had been discarded in the interim, ought it not now to be restored? Did even the bishops of Nicæa have the power to give doctrine a new direction? If they did, then the bishops at subsequent General Councils must also have this power, and, if they did not, the true doctrine was not necessarily what Nicæa had declared it but rather what Nicæa should have declared it. In either case the Nicene decree was presumptive, but in neither case was it conclusive evidence of the true doctrine. Therefore in either case any sub-

---

[6] Cyprian had denied the efficacy of baptism by an heretical priest; Duchesne 1911 I [6] 422.

[7] *De Baptismo* II § 5.

sequent General Council had the power to amend or reverse Nicæa if it chose.

This logic had been employed by the anti-Nicene parties of the middle fourth century. They were not specific about which alternative they adopted because in either case they could, by controlling the decisions of a later General Council, amend the Nicene Creed — to conform either with alleged tradition or with a more correct understanding, And to this logic Augustine also clung. Being a believer in the correctness of the Nicene Creed, he never advocated its revision as a matter of policy; on the other hand he never alleged that merely because he or others thought it accorded with tradition it was forever binding. For in this sense Augustine was enough of a biologist — being a scientist in psychology — to recognize that God's revelation had been gradual, that it came through a teaching which had been accumulating for many centuries, and that through grace, which included a wider human experience, future generations were likely to become susceptible to teaching more advanced than any that had been vouchsafed to him or to any other man of his generation. Therefore the Church must be left free, as Peter had been, to grow in wisdom and understanding. Recall the passage where he says:

If it is considered unseemly to emend anything that Plato has touched, why did Porphyry himself make emendations, and these not a few? [8]

This faith in the progress of the human intellect he applies to his conception of the Church:

Who does not know [a] that the holy canonical Scripture, including the Old Testament as well as the New, is restricted within its own definite boundaries, and that it has such priority over all later texts of bishops that, in regard to the accepted texts, dispute or doubt is not possible — whether anything that has been written in it is true or right; [b] that if, after a canon has been enacted, there be anything in the pastoral letters written or being written by bishops which deviates from the truth, it may be brought into question by the wiser opinion of anyone having more experience in that matter, or by the weightier authority and more learned discretion of other bishops, or by a Council; [c] that . . . regional

[8] *D.C.D.* X 30, quoted p. 125.

or provincial Councils yield without any evasions to the authority of plenary Councils which are formed by delegates from all over the Christian world, and that often the earlier plenary Councils are corrected by later ones — whenever, through some experience of things, that which was obscure is made clear and that which was hidden is revealed; and [d] that [all this has occurred] without any show of unholy pride, without swollen arrogance, without jealous bickering, but rather with holy humility, with Catholic peace, with Christian charity? [9]

That by plenary Councils Augustine means all Councils — General as well as patriarchal — which are more universal than provincial Councils, is clear from this later passage:

For in the eyes of posterity later Councils are given precedence over earlier ones, and it is sound principle that the whole be always preferred to its parts. [10]

The academic but none the less inescapable question now arises of what Augustine would have done had a General Council taken a course of which he, in his conscience, disapproved. Would he, as some Protestants allege, have remained a free lance? No answer can be more than a guess. Augustine believed that his task — as a leading Catholic thinker rather than as bishop of Hippo — was to try to persuade all bishops and laity, [11] all Emperors and even all pagans, of the truth as he saw it. Should it ever come to pass that, in spite of his efforts, a General Council should differ with him, then, and only then, need he decide — according to all the circumstances — whether to submit, or hold out and suffer the consequences. He longed for Catholic unity because he knew that this meant temporal strength as well as the fulfilment of God's will; but he did not on that account forget the example of the martyrs, dying for a lonely truth. Here again, as elsewhere, Augustine was an empiricist. Like the wise judge, he will decide nothing until the actual case with all its own peculiar ramifications — its implications and consequences, its aggravations and extenuations — is presented before his eyes. Only through the concrete case does the abstract principle reveal itself. [12]

---

[9] De Baptismo II § 4.
[10] Ibid. § 14.
[11] For his wide conception of the Church, see Enchiridion 56 & 118.

[12] For the same reason modern courts of law dislike giving a preliminary opinion on the constitutionality of a proposed law.

Augustine was no egoist, no dog-in-the-manger: he was grateful to God for the advance in wisdom that had been vouchsafed him, and he did not begrudge that same engrossing experience to posterity. As he, in his humble way, had conferred some slight benefits on the Church, so might others. Here again is the modesty and determination of the empirical scientist. At every moment, if Augustine is followed to the end of the trail, he will be found about to crack the shell that was shielding him from modernity. His career is the microcosm of which the macrocosm is the intellectual history of Latin Christendom from the eleventh to the eighteenth century. If we may risk a Neoplatonic image, he is the One, out of whose abundance emanated the scholastic νοῦς, out of which in turn emanated the scientific Ψυχή. It is his thought, more than that of any other since the Apostles, which has fertilized Latin Europe and so each of us.

What then was left of the authority of the Roman papacy and the ambitious struggle of Damasus and Siricius to win recognition of its sovereignty? When Pelagius had been condemned by a plenary Council at Carthage and Innocent later confirmed this, Augustine employed the famous phrase *Causa finita est*.[13] But did this mean anything more than that, with Rome supporting Africa, the condemnation was now substantially universal? For remember that the controversy over Pelagius was confined to the West — the East saw nothing in his doctrine that was either heretical or important.[14] Consequently Italy and Africa together had the authority to dictate to the West, and, with the West in accord, it was safe to assume that the East would readily accede. It is very evident, on the other hand, that Augustine regarded the bishop of Rome as the presiding officer of the Church, regarded his opinion as of particular weight and virtually indispensable in order to arrive at that degree of universality which alone could bind.[15] With Rome on the side of the minority, as she was over the question of whether Saturday fasting should be required, Augustine seems to have thought the question still an open one, to be determined at some later time, perhaps, by a judicious compromise. Particularly did he think

[13] *Sermon* # 131 § 10.   [15] Batiffol 1920 192–209.
[14] Haller 1934 I 129.

the opinion of Rome of weight where this concerned the true meaning of a canon of some General Council — as an ad interim authority [16] — but he does not seem to have made the logical inference that Rome could also — pending a decision by a General Council — give the Bible text an authoritative interpretation. Instead he apparently thought that where no canon covered the point at issue, each province — certainly each patriarchate — could do as it pleased.[17]

Just as much has been written on Augustine's idea of Church sovereignty, so has much been written on his idea of the proper relation between Church and State. Here again, although his references to that relationship are rare and haphazard, his extraordinarily incisive empiricism is in evidence. He was certainly opposed to theocracy: his whole conception as expounded in the *City of God* presupposes a radical separation of the twin powers. The ruler may be, as Ambrosiaster termed him, the vicar of God, but only in the sense that the ruler is, like all other human beings, a blind instrument for the accomplishment of the divine purpose, and one of these purposes will be, at the appropriate moment, to chastise the delinquent and to punish the malicious. Thus in 404 Augustine says:

Because even the power of doing harm can come only from God it is therefore written with the tongue of wisdom: *through me kings rule and through me tyrants possess the earth.* And the Apostle also says *there is no power except from God.* Moreover it is written in the Book of Job that *He makes the hypocrites rule on account of the perversity of the people.* And God, speaking of the people of Israel, said *I gave them a king in my wrath.* For it is not unjust that improper persons should receive the power of doing harm, because in this way both the patience of the good is tried and the iniquity of the bad is punished.[18]

And, discussing the same matter many years later, he adds concrete instances:

He who gave power to Marius gave it also to Caius Cæsar: He who gave it to Augustus gave it also to Nero . . . and finally, to avoid the necessity of going over them all, He who gave it to the Christian Constantine gave it also to the apostate Julian.[19]

[16] See *Letter* # 36 § 21.
[17] Caspar 1930 I 332; & cf. 337.

[18] *De Natura Boni* § 32.
[19] *D.C.D.* V 21.

There is nothing original in this view: all Augustine says is
that a bad ruler is imposed on his subjects by God for their
sins.   They may resist him, but only as God wishes they
should resist, by amending their own sinful lives.   This will
either soften God's heart so that He deprives this ruler of his
power — as by death, deposition, or his own amendment —
or will so win public sympathy, as did the martyrs under Diocletian, that the ruler becomes discredited and finally disarmed.

The Church as such, then, is never to use force or violence.
The laity, however, may.   And here we begin to see what
effect persuasion of this laity can properly have.   The Church
may try to persuade a ruler to legislate in her favour and such
legislation will of course be enforced by physical violence.
An indication of how this can come about is the legislation
which Pope Damasus procured from the Emperor Gratian in
378, obliging bishops to abide by appeals to Rome.   If Rome
deposed them then the civil officers would remove them, if
necessary by force.   But it was not the Church that did this;
it was conceivable that the State should decide to persecute
heretics — in order to promote the public order — in spite of
the Church's disapproval.   This was virtually what happened
in the case of Priscillian in 385.   And in 395 a stringent law
against all pagan cults was enacted [20] — perhaps not in the
face of the Pope's disapproval, but certainly in spite of the
many who must still have held to the opinion of Hilary of
Poitiers who, in 360,[21] had pleaded only for fair play and no
favours.   As late as 397 this was still the opinion too of Augustine who, writing to a Manichee, said:

I can on no account rage against you; for I must bear with you as
formerly I had to bear with myself, and I must be patient towards
you as my associates were with me when I went madly and blindly
astray in your beliefs.[22]

Although already bishop in that year [23] it might be thought
that Augustine's reluctance was a personal one, as if he
thought himself still unworthy.   But a letter he wrote to a
Donatist in 408 explains the matter clearly:

---

[20] See p. 21 n. 125.   [23] By 396 at latest: Duchesne 1911
[21] See p. 17.   III [4] 122.
[22] *Contra Epistolam Manichæi* § 3.

Originally my opinion was that no one should be coerced into
unity with Christ, that we must act only by words, fight only by
arguments and prevail only by force of reason, lest we should have
those whom we knew as avowed heretics feigning themselves to be
Catholics. But this opinion of mine was overcome, not by the
words of those who controverted it, but by the conclusive instances
to which they could point. For, in the first place, there was set
over against my opinion my own town, which, although it was
once wholly on the side of Donatus, was brought over to the
Catholic unity by fear of the imperial edicts,[24] and which we now
see filled with such detestation of your ruinous perversity, that it
would scarcely be believed that it had ever been involved in your
error. There were so many others which were mentioned to me
by name that, from the facts themselves, I was made to own that to
this matter the word of Scripture might be understood as applying: *Give opportunity to a wise man and he will grow wiser.*[25]

Fear was an efficacious remedy in the case of the pagans too:

As to the pagans, they may indeed with greater reason reproach us
for the laws which the Christian emperors have enacted against
idolaters; and yet many of these have thereby been, and are now
daily, turned from idols to the living and true God.[26]

Wiser than he was in 408 Augustine never grew: in 418, when
he saw Pope Zosimus on the point of returning Pelagius to
grace, he used his influence at the imperial court in Ravenna
to get a civil law enacted confiscating the property of the
Pelagians and exiling their persons.[27]

   This problem was a most delicate one — and still is today.
Who is so wise as to know whether Hilary or Augustine was
right? Obligatory oaths of allegiance to a nation's laws are
the modern equivalent of religious persecution. Augustine's
answer is perhaps no worse than any other: if compulsion in
belief really does compel it is salutary, if it leads instead to
hypocrisy and treason it is reprehensible — for, in the long
run, only the truth can prevail. As evidence of Augustine's
versatility, he is here less the saint, the jurist, the psychologist, or scientist, than he is the statesman — whose instinct it
is to lead.

   [24] Of 404: Duchesne 1911 III⁴ 132.
Ibid. 130–31 says that Augustine
favoured toleration until shortly after
that year.
   [25] *Letter* # 93 § 17.

   [26] Ibid. § 26.
   [27] Turmel 1931 I 119–20. And in
427 (*Retractationum* II 31) he reiterated his opinion of 408.

D. Africa and Nestorius, 402–432

In 402, when Innocent I became bishop of Rome, the West was still politically intact and, if the Latins recognized Rome's primacy, they did not recognize her sovereignty. But when Innocent died in 417 Gaul, Spain, and Britain were feeling the barbarian yoke and Italy had been ravaged, Rome taken by assault. If the Church did not quickly organize, Roman Catholicism was in jeopardy. Milan's temporary ascendency had survived the death of Ambrose in 397, but did not survive the transfer, under pressure from Alaric, of the Western capital from Milan to Ravenna in 404. Thereafter only Arles, as the Gallic capital, might have resisted Rome's authority in Latin Europe, and only Carthage in Africa. The effort of these two sees to retain their independence failed, as was inevitable, in the years soon to follow. For each barbarian advance forced a corresponding retreat of the Latins towards Rome — a retreat of the beleaguered from the walls to the citadel.

The demand for solidarity which the invasions created served also to break the back of dying paganism. As Catholics in Gaul or Spain must look for guidance to the bishop of Rome,[1] so must the pagan look to the Church — and so to her ranking bishop. No other cohesive force remained. As late as 394 there had been a pagan revival in the city of Rome,[2] yet only sixteen years later, with Alaric at the gates, Pope Innocent deemed it expedient — because safe — to grant the request of pagans that they perform heathen sacrifices.[3] Already then, apparently, were the pagans more to be humoured than feared. And in 416, the year before Innocent died, an imperial decree declared pagans ineligible to hold civil office.[4] By 423 Theodosius II could declare that paganism was virtually extinct — that is, politically inconsequential.[5]

But if the events were playing into Innocent's hands, he did his best to take advantage of them. And this too was

[1] Cf. Batiffol 1924 [2] 196.
[2] Duchesne 1910 II [4] 637–40.
[3] Caspar 1930 I 300.
[4] Dill 1906 [2] 26.
[5] Ibid. 27.

indispensable because the Latins, in order to be reconciled to Rome's sovereignty, must be persuaded that she actually was sovereign. If they wished to be convinced of this, it was none the less Innocent's task to convince them.

At his accession in 402 the General Council was still recognized, even by the Latins, as the Church's sovereign authority — a recognition which was the more insistent because the Creed officially declared at Nicæa seemed to them the true and only Creed. A danger lurked here, however; for a subsequent General Council was presumably at liberty to amend that Creed and substitute another in its place. That any subsequent General Council not only did have, but ought to have, the power to amend the decisions of an earlier one, was the view of Augustine, and his view was certainly the more natural, both logically and pragmatically. Innocent, however, as champion of the claims of the Roman Church, could not safely recognize the sovereignty of the General Council. At the same time he could not deny the sovereignty of the General Council of Nicæa without leaving her Creed at the mercy of future contingencies. The Council of Constantinople of 381 had already declared the Nicene Creed unamendable;[6] Innocent now further declared this to be true of all the Nicene canons as well:

As to the observance of the canons, we say that only those are binding which were enacted at Nicæa, for these alone must the Catholic Church follow and recognize. If, however, other canons are produced by certain persons which deviate from those of Nicæa and are therefore concocted by heretics, they shall be rejected by the Catholic bishops.[7]

And in a later letter he tells us why this is:

This is surely true because, as guardians of the priestly office, you do not believe that the laws of the Fathers are to be trampled upon, and also because they decreed not human but divine ordinances.[8]

Nicæa was thus put in a niche alongside of the Bible.

This being so, and the bishops who had judged at Nicæa

---

[6] In canon # 1 (Hefele 1908 II 2 20), see p. 550 n. 28.

[7] *Letter* # 7 § 3.

[8] *Letter* # 29 § 1.

being all dead, there must be some body with authority to declare exactly what it was that they had declared. When in 404 John Chrysostom had been deposed as bishop of Constantinople, Innocent vainly [9] urged the Emperor to summon a General Council in order to decide whether this had not been done in violation of canon 5 of Nicæa; but from the above quotation he clearly thinks that anything less than a reinstatement of John Chrysostom would constitute a deviation from Nicæa.   Thus Innocent showed outward respect for the General Council while at the same time denying it the smallest sovereign powers.   For it was he himself who was charged with the duty of seeing that no General Council acted beyond its authority.   On what ground did Innocent claim this right?   Surely not in reliance on Nicæa, for canon 6, with the words ' ancient custom shall be preserved in Egypt . . . because there is a similar custom in the case of the city of Rome ', [10] did nothing to prove his case.   Many times Innocent reiterated [11] the Petrine claim as expounded by Damasus. It is evidently out of this, as the following quotations will show, that he was spinning his intricate web.

In the second year of his pontificate he had received a letter from bishop Victricius of the distant diocese of Rouen asking for enlightenment on certain matters of canon law. In his answer Innocent said:

Whenever suits or controversies shall have arisen among the clergy as well of inferior as of superior rank, the dispute shall be settled, as the Council of Nicæa has decreed, by the assembled bishops of that same province; nor is it permissible for anyone (without prejudice, however, to the Roman Church to which deference must be shown in all cases), ignoring the bishops who in that same province govern the Church of God by divine authority, to have recourse to other provinces.[12]

And in the paragraph following he explains the parenthesis:

Where controversies of major importance have become matters of general concern, they shall, after the episcopal judgment, be referred — as holy custom requires — to the apostolic see.[13]

---

[9] Duchesne 1911 III 4 100–03.
[10] See p. 538 n. 17.
[11] Caspar 1930 I 301–02, 322 & 337–38.

[12] *Letter* # 2 §5.
[13] Ibid. § 6.   Haller 1934 I 94 cites this passage as the earliest effort of the papacy to legislate. Cf. p. 537.

The decree of the Council of Nicæa which he refers to is clearly canon 5; yet this, as we know,[14] made no provision for appeals beyond each province. How, then, could Innocent say that controversies of major importance should be referred to the apostolic see? An appeal to Rome had been authorized by the Council of Sardica, and Innocent could properly regard this as binding on the Latin sees. But surely this was an amendment of canon 5 of Nicæa and was, therefore, according to Innocent's own allegation, quite invalid.

We may now see with what ingenuity the Petrine claim was being evolved: from Peter Rome had acquired the right to hear all appeals and to veto the decisions of all General Councils; Nicæa, therefore, could enact only such canons as did not conflict with these Roman rights, and canon 5 was valid only because it did not explicitly forbid appeals beyond the province. It is clear that implicitly it did forbid them — Innocent admitted as much by saying 'nor is it permissible for anyone . . . to have recourse to other provinces' — but he evidently believed that since Nicæa recognized the priority and independence of the Petrine authority her bishops must have meant to say 'to other provinces than Rome'. This was sophistry if you like, but it was perfectly sincere.

In 417 the new Pope was Zosimus. As his name indicates, he was a Greek and, as such, favorably disposed towards the Pelagians. Innocent had readily acceded to the request of the Africans that Rome follow their example and condemn this heresy; but Zosimus tried to reverse this condemnation and was only prevented from doing so by the imperial edict which made that condemnation a part of the civil law.[15] Because the Africans had thus outwitted him he harboured a grudge against them,[16] and it was probably for this reason that when, shortly after this, an African priest, Apiarius, was excommunicated by his bishop for misconduct and appealed to Rome for redress, Zosimus sent over his legate to champion the priest's cause.[17]

By what law did Zosimus claim the right thus to interfere? At the Council of Carthage of 419 his legate first cited a canon

[14] See p. 537 n. 16.   [17] Ibid. 243.
[15] See p. 412 n. 36.
[16] Duchesne 1911 III⁴ 243; & cf.
241.

' decreed in the Council of Nicæa ' which declared that an accused bishop might appeal to Rome.[18] Upon this Alypius, bishop of Tagaste and an old friend of Augustine's, said:

We promise to observe this which was decreed in the Nicene Council. Still, I am moved by the fact that when we examined the Greek copies of this Nicene Council these things, I know not why, were not to be found there.[19]

Another canon, also described as Nicene, was then cited which allowed priests who had been excommunicated by their bishops to appeal to the other bishops of the province.[20] Upon which Augustine said:

We promise to observe this also, while a more diligent investigation of the Nicene Council is being made.[21]

The first canon was not pertinent because Apiarius was not a bishop; [22] the second was pertinent because by African law a priest could not appeal to his provincial Council but only to six bishops of his province [23] who might well be picked by his bishop and therefore sure to uphold his excommunication. Zosimus was doubtless arguing that since the second canon cited was being violated by the Africans, he, as champion of the canons, had the duty to interfere. If the canons cited had been Nicene he would have had a very fair case.

The fact is, however, that these canons which Alypius could not find in the Greek copies of Nicæa have not been found there to this day — for they were nothing else than canons 3 and 14 of the Council of Sardica! [24] Technically, perhaps, the canons of Sardica, although forgotten in Africa,[25] bound the African Church — for it had been a Council of all the West [26] and at least one African bishop had been present.[27] This, however, was not the issue, for Zosimus was submitting them as canons of Nicæa, which were certainly binding, and

---

[18] Chapman 1928 192.
[19] Ibid. 192–93.
[20] Ibid. 193.
[21] Ibid. 194.
[22] Ibid. 199 & 207.
[23] Ibid. 186 n. 6 & 188.
[24] The texts of Sardica are in Hefele 1907 I 2 762–63 & 795–96; the texts cited by the legate in 419 are in Chapman 1928 192–93.

[25] Chapman 1928 208 n. 3 & 209. Although the only *positive* evidence of this is a very ambiguous passage in a letter of Augustine's: see Duchesne 1911 III 4 245 n. 2.
[26] It included a good many Eastern bishops, but only those favourable to Athanasius: Hefele 1907 I 2 749.
[27] Ibid.; & Duchesne 1911 III 4 245 n. 2.

until it should be clear to everyone that they were not Nicene, but Sardican, canons the question of whether the Sardican canons bound Africa was of no concern.[28]

How did Zosimus come to commit what Duchesne has so candidly yet discreetly described as ' a mistake that ought not to have been made '? [29] ' By an unfortunate accident of transcription ', as one scholar has alleged? [30] Since Innocent had properly cited a canon of Sardica as Sardican, the confusion of the two sets of canons cannot have occurred during his pontificate.[31] Zosimus, on the other hand, succeeded Innocent in March 417 and by May 418 [32] he was not only confusing them but was taking conspicuous advantage of this confusion. If the date may thus be fixed we can hazard a further presumption: inasmuch as the imperial edict against the Pelagians was made public in April 418,[33] — or very shortly before the papal legate set sail for Africa — it seems idle to maintain that the confusion occurred merely ' by an unfortunate accident '.

[28] As to whether the canon law of Africa recognized episcopal appeals to Rome, Duchesne 1911 III [4] 242 thinks it did not. Haller 1934 I 108 agrees, as does Seppelt 1931 I 161. But Chapman 1928 189 & 203-07 thinks it did. I do not see, however, how the passage of Alypius, just quoted, bears him out: for the implication is that Africa will recognize this right of appeal only if the canon (# 3 of Sardica) should turn out to be Nicene.

[29] Duchesne 1911 III [4] 244.

[30] Chapman 1928 208.

[31] Chapman 1928 20 n. 4 cites Jerome Letter # 69 § 5, written in 397, as evidence that the confusion had been made before then. Migne P.L. 22 658 (a) is less sure. Nicæa had declared that a bishop was not to be transferred from one see to another; Sardica repeated this and added that this was because avarice might induce a bishop to get transferred to a richer see (canon # 1: Hefele 1907 I [2] 761). But Jerome cites Nicæa to show the evil of a transfer from virginity to adultery, and he did not need the enlightenment offered to stupid or perverse people by Sardica in order to read the Nicene canon, as Sardica had, intelligently.

The confusion, moreover, could hardly have been made by Jerome in 397. It originated in Rome. Now Damasus had been thirty-eight years old when the Sardican Council met, and must, therefore, have remembered what it accomplished. And if he had confused the canons in bad faith he would not have said that the ' Roman Church is not superior because of any decrees of Councils.'

Had Siricius confused them Jerome would never have heard of it, for, disliking Siricius, he had left Rome almost at once, never to return. And Siricius died only in 398.

More than this there was no confusion in Innocent's mind because in Letter # 7 § 3 of 405 (P.L. 20 505A) he referred specifically to a canon of Sardica as such. In Letter # 2 § 5 quoted above p. 573 some MSS. have the words ' sicut synodus statuit ' just before ' as custom requires ', but Caspar 1930 I 603 lines 20-22 says that this is an interpolation suggested by the later confusion.

[32] Chapman 1928 188.

[33] Duchesne 1911 III [4] 238.

But if Zosimus cannot be acquitted, it may be said in extenuation that he was to some extent a victim of a vicious state of mind then prevalent. In the later Roman civil law equitable principles had been widely developed as a reaction against the strict legality of the earlier practice.[34] The strict law certainly has its defects; but a loose equity is not free from them, and one of its principles, that in the interpretation of a text the intent rather than the language governs, was a particularly dangerous one for a people who were not historically minded. Laws are enacted to hinder as well as to help judges, and equity is invented in order to free them from the more awkward of these hindrances. Yet where a judge is asked to look behind the language of an old law in order to unearth its real intent he is being asked to act less as a judge than as an historian.

Possibly it was this principle of Roman equity which led Innocent to his strange interpretation of the fifth canon of Nicæa and which enabled him to make this interpretation in good faith. However that may be, he certainly called attention to a temptation which the more impulsive and irritable Zosimus could not resist. Goaded by the African defiance of Rome, he resorted to a course of action which, as we shall see in a moment, appeared fraudulent even in the eyes of his African contemporaries. Thus, whereas Innocent enhanced the prestige of Rome, Zosimus impaired it.

But that Zosimus acted dishonourably according to the moral standards of his day does not prove that he acted against his conscience. It happens that he was hardly, if at all, younger than Augustine, who, although scrupulous in so many ways, had said that the truth of predestination — even of God's foreknowledge — should be preached only with the greatest circumspection,[35] and, as we know, it was another of his contemporaries, Cassian, who said that

Some have arrived by means of acts in themselves reprehensible at the height of righteousness.[36]

Evidently the notorious doctrine of the sixteenth century that the end justifies the means was not as original as some have

---

[34] See pp. 6 ff.   [36] Quoted p. 481 n. 74.
[35] See p. 401.

supposed. Therefore even though Zosimus meant to deceive the Africans he meant to do this for their own and the Church's ultimate good. He must have believed that because God wished the Church to capture mankind and wished Rome to govern the Church, it was the duty of the Pope to accelerate the fulfilment of His will. For the means to that end could hardly be less holy than the end itself. Surely there were many instances when God Himself, in His age-long struggle against man's rebellious will, had not scrupled to resort to artifices of otherwise doubtful propriety.[37] Poor Zosimus, the irritable Greek facing African complacency; may the lesson which he inadvertently teaches all of us prove his salvation!

In their efforts to bring papal sovereignty into being, both Innocent and Zosimus had adopted the policy of declaring the canons of Nicæa fundamental and then tampering with them. In tampering with the biblical texts to suit their fancy the Priscillianists had merely gone further.[38] Even in those days this was a dangerous game, and Boniface who, when already an old man,[39] succeeded Zosimus in 419, soon had occasion to see its danger. For soon after he was installed he received the reply of the bishops assembled at Carthage regarding the affair of Apiarius — with the signature of Augustine among the others — communicating their doubts about the authenticity of the alleged canons of Nicæa. They said they were writing to some of the Eastern bishops to learn whether their versions of the Nicene Council contained any such canon, and they added that, regardless of the origin of the text and of how it came to be incorporated into the Roman version,

we ought not to be obliged to tolerate such acts as we do not now wish to rehearse, nor ought we to be obliged to suffer such outrages. We trust, however, that, with the help of the mercy of our Lord God, so long as thy holiness [Boniface] presides over the Roman Church we shall not have to put up with such arrogance, and that, as regards us, those things will be heeded which ought — without our being obliged to protest — to be heeded with brotherly charity, and which — according to the wisdom and justice which the All-Highest has conferred on thee — thou too very well

[37] See pp. 84 & 88.   [39] Duchesne 1911 III⁴ 254.
[38] See pp. 341 n. 42, & 459 n. 39.

knowest ought to be heeded — unless the canons of Nicæa should
by chance hold otherwise.[40]

The intimation is plain: unless by some chance there be a
canon of Nicæa authorizing such interference, the African
Church had best be left alone, and if the Roman Church
really has — as she claims — a special gift of wisdom and justice, she should be the first to acknowledge this.

Even if Boniface did not already know that a fraud had
been perpetrated, he knew it now.   He therefore wisely concluded that the less the canons of Councils, whether Nicene,
Sardican, or any other, were relied on by Rome, the safer
would be her prestige.   He therefore writes:

The universal institution of the budding Church acquired her
authority from the honour [granted] to the blessed Peter, on
which rests her rule and her highest power; because from her
fountain-head has emanated the ecclesiastical discipline which has
permeated all the Churches, with the ever-increasing cultivation
of religion.   The decrees of the Nicene Council do not declare
otherwise; nay, that Council did not even presume to decree anything in regard to him because it perceived that nothing could be
conferred on him over and above what his own merit already entitled him to; in short it knew that all things had already been
conceded to him by the words of the Lord.   It is certain, therefore, that this Church bears the same relation to all the other
Churches of the world that the head does to the other members of
the body: whoever cuts himself off from her becomes an exile from
the Christian religion.[41]

Innocent had groped for such an argument.[42]   Now, in the
light of the African exposure of the confusion of the canons,
Boniface made the long-postponed admission that canon 6
of Nicæa decreed nothing in regard to Peter, and nothing,
therefore, in regard to Rome.   Freed at last from all dependence on canons of any kind, the Petrine claim began to assume
a definite shape: Christ knew that a Church must have her
hierarchies and her sovereignty; that is why He delegated
His authority to Peter — in order that Peter and his successors might impose such laws on the Church as they might
from time to time deem expedient.   Boniface therefore says:

---

[40] Included as *Letter* # 2 §5 of   [41] *Letter* # 14 § 1 (ibid. 777).
Boniface (*P.L.* 20 755) .   [42] See pp. 573–74.

He readily submits to discipline who, as he should, acknowledges that discipline. For the whole organization is so constituted that, to the superior parts, those parts which are shown to be subordinate must conform; and on this hierarchy of rules everything depends. Now we are particularly bound to the duty of treating all matters, for it was to us, through the holy apostle Peter, that Christ delegated the duty of leading all; and from among His apostles He did not say who would be lower than the other, but He rather chose him who would be first. Let the rules be our masters; let us not be masters over the rules.[43]

Here, at last, no longer embryonically, is the full declaration of the Petrine claim, here is the final step of this argument. The Roman bishops, whom everyone must acknowledge to be Peter's successors, would be derelict in their duty if they did not, however humbly and even reluctantly, assume this grave responsibility. Indeed the very fact that the Popes have assumed it is added proof that they have conformed themselves to the rules which Christ laid down. When Boniface says ' Let the rules be our masters ' what he means to say is that the papacy has no alternative but to enforce the rules, and to enforce them as she chooses to interpret them.

The papal theory of sovereignty was now clearly outlined on every point but one: if the papacy was bound not only by the laws of God but also by those laws of men which she had deigned to approve, she was to that extent bound by her previous acts. Innocent had said that the Church, and therefore future Popes as well as future General Councils, were bound by the canons of Nicæa. Boniface, perceiving the danger of admitting that the decrees of any General Council, even though they be those of Nicæa, bound the papacy, declared that these Nicene decrees were binding on her only because she had ratified them and that the decrees of future General Councils could only bind her — and hence the Church — should she choose to ratify these too. But because her devotion to Nicæa was on account of the Nicene Creed alone she built up her arguments in order to ensure the permanence of that Creed quite as much as in order to procure her

[43] Given as *Letter* # 3 of Celestine in *P.L.* 50 428. But the letter is probably by Boniface: Caspar 1933 II 81 n. 1, correcting his attribution in his vol. I 381 & 387.

own sovereignty. Because, indeed, her chief incentive in seeking that sovereignty was that she might the better guard the integrity of that Creed, she was satisfied to pose rather as a
judicial than as a legislative authority, to claim the right to
determine not what the law should become but only what it
already was. And, in doing this, she virtually denied her
power to amend or repeal even her own decisions, denied the
existence within the Church of any wholly sovereign power,
and affirmed the fateful principle that the past may bind the
future irrespective of future revelations. This was the law
of the Medes and Persians,[44] in spirit contrary to the evolutionary spirit of the Roman jurists of old. But a time of
ossification was now setting in: as the barbarian pressure increased so did the need not only for a concentration of authority but for a devotion to the past. Just as according to
Valentinian's Constitution of 426 [45] jurists were no longer
allowed to decide a question as they liked, but only as they
should determine what the great jurists of the past had
thought,[46] so now according to Boniface, even the papacy was
not allowed to decide what Christ in fact was, but only what
the bishops assembled at Nicæa had thought He was. It is
true that Church sovereignty was inevitably judicial rather
than legislative, because her fundamental law, the Bible,
could not be amended — as the Manichees apparently believed it could be; but it is also true that all legal sovereignties are subject to analogous restrictions — among them man's
congenital conservatism, which baffles even so sovereign a
body as the British Parliament. In consideration of the
Church's recognition of papal sovereignty, Boniface agreed
that the papacy should be for ever bound, not only by the
Bible and Nicæa, but also by every canon and decree she may
previously have recognized. If this was a natural development it was also one singularly advantageous to the papacy:
a legislative body cannot be infallible, whereas a purely judicial body is virtually obliged to be so. This is why the Roman
Church is the great exhibit of the strength and weakness of
consistency.

[44] Cf. *Daniel* vi 15: ' that no decree
or statute which the king establisheth
may be changed.'
[45] Enacted for the East by the
Theodosian Code of 438; Savigny
1834 I 2 28–29.
[46] Muirhead 1886 390; Jolowicz
1932 468.

Pope Celestine, who succeeded Boniface in 422, seems to have been unusually stupid.[47]   Perhaps Apiarius, the African priest who had been reinstated pending investigation into the authenticity of the so-called Nicene canons, for this very reason waited until Celestine was in office before asking Rome to interfere again in his behalf.   That Celestine could still believe that the Sardican canons were Nicene is almost inconceivable, but the fact remains that Celestine acceded, just as Zosimus had five years before.   Tried before the papal legate and the Council of Carthage of 423, Apiarius broke down and confessed his many outrageous sins.[48]   Whereupon the Africans wrote to Celestine:

That persons may be sent as though on your sanctity's behalf we do not find authorized by any synod of the Fathers: because that which some time ago you sent through our same co-bishop Faustinus, purporting to be an integral part of the canons of Nicæa, in the more authoritative copies of the canons of Nicæa — which we have received from Saint Cyril, our co-bishop of the Church of Alexandria, and from the worthy Atticus, bishop of Constantinople — taken from their authentic copy . . . we have not been able to find any such provision.   Refrain, therefore, from sending your clerics as plenipotentiaries in behalf of anyone applying to you; refrain from acceding; lest we appear to be introducing into the Church of Christ the blinding pride of the temporal world.[49]

It is curious that to these Africans the cardinal sin of Zosimus and Celestine was not deceit but pride.   They failed to see that in a Church where all manifestations of pride were anathema, he who would lead that Church — as someone must — might be obliged to rely on deceit instead.   The Africans were right in seeing the pride through the disguise of deceit; only we should rather have resented the deceit than the pride. Virtues and vices, however, like everything else in this world, are at the mercy of fashion; therefore pride, because it was now the novel vice, was also the most offensive.   Thus awkwardly does man grow in wisdom — in his search for better things discarding many of the good things already won. Before truth revealed truth unrevealed was fleeing; and into the gap thus opened up poured fraud and bias as well as meekness and love.

---

[47] Nestorius spoke of him as a simpleton: Duchesne 1911 III⁴ 336 n. 3.   And cf. pp. 420, & 585 n. 63.

[48] Duchesne 1911 III⁴ 254–55.
[49] Included as *Letter* # 2 §§ 4 & 5 of Celestine (*P.L.* 50 426–27).

In earlier times African resistance to Rome had been less because there had been less to resist. While Ambrose lived informal appeals to Rome or Milan had been frequent,[50] but as Augustine rose to prominence the Africans assumed a more defiant attitude. In the year 411, for instance, a Council of Carthage arranged a settlement of the Donatist controversy, and sought ratification, not from Rome, but from the Emperor.[51] And this same Council condemned the Pelagian Celestius, no one asking either Rome or anyone else for a confirmation.[52] When, somewhat later, Celestius obtained a rehabilitation in the East, the African Church did appeal to Rome for support, and Pope Innocent complied.[53] But, when it was learned that Innocent's successor Zosimus was contemplating a retraction of that compliance, the Africans at once appealed to the Emperor and persuaded him to hale Celestius before a civil court.[54] In 419 and again in 422 African Councils formulated the first Latin code of canon law,[55] and did this without asking Rome's advice or confirmation. These Councils intimated further that there was no appeal from the decisions of a plenary African Council except to a General Council,[56] and in this Pope Celestine now virtually acquiesced.

But this successful resistance to Rome's effort to encroach lasted only until the year 430. It was in that year that Augustine died and that the Vandals became masters of most of the territory. African Catholicism then fell helplessly into the Pope's hands. And for the prestige of the papacy it was most fortunate that this death and this invasion came so soon as they did, for it was in that very year 430 that the Nestorian heresy broke out in the East to menace the integrity of the Nicene Creed. By the time Rome had been informed of this new development and was ready for her reply in defence of Nicæa, she was able to speak not as leader only, but as sovereign, of the whole Latin West. At Sardica nearly a hundred years before, the West had spoken as a unit for Nicæa, but as

---

[50] See pp. 559 n. 75, & 560 n. 77.

[51] Batiffol 1924 ² 232–33. On the Donatist heresy in Africa, which died down after 392, see Tixeront 1921 II ⁶ 223–31.

[52] Ibid. 234.

[53] Ibid. 235–38; Caspar 1930 I 330–32, & 337–38.

[54] Caspar 1930 I 350–60.

[55] Fournier & Le Bras 1931 I 18.

[56] See p. 576 n. 28.

a unit composed of autonomous parts; at the coming Council
of Ephesus the West again spoke as a unit, but this unit was
now a single Western bishop, speaking only incidentally in
the name of all, essentially in the name of Peter.

The disastrously bitter controversy of the fourth century
was now revived again with great intensity by the utterances
of Nestorius who, in 428, as bishop of Constantinople, began
to expound his theory of what was the true essence of Christ.
The Council of Nicæa had declared that Christ was the only-
begotten of the Father, of the essence of and co-substantial
with the Father. Consequently the Virgin had very naturally
come to be called the ' Mother of God.' [57] But, now objected
Nestorius, how, unless in pagan mythology, may a God be
born of a mortal woman? [58] Could there be a more impudent
or sacrilegious conceit? Since, however, the Incarnation is
undeniable, the explanation must be that the human Virgin
merely bore the man-Christ. Thus, according to Pope Leo,
Nestorius believed

that the blessed Virgin Mary conceived a man without a Godhead,
who was created by the Holy Ghost and afterwards assumed the
Word.[59]

Nestorius must admit, of course, that Christ was also uncreated and eternal; consequently there was no moment of
time when Christ the God did not exist. Following the Virgin birth, then, there existed both Christ the man and Christ
the God, so that, until the man assumed the Word, there
were two separate persons. But, if there had been a time
when Christ was two separate persons, it must remain a matter of doubt how, when, and in what degree, these two should
merge into a One. Thus, as Leo later complained, Nestorius
separated ' the Godhead of the Word from the substance of
his assumed manhood,' [60] and thereby ' made the person of
his flesh one thing and that of his Godhead another.' [61] The
union effected by His assumption of the Word was therefore

[57] Duchesne 1911 III 4 324-26; Batiffol 1924 2 345.
[58] The Manichees liked to speak
contemptuously of the Virgin: Stoop
1909 138.

[59] Letter # 59 § 5.
[60] Ibid. # 35 § 1.
[61] Ibid. # 124 § 2.

incomplete, a mere conjunction, rather than a full fusion, of wholly disparate elements.

There now ensued a theological uproar rivalling that which Arius had induced. The opposition to Nestorius was led by the energetic bishop Cyril of Alexandria who at once accused Nestorius of treason to the Nicene Creed and set the wheels in motion for his condemnation. Among other steps he appealed to both the Emperor and Pope Celestine for their support.[62] Celestine, after a first blundering effort to explain what Nicæa had meant to declare,[63] found it discreet to leave his case in the hands of the better qualified Cyril, whom he authorized to act as his agent in any proceedings undertaken against Nestorius.[64] Meanwhile Nestorius in his turn accused Cyril of heresy and persuaded the Emperor to summon a General Council to meet at Ephesus in 431 to settle the dispute.[65] Here Cyril, with the approval of the Emperor and the absent Pope, with a clear majority of the bishops supporting him, and without waiting for the arrival of the hostile delegation from Antioch, procured Nestorius' condemnation.[66] The minority naturally raised the cry of fraud, but the Emperor would not listen to them and Nestorius was accordingly deposed.[67]

Was this a victory for the Roman papacy, or a defeat? It is hard to say. On the one hand Cyril, although incidentally acting as Celestine's agent, acted also as bishop of the ranking see of the East — and so virtually at his own discretion.[68] It was he who presided over the Council, it was he who drafted the text which the Council accepted as the authoritative interpretation of Nicæa,[69] it was he who had the ear of the Emperor. Not only was the Pope not present at Ephesus, not only were his personal delegates too late to take part in the condemnation proceedings,[70] in addition the decision of the Council was determined by neither Cyril's opinion nor Celes-

[62] Batiffol 1924 2 348–49.
[63] Caspar 1930 I 395–98.
[64] Haller 1934 I 140. Celestine sent legates of his own, but these were presumably instructed to follow Cyril's lead. There were also present independent delegates at the Council representing Africa and Illyria: ibid.
[65] Caspar 1930 I 405–07.

[66] Batiffol 1924 2 370–75; Caspar 1930 I 407–08. The majority consisted of 198 bishops, the minority of 53: Batiffol 1924 2 374 n. 4.
[67] Ibid. 273–75 & 392.
[68] Caspar 1930 I 402.
[69] Batiffol 1924 2 370–89; Caspar 1930 I 408.
[70] Caspar 1930 I 412.

tine's, but by the attendant bishops' own opinion of what
Nicæa had in fact declared.[71]   Celestine, moreover, had approved the calling of such Council and had thereby admitted
its independent right to decide for itself what the true doctrine was.[72]   Neither he nor Cyril had claimed the right to
dictate what its judgment should be, nor did Celestine insist
beforehand that any judgment rendered be valid only if Rome
should see fit to ratify it.   Both merely presented their views
for what they were worth.   They assumed the role rather of
prosecuting attorneys than of judges.   For neither dared to
allege, even if he believed, that Church sovereignty lay elsewhere than in the General Council.

Yet if Celestine's part in the decision was negligible he
now, with grave impudence, sought to take the credit for it.
Because the Nicene doctrine had been vindicated, so had the
papal; and, since the East was divided, it might appear that
the Pope had, by holding the balance of power, been the
cause of the victory that ensued.   Actually the Nicene party
was in a majority in the East, actually whatever leadership
there had been belonged to Cyril only.   But so majestically
did Celestine in his letters now boast of the vindication of the
papal claims to supremacy, that not only the West — which
was quite ignorant of the real situation — but the East also,
was half persuaded that Celestine spoke the truth.[73]   If, instead of supporting Cyril, he had held aloof, would the Emperor and the bishops have moved so confidently ahead?[74]
As no one knew, it was easy to be persuaded that perhaps they
would not.

Ephesus soon came to be regarded as even more a victory
for the Virgin.   In the West especially, much was made of
her triumph; and although she was not yet thought of as im-
maculately conceived[75] it was from this time that her cult
began[76] — that cult which gradually transformed her from a

---

[71] Batiffol 1924[2] 373–75; Caspar
1930 I 403 & 407–09.

[72] Caspar 1930 I 404–08.

[73] Batiffol 1924[2] 409–10; Caspar
1930 I 414–22.

[74] Cf. Haller 1934 I 140.

[75] Leo Letter # 28 § 4 (the Tome)
says that 'the Lord assumed his
mother's nature without her faulti-

ness.'   On the suppositions of Ambrose and Augustine, see Dudden
1935 601 & 623.

[76] Dufourcq L'Av. 1910 IV[5] 277–8;
Batiffol 1924[2] 375; Caspar 1930 I
421.   And see p. 590 on the dedica-
tion of the basilica of Liberius by
Pope Sixtus III to the honour of the
Virgin.

daughter of the fallen Adam to the Queen of Heaven. The
first Latin poem written to honour the Virgin is by Caelius
Sedulius, possibly a Roman, who flourished in about 450; it
is called *Salutatio Matris Domini* and runs thus:

All hail, holy parent, thou who hast given birth to the King who
rules heaven and earth throughout the ages and whose name and
dominion, embracing all things in their timeless circuit, abide
without end; thou, who from thy blessed womb hast a mother's
joys yet keepest a virgin's honour, hast shown that there never was
or will be another like thee; thou alone, a woman without counterpart, hast pleased Christ.[77]

Her glory, great as it already is, remains in this poem a reflected, a vicarious glory. Man will only come to love her
in her own right as he comes to love tenderness in its own
right, and man, in the fifth century, was still only half weaned
from the worship of Jove's, or Jehovah's, thunderbolts. Her
day could only come with the day of Aucassin and the trou-
badour.

The Council of Ephesus had condemned the Nestorian
doctrine, enhanced the glory of the Virgin and the prestige of
the Pope. But it did more than this: it dealt a final, mortal
blow to Augustine's doctrine of an evolution in human understanding. Pope Innocent, already slightly younger than
Augustine, had declared the Nicene decrees unamendable; [78]
the Council of Ephesus now ratified that judgment. Human
understanding might still be, as Augustine alleged, a feeble
thing; the bishops assembled at Nicæa in 325, however, had
received a divine revelation which made error there an im-
possibility. Their decision was therefore infallible, just as,
in the realm of civil law, the decisions of the Ulpians and
Papinians were at this moment being also declared infallible.
The bishops assembled at Nicæa were declared by those at
Ephesus to be the Ulpians and Papinians of theology and
canon law. In each case the present was seeking to bind the
future to the authority of the past, seeking to set tradition
above truth. If history is ever to teach us lessons it here
teaches us this: that a present which seeks to bind its future
has no future to bind. The six years 426 to 431 had witnessed

[77] *Paschalis Carminis* II lines 63–   [78] See p. 572 ns. 7 & 8.
69.

the appearance of Valentinian's constitution, Augustine's death, and the decision of Ephesus. Latin-Roman civilization lived until then but did not live longer.[79] It was in 434 that the Semi-Pelagian monk, Vincent of Lerins, wrote this famous passage:

But perhaps someone will say: shall there be no progress in religion within Christ's Church? Certainly; all possible progress. For what being is so ungenerous to man, so full of hatred towards God, that he would seek to forbid it? Yet on condition that it be real progress, not alteration of the faith. For progress requires that the subject be enlarged within itself, alteration that it be transformed into something else. The intelligence, then, the knowledge, the wisdom, as well of individuals as of all, as well of one man as of the whole Church, ought, by successive stages through ages and centuries, to increase and make much and vigorous progress; but yet only in its own kind: that is to say, in the same doctrine, in the same sense, in the same meaning. The growth of religion in the soul must be analogous to the growth of the body, which, although evolving and unfolding its parts with the progress of years, yet remains still the same. There is a wide difference between the flower of youth and the maturity of age; yet they who were once young are still the same now that they have become old.[80]

There had evidently been men who ' viewed with alarm ' the tendency of the Church rather to consolidate her present gains than to seek new ones. Ephesus had only served to confirm their suspicions. Vincent here seeks to allay their uneasiness and his statement is therefore as favourable to the idea of advance as he could conscientiously make it. Nevertheless, his ' same doctrine, in the same sense, in the same meaning ' is the very antithesis of Augustine's view. Vincent confined change to details and thus barred the way to any other kind of variation than an ever increasing complexity — as architecture, if it were forever to remain Gothic, must become ever more intricately flamboyant.[81] Augustine, because he would set no restrictions on change, left the way open for changes in structure. Since it can hardly have escaped his notice that he himself changed almost every matter

[79] See pp. 288-89.
[80] *Commonitorium* § 54.
[81] I should suppose that on the side of Augustine were the scholastic writers like Roger Bacon, Aquinas, Scotus, and Occam, and on the side of Vincent the Popes immediately following him and the bishops attending the Council of Trent.

he touched, it might be argued that he was defending his own cause. But since Vincent may have observed that he himself changed almost nothing he touched was he not defending his cause too? It is true that individuals are inherently different, are not merely the blind products of their generations and are not, therefore, except for time, interchangeable. On the other hand neither is it chronological chance that the child born in 354 was Augustine and the child born in 384 was Vincent.[82]

E. Leo and Eutyches, 432–461

In the year 412 the Visigoths evacuated Italy, and thereafter, for forty years, the peninsula was not invaded.[1] The feeble Emperor Honorius died in 423 and was succeeded by his sister Galla Placidia who ruled in the name of her small son Valentinian III. During these years it might have seemed as if the great days had returned. There were still chronic usurpations[2] and civil wars,[3] but the even tenor of life was largely re-established, and the great accumulation of wealth, although concentrated in a few hands, was still lavishly spent for the glory of the spender and the satisfaction of the populace.[4] The resources of Spain were now lost; so were those of parts of Gaul; in 429 the Vandals invaded Africa, threatening the rich Proconsular province and its great capital Carthage. But in 435 a treaty was signed with the Vandal leader Genseric stipulating that he keep his hands off this part of Africa.[5] Thus for a few more years it could appear that the kernel of Latin civilization, centering around Rome, Carthage, and Arles, was to remain intact. Deceptively serene and uneventful too was the pontificate of Sixtus III, who had succeeded Celestine in 432. His name is more familiar to architects than to theologians, for it was he who built the

---

[82] This date of 384 is an approximation inferred from the only two known dates of Vincent's life: 434, when he wrote the *Commonitorium*, and 450, when he died.

[1] Hodgkin 1892 I 2 819.

[2] That of Joannes: ibid. 845–48.

[3] That between Boniface and Aetius: ibid. 878–79.

[4] Ibid. 883. Salvian *D.G.D.* VI § 49, writing in about 445, says that public games were then being celebrated in Rome and Ravenna.

[5] Hodgkin 1892 II 2 248–49.

great basilica of San Lorenzo and the even more famous
Lateran, and it was he who transformed the modest and dilapi-
dated basilica of Liberius into the glorious church which he
dedicated to the Virgin — known to us as Santa Maria Maggiore.[6]

This happy but ephemeral interlude lasted twenty-seven
years; then, in 439, Genseric broke the treaty, overran Proconsular Africa, took Carthage, and — what was even more
serious to Rome — appropriated the African grain supply
on which much of Italy and the city of Rome especially was
dependent for its food.[7] It was in the very next year, when
the pinch must have been first felt, that the Tuscan [8] Leo became Pope and Rome's second phase — to last over 1400
years — began: henceforth, and at least until 1870, she was
to be the city of the Popes.

And, except in the eyes of scholars, the first real Pope was,
and ever since has been, this Leo, a man universally admired
in his own day and a great name, even to those who know
nothing of him, in ours.[9] As a mind not to be compared to
Augustine, but as a man without a peer. Picturesque details
about him are lacking — for his biography, curiously enough,
was never written — but his character, his inner personality,
is well revealed in his own numerous letters and sermons.
Here force and charm, fierceness and gentleness, dwell together like the wolf with the lamb.[10] Through our confidence in this man we gain confidence in this new civilization which is now concentrating itself around his office, gain
confidence in the Catholic Church as a heritage worthy of the
best that antiquity has bequeathed. Combining the gentleness of Martin, the majesty of Ambrose, and the penetration
of Augustine, he was the first great Latin Christian who felt
wholly at home in his new faith.

As a Christian Leo believed that he knew what the truth
was; as a Roman he dared to demand obedience to that truth.
He did not merely argue his authority, he imposed it; he

---

6 Seppelt 1931 I 189–90. This was
also the time of the first buildings
and mosaics still to be seen at Ravenna: Diehl 1907 24.
7 Hodgkin 1892 I [2] 881–82, & II [2]
250–51.

8 Although he had lived so long
in Rome that he regarded himself
rather as a Roman: Caspar 1930 I
423–24.
9 Cf. Seppelt 1931 I 195.
10 Cf. *Isaiah* xi 6.

gave fewer reasons than had his predecessors, and more commands. When he spoke it was very simply in the name of
Peter,[11] in terms of one divinely inspired.[12] Only from the
assumption of sovereignty did he deign to declare what powers that sovereignty gave him: the right to hear appeals from
all the Churches of East as well as West,[13] the right to declare
as by fiat that the canons of Nicæa must stand unamended
for all time.[14] Gone was the disingenuous apology of a Boniface that necessity obliged him so to act; [15] Leo merely acted
so — not as if impelled from without but as if initiating from
within. That Peter was supreme among the apostles and
that this supremacy was transmitted to Rome alone — all
this Leo took quite for granted. In the same way the see of
Alexandria ranked second because it was the see of Mark.
But even Mark had derived whatever power he had from
Peter [16] just as Cyril's recent manifestation of power had all
been derived from Celestine. Man may hate rank and yet
crave it — for he craves to admire others as well as himself:
the early Christian had been captivated by the revelation
that the ranks of the temporal world had no counterparts in
the spiritual, that Christ was not a subordinate God and that
under God all men were equal. But was not the discarded
Neoplatonism, with its hierarchies, creeping in again? Under
Christ was Peter as his slave, under Peter was Mark as his
slave, under Mark would be more slaves, and below these
slaves again.[17] Is this the best way to run a world? If we
only knew!

In the history of Church discipline the pontificate of Leo
is also of special importance, not because he introduced any
novelties but rather because his judgments were respected
by all the Western dioceses as those of his predecessors had
not been.[18] And that is why very few of his judgments have

---

[11] Caspar 1930 I 428–30.

[12] ' ut revelante Domino . . . re-
scribamus ': *Letter # 6 § 5.*

[13] Caspar 1930 I 457–58.

[14] *Letter # 106 § 2,* quoted p. 611
n. 109.

[15] See pp. 580–81.

[16] Haller 1934 I 146.

[17] The hierarchy ran from top
to bottom about as follows: Pope,
patriarch, archbishop, bishop. Then

priest, archdeacon, deacon, subdea-
con, acolyte, *defensor,* notary, lector,
monk (Langen 1885 171). Then laymen in good standing, those possessed by the devil, the absolved
penitent. Finally those barred from
communion: the catechumen, the
unabsolved penitent, etc. The fe-
male hierarchy would be nun, virgin,
widow, wife, whore.

[18] Haller 1934 I 148 & 197–98. Cf.

been lost: for they were the canon law of the Latin Church. Many of his decrees deal with qualifications for ordination: slaves may not be ordained,[19] nor persons who had married a widow or divorced woman.[20] Others dealt with behaviour after ordination: even a sub-deacon, for instance, could continue to live with his wife only as with a sister,[21] and no priest could practise usury.[22] Clerical promotions must be slow [23] and according to seniority,[24] for a priest must have maturity of judgment and a decent prospect of reward for loyal service. He repeats too, very specifically, how a bishop must be elected: by the local clergy and people as often as this was practicable. And where the archbishop has to interfere this must be rather in order to effect than to thwart the popular will; so that, even when making the nomination himself, he must prefer the most popular rather than the best qualified candidate.[25] At the same time no one could qualify as bishop unless he had already served, as canon law prescribed, in the succession of subordinate offices. Popular choice, but only from among the carefully selected few: what wiser form of government has ever been devised? The conception is of course not Leo's own — it goes back to the earliest Christian times — but how sympathetic he is with this early spirit and purpose, yet how firmly he sets bounds to its enthusiasm! Thus, if in one sense the bishop is the master within his diocese and the rest his servants, in another sense he too is a servant — of the papacy and her canon law. The people are in this way protected in their fundamental rights: they may have whom they will as their bishop, but he must be one who knows, and will respect, their rights. No bishop, for instance, might alienate land belonging to his Church unless not only his clergy but the whole Church approved.[26]

Batiffol 1924 [2] 434, 445–46, 475–76, 480–83 & 488–91; & Caspar 1930 I 441–42 & 469–70; & Leo Letters # 10, 11 & 68.

19 Letter # 4.
20 Ibid.
21 Ibid. # 167. And cf. ibid. # 14.
22 Ibid. # 4.
23 Ibid. # 12.
24 Ibid. # 19.

25 Ibid. # 4. Cf. canon # 54 of the Council of Arles, held in 443 or 452, providing that the archbishop shall nominate three candidates for an episcopal vacancy, the clergy and citizens being obliged to choose among these three: Hefele 1908 II [2] 475.
26 Letter # 17.

Especially in regard to penance and absolution was Leo more specific than his predecessors had been. First, he says, there must be voluntary self-accusation in the confessional.[27] If the sin thus privately confessed were venial — that is, routine — only a private penance of fasting might be imposed and absolution not long deferred.[28] But if the sin confessed were serious — a fornication, a homicide, a worshipping of idols — the priest must impose a public penance [29] which involved a regime not only of fasting but also of constant prayer, shortened sleep, chastity, withdrawal from worldly affairs, almsgiving and the like,[30] to last either — as for fornication — briefly,[31] or for a long term which was sometimes prolonged until imminent death.[32] This penance was rightly called public because it was so, but there was no betrayal of the confessional because the public remained in ignorance of the sin for which the penance was being done.[33] And, since many voluntarily adopted such a regime — as the monks had [34] — either for venial sins or for none at all, the public could not even tell how serious a sin the penitent had committed.[35] A man of evil repute who suddenly adopted such a way of life must, unless he were shamming, have become ashamed of his past; but as to what that past had been no one was now the wiser. Perhaps the heaviness of his guilt had dragged him to remorse, but perhaps too the lightness of his unsuspected innocence had lifted him to grace.

Absolution was forgiveness and it allowed the penitent once more to receive the sacrament of communion and thereby to achieve again, for the moment — as after baptism — a state of grace. For penance the sinner alone was responsible, but for absolution the co-operation of a priest was indispensable. Even then Leo was doubtful whether the abso-

[27] Poschmann 1928 11.
[28] Ibid. 8.
[29] Ibid. Cf. Leo *Letter* # 167 § 19.
[30] Poschmann 1928 23–24. Many of these privations had previously been imposed by Ambrose or earlier Popes.
[31] Usually to end on the Maundy Thursday following: ibid. 34 & 46.
[32] The latter was the usual penance imposed on fornicating monks and nuns: ibid. 131. And the clergy too were of course more severely pe-

nalized than were the laymen: Hefele 1908 II 2 997–98 (on the pertinent canons of the Councils of Toledo in 400 and Agde in 506).
[33] Poschmann 1928 I 11–13. Whether it was ever recognized Church practice to reveal the nature of the sin is not clear: ibid. 14–15.
[34] Monks who joined the army or married could, however, get absolution on their death-beds: Leo *Letter* # 167 § 14.
[35] Poschmann 1928 I 13.

lution would be invariably valid, as where the penance had in fact been inadequate either in time or intensity. But one thing was sure: without the priest no absolution was valid.[36] This brings us to the thorny question of the death-bed repentance. Suppose there had been a most sincere and complete penance but that the penitent, dying violently or at least suddenly, had had no time to call a priest. Was he damned? The most that could be promised was complete uncertainty.[37] Or take the opposite case, of a sinner who had long kept his sins unconfessed, living a gross and impenitent life until the hour of his death, but who then called in a priest, confessed, expressed due remorse, and asked for absolution. The priest could not refuse.[38] If the sinner thereupon died was he surely saved? If not of what use was this death-bed rite?

A further complication arose from the rule that a penitent could be absolved only once — that is, only once after the original absolution conferred by baptism.[39] This second absolution, moreover, unlike the first, did not remove all the disabilities. For not only was further absolution impossible for sins thereafter committed, even the penitent's way of living must be in some degree maintained. What was not a sin for one who had merely been baptized, was a sin for one who, having done penance, had been absolved.[40] Leo said, for instance,

It is altogether contrary to the rules of the Church to return, after doing penance, to the military service in the world, since the Apostle says that *no soldier in God's service entangles himself in the affairs of the world.*[41]

And for the same reason

It is more expedient for a penitent to suffer loss than to be involved in the risks of trafficking, because it is hard for sin not to come into transactions between buyer and seller.[42]

Once a penitent always a penitent is the principle; with the result that absolution, although a re-entry into grace, is a re-

<hr>

36 Poschmann 1928 I 7.
37 *Letter* # 108. Cf. Poschmann 1928 I 39.
38 Poschmann 1928 I 41–44.
39 Ibid. 58.
40 Ibid. 58–59.
41 *Letter* # 167 § 12.
42 Ibid. § 11.

ward to be asked for and accepted at the last possible moment. And the same thing, in a lesser degree, was true of baptism.[43]   Thus a man who is baptized young and, having a delicate conscience, confesses fornication, does his penance, and is absolved, finds himself in a most unenviable situation: he may not join the army, engage in business, marry, or become a priest,[44] for these acts done by a former penitent are not only sins but unforgivable sins!   This is why even the most devout sought to postpone baptism as long as possible; [45] so that, should they sin, they need not confess, do penance, and receive the gloomy sentence of a last absolution.

Of the undue severity of these rules Leo was fully conscious.   He condones the sick man who in his agony calls for a priest to give him absolution but when the priest arrives refuses it because he feels better.[46]   And where a young sinner has, as the result of extreme illness, received absolution, he advises copulation in marriage rather than the risk of fornication, assuring him that if he remains faithful to his wife he will not be damned.[47]

Persons who had thus done penance and been absolved were in theory on the lowest rung of the Church hierarchy, lower, at least, than any but those actually in a state of sin and hence technically outside the Church.   In fact, however, and properly, they came to be considered a privileged class of laymen ranking next below the monks, and they were pointed to as shining examples.[48]   Yet a difficulty remained, all the more awkward if one accepted Augustine's theory of ephemeral grace.   For should grace leave them, as it might through no fault of theirs, they must relapse into a life of sin.   And for this second sin there could be no absolution.   From the point of view of temporal justice these penitents were being rewarded by the regard in which the Church held them; but from the point of view of eternal justice their position could not be more uncomfortable.   Yet to change the rule so that the emphasis should be laid on penance rather than on absolu-

[43] Poschmann 1928 52–54 & 63–64.

[44] Ibid. 62–63.

[45] Ambrose had recommended postponement of confession in such cases: ibid. 64–65.

[46] Ibid. 65–66.

[47] Ibid. 66. Pope Siricius had previously allowed a death-bed absolution in such cases: ibid. 60–61.

[48] Ibid. 67. The catechumens were of course lower still because they were unbaptized.

tion was to reduce the role of the priest and so of the Church to virtual impotence. Unless the Church, rather than God, had the power to bind and loose there was hardly need of any Church, and, without a Church, there would quickly be, as Pope Felix was soon to say,[49] a sterile chaos.

Leo was quite as ready as Ambrose to declare that the canon was superior to, and must therefore invalidate, civil law,[50] and that the physical force of the State was therefore bound to execute the one as well as the other.[51] That such claims could now not only be seriously made but also meekly accepted indicates the growing disintegration of the Latin State and its dependence on the Church.[52] Only in so far as the State acted with the consent of the Church could she now count on the allegiance of her citizens.

For who, if not God, was ruler now? From whom, if not from God, did even the heathen Diocletian derive his authority? Though a scourge, was he not also a servant of God? To admit any other than the divine power was Manichæan. The Emperor must still rule the temporal world, but by what law? Since this must be the law of God, where was it written, in the opinions of the jurists or in those of the Fathers? Where was it revealed, in the mind of the soldier Emperor or in that of the holy priests?[53] The Emperor Julian did God's will only through the medium of the devil. Should such a power be allowed to challenge that of the Fathers, the saints, and the Church? That there were many matters of no concern to Catholics was obvious, and obvious too that it was not always easy to say what these matters in any given case might be; but it was even more obvious that only the Church was competent to determine what these matters were — for she alone could know what things did, and what things did not, concern salvation. Leo, therefore, because through Peter he spoke for God, became sovereign not only of the Latin Church but also of the Latin State. His

49 See p. 627 n. 58.
50 Batiffol 1924 2 548–49. A principle which the Council of Chalcedon was about to affirm: ibid.
51 Cf. ibid. 451–57.
52 Cf. Caspar 1930 I 447.
53 See Voigt 1928 11–12 & 17. Leo's

assertion that the Emperor was inspired by the Holy Ghost was double-edged: if he disagreed with the Pope he was clearly not so inspired and was therefore a false and not the real Emperor. Cf. Carlyle 1927 I 2 162 n. 6 on Ambrose.

will was law, and the civil law was to be respected only in
so far as he respected it.

Leo's proceedings against the Manichees illustrate the real
state of affairs. As alleged magicians this sect had been virtually proscribed ever since Diocletian; [54] yet, with each successive re-enactment of the proscription, enforcement had
grown more lax. After 439, however, there was such an influx
of Manichees from Africa to Italy [55] that in 443 we find Leo
presiding over an assembly composed of laity as well as clergy,
called to ferret out the heretics, to hale them before a civil
court to be tortured, and, upon conviction, to be exiled.[56]
Was Leo acting as Pope, as private informer, or as prosecuting
attorney? We do not know, nor, probably, did he or any
of the others — nor did any of them care. Technically the
ensuing condemnations were for magical acts, actually they
were now for beliefs which Leo, as head of the Church, declared heretical. If the civil authorities were to execute the
laws of the Church it was essential that there be a single body
of law within that Church. Therefore such insubordination
as that now being shown by bishop Hilary of Arles was as
offensive to the Emperor as to the Pope. If bishops did not
take their orders from Rome but instead made their own
laws, enforcement by the State must prove impracticable.
This is why, in 445, Valentinian III re-enacted in stricter form
the decree of Gratian of 378: [57] every ecclesiastical act was
declared illegal if done in defiance of the Pope's authority.
And the reason for this is plainly given:

For only then will the peace of the Churches be everywhere preserved when everyone acknowledges him as leader.[58]

Yet Leo's triumphs were not complete. For the Church,
while ever diligently pursuing her ends in the temporal
world, still professed to despise it. Ever ready to criticize
those undertaking the burden of temporal rule, she was never
quite willing to rule herself. Willing enough to accept the

---

[54] See p. 18 n. 110, & Caspar 1930 I
432.

[55] Batiffol 1924 [2] 434; Caspar 1930
I 432.

[56] Caspar 1930 I 433-35. A law of
Valentinian III ratified the decision
of this assembly: Leo *Letter* # 8.

[57] See p. 547 n. 11.

[58] Incorporated as *Letter* # 11 of
Leo (*P.L.* 54 637). *Leader* is *recto-
rem.*

blessings of temporal welfare, she was not ready to accept the responsibilities that this entailed. With war she would have no dealings, yet she was willing to pray fervently for the blessings that only a bloody victory could procure;[59] with commerce she would have no dealings, yet she unblushingly scrambled for the lion's share of its fruits; she set chastity above the responsibilities of marriage and children, yet she sought to appropriate the children of others as if by right.

Consequently in the centuries now to come the patience even of pious citizens and laymen was often tried by this Church they so loved and feared. For often she fed gluttonously on those very things she most professed to despise. Occasionally, then, the lay world would balk — only in time to repent and submit. Occasionally, too, the Church in her turn would balk — against her own excess. Thus in the year 458 the Emperor Majorian had decreed that all ordinations of priests, if induced by duress, were null and void; that no women under forty years old might take the veil; that all childless widows must marry again within five years or forfeit half their inheritance.[60] Leo not only did not protest, but actually repeated the law regarding nuns, merely adding that the candidate must be a virgin.[61] Evidently Leo too saw the need of putting a brake on Catholic enthusiasm lest it get out of hand and so destroy the very civilization it was designed to regenerate.

Yet how was this compromise with the world to be squared with the Gospels? And pacificism raised the same dilemma as chastity: with the repeal in 440 of the civil law forbidding civilians to arm themselves,[62] with the Attilas and Generics just gone and soon to return, how was the wise Leo blandly to urge that no penitent entangle himself in the military service of this world? Practice here clashed with theory; the duties of the citizen clashed with those of the priest. Under such men as Leo, therefore, there were instances of moderation and compromise, and not for the worldly advantage of the Church but for the bare preservation of the State. Such compromises, however, were vain, because they were haphaz-

---

[59] See p. 377.

[60] Hodgkin 1892 II 2 421; Spreitzenhofer 1894 110.

[61] *Liber Pontificalis* I 90. The alternative reading of LX instead of XL seems most improbable: cf. ibid. 90 & 93.

[62] See p. 277 n. 28.

ard and opportunist, thrust into the breach only in moments
of desperation.   For the Church had evolved no doctrine
or principle of compromise, had rather evolved only doctrines and principles of excess.   If it were good that Catholics fight or marry,[63] it was invariably better that they refrain
from both.   If it were good that the Church lend her assistance to God in His governance of this world, it was better that the individuals composing that Church be otherwise occupied.   To be even so anomalous a statesman as
Leo was seemed little better than to be a soldier or a father.

For according to Catholic philosophy there was a definite
separation of powers: to man was assigned the humble if
difficult task of saving his own soul; to God was assigned
every other responsibility — that of governing on earth as
well as in heaven, and so the tasks at once of soldier, father,
and statesman.   His alone were the worldly concerns; even
were it His judgment that this Roman State, this world of
men, must be destroyed, then let it be so.   It was God Himself who had taught man that happiness, whether on earth or
in heaven, did not depend on prudence, on foresight, on
statecraft, did not even depend — except indirectly — on
justice between man and man; that it depended, merely and
wholly, on individual virtue.   It was no longer man's brain but
his heart that mattered; no longer his appraisal of the outer
world but his perception of the inner.   Thus, as the new
man surveyed the outer world, it faded to a symbol.   What
chance now had the old Rome, the old Rome that scrutinized
unblinkingly the outer world and in it the outer man, that
had sought to build a temporal habitation for the men of
all nations?   The eyes of those Romans who had so long
looked out, looked in now; and their eyes were glazed as
though beholding a vision.

Through the fog of their souls they perceived — dimly but
unmistakably — the soul of Christ, of Him who had come to
save them.   What sort of God was this, who chose to save
men, who came down to suffer as a man, who was willing to
mortify Himself for their sake?   God and yet also man; man

[63] Vigilantius was among the last
to stress the need of propagation:
Tixeront 1921 II 6 249–50.

and yet also God. God by His very definition was Truth and ultimate Reality. Through this incarnated God, through this Christ, one might, by peering intently enough, begin to see how men might be connected with God and so with reality. What other problem was there — could there be — but this? To what end should the State exist? To increase the birthrate [64] that there might be more crops sown and reaped, that there might be more soldiers? Surely not. This was the pagan delusion. Hardly even was it an end of the State to promote social justice among men — such legislation could only be a clumsy human effort to achieve artificially what must inevitably come by divine grace as soon as men deserved such treatment. No, the end of the State was solely to impose the orthodox Catholic faith: that men might be obliged to believe, and so, coming to believe, begin to discipline themselves as that belief prescribed. Men must be forced to look in, forced to learn the true vileness of their souls and so repent; for only as men did repent, did sincerely seek the true virtue which they must, whether they liked it or not, contemplate, could God be moved to mitigate the severity of their temporal life, to transform this age of destruction into an age of construction. That was why the State must humbly serve. That was why the Romans of the West, seeking relief from Attila and Genseric, looked not to their Emperors or Generals, but looked instead to Leo, their priest. And because they looked chiefly to him so he, though a priest, must accept the trust so laid on him, must assume the new weird office of a Catholic temporal leader. He was looked to because he knew God's will, and, because he knew it, knew what the faith was which God had in fact revealed to men, and thus could say what belief was true and so pleasing to God. It might even be said that whereas Athanasius and Damasus had fought the Arians in order to save the Church, Celestine had fought the Nestorians in order to save not the Church alone but also the State. In 370 the State seemed safer than the Church; in 430 it already seemed the other way about. And by 450 this was even

---

[64] Forty years later Pope Gelasius explained all misfortunes as the consequence of sin: *Tract* VI §§ 14–15.

truer: Leo was not so blind as to suppose that the Church
could safely dispense with the help of the State. He therefore wished to save the State — by inducing God to smile
on it. That is why, instead of recruiting armies, he strove
to bring victory to that faith which he believed to be orthodox and true. It was because he thought God's allegiance
to the cause of Rome was the paramount object to be sought
that he chose to fight heresy instead of Hun or Vandal. His
end was still the old Roman end: to preserve the Empire.
It was merely his means, his strategy, that was new.[65] To
Leo [66] the most dangerous invasion of his pontificate was not
the army of Hun or Vandal, but the heresy propounded by
Eutyches, a priest of Constantinople.

Arius had said that Christ was a creature whom God had
infused with divinity; Nicæa had answered that Christ was
an emanation or procreation from the Father who had become incarnated; Nestorius had taught that the Christ who
was born of the Virgin was at that moment wholly man, being
later somehow conjoined with Christ the God. As Arius was
condemned, so was Nestorius; therefore the only remaining
question was, what did Nicæa actually declare? That Christ
was certainly wholly a God, Nicæa, in refuting Arius, had
made very clear; but Nicæa had made it much less clear how
far Christ was also a man. It was this doubt which Eutyches
was now determined to resolve. He said that since Nicæa
defined Christ as of the essence of and co-substantial with the
Father, this could only mean that He was not, and so never
became, of the essence of and co-substantial with man. For
even if one might conceive that He could, by some miracle, be
equally both at once, it was clear from the language of Nicæa
that whereas the completeness of His divinity was made emphatic and categorical the degree of His humanity was left
quite vague. He merely ' made Himself man '. Doubtless if
Nicæa had expressly said that His divinity and humanity were
absolutely equal because both were absolutely complete, Eutyches must have accepted the paradox, but, so long as it was
possible not to suppose this, he thought it more prudent to

[65] Leo's view in this matter is
analogous to that of his contemporary, bishop Maximus of Turin: see
p. 281.

[66] 114 of Leo's 173 letters are concerned with this Christological problem: Caspar 1930 I 462. Cf. Hodgkin
1896 III 2 125.

cling to the rational by assuming that this humanity was partial, applying rather to the body than to the soul. Thus to Eutyches the Christ of Nicæa was a divine soul clothed, or incarnated, in a human body.[67] Consequently it was actually a God who was crucified,[68] a God who was temporarily so disguised that although His form was human His essence remained divine.[69] All of which unfortunately suggested that the Passion was something of a fraud. Now this might be a not irrational gloss on Nicæa; the trouble was that it was a narrow gloss. For on what was Nicæa based if not on the biblical revelation? And, since this was so, it was clear enough that in order to determine the real meaning of Nicæa it was essential to recall the text of which it was itself no more than a gloss. Now in the Gospels Christ was primarily and above all a man — it was precisely His complete humanity which could not be denied. Therefore Nicæa had spoken only in order to affirm Christ's complete divinity and it had chosen to emphasize that, rather than the human, completeness for the simple reason that Arius, whom it was refuting, had already emphasized the opposite. In other words there had, at that time, been no need of a learned Council of theologians in order to assert Christ's humanity — of this the most humble reader of the Gospels was already fully aware.[70] The need had rather been to indicate how, in spite of His humanity, Christ had been none the less also completely a God. Eutyches evidently had a legalistic mind — one which was more stubborn than elastic; as though words were themselves a truth and not its mere ungainly symbols.

The problem raised was therefore one characteristic of this age: of the degree to which ossification may safely be carried. The Gospel doctrine could only be extracted from vivid texts describing the life of a real being; the Nicene Creed was a dry definition in arbitrary words. A living story is easily felt but not easily dissected; a definition, because it is itself a dissection, can be more easily explained than felt or understood. Nicæa, being a revulsion against Arius, diverged too much from Arius; Nestorius, moved by a revul-

---

67 Duchesne 1911 III⁴ 398.
68 Ibid. 400. Cf. ibid. 1925 IV 71.
69 Leo Letter # 28 (the Tome) § 2, & # 59 § 1.

70 Cf. Ambrose Explan. in Psalmorum XII # 61 § 5.

sion against Nicæa, swung back too far towards Arius; now
Eutyches, turning against Nestorius, forced the meaning of
Nicæa. Thus each step was a reaction against the one im-
mediately preceding, so that each — though in an ever di-
minishing degree — rather exploited than illuminated the
Gospel text.

As in 448 the storm broke, appeals from the East poured
in on Leo.[71] Surely because Nestorius was wrong it did not
follow that Eutyches was right. What was Leo's own interpretation of the Nicene Creed? In his famous letter to
bishop Flavian of Constantinople — known as the *Tome* [72] —
he gave his answer. But it was not at all a dissection of the
language, not at all a gloss — which is curious, because Leo,
following the example of his predecessors, usually emphasized
that the text of the Creed was for ever binding and unamendable, whether by Pope or even General Council, and
furthermore that he, as Pope, alone possessed a divine knowledge of what Nicæa meant and was therefore alone qualified
to declare its true meaning. Yet in this *Tome* there is hardly
a reference to Nicæa — hardly a word about the text which
he interprets! Was this because, being inspired by Peter, he
could afford to dispense with it? Or was it because the Creed
lent rather more support to the doctrine of Eutyches than
Leo cared to admit? For both reasons no doubt. But there
was still another reason for the omission: Leo was a Latin, a
Tuscan, a Roman of the old race; he therefore saw things
humanly rather than metaphysically. It was not that he
was, like Pope Celestine, really ignorant of the implications
and technique of Greek philosophy; [73] it was rather that to
him Christ's revelation was of something quite different from
philosophy. He realized that the true Christ was to be far
more adequately comprehended by a humble reading of the
Gospels than by any concoction of dialectic subtleties. Consequently, as the official exponent of what the Nicene Creed
really meant, he dared to look behind its text to the text of
which it was no more than a gloss. In other words, quite
like Augustine, Leo chose his arguments neither from the

[71] Caspar 1930 I 469 & 474.
[72] On the extent of his divergence
from Cyril of Alexandria see Duchesne 1911 III 4 443–45, 451, & 455–

57. A text with parallel English
translation is in *Texts for Students*
29 (London S.P.C.K. 1923).
[73] See p. 582 n. 47.

Fathers nor from the canons, but, quite simply, from the Gospels.

Yet again, even here, because Leo was writing to refute Eutyches, the Gospels were rather exploited than expounded — the emphasis was now chiefly on Christ's manhood [74] because Eutyches had slighted it. Thus to Leo the incarnated Christ became — except for His mortality [75] — another innocent Adam.[76] Just as Adam had it in his power to sin or not to sin, so had Christ; and it was only because Adam did in fact sin and Christ in fact did not that they were counterparts and not repetitions of each other. Above all did Leo insist that not only was Christ's body human in essence as well as in form, but that His soul, too, was completely human.[77] To Leo this Eutychian conception of a human disguise [78] was no other than that of the brazen Manichee.[79] Christ, therefore, was subject not only to hunger, exhaustion, and pain,[80] which are bodily infirmities, but also to sorrow — so that He could 'weep for a dead friend' [81] — and even to humility,[82] both of which are emotions of the soul. Yet He was also — because of the duality of His nature — no less a God. Just as a soul and a body, each of a different nature, are joined in a single person, so in Christ His divine and human natures were so joined.[83] In the *Tome* he says:

The property of each nature and substance remaining, therefore, unimpaired and coming together in one Person, humility was assumed by majesty, weakness by power, mortality by eternity. . . . Thus, in the whole and perfect nature of very man, very God was born — complete in what belonged to Him, complete in what belonged to us. . . .[84]

To hunger, to thirst, to be weary and to sleep, is obviously human; but with five loaves to satisfy five thousand people . . . to walk upon the surface of the sea with feet that do not sink, and to calm the rising waves by rebuking the tempest, is without question divine. As, therefore . . . it does not belong to the same

---

[74] Nestorius, now in exile, declared that the *Tome's* acceptance at Chalcedon had vindicated him: Duchesne 1911 III⁴ 448–49; and bishop Dioscorus of Alexandria had excommunicated Leo in 449 on the ground that his *Tome* was Nestorian: ibid. 477.

[75] See *Letter* # 28 (the *Tome*) § 3. Contrast the predestination view of Augustine: p. 398 n. 51.

[76] *Letter* # 59 § 4.
[77] *Letter* # 35 § 3.
[78] Ibid. § 1.
[79] *Letter* # 15 § 5.
[80] *Tome* § 4.
[81] Ibid.
[82] Ibid. § 3.
[83] *Letter* # 35 § 3.
[84] *Tome* § 3.

nature to weep for a dead friend with emotions of pity, and to recall the same friend from the dead with a word of power . . . so it does not belong to the same nature to say *I and my Father are one,* and to say *My Father is greater than I.*[85]

What are we to make of this apparent confusion, in which Leo, like Augustine before him, leaps cheerfully into the jaws of paradox? Was he not simply cutting the Gordian knot? To the Greeks one thing could not ever be two different things at the same time. Christ might be half divine and half human, or divine at one time and human at another; but He could be two things at once only by ceasing to be one thing. This was sound philosophy no doubt, but the Greeks forgot that Christianity was, among other things, a deliberate denial of the validity of even sound philosophy, and forgot that the Gospels, in describing Christ, made such a denial inevitable. That the Christ of the Gospels appeared to defy logic [86] the Greeks knew well enough, and yet, instead of humbly accepting this as a revelation of the futility of human ratiocination, they struggled by cunning subterfuge to evade it.[87] And, how, moreover, could they expound their faith, how argue others into a conviction of its truth, if it in fact denied that logic on which most men fancy they must rely? It was one thing to swallow one's pride as an individual; quite another to swallow it as a rational human being. But the Fathers, and Augustine especially, had taught Leo this generic humility, this mortification of the whole human race, this inherent incapacity of man to teach himself; had shown how man must instead be taught and, having been taught, must believe and not try to improve on that teaching.[88]

Thus was the Greek of the fifth century like the medieval scholastic: both unweaned from the logic of Aristotle, both clinging to the pagan delusion that in order to be true a thing must be consistent. Truly a very fine, a very masculine conceit; but not good theology. For religion presumes a God

---

[85] *Tome* § 4. And cf. *Letters* # 59 § 5, & # 124 § 5.
[86] Caspar 1930 I 478–79 falls into the same pit that the Greeks had, saying that the *Tome* solved none of the complexities raised by the subtle minds of the East. But Leo did not try to solve them dialectically.

[87] Ibid. 480–81.
[88] Leo might well have argued that whereas logic was an innate human capacity, intuition was an infused grace.

who can do miracles — things surpassing the very capacity
of man's understanding. This God must, therefore, by His
very definition, be chronically defying the laws of logic. To
the Greek too, God could raise the dead because Aristotle had
never denied the logic of it; but God could not make one
thing two things or two things one because Aristotle had
proved that this was impossible. It is commonly alleged [89]
that it was Descartes who first, by repudiating Aristotle, recognized that God's power must necessarily transcend the laws of
human logic. Perhaps Descartes was the first philosopher so
to emancipate himself, but he was hardly the first man. For
every simplest Christian from Peter down had weaned himself
of this delusion, and nowhere is logic defied so lucidly and
convincingly as in this *Tome* of Peter's heir.

A man can have faith in a paradox, moreover, only if he
has reason to think it true: that Christ, because of His complete human nature, had, in contrast to the Father, the freedom to sin, surely was paradoxical; but was it equally so that
He could weep, grieve, suffer, and finally die in agony at the
hand of His creatures? To the Eutychians, as to the Neoplatonists and Manichees, these very capacities must be in
derogation of His dignity. Doubtless they thought that so
anthropomorphic a God was the dream of simple men who
wanted their God, like their friends, to resemble themselves.
They could not conceive, as Leo could, that grief and suffering, although alien to the traditional nature of divinity and
inherent in the nature of man, might be experienced by a
God without impairing His dignity. Yet it was the teaching
of Christ that, although man was in no sense a God, the true
God combined the traditional attribute of dignity with the
unfamiliar attribute of grief; that man must therefore aspire
to God, by cultivating, not divine majesty, but human humility. Christ's two natures, upon which Leo so insisted,
were those of the conventional God and the conventional
man, and His single Person was the unconventional God.
The Man of Sorrows conquered the Roman world, not by
raising men up, but by bringing God down. The Eutychian
was not a Neoplatonist or Manichee, because he did not believe that the human soul was divine; but neither was he

[89] See Gilson 1913 14-32.

truly a Christian, because he still did believe, like his pagan ancestors, that a God was one who could not suffer.

It was in order to expose this error of Eutyches and bring about his condemnation that Leo had written his *Tome*. The Emperor, however, paid it not the slightest attention, but instead summoned a General Council — known as the Robber Council — to meet at Ephesus in 449 for the express purpose of clearing Eutyches, and he managed its proceedings with so high a hand that the assembled bishops had no alternative but to accede.[90]   Leo had sent legates to this Council, but these, especially as they knew no Greek, made no impression.[91] Even their modest demand that the *Tome* be read aloud had been refused — on the pretext that Leo had admitted his bias [92] in the case.   Upon being informed of these arbitrary proceedings, Leo wrote again, begging this time, not for a blind acceptance of the doctrine of the *Tome,* but for some compromise doctrine upon which all parties could agree.[93] Rome's was still the only authoritative judgment; but Rome was nevertheless willing, in forming her final judgment, to give due consideration to the public opinion of the whole Church.   Mindful still of Augustine and of the Roman tradition of statesmanship, Leo chose to pose rather as an indulgent than as an arbitrary despot.

He did demand, however, that the new General Council, which must be at once convoked in order to correct the error committed at Ephesus, should be held, not in the East, but in Rome, as Nicæa had prescribed.[94]   To what **canon of** Nicæa does he refer?   To none other than the notorious canon of Sardica which Zosimus and Celestine had cited to the Africans and whose unauthenticity the Africans had exposed.[95]   That the noble Leo could casually cite this discredited text is the best possible evidence that the Popes of this time could do this sort of thing with a clear conscience. For the Africans' exposure of this so-called Nicene canon occurred only in 423, or seven years before Leo became a power

90 Caspar 1930 I 473.
91 Ibid. 486–87.
92 Ibid. 485–86.
93 Haller 1934 I 166–67.
94 He did not press this demand, however, when Theodosius II in-
sisted that since it was an Eastern controversy it should be settled there: Batiffol 1924 2 520–25; Caspar 1930 I 493–94 & 510–11.
95 Caspar 1930 I 496; Haller 1934 I 165.

in the papal curia. That he was ignorant of this exposure is therefore inconceivable. Evidently Leo regarded this Sardican canon as a valuable emendation of Nicæa because it threw a new and welcome light on the real — though unexpressed — intent of the Nicene bishops. That the Africans had declared it an impertinent variation of Nicæa merely indicated, thought Leo, that they were either ignorant of the extent of Rome's prestige in 325 or jealous of her present prestige. For he thought that to deny Nicæa's recognition of papal sovereignty was virtually to deny that sovereignty.

Before the East had time to consider Leo's suggestions the complexion of affairs suddenly changed. In the year 450 the court of the Western Emperor moved from Ravenna to Rome [96] and Theodosius II, the Eastern Emperor, died. From this moment the West embraced the cause of Leo with enthusiasm, and the East, now in the control of Pulcheria, sister of Theodosius II, did no less.[97] Consequently a General Council was called, although at Chalcedon near Constantinople rather than at Rome, with the avowed purpose of upsetting the decision of Ephesus and condemning Eutyches. Leo's doctrine thereby became the official imperial doctrine; for the moment his will became the law.

Many of the bishops assembled at Chalcedon favoured Eutyches; many favoured Leo; but the majority apparently favoured a middle view which closely resembled that presented by Cyril of Alexandria at the condemnation of Nestorius in 431.[98] Claiming — and not without some reason — to be the most conscientious interpretation of the language of the Nicene Creed, this view, called the Monophysite, while it recognized, as Eutyches did not, that the incarnated Christ was completely human as well as completely divine, alleged that His nature was none the less single.[99] Presumably unwilling to accept the paradox of a single whole containing two wholes, these Monophysites were driven to conceive of the Incarnation somewhat after the manner of Athanasius and Gregory of Nyssa: [100] as having divinized human nature

[96] Haller 1934 I 166.

[97] Duchesne 1911 III 4 424–25; Caspar 1930 I 504–06.

[98] Duchesne 1911 III 4 375 says that Cyril did not quite say what he meant. But would not this be difficult to prove?

[99] Ibid. 457, & 1926 IV 18 n. 1.

[100] See pp. 56 n. 31, & 87 n. 34.

through the magical identification, in Christ, of what had, after the Fall, been two natures. They did not say that the human soul had thereby become indistinguishable from God — this would have been crass Neoplatonism or Manichæism — but they were inclined to think that through the Incarnation human nature became potentially virtuous again — as it had been in the first Adam. And could they not argue that the Virgin's sinlessness was prophetic proof of this?

This Monophysite view tallies closely with the Pelagian view which the East had countenanced a generation earlier. For, if Christ's complete human and complete divine natures were one, human and divine nature must be identical. And since divine nature cannot have been debased human nature must have been ennobled. Man never had, presumably never could, attain a divine perfection on earth, but his failure was henceforth due, not to defect of nature, but to defect of will. Now of this view Augustine's was the antithesis, and on the side of Augustine were all those, whether Ambrosian or Semi-Pelagian, who thought an arbitrary grace indispensable to any substantial degree of human virtue. To Augustine the Incarnation symbolically taught man the love that united divine strength with human weakness — a purely spiritual relationship, marvellous precisely because it was the antithesis of the natural relationship. To him the Incarnation was a union of opposites, not a transmutation producing an identity. Technically Leo probably inclined to the view of Ambrose rather than to that of Augustine, but the Monophysites seemed to be lending countenance to a view which the whole West had bitterly condemned. That Leo so obstinately resisted the Monophysites, therefore, is not to be explained by political reasons. He was fighting for his own personal faith.

Just as in 449 Theodosius II had forced the Council of Ephesus to acquit Eutyches, so Pulcheria in 451 forced the Council of Chalcedon to condemn him.[101] What the decision would have been had no imperial pressure been exerted we cannot tell. But we do know that a compromise was suggested whereby Leo's words ' one person in two natures ' should be amended to read ' one person out of two natures '.[102]

[101] Duchesne 1911 III⁴ 455–56 &   [102] Haller 1934 I 174–75.
464; Caspar 1930 I 509–11.

In spite of the implication here that Christ embodied a single nature composed of two natures it is recorded that Leo's legates were ready to make this concession. Pulcheria, however, would not hear of it: Leo's opinion as expounded in the *Tome* was to be the criterion of orthodoxy and she would tolerate no juggling with that opinion. The only task left to the Council was to paraphrase it in the form of a succinct Creed. It was therefore decreed that, following Leo's gloss on Nicæa,[103]

we believe in Christ, Son, Lord, Monogenous, in two natures, without confusion or change, without division or separation, the differences in the natures being in no wise eliminated by their union, each nature on the contrary preserving its particularity, but both co-operating to form a single person, a single hypostasis.[104]

The decision of Chalcedon had certainly been forced; but because it had not been scandalously forced, because these Eastern bishops knew they were approving a view unanimously held in the West, the triumph of Leo was real and even momentous. On that day papal supremacy over East as well as West was first successfully asserted. A disquieting incident now occurred, however, which indicated that the East was not ready to follow Leo indiscriminately. For when the regular session had been dissolved and the papal legates had retired, the Council re-convened, and decreed a 28th canon providing that, subject to papal ratification,[105] the see of Constantinople be qualified to hear all appeals of the East just as Rome might hear all appeals of the West.[106] Although this had been hinted at by canon 3 of the Council of Constantinople of 381,[107] and also accorded with recent practice,[108] it contradicted not only earlier practice but also the sixth canon of Nicæa — which did not even mention Constantinople. If the Greeks thought that Leo, elated by his triumph in dogma, would good humouredly ratify this amendment to Nicæa in a matter of discipline, they were quickly disabused: for Leo flatly refused his ratification, and

[103] Batiffol 1924 2 545; Caspar 1930 I 517–18.
[104] As quoted in Duchesne 1911 III 4 442. Leo acknowledged its accuracy: ibid. 464.

[105] Caspar 1930 I 530.
[106] Batiffol 1924 2 554–57; Caspar 1930 I 521–22.
[107] See p. 550 n. 31.
[108] Caspar 1930 I 524–29.

his reason was the same as that given by Innocent nearly fifty years before — Nicæa was unamendable because infallible:

Let no synodal Councils flatter themselves on the size of their assemblies, and let not any number of priests, however much larger, dare either to compare or to prefer themselves to those 318 bishops; for the synod of Nicæa is hallowed by God with such privilege that, whether supported by fewer or more ecclesiastical judgments, whatever is opposed to their authority is utterly destitute of authority.[109]

That Leo, having employed a canon of Sardica as if a canon of Nicæa in order to enhance the power of Rome, could now smugly say that the canons of Nicæa were inviolable, shocks us hardly less than his greatness disarms us. And yet, unfair as this may seem — that Rome might amend Nicæa but that Constantinople might not, that Rome might do this covertly whereas Constantinople might not do it openly — Leo's motive, however indelicate, was not ignoble. Leo was God's servant, to do His will on earth. He took it to be God's will that the true faith become the universal faith, and rightly inferred that a centralization of power in Rome under the ægis of Nicæa was the only practicable road to such a universal faith. To our modern consciences it is shocking to impose faith by violence — yet even Augustine succumbed to this temptation. And, if one may properly force a faith out of a reluctant people, may one not also force a meaning out of a reluctant document? Once we grant the principle that it is proper to compromise with the world, we must harden ourselves to whatever compromises the world demands. For it is only in the temporal vacuum of renunciation that reality gives way to conscience. Between the martyr who dies true to his conscience and the ruler who lives true to the outer world there lies an infinite variety of compromises in which the conscience has much free play. But a ruler, if he is to rule, must obey the laws that govern rule. He is a martyr too, perhaps, of a kind: risking, not his earthly, but his eternal life for a cause he deems true. Herein lies the anomaly, not of Leo only, but of the whole Church militant.

If Leo's conscience was clear, that of the Greeks was not:

[109] *Letter* # 106 § 2. Duchesne 1911 III ⁴ 464–65 says that should Leo admit this principle it might not illogically be inferred that Ravenna might come to outrank Rome.

realizing that they had consented to their own defeat they soon became resentful. For the majority of them believed that this Creed of Chalcedon had distorted the true meaning of Nicæa, and the Council had hardly been dissolved when the air was filled again with mutual recriminations. At first Constantinople railed at Rome for not ratifying the canon authorizing her to hear all appeals of the East. When, two years later, Leo found it discreet virtually to ratify this canon,[110] the rest of the East began to rail at Constantinople for acceding to the demands of Pulcheria and Leo. Cyril and Nicæa, they protested, had been betrayed. Pulcheria died in 453, but so long as her husband, the Emperor Marcian, lived, disorder was repressed. Upon his death in 457, however, Leo the Isaurian became Emperor, and this was the signal for an uprising of Monophysites which attained great violence. In Alexandria, Jerusalem, and elsewhere they broke into open rebellion and were suppressed by the imperial troops only after much bloodshed. It is said that in Egypt in 458 ten thousand persons were slaughtered in a single battle, and that most of them were monks fighting in the cause of Cyril.[111] So serious was the turn of affairs [112] that in this same year Leo wrote a long theological letter which, omitting all mention of 'two natures' and speaking instead of 'two qualities', was a clear invitation to a compromise.[113] Nothing had been done, however, when, three years later, Leo died, happy to see the Roman papacy more powerful and respected than she ever previously had been, yet haunted by the knowledge that the real struggle to subdue the East had only begun.

In Leo existed the most perfect fusion of Christian and Roman, of the man of God and the man of the world. As a Christian he despised worldly aims, yet as a Roman he believed that this very unworldliness must lend a new vigour to the earthly life of the Empire. Through the regeneration of the individual will come that of the State.[114] But, be-

[110] Haller 1934 I 181–82.
[111] Duchesne 1911 III⁴ 474–80 & 485.
[112] Batiffol 1924² 583–89 & 618; Caspar 1930 I 547–55.
[113] Duchesne 1911 III⁴ 484; Haller 1934 I 184.
[114] Haller 1934 I 187.

cause this victory must be won, not by cunning or force of arms, but by an increase in faith, in virtue, in renunciation, the cult of weakness is declared to be the new strategy.[115] The Romans have only to exceed other men in meekness and the world will be restored to them. For they are the Chosen People of the New Testament. It is precisely the strategy which was at this moment being advocated in Gaul and Turin by Leo's contemporaries Salvian [116] and Maximus.[117]

Yet because there must be renunciation, because there must above all be fasting, in order to purify ' the reasoning soul ', there was no need of squalor:

For wealth, after its kind and regarded as a means, is good, and is of the greatest advantage to human society provided it is in the hands of the benevolent and open-handed.[118]

And Leo supports the best tradition of Augustinian modera-tion where he says:

We do not bid or advise you to despise God's works or to think there is anything opposed to your faith in what the good God has made good, but to use every kind of creature and the whole furni-ture of this world reasonably and moderately.[119]

The physical world was created by God for the express pur-pose of helping and consoling, even of delighting men. If they will only show their good will its blessings will follow. But if, like Salvian, Leo believed that earthly blessings are be-stowed as a reward of good behaviour,[120] he is, unlike Salvian, full of confidence that the increase in virtue has already taken place and is already reaping the promised reward. For gradu-ally, since the Redemption,

sinfulness returns to innocence and the old nature becomes new; strangers receive adoption and outsiders enter upon an inher-itance. The ungodly begin to be righteous, the miserly benevo-lent, the incontinent chaste, the earthly heavenly.[121]

And he speaks confidently of

[115] Leo *Sermon* # 78 § 1.
[116] See p. 373 n. 3.
[117] See pp. 279–81.
[118] *Sermon* # 10 § 1, quoted p. 371 n. 15.

[119] *Sermon* # 27 § 6, quoted p. 379 n. 18.
[120] See pp. 352–53.
[121] Ibid. § 2, quoted p. 352 n. 86.

these days, in which war is proclaimed against vices, and progress is made in all virtues.[122]

Nor did this optimism ever wholly fail him for, as Genseric departed after the terrible sack of Rome in 455, Leo had defiantly exclaimed,

Who was it that restored this city to safety; that rescued it from captivity; the games of the circus-goers or the care of the saints? [123]

To Leo, indeed, the Redemption was the specific redemption of the Roman people and Roman State; [124] set-backs there had been and would be, but the worst was over provided men clung to and lived by the true faith.   Governed once more by the city as in the great days of the past, a new Roman virtue must triumph, for God had willed it so.   And here, but with a fresh serenity and optimism, Leo echoes the theme of Augustine's *City of God:* Rome had unified the civilized world in order to prepare the diffusion of Christianity; [125] as Nero, no less than Peter, had been a tool in the hand of God,[126] so had Cæsar been, no less than Leo now was.   Each, in conquering, had been guided by God's will, and the means employed in both conquests were God's own means.   And, just as the invasions of Attila and Genseric were caused wholly by God, so were the heresies of Cyril and Eutyches — that out of their errors the truth might be more clearly seen [127] and faith in that truth consolidated.[128]   Man might become a free agent to rule himself, but in any effort he might make to rule others he was a blind agent.

This sense of man's impotence to affect the course of earthly life — except indirectly by adding to the sum total of human virtue — produced a philosophy of history which, even if hypothetical, stirred the human mind to concentrate on the great problem of order in time.[129]   But the idea of man's impotence in the face of nature yielded less happy results when applied to natural science.   Thus Leo believed, for instance, that the moon and sun

---

122 *Sermon* # 40 § 2, quoted p. 352.
123 Ibid. # 84 § 1, quoted pp. 352, 447, & 514.
124 See Haller 1934 I 187.
125 *Sermon* # 82 § 2.

126 Ibid. §§ 3–6.
127 *Letter* # 129, quoting I *Corinthians* xi 19.
128 *Letter* # 104.
129 Out of Bossuet (1627–   ), who

were fashioned for the convenience of man, in order that he who is an animal endowed with reason might be sure of the distinction of the months, the recurrence of the year.[130]

Yet surely there were still many in Leo's day who knew that the moon and sun were themselves the cause of month and year. Nor was Leo less innocent in his explanation of sickness. Those, he says, who profess to cure the sick man are agents, although often deluded agents, of the devil.[131] Since sickness is, like the political tyrant, a visitation of God's wrath, the physician is as unwelcome as the assassin. Galen would have been less shocked than surprised at being coupled with Brutus, but he would have been more shocked than surprised at being coupled with Satan.

Leo disliked natural science even more than had Augustine. But this was a Roman rather than a specifically Christian deficiency. For the only scientific concern of their day was with astrology — that dreariest and most vain of curiosities. If that bastard art was the best that the fifth century could offer, sensible men may well be excused because they turned their attention elsewhere. Just now the clear task was to save Roman civilization — a last and desperate chance — and if the Christians were in error in staking all on the faith that virtue, and virtue alone, could save it, their theory was at least a noble and generous one, inducing a strategy which, although it proved insufficient to save the Roman State, did prove sufficient to save for posterity much of the Roman way of life. For Christianity, and Catholicism especially, was a Roman thing, and this lived on.

All that was now being revealed to these men, by their reading, meditation, and prayer, was not entirely new — nothing is ever that. But the angle from which the old things were now seen was new, and new too was the cogency with which they were comprehended and experienced. In one of Leo's Sermons we read that

the vice of pride is a near neighbour to good deeds, and, hard by virtue, arrogance lies ever in wait. For it is hard for him who lives praiseworthily not to be caught by men's praise.[132]

---

relied on Augustine, came Leibnitz (1646–), Buffon (1705–) and so Lamarck (1744–).

[130] *Sermon* # 27 § 5.
[131] *Sermon* # 3.
[132] *Sermon* # 42 § 3.

The pride so admired by the Stoics had certainly been the butt of pagan sarcasm long before it became known as the sin of Satan, but no pagan ever handled it with the deftness and firmness of an Augustine or a Leo. Nor had there been any pagans — except irresponsible wits — who would have observed, as Leo did quite simply, that

he who glories in the wealth of others is not put to shame by his own poverty.[133]

And no pagan could have said of the poor:

Use loving care and watchfulness in order that we may find him whom modesty conceals and shamefastness keeps back. For there are those who blush to ask openly for what they want and prefer to suffer privation without speaking rather than to be put to shame by a public appeal.[134]

Here already old Rome fades; and, as we read on, she vanishes completely:

and there is nothing more effective, dearly beloved, against the devil's wiles, than kindly mercy and bounteous charity, by which every other sin is either avoided or vanquished.[135]

What wonder that to this new man, to this new City, every Roman turned, in the hope of a new world, a new life!

F. MONOPHYSITES AND FELIX, 461–492

Italy was now suffering acutely from anæmia. Long artificially nourished by the tribute of her provinces, she had become utterly dependent on that tribute. When Diocletian transferred the capital of the Empire to Nicomedia in 284 he also diverted much of the Egyptian grain from Rome to his new city. The economic decline of Italy in the fourth century may have been as much due to imperial neglect as to any internal disease. Agriculturally she had never been able to support the great numbers of aliens who had seeped into

---

[133] *Sermon* # 88 § 4.   [135] *Sermon* # 74 § 5.
[134] *Sermon* # 9 § 3.

Rome, but only when the artificial support began to be with-drawn was this inability apparent.   The civil wars of the fourth century added to her troubles and Alaric's invasion dealt a further most inopportune blow; but the first mortal wound was given by the Vandals when in 439 they overran Proconsular Africa and took Carthage.   With this came con-trol of the sea and thus the end of all grain shipments from Africa to Italy,[1] and this control also enabled them to capture Sicily and Sardinia [2] and threaten the whole sea coast of southern Italy.   On top of these disasters came the destruc-tion of the great city of Aquileia by Attila in 452 [3] and the sack of Rome by the Vandal Genseric in 455.   Italy then gave up the struggle, allowing the barbarian Ricimer, an Arian [4] half Sueve and half Visigoth,[5] to become military dictator.   Contenting himself with the title Patrician,[6] he set up phantom Emperors in order to soothe Roman sensi-bilities and to save himself the drudgery and embarrassment of playing the imperial role.   He governed well and loyally enough: fought off the Vandal raiders,[7] curbed tax extortion,[8] halted the pillaging of public buildings,[9] respected the Church.   But he was quite unqualified to stem the tide of destructive forces and make provision for the future; con-sequently when he died in 472 there followed only an aggra-vation of anarchy.

In the year 476 the Patrician was Orestes, a Roman; the Emperor was his small son, Romulus Augustulus.   But no longer now could any Roman rule with barbarian soldiers. One day these confronted Orestes, demanding one third of the lands of Italy.[10]   When he refused they mutinied under the leadership of the Scyrian [11] Odoacer, leaving Orestes with only a handful of loyal Romans; [12] after offering a brief re-sistance he was taken and murdered, and his child Romulus Augustulus deposed and exiled in Campania.   The western

[1] Duchesne 1911 III [4] 627.
[2] Salvian *D.G.D.* VI § 68; & Hodg-kin 1892 II [2] 253–55.
[3] Hodgkin 1892 II [2] 147–60.
[4] Duchesne 1911 III [4] 478.
[5] Hodgkin 1892 II [2] 389–91.
[6] Ibid. 401.
[7] Ibid. 389, 400, 405, 426–27 & 441.
[8] Ibid. 421–24.
[9] Ibid. 424–25.

[10] Ibid. II [2] 519, & III [2] 123; Hart-mann 1923 I [2] 51–52. The barbarian *foederati* of the Romans had usually received one third of the shelter and yield of the land in the territories as-signed to them, so that this demand of 476 was natural enough: Hart-mann 1923 I [2] 28.
[11] Hartmann 1923 I [2] 51.
[12] Hodgkin 1892 II [2] 521.

half of the Empire, created by Diocletian in 285, thereby ceased to be.

Probably Odoacer commanded hardly more soldiers than were needed to garrison a few cities at strategic points — particularly Milan, Verona,[13] and Ravenna.[14]   Rome was apparently not even worth watching. Odoacer did not presume to pose as an independent sovereign; all he asked was that, in return for his recognition of Zeno as universal Emperor, Zeno would bestow on him the title of Patrician, which gave him the civil as well as the military authority under the Emperor.[15]   Only after the death of the exiled Emperor Nepos four years later did Zeno accede.[16]

Odoacer ruled Italy for fourteen years, ruled it rather after the manner of Ricimer. Also an Arian [17] and a barbarian, he nevertheless left the Romans undisturbed in the civil offices and other occupations. Probably the burden of taxation was lightened: this had been true of the analogous occupations in Gaul and Spain, and it was made the easier because the imperial court had been wiped out and frugal ways of living were the fashion among both the honest barbarians and the honest Christians. Odoacer was at least very ready to grant exemptions from taxation to territories suffering exceptional distress.[18]   He also regained Dalmatia [19] which had slipped off into independence a few years earlier, and, best of all, by negotiation, regained Sicily.[20]   Odoacer doubtless did the best he could; nevertheless his regime, like that of Ricimer, remained of that purely negative kind which nature, in her need for a minimum of law and order, herself provides: the present is rendered tolerable; the future is left to shift for itself.

With these disturbing upheavals the papacy seems to have been curiously unconcerned. The papal records are now unusually scant; nevertheless it is remarkable that there is hardly a reference to the political events of Italy. Evidently it was no empty assurance given by earlier Popes and other leaders

13 Lot 1927 279.
14 Hartmann 1923 I 2 56 & 93–94.
15 Ibid. 52–55.
16 Hodgkin 1896 III 2 129.
17 Ibid. 1892 II 2 515.

18 Ennodius *Life of Epiphanius* (*C.S.E.L.* 6 358).
19 Hartmann 1923 I 2 57.
20 Ibid. 56.

like Ambrose that if the State would keep its hands off spiritual affairs the Church would not meddle in temporal. The
Pope after Leo was Hilary. He reiterated the qualifications
imposed on episcopal aspirants: if they were uneducated or
had ever undergone penance they could not qualify — no
matter how anxiously a diocese might want them.[21] Hilary
also forbad again that any bishop name his own successor.[22]
But on the whole his pontificate was very uneventful. Seven
years later Simplicius followed him. For the first seven years
of this pontificate there are almost no records; [23] then, in the
year 474, the Monophysite heresy burst out again in the East,
forcing the papacy to fight for its life.

Twenty-three years had passed since Chalcedon; yet the
party hostile to it — which Pope Leo had tried to humour
— had lost none of its determination, was still watching for
a chance to renew the combat. The death of the Emperor
Leo in 474 [24] gave it the desired opportunity. His successor, Zeno, was quickly overthrown by the usurper Basiliscus
who, in order to maintain himself, curried favour with the
Monophysites.[25] In the year 475 a formal document repudiating the creed of Chalcedon was meekly signed by no fewer
than six hundred bishops.[26] This trick of Basiliscus, however, probably alienated more people than it conciliated; at
any rate Zeno came back at once to turn him out, whereupon
the same six hundred bishops now obligingly signed an
equally formal document of adherence to Chalcedon.[27]

That Pope Simplicius should have been perturbed by this
display of either cowardice or venality was only natural. His
letters to Zeno and the Patriarch of Constantinople, Acacius,
became abundant and fervid: if these two would only stand
their ground the crisis could be surmounted.[28] This was all
very well, but Zeno could hardly be expected to view with
equanimity a rebellion which was now seething throughout
Syria, Palestine, and Egypt.[29] He cared little or nothing for
Chalcedon or the Roman papacy. They were worth supporting only so long as this seemed good politics. Being an

21 Langen 1885 122.
22 Caspar 1933 II 13.
23 Langen 1885 127.
24 Duchesne 1911 III 4 487.
25 Ibid. 487–88.

26 Caspar 1933 II 15 says 500.
27 Duchesne 1911 III 4 498–99.
28 Langen 1885 128–36.
29 Caspar 1933 II 15.

Isaurian soldier [30] and therefore primarily a man of action,
it must at times have seemed to him that all his subjects were
theologians. His task was to determine how he could best
quiet them, and then proceed accordingly. At least he was
deliberate enough: for the next six years he temporized.
Then, in 482,[31] the situation became intolerable [32] and he decided to act. The result was the publication under his signature of a letter to the bishop of Alexandria, known as the
Henotikon, propounding a compromise view calculated to
appeal to the moderates of both the Chalcedon and Monophysite parties.[33] Probably the real author was Acacius the
patriarch; [34] at all events Acacius lent it his support, thereby
reversing himself and repudiating Chalcedon. To be sure
this *Henotikon* mentioned neither Chalcedon nor Leo and
his *Tome,* and it explicitly condemned the doctrines of both
Nestorius and Eutyches.[35] On the other hand it did declare,
first that the creeds of Nicæa, Constantinople (381), and
Ephesus (431), were each authoritative; [36] secondly, that Mary
actually was the Mother of God; and, thirdly, that the incarnated Son of God was a One and that in His humanity He
was co-substantial with all other men. All idea of division,
confusion, or appearance must therefore be discarded.

Intrinsically this *Henotikon* was vague enough to pass as
innocuous, but practically it served — and intentionally — to
repudiate Chalcedon and hence Leo's Christ-in-two-natures.[37]
Yet, although it went far enough to anger the adherents of
Chalcedon and Rome, it did not go far enough to appease
the Monophysites. This party wanted nothing less than a
categorical declaration that Chalcedon had adopted the doctrine of Nestorius in place of that of Nicæa.[38] Yet these Monophysites did not want a return to the Eutychian view, which
gave Christ a divine soul in a human body. Instead they
argued for the complete identity — in both soul and body
— of both a divine and a human nature.[39] Leo's conception,

30 Duchesne 1911 III 4 486.
31 Ibid. 503 n. 1.
32 Ibid. 500-03. Hordes of Ostrogoths to the north and rebellious
generals within made it imperative to
procure religious peace: Caspar 1933
II 22.
33 Caspar ibid.

34 Duchesne 1911 III 4 500-03.
35 Ibid. 471.
36 Caspar 1933 II 22-23.
37 Duchesne 1911 III 4 503-04; &
cf. ibid. 1925 IV 26 & 30.
38 Ibid. III 4 507-08.
39 Ibid. IV 100.

of two different natures in a single person, was merely paradoxical; but the Monophysite conception, of the complete
identification of the two natures, was less paradoxical than
pagan. For, if Christ had been at the same time both of a
wholly human and of a wholly divine nature, then these natures must be identical: God also a man and man also a
God. To us this can all seem a splitting of hairs unless we
remember that the battle against pagan philosophy which had
been fully won only under the leadership of Augustine, was
essentially a battle to disengage the nature of the human soul
from that of God. Yet, on its face at least, the Monophysite
definition of Christ was a Neoplatonic definition, and Rome
was not reassured by the coincidence that the Monophysite
strength was concentrated in Alexandria, the home of Origen
and Plotinus. And if, at worst, the Monophysite doctrine
was Neoplatonic, at best it was Pelagian: for did not Pelagius
claim that man could, by the intrinsic capacity of his nature,
divest himself of all evil? [40] A Christian did not have to be
an Augustinian in order to believe that the essence of Christ's
revelation was of a love which could bridge two extremes,
two opposites. That Christ had come either to reveal or to
effect a virtual identity could be admitted only by men who
thought God's immense love, grace, and mercy so many mock-
eries to soothe the sentimental. Moreover, if the Redemption had in fact effected all they claimed, why was there still
so much evil in men's hearts? No, the Redemption effected
no magical infusion of the divine nature into the souls of
men; rather it taught men how to see and hate their fallen human nature, in order that they might be wise enough to snatch
at grace when it was offered them. The Monophysites are not
to be blamed for playing with fire — for the subject was infinitely ticklish. But neither is Rome to be blamed, when
she saw they were playing with fire, for begging them, en-
treating them, to desist.

In the following year 483 Simplicius, realizing that his
end was near, persuaded Basilius, the Prætorian Prefect of
Italy, to have a law enacted granting that Prefect a veto power
over papal elections. Simplicius dared not name his own

[40] See p. 410 n. 23.

successor as this was uncanonical, yet he dared not have a free election for fear of *Henotikon* sympathizers. The new Pope must be uncompromising and forceful: let his friend Basilius pick him. No doubt there was already a secret understanding between Basilius and Simplicius as to who was to be picked. Basilius knew well that no opposition need be feared from Odoacer; [41] a Pope eager and willing to champion the independence of Italy and even to impose the will of Italy on the East was the very colleague Odoacer needed. Roman-Italian subservience to the Greek Emperor must eventually lead to barbarian-Italian subservience as well.

That there was an influential *Henotikon* or Greek party in Italy at this time is certain. In fact so keen was the rivalry between the Greek and the Chalcedon parties that Basilius was obliged to re-enforce the laws against the alienation of Church property; apparently it was being illegally sold by both sides in order to raise money for the coming election.[42] We know no details of that election, but we can infer that it was not free and that Basilius, backed by his own law and his own soldiers, chose his own man. For not only was there a suspicious absence of disorder, but the nominee, Felix III, was not the ranking Roman archdeacon, was not even one of the inner group of the papal curia. He was a deacon, but, since he had sons, he must have taken Orders later than was then customary. Furthermore, in contrast to the curia personnel, he was a noble, perhaps of the house of the Anicii.[43] Evidently Basilius, himself an aristocrat,[44] had picked a friend.

It is one of the ironies of history that, at a moment when the old Rome, after all its agonies, now at last appeared to be dead, a Roman noble, as Prætorian Prefect, appears as Italy's executive, and appoints another Roman noble as Pope — a man destined to inaugurate, in the face of apparently insuperable obstacles, a policy which will end in the subjugation of the whole Roman world. That the Prætorian Prefect should have been a noble is not surprising, for the Latin

[41] Cessi 1919 10–11; Caspar 1933 II 23–24.

[42] Hartmann 1923 I 2 56; Duchesne 1925 IV 112; Caspar 1933 II 25.

[43] Cf. Caspar 1933 II 25. It was the family of the pagans Flavian, Probus and Symmachus of before 400: Dill 1906 2 19 & 23. Ambrose was at least a kinsman of Symmachus: Dudden 1935 39.

[44] Caspar 1933 II 24 & 26.

aristocracy had been monopolizing the higher civil offices for many years past.[45] But what suddenly induced Pope Simplicius to break canonical precedent in order to secure a Latin noble as his successor?

The key to the problem must lie in the events of 476 — when the last Western Emperor was whisked away and his place definitely usurped by a barbarian soldier. This Odoacer was recognized by the Emperor Zeno as his legal representative in Italy only in 480 — a scant three years before the bargain struck between Simplicius and Basilius. What must the Latin nobility have thought of this recognition? And what must the Latin Church have thought of it when, only two years later, the *Henotikon* was proclaimed? It must have been obvious then, as it is now, that if Odoacer encountered Latin resistance he must turn to the Greeks for support, and that, in return for that support, he would be asked to provide a Pope favourable to the *Henotikon;* but that if, on the other hand, he received help from the Latins he would gladly join them in defying the Greeks. By opposing Odoacer, therefore, the Latins would be putting both him and themselves at the mercy of the Greeks; by helping him they could save the integrity at once of Chalcedon, of the papacy, and of Italy. In order to achieve this latter purpose, however, a free papal election must be forestalled lest the *Henotikon* party by chance prevail, and a Pope must be chosen who would work hand in glove with the civil authorities. For were the next Pope a man of humble origin he might be intimidated by the East — as Liberius had been [46] — or he might shrink from any alliance with the temporal power. He might even refuse to be courteous to an Arian king. But the alliance of two worldly-wise Latin aristocrats was a fair guarantee of the alliance of Catholic Church and Arian State, and this in turn meant a united Italy which the East was bound to respect.

Is it an anachronism to suggest that patriotism had its part in this affair? The Latin of 483 was certainly readier to die for his faith than for his country — whether this country were the old Empire, the West, Italy, or his native town. But

---

[45] Coster 1935 10; & cf. Hodgkin 1896 III [2] 131-32 & 280-84.   [46] See p. 544 n. 41.

because his patriotism was enfeebled we are not bound to suppose it now negligible. Latin loyalty to the Empire had already weakened before 300; it weakened further after 337, as the Greeks assumed imperial control and Christianity spread. But Latin loyalty to the Latin half and to its smaller units — as to Italy or Rome — fell much less fast. Was the close cooperation between Ambrose of Milan and the Roman Popes a mere coincidence? Was the solidarity of the West under Leo's leadership a matter of chance? If Sidonius could so love his estates, his city Clermont, his province Auvergne, his Gaul, surely other men still shared these very natural sentiments. That the late Romans, although an agricultural people, loved their land so little is marvellous yet true; that they should wholly cease to love it would be a marvel too great to be true. Patriotism, therefore, was surely a motive, not only to the layman Basilius but to the Popes Simplicius and Felix. These Popes cared most to save Chalcedon because they cared most to save truth; but they also cared to save Chalcedon because in doing so they saved Rome too. And if Rome were their heavenly, it was no less their earthly, city, which they loved in part profanely, for its flesh.

Ambrose had issued orders to the Emperor, but he had done this as bishop of the diocese in which the Emperor resided and in a matter more concerned with individual conscience than public policy; [47] Leo had prevailed at Chalcedon, but when he saw danger of a breach with the East his tone became conciliatory; [48] Simplicius had protested against the Emperor's promulgation of the *Henotikon,* but he did nothing more. With the accession of Felix the authoritative voice of Ambrose was heard again,[49] and this time not merely to reprove an act of impetuous violence but to denounce a calculated act of public policy on which the integrity of the Eastern Empire might well depend. For Felix, having summoned bishop Acacius of Constantinople to appear before him in Rome and having received no reply,[50] without further demur declared him and his associates excommunicate [51] — which was a declaration of war against the Eastern State as well as against the Eastern Church.

[47] Caspar 1933 II 25–27.
[48] Ibid. 35–36; & cf. p. 612 n. 113.
[49] Ibid. 35.
[50] Ibid. 29.
[51] Ibid. 32.

On hearing that Felix had excommunicated him, Acacius reciprocated,[52] and the state of war thus begun lasted for the next thirty-five years — until 519. It is usually described as a schism,[53] but Felix would hardly have so described it, for a schism results from a dispute regarding authority and by no stretch of the imagination could it be argued that either the Emperor or the patriarch of Constantinople could repeal the Creed of Chalcedon. Perhaps it did not tally with the Nicene Creed; but Chalcedon had been a General Council — no one disputed that — and it had purported to give Nicæa an official interpretation. Perhaps the bishops at Chalcedon had been wrong, but was it for either the Emperor or his patriarch to judge? Even if the Pope was not qualified to judge, even if Nicæa could not be amended by any subsequent General Council, surely its meaning could be authoritatively interpreted only by another General Council.

Actually there were two issues involved. The first was: who had the authority to decide whether Chalcedon was inconsistent with Nicæa? The second was: who had the authority to decide whether the authority of the one Council or of the other was decisive? The Pope claimed the right to decide both questions, but, as he decided that Chalcedon was not inconsistent with Nicæa, he was able to side-step the embarrassment which the second must cause. The Monophysites and champions of the *Henotikon* claimed that the Pope had no authority to decide the first question, and that on the second Chalcedon must give way to Nicæa. But the weakness of this position was that Nicæa had to be interpreted by someone, and that if neither Chalcedon nor the Pope could do this it must be left either to the Emperor or to each individual. Therefore they were advocating either theocracy or Protestantism.

The folly of the earlier papal argument that Nicæa was unamendable now becomes apparent. For the Monophysites were now alleging that Chalcedon had, however innocently, amended Nicæa, and that such an act, being beyond its powers, was null and void.[54] But what authority did they have to declare that Chalcedon had amended Nicæa? Some power

---

[52] Duchesne 1911 III 4 518.   [54] Ibid. 508.
[53] Ibid. 517.

had to be authorized to declare what Nicæa meant, and this carried with it the additional authority to declare that its own interpretation was correct. Chalcedon therefore did somehow have the right to amend Nicæa, and, if the papacy had the right to ratify Chalcedon, it too had the right to amend Nicæa.

Since by canon law Chalcedon, especially when bolstered by papal ratification, offered the only criterion of orthodoxy, the Monophysites, by preferring their own interpretation of Nicæa, were heretics as well as schismatics. For they not only denied the authority of Chalcedon; they denied the doctrine declared by Chalcedon — denied Christ's two natures. This was not a conclusion of fine logic but of common sense, as was realized by most impartial observers. That is why it was inevitable that Felix should stand his ground, inevitable that ultimately his cause should succeed. Perhaps his view was not that of Nicæa, perhaps it was not even that of the Gospels; but it was that of Chalcedon and so, by canon law, it was the official view of the Church.

Closely related to this was the problem of granting absolution. Here Felix made a distinction between the apostates and the schismatics, between those who frankly and openly accepted a new faith and those who did so under the illusion that they were loyal to Catholic tradition. The African priests who were induced — usually by threats — to forsake the Catholic for the Arian faith of the Vandals were clearly in the former category. Yet in principle how were they to be distinguished from bishop Acacius? The Africans, in repudiating the authority of Nicæa, knew that they were separating themselves from the Catholic communion; but Acacius, if he did not know, should have known, that in repudiating the authority of Chalcedon he was virtually doing the same thing. The apparent contrast between the two repudiations merely results from the constantly decreasing theological momentum: each variation of doctrine, from that of Origen in the third, to the Arian in the fourth, to the Nestorian, Eutychian, Monophysite, and *Henotikon* in the fifth century, was less obvious and more subtle than the one preceding. Thus the Arian seemed much more of a heretic than Acacius and his

Henotikon only because in 335 [55] the doctrine was infinitely more fluid than in 485.

Nor was Felix a man to be taken in by this superficial difference. In regard to the African bishops who had lapsed into Arianism he decreed that, even if this had been induced by threats, their admission of error must be followed by a life-long penance with absolution to be granted only on their death-beds.[56]   And it was this same harsh penance that he declared he must impose on Acacius.[57]   Heresies might differ in degree but not in kind, for, as he elsewhere said,

> If the faith is not one it is nothing.[58]

He did not feel it necessary to argue the discrepancy between the *Henotikon* and Nicæa or between the *Henotikon* and Chalcedon, for Acacius, in refusing to abide by Chalcedon, admitted the discrepancy and hence admitted his heresy.

That the stand taken by Felix was the only sound one, both theologically and canonically, is therefore clear.   But whether it was politically expedient is questionable.   For it was this breach between East and West that suggested to the Vandal Huneric the feasibility of striking a mortal blow at the Roman power in Africa.   We have explained how by this time the power of Roman civilization had become synonymous with the power of the Church.[59]   Huneric was therefore probably right in believing that if he could destroy that African Church he would also be destroying the Roman civilization there. The schism here offered him a promising pretext: for in launching his persecution he could now allege that the African Church, by supporting Felix against the Emperor and the East, was guilty of heresy.[60]   Innocently ignorant, no doubt, of the real issues involved, Huneric took it for granted that the Emperor, as head of the State, was also head of the Church, and that the *Henotikon* was orthodox Catholic doctrine for the simple reason that the Emperor had declared it so.   Since Huneric was seeking to impose the Arian faith rather than

[55] When the controversy reached its peak with the condemnation of Athanasius by the Council of Tyre: see pp. 541–42.

[56] *Letter* # 13 § 2 (Thiel 1868 262–63).

[57] Langen 1885 153.

[58] *Letter* # 13 § 1.

[59] See pp. 304–05, 349, & 596; & Duchesne 1911 III [4] 637–45.

[60] Victor of Vita *H.P.A.P.* III §§ 5 & 12.

that of the *Henotikon,* he could not expect assistance from the Emperor; but, since both to him and to the Emperor he was persecuting, not orthodoxy, but heresy, he could safely count on the Emperor's neutrality. That the African Church, and Roman civilization with it, was effectively destroyed by Huneric while the Emperor sat idly by, may not have been chiefly due to the obstinacy of Felix — for what the Emperor Zeno might have done had Rome been willing to humour him no one can know. Yet in effect Felix did encourage Huneric to persecute and did discourage Zeno from choosing to interfere. Catholicism was perhaps doomed to lose Africa in any case; yet we cannot assume that Felix had any premonition of this. We must conclude that the instinct of the Roman statesman, still alive in Ambrose, in Augustine, and in Leo, was now dead.

These events — the beginning of the schism, and the persecution in Africa — occurred in 484. For Felix and the papacy the crisis was acute, and every effort had to be made to strengthen the position taken. In the argument of Felix there was still one conspicuous weakness: granted that Chalcedon's interpretation of Nicæa was official and binding and that neither Emperor nor Patriarch had any right to flout it, the possibility remained that the Emperor might summon a further General Council which could be persuaded to reverse the interpretation given by Chalcedon. The papacy was now claiming that no decision of a General Council was valid unless and until ratified by Rome, but to claim this was one thing, to prove it convincingly was another. Felix could argue with some plausibility that Chalcedon had been, at the time, generally accepted only because Pope Leo had ratified its interpretation of Nicæa; but it was not so easy to show that Nicæa's interpretation of the Gospel text and of Christian tradition was accepted only because the Nicene Creed had been ratified by Pope Sylvester. On the contrary, there was no textual or traditional record of any such ratification, and, if Nicæa had been generally accepted as valid apart from papal ratification, did not this fact establish the rule that such a ratification as Leo gave Chalcedon was superfluous? And, if this were so, it must be inferred that a subsequent General Council could repeal the Creed of Chalcedon without any ratification by Rome. Manifestly Felix could not afford to allow such an argument to gain currency. Therefore a Roman Council held in 485, after quoting *Matthew* xvi 18–19, declared that

following this voice, the 318 holy fathers gathered at Nicæa signified their confirmation of these facts and also the authority of the holy Roman Church.[61]

This, presumably, referred to a Roman version of Nicæa's canon 6 dating from before the time of Leo, which opens with the words, ' The Roman Church has always enjoyed the primacy.' [62] The accuracy of this version does not seem to have been now questioned by Felix or anybody else. But, if this seemed to show that the bishops of Nicæa recognized Rome as the ranking see of Christendom, it did not in the least suggest that they recognized Rome's right to veto their decrees. Felix, therefore, badly needed a further argument, and not long after,[63] as if by magic, the argument came into being! This consisted of a text purporting to be the acts of a Roman Council of 326, where, sure enough, appeared a formal ratification of Nicæa. In reliance on this text Felix could now argue that both Councils had been ratified by Rome and that this established a binding precedent. *Matthew* xvi 18–19 had raised a presumption that both Councils recognized Rome's veto power, and this fact was now corroborated by texts. Innocent had argued that Nicæa implicitly admitted the fact; Boniface had argued that Nicæa neglected to admit it only because it was already so generally admitted. This latest fabrication vindicated the good judgment of both.

Papal doctrine here takes final shape: Peter transmitted to Rome, not a complete sovereign power, but a veto power. Just as Sylvester might have vetoed the decrees of Nicæa and Leo those of Chalcedon, so might any subsequent Pope veto the decrees of any subsequent General Council. Rome became a Court empowered to decide whether the acts of a General Council accorded or conflicted with the fundamental law.

---

[61] Felix *Letter* # 11 § 4. Cf. Caspar 1930 I 121.

[62] Cf. Batiffol 1924 [2] 148; & Caspar 1930 I 496 n. 4 & 523. Text in Maassen 1870 I 19. See p. 538 n. 17.

[63] Duchesne 1886 cxxxv & cxxxvii says that there is a great contrast in style between this text and a similar one which was fabricated between 501 & 508, and from the superiority of the former's style he concludes that it ' is certainly earlier ' than 501. The text is in Poisnel 1886 VI 4–9.

And because this fundamental law was itself declared un-amendable Rome virtually denied the future all power. This may seem not only a strange but an injudicious doctrine, yet it was a popular one then: for it was one of conserva-tion, of hoarding, at a time when these were wise policies in all spheres, temporal and material as well as ecclesiastical and spiritual. Because this hoarding, whether of gold, law, land, grain, knowledge, or life, was the only prudent course, Rome became, especially in the West, the symbol of the Roman's needs — to cling to the past. That is why Latin civilization hid and hibernated within the Church during the next thou-sand years.

Restriction of sovereignty in terms of time was thus consoli-dated by Felix; but it was not his invention, not even that of Innocent or Boniface,[64] for the germ of the idea lay in the very essence of religion and was inevitably conditioned only by a conception like that which the Jews have always had of the future coming of a Messiah. Thus the idea that Christian doctrine should quickly crystallize into permanent shape must have been a popular idea at an early date, and it was only the creative minds, like those of Origen and Augustine, which pleaded that the door be left open for the sake of com-ing generations. Probably the good fathers assembled at Ni-cæa already shared the belief of the fifth century Popes that a point of doctrine, once it had been discussed and determined, should thereafter remain ever inviolable. Here, then, Felix merely completed a task which his predecessors had long be-fore inaugurated.

And where men's minds are being restricted in time, where, as here, the beliefs of future Christians are being bound by the beliefs of past Christians, may we not expect a restric-tion in space as well? For restrictions are symptoms of con-traction, and one contraction is likely to lead to others. Au-gustine had thought that there should be no restrictions in time — that the future should not be shackled. He also thought that there should be no restrictions in space — that the future should be left in the control of the whole Christian community, the Church being governed by a public opin-ion which individuals should seek rather to persuade than to

64 See pp. 572, & 580.

dragoon. He even thought that the majority should not dragoon the minority except in so far as this pressure promised to bring about a real disintegration of that minority opinion.[65] But Felix, having argued for restriction in time, was likely also to argue for restriction in space.

In his letter of 488 or 489 addressed to the Eastern bishops there is one passage which, taken by itself, may too easily be misunderstood:

Those in the East who hold fast to the Catholic faith do so because they see it defended by me and are heartened by me. Otherwise, either they will also fall because of my fall, or, if I should fall — which God forbid — and they still hold fast, they will rightly damn me before God and men.[66]

Surely this is a surprising statement from Felix: if the Pope should go wrong, that is, prove untrue to Nicæa and Chalcedon, those who remained true to these might properly damn him. The fact that Felix could say such a thing is further proof, if more is needed, that he cared more for the integrity of the doctrine than for the prestige of Rome. But his very sincerity led him into the statement of an absurdity. For who, if not the Pope himself, had the right to declare that he was wrong? That no Emperor, General Council or consensus of opinion had any such right is clear from the passage almost immediately following:

I do not know whether anyone would say that to follow error with the many is more effective than to preserve and cherish truth with the few. Or will error not be such because it is held with the many? And is truth not truth because it is held amongst the few? Error in the many is so much the greater error; truth suffers no harm by smallness because truth stands fixed in any, however few or many, of the parts. It follows that, just as the many do not cause error not to be error, so the few do not cause truth not to be

---

[65] See p. 570.

[66] § 39. This letter is in Thiel 1868 287 ff. and is classified as letter # 1 of Pope Gelasius, although with the date 488–89. Thiel attributes it to Gelasius because its style closely resembles that of the Gelasian letters written after Felix's death in 492: Thiel 1868 21–24. Caspar 1933 II 750–51 approves of this attribution. And Koch 1935 *passim* even traces the influence of Gelasius back to the pontificate of Simplicius! Since Felix was Pope, however, it seems injudicious to infer so much from resemblances in style. Gelasius was Felix's subordinate, and if, as secretary, Gelasius was responsible for the form of the letters, Felix was surely responsible for their substance. A Pope who had defied the whole East, as Felix had, was not likely to leave the determination of substance to any subordinate, however talented.

truth. There are countless examples whereby it may be taught that as error grew thicker truth abode with the few.[67]

Here, for the first time, by Felix, the restriction in space is categorically imposed: not only are future Christians bound to believe what past Christians have believed, all future Christians are also to believe what a single one of them thinks that past Christians have believed.

In this year 489 are we not already on the threshold of the doctrine of papal infallibility? Does this evidence not justify the declaration of 1870 that this doctrine had, in essence, existed since early times? Only one argument, and a bad one, might be raised in objection: could not a subsequent Pope, by repudiating the decision of an earlier one, convict that earlier one, and hence the papacy, of error? Theoretically this certainly could be, but practically it could not: for if a subsequent Pope had the right to declare an earlier one in error, a third Pope could declare the second one in error and so on indefinitely. If any such doctrine were recognized the whole structure of the papal authority would become discredited overnight. Therefore when Felix said that ' if I should fall . . . they will rightly damn me ' he merely meant ' were the Pope not, as he in fact is, infallible '.

Both were great men, Augustine who in 400 [68] trusted not only the future but the popular will of that future, and Felix who in 489 trusted only the past and the judgment of a single living man to interpret that past. Augustine, buoyed up by the false prospect of continuing progress in enlightenment, was willing to gamble on the future; Felix, already witness to a decline of terrible proportions, preferred to hoard what was already in hand. But although Augustine's rashness must appeal more to our impulses than Felix's prudence, mature reflection teaches us that we cannot say which principle was the more wise. For, if Augustine's view is the usual accompaniment of progress, it may also be an organic cause of the termination of that progress; and, if Felix's view is the usual accompaniment of decline, it may also be an organic cause of the termination of that decline. Of causes, effects, and symptoms of social health and disease we as yet know almost nothing. We do not know what corresponds to the

[67] *Letter* # 1 §41.   [68] See p. 566 n. 9.

ruddy cheek which can indicate both health and fever, or what corresponds to that fever which is itself both a symptom and an enemy of disease.

In 488, as Acacius lay dying, the Emperor Zeno still lived. Therefore even if Acacius had wished to make a death-bed confession of error this would not have been easy, for Zeno would have none of it. His successor,[69] Euphemius, was somewhat inclined to sympathize with Felix, and, had the Pope been willing to overlook the past, negotiations leading to a conciliation might have been undertaken and effected. But instead Felix at once ordered Euphemius to strike the name of Acacius from the diptych — which was the official list of his orthodox predecessors — and, since Euphemius did not dare thus to arouse Zeno and the Monophysites, Felix refused to recognize him, thereby leaving the breach still open.[70] It was at this moment that a new factor, destined to prove of the utmost importance, was introduced into the Italian situation: in 489 began the Ostrogothic invasion under the great Theodoric.

It was fortunate for the peace of mind of the Popes of these years that they were not covetous of temporal power, for temporal power just now was not showing very much deference to Catholicism. Arians ruled in Spain and most of Gaul, Arians were the military dictators of Italy; Monophysites had assumed control of the whole eastern half of the Empire and this encouraged Arians in Africa to inaugurate a policy designed to exterminate Catholicism there. Two years after this, in 486, pagan Franks took possession of all that was left of Roman territory in Gaul; and now, in 489, the Ostrogothic nation entered Italy.

Their leader Theodoric, to be sure, had been educated at the court of Constantinople and he was invading Italy with the full authority of the Emperor: ostensibly only in order to oust the recalcitrant Odoacer, but in fact rather in order to regain control over a no less recalcitrant Pope.[71] Never-

[69] There was an intervening bishop who died within four months: Caspar 1933 II 43.
[70] Ibid. 43–44.
[71] Although, as agent of the Emperor, he was of course bound not to deal with the papacy as an Arian might be tempted to: cf. Dumoulin 1911 I 439.

theless it was a question how long he would choose to obey
the Emperor's orders. Theodoric was not merely another
Ricimer or Odoacer, who were soldiers of fortune com-
manding a band of Roman-barbarian mercenaries. The
events of 456 and of 476 had been mere mutinies dignified,
if we choose, with the characterization of *coup d'Etat*. But
this new disturbance of 489 was an invasion by a barbarian
nation consisting of twenty-five thousand[72] men under arms
and women and children in proportion.[73]

Theodoric took four years to complete the conquest of
Italy, but this was rather because he chose to proceed cautiously and perhaps even humanely than because he was anywhere seriously checked. The land the Ostrogoths occupied
was all north and east of Rome.[74] Again one third of the
land was confiscated,[75] but this time, because of the wives and
children, the conquerors became much more an integral part
of the population and paid taxes like the natives.[76] Legally,
of course, Theodoric was an agent of the Emperor; actually
he was no more than an ally, but this status served to maintain the neutrality of the Greek party in Italy and to make
his barbarian regime seem the more palatable. By this means
the eyes of many were for the moment blinded to the fact that
Italy was now definitely going the way of Africa, Spain, and
Gaul.

What did Felix think of this new upheaval? What attitude
did he take towards the new conqueror? We have no record;
and this silence suggests that his indifference was greater than
we could have conceived. On the one hand he was struggling
to prevent a light-headed Emperor from plunging the East
into a disastrous heresy — a crime which must inevitably
bring down the wrath of God on all Romans; on the other
hand he was merely witnessing the latest military upheaval.
The *Henotikon* might taint the Roman faith for the next

---

[72] Hodgkin 1896 III[2] 182, says 40,-
000 men; Lot 1927 280 says 20,000.

[73] Punzi 1927 34 n. 1.

[74] They occupied none near Rome
or in southern Tuscany, but there
were many settlements to the east as
far south as the Abruzzi: Hartmann
1923 I[2] 93–94 & 125; Dopsch 1923
I[2] 206.

[75] Procopius *De Bello Gothico* I
§ 1. Hodgkin 1896 III[2] 273 & Dopsch
1923 I[2] 205 say that it was not in
addition to but in place of the one
third previously taken by Odoacer.

[76] Dumoulin 1911 I 446.

thousand or more years; Theodoric could hardly do more than obstruct the public diffusion of the faith in Italy for the next decade or two. So great had been the progress of the Church in the last century that her annihilation now seemed impossible. The past still bore vivid witness that persecution could only serve to fan the flame of faith. The danger was not, therefore, that ignorant barbarians might destroy the faith; it was rather that sophisticated Greeks might pervert it.

And Felix gauged the situation accurately. For we must remember that in 323, when Christianity first became the religion of the temporal power from Persia to the Atlantic, hardly one person in every ten was a Christian and multitudes of Romans were passionately devoted to other highly evolved beliefs. Until after 378 it was even doubtful whether the Roman world would hold to Catholicism at all. Under these circumstances alliance with the temporal power was a valuable adjunct; nevertheless its very nature was so fleeting and uncertain that any real reliance on it was folly. For the vital thing was to secure the solid Roman citizen — and above all the clergy — in the true faith. If the Pope could really count on these the Emperor might count on whom he pleased. And such was already the situation when, in the year 492, Felix died. The temporal power was nowhere Catholic, but the Roman people were overwhelmingly so. In the East the Monophysites constituted a minority, though a generous one; [77] in the West the Romans, all of whom — except in the isolated regions — were now Catholics, still constituted the vast majority — probably seven for every barbarian.[78] It is, of course, hard to say how many of the earlier barbarian immigrants still clung to their Arian faith, but certainly the actual fifth century invaders did not raise the Arian percentage to threatening proportions. Even the Ostrogoths hardly exceeded 125,000 souls. For two generations these did manage to keep their identity and religion, but this was only because, being segregated as the Italian military unit, they resisted the tendency of the indigenous population to absorb them.

We need not be surprised, therefore, that when Felix died his successor Gelasius quite coolly — and as if as a matter

[77] Duchesne 1911 III 4 505–11.   [78] See p. 290.

of course — proceeded to expound a doctrine which set the Pope up as the true sovereign ruler not only of the whole Church but of the whole temporal world. Monophysite Emperors might rule in the East, Arian kings in Italy or elsewhere; the devil might be particularly active because the end of the world was near. The fact remained that, as Gelasius very well knew, he commanded the obedience of the vast majority of the people living in the Roman world. And he also knew that he commanded a new form of obedience, one infinitely more effective and exacting than any previously imposed.

G. GELASIUS, 492–496

When Felix III died in 492 and the African [1] Gelasius succeeded him, Theodoric had been fighting with Odoacer for three years and did not conquer him until the fourth year. Gelasius assumed office, therefore, in the midst of a violent domestic war which laid most of northern Italy waste. Famine had become chronic [2] and the poverty of the people made it difficult for the Church to feed the starving. And if one quarter or one half — if we include the bishop's own share — was inadequate to supply the people's wants, the rest of the revenue was equally inadequate to maintain the Church buildings and the clergy. Buildings, whether destroyed by time or war, could not be restored; and the clergy, deprived at once of shelter and money,[3] became demoralized and rebellious. Even in the south, as at Nola and Squillace, the clergy, with the acquiescence and collusion of the civil authorities, murdered their bishops.[4] Since money became indispensable there were occasions, as at Volterra, when the bishopric was openly bought by bribing the civil officials.[5] The lesser clergy resorted to every variety of illegal device in order to live. Not only did they cheat the individual of his rightful

---

[1] Duchesne 1925 IV 12; Caspar 1933 II 750.
[2] See Gelasius *Letter* # 14 §1 (Thiel 1868 362).
[3] Onory 1932 177.
[4] Ibid. 166–67.
[5] Ibid. 167–68.

property for their own or the Church's advantage; they also alienated the Church property when a purchaser was to be found and, out of the proceeds, appropriated more than the one quarter to which they were entitled.[6]   Many of the priests having been killed or having fled — from either despair or a wish to make away with ill-gotten gains — it became necessary to fill their places, and with this object serfs were smuggled into the Church to be hastily promoted and ordained before their masters could track down and reclaim them.[7] Nor did the demoralization stop there: for cases are cited where the priests fornicated with nuns [8] or compacted with demons.[9]   And since many of these acts were punishable only by canon and not by civil law, the priests tried to pass themselves off as laymen or serfs of laymen in order to plead exemption from ecclesiastical jurisdiction.[10]   Nor were murder, theft, perjury, fornication, and magic their only offences: more serious perhaps, because fundamental, was their growing insensibility to the purity of the doctrine, revealed by the frequency with which churches were now dedicated to some local worthy or to some heretic.[11]   If we are to judge by the texts of these years the Italian Church had become rotten to the core — hardly any later record equals this one.   But we must remember that honourable Romans, like Gelasius who is our chief informant, had not yet become callous to a state of affairs which at many later times was chronic and normal.   Gelasius could hardly so shock us had he not been so shocked himself.

Immediate needs must be the immediate concern.   Therefore Gelasius devoted himself first to the organization of relief.   With current revenues insufficient and the sale of land forbidden, he raised what money he could by the sale of personal property and remunerative leases.[12]   At first, no doubt, he could not do more than feed the hungry and ransom prisoners of war; later he was able to proceed with more positive assistance, setting up relief rolls of the deserving poor, building granaries to store what was not immediately needed,[13] build-

---

[6] Ibid. 169–70.
[7] Gelasius *Letter* # 20.
[8] Ibid. # 14 § 20.
[9] Ibid. § 19.
[10] Onory 1932 167–68; cf. p. 304.
[11] Gelasius *Letter* # 14 § 25.
[12] Onory 1932 285.
[13] Ibid. 283.

ing hotels or hospitals for the free accommodation of fugitives, pilgrims, and travellers on Church business.[14] Gelasius did not inaugurate any of these relief measures, but he did do much to develop and systematize them.

In these years of violence and confusion one of the greatest obstacles to the administration of justice, whether legal or Christian, was the difficulty of individual identification. Men would turn up, declare they were this or that, and ask for help. Many of them were criminals, many were runaway slaves or serfs, but many too were honourable fugitives whose sad story was quite true. How was the bishop or anyone else to know who spoke the truth, or who, among those not telling the truth, were nevertheless the victims of oppression or violence? Most of the freemen bound to hereditary occupations had already escaped, for their only master was the State and the State had almost disintegrated; but these years of intensive warfare had also given many serfs an opportunity to escape, perhaps from a lay, perhaps from an episcopal, landlord and master, and such masters would be watchful to track them down.

Where could such a runaway better seek refuge than at the feet of a kindly bishop, and what better favour could he ask of this bishop than to be allowed to serve him and his Church? At a time when the need for priests was great such a fugitive could, if presentable and educated, soon qualify for ordination, and this priestly status he was the more eager to acquire because he knew that, once accepted, the Church must refuse to give him back. His plausible story could not be contradicted, his qualifications could not be ignored. Once in Orders he did not care whether his rightful master discovered him or not — he was now a servant of God and not to be detached from that service even by an Emperor. There were borderline cases, however, where the law was not clear. In these Gelasius tried to set up rules which should be fair to all parties. Certainly he had no sentimental weakness for runaways; on the other hand he could not bear to see men forced to return from a holy to an unholy status. He therefore decreed that where a former slave or serf had attained the status of priest he must remain such; but that in order to

14 Onory 1932 284.

compensate the master the culprit must forfeit all his property and other rights.[15] A serf's right as tenant was not likely to have value, but if he owned other property, including rents, reversionary rights, creditor's claims, etc., these must be assigned to the aggrieved master. In most cases the serf probably owned nothing, but Gelasius was as fair as he could be without jeopardizing the very nature of the priest's status. The good faith of Gelasius is best proved by his solution of the deacon's case: if the serf, now a deacon, could find another man willing to take his place and who was acceptable to the master, he might remain a deacon; otherwise he must reassume his servile status.[16]

An analogous problem concerned the right of asylum — which was the right to immunity from immediate arrest or other application of force acquired by anyone who reached the sanctuary of a Church. Such a person became the guest of the Church and the bishop claimed the right to dispose of him as he saw fit. Here, naturally, would come all runaways who had reason to suspect close pursuit. They could not then pose as innocent fugitives, but, when faced with their pursuers, could still allege mistaken identity, cruelty, oppression, or any other abuse of physical force. In such a case the bishop became judge in an informal court. Gelasius, in defending the right of the Church to uphold this immunity, makes it clear that its object is not at all to impede or frustrate the course of justice; on the contrary, its purpose is solely to facilitate justice: to ensure fair play for the fugitive by giving him a chance to be heard.[17] The first question would be, did the pursuers have the right to lay hands on him? If the bishop found that they did, the next question would be whether justice would be done. If, after this preliminary inquisition, the bishop still harboured doubts he would probably release the fugitive on demand, but only upon the claimant's solemn promise that such and such would be done and that the bishop would be kept fully and promptly informed of every step in the proceedings. In this way the Church could act informally as counsel for the defendant, and, in the manor court proceedings with the landlord sitting as

---

[15] Gelasius *Letter* # 14 § 14.   [17] Langen 1885 203–04.
[16] Ibid.

judge, it was comforting for the defendant to know that a representative of the bishop was either present or within call. Too often, no doubt, the episcopal patronage proved a sham. Nevertheless there must have been many occasions when a heartless landlord deemed it discreet to dispense a precise and even a merciful justice.

The fame of the Church of this time as a cohesive force rests on matters of deeper and subtler import than this one of identification and protection. The humbler symbols of power are not, however, to be quite ignored, and it is not an idle detail, therefore, that in these chaotic years the Church instituted a passport system for all who either belonged to or had dealings with her.[18] Civilization has two faces: the grandiose conception and the inconspicuous detail; yet each is an indispensable part of the whole. While the Church was binding men together with the mighty Creed she was also binding them together with passports — the material tie complementary to the spiritual.

Measures to promote relief and the identification of strangers, indispensable as they were, merely laid the foundation for the restoration of the demoralized Church. She particularly needed a larger number of priests and, in order to obtain them, she must do more than feed and house, do more than find out the true name, status, or criminal record. For even the best of the candidates needed training. By canon law promotion in the Church hierarchy was allowed only after prescribed intervals of service in successive grades, so that about ten years of apprenticeship was required before ordination.[19] But so acute now was the need of priests that if this rule were maintained their ranks could not be filled for another decade. No one could have done more for the advancement of the canon law than Gelasius — he was the first to establish it systematically in the West [20] — but he found himself obliged to declare that certain of its provisions must temporarily be suspended; for

unless the ancient intervals fixed for ecclesiastical promotions be soon reduced, the Churches would remain utterly destitute of the holy orders without which they cannot be administered.[21]

18 Onory 1932 282.   20 Fournier & Le Bras 1930 508.
19 See p. 309 n. 44.   21 *Letter* # 14 § 1.

And he made another concession which was equally unconventional and probably even more disturbing to the conserva-
tives.   If, but only if, there be a shortage of priests, he au-
thorizes the prompt ordination of monks, provided that they
have never committed a serious crime, never been married
and abandoned their wives, never been public penitents,
never been slaves or serfs, and provided they are now not
physically mutilated, subject to the burdens of the *curiales,*
or illiterate.[22]   That the priesthood might be recruited from
the monasteries!   Here was a new humiliation.   Yet was
Gelasius not bound to set the monk above the serf, even
above the layman?   That such a decree as this was still possible in Rome fifty years after the monk had assumed the leadership of the Gallic episcopate indicates with what deliberation the papacy had already learned to act.   A monk, says
Gelasius, may conceivably be fit for immediate ordination.
If only we had some record of the comments on this news as it
reached the monastery of Lerins! [23]

Meanwhile the Church was gradually extending her power
over the population.   The State had long professed to act as
the patron of all her citizens,[24] but although this was rather a
boast than a reality it offered a pretext for the Church to
claim a similar relationship to her laity.   Ambrose had declared himself the patron of all widows and orphans; [25] Gelasius extended his patronage to spinsters, to all servants, and
on one occasion assumed the custody of the property of one
lately dead lest the rightful heirs be cheated of their inheritance.[26]   The right of asylum was really nothing more than
the right to claim the bishop's patronage.

All such persons, however, could properly be classified as
oppressed, persons who were, for one or another reason, not
able to protect themselves.   The Church could rightly claim
these as her clients because from the first she had represented
herself as the temporal champion of those in distress.   But
under Gelasius a further important step was taken: every
employee of the Church was declared to be under Church
patronage.[27]   Like so many of the other innovations this one

---

[22] Ibid. § 2. Cf. p. 460 n. 47.
[23] See pp. 488–89.
[24] Onory 1932 301–02.

[25] See p. 258 n. 50.
[26] Onory 1932 299–301.
[27] Onory 1933 204.

was rather the result of natural evolution than of arbitrary usurpation; most of the employees of the Church were workers on the land and most of the land had been obtained from the great landlords whose estates had become self-sufficient economic and legal entities. As the lay landlord had come to be master, patron, and judge, so did the bishop who succeeded to his privileges and responsibilities.[28] Not infrequently, indeed, it was the lay landlord who had become the bishop, and the manager of the lay estate must often have been re-employed as *defensor ecclesiae*. But even to the casual eye a change would be perceptible, for the revenue or income would now be differently expended. Instead of new villas and farm buildings on the land there would be new churches and hostels in the towns; the gold and silver ornament would now decorate the altar rather than the table; the money to pay the courtiers and sycophants would go to pay the clergy; and the poor now got a full quarter of the revenue as a matter not of favour but of right.

It is not wholly clear what services such a client could require of his new patron. Probably he had a prior claim on the one quarter of the revenue set aside for poor relief, although in principle any such discrimination was wrong. Apparently the great advantage to the client was in litigation: if he were sued the *defensor ecclesiae* must see that he was properly defended in court; if he could satisfy the *defensor* that he had a just claim, the *defensor* must bring suit accordingly and prosecute the case.[29] Today free medical assistance is the rule, free legal assistance the exception; in the time of Gelasius it was the other way about.[30]

Still another extension of the *tuitio* or patronage principle was made by Gelasius: he obtained for the bishop the legal right to represent his city in any petition or claim it might wish to make as a unit.[31] The city is not to be confused with the *civitas,* which included the large lay estates as well as the new Gothic settlements; the city was the population which lived within the fortifications, and it was probably for the very reason that the city itself was not recognized as a legal

---

28 Onory 1933 201–03.
29 Onory 1932 147–48.
30 In the fifth, as in the eighteenth,

century, evil was in the soul. In 1900 it was again in matter.
31 Onory 1933 229.

entity under civil law and yet needed such recognition that the bishop was allowed to assume an office which was exclusively civil and temporal.

Theodoric was a much more powerful and able ruler than either Ricimer or Odoacer who were his immediate predecessors. Why was it, then, that the civil power of the Church grew faster after 492 than it ever had before? Gelasius was an unusually able Pope; but this fact alone does not explain the matter. For one thing Theodoric invaded Italy as the technical ally of the Greek Emperor, pledged to rule as the Emperor's representative, pledged specifically to respect and honour the Church.[32] And Theodoric was a man of honour. Unlike Ricimer and Odoacer, moreover, he was not a domestic usurper raised to power by Italy's own army, but a foreign invader conquering with a foreign army. He was therefore an intruder, not a Roman but an outsider; and he was unfamiliar with Italian ways and Italian laws. Having begun to rule he found in the Church a powerful organization entirely ready to co-operate with him in the restoration of law and order, of decency and prosperity. He was therefore only too glad to show her the favour he had promised. If she claimed to possess certain rights and privileges he did not question the claim unless it seemed clearly incompatible with his temporal sovereignty.[33] If she petitioned for new rights and privileges he was ready, provided they seemed innocent and helpful, to grant these too.

A further reason, however, was the condition in which he found the civil government. What little had remained of the civil personnel had been appropriated by Odoacer; when he fell most of this remnant fell with him. Theodoric was himself a literate if not an educated person, but very few of his Gothic followers were fit for administrative responsibility. A Roman civil administration was therefore a thing to be re-created out of virtually nothing — a slow and painful process; whereas the Church organization, though badly shattered, still presented an impressive appearance and evinced an indomitable energy.

Finally it is not to be supposed that because, in his first

³² Ibid. 217.   ³³ Ibid. 204–05.

years, Theodoric did much to extend the temporal power of
the Church he ever did anything to jeopardize his own sovereign authority: he favoured the Church at the expense of the
civil bureaucracy, but not to the extent of subordinating civil
to ecclesiastical power. Gelasius, as we shall see,[34] emphatically reiterated the Church's claim to superiority, yet he apparently did not raise a finger to incorporate this principle
into law. For the law was that the civil courts could alone
declare the extent of ecclesiastical jurisdiction, and could,
therefore, declare that in any given case the ecclesiastical
courts had no jurisdiction. Yet neither did Theodoric change
the law, nor, so far as we know, did Gelasius ask him to change
it. And, as if this check on the Church's power were not
enough, Theodoric enacted a law which gave him the power
to hear all appeals from any court, ecclesiastical as well as
civil.[35]

In 493 Italy needed law and order so badly that all parties
were equally eager to co-operate. Because Theodoric knew
that the Romans must be given a chance to run their own
affairs he rarely interfered in controversies between Church
and civil bureaucracy. In not a few instances the civil courts
resisted the Church's efforts to extend her power. This was
because the civil personnel was fearful that if she were not
checked their offices would soon either be abolished as superfluous or become hopelessly unremunerative.[36] But such
cases were few and unimportant. Gelasius himself was most
careful to respect the civil authorities and civil rights; he
never tried to acquire more powers than Theodoric chose
officially to confer.[37] It would be absurd to suppose that these
two men had identical objectives, or that either was primarily
an Italian patriot. Each knew, however, that his objective
was not to be won without some degree of Italian prosperity,
and each knew that this prosperity could only be won if they
pulled together. If there was already an underlying antagonism it was due rather to presentiments than to actual conflicts. Each knew that loss of temper on the part of either
meant disaster for both.

The restoration of law and order in Italy, and the rehabili-

34 See pp. 651–53.   36 Ibid. 207–08.
35 Onory 1933 206–07.   37 Onory 1932 101–02 & 291–92.

tation of the Church, were to Gelasius serious concerns. They were, however, transitory and hence incidental. As a physical organization the Church could virtually be burnt to ashes and still, like the Phoenix, rise again to new youth and vigour. For mere physical well-being was a matter of God's will, almost of chance. Revelation had taught man that truth and reality lay elsewhere. Undoubtedly there is a Platonic residue here, a contempt for the concrete which the ancient world could never quite shake off. But this contempt was now not absolute but relative, for Christianity gave this concrete an extrinsic significance. The earthly welfare of the Italians thereby acquired such a significance: because the destiny of the Italian souls was somehow conditioned by it. With that sixth sense, which we may call historical, Augustine had recognized the principle of evolution, whereby man rose from a lower to a higher level, with Revelation ever expanding in proportion. Nor was Gelasius without this same sixth sense, only that he perceived, as Augustine could not, that man had, by 492, not only ceased to rise but had begun to fall. Thus if Augustine strove to raise man to a higher level than he had yet attained, Gelasius was no less concerned to hold him at his present level. This present level being symbolized by the Creed, to him, as to his predecessors Simplicius and Felix, the real concern was to defend Chalcedon against the assaults of Emperor and Monophysite.

No more than Simplicius and Felix did Gelasius cast new light on the doctrine — perhaps there was really no more light to cast — but his devotion to the concept of Christ's double nature was on that account none the less intense. Indeed he does add one ramification of his own — prophetic of the symbolic age to come — declaring that although neither the bread nor the wine changes its substance by consecration [38] each through the medium of the Holy Ghost [39] infuses the recipient with a magic quality and that these together form a compound analogous to Christ's two natures. Communion in the bread only was actually a Manichæan practice; [40] how it had come into Catholic use is not clear. Gelasius at all events declared such communion to be sacrilegious and heret-

---

[38] *Tract* III § 14 (Thiel 1868 541–42).

[39] Langen 1885 202.

[40] Stoop 1909 123–24.

ical, and not because it was Manichæan but because it somehow acknowledged the single nature of the Monophysites! [41]

Thus to him as to his predecessors the one vital concern
was to defend the truth, and the truth then was not many
things but one thing: who and what was Christ. Thus Nicæa
was truth and Chalcedon the correct explanation of Nicæa.
Though everything else were lost this truth must be saved,
and no argument, no ingenuity should be spared in order to
save it. His are not the cool arguments of the unscrupulous
professional; they are the fiery arguments of one fighting for
his life. To him the means are indistinguishable from the
end. That is why his argument is at one time prolix, at another fragmentary. This latter type is the more easily quoted:
speaking of the Council of Ephesus which absolved Eutyches
in 449, he says that

an unjust Council ought to give way to a just Council. [42]

And he adds that the decrees of a just Council may not be invalidated by those of a later Council. [43] What he means is
that Ephesus is an unjust, Chalcedon a just, Council. The
Monophysites, however, admitted this principle, only they
declared Ephesus just and Chalcedon unjust. Gelasius therefore begs the real question, which is to prove what body or
authority has the power to decide whether a given Council
be just or unjust.

Elsewhere, of course, he makes it clear that Rome and
Rome alone may decide. Writing of the excommunication
of Acacius and his adherents by Felix he says:

Wherefore we do not fear lest the apostolic decision be dissolved,
which the voice of Christ, the tradition of the Fathers, and the
authority of the canons supports in such wise that it invariably
binds the whole Church. [44]

The voice of Christ is of course *Matthew* xvi 18–19:

No see ought to assert her superiority over any other, except the
first, which ratifies each and every Council by her authority, all
of which she safe-guards with invariable prudence, on account of

---

[41] *Letter* # 37 § 2. Cf. Langen
1885 163–64, 190 & 206.
[42] *Letter* # 26 § 6 (Thiel 1868
401 line 16).

[43] Ibid. (lines 16 ff.).
[44] *Letter* # 10 § 9; & cf. ibid. # 12
§ 9.

her primacy which the blessed Peter took over at the word of the Lord, and which, with the Church following him, he has always held and still retains.[45]

The papal claim is here set forth more uncompromisingly than ever before.   The sees of Alexandria and Antioch are shorn of the powers conceded to them by canon 6 of Nicæa; [46] Nicæa is valid only because Pope Sylvester ratified it; ever since Christ spoke to Peter the Church has recognized the supremacy of Rome.   Of the authority that Rome derives from the canons Gelasius says:

It is the canons themselves which ordered that appeals of the whole Church be referred to the consideration of this see and which decreed that there should absolutely never be appeals from her.[47]

Or again:

The canons intend her to be appealed to from all parts of the world, but that absolutely no one shall appeal from her.[48]

What, if any, canons Gelasius had in mind we can only guess. Surely even the Roman version of canon 6 of Nicæa offered no pretext for such a statement.[49]   Did he then rely on the canon of Sardica which Zosimus had tried to foist on the Africans?   Since this merely authorized the bishop of Rome to order a re-trial at his discretion but did not authorize him to re-try himself,[50] even this text was inadequate.   Still, Pope Leo had cited it and he had also claimed the right of Rome to hear all appeals.[51]   Gelasius was probably relying on the authority of Leo's arguments rather than on any text, and his belief in the accuracy and legality of Leo's claims was probably sincere.   Yet no more than his predecessors may Gelasius be imagined as the victim of earlier propaganda: the false canons purporting to be Sylvester's ratification of Nicæa had been fabricated in Rome after 485,[52] when Gelasius was already influential in the papal curia.   And since he knew that

---

[45] *Letter* # 26 § 3.

[46] Gelasius evidently thought that the bishops of those sees had so often fallen into heresy that they had forfeited whatever special privileges they had originally enjoyed.

[47] *Letter* # 10 § 5.

[48] *Letter* # 26 § 5 (Thiel 1868 399 last line).

[49] See p. 629 n. 62, & Caspar 1933 II 50.

[50] See p. 542 n. 31.

[51] See p. 591 n. 13.

[52] See p. 629.

this document had been fabricated he must have surmised that other documents of the sort had had a similar origin. But he was so firmly convinced of the papacy's divine right according to God's will that he believed a reconstruction of history to correspond with that conviction to be a logical and inescapable corollary. Granting the teleological hypothesis, empirical history was inconceivable. Even in Plato's rational philosophy the concrete fact must be made to fit. How much more must the facts be made to fit where the hypothesis was a Revelation that defied reason!

Gelasius was saying that Rome could hear appeals from the whole Church, yet Felix had excommunicated Acacius merely because Acacius had championed the *Henotikon*. Here Felix was acting, not as a court of appeal, but as a court of first instance. How does Gelasius explain this?

As has been said, the apostolic see has often, by the custom of our ancestors and independently of any previous Council, exercised the power both of absolving those whom a Council had unjustly condemned and of condemning those whom she saw fit to condemn.[53]

And the reason is that,

It is not necessary for the deserved punishment of each transgressor that a new Council be convoked, since, by the course of action which condemned both the error and the author of it, he who, in any way or for any reason, shall have become a sharer of that error in such a way as to be polluted by its contagion, logically shares that same condemnation also, and is bound to suffer the punishment of him whose company he chose.[54]

This, although not recognized by any canon, was a logical enough extension of the papal authority: Chalcedon being the official gloss on Nicæa, anyone who refused to champion Chalcedon was either a Nestorian, a Eutychian, or some other denier of Nicæa and, as such, a heretic like them. Technically Gelasius could not act until the accused had been tried for heresy and acquitted, but where this would be a formality it would naturally be dispensed with — as in the case of Acacius — so that Rome had to act, if at all, of her own initiative.

[53] *Letter* # 26 § 5 (Thiel 1868 400 lines 10–13).

[54] Ibid. § 6 (ibid. 401 lines 22–27). And cf. *Letter* # 26 § 2, & # 27 § 2.

Theoretically this would give the Pope the right to depose any bishop he chose to and veto the nomination of any successor that was chosen; actually, of course, it merely allowed him to depose those bishops who refused to accept Chalcedon. For Gelasius was concentrating all his efforts on this one point, and to this end he claimed the right not only to veto any decree of a Council which in his opinion varied from Chalcedon, but also to pack any future Council with bishops who clung to Chalcedon. This claim in itself was bold enough, but were not its implications even bolder? For if Gelasius had the right to depose bishops as heretics because they denied Chalcedon, did he not also have the right to depose bishops as heretics because they denied some other dogma of which Gelasius approved? The dogma of Chalcedon had acquired a special authority because it had been propounded by a General Council, but it could hardly be alleged that other dogmas were less fundamental. Equally vital, to Rome at any rate, were the dogmas of the Pope as successor of Peter and of the necessity of grace in order to win salvation. Yet neither of these had so far been propounded by any General Council. Innocent had argued that the Council of Nicæa had implicitly recognized the Petrine claim; [55] but Boniface had said that Nicæa

did not even presume to decree anything in regard to him because it perceived that nothing could be conferred on him over and above what his own merit already entitled him to: in short it knew that all things had been conceded to him by the words of the Lord.[56]

To deny *Matthew* xvi 18–19 was therefore a worse heresy than to deny Nicæa, for the former was Revelation itself, the latter a merely human — although divinely inspired — inference from Revelation. If, then, the Pope could depose a bishop who denied Chalcedon, he could also surely depose a bishop who denied Nicæa, and could even more certainly depose a bishop who denied *Matthew* xvi 18–19! And could he not equally depose a bishop who denied any other passage in the Bible?

Fantastic as it may seem that Rome could argue so, the

[55] See pp. 573–74.   [56] See p. 579 n. 41.

truth is that Rome not only did argue so but had long before acted accordingly. For in the year 418 she had deposed all the bishops of Italy who refused to renounce the doctrine of Pelagius.[57] She had not tried to depose such bishops in other lands only because in Africa they already had been deposed and because in Gaul, Spain, and Britain her information as well as her authority were defective. Nevertheless the papacy had shown a disposition to depose any bishop who was a Pelagian, that is, any bishop who misread the true meaning of the Bible on the indispensability of grace. By the same token she could depose any bishop for misreading any other passage of the Bible. In theory, therefore, Rome acquired the power, not only to veto any decree of a General Council, but also, by the deposing of bishops, to appoint as the members of such a Council only those whom she approved.

How could such effrontery pass unchallenged? Because, bold as a lion in claiming power, Rome was as cunning as a fox in exercising it. The very fact that her theoretical power was so complete rendered it imperative that her actual power be small. Like a wise judge she encouraged settlements out of court, postponed her decision, when pressed gave equivocal answers. It was because she had no opinions of her own that her opinions were those of Christendom.

The issue of supremacy as between Church and State was not raised by the defection of Acacius; but it was raised by the Emperor's deposition in 485 of the Catholic bishop of Antioch, Calendio, the pretext being his complicity in a plot to depose the Emperor. The extent of that complicity is here immaterial: as a champion of Chalcedon, Calendio must have been tempted to favour a scheme designed to rid the Empire of the author of the *Henotikon,* but whether his favour amounted to acts of treason is another matter. The serious point was that Calendio, being accused of treason, must be tried, if at all, by a civil court and, if tried and condemned by such a court, must bow to the sentence imposed — which necessarily included his deposition as bishop. But Gelasius refused to recognize the competence of the civil court to depose a bishop for treason,[58] for who was competent

<hr>

[57] See p. 412.   [58] *Letter # 26 § 11.*

to decide what constituted this crime? Was it not rather the Emperor who was guilty of treason — of treason to Chalcedon? And, if so, how could Calendio be guilty of treason in resisting an Emperor who was favouring the heretics and persecuting the Catholics? The real traitors were those who supinely acquiesced. The case of Calendio was not, therefore, a civil but an ecclesiastical concern, and the Church alone had the right to declare this because the Church alone had the right to declare what cases were of civil and what of ecclesiastical concern.

Gelasius is here repeating, although more forcibly and explicitly, the assertion of Ambrose.[59] Writing to his legate in Constantinople, he says:

That in their distraction they do such things is not to be wondered at. Thus are madmen in the habit of either regarding their doctors as enemies or killing them. Yet I ask them where it is possible to conduct the trial which they arrogate to themselves. Can it be among them, with the result that the same men would be at once enemies, witnesses and judges? But to such judges not even human affairs, much less the integrity of the divine law, ought to be entrusted. If, in so far as religion is concerned, the final judgment belongs only to the apostolic see according to the canons, in so far as temporal power is concerned that power ought to find out from the bishops, and especially from the Vicar of the blessed Peter, what are spiritual matters, and ought not to decide this for itself.[60]

And in a letter to the Emperor Anastasius he says:

There are indeed two powers, O august Emperor, by which this world is chiefly governed: the holy authority of the bishops and the royal power. Between these the weight of the bishops is the heavier because at the divine Judgment they must render an account of even the kings of men.[61]

In order to support his theoretical argument Gelasius cites an abundance of precedents: the rebuke of David by Nathan,[62] of Theodosius by Ambrose,[63] of the second Theodosius by Leo, of the Emperor Anthemius by Hilary, and the resistance successfully offered by Simplicius and Felix not only to the usurper Basiliscus but also to the true Emperor Zeno.[64]

---

[59] See pp. 554-55.
[60] Letter # 10 § 9. And cf. Letter # 27 § 8.
[61] Letter # 12 § 2.

[62] II Samuel xii.
[63] See p. 554 n. 47.
[64] Letter # 26 § 11. And cf. ibid. §§ 7 & 12, & Letter # 27 §§ 1 & 2.

These, although well worth repeating, were old arguments furnished by the events of a hundred years before. But there was another argument which Ambrose and the others of his day could not have envisaged but which was patent in 495 to any casual observer: in 395 the temporal power was wielded by a single man over the whole Roman Empire, and this man was the representative of a tradition running back four hundred and even a thousand years. His power seemed universal in its territorial scope and eternal in time. In 495, on the other hand, the temporal power was divided territorially and was proving ephemeral as well. To be sure the East had not changed its political character, but the fall of the West had divided the political control between several barbarians, each of whom held his position rather by force than consent. The change had begun as early as 406 when the Vandals, Suevi, and Alans had occupied Gaul, and had continued as these and other barbarian tribes also occupied Spain and Africa. But Rome did not become aware of this profound transformation until the death of Valentinian III in 454 and the assumption of power by Ricimer two years later. This Ricimer had no real relation to Italy even while he lived, and when, sixteen years later, he died, everything he had done and been died with him. What was already a fact then, became an acknowledged fact a generation later, when bishop Ennodius, writing of those days, spoke quite as a matter of course of the ' purple insignia of ephemeral power '.[65]

And if the career of Ricimer could perhaps be regarded in Italy merely as an insignificant interlude, the career of Odoacer, who abolished the imperial office, could not be. Nor could the similar careers of Euric in Gaul and Huneric in Africa; for these two had inaugurated a violent persecution of all Catholics. That the Church should agree to share the rule over mankind with such upstarts as these was inconceivable; she feared that unless she subjugated them they must subjugate her. These very disasters, therefore, furnished Gelasius with a new and telling argument: how miserable, he says, is the excuse of Acacius that he must accede to the demand of the Emperor:

[65] *Life of Epiphanius* (*C.S.E.L.* VI 346 line 19).

Behold how, only recently, the great man and noble priest Eugenius, bishop of Carthage, and many [other] Catholic priests, resisted with constancy the savage Huneric, king of the Vandals, and, suffering even now the utmost extremities, do not cease to resist their persecutors. It is also evident that we, with God's help, in no way obeyed the barbarian heretic Odoacer, who was then holding the kingdom of Italy, when he ordered that certain things should in no wise be done.[66]

Surely even the Emperor must agree that the Church had the right to resist the attacks of these Arians. Yet what other offence had they been guilty of than that of rejecting Nicæa? The Emperor denied the Church's right to resist his attacks. Yet had he not himself virtually acknowledged that he repudiated Chalcedon? If Gelasius should admit that the Emperor could depose bishops at his pleasure, must he not also have to admit that Theodoric could do likewise? If the Emperor may define heresy at his pleasure, why may not Theodoric? And, should this be, orthodoxy and heresy would vary in each kingdom and under each ruler, without the smallest relation to truth.[67] That is why Gelasius does not hesitate to say that Antichrist is struggling to destroy Christ in the East no less than in Africa,[68] and can further declare that it is the law of God ' which is the highest and the true Emperor '.[69]

By this declaration Gelasius buried the State as an intellectual concept. In so far as its aims did not conform to those of the Church it was no longer a temporal State but a spiritual Antichrist. The State was no longer a subordinate with rights to be respected but a slave to do its master's pleasure. Leo had shown a real concern for the welfare of the temporal State: he had struggled to rid Italy of Attila and Genseric, had enacted laws to discourage a too impetuous renunciation of the world, had even been ready to consider a compromise with the East in the fundamental matter of the two natures. For he felt that the perpetuation of the Roman State was somehow indispensable to the perpetuation of the Church as he conceived her. God had created the Roman Empire as the womb within which the Church should be conceived; because the child was born and grown now should she ungrate-

---

[66] *Letter* # 26 § 11.
[67] Cf. Cessi 1919 46, & p. 597.
[68] *Letter* # 8 § 1.
[69] *Letter* # 10 § 6.

fully spurn her parent? To Leo, much as to Ambrose, the State was inferior to the Church somewhat as the Virgin had been to Christ; inferior in kind, certainly, but not in degree, for both were, in their own way, indispensable and therefore perfect.

But with Gelasius, as with Felix before him, even this lingering civic patriotism died. He did not resent the intrusion of Theodoric as Leo had resented that of Attila or Genseric — he may even have thought a barbarian ruler would trouble the Church less. He did show outward respect for the civil law, but this was rather out of prudence than conviction. That the Italian people be fed, clothed, and housed did seem to him important, but this the Church could attend to as well as could the State; and the things that only the State could properly do did not seem to him worth doing. Felix had said, moreover, that truth is likely to be with the few — political compromise was therefore an absurdity. Both he and Gelasius preferred Chalcedon and the barbarians to the *Henotikon* and the Empire. For to them the doctrine of Christ-in-two-natures was to be defended to the death. Had Gelasius no vision, then, of where barbarian temporal rule might lead? Apparently not; for instead he had another vision: of the State, not as the Virgin, but as the Antichrist, herald to the approaching end of the world.[70]

With Gelasius the frame of the new conception of the world acquires all its four sides. The first side proclaims that all truth lies in the past, the second that the Pope alone may declare what this past truth is; the third proclaims the temporal power's insignificance in space, the fourth its insignificance in time. Just as within the spiritual sphere the future Church was helpless, so within the temporal sphere the future State was helpless. As the spirit must serve the past, so must the flesh — and this past was now the bishop of Rome. This conception — at once sublime and monstrous — may be called ancient Rome's last act: in order to save her soul she destroyed her Empire. Terrifying as a way of life, as a system it is worthy of a place beside the no less

[70] *Letter* # 8 § 1. This conception suggests a tendency to revert to dualism.

terrifying systems of an Augustine or a Newton. For on the one hand there is a strict limitation within time and space — to the past and to the city of Rome; whereas on the other there is infinite extension in both time and space — for the power, thus restricted, spread out to all eternity and over the whole world.[71]

A proud and arrogant claim this can seem; actually it came to be acknowledged because it was humble. For, after all, man being a nothing, to rule him was no great matter. But to be ruled by God was a great matter, and Rome was able to rule because she submitted to being ruled. It was precisely because Rome believed her will to be not her own but Another's that she could make others believe this too. When the Pope spoke, Peter spoke, and Peter spoke for Christ. From a roar Revelation had dwindled to a whisper — into the Pope's ear.

[71] The General Council of the whole Church was called Ecumenical from the Greek οἰκέω (I inhabit), and hence ἡ οἰκουμένη (the whole habitable globe).

TEXTS QUOTED OR CITED

NOTE: This list, arranged alphabetically by author, includes only the texts actually quoted or cited, so that the reader may turn from the abbreviated foot-notes to this unabbreviated record. For systematic bibliographies the reader must refer to such guides as the *Patrologie* of Rauschen (10th and 11th eds. by T. B. Altauer, Freiburg i.B. 1931).

Certain abbreviations in the list below are here given in full:

C.S.E.L.: Corpus Scriptorum Ecclesiasticorum Latinorum, Vienna 1865 ff.
L.C.L.: Loeb Classical Library, London and New York, and Cambridge Mass.
M.G.H., A.A.: Monumenta Germaniae Historica, Auctorum Antiquissimorum, Berlin 1877 ff.
M.G.H., S.R.M.: Monumenta Germaniae Historica, Scriptorum Rerum Merovingicarum, Hannover 1884 ff.
N.&P.N.F.: A Select Library of the Nicene and Post-Nicene Fathers of the Christian Church,
First Series, Philip Schaff ed. Buffalo 1886 ff.
Second Series, Philip Schaff and Henry Wace eds. New York, Oxford & London 1890 ff.
P.G.: Patrologiae Cursus Completus, Series Graeca, accurante J.-P. Migne, Paris 1857 ff.
P.L.: Patrologiae Cursus Completus, Series Prima . . . Ecclesiae Latinae, accurante J.-P. Migne, Paris 1844 ff.
R.E.: Realencyklopädie für protestantische Theologie und Kirche (Albert Hauck ed.) 3rd ed. of J. J. Herzog, Leipsig 1896 ff.

Achelis (Hans): 'Die Martyrologien, ihre Geschichte und ihr Wert'. Article in *Abhandlung der königlichen Gesellschaft der Wissenschaften zu Göttingen,* Philol.-Histor. Klasse, Neue Folge, vol. III pt. 3, Berlin 1900.

Alfaric (Prosper): *L'Evolution intellectuelle de Saint Augustin,* Paris, 1918.

Altamira (y Crevea, Rafael): *Historia de Espana y de la civilizacion espanola,* vol. I 3rd edition, Barcelona 1913.

AMBROSE:

De Apologia Prophetae David, C.S.E.L. vol. 32 part 2, 299 ff.
De Excessu Fratris, P.L. vol. 16 1289 ff.
De Fide ad Gratianum Augustum, P.L. vol. 16 527 ff.
De Jacob, C.S.E.L. vol. 32 part 2, 3 ff.
De Joseph, C.S.E.L. vol. 32 part 2, 72 ff.
De Mysteriis, P.L. vol. 16 389 ff.
De Officiis Ministrorum, P.L. vol. 16 25 ff.
De Virginibus, ad Marcellinam, P.L. vol. 16 187 ff.
Epistolae, P.L. vol. 16 875 ff. (Most of the quotations in the text are from the English translation, *The Letters of S. Ambrose,* by members of the English Church, Oxford 1881).
Exameron, C.S.E.L. vol. 32 part 1, 3 ff.

Explanatio Psalmorum XII, C.S.E.L. vol. 64 3 ff.
Expositio Evangelii secundum Lucam, C.S.E.L. vol. 32 part 4, 3 ff.
Expositio Psalmi CXVIII, C.S.E.L. vol. 62, 3 ff.

AMBROSIASTER:
Commentaria in XIII Epistolas Beati Pauli ad Romanos, P.L. vol. 17 45 ff.
Quaestiones Veteris et Novi Testamenti, C.S.E.L. vol. 50 3 ff.

AMMIANUS (Marcellinus) : *Rerum Gestarum,* ed. V. Gardthausen, Leipsig 1874.

(ANONYMOUS) :
D.P.D.: De Providentia Divina, P.L. vol. 51 617 ff.
De Sancto Marcellino, Acta Sanctorum vol. 10 April 20, 750 ff. ed. Henschenius and Papebrochius, 1675.
De Vocatione omnium gentium, P.L. vol. 51 647 ff.
Hypomnesticon contra Pelagianos et Coelestianos, P.L. 45 1611 ff.
Liber Pontificalis, ed. Louis Duchesne, 2 vols., Paris 1886.
Praeteritorum Sedis Apostolicae Episcoporum Auctoritates, P.L. vol. 51 205 ff.
S. Hilarii Arelatensis Vita, P.L. vol. 50 1219 ff.
Vita Genovefae Virginis Parisiensis, M.G.H., S.R.M. vol. 3 215 ff.
Vita Lupi Episcopi Trecensis, M.G.H., S.R.M. vol. 7 284 ff.

Arnold:
1897: 'Avitus'. Article in *R.E.* vol. 2 317 ff.
1898: 'Claudianus Mamertus'. Article in *R.E.* vol. 4 132 ff.

ATHANASIUS: *Vita et Conversatio S.P.N. Antonii, P.G.* vol. 26 837 ff.

AUGUSTINE:
Confessionum Libri XIII, L.C.L. 'Confessions of St. Augustine' 2 vols. London 1922.
* *Contra Adimantum, C.S.E.L.* vol. 25 part 1 115 ff.
Contra Cresconium, C.S.E.L. vol. 52 325 ff.
* *Contra duas Epistulas Pelagianorum, C.S.E.L.* vol. 60 423 ff.
* *Contra Epistolam Manichæi quam vocant Fundamenti, P.L.* vol. 42 173 ff.
* *Contra Faustum Manichæum, C.S.E.L.* vol. 25 part 1 251 ff.
Contra Mendacium, C.S.E.L. vol. 41 469 ff.
Contra secundam Juliani Responsionem, imperfectum opus, P.L. vol. 45 1049 ff.
* *De Anima et eius Origine, P.L.* vol. 44 475 ff.
De Baptismo, C.S.E.L. vol. 51 145 ff.
De Beata Vita, C.S.E.L. vol. 63 89 ff.
De Bono Conjugali, C.S.E.L. vol. 41 187 ff.
* *D.C.D.: De Civitate Dei,* ed. Dombart & Kalb, 2 vols. Leipsig 1928.
* *De Correptione et Gratia, P.L.* vol. 44 915 ff.

De Cura pro Mortuis Gerenda, C.S.E.L. vol. 41 621 ff.
De Diversis Quaestionibus ad Simplicianum, P.L. vol. 40 101 ff.
* *De Dono Perseverantiae*, P.L. vol. 45 993 ff.
De Genesi ad Litteram, C.S.E.L. vol. 28 3 ff.
De Gestis Pelagii, C.S.E.L. vol. 42 51 ff.
* *De Gratia Christi et de Peccato Originali*, C.S.E.L. vol. 42 125 ff.
* *De Gratia et Libero Arbitrio*, P.L. vol. 44 881 ff.
De Libero Arbitrio Libri tres, P.L. vol. 32 1221 ff.
De Mendacio, C.S.E.L. vol. 41 413 ff.
* *De Natura Boni contra Manichæos*, C.S.E.L. vol. 25 part 2 855 ff.
* *De Natura et Gratia*, C.S.E.L. vol. 60 233 ff.
De Nuptiis et Concupiscentia, C.S.E.L. vol. 42 211 ff.
* *De Peccatorum Meritis et Remissione*, C.S.E.L. vol. 60 3 ff.
De Perfectione Justitiae hominis, C.S.E.L. vol. 42 3 ff.
* *De Praedestinatione Sanctorum*, P.L. vol. 44 959 ff.
* *De Spiritu et Littera*, C.S.E.L. vol. 60 155 ff.
* *De Trinitate*, P.L. vol. 42 819 ff.
Enarrationes in Psalmos, P.L. vol. 36 67 ff.
* *Enchiridion*, P.L. vol. 40 231 ff.
* *Epistulae*, C.S.E.L. vols. 34 (parts 1 & 2), 44 & 62.
Retractationum Libri duo, C.S.E.L. vol. 36 7 ff.
* *Sermones*, P.L. vol. 38 23 ff.

Note: the quotations in the text from the works marked with a star are taken, with a few changes, from the English translations in the *N.&P.N.F.*, First Series, by permission of the publishers Charles Scribner's Sons. The quotations from the *Confessions* are from the *L.C.L.* translation of William Watts of 1631.

Ausonius:
Epistulae, M.G.H., A.A. vol. 5 part 2 157 ff.
Ordo Urbium nobilium, ibid. 98 ff., or *L.C.L.* ' Ausonius ' vol. 1 276 ff.
Avitus (Alcimus Ecdicius) : *Epistularum ad diversos*, M.G.H., A.A. vol. 6 part 2 35 ff.

Babut (Ernest Charles) : *Saint Martin de Tours*, Paris 1912.
Batiffol (Pierre) :
    1920: *Le Catholicisme de Saint Augustin*, 2nd ed. Paris.
    1924: *Le Siège apostolique (359–451)*, 2nd ed. Paris.
Baviera (Giovanni) : ' Concetti e limiti dell' influenza del Cristianismo sul diritto romano '. Article in *Mélanges P. F. Girard*, vol. 1, Paris 1912.
Bayet (C.) : in *Histoire de France*, Lavisse ed. vol. 2 part 1, Paris 1911.
Berry (Arthur) : *A Short History of Astronomy*, London 1898.
Besse (J.-M.) : *Les Moines de l'ancienne France*, being vol. 2 of ' Archives de la France monastique ' Paris 1906.

Bethune-Baker (James Franklin) : *An Introduction to the Early History of Christian Doctrine* etc. 5th ed. London 1933.

Bidez (Joseph) : *La Vie de l'Empereur Julien,* Paris 1930.

Birt (Theodor) : in *M.G.H., A.A.* ed. of *Claudii Claudiani Carmina* vol. 10, Berlin 1892.

Bloch (Gustave) :
1911: in *Histoire de France,* Lavisse ed. vol. 1 part 2, Paris.
1922: *L'Empire romain, Evolution et Décadence,* Paris.

BOETHIUS: *Philosophiae Consolationis, L.C.L.* 'Boethius' 128 ff.

Boissier (Gaston) : *La Fin du Paganisme,* 6th ed. Paris 1909.

BONIFACE: *Epistolae et Decreta, P.L.* vol. 20 750 ff.

Bonwetsch:
1900: 'Hippolytus'. Article in *R.E.* vol. 8 126 ff.
1902: 'Leo I'. Article in *R.E.* vol. 11 367 ff.

Boquet (F.) : *Histoire de l'Astronomie,* Paris 1925.

Bremont (Henri) : *Histoire littéraire du Sentiment religieux en France,* vol. 3, Paris 1921.

Brewster (Edwin Tenney) : *Creation. A History of Non-Evolutionary Theories,* Indianapolis 1927.

Brunner (Heinrich) : *Deutsche Rechtsgeschichte,* vol. 1, 2nd ed. Leipsig 1906.

Buonaiuti (Ernesto) : 'The Genesis of St. Augustine's Idea of Original Sin'. Article in *Harvard Theological Review* vol. 10 159 ff. 1917.

Burkitt (Francis Crawford) : *The Religion of the Manichees,* Cambridge, Eng. 1925.

Butler (Alban) and Thurston (Herbert) : editors of *The Lives of the Saints,* vol. 1, January, London 1926.

Butler (Cuthbert) :
1898: editor of *The Lausiac History of Palladius,* Cambridge Eng.
1924: *Western Mysticism,* New York.

Cappuyns (D. M.) : 'L'Auteur du 'De Vocatione Omnium Gentium''. Article in *Revue Bénédictine* vol. 29 198 ff. 1927.

Carlyle (Robert Warrand and Alexander James) : *A History of Mediaeval Political Theory in the West,* vol. 1 (by A. J. C.) 2nd ed. Edinburgh 1927.

Carré (H.) : in *Histoire de France,* Lavisse ed. vol. 8 part 2, Paris 1911.

Carter (Jesse Benedict) : *The Religious Life of Ancient Rome,* Boston Mass. 1911.

Caspar (Erich) :
1930: *Geschichte des Papsttums,* vol. 1, Tübingen.
1933: ibid. vol. 2.

CASSIAN (Joannes) :
Conlationes XXIIII, C.S.E.L. vol. 13 3 ff.

De Incarnatione Domini contra Nestorium, C.S.E.L. vol. 17 235 ff.

De Institutis Coenobiorum, C.S.E.L. vol. 17 3 ff.

Note: the translations in the text are from the English translations in the Second Series of the *N.&P.N.F.*, by permission of the publishers Charles Scribner's Sons, New York.

Cavallera (Ferd.) : *Saint Jérome, sa vie et son œuvre*, 2 vols. Paris 1922.

CELESTINE: *Epistolae et Decreta, P.L.* vol. 50 417 ff.

Cessi (Roberto) : 'Lo scisma Laurenziano'. Article in *Archivio della R. Societa Romana*, vol. 42, Rome 1919.

Chapman (John) :
  1913: 'On the Decretum Gelasianum'. Two articles in the *Revue Bénédictine* vol. 30.
  1928: *Studies on the Early Papacy*, London.

Charles (Robert Henry) : 'The Book of Revelation'. Article in *Encycl. Brit.* vol. 23 11th ed. 1911.

Cherniss (Harold Fredrik) : 'The Platonism of Gregory of Nyssa'. Article in *University of California Publications in Classical Philology* vol. 11 no. 1, 1930.

CLAUDIAN:
  Carmina Minorum Corpusculum, L.C.L. 'Claudian' vol. 2 174 ff.
  Epithalamium, ibid. vol. 1 242 ff.
  In Eutropium, ibid. vol. 1 138 ff.
  In Rufinum, ibid. vol. 1 24 ff.

CLAUDIANUS MAMERTUS: *De Statu Animae, C.S.E.L.* vol. 11 21 ff.

CODEX THEODOSIANUS, P. Krueger ed. Fasc. I, Liber I–VI, Berlin 1923.

CONSTANTIUS OF LYONS: *Vita Germani Episcopi Autissiodorensis, M.G.H., S.R.M.* vol. 7 part 1 247 ff.

Cooper-Marsdin (A. C.) : *The History of the Islands of Lerins* etc., Cambridge Eng. 1913.

Coster (Charles Henry) : *The Judicium Quinquevirale*, Cambridge Mass. 1935.

Coulange (L.) : pseudonym for Turmel (Joseph) q.v.

Cumont (Franz) :
  1913: *Les Mystères de Mithra*, 3rd ed. Brussels.
  1929: *Les Religions orientales dans le Paganisme romain*, 4th ed. Paris.

Cureton (William) : *History of the Martyrs in Palestine by Eusebius Bishop of Caesarea*, ed. and translated by W. C., London 1861.

CYPRIAN: *Vitae Caesarii episcopi Arelatensis libri duo, M.G.H., S.R.M.* vol. 3 457 ff.

CYRIL OF JERUSALEM: *Catecheses, P.G.* vol. 33 331 ff.

D.P.D.: see ANONYMOUS.

Dalton (Ormonde Maddock) :
  1915: *The Letters of Sidonius,* 2 vols. Oxford. English transla-
    tion by O. M. D. with introduction etc.
  1927: *The History of the Franks by Gregory of Tours,* 2 vols.
    Oxford. English translation by O. M. D. with introduc-
    tion etc.

De Sancto Marcellino: see ANONYMOUS.

De Vocatione: see ANONYMOUS.

Delehaye (Hippolyte) : *Les Légendes hagiographiques,* Brussels
  1905.

Diehl (Charles) : *Ravenne,* Paris 1907.

Diercks (Gustav) : *Geschichte Spaniens von den frühesten Zeiten
  bis auf die Gegenwart,* vol. 1 Berlin 1895.

Dill (Samuel) :
  1906: *Roman Society in the Last Century of the Western Em-
    pire* 2nd ed. London.
  1926: *Roman Society in Gaul in the Merovingian Age,* London.

Dobschütz (Ernst von) : 'Das Decretum Gelasianum'. In *Texte
  und Untersuchungen zur Geschichte der altchristlichen
  Literatur,* 3rd series, vol. 8, 1912.

Dopsch (Alfons) : *Wirtschaftliche und Sociale Grundlagen der
  Europäischen Kulturentwicklung,* vol. 1 2nd ed. Vienna
  1923.

Dourif (J.) : *Du Stoïcisme et du Christianisme,* Paris [1863].

Dreves (Guido Maria) : 'Aurelius Ambrosius "des Vater des
  Kirchengesanges", eine hymnologische Studie'. Article
  in *Stimmen aus Maria-Laach,* vol. 15 58 ff., Freiburg i. B.
  1893.

DU BELLAY (Joachim) : *Deffence et illustration de la Langue
  française,* in the 1549 text, ed. of Léon Séché, vol. 1 5 ff.
  Paris 1903.

Duchesne (Louis) :
  1886: editor of *Liber Pontificalis,* vol. 1 Paris.
  1902: 'Les Canons de Sardique'. Article in *Bessarione,* 2nd
    series, vol. 3, fasc. 68 129 ff.
  1910: *Histoire ancienne de l'Eglise,* vol. 2, 4th ed. Paris.
  1911: ibid. vol. 1, 6th ed.
  1911: ibid. vol. 3, 6th ed.
  1925: *L'Eglise au VIe Siècle,* Paris.

Dudden (F. Holmes) : *The Life and Times of St. Ambrose,* 2 vols.
  Oxford 1935.

Dufourcq (Albert) :
  G.M.R.: Etudes sur les Gesta Martyrum romains, 4 vols. Paris;
    1900: vol. 1.
    1907: vol. 2.
    1907: vol. 3.
    1910: vol. 4.

L'Av.: L'Avenir du Christianisme: part 1: *Le Passé chrétien, vie et pensée,* 7 vols. Paris;
    1908: vol. 1, 5th ed.
    1909: vol. 2, 4th ed.
    1909: vol. 3, 3rd ed.
    1910: vol. 4, 5th ed.
    1911: vol. 5, 3rd ed.
  1904: *Saint Irénée (IIe siècle)*, 3rd ed. Paris.
  1905: *Saint Irénée* (La Pensée chrétienne, textes et études) Paris.
Duhem (Pierre) : *Le Système du Monde,* 5 vols. Paris 1915–17.
Dumoulin (Maurice) : in *Cambridge Medieval History,* vol. 1 Cambridge Eng. 1911.

Ebert (Adolf) : *Allgemeine Geschichte der Literatur des Mittelalters im Abendlande,* vol. 1 2nd ed. Leipsig 1889.
Encyclopaedia Britannica 11th ed. Cambridge Eng. 1910–11.
Engelbrecht (Augustus Godfried) : in *C.S.E.L.* ed. of Faustus of Riez, vol. 21 1891.
Ennodius (Magnus Felix) : *Vita beatissimi viri Epiphani Episcopi Ticinensis Ecclesiae, C.S.E.L.* vol. 6 331 ff.
Eucherius:
De Contemptu Mundi, etc. P.L. vol. 50 711 ff.
Epistula de Laude Heremi, C.S.E.L. vol. 31 177 ff.
Passio Agaunensium, C.S.E.L. vol. 31 165 ff.
Eugippius:
Epistulae, C.S.E.L. vol. 9 part 1, 1 ff.
Vita S. Severini, C.S.E.L. vol. 9 part 2, 13 ff. (The quotations in the text are from the English translation of G. W. Robinson — see below.)
Eusebius of Caesarea:
The Ecclesiastical History, in *Eusebius,* an English translation by H. J. Lawlor & J. E. L. Oulton, vol. 1 3 ff. London 1927.
The Martyrs of Palestine, in ibid. 329 ff.

Faustus of Riez:
Epistulae, C.S.E.L. vol. 21 161 ff.
De Gratia, ibid. 3 ff.
Felix III: *Epistolae et Decreta,* (see Thiel (Andreas) ed. 222 ff.)
Firmicus Maternus:
De Errore Profanarum Religionum, ed. K. Ziegler, Leipsig 1907.
Matheseos Libri VIII, ed. W. Kroll & F. Skutsch, Leipsig 1897.
FitzGerald (Augustine) : editor of *The Essays and Hymns of Synesius of Cyrene,* 2 vols. Oxford 1930.
Fournier (Paul) and LeBras (Gabriel) : *Histoire des Collections canoniques en Occident* etc., vol. 1 Paris 1931.

Franchi dè' Cavalieri (Pio) : *S. Agnese nella tradizione e nella leggenda,* Rome 1899.

Fuller (Benjamin A. G.) :
  1912: *The Problem of Evil in Plotinus,* Cambridge Eng.
  1931: *History of Greek Philosophy,* vol. 3 New York.

Galante (Andreas) ; editor of *Fontes Juris Canonici Selecti,* Innsbruck 1906.

Gebhardt (Bruno) : (*Gebhardts*) *Handbuch der Deutschen Geschichte* 6th ed. by Aloys Meister, Stuttgart 1922.

GELASIUS:
  Epistolae et Decreta, (see Thiel (Andreas) ed. 287 ff.)
  Tract III, ibid. 530 ff.
  Tract V (or *Epistola* #97), *C.S.E.L.* vol. 35 400 ff.
  Tract VI (or *Epistola* #100), *C.S.E.L.* vol. 35 453 ff.

GENNADIUS MASSILIENSIS: (*Liber*) *De Scriptoribus Ecclesiasticis,* *P.L.* vol. 58 1054 ff.

Gerland (Ernst) : *Geschichte der Physik,* Munich 1913.

Gibbon (Edward) : *The Decline and Fall of the Roman Empire* 6 vols. 1776–88. The citations are to Bury's ed., London 1896–1900.

Gilson (Étienne) :
  1913: *La Liberté chez Descartes et la Théologie,* Paris.
  1927: *Le Thomisme. Introduction au Système de Saint Thomas d'Aquin,* 3rd ed. Paris.
  1929: *Introduction à l'Etude de Saint Augustin,* Paris.

Gouilloud (André) : *Saint Eucher. Lérins et l'Eglise de Lyon au Ve siècle,* Lyons 1881.

Goux (Paul) : *Lérins au cinquième Siècle,* Paris 1856.

Goyau (Georges) : *Sainte Melanie (383–439),* 9th ed. Paris 1921.

GREGORY NAZIANZUS: *Orations, P.G.* vol. 35 395 ff.

GREGORY OF TOURS:
  Historia Francorum, M.G.H., S.R.M. vol. 1 31 ff.
  Liber Vitae Patrum, ibid. 661 ff.

Grisar (Hartmann) : *History of Rome and the Popes in the Middle Ages,* English translation, 3 vols. London 1911–1912.

Grützmacher:
  1897: 'Cassianus'. Article in *R.E.* vol. 3 746 ff.
  1902: 'Lerinum'. Article in *R.E.* vol. 11 400 ff.

Grupp (Georg) : *Kulturgeschichte der römische Kaiserzeit,* Munich 1903.

Guitton (Jean) : *Le Temps et l'Eternité chez Plotin et Saint Augustin,* Paris 1933.

Haller (Johannes) : *Das Papsttum; Idee und Wirklichkeit,* vol. 1 Stuttgart 1934.

Hansen (Joseph): *Zauberwahn, Inquisition und Hexenprozess im Mittelalter* etc. Munich 1900.

Harnack (Adolf):
  1897: *Lehrbuch der Dogmengeschichte,* vol. 3 3rd ed. Freiburg i. B.
  1904: 'Optatus'. Article in *R.E.* vol. 14 413 ff.
  1910: 'Origen'. Article in *Encycl. Brit.* vol. 20 11th ed.

Hartmann (Ludo Moritz): *Geschichte Italiens im Mittelalter,* vol. 1 2nd ed. Stuttgart 1923.

Hefele (Charles Joseph):
  1907: *Histoire des Concils,* vol. 1 of the French translation from the 2nd German ed., Paris.
  1908: ibid. vol. 2.

Hennecke: 'Eucherius'. Article in *R.E.* vol. 5 572 ff. 1898.

Heussi (Karl): *Vom Sinn der Geschichte, Augustinus und die Moderne,* Iena 1930.

HILARY OF ARLES: *Sermo de Vita S. Honorati, P.L.* vol. 50 1249 ff.

HILARY OF POITIERS:
  Liber contra Arianos vel Auxentium, P.L. vol. 10 605 ff.
  Liber contra Constantium Imperatorem, P.L. vol. 10 571 ff.

Hodgkin (Robert Howard): *A History of the Anglo-Saxons,* 2 vols. Oxford 1935.

Hodgkin (Thomas):
  1892: *Italy and her Invaders,* vols. 1 & 2, 2nd ed. Oxford.
  1896: ibid. vols. 3 & 4, 2nd ed.

Holmes (Edward): *The Life of Mozart, including his correspondence,* a new ed. by Ebenezer Prout, London 1878.

Hügel (Friedrich von): *The Mystical Element of Religion as studied in Saint Catherine of Genoa and her friends,* 2 vols. London 1909.

HUGO OF SAINT VICTOR: *Eruditionis Didascalicae, P.L.* vol. 176 739 ff. Written about 1150.

Hypomnesticon: see ANONYMOUS.

IGNATIUS: *Epistola ad Romanos, P.G.* vol. 5 685 ff.

INNOCENT I: *Epistolae et Decreta, P.L.* vol. 20 463 ff.

Israël (W.): 'Die Vita S. Hilarionis des Hieronymus'. Article in *Zeitschrift für wissenschaftliche Theologie,* vol. 23 Leipsig 1880.

JEROME:
  Apologia adversus libros Rufini, P.L. vol. 23 397 ff.
  Commentaria in Ezechielem, P.L. vol. 25 15 ff.
  Dialogus adversus Pelagianos, P.L. vol. 23 495 ff.
* *Epistulae, C.S.E.L.* vols. 54–56 (1910–1918).
  Liber contra Vigilantium, P.L. vol. 23 339 ff.
  Libri duo contra Jovinianum, P.L. vol. 23 211 ff.

* *Vita S. Pauli primi eremitae, P.L.* vol. 23 17 ff.
* *Vitae S. Hilarionis eremitae, P.L.* vol. 23 29 ff.

Note: the quotations in the text from the works marked with a star are from the English translations in the Second Series of the *N.&P.N.F.*, by permission of the publishers, Charles Scribner's Sons, New York.

JOHN OF SALISBURY: *Policraticus,* ed. Clement C. I. Webb, 2 vols. Oxford 1909.

Jolowicz (Herbert Felix) : *Historical Introduction to the Study of Roman Law,* Cambridge Eng. 1932.

Jones (Rufus Matthew) : *Studies in Mystical Religion,* London 1923.

Jülicher: 'Vigilantius'. Article in *R.E.* vol. 20 628 ff. 1908.

JULIAN (the Emperor) :
  Letter to the Senate and People of Athens, L.C.L. 'Julian' vol. 2 242 ff.
  Oration #5: Hymn to the Mother of the Gods, ibid. vol. 1 442 ff.

Jullian (Camille) :
  1913: *Histoire de la Gaule,* vol. 4 Paris.
  1920: ibid. vol. 3 2nd ed., & vols. 5 & 6.
  1926: ibid. vols. 7 & 8.

Karlowa (Otto) : *Römische Rechtsgeschichte,* Leipsig 1885.

Kaufmann (Friedrich) : *Aus der Schule des Wulfila,* Strassburg 1899.

Kiepert (Henry) : *Atlas Antiquus. Twelve maps of the Ancient World,* Chicago & New York [1898].

Koch (Hugo) :
  1930: 'Cathedra Petri'. Article in *Beihefte zur Zeitschrift für die neutestamentliche Wissenschaft,* #11.
  1935: 'Gelasius im kirchenpolitischen Dienste seiner Vorgänger, der Päpste Simplicius (468–483) und Felix III (483–492)'. Article in *Sitzungsberichte der Bayerischen Akademie der Wissenschaft,* Philos.-Histor. Abteilung, Heft #6, Munich.

Koeniger (Albert Michael) : *Grundriss einer Geschichte des katholischen Kirchenrechts,* Cologne 1919.

Krüger (Gustav) :
  1906: 'Rufinus'. Article in *R.E.* vol. 17 197 ff.
  1923: *Handbuch der Kirchengeschichte,* vol. 1 2nd ed. Tübingen.

Künstle (Karl) : *Antipriscilliana; dogmengeschichtliche Untersuchungen und Texte aus dem Streite gegen Priscillians Irrlehre,* Freiburg i. B. 1905.

Kuhnmuench (Otto J.) : *Early Christian Latin Poets,* Chicago 1929.

Kurth (Godefroid J. F.) : *Etudes franques,* 2 vols. Paris 1919 [posthumous].

Labriolle (Pierre de) : *La Réaction païenne, étude sur la polémique antichrétienne du Ier au VIe siècle,* Paris 1934.

Lacey (Thomas Alexander) : 'Augustine'. Article in *Encycl. Brit.* vol. 2 14th ed. 1929.

Lagrange (François) : *Histoire de Saint Paulin de Nole,* Paris 1877.

Lanciani (Rodolfo) : *The Destruction of Ancient Rome,* London 1899.

Langen (Joseph) : *Geschichte der römischen Kirche von Leo I bis Nikolaus I,* Bonn 1885.

Lavisse (Ernest) : ' Préliminaires de l'Histoire d'Allemagne '. Article in *Revue des Deux Mondes,* vol. 70 390 ff. (July 15 1885).

Ledlie (James Crawford) : ' Gaius '. Chapter in *Great Jurists of the World,* ed. J. Macdonell & Edw. Manson, Boston Mass. 1914.

Leo I:
  Epistolae, P.L. vol. 54 593 ff.
  Sermones, P.L. vol. 54 137 ff.

Note: the quotations in the text are from the English translations in the Second Series of the *N.&P.N.F.,* by permission of the publishers, Charles Scribner's Sons, New York.

Levison (W.) : Introduction to *Vita Germani* by Constantius in *M.G.H., S.R.M.* vol. 7 part 1.

Levy (Ernest) : ' Westen und Osten in der nachklassischen Entwicklung des römischen Rechts '. Article in *Zeitschrift der Savigny-Stiftung für Rechtsgeschichte,* Romanistische Abteilung vol. 49 230 ff., 1929.

Liber Pontificalis: see Anonymous.

Loofs:
  1904: ' Pelagius '. Article in *R.E.* vol. 15 747 ff.
  1906: ' Semipelagianismus '. Article in *R.E.* vol. 18 192 ff.

Lot (Ferdinand) : *La Fin du Monde antique et le Début du Moyen Age,* Paris 1927.

Maassen (Friedrich) : *Geschichte der Quellen und der Literatur des canonischen Rechts,* vol. 1, Gratz 1870.

Macrobius:
  Commentariorum in Somnium Scipionis, 2nd ed. Franciscus Eyssenhardt, 476 ff., Leipsig 1893.
  Conviviorum Primi Diei Saturnaliorum, ibid. 1 ff.

Malnory (Arthur) : *Saint Césaire, évêque d'Arles, 503-543,* Paris 1894.

Mamertus (see Claudianus Mamertus).

Marignan (Albert) : *Etudes sur la Civilisation française,* 2 vols. Paris 1899.

MARTIANUS CAPELLA: *De Nuptiis Philologiae et Mercurii,* ed. Adolfus Dick, Leipsig 1925.

Martroye (F.) : 'La Répression de la Magie et le Culte des Gentils au IVᵉ Siècle'. Article in *Revue Historique de Droit français et étranger,* 4th series, vol. 9 669 ff., 1930.

Maugain (Gabriel) : *Etude sur l'Evolution intellectuelle de l'Italie de 1657 à 1750 environ,* Paris 1909.

Maurice (Jules) : 'La Terreur de la Magie au IVᵉ Siècle'. Article in *Revue Historique de Droit français et étranger,* 4th series vol. 6 108 ff., 1927.

MAXIMUS OF TURIN:
Homiliae, P.L. vol. 57 221 ff.
Sermones, P.L. vol. 57 531 ff.

Mesnage (J.) : *Le Christianisme en Afrique,* vol. 2 Paris 1915.

Miall (Louis Compton) : *The Early Naturalists,* etc. London 1912.

Migne (Jacques Paul) : *P.L.: Patrologiae Cursus Completus. Series Prima . . . Patres Ecclesiae Latinae,* Paris 1844 ff.

Mommsen (Theodor) : *The History of Rome,* vols. 5 & 6, London 1886.

Monceaux (Paul) :
1894: *Les Africains; étude sur la littérature latine d'Afrique,* Paris.
1926: Introduction to *Saint Martin. Récits de Sulpice Sévère,* Paris.
1932: *Saint Jérome, sa Jeunesse,* 8th ed. Paris.

Montalembert (Charles Forbes René de) : *Les Moines d'Occident,* vol. 1 2nd ed. revised, Paris 1863.

Morin (Germain) :
1904: 'Sanctorum Communionem'. Article in *Revue d'Histoire et de Littérature religieuse,* vol. 9 209 ff.
1913: 'Les Statuta Ecclesiae antiqua'. Article in *Revue Bénédictine,* vol. 30 335 ff.

Muirhead (James) : *Historical Introduction to the Private Law of Rome,* Edinburgh 1886.

Newman (John Henry) : 'The Mission of St. Benedict', 1858. Essay in *Historical Sketches* vol. 2 365 ff. London 1917.

NICOLE (Pierre) : 'Des diverses Manières dont on tente Dieu' and 'De la Charité et de l'Amour-propre'. Essays in *Oeuvres philosophiques et morales de Nicole, comprenant un choix de ses Essais* [of about 1671], ed C. Jourdain Paris 1845, 159 ff. & 179 ff.

Nock (Arthur Darby) : *Conversion,* London 1933.

Nourry (Emile) : *Les Saints successeurs des Dieux,* Paris 1907.

OCCAM (William of) : *Quaestiones et Decisiones in IV Libros Sententiarum,* London 1495 (written in about 1323).

Onory (Sergio Mochi) : ' Vescovi e Città '. Articles in *Rivista di Storia del Diritto Italiano,* 1931–1933.

OPTATUS OF MILEVE: *De Schismate Donatistarum, C.S.E.L.* vol. 26 3 ff.

ORIENTIUS: *Commonitorium, C.S.E.L.* vol. 16 205 ff.

OROSIUS (Paulus) : *H.A.P.: Historiarum adversum Paganos, C.S.E.L.* vol. 5 1 ff.

Pagel (Julius Leopold) : *Einführung in die Geschichte der Medizin,* 2nd ed. Berlin 1915.

PAULINUS OF BEZIERS: *Epigramma, C.S.E.L.* vol. 16 503 ff.

PAULINUS OF MILAN: *Vita Sancti Ambrosii, P.L.* vol. 14 27 ff. (The quotations in the text are based on the English translation by Mary S. Kaniecka, in *The Catholic University of America, Patristic Studies,* vol. 16 Washington D. C. 1928).

PAULINUS OF NOLA: *Carmina, C.S.E.L.* vol. 30 1 ff.

Pauly (Franciscus) :
1883: in *Salvianus, C.S.E.L.* vol. 8.
1914: *Real-encyclopädie der classischen Altertumswissenschaft* 2nd series ed. Georg Wissowa, vol. I Stuttgart 1914.

PELAGIUS:
Commentarii in Epistolas Sancti Pauli, P.L. vol. 30 645 ff.
Libellus Fidei Pelagii ad Innocentiam, P.L. vol. 45 1715 ff.
Pelagii ad Demetriadem Epistola, P.L. vol. 30 15 ff.

PETER CHRYSOLOGUS: *Sermones, P.L.* vol. 52 183 ff.

Pfister (Chr.) : in *Histoire de France,* Lavisse ed. vol. 2 part 1, Paris 1911.

Pickman (E. M.) : ' The Collapse of the Scholastic Hierarchy in Seventeenth-Century France '. Article in *Massachusetts Historical Society Proceedings,* vol. 64, Boston Mass. 1932.

Platenauer (Maurice) : in *L.C.L.* ' *Claudian* ' 2 vols. London 1922.

Plinval (G. de) : ' Recherches sur l'Oeuvre littéraire de Pelage '. Article in *Revue de Philologie, de Littérature et d'Histoire anciennes,* 3rd Series, vol. 8 1934.

PLOTINUS: *Enneads.* In *The Library of Philosophical Translations. Plotinus: the Ethical Treatises,* English translation by Stephen Mackenna, 5 vols. London 1917. (The quotations in the text are from this translation, by permission of Hale, Cushman & Flint, Boston Mass.).

Poisnel (Charles) : ' Un Concile apocryphe du Pape Saint Sylvestre '. Text in *Mélanges d'Archeologie et d'Histoire,* vol. 6 1886.

PONTIUS: *Vita Cypriani,* Harnack ed. in *Texte und Untersuchungen zur Geschichte der altchristlichen Literatur,* vol. 39 heft 3 1913.

PORPHYRY:
Life of Plotinus, see above PLOTINUS: *Enneads,* vol. 1, 1 ff.
On Abstinence from Animal Food, ed. Aug. Nauck, *Porphyrii Philosophi Platonici, Opuscula Selecta,* Leipsig 1886. (The quotations in the text are from the English translation of Thomas Taylor, London 1823).

Poschmann (Bernard) : 'Die abendländische Kirchenbusse im ausgang des christlichen Altertums'. Article in *Münchener Studien zur historischen Theologie,* vol. 7 1928.

POSSIDIUS: *Sancti Augustini Vita,* H. T. Weiskotten ed. Princeton, N. J. 1919.

Praeteritorum: see ANONYMOUS.

Preuschen (Edwin) : *Analecta kürzere Texte zur Geschichte der alten Kirche und des Kanons,* Freiburg i. B. 1893.

PROCOPIUS: *History of the Wars.* Books V–VIII: *The Gothic War, L.C.L.* ' Procopius, ' vols. 3–5.

PROSPER OF AQUITAINE:
Chronicum Integrum, P.L. vol. 51 535 ff.
De Gratia Dei et Libero Arbitrio. Liber contra Collatorem, ibid. 213 ff.
Epistula ad Augustinum, C.S.E.L. vol. 57 454 ff.
Epistola ad Rufinum, P.L. vol. 51 77 ff.
Poema Conjugis ad Uxorem, P.L. vol. 51 611 ff.
Pro Augustino, Responsiones ad Capitula objectionum Gallorum calumniantium, ibid. 155 ff.
Pro Augustino Responsiones ad Excerpta Genuensium, ibid. 187 ff.

PRUDENTIUS:
Contra Symmachum, C.S.E.L. vol. 61 215 ff.
Hamartigenia, ibid. 127 ff.
Peristephanon, ibid. 291 ff.

Punzi (Giuseppe A.) : *L'Italia del VI secolo nelle " Variae " di Cassiodoro,* Aquila 1927.

Rand (Edward Kennard) : *Founders of the Middle Ages,* Cambridge Mass. 1928.

Renan (Ernest) : *Marc-Aurèle,* Paris 1881.

Reymond (Arnold) : *History of the Sciences in Greco-Roman Antiquity,* English translation by R. G. de Bray, New York [1927].

Rivière (Jean) :
1905: *Le Dogme de la Rédemption; essai d'Etude historique,* Paris.
1933: *Le Dogme de la Rédemption chez Saint Augustin,* 3rd ed. Paris.

Rivoira (Giovanni Teresio) : *Roman Architecture,* Oxford 1925.

Robertson (Archibald) : in *N.&P.N.F.* 2nd Series vol. 4, 1892.

Robinson (George W.) : in *The Life of Saint Severinus by Eugippius,* Cambridge Mass. 1914.

Rostovtzeff (Mikhail Ivanovich) : *A History of the Ancient World,* Oxford 1926.

RUFINUS OF AQUILEIA:
 Historia Monachorum, P.L. vol. 21 387 ff.
 Historiae Ecclesiasticae libri duo, ibid. 461 ff.

RURIC OF LIMOGES: *Epistularum libri duo, C.S.E.L.* vol. 21 351 ff.

RUTILIUS NAMATIANUS: *Rut. C. Namat. De Reditu Suo,* ed. Rudolf Helm Heidelberg 1933.

S. Hilarii Arelatensis Vita: see ANONYMOUS.

Saintyves (P.) : pseudonym for Nourry (Emile) , q.v.

SALVIAN:
 Ad Ecclesiam, C.S.E.L. vol. 8 224 ff.
 D.G.D.: De Gubernatione Dei, ibid. 1 ff. (The quotations in the text — except those on pp. 274, 356, 363–64, & 486–87 — are from Sanford's translation — see Sanford (Eva M.) — by permission of the Columbia University Press) .
 Epistulae, ibid. 201 ff.

Sanford (Eva M.) : in *On the Government of God . . . by Salvian,* New York 1930.

Sarton (George) : *Introduction to the History of Science,* vol. 1 Baltimore 1927.

Savigny (Friedrich Carl von) : *Geschichte des römischen Rechts im Mittelalter,* vol. 1 2nd ed. Heidelberg 1834.

Schäfer (Ernst) : *Die Bedeutung der Epigramme des Papstes Damasus I für die Geschichte der Heiligenverehrung,* Rome 1932.

Schaff (Philip) : in *N.&P.N.F.* 1st Series vol. 2 1887.

Schmidt (Carl) : review of Preuschen and of Butler on Palladius in *Göttingische gelehrte Anzeigen,* 161st year, vol. 1 1899.

SEDULIUS (Caelius) : *Paschalis Carminis, C.S.E.L.* vol. 10 14 ff.

Seeberg: 'Faustus von Reji'. Article in *R.E.* vol. 5 782 ff. 1898.

Seppelt (Franz Xaver) : *Der Aufstieg des Papsttums,* vol. 1 Leipsig 1931.

SEVERUS (Sulpicius) :
 Chronica, C.S.E.L. vol. 1 3 ff.
 Dialogi, ibid. 152 ff.
 Epistolae, ibid. 138 ff.
 Life: Vita Sancti Martini, ibid. 109 ff.
 Note: the quotations in the text are from the English translation of M. C. Watt 'St. Martin of Tours' by permission of Sands & Co., the publishers. This translation in turn is from the French of Paul Monceaux 'Saint Martin' 1926, whose publishers, Payot, in Paris, have also allowed my use of that text.

Shepherd (Wm. R.) : *Historical Atlas,* 4th ed. New York 1924.

SIDONIUS:
 Epistolae, M.G.H., A.A. vol. 8 1 ff. (The quotations in the text are from the English translation of O. M. Dalton 1915, q.v.)
 Carmina, L.C.L. ' Sidonius ', vol. 1 2 ff.

SIMPLICIUS: *Epistolae et Decreta* (see Thiel (Andreas) ed. 175 ff.)

Singer (Charles) : *A Short History of Biology. A General Introduction to the Study of Living Things,* Oxford 1931.

SIRICIUS: *Epistolae et Decreta, P.L.* vol. 13 1131 ff.

Speck (Ernst) : *Handelsgeschichte des Altertums,* vol. III part 2 Leipsig 1906.

Spengler (Oswald) : *Der Mensch und die Technik; Beitrag zu einer Philosophie des Lebens,* Munich 1931.

Spreitzenhofer (Ernst) : *Die Entwicklung des alten Mönchthums in Italien,* Vienna 1894.

Steinhausen (Georg) : *Geschichte der Deutschen Kultur,* 2nd ed. Leipsig 1913.

Stoop (Emile de) : *Essai sur la Diffusion du Manichéisme dans l'Empire romain,* Ghent 1909.

SYMMACHUS:
 Epistolae, M.G.H., A.A. vol. 6 part 1, 1 ff.
 Relationes, #3, ibid. 280 ff.

SYNESIUS OF CYRENE: *De Regno, ad Arcadium Imperatorem, P.G.* vol. 66 1053 ff. (See English translation of *The Essays and Hymns* by Augustine Fitzgerald, Oxford 1926) .

Taylor (Henry Osborn) : *The Mediaeval Mind,* 2 vols. 2nd ed. London 1914.

TERTULLIAN: *De Pudicitia, C.S.E.L.* vol. 20 219 ff.

The Book of Saints, a Dictionary etc., compiled by the Benedictine monks of St. Augustine's Abbey, Ramsgate, London 1921.

Thiel (Andreas) : ed. of *Epistolae Romanorum Pontificum Genuinae . . . a S. Hilario usque ad Pelagium II,* vol. 1 Brunsergae 1868.

Thorndike (Lynn) : *A History of Magic and Experimental Science,* vol. 1 New York 1923.

Tixeront (Joseph) :
 1921: *Histoire des Dogmes dans l'Antiquité chrétienne,* vol. 2 6th ed. Paris.
 1924: ibid. vol. 1 9th ed.

Troeltsch (Ernst) : *Augustin, die christliche Antike und das Mittelalter,* Munich 1915.

Turmel (Joseph) :
 1903: ' Le Dogme du Peché original après Saint Augustin dans l'Eglise Latine '. Article in *Revue d'Histoire et de Littérature religieuses,* vol. 8.

1927: *La Messe,* Paris (written under the pseudonym of Louis Coulange).

1931: *Histoire des Dogmes,* vol. 1 Paris.

1933: ibid. vol. 3.

Turner (Cuthbert Hamilton): in *Cambridge Medieval History,* vol. 1 Cambridge Eng. 1911.

Ueberweg (Friedrich): *Grundriss der Geschichte der Philosophie,* Part 2 10th ed. (Matthias Baumgartner) Berlin 1915.

URANIUS: *Epistola . . . de Obitu S. Paulini, P.L.* vol. 53 859 ff.

VICTOR OF VITA: *H.P.A.P.: Historia Persecutionis Africanae Provinciae, C.S.E.L.* vol. 7 1 ff.

VICTORINUS: *Liber ad Justinum Manichæum, P.L.* vol. 8 999 ff.

VINCENT OF LERINS: *Commonitorium,* 2nd ed. Adolf Jülicher, Tübingen 1925.

Vita Genovefae: see ANONYMOUS.

Vita Lupi: see ANONYMOUS.

Voigt (Karl): 'Papst Leo der Grosse und die "Unfehlbarkeit" des oströmischen Kaisers'. Article in *Zeitschrift für Kirchengeschichte,* vol. 47 1928.

Ward (John): *The Roman Era in Britain,* London 1911.

Weber (Alfred): *History of Philosophy,* English translation from the 5th French ed., New York 1906.

Weiskotten (Herbert T.): in *Sancti Augustini vita scripta a Possidio episcopo,* Princeton N. J. 1919.

Wesendonk (Otto Günther von): *Die Lehre des Mani,* Leipsig 1922.

Wetter (Gillis P: son): *Phôs; eine Untersuchung über hellenistische Frömmigkeit zugleich im Beitrag zum Verständnis des Manichäismus,* Upsala 1915.

Whittaker (Thomas):

1901: *The NeoPlatonists,* Cambridge Eng.

1923: *Macrobius, or Philosophy, Science and Letters in the year 400,* Cambridge Eng.

Wörter (Friedrich):

1898: *Beiträge zur Dogmengeschichte des Semipelagianismus,* Paderborn.

1899: *Zur Dogmengeschichte des Semipelagianismus,* Münster i. W.

Wright (Wilmer Cave): in *L.C.L.,* 'Philostratus and Eunapius,' 1922.

Young (George Frederick): *East and West through Fifteen Centuries,* 2 vols. London 1916.

Yule (Henry): 'China'. Article in *Encycl. Brit.* vol. 6 11th ed. 1910.

Zeiller (J.) : 'La Conception de l'Eglise aux quatre premiers Siècles'. Two articles in *Revue d'Histoire ecclésiastique,* vol. 29 1933.

Ziegler (Aloysius K.) : *Church and State in Visigothic Spain,* Washington D. C. 1930.

Zöckler: 'Palladius'. Article in *R.E.* vol. 14 609 ff. 1904.

ZOSIMUS: *Historia Nova,* ed. Ludovicus Mendelssohn, Leipsig 1887. (Cf. German translation *Geschichte des Zosimus* by Seybold and Heyler, Frankfurt-on-Main 1802).

INDEX

235 n. 57, 259 n. 55, 261, 264,
268, 316, 358, 360, 367, 443, 454,
536, 540.
Constantinople,
capital, 2, 229, 245, 540, 551.
rivals of, 540–1, 550, 610–1.
Constantius II, 2, 17, 22 n. 131, 544,
553.
Constantius (of Lauriacum), 295.
Constantius (of Lyons), 308, 518–21,
526–7.
Constantius (patrician), 312 n. 62.
contemplation, [Martha and Mary,
mysticism], 310.
contract,
of agency, 57 n. 33.
civil law, 7–8.
devil & God, [devil-*pact*].
for happiness, 319.
man & devil, [devil-*pact*].
man & God, 353.
saint & God, 185.
saint & peasant, 183–4.
in theology, 55–7.
contraction, 65, 177, 315, 332, 369, 385,
467, 611, 630–1.
contrition, [penance],
baptism, 87, 393–4.
charity, 371 n. 17.
Christian, 51, 600.
death-bed, [penance].
devil's, 187.
grace of, 393.
infant baptism, 393 n. 23, 395.
miracle caused by, 172–3.
in Old Testament, 58, 380.
pardon, 76, 87, 91 n. 54.
Pelagius, 408.
pre-existence &, 381–2.
punishment postponed invites, 327.
Redemption &, 90–3.
suppliant's, 200.
teaching, 90–3, 343.
teleology of, 321 n. 29.
conversion,
aristocrats', 306–7, 490 n. 47.
Church Fathers', 26.
cures promote, 175.
duress, 302–3, 569–70, [persecution].
Eucherius argues for, 490–3.
in 416: 337, 372.
in 450: 512–4.
justice on earth as price of, 351.
logic to win, 51, 605.
Martin, 186, 190.
moral incentive to, 140.
pagan, 13.
risk of, 429.
worldly advantage of, 61, 268–9,
337, 372, 377, 382, 454, 536.

co-operation, [will],
in governing, 541.
with God,
by Church, 350, 541, 578.
by individual, 91–2, 279–81,
398–9, 403–4, 416–7, 434.
for justice on earth, 279–81, 354,
494.
Copernicus, 45, 108, 208 n. 58, 209.
copulation, [marriage, Virgin]; (in
creationism) 81, 384, 437.
corruption, [matter, soul],
Arian, of the faith, 294 n. 49.
Church, 253, 268, 311.
civic, 235, 250, 257–9, 268.
judicial, 239, 257–9, 284–5, 304.
of sub-lunar world, 118–19, 133.
Corsica, 286, 303.
cosmology,
antipodes, 206.
Aristotle, 106–7, 208, 215.
baptism evades, 444.
Christian & Neoplatonic, 48–9,
205–6.
Claudian's, 314.
earth in, 111, 128–9, 207.
evasion of, 444.
First Mover, 214.
justice in, 84.
Mithraic, 31–3, 121–2.
orderly, 13–15, 19, 205.
pagan, 38–9, 101–2, 118–21, 314.
perfection in, of Plato, 27.
Redemption, 82–94, 344, 407–8, 421,
479–80.
significance of, 111.
stars, 209.
sun, 207–8.
symbolic, 111–4.
[war].
costume of,
clergy, 312 n. 63, 465, 490.
laity, 379.
monks, 454, 457, 470, 490, 492.
saints in heaven, 151, 521.
Council,
Agade in 506: 593 n. 32.
Antioch in 341: 371 n. 19.
Aquileia in 381: 548–50, 552, 558–9.
Arles in 315: 233 n. 37,
in 443 or 452: 592.
in 453: 500–1, 513.
in 475: 531–2
Carthage in 398: 251, 394 n. 25, 458
n. 29, 464 n. 62.
in 401: 221.
in 411: 412, 583.
in 416: 412, 567.
in 418: 412, 567.
in 419: 574–5, 583.

influence over, 14.
injustice of, 347 n. 74.
lightness of, 38.
local, 513.
miracles of, 224–5, 227.
[Mithraic].
morality of, 469.
multiplicity of, 162, 205–6, 390.
Oriental, 30–1.
peasants, 512–3.
Punic, 272 n. 12.
[Stoic].
[sun].
of Thunder, 160.
unknowability, 42.
victory as a, 317.
good,
    actualized, 147.
    evil &, 26–7, 30–5, 48, 69 n. 28,
       95–6.
    evil without, 30 n. 18, 46 n. 38, 95–6.
    out of evil, 54, 92, 109, 120.
government, [civil administration,
       State],
    analogy to U.S., 542.
    bad, 247–8.
    Christian theory of, 139–40, 147,
       188.
    Christianity enters, 270, 498.
    Christianity suits, 19–21.
    [Church].
    decline of, 288.
    despotic, 11 n. 74.
    fortuitous, 234–5.
    God's, 45 n. 34, 50, 211–2, 220.
grace,
    abandoned by man, 434.
    absolution &, 593.
    Adam's, 62, 390.
    analogy to music, 399.
    baptism depends on, 60, 342.
    baptism gives, 59.
    of contrition, 393–5.
    [co-operation].
    defined, 435.
    degrees of, 392–7.
    denial of, 409, 411, 414, 439.
    dispensable, 410–11, 609.
    ephemeral, 396, 416, 595.
    free, 383, 385–6, 397–8, 415–6, 434,
       531.
    free will &, 130, 390.
    freedom &, 391, 398–9, 438 n. 13.
    grace for, 396–8, 410, 416, 434–5.
    of Holy Ghost, 393–7.
    incentive of, 61 n. 43.
    incipient, 400.
    indispensable, 147, 391–2, 425, 428,
       532, 649–50.
    ineffectual, 403–4.

inner, 130–1, (395–6), 409, 411, 414,
    439.
intuition as, 130, 605 n. 88.
irresistible, 130, 388 n. 33, 396,
    415–7, 428.
of learning, 393.
magic &, 182.
merit earns, 52, 59, 75, 308, 386, 398,
    408, 410, 414–7, 434–5, 439, 531.
natural, 392–5, 414, 435, 437, 438
    n. 13, 440, 441 n. 27.
Origen on, 52.
outer, [inner].
passive waiting for, 420.
persevering, 95, 396–7, 417, 421
    n. 13, 428 n. 45, 476, 495–6.
physiological, 91 n. 54, 135 n. 5.
preliminary, 392–5, 414.
pre-Redemption, 54, 91.
prevenient, 60 n. 41, 383–5, 407,
    418 n. 3, 420, 426–7, 433, 439,
    441–2, 530–2.
reason as, 135 n. 5, 392.
Redemption &, 87, 92, 94, 212, 342.
resistible, 386 n. 27, 415–7, 427–8,
    432, 434, 438 n. 13.
saints dispense, 156.
salvation &, 313 n. 66.
saving, [persevering], 428 n. 45, 434,
    441 n. 27.
State to be saved by, 140, 280–1.
teaching as, 408–9.
transmission of, 110.
varieties of, 391–8, 400.
grain, 4, 242, 286, 297–9, 590, 616–7,
    637.
Gratian, 546–8.
    assassination, 317, 325–6, 552.
    decree of, 547, 550, 560, 569, 597.
gravitation, 215 n. 20, 223.
Great Year, 119–20, 209 n. 64.
Greeks (early),
    on evil, 30.
    on fate, 390.
    on history, 119–21, 123.
    in 300 B.C., 116, 247–8.
    on man and nature, 104.
    philosophy of, 27–9, 40, 66, 106–8,
       115, 118–9.
    soul, 27, 377.
Greeks (Eastern Empire), [Arius,
    Eutyches, Henotikon, Mo-
    nophysites, Nestorius],
    Cassian &, 413, 484.
    in 475: 531.
    in 489: 535.
    Latins vs., 245–6.
    Lerins &, 484 n. 6.
    monks, 461.
    morals of, 139.

miracles, *149–228, 503–524,*
  abundance of, [*faith in*].
  barbarians demand, 513.
  biblical, 161, 198, 223–4, 459.
  Christ's, 135, 194, 501, 604.
  confessors', 176–93, 520–1.
  contemporary, 226–7.
  conventional view of, 210.
  craving for, [*demand*].
  Creation as supreme, 218.
  [*credulity*].
  [*cures*].
  [*dead*].
  decline of? 161, 164–5.
  demand for, 149–62, 170–1, 182–4,
    524.
  didactic, 504.
  [*Epicureans*].
  Eusebius on, 162–4.
  every event a, 123, 162, 216, 219,
    403–4.
  experience of, 505.
  faith in, 179, [Martin], 221–2, 227,
    508, 514–6, 525.
  familiarity as test, 217–8.
  free will &, 129, 503–4, 504 n. 5.
  geography of, 220–1.
  God acts only by, 516.
  [*hermits*].
  initiative in, 182–4, 440, 462, 510,
    521–2.
  justice on earth &, 328, 335, 376,
    493, 503–4.
  magic vs., 181–2.
  Martin's, 189–93, 456–60.
  martyrs', 162–75, 225–6, 514–6.
  material, [*physical*].
  military, 317 n. 13.
  monastic, 177–85, 463.
  natural events vs., 129, 161, 210–12,
    503.
  one kind of event, [*every event*].
  pagan, 170, 224–5.
  papacy's rise as a, 539.
  ' parvenu ', 193.
  peasant's demand for, 182–4, 513.
  physical, 160, 168–70, 178, 189–93,
    223–7.
  physics of, 173.
  prayer &, 221–2.
  predestination &, 504.
  pride in, 181.
  primitive analysis of, 160, 170.
  prodigies, 491.
  prove,
    divinity of Christ, 135, 501, 604.
    holiness, 177 n. 13, 507.
    truth of Revelation, 135.
  Prudentius on, 168–70.
  purpose of, 198, 515.

renunciation, 503.
saints', 182–4.
scarcity of, 161, 164–5, 171, 217–8,
  458.
scepticism of, 165, 193–205, 466,
  505, 508 n. 21, 508–12, 521–2,
  524.
science vs., 523.
[*Sign*].
spiritual, 158–60.
surrender to, 515.
survival of Christianity as a, 376.
[*telepathy*].
triumph of, 518, 522–4.
unreliable, 199–200.
utility of, 90.
virtue causes, 462.
vision as a, 178, 508.
vogue of, 518, 522–4.
misery, [suffering].
missionaries, 25 n. 146, 143, 150,
  176, 514–15.
Mithraism,
  astrology, 18.
  civic virtues, 32.
  compromise, 145.
  cosmology, 101, 121–2.
  defect of, 33, 38.
  democratic, 149.
  demons in, 18, 31–2, 36, 43.
  Diocletian &, 16, 31, 137–8.
  dualism of, 18, 31–3, 36, 38, 43, 55,
    365.
  emanation, 45–6.
  failure of, 138, 145.
  Fall of man, 31, 41.
  fatalism of, 32–3, 64.
  God of, 33.
  history to, 121–3.
  humanitarianism, 13 n. 88.
  incarnation of man, 31, 110 n. 25.
  justice on earth, [*dualism*].
  light, 31.
  matter, 38, 121, 149.
  morality of, 12 n. 78, 13 n. 88.
  nature, 31.
  opposition to, 31, 138.
  optimism, 31–2.
  Redemption in, 41.
  sacrifice is carnal, 32 n. 35.
  souls, 31.
  sun, 31, 39–40.
  symbolism, 111, 114.
  Trinity in, 41.
  war in, 12 n. 78, 31–2, 58, 64, 149.
  works required, 32, 110 n. 25.
modesty, [chastity, humility], 136,
  142–3, 185 n. 52, 192, 310.
modus vivendi, 303, 643–4, 654.
Moesia, 25 n. 146, 159, 165, 548.

Mohammedan, 288.
monasticism, [Cassian, Eutyches, hermits, Jerome, Jovinian, Lerins, Rufinus, Vincent of Lerins].
[abbot].
African, 486.
agriculture, 471.
aristocrats in, 310 n. 46, 461, 512.
asceticism, 473.
Basil, 463, 473.
beauty, cult of, 526.
bishops &, 354, 488–90, 500–1.
canon law &, 464.
cenobites, 471, 473.
charity, 471.
clergy &, 460–1, 464–5, 641.
Council of Chalcedon on, 500.
Council open to, 499.
economics of, 471–2.
Egyptian, 176–81, 463, 612.
free will &, 495.
fugitives, 502.
Gallic foundations, 485, 489.
Gelasius, 641.
gifts to, 455.
Greeks &, 455.
happiness of, 479, 493.
harshness of, 482.
hereditary vocations, 464, 500.
[hermits].
inheritances, 472, 499–500, 502.
invasions &, 485.
Italian, 466.
itinerant, 295, 460–1, 500.
justice on earth &, 317, *328–36*, 366 n. 43, 493–5, 525.
laity vs., 486–7.
legislation on, 461, 464, 472, 499–500, 502.
manual labour, 457.
martyr supplanted by, 176.
medicine, 457, 478.
medieval, 313.
military, 136–7.
miracles, 177–85, 503, 523.
nun, 307, 455, 460, 462, 464–5, 466 n. 79, 473, 591 n. 17, 598, 637.
obedience, 470, 473.
Orders, 460 n. 47, 641.
penance of, 593 ns. 32 & 33.
persecution of, 486–7.
poverty of, 471.
prejudice v., 460–1, 466, 485–8, 490, 503.
prestige of, 462, 488–90, 499–502.
punishment of, 500, 502.
rank, 591 n. 17.
rights of, 473, 500.
Rules, 457, 462–3, *473*, 484–5, 500.

sacrifice, 494–5.
Salvian on African, 486.
science of, 478.
security of, 491, 493, 496.
serenity of, 479, 493.
Severinus, 294–6.
simplification, 479, 492–3.
Siricius, 460.
Sixtus III, 499.
statescraft of Christian, 148.
teaching of, 476–7.
triumph of, 461–2, 488–9.
truth, 480–1, 493.
[ugliness].
Vigilantius on, 197, 465–6.
vow, 455, 456 n. 11, 460, 464–5, *470*, 472–3, 500, 502.
wealth of, 471–2, 493.
worldly advantage, 330–1.
Monica, 63, 100 n. 83.
monism, 20–1, 123, 128, 204–6.
Monophysites, *608–9*, 612, 619–21, 624–7, 633, 635–6, 645–6.
Montaigne, 103.
moon, 108, 118, 208, 224, 614–5.
morals, [sin, virtue],
absolute vs. relative, 477–8.
Cassian's, 475–7.
Christian, 40, 111, 140–8, 261, 265, 477–8, 493.
[deceit].
equality in, 75 n. 18, 91 n. 51, 397, 399.
evolution of, 125.
Greek, 27–9, 40.
Latin vs. Eastern, 139.
laws on, 138–9.
Mithraic, 12 n. 78.
monastic, 493.
pagan-Roman, 29, 477.
popularized, 477.
principle vs. expediency, 477–8.
science &, 27–9, 40, 103.
Spain, 29.
survival value, 376–9.
temporal world &, 113.
wealth &, 371.
morrow (thought for), 284, 297, (299), 377, 479, 493, 618, 637.
mortgage, 8.
Moselle, 231–2, 274, 285, 499 n. 86.
Moses, [Bible-*O. & N. L.*], 335, 355.
motion, 44 n. 33, 115 n. 52, 119, 206, 208–9, 346 n. 68, [First Mover].
Mozart, 48, 127 n. 39.
murder, 79, 151, 313, 537 n. 12, 545–6, 593, 636.
Mursa (battle of), 233 n. 40.
music, 101 n. 85, 127, 242, 336, 399, 468.

popular, 549, 560–3.
provincial Council, 537.
Church vs. State, [Church-*State
&*-].
cosmological, [fate, God-*omnipotence*].
of episcopal electorate, 312.
State vs. local, [patriotism-*to city,
& Italian*].
Sozomen, 517.
space, 66, 498–9, 529–30, 630–2,
652–5.
Spain,
communication with, 230, 232,
300.
economics, 3–4.
in 406: [Vandals].
in 414: 271.
in 428: 272, 286 n. 11.
in 456: 286 n. 11.
in 469: 287 n. 16.
in 8th C., 288.
in 17th C., 248.
invasions of, 271–3, 286 n. 11, 288.
moralists, 29.
patriotism, 246 n. 132, 268 n. 95.
population, 247 n. 136.
Spengler, 234 n. 50, 376.
Spinoza, 220.
spiritual, [otherworldliness, temporal
responsibilities].
Squillace, 636.
stars, 209–10, 215, 341, 449–50.
State, [Emperor, Greeks (Eastern
Empire), fall of Western Empire],
Anti-Christ as, 653–4.
attitude of Romans to, 28–9, 136–
40, 240 n. 90.
bishop as agent of, 266.
buried, 653.
[Church-*State &*].
confidence in, 10–1.
despotism of, 11 n. 74, 240–4, 256,
258.
ephemeral, 652.
Gelasius on, 653.
individual vs., 5–13, 130–40, 239–
42.
insignificance of, 654.
justice &, 58.
justice on earth &, 322.
legislation 443 to 452: 283–5.
magic &, 17–21.
monastery is ideal of, 148.
monasticism &, 464.
otherworldliness &, 133–4, 349.
parasite, 239.
patronage, 641.
perfection of, 654.

philosophy for, 445.
as plaintiff, 260.
purpose of, 600.
responsibility, [temporal resp.].
[rise of Roman Empire].
Roman view of, 28–9, 136–40, 240
n. 90.
saint succeeds to, 188.
serfs of, 241–2.
split in, 229–30.
symbolism of, 137.
universality of, 545 n. 55, 652.
statesmanship, [strategy], 28, 148,
554–5, 570, 599, 607, 611, 628.
Stephen (Pope), 543, 564.
Stephen (martyr), 221, 221 n. 45.
Stilicho, 5, 377.
Stoics,
anthropocentric, 109–10.
aristocratic, 149.
on the body, 117 n. 55.
[Cicero].
contraction, 65, 332, 369, 379 n. 17.
cycles, 119–20.
failure of, 314–5, 324.
fatalism, 128 n. 41.
God of, 30, 33–4, (cf. 219–20), 345
n. 66.
justice on earth, 314, 322, 364–6.
matter, 100, 365.
misery, 320, 324, 360.
monasticism, 177–8.
monism, 204.
nature, 30, 33–4, (cf. 219–20).
pride, 333.
Providence, 314, 345 n. 66.
Romans (early), 29.
[Seneca].
sorrow, 320, 324.
transmigration, 119–20.
virtue as an end, 374.
storms, 191.
Strabo, 289.
strangers, [fugitives], 372, 490.
strategy,
Church, in 378–82: 549–50, 551
n. 32.
Church, in 450: 513–4.
of compromise, 413–4, 607.
of God, 45–7, 61–2, 83–4, 87–92,
316.
martyrs', 367.
military, 6, 279, 296, 367.
[papacy-*claims*].
of persecution, 569–70.
of prayer, 279, 296, 368, 370.
temporal, 14, 140, 147–8, 280–1,
367–9, 600–1, 612–15.
sub-deacon, 591 n. 17, 592 n. 21.
Sueve, (in 406) 271–2, 286 n. 11,